Welcome to ECONOMICS [obscured by sticker] The Micro View

UPDATED WITH

IMPORTANT

Your Student Access Code for MyEconLab

INSTRUCTIONS

1. Ask your instructor for your **MyEconLab Course ID** and record it here: ______________

2. Go to **http://www.myeconlab.com** and follow the instructions for getting started, installation, and registration for your course. You will need your **Course ID** and your **Student Access Code** only the first time you register for your course.

3. If you need help at any time during the registration process, please send an email to support@coursecompass.com or simply click on the Need Help? Icon.

Your unique **Student Access Code** is:

WSCDFT-BREWS-ORIEL-BLUED-HELOT-OBESE

This Access Code can be used only once to register for your course. Your registration is not transferable. If you did not purchase a new textbook, your Access Code may not be valid.

ECONOMICS TODAY

The Micro View

The Addison-Wesley Series in Economics

Abel/Bernanke
Macroeconomics

Bade/Parkin
Foundations of Microeconomics

Bade/Parkin
Foundations of Macroeconomics

Bierman/Fernandez
Game Theory with Economic Applications

Binger/Hoffman
Microeconomics with Calculus

Boyer
Principles of Transportation Economics

Branson
Macroeconomic Theory and Policy

Bruce
Public Finance and the American Economy

Byrns/Stone
Economics

Carlton/Perloff
Modern Industrial Organization

Caves/Frankel/Jones
World Trade and Payments: An Introduction

Chapman
Environmental Economics: Theory, Application, and Policy

Cooter/Ulen
Law and Economics

Downs
An Economic Theory of Democracy

Eaton/Mishkin
Online Readings to Accompany The Economics of Money, Banking, and Financial Markets

Ehrenberg/Smith
Modern Labor Economics

Ekelund/Tollison
Economics: Private Markets and Public Choice

Fusfeld
The Age of the Economist

Gerber
International Economics

Ghiara
Learning Economics: A Practical Workbook

Gordon
Macroeconomics

Gregory
Essentials of Economics

Gregory/Stuart
Russian and Soviet Economic Performance and Structure

Hartwick/Olewiler
The Economics of Natural Resource Use

Hubbard
Money, the Financial System, and the Economy

Hughes/Cain
American Economic History

Husted/Melvin
International Economics

Jehle/Reny
Advanced Microeconomic Theory

Klein
Mathematical Methods for Economics

Krugman/Obstfeld
International Economics: Theory and Policy

Laidler
The Demand for Money: Theories, Evidence, and Problems

Leeds/von Allmen
The Economics of Sports

Lipsey/Courant/Ragan
Economics

McCarty
Dollars and Sense: An Introduction to Economics

Melvin
International Money and Finance

Miller
Economics Today

Miller/Benjamin/North
The Economics of Public Issues

Mills/Hamilton
Urban Economics

Mishkin
The Economics of Money, Banking, and Financial Markets

Parkin
Economics

Parkin/Bade
Economics in Action Software

Perloff
Microeconomics

Phelps
Health Economics

Riddell/Shackelford/Stamos/Schneider
Economics: A Tool for Critically Understanding Society

Ritter/Silber/Udell
Principles of Money, Banking, and Financial Markets

Rohlf
Introduction to Economic Reasoning

Ruffin/Gregory
Principles of Economics

Sargent
Rational Expectations and Inflation

Scherer
Industry Structure, Strategy, and Public Policy

Schotter
Microeconomics: A Modern Approach

Stock/Watson
Introduction to Econometrics

Studenmund
Using Econometrics: A Practical Guide

Tietenberg
Environmental and Natural Resource Economics

Tietenberg
Environmental Economics and Policy

Todaro/Smith
Economic Development

Waldman/Jensen
Industrial Organization: Theory and Practice

Williamson
Macroeconomics

ECONOMICS TODAY

The Micro View

2001–2002 EDITION
MYECONLAB.COM UPDATE

Roger LeRoy Miller
Institute for University Studies, Arlington, Texas

Boston San Francisco New York
London Toronto Sydney Tokyo Singapore Madrid
Mexico City Munich Paris Cape Town Hong Kong Montreal

Photo Credits
Pages 3 and 14, ©Grant LeDuc/Stock Boston; pages 26 and 43, ©Annie Griffiths Belt/CORBIS; pages 48 and 71, ©Keren Su/Stock Boston; pages 75 and 90, ©Tony Freeman/Photo Edit; pages 95 and 115, ©Bill Aron/Photo Edit; pages 120 and 135, ©CORBIS; pages 455 and 468, ©Susan Van Etten; pages 482 and 501, ©Susan Van Etten; pages 505 and 520, Stephen Ferry/Gamma Liaison; pages 531 and 555, *Chicago Tribune* photo by Bill Hogan; pages 560 and 582, ©Richard Hutchings/Photo Edit; pages 588 and 608, ©Martin Rogers/Tony Stone Images/Chicago Inc.; pages 612 and 634, permission granted by Lands' End.com; pages 638 and 656, ©Todd Gipstein/CORBIS; pages 665 and 684, ©Susan Van Etten; pages 689 and 707, ©Bettmann/CORBIS; pages 712 and 727, Copyright 2000–Wisconsin Department of Revenue–Lottery Division; pages 731 and 755, ©Ted Spiegel/CORBIS; pages 759 and 774, ©Jorie Butler Kent/Abercrombie & Kent; pages 783 and 800, ©Paul Conklin/Photo Edit; pages 805 and 827, ©Miladinovic/Sygma CORBIS.

Editor-in-Chief: Denise Clinton
Acquisitions Editor: Victoria Warneck
Developmental Editor: Rebecca Ferris
Web Project Manager: Karen Schmitt
Associate Editor: Roxanne Hoch
Managing Editor: James Rigney
Production Supervisor: Katherine Watson
Marketing Manager: Adrienne D'Ambrosio
Senior Media Producer: Melissa Honig
Design Manager: Regina Kolenda
Cover Designer: Regina Kolenda and Joyce Cosentino Wells
Senior Manufacturing Buyer: Hugh Crawford
Cover Collage Images: ©Digital Vision/PictureQuest; © Robert Cattan/Index Stock Imagery; ©PhotoDisc.
Compositor: Lynn Lowell
Art Studio: ElectraGraphics, Inc.
Printer and Binder: Quebecor World
Cover Printer: Coral Graphic Services, Inc.

ISBN 0-201-78617-6
12345678910—QWT—0605040302

To Jenna and Bob Hall,

You make the Valley
a better place in which
to live.

R. L. M.

Contents in Brief

CONTENTS IN DETAIL

Acknowledgments

I am the most fortunate of economics textbook writers, for I receive the benefit of literally hundreds of suggestions from those of you who use *Economics Today*. I continue to be fully appreciative of the constructive criticisms that you offer. There are some professors who have been asked by my publisher to participate in a more detailed reviewing process of this edition. I list them below. I hope that each one of you so listed accepts my sincere appreciation for the fine work that you have done.

Bill Adamson, South Dakota State University
John Allen, Texas A&M University
John Baffoe-Bonnie, Pennsylvania State University
Kevin Baird, Montgomery County Community College
Daniel Benjamin, Clemson University
Abraham Bertisch, Nassau Community College
John Bethune, University of Tennessee
R. A. Blewett, St. Lawrence University
Melvin Borland, Western Kentucky University
James Carlson, Manatee Community College
Robert Carlsson, University of South Carolina
K. Merry Chambers, Central Piedmont Community College
Catherine Chambers, Central Missouri State University
Marc Chopin, Louisiana Tech University
Curtis Clarke, Mountain View College
Jerry Crawford, Arkansas State University
Andrew J. Dane, Angelo State University
Carl Enomoto, New Mexico State University
Abdollah Ferdowsi, Ferris State University
James Gale, Michigan Technical University
Neil Garston, California State University, Los Angeles
Paul Graf, Penn State University
William Henderson, Franklin University
Charles W. Hockert, Oklahoma City Community College
Yu Hsing, Southeastern Louisiana University
Scott Hunt, Columbus State Community College
Joseph W. Hunt Jr., Shippensburg University of Pennsylvania
John Ifediora, University of Wisconsin, Platteville
Allan Jenkins, University of Nebraska, Kearney
Alan Kessler, Providence College
Marie Kratochvil, Nassau Community College
James C. McBrearty, University of Arizona
Diego Méndez-Carbajo, Florida International University
Khan Mohabbat, Northern Illinois University
Zuohong Pan, Western Connecticut State University
Ginger Parker, Miami-Dade Community College
Bruce Pietrykowski, University of Michigan, Dearborn
Mannie Poen, Houston Community College
Robert Posatko, Shippensburg University of Pennsylvania
Jaishankar Raman, Valparaiso University
Richard Rawlins, Missouri Southern State College
Charles Roberts, Western Kentucky University
Larry Ross, University of Alaska, Anchorage
Stephen Rubb, Providence College
Henry Ryder, Gloucester County College
Swapan Sen, Christopher Newport University
Garvin Smith, Daytona Beach Community College
Alan Stafford, Niagara County College
Thomas Swanke, West Virginia State College
Lea Templer, College of the Canyons
David VanHoose, University of Alabama
Craig Walker, Delta State University
Mark Wohar, University of Nebraska, Omaha
Tim Wulf, Parkland College
Alex Yguado, Los Angeles Mission College

I also thank the reviewers of previous editions:

Esmond Adams
John Adams
John R. Aidem
Mohammed Akacem
M. C. Alderfer
Ann Al-Yasiri
Leslie J. Anderson
Fatima W. Antar
Aliakbar Ataiifar
Leonard Atencio
Glen W. Atkinson
Thomas R. Atkinson
James Q. Aylesworth
Charley Ballard
Maurice B. Ballabon
G. Jeffrey Barbour
Daniel Barszcz
Robin L. Bartlett
Kari Battaglia
Robert Becker
Charles Beem
Glen Beeson
Charles Berry
Scott Bloom
M. L. Bodnar
Mary Bone
Karl Bonnhi
Thomas W. Bonsor
John M. Booth
Wesley F. Booth
Thomas Borcherding
Tom Boston
Barry Boyer
Maryanna Boynton
Ronald Brandolini
Fenton L. Broadhead
Elba Brown
William Brown
Michael Bull
Maureen Burton
Conrad P. Caligaris
Kevin Carey
Dancy R. Carr
Doris Cash
Thomas H. Cate
Richard J. Cebula
Richard Chapman
Young Back Choi
Carol Cies
Joy L. Clark
Gary Clayton
Marsha Clayton
Warren L. Coats
Ed Coen
Pat Conroy
James Cox
Stephen R. Cox
Eleanor D. Craig
Joanna Cruse
John P. Cullity
Thomas Curtis
Mahmoud Davoudi
Edward Dennis
Carol Dimamro
William Dougherty
Barry Duman
Diane Dumont
Floyd Durham
G. B. Duwaji
James A. Dyal
Ishita Edwards
Robert P. Edwards
Alan E. Ellis
Mike Ellis
Steffany Ellis
Frank Emerson
Zaki Eusufzai
Sandy Evans
John L. Ewing-Smith
Frank Falero
Frank Fato
Grant Ferguson
David Fletcher
James Foley
John Foreman
Ralph G. Fowler
Arthur Friedberg
Peter Frost
E. Gabriel
Steve Gardner
Peter C. Garlick
Alexander Garvin
Joe Garwood
J. P. Gilbert
Otis Gilley
Frank Glesber
Jack Goddard
Allen C. Goodman
Richard J. Gosselin
Edward Greenberg
Gary Greene
Nicholas Grunt
William Gunther
Kwabena Gyimah-Brempong
Demos Hadjiyanis
Martin D. Haney
Mehdi Haririan
Ray Harvey
E. L. Hazlett
Sanford B. Helman
John Hensel
Robert Herman
Gus W. Herring
Charles Hill
John M. Hill
Morton Hirsch
Benjamin Hitchner
R. Bradley Hoppes
James Horner
Grover Howard
Nancy Howe-Ford
R. Jack Inch
Christopher Inya
Tomotaka Ishimine
E. E. Jarvis

Parvis Jenab
Mark Jensen
S. D. Jevremovic
J. Paul Jewell
Frederick Johnson
David Jones
Lamar B. Jones
Paul A. Joray
Daniel A. Joseph
Craig Justice
Septimus Kai Kai
Devajyoti Kataky
Timothy R. Keely
Ziad Keilany
Norman F. Keiser
Randall G. Kesselring
E. D. Key
M. Barbara Killen
Bruce Kimzey
Philip G. King
Terrence Kinal
E. R. Kittrell
David Klingman
Charles Knapp
Jerry Knarr
Faik Koray
Janet Koscianski
Peter Kressler
Michael Kupilik
Larry Landrum
Margaret Landman
Keith Langford
Anthony T. Lee
George Lieu
Stephen E. Lile
Lawrence W. Lovick
Akbar Marvasti
Warren T. Matthews
Robert McAuliffe
Howard J. McBride
Bruce McClung
John McDowell
E. S. McKuskey
James J. McLain
John L. Madden
Mary Lou Madden
Glen Marston
John M. Martin
Paul J. Mascotti
James D. Mason
Paul M. Mason
Tom Mathew
Warren Matthews
G. Hartley Mellish
Mike Melvin
Dan C. Messerschmidt
Michael Metzger
Herbert C. Milikien
Joel C. Millonzi
Glenn Milner
Thomas Molloy
Margaret D. Moore
William E. Morgan
Stephen Morrell
Irving Morrissett
James W. Moser
Martin F. Murray
George L. Nagy
Jerome Neadly
James E. Needham
Claron Nelson
Douglas Nettleton
Gerald T. O'Boyle
Lucian T. Orlowski
Diane S. Osborne
Jan Palmer
Gerald Parker
Randall E. Parker
Norm Paul
Raymond A. Pepin
Martin M. Perline
Timothy Perri
Jerry Petr
Maurice Pfannesteil
James Phillips
Raymond J. Phillips
I. James Pickl
Dennis Placone
William L. Polvent
Reneé Prim
Robert W. Pulsinelli
Rod D. Raehsler
Kambriz Raffiee
Sandra Rahman
John Rapp
Gautam Raychaudhuri
Ron Reddall
Mitchell Redlo
Charles Reichhelu
Robert S. Rippey
Ray C. Roberts
Richard Romano
Duane Rosa
Richard Rosenberg
Barbara Ross-Pfeiffer
Philip Rothman
John Roufagalas
Patricia Sanderson
Thomas N. Schaap
William A. Schaeffer
William Schaniel
David Schauer
A. C. Schlenker
Scott J. Schroeder
William Scott
Dan Segebarth
Augustus Shackelford
Richard Sherman Jr.
Liang-rong Shiau
David Shorow
Vishwa Shukla
R. J. Sidwell
David E. Sisk
Alden Smith
Howard F. Smith
Lynn A. Smith
Phil Smith
Steve Smith
William Doyle Smith
Lee Spector
George Spiva
Richard L. Sprinkle
Herbert F. Steeper
Columbus Stephens
William Stine
Allen D. Stone
Osman Suliman
J. M. Sullivan
Rebecca Summary
Joseph L. Swaffar
Frank D. Taylor
Daniel Teferra
Gary Theige
Robert P. Thomas
Deborah Thorsen
Richard Trieff
George Troxler
William T. Trulove
William N. Trumbull
Arianne K. Turner
Kay Unger
John Vahaly
Jim Van Beek
Lee J. Van Scyoc
Roy Van Til
Robert F. Wallace
Henry C. Wallich
Milledge Weathers
Robert G. Welch
Terence West
Wylie Whalthall
Everett E. White
Michael D. White
Mark A. Wilkening
Raburn M. Williams
James Willis
George Wilson
Travis Wilson
Ken Woodward
Peter R. Wyman
Whitney Yamamura
Donald Yankovic
Paul Young
Shik Young
Mohammed Zaheer
Ed Zajicek
Paul Zarembka
William J. Zimmer Jr.

This MyEconLab.com update required the labor of dozens of individuals and groups. Of course, I continue to be in debt to those who helped me on the original, underlying edition on which this version is based. In addition, the multimedia project manager, Karen Schmitt, made sure that all of the myriad elements of this extraordinary enterprise worked together. I thank her for the countless nights and weekends she devoted to this project. Melissa Honig helped with the technology every step of the way, as always. Rebecca Ferris, my ever-present developmental editor, conceptualized the project and stepped in on numerous occasions to make sure that the print and multimedia elements worked well together and came out on time. Victoria Warneck and Denise Clinton on the Addison-Wesley team supported this work from the very beginning. Others at Addison-Wesley who lent an invaluable hand included Katherine Watson, Production Supervisor, Scott Silva, Composition Manager, Lynn Lowell, Electronic Publisher, and Mansour Bethoney, Senior Web Designer.

The creators of the major animations, Ben Mallory, Matt Hampton, and Chris Bassolino of Fuse5, put in a lot more effort than planned, but came through with superb results. Dave VanHoose wrote the major scripts for all of the Economics in Motion features, while Debbie Mullen of the University of Colorado scripted the Graphs in Motion animations. All of the animations were scrutinized by our dedicated team of reviewers, including Paul Graf, Scott Hunt, Marie Kratochvil, Garvin Smith, Tim Wulf, and James Carlson.

I am also indebted to Steve Melzer of VidBoston and his top-notch crew, as well as Ken Kavanah of Newbury Sound and our voice talent, Ray Childs and Mary Ellen Whitaker, for their contributions. Thanks also to Henry Ryder and Debbie Mullin for their work preparing scripts for the glossary terms.

So, from the true bottom of my heart, I extend my appreciation to the above-mentioned individuals and companies. Putting together a regular book requires more effort than most imagine. Putting together a multimedia version extends the limits of such effort beyond reason. But the end result is, I am sure you will agree, worthy of a great team's travails.

I plan to add to this multimedia, interactive version of the *Economics Today* text. Please let me know what I can do to improve this project.

Roger LeRoy Miller

Preface

Economics Today has long led the field in offering students and instructors a dynamic, application-rich approach to learning and teaching economics. Often imitated but never duplicated, Miller remains on the cutting edge of economic teaching, defining what it means for a text to be user-friendly and student-oriented. With the introduction of the MyEconLab.com, powered by CourseCompass, it again zooms ahead of the pack.

The MyEconLab.com update presents an unprecedented wealth of specially designed multimedia resources, all available in an easy-to-use Web-based environment. It is contained within Addison-Wesley's premier Blackboard-based course management system, CourseCompass, allowing instructors to incorporate technology into the classroom with unprecedented ease.

Those of you who already teach from Miller's *Economics Today* will quickly notice the multimedia icons that have been inserted at strategic points throughout every textbook chapter. To view these new multimedia resources and see how effortlessly they will enhance your students' learning experience, please visit the MyEconLab.com Web site at **http://www.myeconlab.com**.

- **Flip and fumble no more.** Let's face it: Most introductory textbooks now come with a mind-boggling array of ancillary learning tools, both print and electronic. But do your students *use* those tools? Do they know what they are, or how they tie into their textbook? If not, how many take the time to find out? If your students are like most students, they will flip and fumble for a few minutes at most before giving up.

With MyEconLab.com, they don't need to search any further than the textbook page itself. The familiar design of their printed textbook — with the same layout, the same font, even the same page numbers—is a navigational tool that allows your students to painlessly access a wide array of video and audio clips, moving graphs, and full-scale animations of key concepts. All your students need to do is point and click. It's all at their fingertips!

NEW MULTIMEDIA ENHANCEMENTS

MyEconLab.com is tailored to match the *Economics Today* textbook; the Web site features an electronic version of the textbook that serves as a navigational tool for students to access animations, video clips, audio narration, and Internet activities. The goal of these multimedia features is to sharpen students' overall mastery of economics by reinforcing their command of economic theory and bolstering their ability to analyze graphs.

- **Seamless integration of the text and Web site.** Students experience multimedia content in the context of what they are learning in the textbook. Available in PDF format, the complete online textbook has the exact same layout as the printed version. Within each chapter PDF file, students can:
  - Preview the most critical concepts in an audio introduction by the author, Roger LeRoy Miller
  - Use the chapter outline to jump to a particular section
  - View animated graphs
  - Gauge their mastery of concepts in chapter quizzes
  - Link to Web sites cited in the Econ on the Net Internet Activities
  - View videos featuring the author, Roger LeRoy Miller, or

- Link to the Econ Tutor Center, where qualified instructors are on call five days a week to answer questions.

- **Media-rich learning resources.** The online version of the textbook includes a system of icons indicating the availability of innovative media tools:

  In video clips, the author stresses the key points in every chapter and further clarifies concepts that students find most difficult to grasp.

  To simplify the task of learning the vocabulary of economics, the key terms printed in bold type and defined in the text margin are available as audio clips. In addition to the definition, each clip includes an illuminating, relevant example or that extra word of explanation needed to cement students' understanding.

  Each chapter also includes an upbeat audio introduction by the author during which he discusses the chapter topics and focuses student attention on the most critical concepts.

  We have identified the ten key economic ideas in the textbook that are ideally suited to animated presentations. These *Economics in Motion* features are in-depth animations that guide students through these precise graphical presentations with detailed audio explanations. The step-by-step approach guides students through the action and makes clear the underlying economic theory. A Contents Guide in each animation allows students to focus in on the ideas that they are struggling with most.

  Beginning students of economics are often apprehensive about working with graphs. Using the *Graphs in Motion* feature, with a click of the mouse curves shift, graphs come to life, and students' confidence builds. These animated graphs in every chapter foster graph-analyzing capabilities as points are plotted, curves are drawn, movement is simulated, and intersection points are called out.

  Economics in Action, the market-leading interactive tutorial software in principles of economics, is now available via the Web. Icons in the text indicate the availability of modules that aid students' mastery of concepts through review, demonstration, and interaction. In-depth tutorials guide students in their discovery of the relationship between economic theory and real-world applications, while the Draw Graph palette lets them test their graphing abilities.

  Four ten-question quizzes per chapter with tutorial feedback allow students to gauge their understanding of the material.

  One more tool to encourage students to succeed at economics is the Study Guide. Students can download a PDF version of the material from the print Study Guide for every chapter, all for no additional cost.

  MyEconLab.com gives your students complimentary access to help from qualified economics instructors when you are not available. Five days a week, tutors answer questions via phone, fax, and e-mail.

THE COURSECOMPASS ADVANTAGE

MyEconLab.com is powered by CourseCompass. It allows you to easily build and manage online course materials that enhance your classroom teaching time. If you have an Internet connection and a Web browser, you can use CourseCompass. Because CourseCompass is nationally hosted, there is no need for anyone at your academic institution to have to set up and maintain CourseCompass.

Powered by the Blackboard online learning system, CourseCompass includes all the powerful Blackboard features for teaching and learning. Additionally, MyEconLab.com comes with preloaded, state-of-art course materials provided by Addison-Wesley. These course materials include a complete version of the textbook and study guide, extensive animations, video and audio clips, and more.

The advantages of CourseCompass include:

- **Flexibility**. CourseCompass lets you add files of any type to your course, from simple text documents to complex slide presentations and animations.
- **Automated grading**. CourseCompass grades student assessments as students complete them, and automatically posts scores to an online gradebook. As a result, you can spend more time teaching and less time grading.
- **Superior customer support.** CourseCompass provides customer support as well as an *Instructor Quick Start Guide* and comprehensive online Help system tailored to your needs. CourseCompass also includes a *Student Quick Start Guide* and online Help for students, so you can focus on teaching your course, not on teaching CourseCompass.

As an instructor, you will have a wealth of content and resources and powerful tools preloaded on to a customizable course that you download. In addition to the Multimedia Edition, you can:

- Access all of the supplementary items available with the text, including PowerPoint, Test Banks, and Instructor's Manual
- Set up a course calendar to post assignments and assess student performance with the gradebook
- Assign quizzes to students with time limits
- Add post-it notes to the online version of the text to point out particular items or to incorporate a favorite example
- Use communication tools such as e-mail and a course discussion board
- Direct students to submit documents electronically in the digital drop box.

And students can view announcements from the instructor, track their progress on testing features, or contribute to an online discussion board.

- **Value-added material.** For no additional cost, students who purchase the MyEconLab.com Update Edition receive access to the latest release of the Economics in Action software, an electronic version of the printed Study Guide, and access to the Addison-Wesley Tutor Center.

PEDAGOGY WITH PURPOSE

Economics Today, 2001–2002 Edtion, provides a fine-tuned teaching and learning system. This system is aimed at capturing student interest through the infusion of examples that capture the vitality of economics. Each of the following features has been carefully crafted to enhance the learning process:

- **Chapter-Opening Issues** Each chapter-opening issue whets student interest in core chapter concepts with compelling examples.

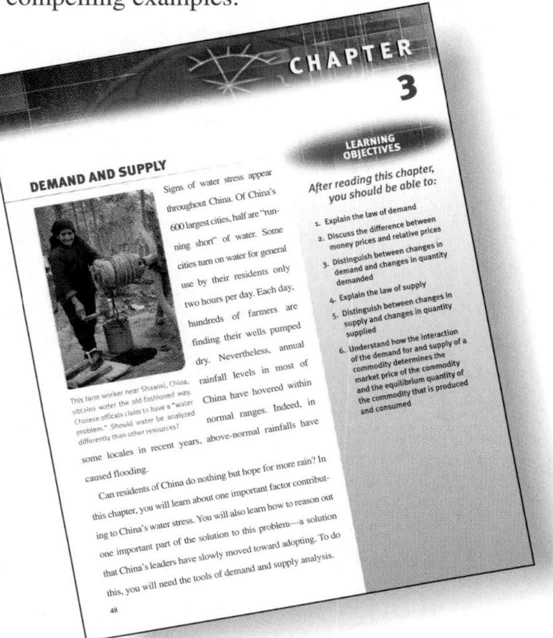

CHAPTER 3

DEMAND AND SUPPLY

Signs of water stress appear throughout China. Of China's 600 largest cities, half are "running short" of water. Some cities turn on water for general use by their residents only two hours per day. Each day, hundreds of farmers are finding their wells pumped dry. Nevertheless, annual rainfall levels in most of China have hovered within normal ranges. Indeed, in some locales in recent years, above-normal rainfalls have caused flooding.

Can residents of China do nothing but hope for more rain? In this chapter, you will learn about one important factor contributing to China's water stress. You will also learn how to reason out one important part of the solution to this problem—a solution that China's leaders have slowly moved toward adopting. To do this, you will need the tools of demand and supply analysis.

This farm worker near Shaanxi, China, obtains water the old fashioned way. Chinese officials claim to have a "water problem." Should water be analyzed differently than other resources?

LEARNING OBJECTIVES

After reading this chapter, you should be able to:

1. Explain the law of demand
2. Discuss the difference between money prices and relative prices
3. Distinguish between changes in demand and changes in quantity demanded
4. Explain the law of supply
5. Distinguish between changes in supply and changes in quantity supplied
6. Understand how the interaction of the demand for and supply of a commodity determines the market price of the commodity and the equilibrium quantity of the commodity that is produced and consumed

48

- **Did You Know That . . . ?** Each chapter starts with a provocative question to engage students and to lead them into the content of the chapter.

Did You Know That... more than 75 million people currently own portable cellular phones? This is a huge jump from the mere 200,000 who owned them in 1985. Since 1992, two out of every three new telephone numbers have been assigned to cellular phones. There are several reasons for the growth of cellular phones, not the least being the dramatic reduction in both price and size due to improved and cheaper computer chips that go into making them. There is something else at work, though. It has to do with crime. In a recent survey, 46 percent of new cellular phone users said that personal safety was the main reason they bought a portable phone. In Florida, for example, most cellular phone companies allow users simply to dial *FHP to reach the Florida Highway Patrol. The rush to cellular phones is worldwide. Over the past decade, sales have grown by nearly 50 percent every year outside the United States.

We could attempt to explain the phenomenon by saying that more people like to use portable phones. But that explanation is neither satisfying nor entirely accurate. If we use the economist's primary set of tools, *demand and supply,* we will have a better understanding of the cellular phone explosion, as well as many other phenomena in our world. Demand and supply are two ways of categorizing the influences on the price of goods that you buy and the quantities available. As such, demand and supply form the basis of virtually all economic analysis of the world around us.

As you will see throughout this text, the operation of the forces of demand and supply take place in *markets.* A **market** is an abstract concept referring to all the arrangements individuals have for exchanging with one another. Goods and services are sold in markets, such as the automobile market, the health market, and the compact disc market. Workers offer their services in the labor market. Companies, or firms, buy workers' labor services in the labor market. Firms also buy other inputs in order to produce the goods and services that you buy as a consumer. Firms purchase machines, buildings, and land. These markets are in operation at all times. One of the most important activities in these markets is the setting of the prices of all of the inputs and outputs that are bought and sold in our complicated economy. To understand the determination of prices, you first need to look at the law of demand.

- **Learning Objectives** A clear statement of learning objectives on the first page of the chapter focuses students' studies.
- **Chapter Outline** The outline serves as a guide to the chapter coverage.
- **Graphs** Precise, four-color graphs clearly illustrate key concepts.
- **Key Terms** To simplify the task of learning the vocabulary of economics, key terms are printed in bold type and defined in the margin of the text the first time they appear.
- **Policy Examples** Students are exposed to important policy questions on both domestic and international fronts in over 40 policy examples.

POLICY EXAMPLE

Should Shortages in the Ticket Market Be Solved by Scalpers?

If you have ever tried to get tickets to a playoff game in sports, a popular Broadway play, or a superstar's rock concert, you know about "shortages." The standard ticket situation for a Super Bowl is shown in Figure 3-12. At the face-value price of Super Bowl tickets (P_1), the quantity demanded (Q_2) greatly exceeds the quantity supplied (Q_1). Because shortages last only so long as prices and quantities do not change, markets tend to exhibit a movement out of this disequilibrium toward equilibrium. Obviously, the quantity of Super Bowl tickets cannot change, but the price can go as high as P_2.

Enter the scalper. This colorful term is used because when you purchase a ticket that is being resold at a price that is higher than face value, the seller is skimming an extra profit off the top. If an event sells out, ticket prices by definition have been lower than market clearing prices. People without tickets may be willing to buy high-priced tickets because they place a greater value on the entertainment event than the face value of the ticket. Without scalpers, those individuals would not be able to attend the event. In the case of the Super Bowl, various forms of scalping occur nationwide. Tickets for a seat on the 50-yard line have been sold for more than $2,000 a piece. In front of every Super Bowl arena, you can find ticket scalpers hawking their wares.

In most states, scalping is illegal. In Pennsylvania, convicted scalpers are either fined $5,000 or sentenced to two years behind bars. For an economist, such legislation seems strange. As one New York ticket broker said, "I look at scalping like working as a stockbroker, buying low and selling high. If people are willing to pay me the money, what kind of problem is that?"

For Critical Analysis

What happens to ticket scalpers who are still holding tickets after an event has started?

S
P_2
Price per Ticket
P_1
D
Excess quantity demanded (shortage at price P_1)
Q_1
Q_2
Quantity of Super Bowl Tickets

FIGURE 3-12
Shortages of Super Bowl Tickets
The quantity of tickets for any one Super Bowl is fixed at Q_1. At the price per ticket of P_1, the quantity demanded is Q_2, which is greater than Q_1. Consequently, there is an excess quantity demanded at the below-market-clearing price. Prices can go as high as P_2 in the scalpers' market.

- **International Examples** Over 30 international examples emphasize the interconnections of today's global economy.

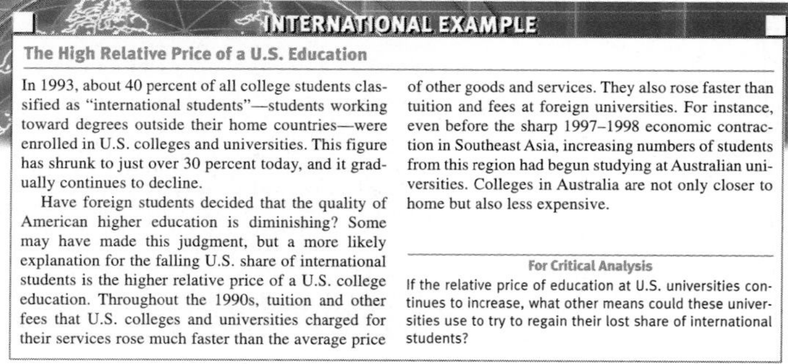

INTERNATIONAL EXAMPLE

The High Relative Price of a U.S. Education

In 1993, about 40 percent of all college students classified as "international students"—students working toward degrees outside their home countries—were enrolled in U.S. colleges and universities. This figure has shrunk to just over 30 percent today, and it gradually continues to decline.

Have foreign students decided that the quality of American higher education is diminishing? Some may have made this judgment, but a more likely explanation for the falling U.S. share of international students is the higher relative price of a U.S. college education. Throughout the 1990s, tuition and other fees that U.S. colleges and universities charged for their services rose much faster than the average price of other goods and services. They also rose faster than tuition and fees at foreign universities. For instance, even before the sharp 1997–1998 economic contraction in Southeast Asia, increasing numbers of students from this region had begun studying at Australian universities. Colleges in Australia are not only closer to home but also less expensive.

For Critical Analysis

If the relative price of education at U.S. universities continues to increase, what other means could these universities use to try to regain their lost share of international students?

- **Examples** More than 50 thought-provoking and relevant examples highlight U.S. current events and demonstrate economic principles.

EXAMPLE

Garth Brooks, Used CDs, and the Law of Demand

A few years ago, country singer Garth Brooks tried to prevent his latest album from being sold to any chain or store that also sells used CDs. His argument was that the used-CD market deprived labels and artists of earnings. His announcement came after Wherehouse Entertainment, Inc., a 339-store retailer based in Torrance, California, started selling used CDs side by side with new releases, at half the price. Brooks, along with the distribution arms of Sony, Warner Music, Capitol-EMI, and MCA, was trying to quash the used-CD market. By so doing, it appears that none of these parties understands the law of demand.

Let's say the price of a new CD is $15. The existence of a secondary used-CD market means that to people who choose to resell their CDs for $5, the cost of a new CD is in fact only $10. Because we know that quantity demanded is inversely related to price, we know that more of a new CD will be sold at a price of $10 than of the same CD at a price of $15. Taking only this force into account, eliminating the used-CD market tends to reduce sales of new CDs.

But there is another force at work here, too. Used CDs are substitutes for new CDs. If used CDs are not available, some people who would have purchased them will instead purchase new CDs. If this second effect outweighs the incentive to buy less because of the higher effective price, then Brooks is behaving correctly in trying to suppress the used CD market.

For Critical Analysis

Can you apply this argument to the used-book market, in which both authors and publishers have long argued that used books are "killing them"?

- **For Critical Analysis** At the end of each example, students are asked to "think like economists" to answer the critical analysis questions. The answers to all questions are found in the Instructor's Manual.
- **Concepts in Brief** Following each major section, "Concepts in Brief" summarizes the main points of the section to reinforce learning and to encourage rereading of any difficult material.
- **FAQ** All-new sidebars encourage analysis by providing answers to frequently asked questions based on economic reasoning.

FAQ

Isn't postage a lot more expensive than it used to be?

No, in reality, the *relative price* of postage in the United States has fallen steadily over the years. The absolute dollar price of a first-class stamp rose from 3 cents in 1940 to 33 cents at the beginning of the twenty-first century. Nevertheless, the price of postage relative to the average of all other prices has declined since reaching a peak in 1975.

Click here to see how the U.S. Department of Agriculture seeks to estimate demand and supply conditions for major agricultural products.

- **Internet Resources** Margin notes link directly to interesting Web sites that illustrate chapter topics, giving students the opportunity to build their economic research skills by accessing the latest information on the national and global economy.

Market Equilibrium
Click here study market equilibrium in greater detail.

- **Economics in Action Icon** This marginal element directs students to "Economics in Action" modules corresponding to chapter content.

- **Netnomics** The new "Netnomics" feature explores how innovations in information technology are changing economic theory and behavior.

NETNOMICS

Stealth Attacks by New Technologies

Successful new products often get off to a slow start. Eventually, however, consumers substitute away from the old products to the point at which demand for the old products effectively disappears. Consider handwritten versus printed manuscripts. For several years in the mid-fifteenth century, printed books were a rarity, and manuscript-copying monks and scribes continued to turn out the bulk of written forms of communication. By the 1470s, however, printed books were more common than handwritten manuscripts. By the end of the fifteenth century, manuscripts had become the rare commodity.

A more recent example involves train engines. Just before 1940, after the diesel-electric engine for train locomotives was invented, an executive of a steam-engine company declared, "They'll never replace the steam locomotive." In fact, it only took 20 years to prove the executive wrong. By 1960, steam engines were regarded as mechanical dinosaurs.

To generate the bulk of its profits, the U.S. Postal Service relies on revenues from first-class mail. To keep its first-class customers satisfied, it recently deployed a $5 billion automation system that reads nine addresses per second and paints envelopes with bar codes to speed sorting. Yet the postal service has lost about $4 billion in first-class mail business since 1994. Around that time, people began to compare the 25-cent cost of a one-minute phone call with the 32-cent cost of first-class postage. Then they began to substitute away from first-class letters to faxes. Other people got access to the Internet and began to send messages by electronic mail, at no additional charge. First-class mail increasingly looks like a steam-engine dinosaur.

Some observers of the software industry think the same sort of thing could happen to a powerhouse of the present: Microsoft Windows. Today the code for this program is on most personal computers on the planet. Competing operating system applications offered by Sun Microsystems's Java software and others currently run more slowly than Windows. But they consume many fewer lines of computer code and hence promise swift accessibility via the Internet. It is conceivable that someday people may log on to the Internet and pay by the minute to use such software to run their computers, thereby freeing up their hard drives for other uses. Thus today's dominant operating system may someday look a lot like a handwritten manuscript does to generations accustomed to reading printed books instead of handwritten manuscripts.

- **Issues and Applications** Linked to the chapter-opening issue, the all-new "Issues and Applications" features are designed to encourage students to apply economic concepts to real-world situations. Each outlines the concepts being applied in the context of a particular issue and is followed by several critical thinking questions that may be used to prompt in-class discussion. Suggested answers to the critical thinking questions appear in the Instructor's Manual.

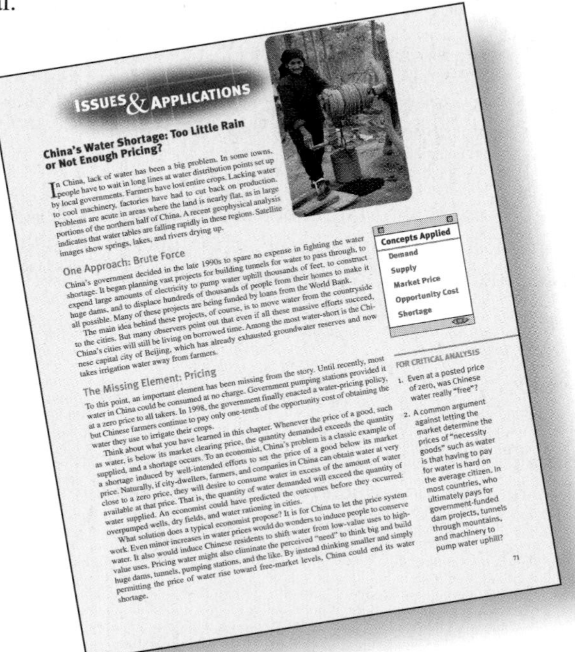

ISSUES & APPLICATIONS

China's Water Shortage: Too Little Rain or Not Enough Pricing?

In China, lack of water has been a big problem. In some towns, people have to wait in long lines at water distribution points set up by local governments. Farmers have lost entire crops. Lacking water to cool machinery, factories have had to cut back on production. Problems are acute in areas where the land is nearly flat, as in large portions of the northern half of China. A recent geophysical analysis indicates that water tables are falling rapidly in these regions. Satellite images show springs, lakes, and rivers drying up.

One Approach: Brute Force

China's government decided in the late 1990s to spare no expense in fighting the water shortage. It began planning vast projects for building tunnels for water to pass through, to expend large amounts of electricity to pump water uphill thousands of feet, to construct huge dams, and to displace hundreds of thousands of people from their homes to make it all possible. Many of these projects are being funded by loans from the World Bank.

The main idea behind these projects, of course, is to move water from the countryside to the cities. But many observers point out that even if all these massive efforts succeed, China's cities will still be living on borrowed time. Among the most water-short is the Chinese capital city of Beijing, which has already exhausted groundwater reserves and now takes irrigation water away from farmers.

The Missing Element: Pricing

To this point, an important element has been missing from the story. Until recently, most water in China could be consumed at no charge. Government pumping stations provided it at a zero price to all takers. In 1998, the government finally enacted a water-pricing policy, but Chinese farmers continue to pay only one-tenth of the opportunity cost of obtaining the water they use to irrigate their crops.

Think about what you have learned in this chapter. Whenever the price of a good, such as water, is below its market clearing price, the quantity demanded exceeds the quantity supplied, and a shortage occurs. To an economist, China's problem is a classic example of a shortage induced by well-intended efforts to set the price of a good below its market price. Naturally, if city-dwellers, farmers, and companies in China can obtain water at very close to a zero price, they will desire to consume water in excess of the amount of water available at that price. That is, the quantity of water demanded will exceed the quantity of water supplied. An economist could have predicted the outcomes before they occurred: overpumped wells, dry fields, and water rationing in cities.

What solution does a typical economist propose? It is for China to let the price system work. Even minor increases in water prices would do wonders to induce people to conserve water. It also would induce Chinese residents to shift water from low-value uses to high-value uses. Pricing water might also eliminate the perceived "need" to think big and build huge dams, tunnels, pumping stations, and the like. By instead thinking smaller and simply permitting the price of water rise toward free-market levels, China could end its water shortage.

Concepts Applied

Demand
Supply
Market Price
Opportunity Cost
Shortage

FOR CRITICAL ANALYSIS

1. Even at a posted price of zero, was Chinese water really "free"?
2. A common argument against letting the market determine the prices of "necessity goods" such as water is that having to pay for water is hard on the average citizen. In most countries, who ultimately pays for government-funded dam projects, tunnels through mountains, and machinery to pump water uphill?

71

- **Summary Discussion of Learning Objectives** Every chapter ends with a concise, thorough summary of the important concepts organized around the learning objectives presented at the beginning of each chapter.
- **Key Terms** A list of key terms with page references is a handy study device.
- **Problems** A variety of problems support each chapter. Answers for all odd-numbered problems are provided at the back of the textbook.
- **Economics on the Net** Internet activities are designed to build student research skills and reinforce key concepts. The activities guide students to a Web site and provide a structured assignment for both individual and group work.

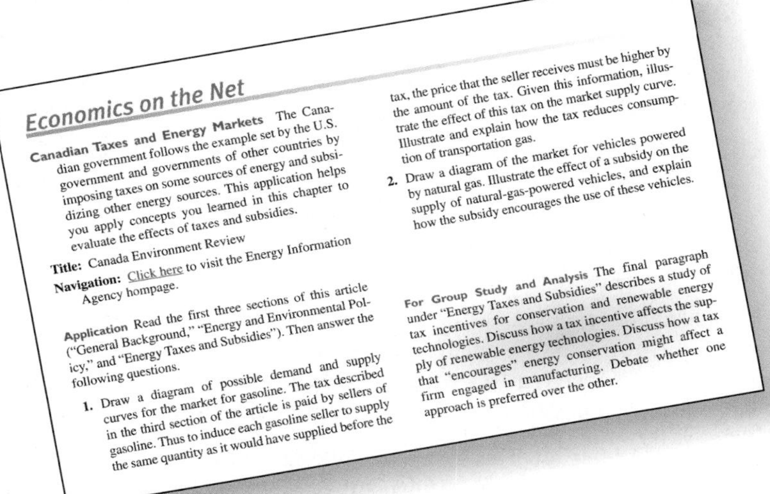

Economics on the Net

Canadian Taxes and Energy Markets The Canadian government follows the example set by the U.S. government and governments of other countries by imposing taxes on some sources of energy and subsidizing other energy sources. This application helps you apply concepts you learned in this chapter to evaluate the effects of taxes and subsidies.

Title: Canada Environment Review

Navigation: Click here to visit the Energy Information Agency hompage.

Application Read the first three sections of this article ("General Background," "Energy and Environmental Policy," and "Energy Taxes and Subsidies"). Then answer the following questions.

1. Draw a diagram of possible demand and supply curves for the market for gasoline. The tax described in the third section of the article is paid by sellers of gasoline. Thus to induce each gasoline seller to supply the same quantity as it would have supplied before the tax, the price that the seller receives must be higher by the amount of the tax. Given this information, illustrate the effect of this tax on the market supply curve. Illustrate and explain how the tax reduces consumption of transportation gas.
2. Draw a diagram of the market for vehicles powered by natural gas. Illustrate the effect of a subsidy on the supply of natural-gas-powered vehicles, and explain how the subsidy encourages the use of these vehicles.

For Group Study and Analysis The final paragraph under "Energy Taxes and Subsidies" describes a study of tax incentives for conservation and renewable energy technologies. Discuss how a tax incentive affects the supply of renewable energy technologies. Discuss how a tax that "encourages" energy conservation might affect a firm engaged in manufacturing. Debate whether one approach is preferred over the other.

- **Tying It All Together** This new feature captures the themes of each part in an extensive case application that demonstrates the relevance of concepts in a business decision-making context. Accompanying questions probe students to assess key issues and do additional research on the Internet. (The answers to all questions are found in the Instructor's Manual.)

TYING IT ALL TOGETHER

Part One Case Problem

Case Background

Cyber Dynamics International Corporation (CDI) is engaged in both business-to-consumer and business-to-business Internet applications as well as the production and distribution of new software programs. CDI is based in Singapore, but it sells its products and services throughout the world, including in the United States.

The management of CDI is well aware of the fact that in the Internet world everything happens at, well, Internet speed. New competitors are getting stronger every day. One of them appears to be Global Online Services. Indeed, in a recent planning meeting at CDI, the chief executive officer asked her management team to look into expanding into new areas on the Internet, new software applications, and new countries.

A week later the various officers and managers of the company have come forth with the following recommendations:

1. Lower the price of Internet access to compete more aggressively with Global Online Services and America Online.
2. Add numerous new features to the company's existing popular business accounting program and raise its price.
3. Break up the existing advertising and sales division into two separate divisions.
4. Open a major software manufacturing plant somewhere in the United States.
5. Enter into a partnership with a software company in the People's Republic of China.
6. Create a new employee's benefit in the form of a pension plan that will pay loyal workers a certain sum of money every month after they retire.

Points to Analyze

1. Do you think it matters that CDI's headquarters are in Singapore? To whom might it matter and why?
2. In recommendation number 1 above, a manager suggested that the company lower its price of Internet access. If it does, will the number of Internet access subscribers increase or decrease? Under what circumstances will total revenues increase? Decrease?
3. If the company's accounting program is enhanced, under what circumstances might it be able to raise the price and actually sell more copies?
4. Recommendation number 3 argues in favor of splitting up a division into two separate parts. What famous economist might applaud this action and why?
5. If you were in charge of deciding whether to support the recommendation that a software manufacturing plant be located in the United States, what are some of the factors that you might want to analyze to reach your conclusion? One might be the going wage rate that would have to be paid to new workers. But there is another key cost for companies doing business in the United States. What is it?
6. While you might be convinced that entering the marketplace in the People's Republic of China is an exciting prospect ("everybody's doing it") there might be some problems with going into partnership with an existing Chinese company. Think about the economic functions of government that you learned in Chapter 5. Which function (or lack thereof) might create the biggest problem for your company's new partnership in China?
7. While the suggestion to create a new employee benefit involving a retirement system might seem appealing because it would attract more and better workers, would you want to offer the same retirement plan to your workers in all countries? What government-funded institution should you examine first in each country before you make such a decision?

Casing the Internet

1. Click here to go to the Web site of Global Online Services. Once on this site, navigate through some of the sections.
   a. What part of the world is the main focus of the activities of this company?
   b. What various types of products does this company produce?
   c. Why do you suppose that there are so many informational Web pages located at this company's home page?
   d. The advertisements at this Web site relate to this company only. Could Global Online Services gain from allowing others to place advertisements at its site?
   e. Is it likely that other companies would want to place ads at this Web site? Why or why not?
2. Now click here to go to the Web site for Global Online Electronic Services.
   a. Do you think that this company competes directly with Global Online Services? Why or why not?
   b. To what audience is that Web site addressing itself?
   c. Under what circumstances would you want to purchase the services of Global Online Electronic Services?
3. Go to any popular search engine, such as Yahoo.com, Profusion.com, Google.com, or Lycos.com. Type in the word "global" and see what happens.
   a. Why do you think so many companies include the word global in their names today?

   Do the same thing with typing the word "online" and see what happens.
   b. Why do so many companies what to include the word online in their names today?

140

141

AN EXPANSIVE, INNOVATIVE TEACHING AND LEARNING PACKAGE

Economics Today is accompanied by a variety of technologically innovative and useful supplements for instructors and students.

TO THE INSTRUCTOR

The following supplementary materials are available to help busy instructors teach more effectively and to incorporate technological resources into their principles courses.

- **Instructor's Resource Disk (IRD) with PowerPoint Lecture Presentation** Fully compatible with the Windows NT, 95, and 98, and Macintosh computers, this CD-ROM provides numerous resources.

- The PowerPoint Lecture Presentation was developed by Jeff Caldwell, Steve Smith, and Mark Mitchell of Rose State College and revised by Andrew J. Dane of Angelo State University. With nearly 100 slides per chapter, the PowerPoint Lecture Presentation animates graphs from the text; outlines key terms, concepts, and figures; and provides direct links for in-class Internet activities.

- For added convenience, the IRD also includes Microsoft Word files for the entire content of the Instructor's Manual and Computerized Test Bank files. The easy-to-use testing software (**TestGen-EQ with QuizMaster-EQ** for Windows and Macintosh) is a valuable test preparation tool that allows professors to view, edit, and add questions.

- **Economics in Action** This interactive tutorial software has been developed by Michael Parkin and Robin Bade of the University of Western Ontario and adapted by David VanHoose of the University of Alabama for use with *Economics Today*. Available through **MyEconLab.com**, Economics in Action aids students' mastery of concepts through review, demonstration, and interaction. Step-by-step tutorials guide students in their discovery of the relationship between economic theory and real-world applications, while the Draw Graph palette tests their graphing abilities. Detailed, customizable quizzes help students prepare for exams by testing their grasp of concepts.

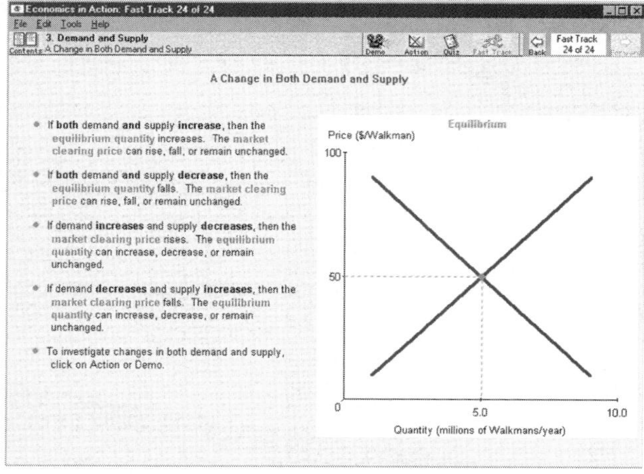

- **Instructor's Manual** Prepared by Andrew J. Dane of Angelo State University, the Instructor's Manual provides the following materials:
  - Chapter overviews, objectives, and outlines
  - Points to emphasize for those who wish to stress theory
  - Answers to "Issues and Applications" critical thinking questions
  - Further questions for class discussion
  - Answers to even-numbered end-of-chapter problems
  - Detailed step-by-step analysis of end-of-chapter problems
  - Suggested answers to "Tying It All Together" case questions
  - Annotated answers to selected student learning questions
  - Selected references

- **Test Bank 1** This Test Bank provides over 3,000 multiple-choice questions and more than 250 short-essay questions with answers. Revised by John Ifediora of the University of Wisconsin, the questions have been extensively classroom-tested for a number of years.
- **Test Bank 2** Revised by James R. Carlson of Manatee Community College, this test bank includes over 3,000 multiple-choice questions and more than 250 short-essay questions. These questions have been class-tested by many professors, including Clark G. Ross, coauthor of the National Competency Test for economics majors for the Educational Testing Service in Princeton, New Jersey.
- **Wired Test Bank** This all-new, innovative supplement is an indispensable aid for professors who are incorporating *Economics Today*'s many technology resources into their courses. It includes questions that allow you to test students on the "Economics in Action" modules, end-of-chapter "Economics on the Net" activities, and "Tying It All Together" cases' Internet feature.

- **Lecture Outlines with Transparency Masters** Prepared by Andrew J. Dane of Angelo State University, this lecture system features more than 500 pages of lecture outlines and text illustrations, including numerous tables taken from the text. Its pages can be made into transparencies or handouts to assist student note taking.
- **Four-Color Overhead Transparencies** One hundred of the most important graphs from the textbook are reproduced as full-color transparency acetates. Many contain multiple overlays.

- **Economics Experiments in the Classroom** Developed by Denise Hazlett of Whitman College, these economics experiments involve students in actively testing economic theory. In addition to providing a variety of micro and macro experiments, this supplement offers step-by-step guidelines for successfully running experiments in the classroom.
- **Additional Homework Problems** For each text chapter, more than 20 additional problems are provided in two separate sets of homework assignments that are available for download from **www.myeconlab.com**. Each homework problem is accompanied by suggested answers.
- **Regional Case Studies for the East Coast, Texas, and California** Additional case studies, available at **www.myeconlab.com**, can be used for in-class team exercises or for additional homework assignments.

- **Pocket Guide to Economics Today for Printed and Electronic Supplements** The Pocket Guide is designed to coordinate the extensive teaching and learning package that accompanies *Economics Today.* For each chapter heading, the author has organized a list of print and electronic ancillaries with page references to help organize lectures, develop class assignments, and prepare examinations.

- **Econ Tutor Center** Order the Econ Tutor Center Edition of *Economics Today* to give your students help when you are not available. Five days a week, qualified economics instructors answer questions via phone, fax, and e-mail, all at no additional cost for students who purchase a new textbook. Contact your local sales representative for details.

TO THE STUDENT

The following supplementary materials are available to aid and enhance students' mastery of concepts.

- **Study Guide** The Study Guide has been written by the author and updated by David VanHoose. This valuable guide offers the practice and review students need to succeed. It has been thoroughly revised to take into account the significant changes in many of the chapters of the 2001–2002 Edition. Review questions now are focused on issues appropriate for the 2000s, and the Study Guide is firmly oriented toward helping students learn what they need to know to succeed in the course—and in life. An electronic version of the Study Guide is available at the MyEconLab.com Web site.
- **Student Study Notes for PowerPoint Lecture Presentation** Developed by Jeff Caldwell of Rose State College and updated by Andrew J. Dane of Angelo State University, the Student Study Notes are a valuable note-taking and study device.

- **Economics in Action, 2001–2002 Edition** This interactive tutorial software is available at **www.myeconlab.com**. The market leader in principles of economics software, Economics in Action aids mastery of concepts through review, demonstration, and interaction. See how changing conditions cause curves to shift. Test your graphing abilities with the Draw Graph palette. And prepare for exams with detailed, customizable quizzes.
- **Your Economic Life** Available at **www.myeconlab.com**, this booklet offers numerous practical applications of economics and guidance for analyzing economic news.

Part 1
Introduction

CHAPTER

1

THE NATURE OF ECONOMICS

Men who are married earn, on average, higher incomes than those who are not married. Does this marriage premium mean that if you are single and decide to get married, you will automatically make a higher income?

In 1911, Edgar Watson Howe wrote, "Marriage is a good deal like a circus: There is not as much in it as is represented by the advertising." Nevertheless, for men (but not, apparently, for women), marriage has a concrete payoff: earnings 10 to 20 percent higher than those of unmarried men. Economists call this wage differential the "marriage premium."

One rationale for the marriage premium is that by settling down, men are able to be more successful in their careers. Another theory, however, is that the women do a good job of selecting their husbands. That is, women choose to marry men who are more successful than the men they choose not to marry.

Whether it is men deciding to marry for the good of their careers or women selecting a successful marriage partner, both make *choices*. A fundamental aspect of the science of economics is seeking to understand how people make choices.

LEARNING OBJECTIVES

After reading this chapter, you should be able to:

1. **Discuss the difference between microeconomics and macroeconomics**
2. **Evaluate the role that rational self-interest plays in economic analysis**
3. **Explain why the study of economics is a science**
4. **Distinguish between positive and normative economics**

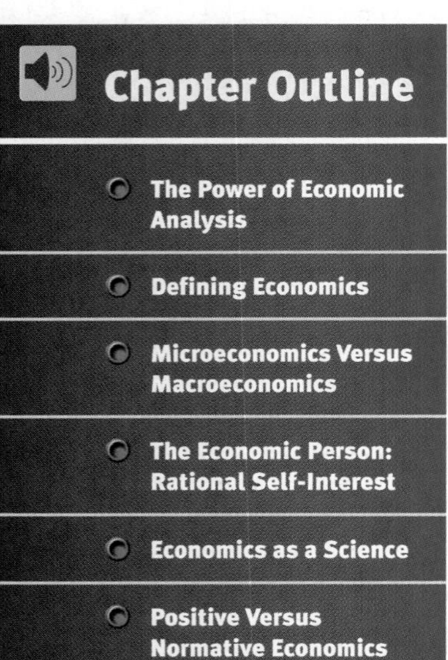

Did You Know That... since 1989, the number of fax machines in U.S. offices and homes has increased by over 10,000 percent? During the same time period, the number of bike messengers in downtown New York City *decreased* by over 65 percent. The world around us is definitely changing. Much of that change is due to the dramatically falling cost of communications and information technology. Today the computers inside video games cost only about $100 yet have 50 times the processing power that a $10 million IBM mainframe had in 1975. Not surprisingly, American firms have been spending more on communications equipment and computers than on new construction and heavy machinery.

Cyberspace, the Internet, the World Wide Web—call it what you want, but your next home (if not your current one) will almost certainly have an address on it. The percentage of U.S. households that have at least one telephone is close to 100 percent, and those that have video game players is over 50 percent. Over half of homes have personal computers, and more than two-thirds of those machines are set up to receive and access information via phone lines. Your decisions about such things as when and what type of computer to buy, whether to accept a collect call from a friend traveling in Europe, and how much time you should invest in learning to use the latest Web browser involve an untold number of variables: where you live, the work your parents do, what your friends think, and so on. But as you will see, there are economic underpinnings for nearly all the decisions you make.

THE POWER OF ECONOMIC ANALYSIS

Knowing that an economic problem exists every time you make a decision is not enough. You also have to develop a framework that will allow you to analyze solutions to each economic problem—whether you are trying to decide how much to study, which courses to take, whether to finish school, or whether America should send troops abroad or raise tariffs. The framework that you will learn in this text is based on the *economic way of thinking.*

This framework gives you power—the power to reach informed conclusions about what is happening in the world. You can, of course, live your life without the power of economic analysis as part of your analytical framework. Indeed, most people do. But economists believe that economic analysis can help you make better decisions concerning your career, your education, financing your home, and other important matters. In the business world, the power of economic analysis can help you increase your competitive edge as an employee or as the owner of a business. As a voter, for the rest of your life you will be asked to make judgments about policies that are advocated by a particular political party. Many of these policies will deal with questions related to international economics, such as whether the U.S. government should encourage or discourage immigration, prevent foreigners from investing in domestic TV stations and newspapers, or restrict other countries from selling their goods here. Finally, just as taking an art, music, or literature appreciation class increases the pleasure you receive when you view paintings, listen to concerts, or read novels, taking an economics course will increase your understanding when watching the news on TV or reading the newspaper.

DEFINING ECONOMICS

What is economics exactly? Some cynics have defined *economics* as "common sense made difficult." But common sense, by definition, should be within everyone's grasp. You will encounter in the following pages numerous examples that show that economics is, in fact, pure and simple common sense.

Economics is part of the social sciences and as such seeks explanations of real events. All social sciences analyze human behavior, as opposed to the physical sciences, which generally analyze the behavior of electrons, atoms, and other nonhuman phenomena.

Economics is the study of how people allocate their limited resources in an attempt to satisfy their unlimited wants. As such, economics is the study of how people make choices.

Economics 
The study of how people allocate their limited resources to satisfy their unlimited wants.

To understand this definition fully, two other words need explaining: *resources* and *wants*. **Resources** are things that have value and, more specifically, are used to produce things that satisfy people's wants. **Wants** are all of the things that people would consume if they had unlimited income.

Resources 
Things used to produce other things to satisfy people's wants.

Wants 
What people would buy if their incomes were unlimited.

Whenever an individual, a business, or a nation faces alternatives, a choice must be made, and economics helps us study how those choices are made. For example, you have to choose how to spend your limited income. You also have to choose how to spend your limited time. You may have to choose how much of your company's limited funds to spend on advertising and how much to spend on new-product research. In economics, we examine situations in which individuals choose how to do things, when to do things, and with whom to do them. Ultimately, the purpose of economics is to explain choices.

MICROECONOMICS VERSUS MACROECONOMICS 

Economics is typically divided into two types of analysis: **microeconomics** and **macroeconomics.**

Microeconomics is the part of economic analysis that studies decision making undertaken by individuals (or households) and by firms. It is like looking through a microscope to focus on the small parts of our economy.

Microeconomics 
The study of decision making undertaken by individuals (or households) and by firms.

Macroeconomics is the part of economic analysis that studies the behavior of the economy as a whole. It deals with economywide phenomena such as changes in unemployment, the general price level, and national income.

Macroeconomics 
The study of the behavior of the economy as a whole, including such economywide phenomena as changes in unemployment, the general price level, and national income.

Microeconomic analysis, for example, is concerned with the effects of changes in the price of gasoline relative to that of other energy sources. It examines the effects of new taxes on a specific product or industry. If price controls were reinstituted in the United States, how individual firms and consumers would react to them would be in the realm of microeconomics. The raising of wages by an effective union strike would also be analyzed using the tools of microeconomics.

By contrast, issues such as the rate of inflation, the amount of economywide unemployment, and the yearly growth in the output of goods and services in the nation all fall into the realm of macroeconomic analysis. In other words, macroeconomics deals with **aggregates,** or totals—such as total output in an economy.

Aggregates 
Total amounts or quantities; aggregate demand, for example, is total planned expenditures throughout a nation.

Be aware, however, of the blending of microeconomics and macroeconomics in modern economic theory. Modern economists are increasingly using microeconomic analysis—the study of decision making by individuals and by firms—as the basis of macroeconomic analysis. They do this because even though in macroeconomic analysis aggregates are being examined, those aggregates are the result of choices made by individuals and firms.

THE ECONOMIC PERSON: RATIONAL SELF-INTEREST 

Economists assume that individuals act *as if* motivated by self-interest and respond predictably to opportunities for gain. This central insight of economics was first clearly articulated by Adam Smith in 1776. Smith wrote in his most famous book, *An Inquiry into the*

Click here to explore whether it is in a consumer's self-interest to shop on the Internet. Click on "To e-shoppers".

Nature and Causes of the Wealth of Nations, that "it is not from the benevolence of the butcher, the brewer, or the baker that we expect our dinner, but from their regard to their own interest." Otherwise stated, the typical person about whom economists make behavioral predictions is assumed to act as though motivated by self interest. Because monetary benefits and costs of actions are often the most easily measured, economists most often make behavioral predictions about individuals' responses to ways to increase their wealth, measured in money terms. Let's see if we can apply the theory of rational self-interest to explain an anomaly concerning the makeup of the U.S. population.

EXAMPLE

The Increasing Native American Population

Look at Figure 1-1. You see that the proportion of Native Americans increased quite dramatically from 1970 to 1990. Can we use Adam Smith's ideas to understand why so many Native Americans have decided to rejoin their tribes? Perhaps. Consider the benefits of being a member of the Mdewakanton *(bday-WAH-kan-toon),* a tribe of about 100 that runs a casino in which gamblers in a recent year wagered over $500 million. Each member of the tribe received over $400,000 from the casino's profits. There is now a clear economic reason for Native Americans to return home. Over 200 of the nation's 544 tribes have introduced gambling of some sort, and almost half of those have big-time casinos. Reservations are grossing almost $6 billion a year from gaming. Tribe members sometimes get direct payments and others get the benefits of better health care, subsidized mortgages, and jobs. Self-identified Native Americans increased in number by 150 percent between 1970 and 2000.

For Critical Analysis

What nonmonetary reasons are there for Native Americans to rejoin their tribes?

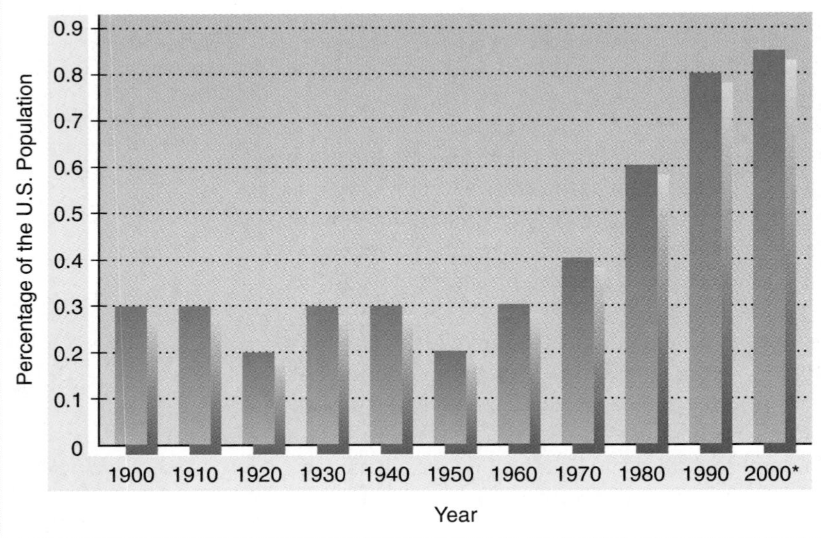

FIGURE 1-1
Native American Population of the United States
The percentage of the U.S. population identifying itself as Native American has increased substantially in recent decades. Is there an economic explanation for this demographic trend?

* Data for 2000 based on author's estimate

The Rationality Assumption

Rationality assumption 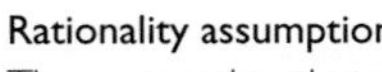
The assumption that people do not intentionally make decisions that would leave them worse off.

The **rationality assumption** of economics, simply stated, is as follows:

> We assume that individuals do not intentionally make decisions that would leave them worse off.

The distinction here is between what people may think—the realm of psychology and psychiatry and perhaps sociology—and what they do. Economics does *not* involve itself in analyzing individual or group thought processes. Economics looks at what people actually do in life with their limited resources. It does little good to criticize the rationality assumption by stating, "Nobody thinks that way" or "I never think that way" or "How unrealistic! That's as irrational as anyone can get!"

Take the example of driving. When you consider passing another car on a two-lane highway with oncoming traffic, you have to make very quick decisions: You must estimate the speed of the car that you are going to pass, the speed of the oncoming cars, the distance between your car and the oncoming cars, and your car's potential rate of acceleration. If we were to apply a model to your behavior, we would use the rules of calculus. In actual fact, you and most other drivers in such a situation do not actually think of using the rules of calculus, but to predict your behavior, we could make the prediction *as if* you understood the rules of calculus.

In any event, when you observe behavior around you, what may seem irrational often has its basis in the rationality assumption, as you can see by the following example.

EXAMPLE

When It May Be Rational *Not* to Learn New Technology

The standard young person's view of older people (particularly one's parents) is that they're reluctant to learn new things. The saying "You can't teach an old dog new tricks" seems to apply. Young people, in contrast, seem eager to learn about new technology—mastering computers and multimedia, playing interactive games, surfing the Internet. But there can be a rational reason for older people's reduced willingness to learn new technologies. If you are 20 years old and learn a new skill, you will be able to gain returns from your investment in learning over the course of many decades. If you are 60, however, and invest the same amount of time and effort learning the same skill, you will almost certainly not be able to reap those returns for as long a time period. Hence it can be perfectly rational for "old dogs" not to want to learn new tricks.

For Critical Analysis

Some older people do learn to use new technologies as they emerge. What might explain this behavior?

Responding to Incentives

If it can be assumed that individuals never intentionally make decisions that would leave them worse off, then almost by definition they will respond to different incentives. We define **incentives** as the potential rewards available if a particular activity is undertaken. Indeed, much of human behavior can be explained in terms of how individuals respond to changing incentives over time.

Incentives Rewards for engaging in a particular activity.

Schoolchildren are motivated to do better by a variety of incentive systems, ranging from gold stars and certificates of achievement when they are young to better grades with accompanying promises of a "better life" as they get older. There are, of course, negative incentives that affect our behavior, too. Children who disrupt the class are given after-school detention or sent to the vice principal for other punishment. Young people, like adults, respond to incentives.

For instance, consider the juvenile criminal justice system. Between the late 1970s and the mid-1990s, the number of arrests of adults for murder fell by 7 percent, but juvenile murder arrests increased by 177 percent. Arrests of juveniles for all violent crimes rose by 79 percent during the period, nearly three times the increase in adult arrests for these crimes.

Steven Levitt of the University of Chicago examined the incentives that juvenile criminals face. While the average number of adults incarcerated per violent crime rose by

60 percent over the same period, the corresponding ratio of juveniles imprisoned in youth detention centers *declined* by 20 percent. Levitt concluded that the probability of a juvenile offender's being jailed was less than half the probability of imprisonment that an adult faced.

Levitt also found changes in criminal behavior when youths face adult criminal justice at age 18. In states where incarceration rates for youths are high but those for adults are low, violent crimes committed by 18-year-olds rise by 23 percent. But crimes committed by 18-year-olds *fall* by 4 percent in states where incarceration rates for adults are relatively high.

Implicitly, all people, including juveniles contemplating crime, react to changing incentives after they have done some sort of rough comparison of the costs and benefits of various courses of action. In fact, making rational choices invariably involves balancing costs and benefits.

The linked concepts of incentives and costs and benefits can be used to explain much human behavior in the world around us. It can also explain how government policies can *induce* people to break the law.

INTERNATIONAL POLICY EXAMPLE

Chinese Smuggling

Recently, China's leaders announced the formation of a new antismuggling police force to try to stop the annual flow of tens of billions of dollars in illegal contraband.

One example of "illegal contraband" is cigarettes. Domestic taxes on cigarettes are so high that many Chinese cigarette manufacturers export half of their output, which they then smuggle back into China. Another example is diesel oil, the price of which the Chinese government sets at levels above prices elsewhere in the world. This gives consumers of diesel oil an incentive to smuggle foreign-produced diesel oil into the country.

Why does China need an antismuggling police force when it already has an army of border guards and customs inspectors? The answer is that the returns to smuggling are so high that many existing border guards and customs inspectors have become smugglers themselves. Thus the government feels that new police are needed in part to watch over the existing cadre of "law enforcers."

For Critical Analysis

What actions could the government take to end the incentives to smuggle cigarettes and diesel oil?

Defining Self-Interest

Self-interest does not always mean increasing one's wealth measured in dollars and cents. We assume that individuals seek many goals, not just increased wealth measured in monetary terms. Thus the self-interest part of our economic-person assumption includes goals relating to prestige, friendship, love, power, helping others, creating works of art, and many other matters. We can also think in terms of enlightened self-interest whereby individuals, in the pursuit of what makes them better off, also achieve the betterment of others around them. In brief, individuals are assumed to want the right to further their goals by making decisions about how things around them are used. The head of a charitable organization will usually not turn down an additional contribution because accepting it gains control over how that money is used, even if it is for other people's benefit.

Otherwise stated, charitable acts are not ruled out by self-interest. Giving gifts to relatives can be considered a form of charity that is nonetheless in the self-interest of the giver. But how efficient is such gift giving?

EXAMPLE

The Perceived Value of Gifts

Every holiday season, aunts, uncles, grandparents, mothers, and fathers give gifts to their college-aged loved ones. Joel Waldfogel, an economist at Yale University, surveyed several thousand college students after Christmas to find out the value of holiday gifts. He found that compact discs and outerwear (coats and jackets) had a perceived intrinsic value about equal to their actual cash equivalent. By the time he got down the list to socks, underwear, and cosmetics, the students' valuation was only about 85 percent of the cash value of the gift. He found out that aunts, uncles, and grandparents gave the "worst" gifts and friends, siblings, and parents gave the "best."

For Critical Analysis

What argument could you use against the idea of substituting cash or gift certificates for physical gifts?

CONCEPTS IN BRIEF

- Economics is a social science that involves the study of how individuals choose among alternatives to satisfy their wants, which are what people would buy if their incomes were unlimited.
- Microeconomics, the study of the decision-making processes of individuals (or households) and firms, and macroeconomics, the study of the performance of the economy as a whole, are the two main branches into which the study of economics is divided.
- In economics, we assume that people do not intentionally make decisions that will leave them worse off. This is known as the rationality assumption.
- Self-interest is not confined to material well-being but also involves any action that makes a person feel better off, such as having more friends, love, power, affection, or providing more help to others.

ECONOMICS AS A SCIENCE

Economics is a social science that employs the same kinds of methods used in other sciences, such as biology, physics, and chemistry. Like these other sciences, economics uses models, or theories. Economic **models,** or **theories,** are simplified representations of the real world that we use to help us understand, explain, and predict economic phenomena in the real world. There are, of course, differences between sciences. The social sciences—especially economics—make little use of laboratory methods in which changes in variables can be explained under controlled conditions. Rather, social scientists, and especially economists, usually have to examine what has already happened in the real world in order to test their models, or theories.

Models, or **theories**
Simplified representations of the real world used as the basis for predictions or explanations.

Models and Realism

At the outset it must be emphasized that no model in *any* science, and therefore no economic model, is complete in the sense that it captures *every* detail or interrelationship that exists. Indeed, a model, by definition, is an abstraction from reality. It is conceptually impossible to construct a perfectly complete realistic model. For example, in physics we cannot account for every molecule and its position and certainly not for every atom and subparticle. Not only is such a model impossibly expensive to build, but working with it would be impossibly complex.

The nature of scientific model building is such that the model should capture only the *essential* relationships that are sufficient to analyze the particular problem or answer the particular question with which we are concerned. *An economic model cannot be faulted as unrealistic simply because it does not represent every detail of the real world.* A map of a city that shows only major streets is not necessarily unrealistic if, in fact, all you need to know is how to pass through the city using major streets. As long as a model is realistic in terms of shedding light on the *central* issue at hand or forces at work, it may be useful.

A map is the quintessential model. It is always a simplified representation. It is always unrealistic. But it is also useful in making (refutable) predictions about the world. If the model—the map—predicts that when you take Campus Avenue to the north, you always run into the campus, that is a (refutable) prediction. If our goal is to explain observed behavior, the simplicity or complexity of the model we use is irrelevant. If a simple model can explain observed behavior in repeated settings just as well as a complex one, the simple model has some value and is probably easier to use.

Assumptions

Every model, or theory, must be based on a set of assumptions. Assumptions define the set of circumstances in which our model is most likely to be applicable. When scientists predicted that sailing ships would fall off the edge of the earth, they used the *assumption* that the earth was flat. Columbus did not accept the implications of such a model. He assumed that the world was round. The real-world test of his own model refuted the flat-earth model. Indirectly, then, it was a test of the assumption of the flat-earth model.

EXAMPLE

Getting Directions

Assumptions are a shorthand for reality. Imagine that you have decided to drive from your home in San Diego to downtown San Francisco. Because you have never driven this route, you decide to get directions from the local office of the American Automobile Association (AAA).

When you ask for directions, the travel planner could give you a set of detailed maps that shows each city through which you will travel—Oceanside, San Clemente, Irvine, Anaheim, Los Angeles, Bakersfield, Modesto, and so on—and then, opening each map, show you exactly how the freeway threads through each of these cities. You would get a nearly complete description of reality because the AAA travel planner will not have used many simplifying assumptions. It is more likely, however, that the travel planner will simply say, "Get on Interstate 5 going north. Stay on it for about 500 miles. Follow the signs for San Francisco. After crossing the toll bridge, take any exit marked 'Downtown.'" By omitting all of the trivial details, the travel planner has told you all that you really need and want to know. The models you will be using in this text are similar to the simplified directions on how to drive from San Diego to San Francisco—they focus on what is relevant to the problem at hand and omit what is not.

For Critical Analysis

In what way do small talk and gossip represent the use of simplifying assumptions?

Ceteris paribus [KAY-ter-us PEAR-uh-bus] assumption
The assumption that nothing changes except the factor or factors being studied.

The *Ceteris Paribus* Assumption: All Other Things Being Equal. Everything in the world seems to relate in some way to everything else in the world. It would be impossible to isolate the effects of changes in one variable on another variable if we always had to worry about the many other variables that might also enter the analysis. As in other sciences, economics uses the ***ceteris paribus*** **assumption.** *Ceteris paribus* means "other things constant" or "other things equal."

Consider an example taken from economics. One of the most important determinants of how much of a particular product a family buys is how expensive that product is relative to other products. We know that in addition to relative prices, other factors influence decisions about making purchases. Some of them have to do with income, others with tastes, and yet others with custom and religious beliefs. Whatever these other factors are, we hold them constant when we look at the relationship between changes in prices and changes in how much of a given product people will purchase.

Deciding on the Usefulness of a Model

We generally do not attempt to determine the usefulness, or "goodness," of a model merely by evaluating how realistic its assumptions are. Rather, we consider a model good if it yields usable predictions and implications for the real world. In other words, can we use the model to predict what will happen in the world around us? Does the model provide useful implications of how things happen in our world?

Once we have determined that the model does predict real-world phenomena, the scientific approach to the analysis of the world around us requires that we consider evidence. Evidence is used to test the usefulness of a model. This is why we call economics an **empirical** science, *empirical* meaning that evidence (data) is looked at to see whether we are right. Economists are often engaged in empirically testing their models.

Empirical
Relying on real-world data in evaluating the usefulness of a model.

Consider two competing models for the way students act when doing complicated probability problems to choose the best gambles. One model predicts that based on the assumption of rational self-interest, students who are paid more money for better performance will in fact perform better on average during the experiment. A competing model might be that students whose last names start with the letters *A* through *L* will do better than students with last names starting with *M* through *Z*, irrespective of how much they are paid. The model that consistently predicts more accurately is the model that we would normally choose. In this example, the "alphabet" model did not work well: The first letter of the last name of the students who actually did the experiment at UCLA was irrelevant in predicting how well they would perform the mathematical calculations necessary to choose the correct gambles. On average, students who received higher cash payments for better gambles did choose a higher percentage of better gambles. Thus the model based on rational self-interest predicted well.

Models of Behavior, Not Thought Processes

Take special note of the fact that economists' models do not relate to the way people *think;* they relate to the way people *act,* to what they do in life with their limited resources. Models tend to generalize human behavior. Normally, the economist does not attempt to predict how people will think about a particular topic, such as a higher price of oil products, accelerated inflation, or higher taxes. Rather, the task at hand is to

FAQ

Can economists rely on opinion polls to understand what motivates behavior?

No, most economists are leery of trying to glean much from opinion polls. For instance, a psychology study once revolved around polls asking people at various income levels how "happy" they were, based on a scale of 1 to 10. The researchers who conducted the study received responses that appeared to indicate that many rich people were less happy, leading the researchers to conclude that wealth can be associated with lower satisfaction. Economics is a science of *revealed* preferences, however. We find out virtually no useful information by asking people to rate their happiness levels on an arbitrary scale. In response to this particular study, a typical economist would note that if "too much" wealth makes people unhappy, they can always give it away. No one forces them to keep it. The fact that we rarely observe people disposing of their wealth causes an economist to infer that higher wealth must be preferred to lower wealth.

predict how people will act, which may be quite different from what they *say* they will do (much to the consternation of poll takers and market researchers). The people involved in examining thought processes are psychologists and psychiatrists, not typically economists.

EXAMPLE

Incentives Work for Pigeons and Rats, Too

Researchers at Texas A&M University did a series of experiments with pigeons and rats. They allowed them to "purchase" food and drink by pushing various levers. The "price" was the number of times a lever had to be pushed. A piece of cheese required 10 pushes, a drop of root beer only one. The "incomes" that the animals were given equaled a certain number of total pushes per day. Once the income was used up, the levers did not work. The researchers discovered that holding income constant, when the price of cheese went down, the animals purchased more cheese. Similarly, they found that when the price of root beer was increased, the animals purchased less root beer. These are exactly the predictions that we make about human behavior.

For Critical Analysis

"People respond to incentives." Is this assumption also usable in the animal world?

POSITIVE VERSUS NORMATIVE ECONOMICS 

Economics uses *positive analysis,* a value-free approach to inquiry. No subjective or moral judgments enter into the analysis. Positive analysis relates to statements such as "If A, then B." For example, "If the price of gasoline goes up relative to all other prices, then the amount of it that people will buy will fall." That is a positive economic statement. It is a statement of *what is.* It is not a statement of anyone's value judgment or subjective feelings. For many problems analyzed in the hard sciences such as physics and chemistry, the analyses are considered to be virtually value-free. After all, how can someone's values enter into a theory of molecular behavior? But economists face a different problem. They deal with the behavior of individuals, not molecules. That makes it more difficult to stick to what we consider to be value-free or **positive economics** without reference to our feelings.

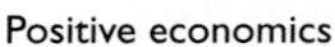
Positive economics 
Analysis that is strictly limited to making either purely descriptive statements or scientific predictions; for example, "If A, then B." A statement of *what is.*

Normative economics 
Analysis involving value judgments about economic policies; relates to whether things are good or bad. A statement of *what ought to be.*

When our values are interjected into the analysis, we enter the realm of **normative economics,** involving *normative analysis.* A positive economic statement is "If the price of gas rises, people will buy less." If we add to that analysis the statement "so we should not allow the price to go up," we have entered the realm of normative economics—we have expressed a value judgment. In fact, any time you see the word *should,* you will know that values are entering into the discussion. Just remember that positive statements are concerned with *what is,* whereas normative statements are concerned with *what ought to be.*

Each of us has a desire for different things. That means that we have different values. When we express a value judgment, we are simply saying what we prefer, like, or desire. Because individual values are diverse, we expect—and indeed observe—people expressing widely varying value judgments about how the world ought to be.

A Warning: Recognize Normative Analysis

It is easy to define positive economics. It is quite another matter to catch all unlabeled normative statements in a textbook, even though an author goes over the manuscript many times before it is printed. Therefore, do not get the impression that a textbook author will be able to keep all personal values out of the book. They will slip through. In fact, the very choice of which topics to include in an introductory textbook involves normative economics. There is no value-free, or objective, way to decide which topics to use in a textbook. The author's values ultimately make a difference when choices have to be made. But from your own standpoint, you might want to be able to recognize when you are engaging in normative as opposed to positive economic analysis. Reading this text will help equip you for that task.

CONCEPTS IN BRIEF

- A model, or theory, uses assumptions and is by nature a simplification of the real world. The usefulness of a model can be evaluated by bringing empirical evidence to bear on its predictions.
- Models are not necessarily deficient simply because they are unrealistic and use simplifying assumptions, for every model in every science requires simplification compared to the real world.
- Most models use the *ceteris paribus* assumption, that all other things are held constant, or equal.
- Positive economics is value-free and relates to statements that can be refuted, such as "If A, then B." Normative economics involves people's values, and normative statements typically contain the word *should.*

NETNOMICS

Is It Irrational for People to Pay Amazon.com More for a Book They Can Buy for Less at Books.com?

To try to understand how consumers respond to changing incentives they face now that they can purchase goods and services on the Internet, Erik Brynjolfsson and Michael Smith of the Massachusetts Institute of Technology gathered more than 10,000 observations of the prices charged by traditional brick-and-mortar bookstores and Internet booksellers. What they found was what most economists would predict: The lower costs faced by Internet booksellers allowed them to charge about 8 percent less for a given book than traditional bookstores. Furthermore, the cost advantage of Internet booksellers allowed them to gain market share at the expense of traditional stores. (Indeed, some brick-and-mortar bookstores initially included in the study went out of business before the study ended.)

One finding seemed surprising, however. Amazon.com, which garnered an 80 percent share of all Internet-based book sales, charged an average of $1.60 more per book than Books.com, another Internet bookseller (now part of barnesandnoble.com). Yet Books.com could not seem to push its market share much above 2 percent during the period of the study. On the surface, this seemed to imply irrational consumers. After all, wouldn't everyone want to choose Books.com and save $1.60 per book?

As the authors point out, this would be true only if the *ceteris paribus* assumption had been satisfied. In their study, however, it was not. For one thing, Amazon.com spent a considerable amount on advertising and got a jump start on its Internet competitors. Indeed, even today, a great many Internet users have heard of Amazon.com but are unfamiliar with its competitors. This made Brynjolfsson and Smith wonder if perhaps people felt confident that Amazon.com really would deliver but might not have as much faith in less well-known Internet companies. Thus part of the $1.60 difference in the average price of a book might amount to a "trust premium." Furthermore, Brynjolfsson and Smith's study did not take into account differences in features of the two companies' Web sites. If people already knew how to use the Amazon.com Web site, then a legitimate question to ask is, would the average person consider $1.60 enough to compensate for having to learn how to order a book from another Web site?

ISSUES & APPLICATIONS

Marriage Isn't a Marxist Utopia, but It Can Pay Off

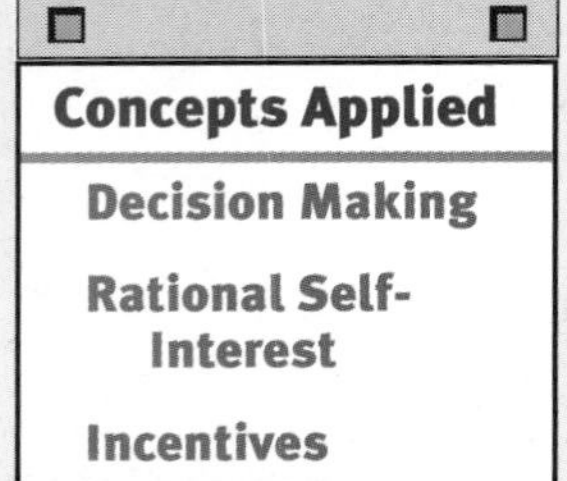

Concepts Applied
Decision Making
Rational Self-Interest
Incentives

Karl Marx was a German economist who wrote a treatise called *Das Kapital* (Capital), in which he proposed that labor is the fundamental source of all value. With Friedrich Engels, he wrote an even more famous book, *The Communist Manifesto,* in which he promoted the virtues of state socialism. Economists largely have rejected his theory of value as overly narrow, and communism is on the decline worldwide. Nevertheless, Marx left a lasting legacy: the idea that people could achieve a perfect world, commonly called a *utopia.* The word was coined by Sir Thomas More in his book about a fictitious island by that name. More called his land Utopia (Greek for "no place") because he knew that a perfect world is impossible to achieve.

Nevertheless, on their wedding day, many women and men think they are entering a personal utopia: They convince themselves that they are embarking on the "perfect marriage." Jennifer Roback Morse of the Hoover Institution has written, "Utopianism in politics is destructive: Perfectionism in human relationships can be, too. The Marxist search for a perfect society has cost millions of lives. The American yearning for perfect marriages probably has ruined many lives."

Marriage as an Exercise in Self-Interest

A number of couples, however, remain married for decades even when they know that their marriages are imperfect. To outsiders looking at such a married couple and observing one spouse silently suffering for years while the other spouse continually behaves in some socially unacceptable manner, the rationality of the marriage can be hard to fathom. To an economist, this makes the institution of marriage an especially interesting case study of human choice.

Throughout history, literally billions of people have chosen to be married and to put up with the faults of their matrimonial partners. Why do they do this? One reason that economists have offered is that spouses show consideration for their marriage partners in the hope or expectation that the favor will be returned. This is self-interest at work. In addition, by entering into and staying faithful to a marriage, one spouse establishes a reputation with the other. By honoring their commitment to the marriage, they show more broadly that they are not afraid of commitments. This gives both a greater incentive to trust each other when they make joint financial decisions. By pooling their resources, both marriage partners can thereby make themselves better off than they would be alone. This is also an example of people responding in a self-interested way to incentives they face.

"Shotgun Weddings" and the Marriage Premium

Economists have evidence that there is something to this story. Recall from the opening to this chapter that most married men earn more than unmarried men. Donna Ginther of Washington University and Madeline Zavodny of the Federal Reserve Bank of Atlanta tried to evaluate whether this marriage premium is simply due to beneficial effects of marriage for men or instead results from careful spousal choices by women seeking committed husbands. To do this, they compared the wages of men married in so-called shotgun weddings—marriages followed within, say, seven months by the birth of a child—with the wages of men whose wives did not bear children until later on. After controlling for other factors, they found that men married in shotgun weddings typically did not earn a marriage premium. Presumably, many men in such situations are less committed to the marriage. Nevertheless, women expecting children may feel that their choices are constrained, so they are less likely to reject the marriage partner in a shotgun wedding. Thus it appears that in most instances, the marriage premium applies to the husbands of women who feel less constrained in choosing their mates.

FOR CRITICAL ANALYSIS

1. So far there is little evidence of a marriage premium for women. Can you think of any reasons why this is so?
2. What is the economic role of love in marriage?

SUMMARY DISCUSSION OF LEARNING OBJECTIVES

1. **Microeconomics Versus Macroeconomics:** In general, economics is the study of how individuals make choices to satisfy wants. Economics is usually divided into microeconomics, which is the study of individual decision making by households and firms, and macroeconomics, which is the study of nationwide phenomena, such as inflation and unemployment.
2. **Self-Interest in Economic Analysis:** Rational self-interest is the assumption that individuals behave in a reasonable (rational) way in making choices to further their interests. That is, economists assume that individuals never intentionally make decisions that would leave them worse off. Instead, they are motivated primarily by their self-interest, keeping in mind that self-interest can relate to monetary and nonmonetary objectives, such as love, prestige, and helping others.
3. **Economics as a Science:** Like other scientists, economists use models, or theories, that are simplified representations of the real world to analyze and make predictions about the real world. Economic models are never completely realistic because by definition they are simplifications using assumptions that are not directly testable. Nevertheless, economists can subject the predictions of economic theories to empirical tests in which real-world data are used to decide whether or not to reject the predictions.
4. **The Difference Between Positive and Normative Economics:** Positive economics deals with *what is,* whereas normative economics deals with *what ought to be.* Positive economic statements are of the "if . . . then" variety; they are descriptive and predictive and are not related to what "should" happen. By contrast, whenever statements embodying values are made, we enter the realm of normative economics, or how individuals and groups think things ought to be.

Key Terms and Concepts

Aggregates (5)
Ceteris paribus assumption (10)
Economics (5)
Empirical (11)
Incentives (7)
Macroeconomics (5)
Microeconomics (5)
Models, or theories (9)
Normative economics (12)
Positive economics (12)
Rationality assumption (6)
Resources (5)
Wants (5)

Problems

Answers to the odd-numbered problems appear at the back of the book.

1-1. Some people claim that the "economic way of thinking" does not apply to issues such as health care. Explain how economics does apply to this issue by developing a "model" of an individual's choice.

1-2. In a single sentence, contrast microeconomics and macroeconomics. Next, categorize the following issues as either a microeconomic issue, a macroeconomic issue, or not an economic issue.

- **a.** The national unemployment rate
- **b.** The decision of a worker to work overtime or not
- **c.** A family's choice of having a baby
- **d.** The rate of growth of the money supply
- **e.** The national government's budget deficit
- **f.** A student's allocation of study time across two subjects

1-3. One of your classmates, Sally, is a hardworking student, serious about her classes, and conscientious about her grades. Sally is also involved, however, in volunteer activities and an extracurricular sport. Is Sally displaying rational behavior? Based on what you read in this chapter, construct an argument supporting the conclusion that she is.

1-4. You have 10 hours in which to study for both a French test and an economics test. Construct a model to determine your allocation of study hours. Include as assumptions the points you "gain" from an hour of study time in each subject and your desired outcome on each test.

1-5. Use the model you constructed in Problem 1-4 to determine the allocation of study time across subjects.

1-6. Suppose you followed the model you constructed in Problem 1-4. Explain how you would "grade" the model.

1-7. Write a sentence contrasting positive and normative economic analysis.

1-8. Based on your answer to Problem 1-7, categorize the following conclusions as the result of positive analysis or normative analysis.

- **a.** Increasing the minimum wage will reduce minimum wage employment opportunities.
- **b.** Increasing the prospects of minimum wage employees is desirable, and raising the minimum wage is the best way to accomplish this.
- **c.** Everyone should enjoy open access to health care.
- **d.** Heath care subsidies will increase the demands for health care.

1-9. Consider the following statements, based on a positive economic analysis that assumes that all other things remain constant. List one other thing that might change and offset the outcome stated.

- **a.** Increased demand for laptop computers will drive up their price.
- **b.** Falling gasoline prices will result in additional vacation travel.
- **c.** A reduction of income tax rates will result in more people working.

1-10. Alan Greenspan, chairman of the U.S. Federal Reserve, referred to the high stock market prices of the late 1990s as a result of "irrational exuberance." Counter this statement by considering the rationality of stock market investors.

Economics on the Net

The Usefulness of Studying Economics This application helps you see how accomplished people benefited from their study of economics. It also explores ways in which these people feel others of all walks of life can gain from learning more about the economics field.

Navigation: Click here to visit the the Federal Reserve Bank of Minneapolis homepage. To access eonomics in *The Region* on Their Student Experiences and the Need for Economic Literacy, under Publications, click on *The Region.* Select the index of all issues and click on December 1998. Select the last article of the issue, Economics in *The Region* on Their Student Experiences and the Need for Economic Literacy.

Application Read the interviews of the six economists, and answer the following questions.

1. Based on your reading, what economists do you think other economists regard as influential? What educational institutions do you think are the most influential in economics?
2. Which economists do you think were attracted to microeconomics and which to macroeconomics?

For Group Study and Analysis Divide the class into three groups, and assign the groups the Blinder, Yellen, and Rivlin interviews. Have each group use the content of its assigned interview to develop a statement explaining why the study of economics is important, regardless of a student's chosen major.

APPENDIX A

READING AND WORKING WITH GRAPHS

Independent variable 
A variable whose value is determined independently of, or outside, the equation under study.

Dependent variable 
A variable whose value changes according to changes in the value of one or more independent variables.

A graph is a visual representation of the relationship between variables. In this appendix, we'll stick to just two variables: an **independent variable,** which can change in value freely, and a **dependent variable,** which changes only as a result of changes in the value of the independent variable. For example, if nothing else is changing in your life, your weight depends on the amount of food you eat. Food is the independent variable and weight the dependent variable.

A table is a list of numerical values showing the relationship between two (or more) variables. Any table can be converted into a graph, which is a visual representation of that list. Once you understand how a table can be converted to a graph, you will understand what graphs are and how to construct and use them.

Consider a practical example. A conservationist may try to convince you that driving at lower highway speeds will help you conserve gas. Table A-1 shows the relationship between speed—the independent variable—and the distance you can go on a gallon of gas at that speed—the dependent variable. This table does show a pattern of sorts. As the data in the first column get larger in value, the data in the second column get smaller.

Now let's take a look at the different ways in which variables can be related.

TABLE A-1
Gas Mileage as a Function of Driving Speed

Miles per Hour	Miles per Gallon
45	25
50	24
55	23
60	21
65	19
70	16
75	13

DIRECT AND INVERSE RELATIONSHIPS

Direct relationship 
A relationship between two variables that is positive, meaning that an increase in one variable is associated with an increase in the other and a decrease in one variable is associated with a decrease in the other.

Inverse relationship 
A relationship between two variables that is negative, meaning that an increase in one variable is associated with a decrease in the other and a decrease in one variable is associated with an increase in the other.

Two variables can be related in different ways, some simple, others more complex. For example, a person's weight and height are often related. If we measured the height and weight of thousands of people, we would surely find that taller people tend to weigh more than shorter people. That is, we would discover that there is a **direct relationship** between height and weight. By this we simply mean that an *increase* in one variable is usually associated with an *increase* in the related variable. This can easily be seen in panel (a) of Figure A-1.

Let's look at another simple way in which two variables can be related. Much evidence indicates that as the price of a specific commodity rises, the amount purchased decreases—there is an **inverse relationship** between the variable's price per unit and quantity purchased. A table listing the data for this relationship would indicate that for higher and higher prices, smaller and smaller quantities would be purchased. We see this relationship in panel (b) of Figure A-1.

FIGURE A-1
Relationships

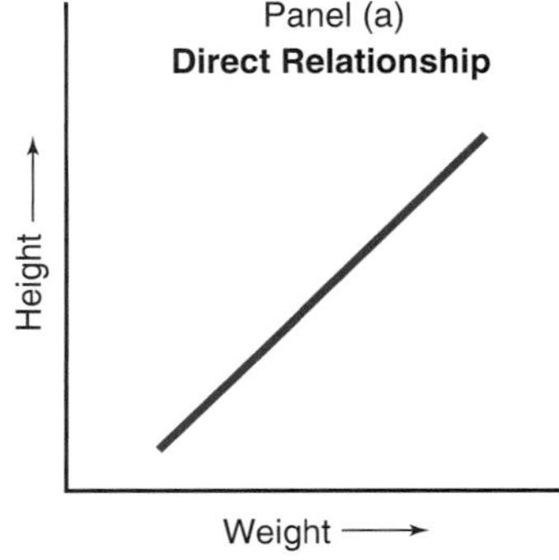

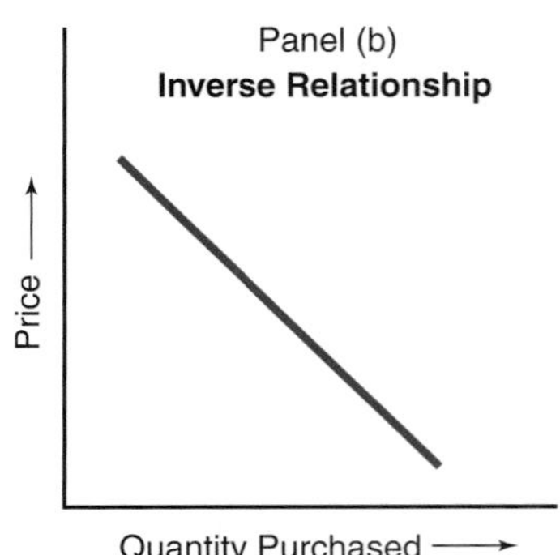

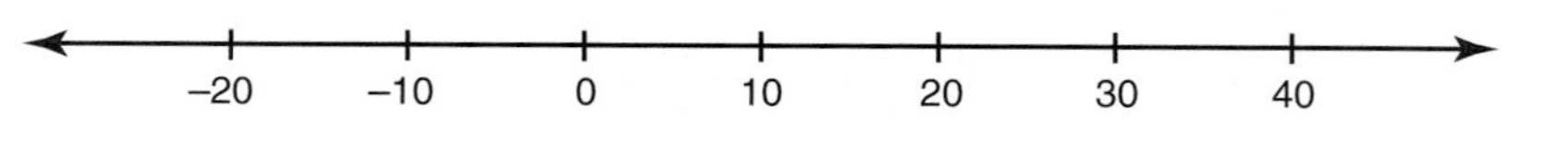

FIGURE A-2
Horizontal Number Line

CONSTRUCTING A GRAPH

Let us now examine how to construct a graph to illustrate a relationship between two variables.

A Number Line

The first step is to become familiar with what is called a **number line.** One is shown in Figure A-2. There are two things that you should know about it.

Number line
A line that can be divided into segments of equal length, each associated with a number.

1. The points on the line divide the line into equal segments.
2. The numbers associated with the points on the line increase in value from left to right; saying it the other way around, the numbers decrease in value from right to left. However you say it, what we're describing is formally called an *ordered set of points.*

On the number line, we have shown the line segments—that is, the distance from 0 to 10 or the distance between 30 and 40. They all appear to be equal and, indeed, are equal to $\frac{1}{2}$ inch. When we use a distance to represent a quantity, such as barrels of oil, graphically, we are *scaling* the number line. In the example shown, the distance between 0 and 10 might represent 10 barrels of oil, or the distance from 0 to 40 might represent 40 barrels. Of course, the scale may differ on different number lines. For example, a distance of 1 inch could represent 10 units on one number line but 5,000 units on another. Notice that on our number line, points to the left of 0 correspond to negative numbers and points to the right of 0 correspond to positive numbers.

Of course, we can also construct a vertical number line. Consider the one in Figure A-3. As we move up this vertical number line, the numbers increase in value; conversely, as we descend, they decrease in value. Below 0 the numbers are negative, and above 0 the numbers are positive. And as on the horizontal number line, all the line segments are equal. This line is divided into segments such that the distance between −2 and −1 is the same as the distance between 0 and 1.

FIGURE A-3
Vertical Number Line

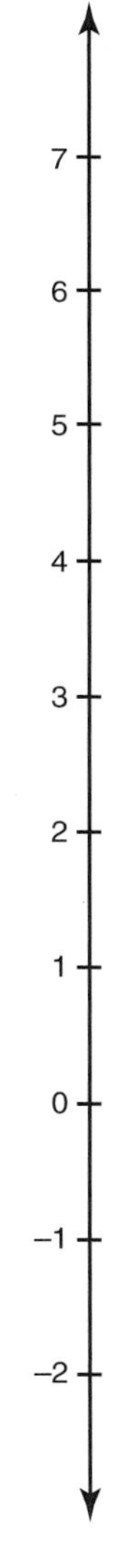

Combining Vertical and Horizontal Number Lines

By drawing the horizontal and vertical lines on the same sheet of paper, we are able to express the relationships between variables graphically. We do this in Figure A-4.

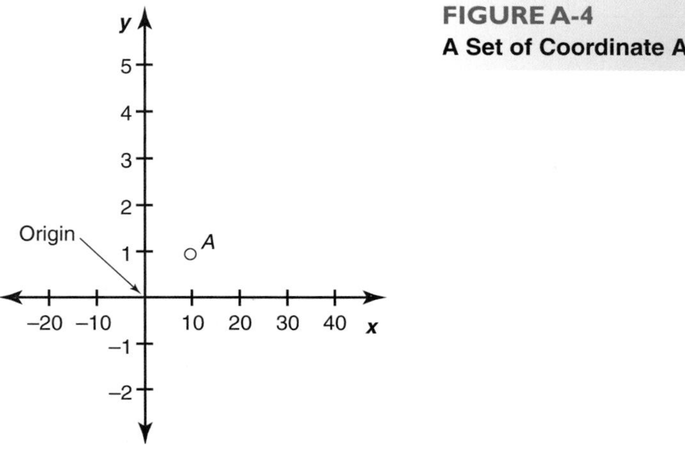

FIGURE A-4
A Set of Coordinate Axes

We draw them (1) so that they intersect at each other's 0 point and (2) so that they are perpendicular to each other. The result is a set of coordinate axes, where each line is called an *axis*. When we have two axes, they span a *plane*.

For one number line, you need only one number to specify any point on the line; equivalently, when you see a point on the line, you know that it represents one number or one value. With a coordinate value system, you need two numbers to specify a single point in the plane; when you see a single point on a graph, you know that it represents two numbers or two values.

y axis The vertical axis in a graph.

x axis The horizontal axis in a graph.

Origin The intersection of the *y* axis and the *x* axis in a graph.

The basic things that you should know about a coordinate number system are that the vertical number line is referred to as the ***y* axis,** the horizontal number line is referred to as the ***x* axis,** and the point of intersection of the two lines is referred to as the **origin.**

Any point such as *A* in Figure A-4 represents two numbers—a value of *x* and a value of *y*. But we know more than that; we also know that point *A* represents a positive value of *y* because it is above the *x* axis, and we know that it represents a positive value of *x* because it is to the right of the *y* axis.

Point *A* represents a "paired observation" of the variables *x* and *y;* in particular, in Figure A-4, *A* represents an observation of the pair of values $x = 10$ and $y = 1$. Every point in the coordinate system corresponds to a paired observation of *x* and *y,* which can be simply written (x, y)—the *x* value is always specified first, then the *y* value. When we give the values associated with the position of point *A* in the coordinate number system, we are in effect giving the coordinates of that point. *A*'s coordinates are $x = 10$, $y = 1$, or (10, 1).

TABLE A-2
T-Shirts Purchased

(1) Price of T-Shirts	(2) Number of T-Shirts Purchased per Week
$10	20
9	30
8	40
7	50
6	60
5	70

GRAPHING NUMBERS IN A TABLE

Consider Table A-2. Column 1 shows different prices for T-shirts, and column 2 gives the number of T-shirts purchased per week at these prices. Notice the pattern of these numbers. As the price of T-shirts falls, the number of T-shirts purchased per week increases. Therefore, an inverse relationship exists between these two variables, and as soon as we represent it on a graph, you will be able to see the relationship. We can graph this relationship using a coordinate number system—a vertical and horizontal number line for each of these two variables. Such a graph is shown in panel (b) of Figure A-5.

FIGURE A-5
Graphing the Relationship Between T-Shirts Purchased and Price

Panel (a)

Price per T-Shirt	T-Shirts Purchased per Week	Point on Graph
$10	20	*I* (20, 10)
9	30	*J* (30, 9)
8	40	*K* (40, 8)
7	50	*L* (50, 7)
6	60	*M* (60, 6)
5	70	*N* (70, 5)

Panel (b)

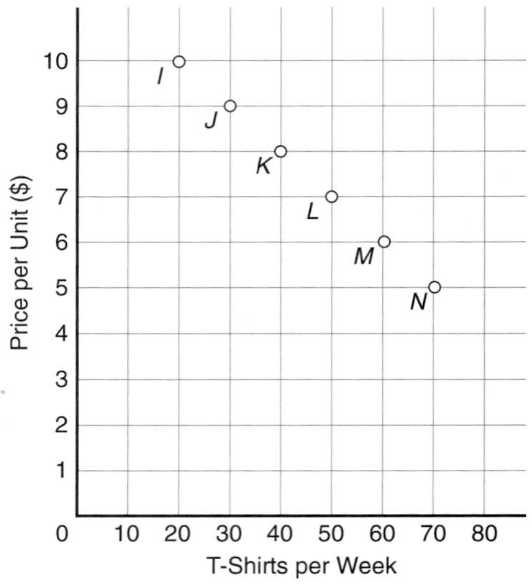

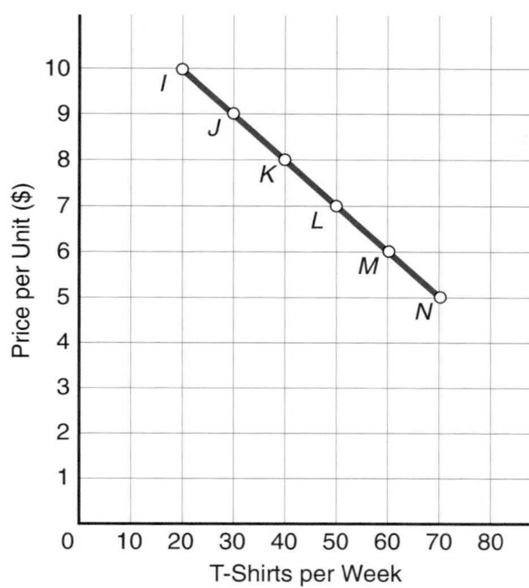

FIGURE A-6
Connecting the Observation Points

In economics, it is conventional to put dollar values on the *y* axis. We therefore construct a vertical number line for price and a horizontal number line, the *x* axis, for quantity of T-shirts purchased per week. The resulting coordinate system allows the plotting of each of the paired observation points; in panel (a), we repeat Table A-2, with a column added expressing these points in paired-data (*x, y*) form. For example, point *J* is the paired observation (30, 9). It indicates that when the price of a T-shirt is $9, 30 will be purchased per week.

If it were possible to sell parts of a T-shirt ($\frac{1}{2}$ or $\frac{1}{20}$ of a shirt), we would have observations at every possible price. That is, we would be able to connect our paired observations, represented as lettered points. Let's assume that we can make T-shirts perfectly divisible so that the linear relationship shown in Figure A-5 also holds for fractions of dollars and T-shirts. We would then have a line that connects these points, as shown in the graph in Figure A-6.

In short, we have now represented the data from the table in the form of a graph. Note that an inverse relationship between two variables shows up on a graph as a line or curve that slopes *downward* from left to right. (You might as well get used to the idea that economists call a straight line a "curve" even though it may not curve at all. Much of economists' data turn out to be curves, so they refer to everything represented graphically, even straight lines, as curves.)

THE SLOPE OF A LINE (A LINEAR CURVE)

An important property of a curve represented on a graph is its *slope*. Consider Figure A-7, which represents the quantities of shoes per week that a seller is willing to offer at different prices. Note that in panel (a) of Figure A-7, as in Figure A-5, we have expressed the coordinates of the points in parentheses in paired-data form.

Slope 
The change in the *y* value divided by the corresponding change in the *x* value of a curve; the "incline" of the curve.

The **slope** of a line is defined as the change in the *y* values divided by the corresponding change in the *x* values as we move along the line. Let's move from point *E* to point *D* in panel (b) of Figure A-7. As we move, we note that the change in the *y* values, which is the change in price, is +$20, because we have moved from a price of $20 to a price of $40 per pair. As we move from *E* to *D,* the change in the *x* values is +80; the number of pairs of shoes willingly offered per week rises from 80 to 160 pairs. The slope calculated as a change in the *y* values divided by the change in the *x* values is therefore

$$\frac{20}{80} = \frac{1}{4}$$

FIGURE A-7
A Positively Sloped Curve

Panel (a)

Price per Pair	Pairs of Shoes Offered per Week	Point on Graph
$100	400	*A* (400,100)
80	320	*B* (320, 80)
60	240	*C* (240, 60)
40	160	*D* (160, 40)
20	80	*E* (80, 20)

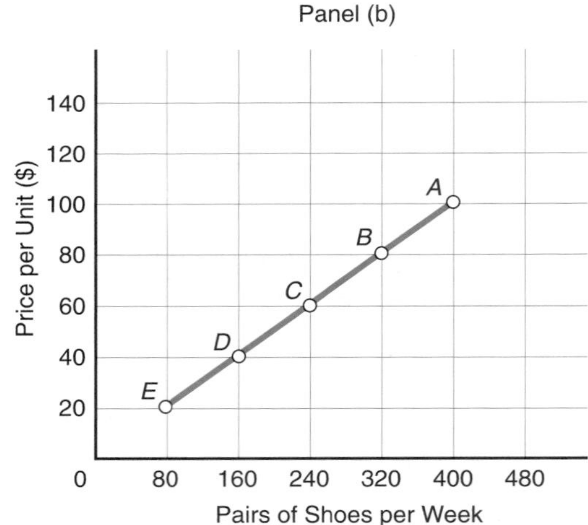

It may be helpful for you to think of slope as a "rise" (movement in the vertical direction) over a "run" (movement in the horizontal direction). We show this abstractly in Figure A-8. The slope is measured by the amount of rise divided by the amount of run. In the example in Figure A-8, and of course in Figure A-7, the amount of rise is positive and so is the amount of run. That's because it's a direct relationship. We show an inverse relationship in Figure A-9. The slope is still equal to the rise divided by the run, but in this case the rise and the run have opposite signs because the curve slopes downward. That means that the slope will have to be negative and that we are dealing with an inverse relationship.

Now let's calculate the slope for a different part of the curve in panel (b) of Figure A-7. We will find the slope as we move from point *B* to point *A*. Again, we note that the slope, or rise over run, from *B* to *A* equals

$$\frac{20}{80} = \frac{1}{4}$$

A specific property of a straight line is that its slope is the same between any two points; in other words, the slope is constant at all points on a straight line in a graph.

We conclude that for our example in Figure A-7, the relationship between the price of a pair of shoes and the number of pairs of shoes willingly offered per week is *linear,* which simply means "in a straight line," and our calculations indicate a constant slope. Moreover, we calculate a direct relationship between these two variables, which turns out to be an

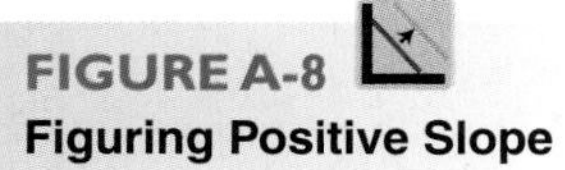

FIGURE A-8
Figuring Positive Slope

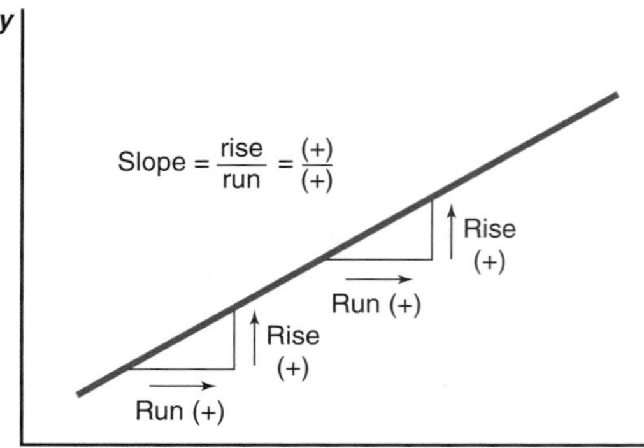

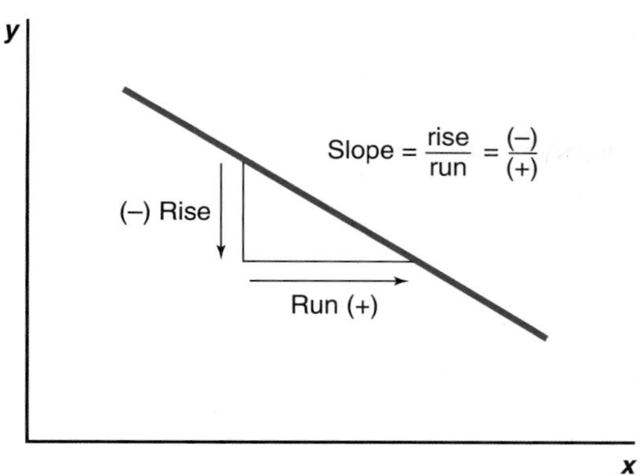

FIGURE A-9
Figuring Negative Slope

upward-sloping (from left to right) curve. Upward-sloping curves have positive slopes—in this case, it is $+\frac{1}{4}$.

We know that an inverse relationship between two variables shows up as a downward-sloping curve—rise over run will be a negative slope because the rise and run have opposite signs, as shown in Figure A-9. When we see a negative slope, we know that increases in one variable are associated with decreases in the other. Therefore, we say that downward-sloping curves have negative slopes. Can you verify that the slope of the graph representing the relationship between T-shirt prices and the quantity of T-shirts purchased per week in Figure A-6 is $-\frac{1}{10}$?

Slopes of Nonlinear Curves

The graph presented in Figure A-10 indicates a *nonlinear* relationship between two variables, total profits and output per unit of time. Inspection of this graph indicates that at first, increases in output lead to increases in total profits; that is, total profits rise as output increases. But beyond some output level, further increases in output cause decreases in total profits.

Can you see how this curve rises at first, reaches a peak at point *C*, and then falls? This curve relating total profits to output levels appears mountain-shaped.

Considering that this curve is nonlinear (it is obviously not a straight line), should we expect a constant slope when we compute changes in *y* divided by corresponding changes in *x* in moving from one point to another? A quick inspection, even without specific numbers, should lead us to conclude that the slopes of lines joining different points in this curve, such as between *A* and *B*, *B* and *C*, or *C* and *D*, will *not* be the same. The curve slopes upward (in a positive direction) for some values and downward (in a negative direction) for

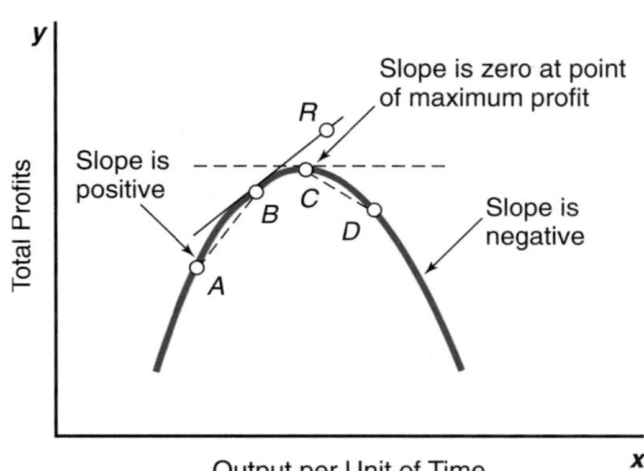

FIGURE A-10
The Slope of a Nonlinear Curve

other values. In fact, the slope of the line between any two points on this curve will be different from the slope of the line between any two other points. Each slope will be different as we move along the curve.

Instead of using a line between two points to discuss slope, mathematicians and economists prefer to discuss the slope *at a particular point.* The slope at a point on the curve, such as point *B* in the graph in Figure A-10, is the slope of a line *tangent* to that point. A tangent line is a straight line that touches a curve at only one point. For example, it might be helpful to think of the tangent at *B* as the straight line that just "kisses" the curve at point *B.*

To calculate the slope of a tangent line, you need to have some additional information besides the two values of the point of tangency. For example, in Figure A-10, if we knew that the point *R* also lay on the tangent line and we knew the two values of that point, we could calculate the slope of the tangent line. We could calculate rise over run between points *B* and *R,* and the result would be the slope of the line tangent to the one point *B* on the curve.

Appendix Summary

1. Direct relationships involve a dependent variable changing in the same direction as the change in the independent variable.
2. Inverse relationships involve the dependent variable changing in the opposite direction of the change in the independent variable.
3. When we draw a graph showing the relationship between two economic variables, we are holding all other things constant (the Latin term for which is *ceteris paribus*).
4. We obtain a set of coordinates by putting vertical and horizontal number lines together. The vertical line is called the *y* axis; the horizontal line, the *x* axis.
5. The slope of any linear (straight-line) curve is the change in the *y* values divided by the corresponding change in the *x* values as we move along the line. Otherwise stated, the slope is calculated as the amount of rise over the amount of run, where rise is movement in the vertical direction and run is movement in the horizontal direction.
6. The slope of a nonlinear curve changes; it is positive when the curve is rising and negative when the curve is falling. At a maximum or minimum point, the slope of the nonlinear curve is zero.

Key Terms and Concepts

Dependent variable (18)
Direct relationship (18)
Independent variable (18)
Inverse relationship (18)
Number line (19)
Origin (20)
Slope (21)
x axis (20)
y axis (20)

Problems Test

Answers to the odd-numbered problems appear at the back of the book.

A-1. Explain which is the independent variable and which is the dependent variable for the following examples.

a. Once you determine the price of a notebook at the college bookstore, you will decide how many notebooks to buy.

b. You will decide how many credit hours to register for this semester once the university tells you how many work-study hours you will be assigned.

c. You are anxious to receive your economics exam grade because you studied many hours in the weeks preceding the exam.

A-2. For the following items, state whether a direct or an inverse relationship is likely to exist.

a. The number of hours you study for an exam and your exam score
b. The price of pizza and the quantity purchased
c. The number of games the university basketball team won last year and the number of season tickets sold this year

A-3. Review Figure A-4, and then state whether the following paired observations are on, above, or below the x axis and on, to the left of, or to the right of the y axis.

a. $(-10, 4)$
b. $(20, -2)$
c. $(10, 0)$

A-4. State whether the following functions are linear or nonlinear.

a. $y = 5x$
b. $y = 5x^2$
c. $y = 3 + x$
d. $y = -3x$

A-5. Given the function $y = 5x$, complete the following schedule and plot the curve.

y	x
	-4
	-2
	0
	2
	4

A-6. Given the function $y = 5x^2$, complete the following schedule and plot the curve.

y	x
	-4
	-2
	0
	2
	4

A-7. Calculate the slope of the function you graphed in Problem A-5.

A-8. Indicate at each ordered pair whether the slope of the curve you plotted in Problem A-6 is positive, negative, or zero.

A-9. State whether the following functions imply a positive or negative relationship between x and y.

a. $y = 5x$
b. $y = 3 + x$
c. $y = -3x$

CHAPTER

2

SCARCITY AND THE WORLD OF TRADE-OFFS

This harried father tries to balance the demands of work with those of child rearing. Why does it typically cost more for higher-income-earning parents to raise children than for those earning less income?

In Chapter 1, you learned that men and women can have good economic reasons to marry. Because children traditionally shared the family workload, couples have also had a strong incentive to have children. In most developed nations, however, this incentive for having children has largely disappeared. Even on today's "family farms," many tasks are now mechanized and even automated.

At the same time, the costs of raising children have increased. Of course, parents have always housed, fed, and clothed their children. In addition, they have sacrificed to provide "quality time" with their children. For many people today, the value of that time is greater than it was in years past. In this chapter you will learn how to put a value on time spent with children. This will help you understand why children are a more costly "commodity" than they used to be.

LEARNING OBJECTIVES

After reading this chapter, you should be able to:

1. Evaluate whether even affluent people face the problem of scarcity
2. Understand why economics considers individuals' "wants" but not their "needs"
3. Explain why the scarcity problem induces individuals to consider opportunity costs
4. Discuss why obtaining increasing increments of any particular good typically entails giving up more and more units of other goods
5. Explain why society faces a trade-off between consumption goods and capital goods
6. Distinguish between absolute and comparative advantage

Did You Know That... Chris Van Horn, president of CVK Group in Washington, D.C., grosses over $200,000 a year for having people wait in line? Adam Goldin loves working as a "line waiter" because he gets paid for "doing nothing." His job is to arrive early in the morning on Capitol Hill to hold places for lobbyists who must attend congressional hearings. Van Horn charges his more than 100 lobbyists and law firm clients $27 an hour and pays his part-time line waiters like Mr. Goldin $10 an hour. For example, when Congress was going to hold hearings for the proposed 1997 tax cut, $10-an-hour professional standees arrived to hold places for $300-an-hour lobbyists who would not show up until hours later. After all, lobbyists do not have an unlimited amount of time. Their time is scarce. It is worth more than what they are charged to "save" it.

Chapter Outline

SCARCITY

Whenever individuals or communities cannot obtain everything they desire simultaneously, choices occur. Choices occur because of *scarcity.* **Scarcity** is the most basic concept in all of economics. Scarcity means that we do not ever have enough of everything, including time, to satisfy our *every* desire. Scarcity exists because human wants always exceed what can be produced with the limited resources and time that nature makes available.

Scarcity 
A situation in which the ingredients for producing the things that people desire are insufficient to satisfy all wants.

What Scarcity Is Not

Scarcity is not a shortage. After a hurricane hits and cuts off supplies to a community, TV newscasts often show people standing in line to get minimum amounts of cooking fuel and food. A news commentator might say that the line is caused by the "scarcity" of these products. But cooking fuel and food are always scarce—we cannot obtain all that we want at a zero price. Therefore, do not confuse the concept of scarcity, which is general and all-encompassing, with the concept of shortages as evidenced by people waiting in line to obtain a particular product.

Scarcity is not the same thing as poverty. Scarcity occurs among the poor and among the rich. Even the richest person on earth faces scarcity because available time is limited. Low income levels do not create more scarcity. High income levels do not create less scarcity.

Scarcity is a fact of life, like gravity. And just as physicists did not invent gravity, economists did not invent scarcity—it existed well before the first economist ever lived. It exists even when we are not using all of our resources.

Scarcity and Resources 

The scarcity concept arises from the fact that resources are insufficient to satisfy our every desire. Resources are the inputs used in the production of the things that we want. **Production** can be defined as virtually any activity that results in the conversion of resources into products that can be used in consumption. Production includes delivering things from one part of the country to another. It includes taking ice from an ice tray to put it in your soft-drink glass. The resources used in production are called *factors of production,* and some economists use the terms *resources* and *factors of production* interchangeably. The total quantity of all resources that an economy has at any one time determines what that economy can produce.

Production 
Any activity that results in the conversion of resources into products that can be used in consumption.

Land 
The natural resources that are available from nature. Land as a resource includes location, original fertility and mineral deposits, topography, climate, water, and vegetation.

Labor  
Productive contributions of humans who work, involving both mental and physical activities.

Physical capital 
All manufactured resources, including buildings, equipment, machines, and improvements to land that is used for production.

Human capital 
The accumulated training and education of workers.

Entrepreneurship 
The factor of production involving human resources that perform the functions of raising capital, organizing, managing, assembling other factors of production, and making basic business policy decisions. The entrepreneur is a risk taker.

Factors of production can be classified in many ways. Here is one such classification:

1. Land. **Land** encompasses all the nonhuman gifts of nature, including timber, water, fish, minerals, and the original fertility of land. It is often called the *natural resource.*
2. Labor. **Labor** is the human resource, which includes all productive contributions made by individuals who work, such as steelworkers, ballet dancers, and professional baseball players.
3. Physical capital. **Physical capital** consists of the factories and equipment used in production. It also includes improvements to natural resources, such as irrigation ditches.
4. Human capital. **Human capital** is the economic characterization of the education and training of workers. How much the nation produces depends not only on how many hours people work but also on how productive they are, and that in turn depends in part on education and training. To become more educated, individuals have to devote time and resources, just as a business has to devote resources if it wants to increase its physical capital. Whenever a worker's skills increase, human capital has been improved.
5. Entrepreneurship. The factor of production known as **entrepreneurship** (actually a subdivision of labor) involves human resources that perform the functions of organizing, managing, and assembling the other factors of production to make business ventures. Entrepreneurship also encompasses taking risks that involve the possibility of losing large sums of wealth on new ventures. It includes new methods of doing common things and generally experimenting with any type of new thinking that could lead to making more money income. Without entrepreneurship, virtually no business organization could operate.

Goods Versus Economic Goods

Goods 
All things from which individuals derive satisfaction or happiness.

Economic goods 
Goods that are scarce, for which the quantity demanded exceeds the quantity supplied at a zero price.

Services 
Mental or physical labor or help purchased by consumers. Examples are the assistance of doctors, lawyers, dentists, repair personnel, housecleaners, educators, retailers, and wholesalers; things purchased or used by consumers that do not have physical characteristics.

Goods are defined as all things from which individuals derive satisfaction or happiness. Goods therefore include air to breathe and the beauty of a sunset as well as food, cars, and CD players.

Economic goods are a subset of all goods—they are goods derived from scarce resources about which we must constantly make decisions regarding their best use. By definition, the desired quantity of an economic good exceeds the amount that is directly available at a zero price. Virtually every example we use in economics concerns economic goods—cars, CD players, computers, socks, baseball bats, and corn. Weeds are a good example of *bads*—goods for which the desired quantity is much *less* than what nature provides at a zero price.

Sometimes you will see references to "goods and services." **Services** are tasks that are performed for someone else, such as laundry, cleaning, hospital care, restaurant meal preparation, car polishing, psychological counseling, and teaching. One way of looking at services is thinking of them as *intangible goods.*

WANTS AND NEEDS

Wants are not the same as needs. Indeed, from the economist's point of view, the term *needs* is objectively undefinable. When someone says, "I need some new clothes," there is no way to know whether that person is stating a vague wish, a want, or a lifesaving necessity. If the individual making the statement were dying of exposure in a northern country during the winter, we might argue that indeed the person does need clothes—perhaps not new ones, but at least some articles of warm clothing. Typically, however, the term *need* is used very casually in most conversations. What people mean, usually, is that they want something that they do not currently have.

Humans have unlimited wants. Just imagine if every single material want that you might have were satisfied. You can have all of the clothes, cars, houses, CDs, tickets to concerts, and other things that you want. Does that mean that nothing else could add to your total level of happiness? Probably not, because you might think of new goods and services that you could obtain, particularly as they came to market. You would also still be lacking in fulfilling all of your wants for compassion, friendship, love, affection, prestige, musical abilities, sports abilities, and so on.

In reality, every individual has competing wants but cannot satisfy all of them, given limited resources. This is the reality of scarcity. Each person must therefore make choices. Whenever a choice is made to do or buy something, something else that is also desired is not done or not purchased. In other words, in a world of scarcity, every want that ends up being satisfied causes one or more other wants to remain unsatisfied or to be forfeited.

CONCEPTS IN BRIEF

- Scarcity exists because human wants always exceed what can be produced with the limited resources and time that nature makes available.
- We use scarce resources, such as land, labor, physical and human capital, and entrepreneurship, to produce economic goods—goods that are desired but are not directly obtainable from nature to the extent demanded or desired at a zero price.
- Wants are unlimited; they include all material desires and all nonmaterial desires, such as love, affection, power, and prestige.
- The concept of need is difficult to define objectively for every person; consequently, we simply consider that every person's wants are unlimited. In a world of scarcity, satisfaction of one want necessarily means nonsatisfaction of one or more other wants.

SCARCITY, CHOICE, AND OPPORTUNITY COST

The natural fact of scarcity implies that we must make choices. One of the most important results of this fact is that every choice made (or not made, for that matter) means that some opportunity had to be sacrificed. Every choice involves giving up another opportunity to do or use something else.

Consider a practical example. Every choice you make to study one more hour of economics requires that you give up the opportunity to do any of the following activities: study more of another subject, listen to music, sleep, browse at a local store, read a novel, or work out at the gym. Many more opportunities are forgone also if you choose to study economics an additional hour.

Because there were so many alternatives from which to choose, how could you determine the value of what you gave up to engage in that extra hour of studying economics? First of all, no one else can tell you the answer because only you can *subjectively* put a value on the alternatives forgone. Only you know what is the value of another hour of sleep or of an hour looking for the latest CDs. That means that only you can determine the highest-valued, next-best alternative that you had to sacrifice in order to study economics one more hour. It is you who come up with the *subjective* estimate of the expected value of the next-best alternative.

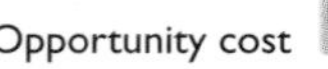

Opportunity cost
The highest-valued, next-best alternative that must be sacrificed to obtain something or to satisfy a want.

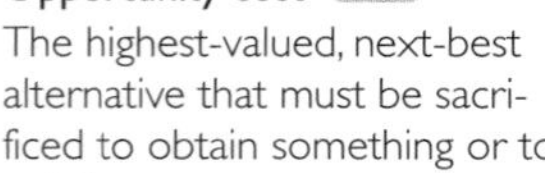

The value of the next-best alternative is called **opportunity cost.** The opportunity cost of any action is the value of what is given up—the next-highest-ranked alternative—because a choice was made. When you study one more hour, there may be many alternatives available for the use of that hour, but assume that you can do only one other thing in that hour—your next-highest-ranked alternative. What is important is the choice that you would have made if you hadn't studied one more hour. Your opportunity cost is the *next-highest-ranked* alternative, not *all* alternatives.

In economics, cost is always a forgone opportunity.

One way to think about opportunity cost is to understand that when you choose to do something, you lose. What you lose is being able to engage in your next-highest-valued alternative. The cost of your choice is what you lose, which is by definition your next-highest-valued alternative. This is your opportunity cost.

Let's consider a real-world example: the opportunity cost of a national monument.

POLICY EXAMPLE

The Trillion-Dollar Canyon

In September 1996, the U.S. government established the Grand Staircase/Escalante National Monument. If you visit the Monument's Web page (click here to visit the site), you will learn all about various activities available to visitors to the cliffs and canyons encompassed within the monument.

What the Web page does not tell you is that this 1.8 million-acre park in the southern Utah desert lies above the largest known reserve of coal in the United States: an underground bank of nearly 7 billion tons of coal with an estimated market value of about $1 trillion. That is the opportunity cost of this particular national monument.

For Critical Analysis

Recall that opportunity cost is the value of the next-best alternative. What does this tell us about the perceived social value of the Grand Staircase/Escalante National Monument?

THE WORLD OF TRADE-OFFS

Whenever you engage in any activity using any resource, even time, you are *trading off* the use of that resource for one or more alternative uses. The value of the trade-off is represented by the opportunity cost. The opportunity cost of studying economics has already been mentioned—it is the value of the next-best alternative. When you think of any alternative, you are thinking of trade-offs.

Let's consider a hypothetical example of a one-for-one trade-off between the results of spending time studying economics and accounting. For the sake of this argument, we will assume that additional time studying either economics or accounting will lead to a higher grade in the subject studied more. One of the best ways to examine this trade-off is with a graph. (If you would like a refresher on graphical techniques, study Appendix A at the end of Chapter 1 before going on.)

Graphical Analysis

In Figure 2-1, the expected grade in accounting is measured on the vertical axis of the graph, and the expected grade in economics is measured on the horizontal axis. We simplify the world and assume that you have a maximum of 10 hours per week to spend studying these two subjects and that if you spend all 10 hours on economics, you will get an A in the course. You will, however, fail accounting. Conversely, if you spend all of your 10 hours studying accounting, you will get an A in that subject, but you will flunk economics. Here the trade-off is a special case: one to one. A one-to-one trade-off means that the opportunity cost of receiving one grade higher in economics (for example, improving from a C to a B) is one grade lower in accounting (falling from a C to a D).

The Production Possibilities Curve (PPC)

The graph in Figure 2-1 illustrates the relationship between the possible results that can be produced in each of two activities, depending on how much time you choose to devote to each activity. This graph shows a representation of a **production possibilities curve (PPC).**

Production possibilities curve (PPC) A curve representing all possible combinations of total output that could be produced assuming (1) a fixed amount of productive resources of a given quality and (2) the efficient use of those resources.

Consider that you are producing a grade in economics when you study economics and a grade in accounting when you study accounting. Then the graph in Figure 2-1 can be related to the production possibilities you face. The line that goes from A on one axis to A on the other axis therefore becomes a production possibilities curve. It is defined as the maximum quantity of one good or service that can be produced, given that a specific quantity of another is produced. It is a curve that shows the possibilities available for increasing the output of one good or service by reducing the amount of another. In the example in Figure 2-1, your time for studying was limited to 10 hours per week. The two possible outputs were grades in accounting and grades in economics. The particular production possibilities curve presented in Figure 2-1 is a graphical representation of the opportunity cost of studying one more hour in one subject. It is a *straight-line production possibilities curve,* which is a special case. (The more general case will be discussed next.) If you decide to be at point *x* in Figure 2-1, 5 hours of study time will be spent on accounting and 5 hours will be spent on economics. The expected grade in each course will be a C. If you are more interested in getting a B in economics, you will go to point *y* on the production possibilities curve, spending only 2.5 hours

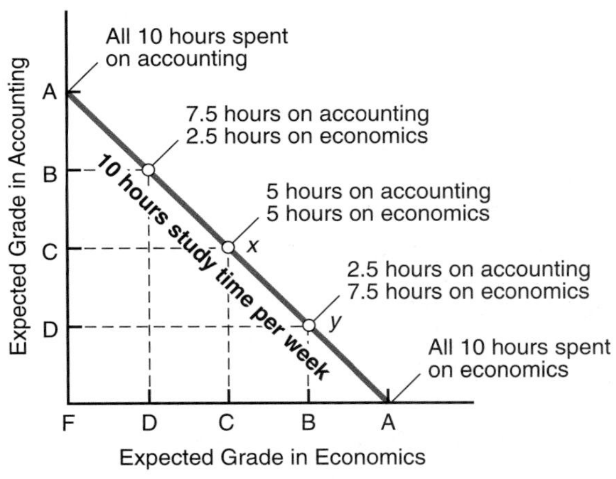

FIGURE 2-1
Production Possibilities Curve for Grades in Accounting and Economics (Trade-Offs)
We assume that only 10 hours can be spent per week on studying. If the student is at point *x*, equal time (5 hours a week) is spent on both courses and equal grades of C will be received. If a higher grade in economics is desired, the student may go to point *y*, thereby receiving a B in economics but a D in accounting. At point *y*, 2.5 hours are spent on accounting and 7.5 hours on economics.

on accounting but 7.5 hours on economics. Your expected grade in accounting will then drop from a C to a D.

Note that these trade-offs between expected grades in accounting and economics are the result of *holding constant* total study time as well as all other factors that might influence a student's ability to learn, such as computerized study aids. Quite clearly, if you wished to spend more total time studying, it would be possible to have higher grades in both economics and accounting. In that case, however, we would no longer be on the specific production possibilities curve illustrated in Figure 2-1. We would have to draw a new curve, farther to the right, to show the greater total study time and a different set of possible trade-offs.

CONCEPTS IN BRIEF

- Scarcity requires us to choose. Whenever we choose, we lose the next-highest-valued alternative.
- Cost is always a forgone opportunity.
- Another way to look at opportunity cost is the trade-off that occurs when one activity is undertaken rather than the next-best alternative activity.
- A production possibilities curve (PPC) graphically shows the trade-off that occurs when more of one output is obtained at the sacrifice of another. The PPC is a graphical representation of, among other things, opportunity cost.

THE CHOICES SOCIETY FACES

The straight-line production possibilities curve presented in Figure 2-1 can be generalized to demonstrate the related concepts of scarcity, choice, and trade-offs that our entire nation faces. As you will see, the production possibilities curve is a simple but powerful economic model because it can demonstrate these related concepts. The example we will use is the choice between the production of network computers and digital televisions (DTVs). We assume for the moment that these are the only two goods that can be produced in the nation. Panel (a) of Figure 2-2 gives the various combinations of computers and DTVs that are possible. If all resources are devoted to computer production, 25 million per year can be produced. If all resources are devoted to DTV production, 30 million per year can be produced. In between are various possible combinations. These combinations are plotted as points *A, B, C, D, E, F,* and *G* in panel (b) of Figure 2-2. If these points are connected with a smooth curve, the nation's production possibilities curve is shown, demonstrating the trade-off between the production of computers and DTVs. These trade-offs occur *on* the production possibilities curve.

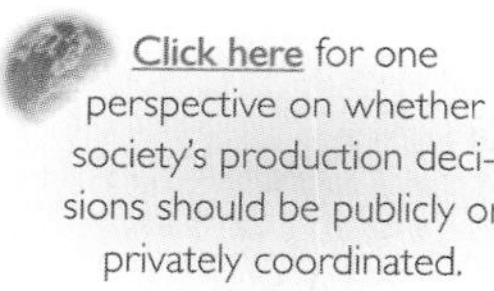
Click here for one perspective on whether society's production decisions should be publicly or privately coordinated.

Notice the major difference in the shape of the production possibilities curves in Figures 2-1 and 2-2. In Figure 2-1, there is a one-to-one trade-off between grades in economics and in accounting. In Figure 2-2, the trade-off between computer production and DTV production is not constant, and therefore the PPC is a *bowed* curve. To understand why the production possibilities curve for a society is typically bowed outward, you must understand the assumptions underlying the PPC.

Assumptions Underlying the Production Possibilities Curve

When we draw the curve that is shown in Figure 2-2, we make the following assumptions:

1. Resources are fully employed.
2. We are looking at production over a specific time period—for example, one year.

FIGURE 2-2

Society's Trade-Off Between Network Computers and Digital Televisions

The production of network computers and digital televisions are measured in millions of units per year. The various combinations are given in panel (a) and plotted in panel (b). Connecting the points *A–G* with a relatively smooth line gives the society's production possibilities curve for network computers and digital televisions. Point *R* lies outside the production possibilities curve and is therefore unattainable at the point in time for which the graph is drawn. Point *S* lies inside the production possibilities curve and therefore represents an inefficient use of available resources.

Panel (a)

Combination	Network Computers (millions per year)	Digital Televisions (millions per year)
A	25.00	0
B	24.00	5
C	22.50	10
D	20.00	15
E	16.50	20
F	11.25	25
G	0	30

Panel (b)

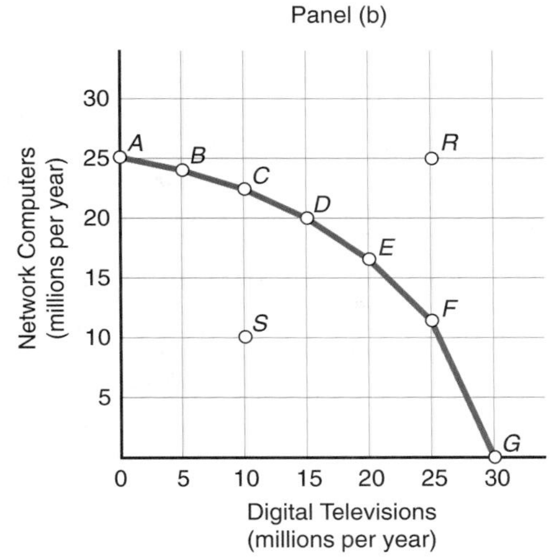

3. The resource inputs, in both quantity and quality, used to produce computers or digital televisions are fixed over this time period.
4. Technology does not change over this time period.

Technology is defined as society's pool of applied knowledge concerning how goods and services can be produced by managers, workers, engineers, scientists, and artisans, using land and capital. You can think of technology as the formula or recipe used to combine factors of production. (When better formulas are developed, more production can be obtained from the same amount of resources.) The level of technology sets the limit on the amount and types of goods and services that we can derive from any given amount of resources. The production possibilities curve is drawn under the assumption that we use the best technology that we currently have available and that this technology doesn't change over the time period under study.

Technology
Society's pool of applied knowledge concerning how goods and services can be produced.

Production Possibilities Curve
Practice with the production possibilities curve.

Being off the Production Possibilities Curve

Look again at panel (b) of Figure 2-2. Point *R* lies *outside* the production possibilities curve and is *impossible* to achieve during the time period assumed. By definition, the production possibilities curve indicates the *maximum* quantity of one good given some quantity of the other.

It is possible, however, to be at point *S* in Figure 2-2. That point lies beneath the production possibilities curve. If the nation is at point *S,* it means that its resources are not being fully utilized. This occurs, for example, during periods of unemployment. Point *S* and all such points within the production possibilities curve are always attainable but usually not desirable.

Efficiency

The production possibilities curve can be used to define the notion of efficiency. Whenever the economy is operating on the PPC, at points such as *A, B, C,* or *D,* we say that its production is efficient. Points such as *S* in Figure 2-2, which lie beneath the production possibilities curve, are said to represent production situations that are not efficient.

Efficiency can mean many things to many people. Even within economics, there are different types of efficiency. Here we are discussing productive efficiency. An economy is productively efficient whenever it is producing the maximum output with given technology and resources.

Efficiency
The case in which a given level of inputs is used to produce the maximum output possible. Alternatively, the situation in which a given output is produced at minimum cost.

A simple commonsense definition of efficiency is getting the most out of what we have as an economy. Clearly, we are not getting the most that we have if we are at point *S* in panel (b) of Figure 2-2. We can move from point *S* to, say, point *C,* thereby increasing the total quantity of network computers produced without any decrease in the total quantity of digital televisions produced. We can move from point *S* to point *E,* for example, and have both more computers and more DTVs. Point *S* is called an **inefficient point,** which is defined as any point below the production possibilities curve.

Inefficient point
Any point below the production possibilities curve at which resources are being used inefficiently.

We can relate the concept of economic efficiency to how goods are distributed among different individuals and entities. In an efficient economy, people who value specific goods relatively the most end up with those goods. If you own a vintage electric Fender guitar but I value it more than you, I can buy it from you. Such trading benefits you and me mutually. In the process, the economy becomes more efficient. The maximum efficiency an economy can reach is when all such mutual benefits through trade have been exhausted.

The Law of Increasing Relative Cost

In the example in Figure 2-1, the trade-off between a grade in accounting and a grade in economics is one to one. The trade-off ratio was fixed. That is to say, the production possibilities curve was a straight line. The curve in Figure 2-2 is a more general case. We have re-created the curve in Figure 2-2 as Figure 2-3. Each combination, *A* through *G,* of network computers and digital televisions is represented on the production possibilities curve. Starting with the production of zero DTVs, the nation can produce 25 million units of computers with its available resources and technology. When we increase production of DTVs from zero to 5 million per year, the nation has to give up in computers that first vertical arrow, *Aa.* From panel (a) of Figure 2-2 you can see that this is 1 mil-

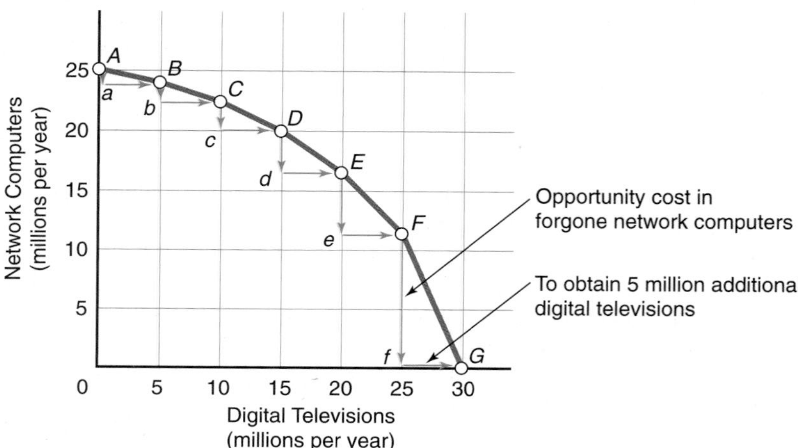

FIGURE 2-3
The Law of Increasing Relative Cost
Consider equal increments of digital television production, as measured on the horizontal axis. All of the horizontal arrows—*aB, bC,* and so on—are of equal length (5 million). The opportunity cost of going from 25 million DTVs per year to 30 million (*Ff*) is much greater than going from zero units to 5 million (*Aa*). The opportunity cost of each additional equal increase in DTV production rises.

lion computers a year (25 million − 24 million). Again, if we increase production of DTVs by 5 million units per year, we go from *B* to *C*. In order to do so, the nation has to give up the vertical distance *Bb,* or 1.5 million computers a year. By the time we go from 25 million to 30 million digital televisions, to obtain that 5 million increase, we have to forgo the vertical distance *Ff,* or 11.25 million computers. In other words, we see an increase in the opportunity cost of the last 5 million digital televisions—11.25 million computers—compared to an equivalent increase in DTVs when we started with none being produced at all—1 million computers.

What we are observing is called the **law of increasing relative cost.** When society takes more resources and applies them to the production of any specific good, the opportunity cost increases for each additional unit produced. The reason that, as a nation, we face the law of increasing relative cost (which causes the production possibilities curve to bow outward) is that certain resources are better suited for producing some goods than they are for other goods. Resources are generally not *perfectly* adaptable for alternative uses. When increasing the output of a particular good, producers must use less suitable resources than those already used in order to produce the additional output. Hence the cost of producing the additional units increases. With respect to our hypothetical example here, at first the computer hardware specialists at computer firms would shift over to producing digital televisions. After a while, though, computer networking technicians, workers who normally build hard drives, and others would be asked to help design and manufacture television components. Clearly, they would be less effective in making televisions than the people who specialize in this task.

Law of increasing relative cost
The observation that the opportunity cost of additional units of a good generally increases as society attempts to produce more of that good. This accounts for the bowed-out shape of the production possibilities curve.

As a rule of thumb, *the more specialized the resources, the more bowed the production possibilities curve.* At the other extreme, if all resources are equally suitable for digital-television production or network computer production, the curves in Figures 2-2 and 2-3 would approach the straight line shown in our first example in Figure 2-1.

CONCEPTS IN BRIEF

- Trade-offs are represented graphically by a production possibilities curve showing the maximum quantity of one good or service that can be produced, given a specific quantity of another, from a given set of resources over a specified period of time—for example, one year.
- A PPC is drawn holding the quantity and quality of all resources fixed over the time period under study.
- Points outside the production possibilities curve are unattainable; points inside are attainable but represent an inefficient use or underuse of available resources.
- Because many resources are better suited for certain productive tasks than for others, society's production possibilities curve is bowed outward, following the law of increasing relative cost.

The Bowed-Out Curve
Practice with the concept of the law of increasing relative cost.

ECONOMIC GROWTH AND THE PRODUCTION POSSIBILITIES CURVE

Over any particular time period, a society cannot be outside the production possibilities curve. Over time, however, it is possible to have more of everything. This occurs through economic growth. (An important reason for economic growth, capital accumulation, is discussed next. A more complete discussion of why economic growth occurs is discussed in Chapter 9). Figure 2-4 shows the production possibilities curve for network computers and digital televisions shifting outward. The two additional curves shown represent new choices open to an economy that has experienced economic growth. Such economic growth

FIGURE 2-4

Economic Growth Allows for More of Everything

If the nation experiences economic growth, the production possibilities curve between network computers and digital televisions will move out, as is shown. This takes time, however, and it does not occur automatically. This means, therefore, that we can have more network computers and more DTVs only after a period of time during which we have experienced economic growth.

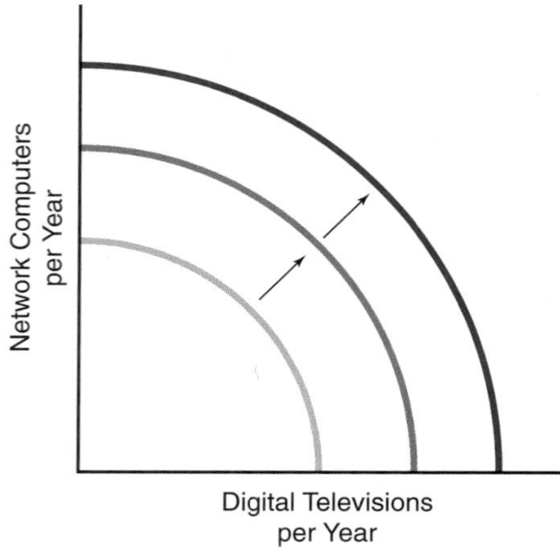

occurs because of many things, including increases in the number of workers and productive investment in equipment.

Scarcity still exists, however, no matter how much economic growth there is. At any point in time, we will always be on some production possibilities curve; thus we will always face trade-offs. The more we want of one thing, the less we can have of others.

If a nation experiences economic growth, the production possibilities curve between network computers and digital televisions will move outward, as shown in Figure 2-4. This takes time and does not occur automatically. One reason it will occur involves the choice about how much to consume today.

THE TRADE-OFF BETWEEN THE PRESENT AND THE FUTURE

Consumption 
The use of goods and services for personal satisfaction.

The production possibilities curve and economic growth can be used to examine the trade-off between present **consumption** and future consumption. When we consume today, we are using up what we call consumption or consumer goods—food and clothes, for example. And we have already defined physical capital as the manufactured goods, such as machines and factories, used to make other goods and services.

Why We Make Capital Goods

Why would we be willing to use productive resources to make things—capital goods—that we cannot consume directly? For one thing, capital goods enable us to produce larger quantities of consumer goods or to produce them less expensively than we otherwise could. Before fish are "produced" for the market, equipment such as fishing boats, nets, and poles are produced first. Imagine how expensive it would be to obtain fish for market without using these capital goods. Catching fish with one's hands is not an easy task. The price per fish would be very high if capital goods weren't used.

Forgoing Current Consumption

Whenever we use productive resources to make capital goods, we are implicitly forgoing current consumption. We are waiting for some time in the future to consume the fruits that will be reaped from the use of capital goods. In effect, when we forgo current consumption to invest in capital goods, we are engaging in an economic activity that is forward-looking—we do not get instant utility or satisfaction from our activity. Indeed, if we were to produce only consumer goods now and no capital goods, our capacity to produce consumer goods in the future would suffer. Here we see a trade-off.

The Trade-Off Between Consumption Goods and Capital Goods

To have more consumer goods in the future, we must accept fewer consumer goods today. In other words, an opportunity cost is involved. Every time we make a choice for more goods today, we incur an opportunity cost of fewer goods tomorrow, and every time we make a choice of more goods in the future, we incur an opportunity cost of fewer goods today. With the resources that we don't use to produce consumer goods for today, we invest in capital goods that will produce more consumer goods for us later. The trade-off is shown in Figure 2-5. On the left in panel (a), you can see this trade-off depicted as a production possibilities curve between capital goods and consumption goods.

Assume that we are willing to give up $1 trillion worth of consumption today. We will be at point *A* in the left-hand diagram of panel (a). This will allow the economy to grow. We will have more future consumption because we invested in more capital goods today. In the right-hand diagram of panel (a), we see two goods represented, food and recreation. The production possibilities curve will move outward if we collectively decide to restrict consumption each year and invest in capital goods.

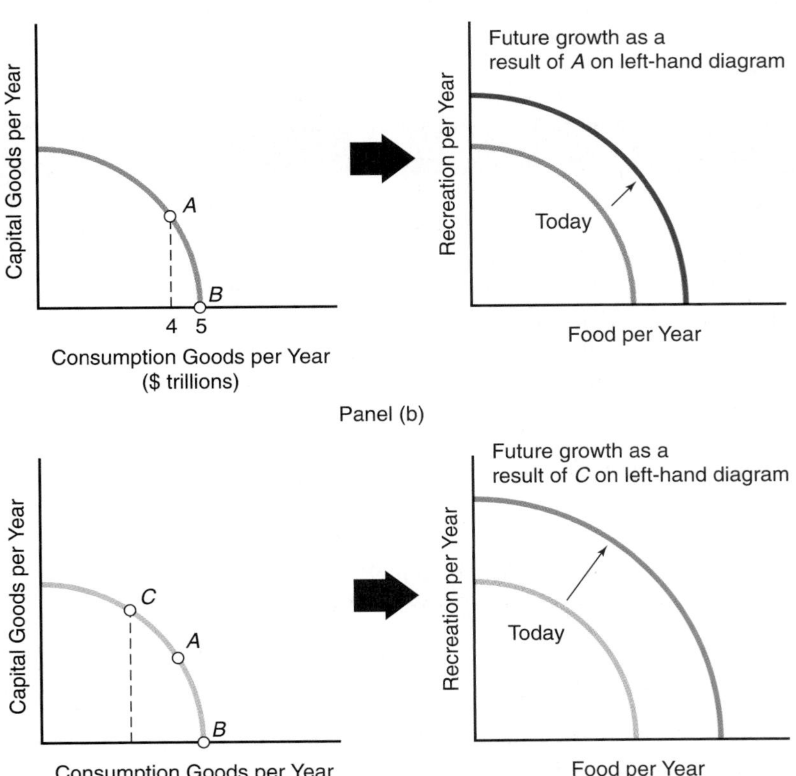

FIGURE 2-5
Capital Goods and Growth
In panel (a), the nation chooses not to consume $1 trillion, so it invests that amount in capital goods. In panel (b), it chooses even more capital goods. The PPC moves even more to the right on the right-hand diagram in panel (b) as a result.

In panel (b), we show the results of our willingness to forgo more current consumption. We move to point *C,* where we have many fewer consumer goods today but produce a lot more capital goods. This leads to more future growth in this simplified model, and thus the production possibilities curve in the right-hand side of panel (b) shifts outward more than it did in the right-hand side of panel (a).

In other words, the more we give up today, the more we can have tomorrow, provided, of course, that the capital goods are productive in future periods.

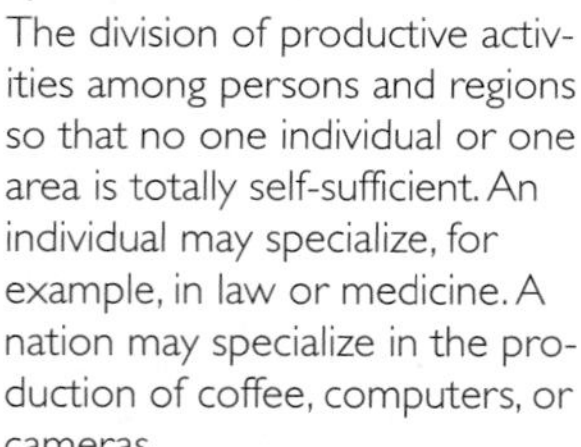

- The use of capital requires using productive resources to produce capital goods that will later be used to produce consumer goods.
- A trade-off is involved between current consumption and capital goods or, alternatively, between current consumption and future consumption because the more we invest in capital goods today, the greater the amount of consumer goods we can produce in the future and the smaller the amount of consumer goods we can produce today.

SPECIALIZATION AND GREATER PRODUCTIVITY

Specialization
The division of productive activities among persons and regions so that no one individual or one area is totally self-sufficient. An individual may specialize, for example, in law or medicine. A nation may specialize in the production of coffee, computers, or cameras.

Specialization involves working at a relatively well-defined, limited endeavor, such as accounting or teaching. It involves a division of labor among different individuals and regions. Most individuals do specialize. For example, you could change the oil in your car if you wanted to. Typically, though, you take your car to a garage and let the mechanic change the oil. You benefit by letting the garage mechanic specialize in changing the oil and in doing other repairs on your car. The specialist will get the job finished sooner than you could and has the proper equipment to make the job go more smoothly. Specialization usually leads to greater productivity, not only for each individual but also for the nation.

Specialization pays off for companies around the globe. This often has proved true in the automotive industry.

INTERNATIONAL POLICY EXAMPLE

Why the Light Turned Green Once the Trabi Was Parked

Among residents of eastern Germany, one of the best-recalled failures of communist rule was a little auto known as the "Trabi." Years after the reunification of Germany, people still joke about the car. For instance, "Why didn't the Trabi move when the light turned green? Because its tire got stuck on a piece of gum." Or "Why do deluxe Trabis have heated rear windows? To keep your hands warm as you push it." Another goes "How do you double a Trabi's value? Fill the gasoline tank."

Today the punch line is different, however. The company that once manufactured Trabis now has a booming business. The key to its success is that it no longer builds cars. Instead, it supplies auto parts to General Motors, Volkswagen, and DaimlerChrysler. What the company learned was that it was better off specializing in making auto parts—and leaving assembly of the parts to someone else.

For Critical Analysis

How do General Motors, Volkswagen, and DaimlerChrysler gain from specialization?

Absolute Advantage 

Specialization occurs because different individuals and different nations have different skills. Sometimes it seems that some individuals are better at doing everything than anyone else. A president of a large company might be able to type better than any of the typists, file better than any of the file clerks, and wash windows better than any of the window washers. The president has an **absolute advantage** in all of these endeavors—if he were to spend a given amount of time in one of these activities, he could produce more than anyone else in the company. The president does not, however, spend his time doing those other activities. Why not? Because he is being paid the most for undertaking the president's managerial duties. The president specializes in one particular task in spite of having an absolute advantage in all tasks. Indeed, absolute advantage is irrelevant in predicting how he uses his time; only *comparative advantage* matters.

Absolute advantage 
The ability to produce more units of a good or service using a given quantity of labor or resource inputs. Equivalently, the ability to produce the same quantity of a good or service using fewer units of labor or resource inputs.

Comparative Advantage

Comparative advantage is the ability to perform an activity at a lower opportunity cost. You have a comparative advantage in one activity whenever you have a lower opportunity cost of performing that activity. Comparative advantage is always a *relative* concept. You may be able to change the oil in your car; you might even be able to change it faster than the local mechanic. But if the opportunity cost you face by changing the oil exceeds the mechanic's opportunity cost, the mechanic has a comparative advantage in changing the oil. The mechanic faces a lower opportunity cost for that activity.

Comparative advantage 
The ability to produce a good or service at a lower opportunity cost compared to other producers.

You may be convinced that everybody can do everything better than you. In this extreme situation, do you still have a comparative advantage? The answer is yes. What you need to do to discover your comparative advantage is to find a job in which your *disadvantage* relative to others is smaller. You do not have to be a mathematical genius to figure this out. The market tells you very clearly by offering you the highest income for the job for which you have a smaller disadvantage compared to others. Stated differently, to find your comparative advantage no matter how much better everybody else can do the jobs that you want to do, you simply find which job maximizes your income.

The coaches of sports teams are constantly faced with determining each player's comparative advantage. Babe Ruth was originally one of the best pitchers in professional baseball when he played for the Boston Red Sox. After he was traded to the New York Yankees, the owner and the coach decided to make him an outfielder, even though he was a better pitcher than anyone else on the team roster. They wanted "The Babe" to concentrate on his hitting. Good pitchers do not bring in as many fans as home-run kings. Babe Ruth's comparative advantage was clearly in hitting homers rather than practicing and developing his pitching game.

Scarcity, Self-Interest, and Specialization

In Chapter 1, you learned about the assumption of rational self-interest. To repeat, for the purposes of our analyses we assume that individuals are rational in that they will do what is in their own self-interest. They will not consciously carry out actions that will make them worse off. In this chapter, you learned that scarcity requires people to make choices. We assume that they make choices based on their self-interest. When they make these choices, they attempt to maximize benefits net of opportunity cost. In so doing, individuals choose their comparative advantage and end up specializing. Ultimately, when people specialize, they increase the money income they make and therefore become richer. When all individuals and businesses specialize simultaneously, the gains are seen in greater material well-being. With any given set of resources, specialization will result in higher output.

INTERNATIONAL EXAMPLE

Why Foreign Graduate Students Specialize When Studying in the United States

Specialization is evident in the fields of endeavor that foreign students choose when they come to the United States for graduate studies. Consider the following statistics: More than 60 percent of U.S. doctorates in engineering and 55 percent of those in mathematics, computer science, and the physical sciences are earned by foreign-born students. Yet foreign nationals are awarded relatively few advanced degrees in business, law, or medicine. The reason has nothing to do with intelligence or giftedness; it is simply that many more of the best American students choose schools in these professional fields rather than ones offering science and engineering programs.

Why does this specialization occur? For American students, the greatest returns for about the same effort come from business, law, and medicine. In contrast, foreign-born graduate students face fewer language and cultural obstacles (and hence better job prospects) if they choose technical subjects.

When students from foreign countries come to American graduate schools to obtain their Ph.D. degrees, more than 70 percent of them remain in the United States after graduation, thereby augmenting America's supply of engineers and scientists. Such specialization has helped the United States maintain its leadership in both the technoscientific and sociocultural areas.

For Critical Analysis

What type of capital do foreign-born students bring with them to the United States?

THE DIVISION OF LABOR

Division of labor 
The segregation of a resource into different specific tasks; for example, one automobile worker puts on bumpers, another doors, and so on.

In any firm that includes specialized human and nonhuman resources, there is a **division of labor** among those resources. The best-known example comes from Adam Smith, who in *The Wealth of Nations* illustrated the benefits of a division of labor in the making of pins, as depicted in the following example:

> One man draws out the wire, another straightens it, a third cuts it, a fourth points it, a fifth grinds it at the top for receiving the head; to make the head requires two or three distinct operations; to put it on is a peculiar business, to whiten the pins is another; it is even a trade by itself to put them into the paper.

Making pins this way allowed 10 workers without very much skill to make almost 48,000 pins "of a middling size" in a day. One worker, toiling alone, could have made perhaps 20 pins a day; therefore, 10 workers could have produced 200. Division of labor allowed for an increase in the daily output of the pin factory from 200 to 48,000! (Smith did not attribute all of the gain to the division of labor according to talent but credited also the use of machinery and the fact that less time was spent shifting from task to task.)

What we are discussing here involves a division of the resource called labor into different kinds of labor. The different kinds of labor are organized in such a way as to increase the amount of output possible from the fixed resources available. We can therefore talk about an organized division of labor within a firm leading to increased output.

COMPARATIVE ADVANTAGE AND TRADE AMONG NATIONS

Click here to find out about how much international trade takes place. Click on "Statistics" in the "A-Z list".

Though most of our analysis of absolute advantage, comparative advantage, and specialization has dealt with individuals, it is equally applicable to nations. First consider the United States. The Plains states have a comparative advantage in the production of grains and other agricultural goods. The states to the north and east tend to specialize in industrialized production, such as automobiles. Not surprisingly, grains are shipped from the Plains states to the northern states, and automobiles are shipped in the reverse direction. Such specialization and trade allow for higher incomes and standards of living. If both the Plains states and the northern states were politically defined as separate nations, the same analysis would still hold, but we would call it international trade. Indeed, Europe is comparable to the United States in area and population, but instead of one nation, Europe has 15. What in America we call *interstate* trade, in Europe they call *international* trade. There is no difference, however, in the economic results—both yield greater economic efficiency and higher average incomes.

Political problems that do not normally arise within a particular nation often do between nations. For example, if California avocado growers develop a cheaper method than growers in southern Florida to produce a tastier avocado, the Florida growers will lose out. They cannot do much about the situation except try to lower their own costs of production or improve their product. If avocado growers in Mexico, however, develop a cheaper method to produce better-tasting avocados, both California and Florida growers can (and likely will) try to raise political barriers that will prevent Mexican avocado growers from freely selling their product in America. U.S. avocado growers will use such arguments as "unfair" competition and loss of American jobs. In so doing, they are only partly right: Avocado-growing jobs may decline in America, but jobs will not necessarily decline overall. If the argument of U.S. avocado growers had any validity, every time a region in the United States developed a better way to produce a product manufactured somewhere else in the country, employment in America would decline. That has never happened and never will.

FAQ

Isn't too much international trade bad for the U.S. economy?

No, despite what you may read or hear, international trade is just like any other economic activity. Indeed, you can think of international trade as a production process that transforms goods that we sell to other countries (exports) into goods that we buy from other countries (imports). This process is a mutually beneficial exchange that takes place across political borders. Because international trade occurs only because it is in the interests of both buyers and sellers, people in both nations gain from trade.

When nations specialize where they have a comparative advantage and then trade with the rest of the world, the average standard of living in the world rises. In effect, international trade allows the world to move from inside the global production possibilities curve toward the curve itself, thereby improving worldwide economic efficiency.

CONCEPTS IN BRIEF

- With a given set of resources, specialization results in higher output; in other words, there are gains to specialization in terms of greater material well-being.
- Individuals and nations specialize in their areas of comparative advantage in order to reap the gains of specialization.
- Comparative advantages are found by determining which activities have the lowest opportunity cost—that is, which activities yield the highest return for the time and resources used.
- A division of labor occurs when different workers are assigned different tasks. Together, the workers produce a desired product.

NETNOMICS

Allocating Scarce Space on the Web

Nearly half of all users of the World Wide Web visit fewer than 10 Internet sites per month. Companies that want to sell their products on the Internet know this. They also know that when individuals access the Internet, their homepage is typically that of their Internet service provider (Netscape, Explorer) or a search engine such as Yahoo! Consequently, many companies advertise on those Web pages.

This is why each time you access the Net, you see advertising—banners, buttons, keywords, hot links, and other promotions. Some of the biggest advertisers on the Web are Microsoft, Toyota, General Motors, Disney, IBM, AT&T, and American Express. Internet-based companies such as Amazon.com also are major Web advertisers. It is estimated that by 2005, advertisers will be spending more than $25 billion a year on the Web.

The owner of any Web page that carries advertising faces an opportunity cost. For example, advertisers widely consider the opening page of the Yahoo! search engine "prime real estate" because so many people see it each day. But there is relatively little space on the screen. Thus when Yahoo! allocates space to promote its own services and products, it gives up space it could sell. But if it fills up too much of the screen with ads, some users will switch to a less cluttered search engine. That fact makes Web page design a crucial business concern.

Issues & Applications

The Costs of Raising a Child Are Not the Same for Everyone

> **Concepts Applied**
> - Scarcity
> - Choice
> - Opportunity Cost

The U.S. Department of Agriculture (USDA) has estimated the costs of raising a child. These include explicit expenses parents incur in providing the child with housing, food, clothing, day care, education, health care, and transportation. Panel (a) of Figure 2-6 shows the USDA's estimates of these expenses that typical American parents in upper-, middle-, and lower-income families with only one child born in 1997 will incur during each of the first 17 years of the child's life. (These estimates take into account projected inflation. Also, note that a wife often reduces or halts her income-earning activities before a child is born, so there is also an "age 0" in the chart.) As you might expect, higher-income parents incur greater direct expenses; they are more likely to buy high-tech toys and trendy clothing.

"Quality Time" with Kids Has a Market Value

Another key component of the cost of raising a child, however, is the wages that parents forgo when they spend time taking kids to school, the doctor, soccer games, and so on. In some families, one spouse stays home most of the time to provide these services. In others, both parents work but take turns allocating some of their time each day to these duties. No matter how they choose to balance the time, parents forgo wages they

FIGURE 2-6
The Full Cost of Raising a Child
As shown in panel (a), the dollar cost of raising a child increases with the child's age and is more for higher-income parents. The same is true of opportunity cost, as shown in panel (b). Panel (c) reveals that forgone wages (opportunity cost) make up the largest part of total child-rearing expenses.

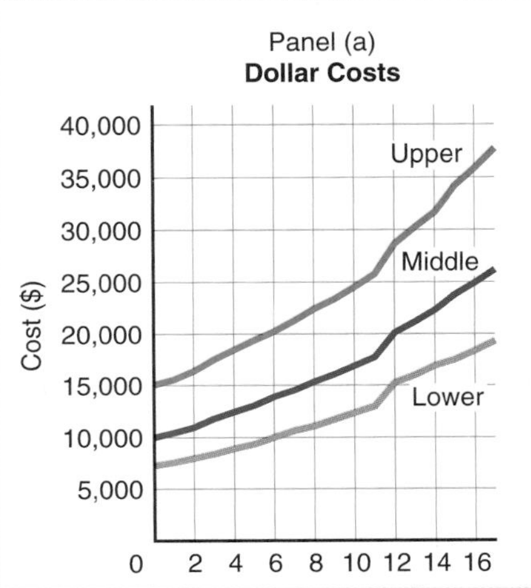

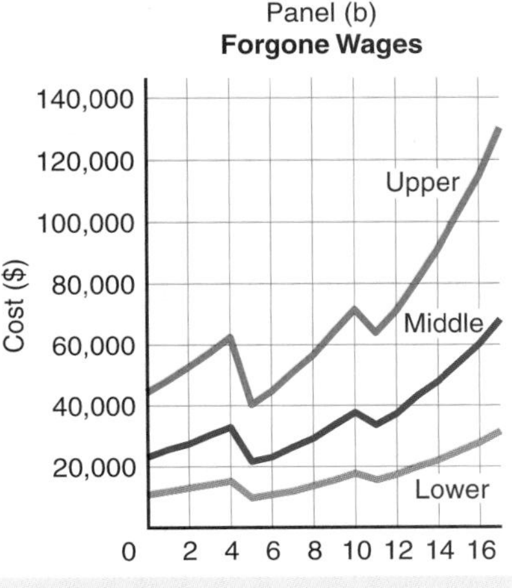

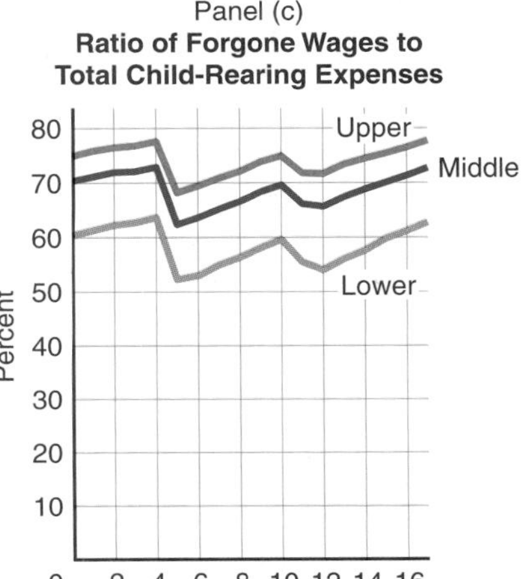

FOR CRITICAL ANALYSIS

1. Note in panel (b) that the forgone-wage component of the opportunity cost of child raising drops when a child reaches the age of 5 and then dips again slightly around age 11. What institutional factors do you suppose might account for this pattern?
2. In recent decades, population growth in lower-income countries has exceeded population growth in higher-income countries. Based on our discussion, can you provide a hypothesis explaining why?

otherwise could have earned if they had allocated their time to income-generating activities.

Panel (b) shows the USDA's estimates of forgone wages for parents in a typical one-child family. Not surprisingly, the forgone wages are much higher for upper-income parents than for parents in middle- and lower-income families.

Forgone Wages and the Opportunity Cost of Raising a Child

The sum of explicit expenses and forgone wages constitutes the total opportunity cost of raising a child. Thus adding together the costs at each age in panels (a) and (b) would give the amounts that couples forgo by engaging in the activity of parenting rather than earning the highest possible wages and allocating their incomes to other activities. If you compare the dollar amounts in panels (a) and (b), however, it is clear that forgone wages are the key component of the total opportunity cost of child raising. Panel (c) verifies this fact. It shows the ratio of forgone wages to total child-raising expenses for each parental income category. Within each income group, and at each age of the child, forgone wages consistently exceed half the total opportunity cost of raising a child. For higher-income parents, forgone wages are consistently in excess of two-thirds of the total opportunity cost.

We can infer an important fact from Figure 2-6. When people acquire more training and education and move into higher-wage occupations, the opportunity cost of raising a child rises significantly. Other things being equal—for instance, if we assume that parents derive roughly the same satisfaction from raising children irrespective of their income—this is likely to induce higher-income people to have fewer children.

SG

SUMMARY DISCUSSION OF LEARNING OBJECTIVES

1. **The Problem of Scarcity, Even for the Affluent:** Scarcity is very different from poverty. No one can obtain all one desires from nature without sacrifice. Thus even the richest people face scarcity, because they have to make choices among alternatives. Despite their high levels of income or wealth, affluent people, like everyone else, typically want more than they can have (in terms of goods, power, prestige, and so on).
2. **Why Economists Consider Individuals' Wants but Not Their "Needs":** Goods are all things from which individuals derive satisfaction. Economic goods are those for which the desired quantity exceeds that amount that is directly available from nature at a zero price. The goods that we want are not necessarily those that we need. To economists, the term *need* is undefinable, whereas humans have unlimited *wants,* which are defined as the goods and services on which we place a positive value.
3. **Why Scarcity Leads People to Evaluate Opportunity Costs:** We measure the opportunity cost of anything by the highest-valued alternative that one must give up to obtain it. The trade-offs that we face as individuals and as a society can be represented by a production possibilities curve (PPC), and moving from one point on a PPC to another entails incurring an opportunity cost. The reason is that along a PPC, all currently available resources and technology are being used, so obtaining more of one good requires shifting resources to production of that good and away from production of another. That is, there is an opportunity cost of allocating scarce resource toward producing one good instead of another good.

4. **Why Obtaining Increasing Increments of a Good Requires Giving Up More and More Units of Other Goods:** Typically, resources are specialized. Thus when society allocates additional resources to producing more and more of a single good, it must increasingly employ resources that would be better suited for producing other goods. As a result, the law of increasing relative cost holds. Each additional unit of a good can be obtained only by giving up more and more of other goods, which means that the production possibilities curve that society faces is bowed outward.
5. **The Trade-Off Between Consumption Goods and Capital Goods:** If we allocate more resources to producing capital goods today, then, other things being equal, the economy will grow by a larger amount. Thus the production possibilities curve will shift outward by a larger amount in the future, which means that we can have more consumption goods in the future. The trade-off, however, is that producing more capital goods today entails giving up consumption goods today.
6. **Absolute Advantage Versus Comparative Advantage:** A person has an absolute advantage if she can produce more of a specific good than someone else who uses the same amount of resources. This also means that she can produce the same amount of that good using fewer resources. Nevertheless, the individual may be better off producing a different good if she has a comparative advantage in producing the other good, meaning that she can produce the other good at lower opportunity cost than someone else. By specializing in producing the good for which she has a comparative advantage, she assures herself of reaping gains from specialization in the form of a higher income.

Key Terms and Concepts

Absolute advantage (39)
Comparative advantage (39)
Consumption (36)
Division of labor (40)
Economic goods (28)
Efficiency (34)
Entrepreneurship (28)
Goods (28)
Human capital (28)
Inefficient point (34)
Labor (28)
Land (28)
Law of increasing relative cost (35)
Opportunity cost (30)
Physical capital (28)
Production (27)
Production possibilities curve (PPC) (31)
Scarcity (27)
Services (28)
Specialization (38)
Technology (33)

Problems

Answers to the odd-numbered problems appear at the back of the book.

2-1. The following table illustrates the points a student can earn on examinations in economics and biology if the student uses all available hours for study.

Economics	Biology
100	40
90	50
80	60
70	70
60	80
50	90
40	100

Plot this student's production possibilities curve. Does the PPC illustrate increasing or decreasing opportunity costs?

2-2. Based on the information provided in Problem 2-1, what is the opportunity cost to this student of allocating sufficient additional study time on economics to move her grade up from a 90 to a 100?

2-3. Consider the following costs that a student incurs by attending a public university for one semester: $3,000 for tuition, $1,000 for room and board, $500 for books, $3,000 in wages lost that the student could have earned working, and 3 percent interest lost on the $4,500 paid for tuition, room and board, and books. Calculate the total opportunity cost that the student incurs by attending college for one semester.

2-4. Consider a change in the table in Problem 2-2. The student's set of opportunities is now as follows:

Economics	Biology
100	40
90	60
80	75
70	85
60	93
50	98
40	100

Plot this student's production possibilities curve. Does the PPC illustrate increasing or decreasing opportunity costs? What is the opportunity cost to this student for the additional amount of study time on economics required to move his grade from 60 to 70? From 90 to 100?

2-5. Construct a production possibilities curve for a nation facing increasing opportunity costs for producing food and video games. Show how the PPC changes given the following events.

a. A new and better fertilizer is invented.

b. There is a surge in labor, which can be employed in both the agricultural sector and the video game sector.

c. A new programming language is invented that is less costly to code and is more memory-efficient, enabling the use of smaller games cartridges.

d. A heat wave and drought results in a 10 percent decrease in usable farmland.

2-6. The president of a university announces to the local media that the university was able to construct its sports complex at a lower cost than it had previously projected. The president argues that the university can now purchase a yacht for the president at no additional cost. Explain why this statement is false by considering opportunity cost.

2-7. You can wash, fold, and iron a basket of laundry in two hours and prepare a meal in one hour. Your roommate can wash, fold, and iron a basket of laundry in three hours and prepare a meal in one hour. Who has the absolute advantage in laundry, and who has an absolute advantage in meal preparation? Who has the comparative advantage in laundry, and who has a comparative advantage in meal preparation?

2-8. Based on the information in Problem 2-7, should you and your roommate specialize in a particular task? Why? And if so, who should specialize in which task? Show how much labor time you save if you choose to "trade" an appropriate task with your roommate as opposed to doing it yourself.

2-9. On the one hand, Canada goes to considerable lengths to protect its television program and magazine producers from U.S. competitors. The United States, on the other hand, often seeks protection from food imports from Canada. Construct an argument showing that from an economywide viewpoint, these efforts are misguided.

2-10. Using only the concept of comparative advantage, evaluate this statement: "A professor with a Ph.D. in economics should never mow his or her own lawn, because this would fail to take into account the professor's comparative advantage."

2-11. Country A and country B produce the same consumption goods and capital goods and currently have *identical* production possibilities curves. They also have the same resources at present, and they have access to the same technology.

a. At present, does either country have a comparative advantage in producing capital goods? Consumption goods?

b. Currently, country A has chosen to produce more consumption goods, compared with country B. Other things being equal, which will experience the larger outward shift of its PPC during the next year?

c. Suppose that a year passes with no changes in technology or in factors other than the capital goods and consumption goods choices the countries initially made. Both countries' PPCs have shifted outward from their initial positions, but not in a parallel fashion. Country B's opportunity cost of producing consumption goods is now higher than in country A. Does either country have a comparative advantage in producing capital goods? Consumption goods?

Economics on the Net

Opportunity Cost and Labor Force Participation Many students choose to forgo full-time employment to concentrate on their studies, thereby incurring a sizable opportunity cost. This application explores the nature of this opportunity cost.

Title: College Enrollment and Work Activity of High School Graduates

Navigation: Click here to visit the Bureau of Labor Statistics (BLS) hompage. Select Topics A-Z, then click on Educational attainment, statistics. Finally, click on College Enrollment and Work Activity of High School Graduates.

Application Read the abbreviated report on college enrollment and work activity of high school graduates. Then answer the following questions.

1. Based on the article, explain who the BLS considers to be in the labor force and who it does not view as part of the labor force.
2. What is the difference in labor force participation rates between high school students entering four-year universities and those entering two-year universities? Using the concept of opportunity cost, explain the difference.
3. What is the difference in labor force participation rates between part-time college students and full-time college students? Using the concept of opportunity cost, explain the difference.

For Group Study and Analysis Read the last paragraph of the article, and then divide the class into two groups. The first group should explain, based on the concept of opportunity cost, the difference in labor force participation rates between youths not in school but with a high school diploma and youths not in school and without a high school diploma. The second half should explain, based on opportunity cost, the difference in labor force participation rates between men and women not in school but with a high school diploma and between men and women not in school and without a high school diploma.

CHAPTER 3

DEMAND AND SUPPLY

This farm worker near Shaanxi, China, obtains water the old-fashioned way. Chinese officals claim to have a "water problem." Should water be analyzed differently than other resources?

Signs of water stress appear throughout China. Of China's 600 largest cities, half are "running short" of water. Some cities turn on water for general use by their residents only two hours per day. Each day, hundreds of farmers are finding their wells pumped dry. Nevertheless, annual rainfall levels in most of China have hovered within normal ranges. Indeed, in some locales in recent years, above-normal rainfalls have caused flooding.

Can residents of China do nothing but hope for more rain? In this chapter, you will learn about one important factor contributing to China's water stress. You will also learn how to reason out one important part of the solution to this problem—a solution that China's leaders have slowly moved toward adopting. To do this, you will need the tools of demand and supply analysis.

LEARNING OBJECTIVES

After reading this chapter, you should be able to:

1. Explain the law of demand
2. Discuss the difference between money prices and relative prices
3. Distinguish between changes in demand and changes in quantity demanded
4. Explain the law of supply
5. Distinguish between changes in supply and changes in quantity supplied
6. Understand how the interaction of the demand for and supply of a commodity determines the market price of the commodity and the equilibrium quantity of the commodity that is produced and consumed

Did You Know That... more than 75 million people currently own portable cellular phones? This is a huge jump from the mere 200,000 who owned them in 1985. Since 1992, two out of every three new telephone numbers have been assigned to cellular phones. There are several reasons for the growth of cellular phones, not the least being the dramatic reduction in both price and size due to improved and cheaper computer chips that go into making them. There is something else at work, though. It has to do with crime. In a recent survey, 46 percent of new cellular phone users said that personal safety was the main reason they bought a portable phone. In Florida, for example, most cellular phone companies allow users simply to dial *FHP to reach the Florida Highway Patrol. The rush to cellular phones is worldwide. Over the past decade, sales have grown by nearly 50 percent every year outside the United States.

We could attempt to explain the phenomenon by saying that more people like to use portable phones. But that explanation is neither satisfying nor entirely accurate. If we use the economist's primary set of tools, *demand and supply,* we will have a better understanding of the cellular phone explosion, as well as many other phenomena in our world. Demand and supply are two ways of categorizing the influences on the price of goods that you buy and the quantities available. As such, demand and supply form the basis of virtually all economic analysis of the world around us.

As you will see throughout this text, the operation of the forces of demand and supply take place in *markets.* A **market** is an abstract concept referring to all the arrangements individuals have for exchanging with one another. Goods and services are sold in markets, such as the automobile market, the health market, and the compact disc market. Workers offer their services in the labor market. Companies, or firms, buy workers' labor services in the labor market. Firms also buy other inputs in order to produce the goods and services that you buy as a consumer. Firms purchase machines, buildings, and land. These markets are in operation at all times. One of the most important activities in these markets is the setting of the prices of all of the inputs and outputs that are bought and sold in our complicated economy. To understand the determination of prices, you first need to look at the law of demand.

Chapter Outline 

Market 
All of the arrangements that individuals have for exchanging with one another. Thus we can speak of the labor market, the automobile market, and the credit market.

THE LAW OF DEMAND

Demand has a special meaning in economics. It refers to the quantities of specific goods or services that individuals, taken singly or as a group, will purchase at various possible prices, other things being constant. We can therefore talk about the demand for microprocessor chips, French fries, compact disc players, children, and criminal activities.

Associated with the concept of demand is the **law of demand,** which can be stated as follows:

> When the price of a good goes up, people buy less of it, other things being equal.
> When the price of a good goes down, people buy more of it, other things being equal.

The law of demand tells us that the quantity demanded of any commodity is inversely related to its price, other things being equal. In an inverse relationship, one variable moves up in value when the other moves down. The law of demand states that a change in price causes a change in the quantity demanded in the *opposite* direction.

Notice that we tacked on to the end of the law of demand the statement "other things being equal." We referred to this in Chapter 1 as the *ceteris paribus* assumption. It means, for example, that when we predict that people will buy fewer DVD (digital videodisk)

Demand 
A schedule of how much of a good or service people will purchase at any price during a specified time period, other things being constant.

Law of demand 
The observation that there is a negative, or inverse, relationship between the price of any good or service and the quantity demanded, holding other factors constant.

players if their price goes up, we are holding constant the price of all other goods in the economy as well as people's incomes. Implicitly, therefore, if we are assuming that no other prices change when we examine the price behavior of DVD players, we are looking at the *relative* price of DVD players.

The law of demand is supported by millions of observations of people's behavior in the marketplace. Theoretically, it can be derived from an economic model based on rational behavior, as was discussed in Chapter 1. Basically, if nothing else changes and the price of a good falls, the lower price induces us to buy more over a certain period of time because we can enjoy additional net gains that were unavailable at the higher price. For the most part, if you examine your own behavior, you will see that it generally follows the law of demand.

Relative Prices Versus Money Prices 

Relative price 
The price of one commodity divided by the price of another commodity; the number of units of one commodity that must be sacrificed to purchase one unit of another commodity.

Money price 
The price that we observe today, expressed in today's dollars. Also called the *absolute* or *nominal price.*

The **relative price** of any commodity is its price in terms of another commodity. The price that you pay in dollars and cents for any good or service at any point in time is called its **money price.** Consider an example that you might hear quite often around parents and grandparents. "When I bought my first new car, it cost only fifteen hundred dollars." The implication, of course, is that the price of cars today is outrageously high because the average new car might cost $25,000. But that is not an accurate comparison. What was the price of the average house during that same year? Perhaps it was only $12,000. By comparison, then, given that houses today average about $175,000, the price of a new car today doesn't sound so far out of line, does it?

The point is that money prices during different time periods don't tell you much. You have to find out relative prices. Consider an example of the price of CDs versus cassettes from last year and this year. In Table 3-1, we show the money price of CDs and cassettes for two years during which they have both gone up. That means that we have to pay out in today's dollars and cents more for CDs and more for cassettes. If we look, though, at the relative prices of CDs and cassettes, we find that last year, CDs were twice as expensive as cassettes, whereas this year they are only $1\frac{3}{4}$ times as expensive. Conversely, if we compare cassettes to CDs, last year they cost only half

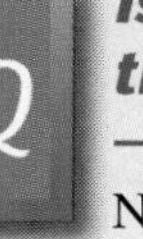

Isn't postage a lot more expensive than it used to be?

No, in reality, the *relative price* of postage in the United States has fallen steadily over the years. The absolute dollar price of a first-class stamp rose from 3 cents in 1940 to 33 cents at the beginning of the twenty-first century. Nevertheless, the price of postage relative to the average of all other prices has declined since reaching a peak in 1975.

TABLE 3-1
Money Price Versus Relative Price
The money price of both compact disks (CDs) and cassettes has risen. But the relative price of CDs has fallen (or conversely, the relative price of cassettes has risen).

	Money Price		Relative Price	
	Price Last Year	Price This Year	Price Last Year	Price This Year
CDs	$12	$14	$\frac{\$12}{\$6} = 2.0$	$\frac{\$14}{\$8} = 1.75$
Cassettes	$ 6	$ 8	$\frac{\$6}{\$12} = 0.5$	$\frac{\$8}{\$14} = 0.57$

as much as CDs, but today they cost about 57 percent as much. In the one-year period, though both prices have gone up in money terms, the relative price of CDs has fallen (and equivalently, the relative price of cassettes has risen).

INTERNATIONAL EXAMPLE

The High Relative Price of a U.S. Education

In 1993, about 40 percent of all college students classified as "international students"—students working toward degrees outside their home countries—were enrolled in U.S. colleges and universities. This figure has shrunk to just over 30 percent today, and it gradually continues to decline.

Have foreign students decided that the quality of American higher education is diminishing? Some may have made this judgment, but a more likely explanation for the falling U.S. share of international students is the higher relative price of a U.S. college education. Throughout the 1990s, tuition and other fees that U.S. colleges and universities charged for their services rose much faster than the average price of other goods and services. They also rose faster than tuition and fees at foreign universities. For instance, even before the sharp 1997–1998 economic contraction in Southeast Asia, increasing numbers of students from this region had begun studying at Australian universities. Colleges in Australia are not only closer to home but also less expensive.

For Critical Analysis

If the relative price of education at U.S. universities continues to increase, what other means could these universities use to try to regain their lost share of international students?

CONCEPTS IN BRIEF

- The law of demand posits an inverse relationship between the quantity demanded of a good and its price, other things being equal.
- The law of demand applies when other things, such as income and the prices of all other goods and services, are held constant.

THE DEMAND SCHEDULE

Let's take a hypothetical demand situation to see how the inverse relationship between the price and the quantity demanded looks (holding other things equal). We will consider the quantity of minidisks demanded *per year.* Without stating the *time dimension,* we could not make sense out of this demand relationship because the numbers would be different if we were talking about the quantity demanded per month or the quantity demanded per decade.

In addition to implicitly or explicitly stating a time dimension for a demand relationship, we are also implicitly referring to *constant-quality units* of the good or service in question. Prices are always expressed in constant-quality units in order to avoid the problem of comparing commodities that are in fact not truly comparable.

In panel (a) of Figure 3-1 on page 52, we see that if the price were $1 per minidisk, 50 disks would be bought each year by our representative individual, but if the price were $5 per disk, only 10 minidisks would be bought each year. This reflects the law of demand. Panel (a) is also called simply demand, or a *demand schedule,* because it gives a schedule of alternative quantities demanded per year at different possible prices.

FIGURE 3-1
The Individual Demand Schedule and the Individual Demand Curve
In panel (a), we show combinations *A* through *E* of the quantities of minidisks demanded, measured in constant-quality units at prices ranging from $5 down to $1 per disk. In panel (b), we plot combinations *A* through *E* on a grid. The result is the individual demand curve for minidisks.

Panel (a)

Combination	Price per Constant-Quality Minidisks	Quantity of Constant-Quality Minidisks per Year
A	$5	10
B	4	20
C	3	30
D	2	40
E	1	50

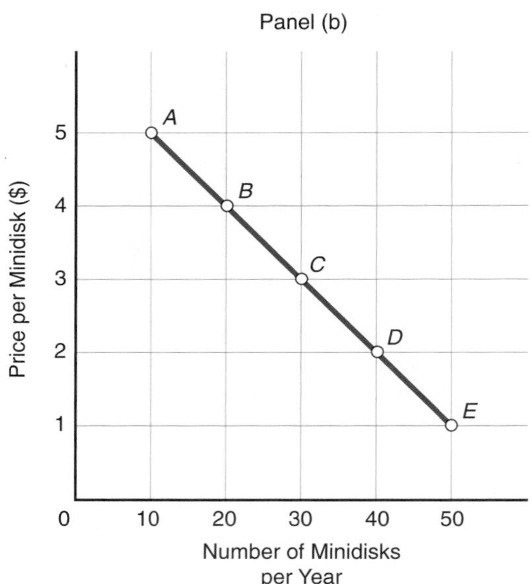

The Demand Curve

Tables expressing relationships between two variables can be represented in graphical terms. To do this, we need only construct a graph that has the price per constant-quality minidisk on the vertical axis and the quantity measured in constant-quality minidisks per year on the horizontal axis. All we have to do is take combinations *A* through *E* from panel (a) of Figure 3-1 and plot those points in panel (b). Now we connect the points with a smooth line, and *voilà,* we have a **demand curve.*** It is downward-sloping (from left to right) to indicate the inverse relationship between the price of minidisks and the quantity demanded per year. Our presentation of demand schedules and curves applies equally well to all commodities, including toothpicks, hamburgers, textbooks, credit, and labor services. Remember, the demand curve is simply a graphical representation of the law of demand.

Demand curve 
A graphical representation of the demand schedule; a negatively sloped line showing the inverse relationship between the price and the quantity demanded (other things being equal).

Individual Versus Market Demand Curves

The demand schedule shown in panel (a) of Figure 3-1 and the resulting demand curve shown in panel (b) are both given for an individual. As we shall see, the determination of price in the marketplace depends on, among other things, the **market demand** for a particular commodity. The way in which we measure a market demand schedule and derive a market demand curve for minidisks or any other commodity is by summing (at each price) the individual demand for all buyers in the market. Suppose that the market demand for minidisks consists of only two buyers: buyer 1, for whom we've already shown the demand schedule, and buyer 2, whose demand schedule is displayed in column 3 of panel (a) of

Market demand 
The demand of all consumers in the marketplace for a particular good or service. The summing at each price of the quantity demanded by each individual.

*Even though we call them "curves," for the purposes of exposition we often draw straight lines. In many real-world situations, demand and supply curves will in fact be lines that do curve. To connect the points in panel (b) with a line, we assume that for all prices in between the ones shown, the quantities demanded will be found along that line.

FIGURE 3-2

The Horizontal Summation of Two Demand Schedules

Panel (a) shows how to sum the demand schedule for one buyer with that of another buyer. In column 2 is the quantity demanded by buyer 1, taken from panel (a) of Figure 3-1. Column 4 is the sum of columns 2 and 3. We plot the demand curve for buyer 1 in panel (b) and the demand curve for buyer 2 in panel (c). When we add those two demand curves horizontally, we get the market demand curve for two buyers, shown in panel (d).

Panel (a)

(1) Price per Minidisk	(2) Buyer 1's Quantity Demanded	(3) Buyer 2's Quantity Demanded	(4) = (2) + (3) Combined Quantity Demanded per Year
$5	10	10	20
4	20	20	40
3	30	40	70
2	40	50	90
1	50	60	110

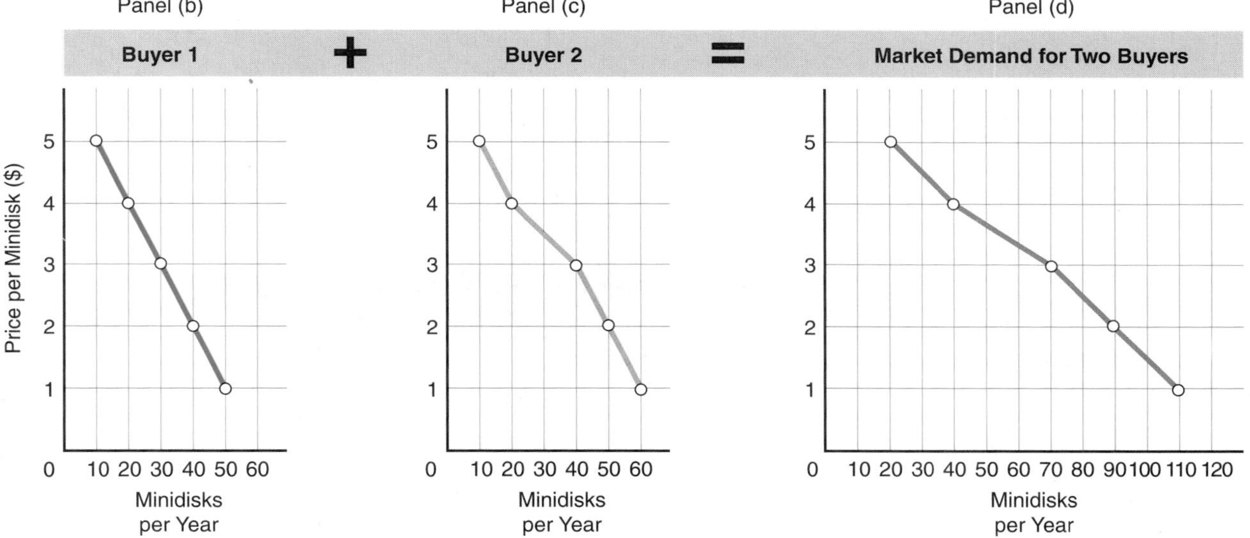

Figure 3-2. Column 1 shows the price, and column 2 shows the quantity demanded by buyer 1 at each price. These data are taken directly from Figure 3-1. In column 3, we show the quantity demanded by buyer 2. Column 4 shows the total quantity demanded at each price, which is obtained by simply adding columns 2 and 3. Graphically, in panel (d) of Figure 3-2, we add the demand curves of buyer 1 [panel (b)] and buyer 2 [panel (c)] to derive the market demand curve.

There are, of course, numerous potential consumers of minidisks. We'll simply assume that the summation of all of the consumers in the market results in a demand schedule, given in panel (a) of Figure 3-3 on page 54, and a demand curve, given in panel (b). The quantity demanded is now measured in millions of units per year. Remember, panel (b) in Figure 3-3 shows the market demand curve for the millions of users of minidisks. The "market" demand curve that we derived in Figure 3-2 was undertaken assuming that there were only two buyers in the entire market. That's why the "market" demand curve for two buyers in panel (d) of Figure 3-2 is not a smooth line, whereas the true market demand curve in panel (b) of Figure 3-3 is a smooth line with no kinks.

Now consider some special aspects of the market demand curve for compact disks.

The Demand for Walkmans

Practice working with demand schedules.

FIGURE 3-3
The Market Demand Schedule for Minidisks
In panel (a), we add up the existing demand schedules for minidisks. In panel (b), we plot the quantities from panel (a) on a grid; connecting them produces the market demand curve for minidisks.

Panel (a)

Price per Constant-Quality Minidisk	Total Quantity Demanded of Constant-Quality Minidisks per Year (millions)
$5	2
4	4
3	6
2	8
1	10

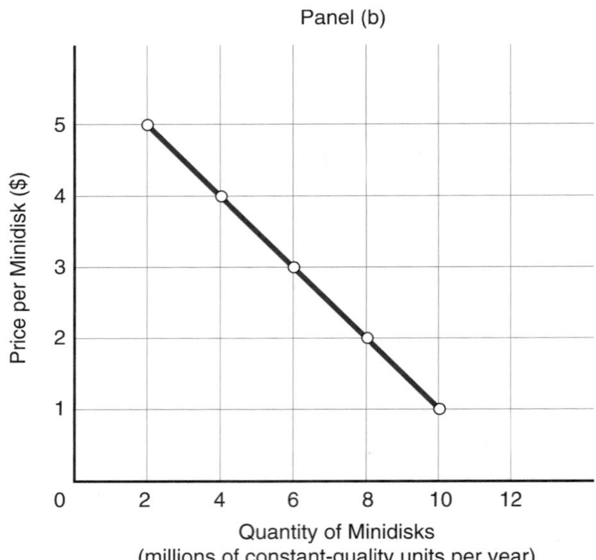

EXAMPLE

Garth Brooks, Used CDs, and the Law of Demand

A few years ago, country singer Garth Brooks tried to prevent his latest album from being sold to any chain or store that also sells used CDs. His argument was that the used-CD market deprived labels and artists of earnings. His announcement came after Wherehouse Entertainment, Inc., a 339-store retailer based in Torrance, California, started selling used CDs side by side with new releases, at half the price. Brooks, along with the distribution arms of Sony, Warner Music, Capitol-EMI, and MCA, was trying to quash the used-CD market. By so doing, it appears that none of these parties understands the law of demand.

Let's say the price of a new CD is $15. The existence of a secondary used-CD market means that to people who choose to resell their CDs for $5, the cost of a new CD is in fact only $10. Because we know that quantity demanded is inversely related to price, we know that more of a new CD will be sold at a price of $10 than of the same CD at a price of $15. Taking only this force into account, eliminating the used-CD market tends to reduce sales of new CDs.

But there is another force at work here, too. Used CDs are substitutes for new CDs. If used CDs are not available, some people who would have purchased them will instead purchase new CDs. If this second effect outweighs the incentive to buy less because of the higher effective price, then Brooks is behaving correctly in trying to suppress the used CD market.

For Critical Analysis

Can you apply this argument to the used-book market, in which both authors and publishers have long argued that used books are "killing them"?

CONCEPTS IN BRIEF

- We measure the demand schedule in terms of a time dimension and in constant-quality units.
- The market demand curve is derived by summing the quantity demanded by individuals at each price. Graphically, we add the individual demand curves horizontally to derive the total, or market, demand curve.

SHIFTS IN DEMAND

Assume that the federal government gives every student registered in a college, university, or technical school in the United States a minidisk player-recorder. The demand curve presented in panel (b) of Figure 3-3 would no longer be an accurate representation of total market demand for minidisks. What we have to do is shift the curve outward, or to the right, to represent the rise in demand. There will now be an increase in the number of minidisks demanded at *each and every possible price.* The demand curve shown in Figure 3-4 will shift from D_1 to D_2. Take any price, say, $3 per minidisk. Originally, before the federal government giveaway of player-recorders, the amount demanded at $3 was 6 million minidisks per year. After the government giveaway, however, the new amount demanded at $3 is 10 million minidisks per year. What we have seen is a shift in the demand for minidisks.

The shift can also go in the opposite direction. What if colleges uniformly outlawed the use of minidisk players by any of their students? Such a regulation would cause a shift inward—to the left—of the demand curve for minidisks. In Figure 3-4, the demand curve would shift to D_3; the amount demanded would now be less at each and every possible price.

The Other Determinants of Demand

The demand curve in panel (b) of Figure 3-3 is drawn with other things held constant, specifically all of the other factors that determine how much will be bought. There are many such determinants. The major other determinants are income; tastes and preferences; the prices of related goods; expectations regarding future prices, future incomes, and future product availability; and market size (number of buyers). Let's examine each determinant more closely.

Income. For most goods, an increase in income will lead to an increase in demand. The expression *increase in demand* always refers to a comparison between two different demand curves. Thus for most goods, an increase in income will lead to a rightward shift in the position of the demand curve from, say, D_1 to D_2 in Figure 3-4. You can avoid confusion about shifts in curves by always relating a rise in demand to a rightward shift in the

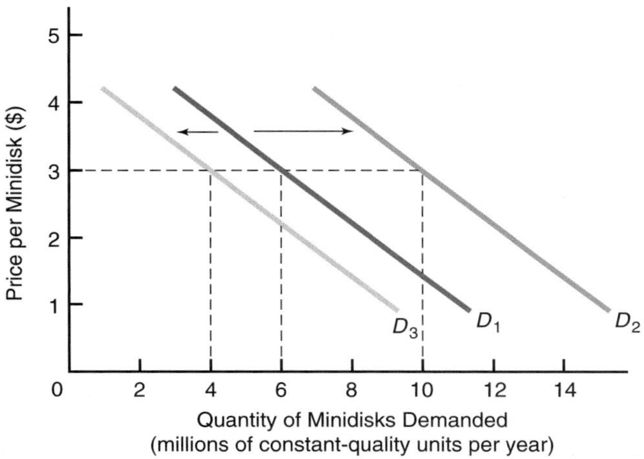

FIGURE 3-4

A Shift in the Demand Curve

If some factor other than price changes, the only way we can show its effect is by moving the entire demand curve, say, from D_1 to D_2. We have assumed in our example that the move was precipitated by the government's giving a free minidisk player-recorder to every registered college student in America. That meant that at *all* prices, a larger number of minidisks would be demanded than before. Curve D_3 represents reduced demand compared to curve D_1, caused by a law prohibiting computers on campus.

Normal goods 
Goods for which demand rises as income rises. Most goods are considered normal.

Inferior goods 
Goods for which demand falls as income rises.

demand curve and a fall in demand to a leftward shift in the demand curve. Goods for which the demand rises when income rises are called **normal goods.** Most goods, such as shoes, computers, and CDs, are "normal goods." For some goods, however, demand *falls* as income rises. These are called **inferior goods.** Beans might be an example. As households get richer, they tend to spend less and less on beans and more and more on meat. (The terms *normal* and *inferior* are merely part of the economist's lexicon; no value judgments are associated with them.)

Remember, a shift to the left in the demand curve represents a fall in demand, and a shift to the right represents a rise, or increase, in demand.

EXAMPLE

Is Dental Care Becoming an Inferior Good?

A British health minister once claimed that the demand for health care is infinite because in the end everyone is in a losing battle against death. This is not so for American dentistry, however. As aggregate U.S. income levels have risen during the past 25 years, overall spending on dental care services has declined.

It isn't that fewer Americans are seeing dentists each year. They just do not require as many fillings or extractions. As incomes rose across the land, people purchased more expensive and effective toothpastes. More towns, cities, and counties began to fluoridate their water as the relative price of this anticavity agent declined, so changing relative prices have also played a role. And higher incomes of their residents have permitted more municipalities to purchase fluoridation systems.

At every age, the average American now has about two more teeth than 25 years ago. Unfortunately for dentists who specialize in treating decaying and diseased teeth, Americans' teeth are healthier than ever before.

For Critical Analysis

Many fledgling dentists have begun specializing in "cosmetic dentistry" desired by clients with healthy but less than beautiful teeth. Compared to traditional dental care services, is cosmetic dentistry more or less likely to be a normal good?

Tastes and Preferences. A change in consumer tastes in favor of a good can shift its demand curve outward to the right. When Frisbees® became the rage, the demand curve for them shifted outward to the right; when the rage died out, the demand curve shifted inward to the left. Fashions depend to a large extent on people's tastes and preferences. Economists have little to say about the determination of tastes; that is, they don't have any "good" theories of taste determination or why people buy one brand of product rather than others. Advertisers, however, have various theories that they use to try to make consumers prefer their products over those of competitors.

Prices of Related Goods: Substitutes and Complements. Demand schedules are always drawn with the prices of all other commodities held constant. That is to say, when deriving a given demand curve, we assume that only the price of the good under study changes. For example, when we draw the demand curve for butter, we assume that the price of margarine is held constant. When we draw the demand curve for stereo speakers, we assume that the price of stereo amplifiers is held constant. When we refer to *related goods,* we are talking about goods for which demand is interdependent. If a change in the price of one good shifts the demand for another good, those two goods are related. There are two types of related goods: *substitutes* and *complements.* We can define and distinguish between substitutes and complements in terms of how the change in price of one commodity affects the demand for its related commodity.

Butter and margarine are **substitutes.** Either can be consumed to satisfy the same basic want. Let's assume that both products originally cost \$2 per pound. If the price of butter remains the same and the price of margarine falls from \$2 per pound to \$1 per pound, people will buy more margarine and less butter. The demand curve for butter will shift inward to the left. If, conversely, the price of margarine rises from \$2 per pound to \$3 per pound, people will buy more butter and less margarine. The demand curve for butter will shift outward to the right. In other words, an increase in the price of margarine will lead to an increase in the demand for butter, and an increase in the price of butter will lead to an increase in the demand for margarine. For substitutes, a price change in the substitute will cause a change in demand *in the same direction.*

Substitutes 

Two goods are substitutes when either one can be used for consumption to satisfy a similar want—for example, coffee and tea. The more you buy of one, the less you buy of the other. For substitutes, the change in the price of one causes a shift in demand for the other in the same direction as the price change.

For **complements,** goods typically consumed together, the situation is reversed. Consider stereo speakers and stereo amplifiers. We draw the demand curve for speakers with the price of amplifiers held constant. If the price per constant-quality unit of stereo amplifiers decreases from, say, \$500 to \$200, that will encourage more people to purchase component stereo systems. They will now buy more speakers, at any given speaker price, than before. The demand curve for speakers will shift outward to the right. If, by contrast, the price of amplifiers increases from \$200 to \$500, fewer people will purchase component stereo systems. The demand curve for speakers will shift inward to the left. To summarize, a decrease in the price of amplifiers leads to an increase in the demand for speakers. An increase in the price of amplifiers leads to a decrease in the demand for speakers. Thus for complements, a price change in a product will cause a change in demand *in the opposite direction.*

Complements 

Two goods are complements if both are used together for consumption or enjoyment—for example, coffee and cream. The more you buy of one, the more you buy of the other. For complements, a change in the price of one causes an opposite shift in the demand for the other.

Are new learning technologies complements or substitutes for college instructors? Read on.

EXAMPLE

Getting Your Degree via the Internet

In this class and in others, you have most likely been exposed to such instructional technologies as films, videos, and interactive CD-ROM learning systems. The future for some of you, or at least the next few generations, may be quite different. All of the instructional technology that your professor provides may be packaged in the form of on-line courses. Many institutions of higher learning are now using the Internet to provide full instruction. It is called *distance learning* or *distributive learning.* And it is worldwide. For example, the University of Michigan, in conjunction with companies in Hong Kong, South Korea, and Europe, offers a global M.B.A. through the Internet. A professor teaches a course "live" via video and uses the software program Lotus Notes, which allows course information to be sent via the Internet. Students submit their homework assignments the same way. Duke University runs the Global Executive M.B.A. program, in which students "attend" CD-ROM video lectures, download additional video and audio materials, and receive interactive study aids, all via the Internet.

Virtually all major college publishers now have projects to develop distance learning via the Internet. In addition, a consortium of over 100 universities has put in place what is called Internet II. Internet II permits full-motion video and virtually instantaneous interactivity for participating universities. The age of fully interactive distance learning with full-motion video is not far off. Certainly, even better technology, as yet undeveloped, will speed up this process.

For Critical Analysis

What do you predict will happen to the demand curve for college professors in the future?

Expectations. Consumers' expectations regarding future prices, future incomes, and future availability may prompt them to buy more or less of a particular good without a change in its current money price. For example, consumers getting wind of a scheduled 100 percent price increase in minidisks next month may buy more of them today at today's prices. Today's demand curve for minidisks will shift from D_1 to D_2 in Figure 3-4. The opposite would occur if a decrease in the price of minidisks were scheduled for next month.

Expectations of a rise in income may cause consumers to want to purchase more of everything today at today's prices. Again, such a change in expectations of higher future income will cause a shift in the demand curve from D_1 to D_2 in Figure 3-4.

Finally, expectations that goods will not be available at any price will induce consumers to stock up now, increasing current demand.

Market Size (Number of Buyers). An increase in the number of buyers (holding per capita income constant) shifts the market demand curve outward. Conversely, a reduction in the number of buyers shifts the market demand curve inward.

Changes in Demand Versus Changes in Quantity Demanded 

We have made repeated references to demand and to quantity demanded. It is important to realize that there is a difference between a *change in demand* and a *change in quantity demanded.*

Demand refers to a schedule of planned rates of purchase and depends on a great many nonprice determinants. Whenever there is a change in a nonprice determinant, there will be a change in demand—a shift in the entire demand curve to the right or to the left.

A quantity demanded is a specific quantity at a specific price, represented by a single point on a demand curve. When price changes, quantity demanded changes according to the law of demand, and there will be a movement from one point to another along the same demand curve. Look at Figure 3-5. At a price of $3 per minidisk, 6 million disks per year are demanded. If the price falls to $1, quantity demanded increases to 10 million per year. This movement occurs because the current market price for the product changes. In Figure 3-5, you can see the arrow pointing down the given demand curve *D.*

FIGURE 3-5
Movement Along a Given Demand Curve
A change in price changes the quantity of a good demanded. This can be represented as movement along a given demand schedule. If, in our example, the price of minidisks falls from $3 to $1 apiece, the quantity demanded will increase from 6 million to 10 million units per year.

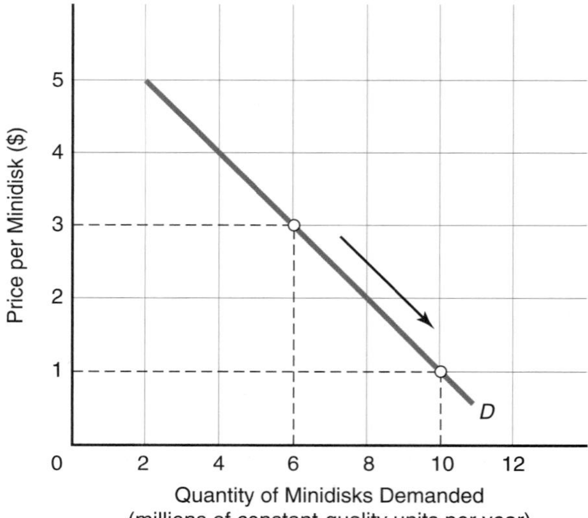

When you think of demand, think of the entire curve. Quantity demanded, in contrast, is represented by a single point on the demand curve.

> A change or shift in demand causes the *entire* curve to move. The *only* thing that can cause the entire curve to move is a change in a determinant *other than its own price.*

In economic analysis, we cannot emphasize too much the following distinction that must constantly be made:

> A change in a good's own price leads to a change in quantity demanded, for any given demand curve, other things held constant. This is a movement *on* the curve.
>
> A change in any other determinant of demand leads to a change in demand. This causes a movement *of* the curve.

CONCEPTS IN BRIEF

- Demand curves are drawn with determinants other than the price of the good held constant. These other determinants are (1) income; (2) tastes and preferences; (3) prices of related goods; (4) expectations about future prices, future incomes, and future availability of goods; and (5) market size (the number of buyers in the market). If any one of these determinants changes, the demand schedule will shift to the right or to the left.
- A change in demand comes about only because of a change in the other determinants of demand. This change in demand shifts the demand curve to the left or to the right.
- A change in the quantity demanded comes about when there is a change in the price of the good (other things held constant). Such a change in quantity demanded involves a movement along a given demand curve.

THE LAW OF SUPPLY

The other side of the basic model in economics involves the quantities of goods and services that firms will offer for sale to the market. The **supply** of any good or service is the amount that firms will produce and offer for sale under certain conditions during a specified time period. The relationship between price and quantity supplied, called the **law of supply,** can be summarized as follows:

Supply 
A schedule showing the relationship between price and quantity supplied for a specified period of time, other things being equal.

Law of Supply 
The observation that the higher the price of a good, the more of that good sellers will make available over a specified time period, other things being equal.

> At higher prices, a larger quantity will generally be supplied than at lower prices, all other things held constant. At lower prices, a smaller quantity will generally be supplied than at higher prices, all other things held constant.

There is generally a direct relationship between quantity supplied and price. For supply, as the price rises, the quantity supplied rises; as price falls, the quantity supplied also falls. Producers are normally willing to produce and sell more of their product at a higher price than at a lower price, other things being constant. At $5 per minidisk, manufacturers would almost certainly be willing to supply a larger quantity than at $1 per unit, assuming, of course, that no other prices in the economy had changed.

As with the law of demand, millions of instances in the real world have given us confidence in the law of supply. On a theoretical level, the law of supply is based on a model in which producers and sellers seek to make the most gain possible from their a ctivities. For example, as a minidisk manufacturer attempts to produce more and more minidisks over the same time period, it will eventually have to hire more workers, pay overtime wages (which are higher), and overutilize its machines. Only if offered a higher price per minidisk will the minidisk manufacturer be willing to incur these higher costs. That is why the law of supply implies a direct relationship between price and quantity supplied.

The Law of Supply
Gain more experience with the concept of the law of supply.

THE SUPPLY SCHEDULE

Just as we were able to construct a demand schedule, we can construct a *supply schedule,* which is a table relating prices to the quantity supplied at each price. A supply schedule can also be referred to simply as *supply.* It is a set of planned production rates that depends on the price of the product. We show the individual supply schedule for a hypothetical producer in panel (a) of Figure 3-6. At $1 per minidisk, for example, this producer will supply 20,000 minidisks per year; at $5, this producer will supply 55,000 minidisks per year.

The Supply Curve

Supply curve
The graphical representation of the supply schedule; a line (curve) showing the supply schedule, which generally slopes upward (has a positive slope), other things being equal.

We can convert the supply schedule in panel (a) of Figure 3-6 into a **supply curve,** just as we earlier created a demand curve in Figure 3-1. All we do is take the price-quantity combinations from panel (a) of Figure 3-6 and plot them in panel (b). We have labeled these combinations *F* through *J.* Connecting these points, we obtain an upward-sloping curve that shows the typically direct relationship between price and quantity supplied. Again, we have to remember that we are talking about quantity supplied *per year,* measured in constant-quality units.

The Market Supply Curve

Just as we had to sum the individual demand curves to get the market demand curve, we need to sum the individual producers' supply curves to get the market supply curve. Look at Figure 3-7, in which we horizontally sum two typical minidisk manufacturers' supply curves. Supplier 1's data are taken from Figure 3-6; supplier 2 is added. The numbers are presented in panel (a). The graphical representation of supplier 1 is in panel (b), of supplier 2 in panel (c), and of the summation in panel (d). The result, then, is the supply curve for minidisks for suppliers 1 and 2. We assume that there are more suppliers of minidisks, however. The total market supply schedule and total market demand curve for minidisks are represented in Figure 3-8, with the curve in panel (b) obtained by adding all of the supply

FIGURE 3-6
The Individual Producer's Supply Schedule and Supply Curve for Minidisks
Panel (a) shows that at higher prices, a hypothetical supplier will be willing to provide a greater quantity of minidisks. We plot the various price-quantity combinations in panel (a) on the grid in panel (b). When we connect these points, we find the individual supply curve for diskettes. It is positively sloped.

Panel (a)

Combination	Price per Constant-Quality Minidisk	Quantity of Minidisks Supplied (thousands of constant-quality units per year)
F	$5	55
G	4	40
H	3	35
I	2	25
J	1	20

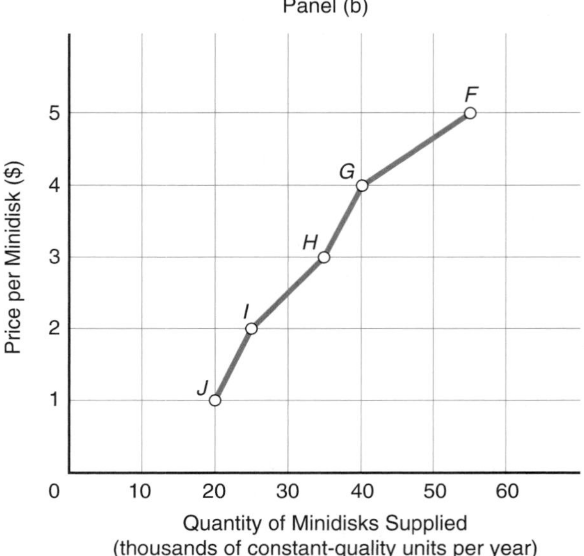

Panel (a)

(1) Price per Minidisk	(2) Supplier 1's Quantity Supplied (thousands)	(3) Supplier 2's Quantity Supplied (thousands)	(4) = (2) + (3) Combined Quantity Supplied per Year (thousands)
$5	55	35	90
4	40	30	70
3	35	20	55
2	25	15	40
1	20	10	30

FIGURE 3-7

Horizontal Summation of Supply Curves

In panel (a), we show the data for two individual suppliers of minidisks. Adding how much each is willing to supply at different prices, we come up with the combined quantities supplied in column 4. When we plot the values in columns 2 and 3 on grids in panels (b) and (c) and add them horizontally, we obtain the combined supply curve for the two suppliers in question, shown in panel (d).

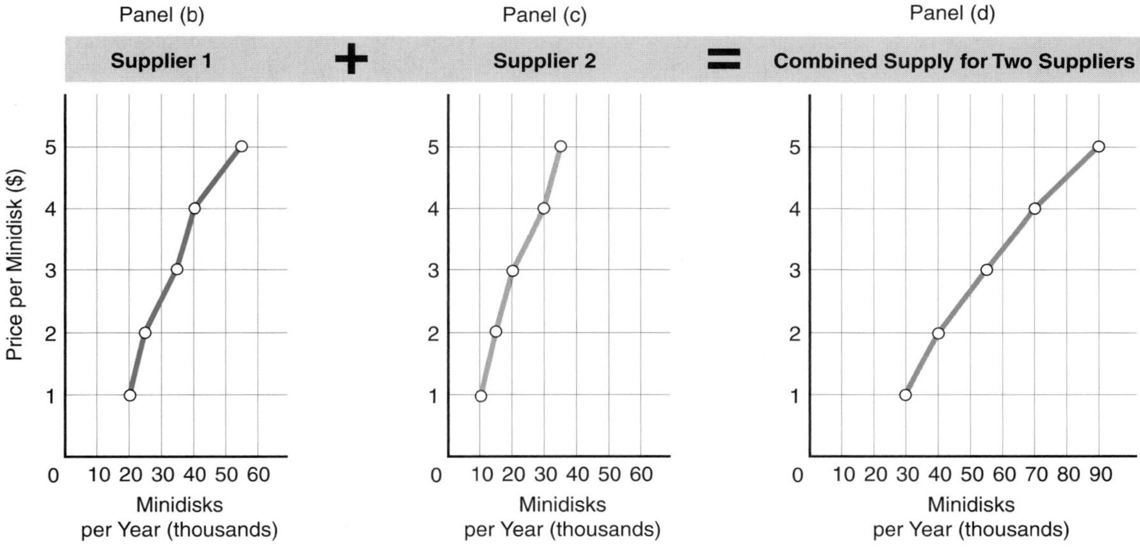

FIGURE 3-8

The Market Supply Schedule and the Market Supply Curve for Minidisks

In panel (a), we show the summation of all the individual producers' supply schedules; in panel (b), we graph the resulting supply curve. It represents the market supply curve for diskettes and is upward-sloping.

Panel (a)

Price per Constant-Quality Minidisk	Quantity of Minidisks Supplied (millions of constant-quality units per year)
$5	10
4	8
3	6
2	4
1	2

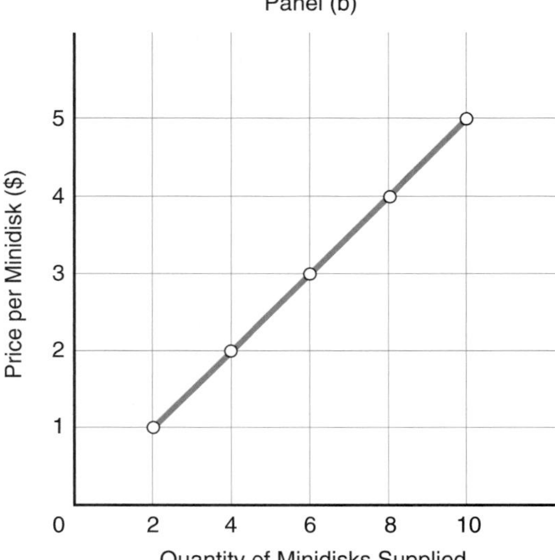

curves such as those shown in panels (b) and (c) of Figure 3-7. Notice the difference between the market supply curve with only two suppliers in Figure 3-7 and the one with a large number of suppliers—the entire true market—in panel (b) of Figure 3-8. We assume that the true total market supply curve is a straight line.

Notice what happens at the market level when price changes. If the price is $3, the quantity supplied is 6 million. If the price goes up to $4, the quantity supplied increases to 8 million per year. If the price falls to $2, the quantity supplied decreases to 4 million per year. Changes in quantity supplied are represented by movements along the supply curve in panel (b) of Figure 3-8.

CONCEPTS IN BRIEF

- There is normally a direct, or positive, relationship between price and quantity of a good supplied, other things held constant.
- The supply curve normally shows a direct relationship between price and quantity supplied. The market supply curve is obtained by horizontally adding individual supply curves in the market.

SHIFTS IN SUPPLY

When we looked at demand, we found out that any change in anything relevant besides the price of the good or service caused the demand curve to shift inward or outward. The same is true for the supply curve. If something besides price changes and alters the willingness of suppliers to produce a good or service, then we will see the entire supply curve shift.

Consider an example. A new method of coating minidisks has been invented. It reduces the cost of production by 50 percent. In this situation, minidisk producers will supply more product at *all* prices because their cost of so doing has fallen dramatically. Competition among manufacturers to produce more at each and every price will shift the supply schedule outward to the right from S_1 to S_2 in Figure 3-9. At a price of $3, the quantity supplied was originally 6 million per year, but now the quantity supplied (after the reduction in the costs of production) at $3 a minidisk will be 9 million a year. (This is similar to what has happened to the supply curve of personal computers and fax machines in recent years as computer memory chip prices have fallen.)

Consider the opposite case. If the cost of making minidisks doubles, the supply curve in Figure 3-9 will shift from S_1 to S_3. At each and every price, the number of minidisks supplied will fall due to the increase in the price of raw materials.

FIGURE 3-9
A Shift in the Supply Schedule
If the cost of producing minidisks were to fall dramatically, the supply schedule would shift rightward from S_1 to S_2 such that at all prices, a larger quantity would be forthcoming from suppliers. Conversely, if the cost of production rose, the supply curve would shift leftward to S_3.

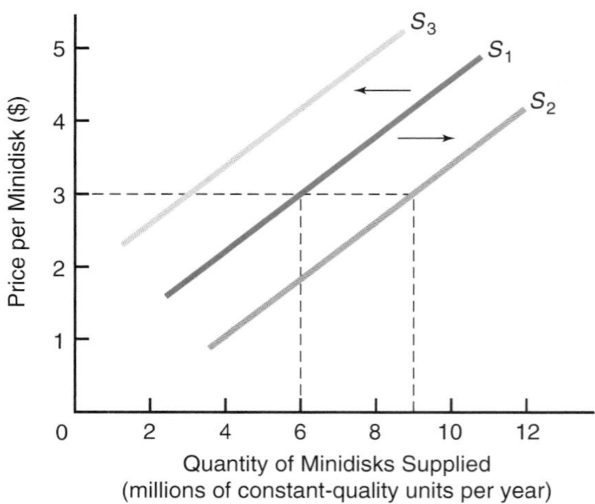

The Other Determinants of Supply

When supply curves are drawn, only the price of the good in question changes, and it is assumed that other things remain constant. The other things assumed constant are the costs of resources (inputs) used to produce the product, technology and productivity, taxes and subsidies, producers' price expectations, and the number of firms in the industry. These are the major nonprice determinants of supply. If *any* of them changes, there will be a shift in the supply curve.

Cost of Inputs Used to Produce the Product. If one or more input prices fall, the supply curve will shift outward to the right; that is, more will be supplied at each and every price. The opposite will be true if one or more inputs become more expensive. For example, when we draw the supply curve of new cars, we are holding the cost of steel (and other inputs) constant. When we draw the supply curve of blue jeans, we are holding the cost of cotton fabric fixed. Likewise, when we draw a supply curve for caviar, we are holding constant the cost of obtaining a fundamental input—a particular kind of fish.

INTERNATIONAL EXAMPLE

Caviar Poaching Is Making a Pricey Delicacy Even Pricier

You've probably heard that caviar is nothing but fish eggs. That is true, but the best caviar comes from a fish called the sturgeon, which thrives in the waters of the Volga River in Russia and the Caspian Sea. Caviar is a big but dwindling business. The reason is that in years past, poachers have removed so many sturgeon from their watery home that their population today is lower than in prior years.

The immediate effect? A leftward shift in the market supply curve. The market outcome? A big increase in the market price of caviar. In 1998, an ounce of prized caviar from a particular sturgeon, the beluga, sold for $55 in New York caviar boutiques. Since then, the market price has steadily risen, and within a few years it is expected to top $100 per ounce.

For Critical Analysis

The Russian government is trying to beef up its fisheries police force that patrols the Volga River, and nations bordering the Caspian Sea are working on a way to enforce the ban on poaching. If successful, how are these policies likely to affect the market price of caviar?

Technology and Productivity. Supply curves are drawn by assuming a given technology, or "state of the art." When the available production techniques change, the supply curve will shift. For example, when a better production technique for minidisks becomes available, the supply curve will shift to the right. A larger quantity will be forthcoming at each and every price because the cost of production is lower.

Taxes and Subsidies. Certain taxes, such as a per-unit tax, are effectively an addition to production costs and therefore reduce the supply. If the supply curve were S_1 in Figure 3-9, a per-unit tax increase would shift it to S_3. A **subsidy** would do the opposite; it would shift the curve to S_2. Every producer would get a "gift" from the government of a few cents for each unit produced.

Subsidy
A negative tax; a payment to a producer from the government, usually in the form of a cash grant.

Price Expectations. A change in the expectation of a future relative price of a product can affect a producer's current willingness to supply, just as price expectations affect a consumer's current willingness to purchase. For example, minidisk suppliers may withhold from the market part of their current supply if they anticipate higher prices in the future. The current amount supplied at each and every price will decrease.

Number of Firms in the Industry. In the short run, when firms can only change the number of employees they use, we hold the number of firms in the industry constant. In the long run, the number of firms (or the size of some existing firms) may change. If the number of firms increases, the supply curve will shift outward to the right. If the number of firms decreases, it will shift inward to the left.

Changes in Supply Versus Changes in Quantity Supplied 

We cannot overstress the importance of distinguishing between a movement along the supply curve—which occurs only when the price changes for a given supply curve—and a shift in the supply curve—which occurs only with changes in other nonprice factors. A change in price always brings about a change in quantity supplied along a given supply curve. We move to a different coordinate on the existing supply curve. This is specifically called a *change in quantity supplied.* When price changes, quantity supplied changes, and there will be a movement from one point to another along the same supply curve.

When you think of *supply,* think of the entire curve. Quantity supplied is represented by a single point on the supply curve.

> A change or shift in supply causes the entire curve to move. The *only* thing that can cause the entire curve to move is a change in a determinant *other than price.*

Consequently,

> A change in the price leads to a change in the quantity supplied, other things being constant. This is a movement *on* the curve.
>
> A change in any other determinant of supply leads to a change in supply. This causes a movement *of* the curve.

CONCEPTS IN BRIEF

- If the price changes, we *move along* a curve—there is a change in quantity demanded or supplied. If some other determinant changes, we *shift* a curve—there is a change in demand or supply.
- The supply curve is drawn with other things held constant. If other determinants of supply change, the supply curve will shift. The other major determinants are (1) input costs, (2) technology and productivity, (3) taxes and subsidies, (4) expectations of future relative prices, and (5) the number of firms in the industry.

PUTTING DEMAND AND SUPPLY TOGETHER

In the sections on supply and demand, we tried to confine each discussion to supply or demand only. But you have probably already realized that we can't view the world just from the supply side or just from the demand side. There is an interaction between the two. In this section, we will discuss how they interact and how that interaction determines the prices that prevail in our economy. Understanding how demand and supply interact is essential to understanding how prices are determined in our economy and other economies in which the forces of supply and demand are allowed to work.

Let's first combine the demand and supply schedules and then combine the curves.

Click here to see how the U.S. Department of Agriculture seeks to estimate demand and supply conditions for major agricultural products.

Demand and Supply Schedules Combined

Let's place panel (a) from Figure 3-3 (the market demand schedule) and panel (a) from Figure 3-8 (the market supply schedule) together in panel (a) of Figure 3-10. Column 1 shows the price; column 2, the quantity supplied per year at any given price; and column 3,

FIGURE 3-10

Putting Demand and Supply Together

In panel (a), we see that at the price of $3, the quantity supplied and the quantity demanded are equal, resulting in neither an excess in the quantity demanded nor an excess in the quantity supplied. We call this price the equilibrium, or market clearing, price. In panel (b), the intersection of the supply and demand curves is at *E,* at a price of $3 and a quantity of 6 million per year. At point *E,* there is neither an excess in the quantity demanded nor an excess in the quantity supplied. At a price of $1, the quantity supplied will be only 2 million per year, but the quantity demanded will be 10 million. The difference is excess quantity demanded at a price of $1. The price will rise, so we will move from point *A* up the supply curve and point *B* up the demand curve to point *E.* At the other extreme, $5 elicits a quantity supplied of 10 million but a quantity demanded of only 2 million. The difference is excess quantity supplied at a price of $5. The price will fall, so we will move down the demand curve and the supply curve to the equilibrium price, $3 per minidisk.

Panel (a)

(1) Price per Constant-Quality Minidisk	(2) Quantity Supplied (minidisks per year)	(3) Quantity Demanded (minidisks per year)	(4) Difference (2) − (3) (minidisks per year)	(5) Condition
$5	10 million	2 million	8 million	Excess quantity supplied (surplus)
4	8 million	4 million	4 million	Excess quantity supplied (surplus)
3	6 million	6 million	0	Market clearing price—equilibrium (no surplus, no shortage)
2	4 million	8 million	–4 million	Excess quantity demanded (shortage)
1	2 million	10 million	–8 million	Excess quantity demanded (shortage)

Panel (b)

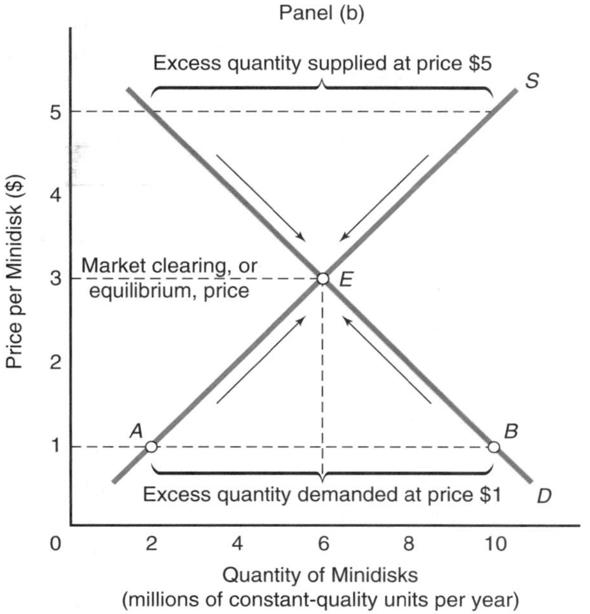

the quantity demanded. Column 4 is merely the difference between columns 2 and 3, or the difference between the quantity supplied and the quantity demanded. In column 5, we label those differences as either excess quantity supplied (called a *surplus,* which we shall discuss shortly) or excess quantity demanded (a commonly known as a *shortage,* discussed shortly). For example, at a price of $1, only 2 million minidisks would be supplied, but the quantity demanded would be 10 million. The difference would be -8 million, which we label excess quantity demanded (a shortage). At the other end of the scale, a price of $5 would elicit 10 million in quantity supplied, but quantity demanded would drop to 2 million, leaving a difference of +8 million units, which we call excess quantity supplied (a surplus).

Market clearing, or equilibrium, price 
The price that clears the market, at which quantity demanded equals quantity supplied; the price where the demand curve intersects the supply curve.

Now, do you notice something special about the price of $3? At that price, both the quantity supplied and the quantity demanded per year are 6 million. The difference then is zero. There is neither excess quantity demanded (shortage) nor excess quantity supplied (surplus). Hence the price of $3 is very special. It is called the **market clearing price—**it clears the market of all excess supply or excess demand. There are no willing consumers who want to pay $3 per minidisk but are turned away by sellers, and there are no willing suppliers who want to sell minidisks at $3 who cannot sell all they want at that price. Another term for the market clearing price is the **equilibrium price,** the price at which there is no tendency for change. Consumers are able to get all they want at that price, and suppliers are able to sell the amount that they want at that price.

Equilibrium

Equilibrium 
The situation when quantity supplied equals quantity demanded at a particular price.

We can define **equilibrium** in general as a point at which quantity demanded equals quantity supplied at a particular price. There tends to be no movement away from this point unless demand or supply changes. Any movement away from this point will set into motion certain forces that will cause movement back to it. Therefore, equilibrium is a stable point. Any point that is not at equilibrium is unstable and cannot be maintained.

The equilibrium point occurs where the supply and demand curves intersect. The equilibrium price is given on the vertical axis directly to the left of where the supply and demand curves cross. The equilibrium quantity demanded and supplied is given on the horizontal axis directly underneath the intersection of the demand and supply curves. Equilibrium can change whenever there is a *shock.*

A shock to the supply-and-demand system can be represented by a shift in the supply curve, a shift in the demand curve, or a shift in both curves. Any shock to the system will result in a new set of supply-and-demand relationships and a new equilibrium; forces will come into play to move the system from the old price-quantity equilibrium (now a disequilibrium situation) to the new equilibrium, where the new demand and supply curves intersect.

Putting Demand and Supply Together
Study market equilibrium in more detail.

Panel (b) in Figure 3-3 and panel (b) in Figure 3-8 are combined as panel (b) in Figure 3-10. The only difference now is that the horizontal axis measures both the quantity supplied and the quantity demanded per year. Everything else is the same. The demand curve is labeled *D,* the supply curve *S.* We have labeled the intersection of the supply curve with the demand curve as point *E,* for equilibrium. That corresponds to a market clearing price of $3, at which both the quantity supplied and the quantity demanded are 6 million units per year. There is neither excess quantity supplied nor excess quantity demanded. Point *E,* the equilibrium point, always occurs at the intersection of the supply and demand curves. This is the price toward which the market price will automatically tend to gravitate.

EXAMPLE

Why Babysitters Are Earning More

Though good data are hard to come by, parents today agree that the market price of babysitting is way up. Two factors have worked together to bring this about. To see how, take a look at Figure 3-11. There you see the original supply and demand curves for babysitting services in the early 1980s, labeled S_1 and D_1. The market price is P_1, and the equilibrium quantity is Q_1. Now let's think about two events that occurred in the 1990s and early 2000s.

First, there was a population shift. In 1980, there were about 39 million Americans aged 10 to 19, the typical age of babysitters. By the early 2000s, there were about 5 percent fewer people in this age group. Thus the number of suppliers of babysitting services declined at any given price; the market supply schedule shifted leftward, from S_1 to S_2.

At the same time, the number of children younger than 10 rose from 33 million in 1980 to nearly 40 million in the early 2000s. Furthermore, U.S. incomes rose, so more parents desired to eat out and be entertained without their children in tow. These two factors together increased the demand for babysitting services in the 2000s. That is, at any given price, the quantity of babysitting services demanded rose. The demand curve shifted from D_1 to D_2.

As you can see in Figure 3-11, the net effect of these two shifts is an unambiguous rise in the market price of babysitting services, from P_1 to P_2. The equilibrium quantity of babysitting services may increase or decrease. We have illustrated a situation in which it does not change. That is, it is entirely possible that parents in the 2000s are paying a lot more for exactly the same amount of babysitting services that parents purchased at a lower price in the 1980s.

For Critical Analysis

Suppose that in a few years, retiring baby boomers decide to earn extra income by offering to spend some of their time babysitting. What would happen to the equilibrium price of babysitting services? Why?

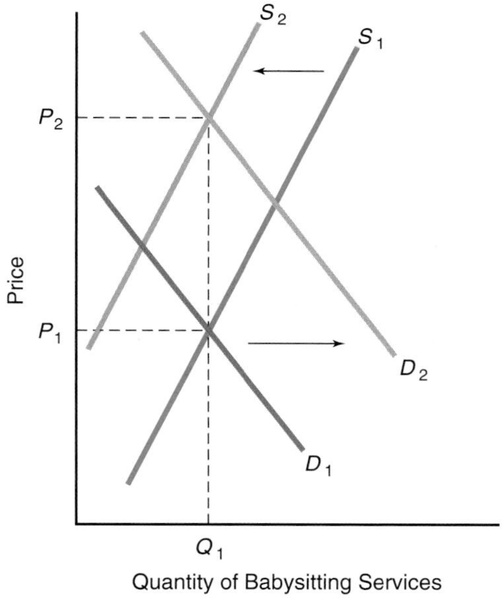

FIGURE 3-11

The Changing Price of Babysitting Services

Simultaneous shifts in the demand curve for babysitting services from D_1 to D_2 and in the supply curve for babysitting services from S_1 to S_2 will cause the equilibrium price of babysitting services to rise from P_1 to P_2. The equilibrium quantity may increase, decrease, or, as illustrated, remain unchanged.

Shortages

The demand and supply curves depicted in Figure 3-10 represent a situation of equilibrium. But a non-market-clearing, or disequilibrium, price will put into play forces that cause the price to change toward the market clearing price at which equilibrium will again be sustained. Look again at panel (b) in Figure 3-10 on page 65. Suppose that instead of being at the market clearing price of $3, for some reason the market price is $1. At this price, the quantity demanded exceeds the quantity supplied, the former being 10 million per year and the latter, 2 million per year. We have a situation of excess quantity demanded at the price of $1. This is usually called a **shortage.** Consumers of minidisks would find that they could not buy all that they wished at $1 apiece. But forces will cause the price to rise: Competing consumers will bid up the price, and suppliers will raise the price and increase output, whether explicitly or implicitly. (Remember, some buyers would pay $5 or more rather than do without minidisks. They do not want to be left out.) We would move from points *A* and *B* toward point *E*. The process would stop when the price again reached $3 per minidisk.

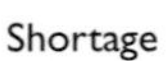
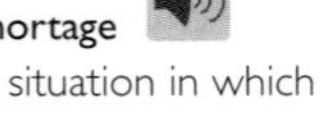

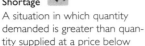

Shortage
A situation in which quantity demanded is greater than quantity supplied at a price below the market clearing price.

At this point, it is important to recall a distinction made in Chapter 2:

Shortages and scarcity are not the same thing.

A shortage is a situation in which the quantity demanded exceeds the quantity supplied at a price *below* the market clearing price. Our definition of scarcity was much more general and all-encompassing: a situation in which the resources available for producing output are insufficient to satisfy all wants. Any choice necessarily costs an opportunity, and the opportunity is lost. Hence we will always live in a world of scarcity because we must constantly make choices, but we do not necessarily have to live in a world of shortages.

Surpluses

Now let's repeat the experiment with the market price at $5 rather than at the market clearing price of $3. Clearly, the quantity supplied will exceed the quantity demanded at that price. The result will be an excess quantity supplied at $5 per unit. This excess quantity supplied is often called a **surplus.** Given the curves in panel (b) in Figure 3-10, however, there will be forces pushing the price back down toward $3 per minidisk: Competing suppliers will attempt to reduce their inventories by cutting prices and reducing output, and consumers will offer to purchase more at lower prices. Suppliers will want to reduce inventories, which will be above their optimal level; that is, there will be an excess over what each seller believes to be the most profitable stock of minidisks. After all, inventories are costly to hold. But consumers may find out about such excess inventories and see the possibility of obtaining increased quantities of minidisks at a decreased price. It behooves consumers to attempt to obtain a good at a lower price, and they will therefore try to do so. If the two forces of supply and demand are unrestricted, they will bring the price back to $3 per minidisk.

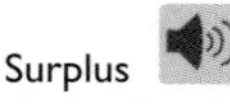

Surplus
A situation in which quantity supplied is greater than quantity demanded at a price above the market clearing price.

Shortages and surpluses are resolved in unfettered markets—markets in which price changes are free to occur. The forces that resolve them are those of competition: In the case of shortages, consumers competing for a limited quantity supplied drive up the price; in the case of surpluses, sellers compete for the limited quantity demanded, thus driving prices down to equilibrium. The equilibrium price is the only stable price, and all (unrestricted) market prices tend to gravitate toward it.

What happens when the price is set below the equilibrium price? Here come the scalpers.

POLICY EXAMPLE

Should Shortages in the Ticket Market Be Solved by Scalpers?

If you have ever tried to get tickets to a playoff game in sports, a popular Broadway play, or a superstar's rock concert, you know about "shortages." The standard ticket situation for a Super Bowl is shown in Figure 3-12. At the face-value price of Super Bowl tickets (P_1), the quantity demanded (Q_2) greatly exceeds the quantity supplied (Q_1). Because shortages last only so long as prices and quantities do not change, markets tend to exhibit a movement out of this disequilibrium toward equilibrium. Obviously, the quantity of Super Bowl tickets cannot change, but the price can go as high as P_2.

Enter the scalper. This colorful term is used because when you purchase a ticket that is being resold at a price that is higher than face value, the seller is skimming an extra profit off the top. If an event sells out, ticket prices by definition have been lower than market clearing prices. People without tickets may be willing to buy high-priced tickets because they place a greater value on the entertainment event than the face value of the ticket. Without scalpers, those individuals would not be able to attend the event. In the case of the Super Bowl, various forms of scalping occur nationwide. Tickets for a seat on the 50-yard line have been sold for more than $2,000 a piece. In front of every Super Bowl arena, you can find ticket scalpers hawking their wares.

In most states, scalping is illegal. In Pennsylvania, convicted scalpers are either fined $5,000 or sentenced to two years behind bars. For an economist, such legislation seems strange. As one New York ticket broker said, "I look at scalping like working as a stockbroker, buying low and selling high. If people are willing to pay me the money, what kind of problem is that?"

For Critical Analysis

What happens to ticket scalpers who are still holding tickets after an event has started?

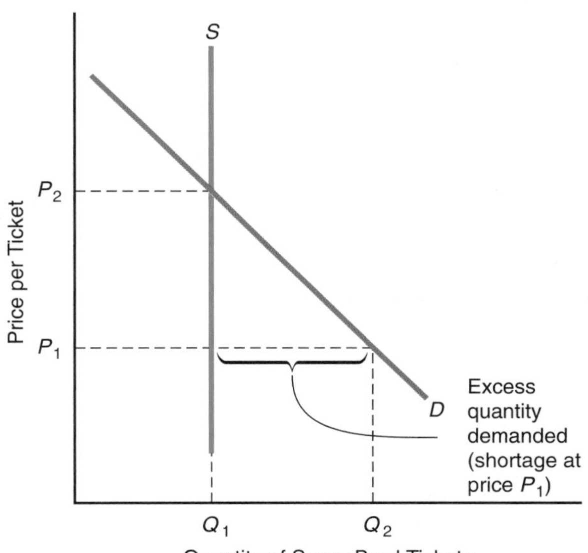

FIGURE 3-12

Shortages of Super Bowl Tickets

The quantity of tickets for any one Super Bowl is fixed at Q_1. At the price per ticket of P_1, the quantity demanded is Q_2, which is greater than Q_1. Consequently, there is an excess quantity demanded at the below-market-clearing price. Prices can go as high as P_2 in the scalpers' market.

CONCEPTS IN BRIEF

- The market clearing price occurs at the intersection of the market demand curve and the market supply curve. It is also called the equilibrium price, the price from which there is no tendency to change unless there is a change in demand or supply.
- Whenever the price is greater than the equilibrium price, there is an excess quantity supplied (a surplus).
- Whenever the price is less than the equilibrium price, there is an excess quantity demanded (a shortage).

NETNOMICS

Stealth Attacks by New Technologies

Successful new products often get off to a slow start. Eventually, however, consumers substitute away from the old products to the point at which demand for the old products effectively disappears. Consider handwritten versus printed manuscripts. For several years in the mid-fifteenth century, printed books were a rarity, and manuscript-copying monks and scribes continued to turn out the bulk of written forms of communication. By the 1470s, however, printed books were more common than handwritten manuscripts. By the end of the fifteenth century, manuscripts had become the rare commodity.

A more recent example involves train engines. Just before 1940, after the diesel-electric engine for train locomotives was invented, an executive of a steam-engine company declared, "They'll never replace the steam locomotive." In fact, it only took 20 years to prove the executive wrong. By 1960, steam engines were regarded as mechanical dinosaurs.

To generate the bulk of its profits, the U.S. Postal Service relies on revenues from first-class mail. To keep its first-class customers satisfied, it recently deployed a $5 billion automation system that reads nine addresses per second and paints envelopes with bar codes to speed sorting. Yet the postal service has lost about $4 billion in first-class mail business since 1994. Around that time, people began to compare the 25-cent cost of a one-minute phone call with the 32-cent cost of first-class postage. Then they began to substitute away from first-class letters to faxes. Other people got access to the Internet and began to send messages by electronic mail, at no additional charge. First-class mail increasingly looks like a steam-engine dinosaur.

Some observers of the software industry think the same sort of thing could happen to a powerhouse of the present: Microsoft Windows. Today the code for this program is on most personal computers on the planet. Competing operating system applications offered by Sun Microsystems's Java software and others currently run more slowly than Windows. But they consume many fewer lines of computer code and hence promise swift accessibility via the Internet. It is conceivable that someday people may log on to the Internet and pay by the minute to use such software to run their computers, thereby freeing up their hard drives for other uses. Thus today's dominant operating system may someday look a lot like a handwritten manuscript does to generations accustomed to reading printed books instead of handwritten manuscripts.

ISSUES & APPLICATIONS

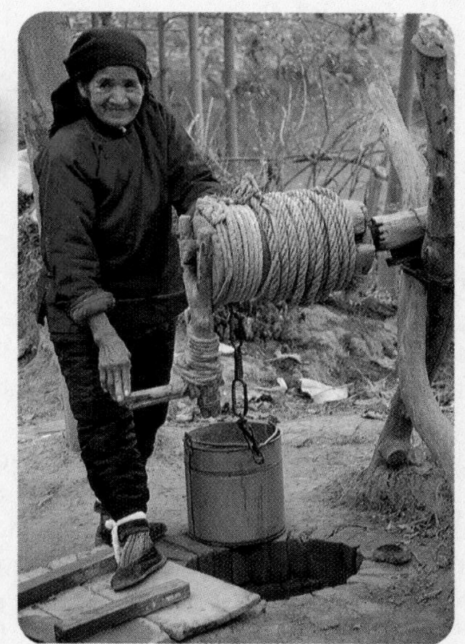

China's Water Shortage: Too Little Rain or Not Enough Pricing?

In China, lack of water has been a big problem. In some towns, people have to wait in long lines at water distribution points set up by local governments. Farmers have lost entire crops. Lacking water to cool machinery, factories have had to cut back on production. Problems are acute in areas where the land is nearly flat, as in large portions of the northern half of China. A recent geophysical analysis indicates that water tables are falling rapidly in these regions. Satellite images show springs, lakes, and rivers drying up.

One Approach: Brute Force

China's government decided in the late 1990s to spare no expense in fighting the water shortage. It began planning vast projects for building tunnels for water to pass through, to expend large amounts of electricity to pump water uphill thousands of feet, to construct huge dams, and to displace hundreds of thousands of people from their homes to make it all possible. Many of these projects are being funded by loans from the World Bank.

The main idea behind these projects, of course, is to move water from the countryside to the cities. But many observers point out that even if all these massive efforts succeed, China's cities will still be living on borrowed time. Among the most water-short is the Chinese capital city of Beijing, which has already exhausted groundwater reserves and now takes irrigation water away from farmers.

The Missing Element: Pricing

To this point, an important element has been missing from the story. Until recently, most water in China could be consumed at no charge. Government pumping stations provided it at a zero price to all takers. In 1998, the government finally enacted a water-pricing policy, but Chinese farmers continue to pay only one-tenth of the opportunity cost of obtaining the water they use to irrigate their crops.

Think about what you have learned in this chapter. Whenever the price of a good, such as water, is below its market clearing price, the quantity demanded exceeds the quantity supplied, and a shortage occurs. To an economist, China's problem is a classic example of a shortage induced by well-intended efforts to set the price of a good below its market price. Naturally, if city-dwellers, farmers, and companies in China can obtain water at very close to a zero price, they will desire to consume water in excess of the amount of water available at that price. That is, the quantity of water demanded will exceed the quantity of water supplied. An economist could have predicted the outcomes before they occurred: overpumped wells, dry fields, and water rationing in cities.

What solution does a typical economist propose? It is for China to let the price system work. Even minor increases in water prices would do wonders to induce people to conserve water. It also would induce Chinese residents to shift water from low-value uses to high-value uses. Pricing water might also eliminate the perceived "need" to think big and build huge dams, tunnels, pumping stations, and the like. By instead thinking smaller and simply permitting the price of water rise toward free-market levels, China could end its water shortage.

Concepts Applied

- Demand
- Supply
- Market Price
- Opportunity Cost
- Shortage

FOR CRITICAL ANALYSIS

1. Even at a posted price of zero, was Chinese water really "free"?
2. A common argument against letting the market determine the prices of "necessity goods" such as water is that having to pay for water is hard on the average citizen. In most countries, who ultimately pays for government-funded dam projects, tunnels through mountains, and machinery to pump water uphill?

SUMMARY DISCUSSION OF LEARNING OBJECTIVES

1. **The Law of Demand:** According to the law of demand, other things being equal, individuals will purchase fewer units of a commodity at a higher price, and they will purchase more units of the commodity at a lower price.
2. **Relative Prices Versus Money Prices:** When determining the quantity of a commodity to purchase, people respond to changes in its relative price, the price of the commodities in terms of other commodities, rather than a change in the commodity's money price expressed in today's dollars. If the price of a CD rises by 50 percent next year while at the same time all other prices, including your wages, also increase by 50 percent, then the relative price of the CD has not changed. Thus in a world of generally rising prices, you have to compare the price of one good with the general level of prices of other goods in order to decide whether the relative price of that one good has gone up, gone down, or stayed the same.
3. **A Change in Quantity Demanded Versus a Change in Demand:** The demand schedule shows the relationship between various possible prices and respective quantities purchased per unit of time. Graphically, the demand schedule is a downward-sloping demand curve. A change in the price of the good generates a change in the quantity demanded, which is a movement along the demand curve. The determinants of the demand for a good other than the price of the good are (a) income, (b) tastes and preferences, (c) the prices of related goods, (d) expectations, and (e) market size (the number of buyers). Whenever any of these determinants of demand changes, there is a change in the demand for the good, and the demand curve shifts to a new position.
4. **The Law of Supply:** According to the law of supply, sellers will produce and offer for sale more units of a commodity at a higher price, and they will produce and offer for sale fewer units of the commodity at a lower price.
5. **A Change in Quantity Supplied Versus a Change in Supply:** The supply schedule shows the relationship between various possible prices and respective quantities produced and sold per unit of time. On a graph, the supply schedule is a supply curve that slopes upward. A change in the price of the good generates a change in the quantity supplied, which is a movement along the supply curve. The determinants of the supply of a good other than the price of the good are (a) input costs, (b) technology and productivity, (c) taxes and subsidies, (d) price expectations, and (e) the number of sellers. Whenever any of these determinants of supply changes, there is a change in the supply of the good, and the supply curve shifts to a new position
6. **Determining the Market Price and the Equilibrium Quantity:** The market price of a commodity and equilibrium quantity of the commodity that is produced and sold are determined by the intersection of the demand and supply curves. At this intersection point, the quantity demanded by buyers of the commodity just equals the quantity supplied by sellers. At the market price at this point of intersection, the plans of buyers and sellers mesh exactly. Hence there is neither an excess quantity of the commodity supplied (surplus) nor an excess quantity of the commodity demanded (shortage) at this equilibrium point.

Key Terms and Concepts

Complements (57)
Demand (49)
Demand curve (52)
Equilibrium (66)
Inferior goods (56)
Law of demand (49)
Law of supply (59)
Market (49)
Market clearing, or equilibrium, price (66)
Market demand (52)
Money price (50)
Normal goods (56)
Relative price (50)
Shortage (68)
Subsidy (63)
Substitutes (57)
Supply (59)
Supply curve (60)
Surplus (68)

Problems

Answers to the odd-numbered problems appear at the back of the book.

3-1. Suppose that in a recent market period, an industrywide survey determined the following relationship between the price of rock music CDs and the quantity supplied and quantity demanded.

Price	Quantity Demanded	Quantity Supplied
$9	100 million	40 million
$10	90 million	60 million
$11	80 million	80 million
$12	70 million	100 million
$13	60 million	120 million

Illustrate the supply and demand curves for rock CDs given the information in the table. What are the equilibrium price and quantity? If the industry price is $10, is there a shortage or surplus of CDs? How much is the shortage or surplus?

3-2. Suppose that a survey for a later market period indicates that the quantities supplied in the table in Problem 3-1 are unchanged. The quantity demanded, however, has increased by 30 million at each price. Construct the resulting demand curve in the illustration you made for Problem 3-1. Is this an increase or a decrease in demand? What are the new equilibrium quantity and the new market price? Give two examples that might cause such a change.

3-3. In the market for rock music CDs, explain whether the following event would cause an increase or a decrease in demand or an increase or a decrease in the quantity demanded. Also explain what happens to the equilibrium quantity and the market price.

a. The price of CD packaging material declines.
b. The price of CD players declines.
c. The price of cassette tapes increases dramatically.
d. A booming economy increases the income of the typical CD buyer.
e. Many rock fans suddenly develop a fondness for country music.

3-4. Give an example of a complement and a substitute in consumption for each of the following items.

a. Bacon
b. Tennis racquets
c. Coffee
d. Automobiles

3-5. At the end of the 1990s, the United States imposed high taxes on a number of European goods due to a trade dispute. One of these goods was Roquefort cheese. Show how this tax affects the market for Roquefort cheese, shifting the appropriate curve and indicating a new equilibrium quantity and market price.

3-6. Problem 3-5 described a tax imposed on Roquefort cheese. Illustrate the effect of the tax on Roquefort cheese on other types of blue cheese, shifting the appropriate curve and indicating a new equilibrium quantity and market price.

3-7. Consider the market for laptop computers. Explain whether the following events would cause an increase or a decrease in supply or an increase or a decrease in the quantity supplied. Illustrate each, and show what would happen to the equilibrium quantity and the market price.

a. The price of memory chips used in laptop computers declines.
b. The price of memory chips used in desktop personal computers declines.
c. The number of manufactures of laptop computers increases.
d. The price of computer peripherals, printers, fax-modems, and scanners decreases.

3-8. The United States offers significant subsidy payments to U.S. sugar growers. Describe the effects of the introduction of such subsidies on the market for sugar and the market for artificial sweeteners. Explain whether the demand curve or supply curve shifts in each market, and if so, in which direction. Also explain what happens to the equilibrium quantity and the market price in each market.

3-9. The supply curve for season tickets for basketball games for your school's team is vertical because there are a fixed number of seats in the school's gymnasium. Before preseason practice sessions begin, your school's administration commits itself to selling season tickets the day before the first basketball game at a predetermined price that it believes to be equal to the market price. The school will not change that price at any time prior to and including the day tickets go on sale. Illustrate, within a supply and demand framework, the effect of each of the following events on the market for season tickets on the day the school opens ticket sales, and indicate whether a surplus or a shortage would result.

a. The school's star player breaks a leg during preseason practice.

b. During preseason practice, a published newspaper poll of coaches of teams in your school's conference surprises everyone by indicating that your school's team is in the running to win the conference championship.

c. At a preseason practice session that is open to the public, the school president announces that all refreshments served during games will be free of charge throughout the season.

d. Most of your school's basketball fans enjoy an up-tempo, "run and gun" approach to basketball, but after the team's coach quits following the first preseason practice, the school's administration immediately hires a new coach who believes in a deliberate style of play that relies heavily on slow-tempo, four-corners offense.

3-10. Advances in computer technology allow individuals to purchase and download music from the Internet. Buyers may download single songs or complete tracks of songs that are also sold on CDs. Explain the impact of this technological advance on the market for CDs sold in retail stores.

Economics on the Net

Canadian Taxes and Energy Markets The Canadian government follows the example set by the U.S. government and governments of other countries by imposing taxes on some sources of energy and subsidizing other energy sources. This application helps you apply concepts you learned in this chapter to evaluate the effects of taxes and subsidies.

Title: Canada Environment Review

Navigation: Click here to visit the Energy Information Agency hompage.

Application Read the first three sections of this article ("General Background," "Energy and Environmental Policy," and "Energy Taxes and Subsidies"). Then answer the following questions.

1. Draw a diagram of possible demand and supply curves for the market for gasoline. The tax described in the third section of the article is paid by sellers of gasoline. Thus to induce each gasoline seller to supply the same quantity as it would have supplied before the tax, the price that the seller receives must be higher by the amount of the tax. Given this information, illustrate the effect of this tax on the market supply curve. Illustrate and explain how the tax reduces consumption of transportation gas.
2. Draw a diagram of the market for vehicles powered by natural gas. Illustrate the effect of a subsidy on the supply of natural-gas-powered vehicles, and explain how the subsidy encourages the use of these vehicles.

For Group Study and Analysis The final paragraph under "Energy Taxes and Subsidies" describes a study of tax incentives for conservation and renewable energy technologies. Discuss how a tax incentive affects the supply of renewable energy technologies. Discuss how a tax that "encourages" energy conservation might affect a firm engaged in manufacturing. Debate whether one approach is preferred over the other.

CHAPTER

4

EXTENSIONS OF DEMAND AND SUPPLY ANALYSIS

A basic principle in economics is that people respond to incentives. Why might this young person quit school to become a systems programmer?

A few years ago, after a top-flight college athlete turned professional following his sophomore season, a television news commentator called for a law prohibiting college stars from becoming pros "too soon." "He's too young to know what's in his own best interest," the commentator said, without noting that the athlete's salary would dwarf his own.

Other student stars, this time in the academic sphere, have also been responding to market incentives. In the face of soaring entry-level salaries, hordes of computer science students have been dropping their studies in favor of high-paying jobs. College deans and presidents have decried this trend, arguing that ultimately market salaries will fall. The students, they say, are grabbing near-term gains, but lacking degrees, they eventually face the prospect of lower future earnings. Do these academic naysayers have a point? To answer this question, you must learn more about how markets work.

LEARNING OBJECTIVES

After reading this chapter, you should be able to:

1. Discuss the essential features of the price system
2. Evaluate the effects on the market price and equilibrium quantity of changes in demand and supply
3. Understand the rationing function of prices
4. Explain the effects of price ceilings
5. Explain the effects of price floors
6. Describe various types of government-imposed quantity restrictions on markets

Chapter Outline

Did You Know That... according to the U.S. Customs Service, the second most serious smuggling problem along the Mexican border, just behind drugs, involves the refrigerant Freon? Selling Freon is more profitable than dealing in cocaine, and illegal Freon smuggling is a bigger business than gunrunning. Freon is used in many air conditioners in cars and homes. Its use is already illegal in the United States, but residents of developing countries may legally use it until the year 2005. When an older U.S. air conditioner needs fixing, it is often cheaper to pay a relatively high price for illegally smuggled Freon than to modify the unit to use a replacement coolant. You can analyze illegal markets, such as the one for Freon, using the supply and demand analysis you learned in Chapter 3. Similarly, you can use this analysis to examine legal markets and the "shortage" of skilled information technology specialists, the "shortage" of apartments in certain cities, and many other phenomena. All of these examples are part of our economy, which we characterize as a *price system.*

THE PRICE SYSTEM

A **price system,** otherwise known as a *market system,* is one in which relative prices are constantly changing to reflect changes in supply and demand for different commodities. The prices of those commodities are the signals to everyone within the system as to what is relatively scarce and what is relatively abundant. Indeed, it is the *signaling* aspect of the price system that provides the information to buyers and sellers about what should be bought and what should be produced. In a price system, there is a clear-cut chain of events in which any changes in demand and supply cause changes in prices that in turn affect the opportunities that businesses and individuals have for profit and personal gain. Such changes influence our use of resources.

Price system 
An economic system in which relative prices are constantly changing to reflect changes in supply and demand for different commodities. The prices of those commodities are signals to everyone within the system as to what is relatively scarce and what is relatively abundant.

EXCHANGE AND MARKETS

The price system features **voluntary exchange,** acts of trading between individuals that make both parties to the trade subjectively better off. The **terms of exchange**—the prices we pay for the desired items—are determined by the interaction of the forces underlying supply and demand. In our economy, the majority of exchanges take place voluntarily in markets. A market encompasses the exchange arrangements of both buyers and sellers that underlie the forces of supply and demand. Indeed, one definition of a market is a low-cost institution for facilitating exchange. A market increases incomes by helping resources move to their highest-valued uses by means of prices. Prices are the providers of information.

Voluntary exchange 
An act of trading, done on a voluntary basis, in which both parties to the trade are subjectively better off after the exchange.

Terms of exchange 
The terms under which trading takes place. Usually the terms of exchange are equal to the price at which a good is traded.

Transaction Costs

Individuals turn to markets because markets reduce the cost of exchanges. These costs are sometimes referred to as **transaction costs,** which are broadly defined as the costs associated with finding out exactly what is being transacted as well as the cost of enforcing contracts. If you were Robinson Crusoe and lived alone on an island, you would never incur a transaction cost. For everyone else, transaction costs are just as real as the costs of production. High-speed large-scale computers have allowed us to reduce transaction costs by increasing our ability to process information and keep records.

Consider some simple examples of transaction costs. The supermarket reduces transaction costs relative to your having to go to numerous specialty stores to obtain the items you desire. Organized stock exchanges, such as the New York Stock Exchange, have reduced transaction costs of buying and selling stocks and bonds. In general, the more organized the market, the lower the transaction costs. One group of individuals who constantly attempt to lower transaction costs are the much maligned middlemen.

Transaction costs 
All of the costs associated with exchanging, including the informational costs of finding out price and quality, service record, and durability of a product, plus the cost of contracting and enforcing that contract.

The Role of Middlemen

As long as there are costs to bringing together buyers and sellers, there will be an incentive for intermediaries, normally called middlemen, to lower those costs. This means that middlemen specialize in lowering transaction costs. Whenever producers do not sell their products directly to the final consumer, there are, by definition, one or more middlemen involved. Farmers typically sell their output to distributors, who are usually called wholesalers, who then sell those products to supermarkets.

Recently, technology has changed the way middlemen work.

EXAMPLE

Middlemen Flourish on the Internet

At one time, people speculated that the Internet would be bad news for middlemen. People would just click their mouse to head to a Web site where they could deal directly with a company. In fact, every day there are new companies establishing middleman sites all over the Web. For instance, one Web site, Kelley Blue Book (www.kbb.com), allows you to get exact dealer invoice prices and destination charges for automobiles so that you can learn what wholesale prices car dealers pay for the cars. You can even find out the prices of optional equipment.

To help consumers locate harder-to-find items, software companies have developed *intelligent shopping agents,* sometimes called "shopbots," which are programs that search the Web to find specific items. Even though human beings are not the middlemen in this instance, the software companies provide middleman services by offering to sell or lease these programs.

For Critical Analysis

Any of us connected to the Internet can find the same information that an Internet middleman (or shopbot, for that matter) can find. Why, then, would someone pay for the services of an Internet middleman?

CHANGES IN DEMAND AND SUPPLY

It is in markets that we see the results of changes in demand and supply. In certain situations, it is possible to predict what will happen to equilibrium price and equilibrium quantity when a change occurs in demand or supply. Specifically, whenever one curve is stable while the other curve shifts, we can tell what will happen to price and quantity. Consider the four possibilities in Figure 4-1 (p. 78). In panel (a), the supply curve remains stable but demand increases from D_1 to D_2. Note that the result is both an increase in the market clearing price from P_1 to P_2 and an increase in the equilibrium quantity from Q_1 to Q_2.

In panel (b), there is a decrease in demand from D_1 to D_3. This results in a decrease in both the relative price of the good and the equilibrium quantity. Panels (c) and (d) show the effects of a shift in the supply curve while the demand curve is stable. In panel (c), the supply

FIGURE 4-1

Shifts in Demand and in Supply: Determinate Results

In panel (a), the supply curve is stable at S. The demand curve shifts outward from D_1 to D_2. The equilibrium price and quantity rise from P_1, Q_1 to P_2, Q_2, respectively. In panel (b), again the supply curve remains stable at S. The demand curve, however, shifts inward to the left, showing a decrease in demand from D_1 to D_3. Both equilibrium price and equilibrium quantity fall. In panel (c), the demand curve now remains stable at D. The supply curve shifts from S_1 to S_2. The equilibrium price falls from P_1 to P_2. The equilibrium quantity increases, however, from Q_1 to Q_2. In panel (d), the demand curve is stable at D. Supply decreases as shown by a leftward shift of the supply curve from S_1 to S_3. The market clearing price increases from P_1 to P_3. The equilibrium quantity falls from Q_1 to Q_3.

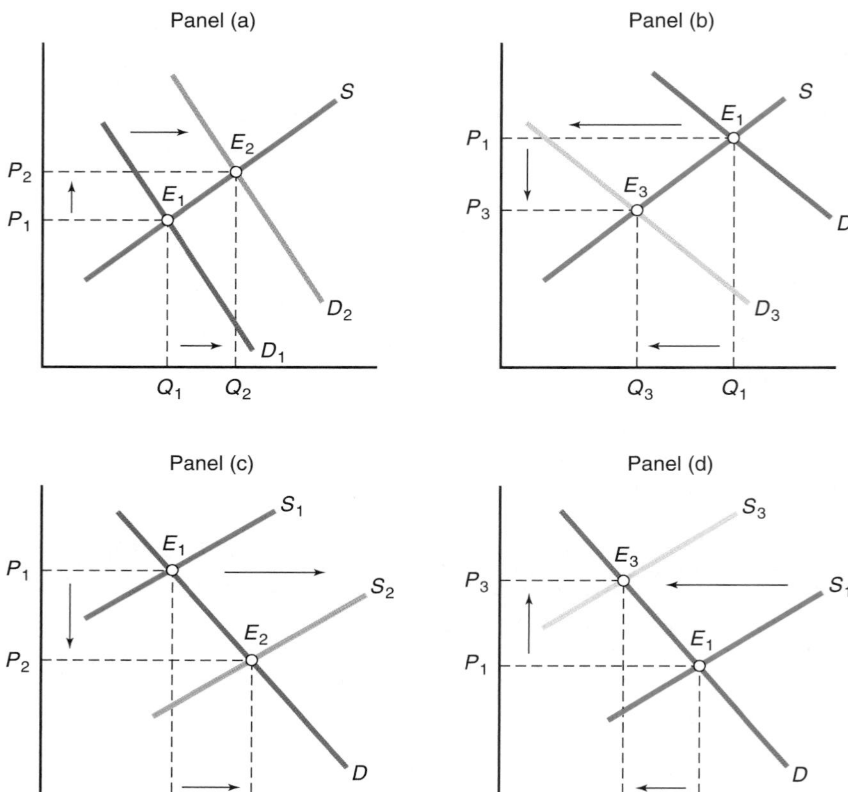

curve has shifted rightward. The relative price of the product falls; the equilibrium quantity increases. In panel (d), supply has shifted leftward—there has been a supply decrease. The product's relative price increases; the equilibrium quantity decreases.

EXAMPLE

The Upside of the Yo-Yo Cycle

Toymaking is a big business. It is also a volatile business. Consider the simple yo-yo. For years, kids couldn't get enough yo-yos, and the industry boomed. Then it fell on hard times—how could pieces of wood or plastic attached to a string compete with action figures and video games? But after years of dormant sales, yo-yos suddenly are hot again in places such as Australia, Japan, and the United Kingdom. Companies that manufacture yo-yos have found that they cannot keep up with this increasing worldwide demand at prevailing prices. Toy retailers can't keep yo-yos in stock. One San Francisco store maintains a yo-yo waiting list that runs to 200 names.

We can turn to demand and supply to see why this situation has arisen in the market for yo-yos. As you can see in Figure 4-2, when the demand schedule for yo-yos shifts rightward, the quantity of yo-yos demanded exceeds the quantity supplied, so at the initial market price, a shortage of yo-yos results. Adjustment to market equilibrium will entail a rise in the market price of yo-yos, which will raise the quantity of yo-yos supplied toward equality with the quantity demanded. Consistent

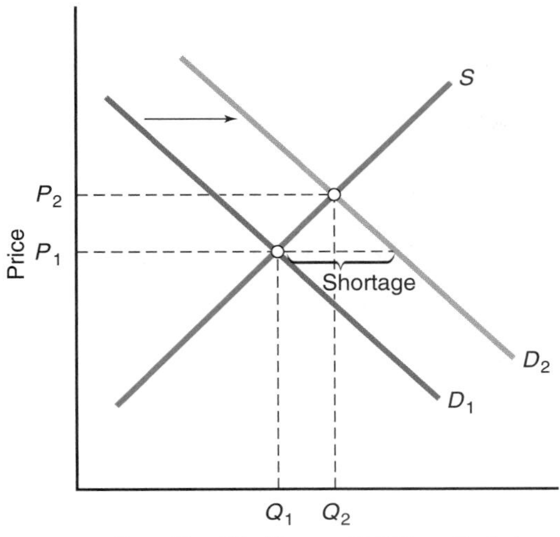

FIGURE 4-2

Responses to a Shift in Yo-Yo Demand

When demand shifts to D_2 but supply stays the same, there will be shortages at the prevailing price P. Eventually, price will rise to P_2 and equilibrium will occur at Q_2.

with this prediction, some yo-yo manufacturers report that their existing plants now run 24 hours a day, seven days a week. Many producers are opening new production lines. In the meantime, yo-yo prices have risen considerably at toy stores around the globe.

For Critical Analysis

The current yo-yo craze is unlikely to last. When it ends, what kinds of adjustments are likely to occur in the market for yo-yos?

When Both Demand and Supply Shift

The examples given in Figure 4-1 each showed a theoretically determinate outcome of a shift in either the demand curve holding the supply curve constant or the supply curve holding the demand curve constant. When both supply and demand curves change, the outcome is indeterminate for either equilibrium price or equilibrium quantity.

Predicting Changes in Price and Quantities

Improve your ability to reason through the effects of shifts in demand and supply.

When both demand and supply increase, all we can be certain of is that equilibrium quantity will increase. We do not know what will happen to equilibrium price until we determine whether demand increased relative to supply (equilibrium price will rise) or supply increased relative to demand (equilibrium price will fall). The same analysis applies to decreases in both demand and supply, except that in this case equilibrium quantity falls.

We can be certain that when demand decreases and supply increases, the equilibrium price will fall, but we do not know what will happen to the equilibrium quantity unless we actually draw the new curves. If supply decreases and demand increases, we can be sure that equilibrium price will rise, but again we do not know what happens to equilibrium quantity without drawing the curves. In every situation in which both supply and demand change, you should always draw graphs to determine the resulting change in equilibrium price and quantity.

PRICE FLEXIBILITY AND ADJUSTMENT SPEED

We have used as an illustration for our analysis a market in which prices are quite flexible. Some markets are indeed like that. In others, however, price flexibility may take the form of indirect adjustments such as hidden payments or quality changes. For example, although the published price of bouquets of flowers may stay the same, the freshness of the flowers may change, meaning that the price per constant-quality unit changes. The published price of French bread might stay the same, but the quality could go up or down, thereby changing the price per constant-quality unit. There are many ways to change prices without actually changing the published price for a *nominal* unit of a product or service.

We must also consider the fact that markets do not return to equilibrium immediately. There must be an adjustment time. A shock to the economy in the form of an oil embargo, a drought, or a long strike will not be absorbed overnight. This means that even in unfettered market situations, in which there are no restrictions on changes in prices and quantities, temporary excess quantities supplied and excess quantities demanded may appear. Our analysis simply indicates what the market clearing price ultimately will be, given a demand curve and a supply curve. Nowhere in the analysis is there any indication of the speed with which a market will get to a new equilibrium if there has been a shock. The price may overshoot the equilibrium level. Remember this warning when we examine changes in demand and in supply due to changes in their nonprice determinants.

CONCEPTS IN BRIEF

- The terms of exchange in a voluntary exchange are determined by the interaction of the forces underlying demand and supply. These forces take place in markets, which tend to minimize transaction costs.
- When the demand curve shifts outward or inward with a stable supply curve, equilibrium price and quantity increase or decrease, respectively. When the supply curve shifts outward or inward given a stable demand curve, equilibrium price moves in the direction opposite of equilibrium quantity.
- When there is a shift in demand or supply, the new equilibrium price is not obtained instantaneously. Adjustment takes time.

THE RATIONING FUNCTION OF PRICES 

A shortage creates a situation that forces price to rise toward a market clearing, or equilibrium, level. A surplus brings into play forces that cause price to fall toward its market clearing level. The synchronization of decisions by buyers and sellers that creates a situation of equilibrium is called the *rationing function of prices.* Prices are indicators of relative scarcity. An equilibrium price clears the market. The plans of buyers and sellers, given the price, are not frustrated.* It is the free interaction of buyers and sellers that sets the price that eventually clears the market. Price, in effect, rations a commodity to demanders who are willing and able to pay the highest price. Whenever the rationing function of prices is frustrated by government-enforced price ceilings that set prices below the market clearing level, a prolonged shortage situation is not allowed to be corrected by the upward adjustment of the price.

*There is a difference between frustration and unhappiness. You may be unhappy because you can't buy a Rolls Royce, but if you had sufficient income, you would not be frustrated in your attempt to purchase one at the current market price. By contrast, you would be frustrated if you went to your local supermarket and could get only two cans of your favorite soft drink when you had wanted to purchase a dozen and had the necessary funds.

There are other ways to ration goods. *First come, first served* is one method. *Political power* is another. *Physical force* is yet another. Cultural, religious, and physical differences have been and are used as rationing devices throughout the world.

Consider first come, first served as a rationing device. In countries that do not allow prices to reflect true relative scarcity, first come, first served has become a way of life. We call this *rationing by queues,* where *queue* means "line," as in Britain. Whoever is willing to wait in line the longest obtains meat that is being sold at less than the market clearing price. All who wait in line are paying a higher *total* price than the money price paid for the meat. Personal time has an opportunity cost. To calculate the total price of the meat, we must add up the money price plus the opportunity cost of the time spent waiting.

Lotteries are another way to ration goods. You may have been involved in a rationing-by-lottery scheme during your first year in college when you were assigned a university-provided housing unit. Sometimes for popular classes, rationing by lottery is used to fill the available number of slots.

Rationing by *coupons* has also been used, particularly during wartime. In the United States during World War II, families were allotted coupons that allowed them to purchase specified quantities of rationed goods, such as meat and gasoline. To purchase such goods, you had to pay a specified price *and* give up a coupon.

Rationing by waiting may occur in situations in which entrepreneurs are free to change prices to equate quantity demanded with quantity supplied but choose not to do so. This results in queues of potential buyers. The most obvious conclusion seems to be that the price in the market is being held below equilibrium by some noncompetitive force. That is not true, however.

The reason is that queuing may also arise when the demand characteristics of a market are subject to large or unpredictable fluctuations, and the additional costs to firms (and ultimately to consumers) of constantly changing prices or of holding sufficient inventories or providing sufficient excess capacity to cover these peak demands are greater than the costs to consumers of waiting for the good. This is the usual case of waiting in line to purchase a fast-food lunch or to purchase a movie ticket a few minutes before the next show.

The Essential Role of Rationing

In a world of scarcity, there is, by definition, competition for what is scarce. After all, any resources that are not scarce can be had by everyone at a zero price in as large a quantity as everyone wants, such as air to burn in internal combustion engines. Once scarcity arises, there has to be some method to ration the available resources, goods, and services. The price system is one form of rationing; the others that we mentioned are alternatives. Economists cannot say which system of rationing is best. They can, however, say that rationing via the price system leads to the most efficient use of available resources. This means that generally in a price system, further trades could not occur without making somebody worse off. In other words, in a freely functioning price system, all of the gains from mutually beneficial trade will be exhausted.

CONCEPTS IN BRIEF

- Prices in a market economy perform a rationing function because they reflect relative scarcity, allowing the market to clear. Other ways to ration goods include first come, first served; political power; physical force; lotteries; and coupons.
- Even when businesspeople can change prices, some rationing by waiting will occur. Such queuing arises when there are large unexpected changes in demand coupled with high costs of satisfying those changes immediately.

THE POLICY OF GOVERNMENT-IMPOSED PRICE CONTROLS

Price controls 
Government-mandated minimum or maximum prices that may be charged for goods and services.

Price ceiling 
A legal maximum price that may be charged for a particular good or service.

Price floor 
A legal minimum price below which a good or service may not be sold. Legal minimum wages are an example.

Nonprice rationing devices 
All methods used to ration scarce goods that are price-controlled. Whenever the price system is not allowed to work, nonprice rationing devices will evolve to ration the affected goods and services.

Black market 
A market in which goods are traded at prices above their legal maximum prices or in which illegal goods are sold.

The rationing function of prices is often not allowed to operate when governments impose price controls. **Price controls** typically involve setting a **price ceiling**—the maximum price that may be allowed in an exchange. The world has had a long history of price ceilings applied to some goods, wages, rents, and interest rates, among other things. Occasionally a government will set a **price floor**—a minimum price below which a good or service may not be sold. These have most often been applied to wages and agricultural products. Let's consider price controls in terms of price ceilings.

Price Ceilings and Black Markets

As long as a price ceiling is below the market clearing price, imposing a price ceiling creates a shortage, as can be seen in Figure 4-3. At any price below the market clearing, or equilibrium, price of P_e, there will always be a larger quantity demanded than quantity supplied—a shortage, as you will recall from Chapter 3. Normally, whenever a shortage exists, there is a tendency for price and output to rise to equilibrium levels. This is exactly what we pointed out when discussing shortages in the labor market. But with a price ceiling, this tendency cannot be fully realized because everyone is forbidden to trade at the equilibrium price.

The result is fewer exchanges and **nonprice rationing devices.** In Figure 4-3, at an equilibrium price of P_e, the equilibrium quantity demanded and supplied (or traded) is Q_e. But at the price ceiling of P_1, the equilibrium quantity offered is only Q_s. What happens if there is a shortage? The most obvious nonprice rationing device to help clear the market is queuing, or long lines, which we have already discussed.

Typically, an effective price ceiling leads to a **black market.** A black market is a market in which the price-controlled good is sold at an illegally high price through various methods. For example, if the price of gasoline is controlled at lower than the market clearing price, a gas station attendant may take a cash payment on the side in order to fill up a driver's car (as happened in the 1970s in the United States during price controls on gasoline). If the price of beef is controlled at below its market clearing price, the butcher may give special service to a customer who offers the butcher great seats at an upcoming foot-

FIGURE 4-3 
Black Markets
The demand curve is D. The supply curve is S. The equilibrium price is P_e. The government, however, steps in and imposes a maximum price of P_1. At that lower price, the quantity demanded will be Q_d, but the quantity supplied will only be Q_s. There is a "shortage." The implicit price (including time costs) tends to rise to P_2. If black markets arise, as they generally will, the equilibrium black market price will end up somewhere between P_1 and P_2.

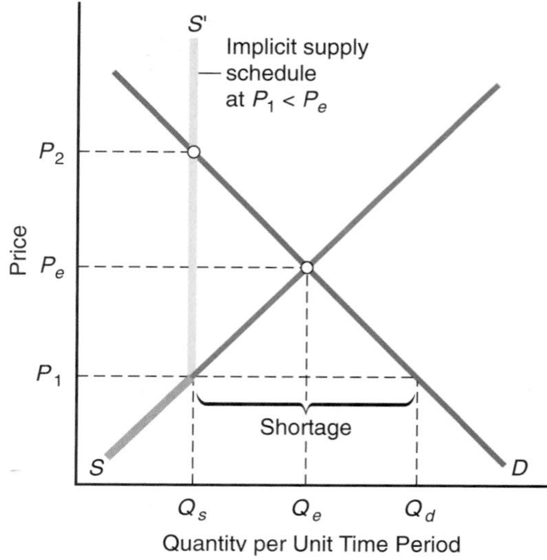

ball game. Indeed, the number of ways in which the true implicit price of a price-controlled good or service can be increased is infinite, limited only by the imagination. (Black markets also occur when goods are made illegal—their legal price is set at zero.)

Whenever a nation attempts to freeze all prices, a variety of problems arise. Many of them occurred a few years ago in one African country, Sierra Leone.

INTERNATIONAL EXAMPLE

Price Controls in Sierra Leone

Lisa Walker spent a year as a Peace Corps volunteer in Sierra Leone, West Africa, and she kept a diary of her experiences. One thing she wrote about was what happened when the government imposed price controls on many common items: "For the last five days," she wrote, "nobody has sold cigarettes, kerosene, Maggi [bouillon] cubes, or rice here . . . . This is the result of the government's new order. The government says that Maggi cubes have to be sold for 30 cents, but sellers bought them for 50 cents, so when military men enter the village to enforce the government price, those with Maggis hide them. Same story for cigarettes and kerosene. The rice supplies are now hidden because of government prices. Unless one is willing to pay an outrageous price, it is impossible to buy rice in the marketplace. The only way to get rice legally is to buy it from the government. This means standing in long lines for many hours to get a rationed amount. I don't know how Sierra Leoneans are managing or how long this artificial rice shortage will last."

For Critical Analysis

How would you graphically illustrate the market for rice in Sierra Leone in the presence of price controls?

CONCEPTS IN BRIEF

- Government policy can impose price controls in the form of price ceilings and price floors.
- An effective price ceiling is one that sets the legal price below the market clearing price and is enforced. Effective price ceilings lead to nonprice rationing devices and black markets.

THE POLICY OF CONTROLLING RENTS

Over 200 American cities and towns, including Berkeley and New York City, operate under some kind of rent control. **Rent control** is a system under which the local government tells building owners how much they can charge their tenants in rent. In the United States, rent controls date back to at least World War II. The objective of rent control is to keep rents below levels that would be observed in a freely competitive market.

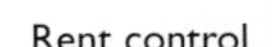

Rent control The placement of price ceilings on rents in particular cities.

The Functions of Rental Prices

In any housing market, rental prices serve three functions: (1) to promote the efficient maintenance of existing housing and stimulate the construction of new housing, (2) to allocate existing scarce housing among competing claimants, and (3) to ration the use of existing housing by current demanders.

<u>Competitive Housing Market</u>
Get practice examining the effects of rent controls.

Rent Controls and Construction. Rent controls have discouraged the construction of new rental units. Rents are the most important long-term determinant of profitability, and rent controls have artificially depressed them. Consider some examples. In a recent year in

Dallas, Texas, with a 16 percent rental vacancy rate but no rent control laws, 11,000 new rental housing units were built. In the same year in San Francisco, California, only 2,000 units were built. The major difference? San Francisco has only a 1.6 percent vacancy rate but stringent rent control laws. In New York City, until a change in the law in 1997, the only rental units being built were luxury units, which were exempt from controls.

Effects on the Existing Supply of Housing. When rental rates are held below equilibrium levels, property owners cannot recover the cost of maintenance, repairs, and capital improvements through higher rents. Hence they curtail these activities. In the extreme situation, taxes, utilities, and the expenses of basic repairs exceed rental receipts. The result is abandoned buildings. Numerous buildings have been abandoned in New York City. Some owners have resorted to arson, hoping to collect the insurance on their empty buildings before the city claims them for back taxes.

Rationing the Current Use of Housing. Rent controls also affect the current use of housing because they restrict tenant mobility. Consider the family whose children have gone off to college. That family might want to live in a smaller apartment. But in a rent-controlled environment, there can be a substantial cost to giving up a rent-controlled unit. In most rent-controlled cities, rents can be adjusted only when a tenant leaves. That means that a move from a long-occupied rent-controlled apartment to a smaller apartment can involve a hefty rent hike. This artificial preservation of the status quo became known in New York as "housing gridlock."

Attempts at Evading Rent Controls

The distortions produced by rent controls lead to efforts by both property owners and tenants to evade the rules. This leads to the growth of expensive government bureaucracies whose job it is to make sure that rent controls aren't evaded. In New York City, property owners have had an incentive to make life unpleasant for tenants to drive them out or to evict them on the slightest pretense as the only way to raise the rent. The city has responded by making evictions extremely costly for property owners. Eviction requires a tedious and expensive judicial proceeding. Tenants, for their part, routinely try to sublet all or part of their rent-controlled apartments at fees substantially above the rent they pay to the owner. Both the city and the property owners try to prohibit subletting and typically end up in the city's housing courts—an entire judicial system developed to deal with disputes involving rent-controlled apartments. The overflow and appeals from the city's housing courts is now clogging the rest of New York's judicial system.

Who Gains and Who Loses from Rent Controls?

The big losers from rent controls are clearly property owners. But there is another group of losers—low-income individuals, especially single mothers, trying to find their first apartment. Some observers now believe that rent controls have worsened the problem of homelessness in such cities as New York.

Typically, owners of rent-controlled apartments often charge "key money" before a new tenant is allowed to move in. This is a large up-front cash payment, usually illegal but demanded nonetheless—just one aspect of the black market in rent-controlled apartments. Poor individuals cannot afford a hefty key money payment, nor can they assure the owner that their rent will be on time or even paid each month. Because controlled rents are usually below market clearing levels, there is little incentive for apartment owners to take any risk on low-income-earning individuals as tenants. This is particularly true when a prospective tenant's chief source of income is a welfare check. Indeed, a large number of the litigants in the New York housing courts are welfare mothers who have missed their rent payments due to emergency expenses or delayed welfare checks. Often their appeals end in evictions and a new home in a temporary public shelter—or on the streets.

Who benefits from rent control? Ample evidence indicates that upper-income professionals benefit the most. These are the people who can use their mastery of the bureaucracy and their large network of friends and connections to exploit the rent control system. Consider that in New York, actresses Mia Farrow and Cicely Tyson live in rent-controlled apartments, paying well below market rates. So do State Senate Democratic leader Manfred Ohrenstein, the director of the Metropolitan Museum of Art, the chairman of Pathmark Stores, and writer Alistair Cooke.

INTERNATIONAL EXAMPLE

The End of Rent Controls in Egypt

Since Gamal Abdel Nasser's efforts to recast Egypt along socialist lines in the 1950s, farmland in this nation was subject to strict rent controls. Consequently, for more than 40 years, rents paid by tenant farmers—roughly 10 percent of the Egyptian populace—were frozen. Due to the considerable inflation that took place in Egypt during this period, the relative rental price of land was rapidly approaching zero. Tenants effectively took over lands they did not own, practically free of charge. A consequence was that the value of the land was very low to its owners, and this discouraged the adoption of modern cultivation techniques. Many tenant farmers in Egypt continued to plant only subsistence crops using their hands, hoes, and water buffaloes.

In 1992, Egypt adopted a law that reversed its rent controls. It phased in the law very gradually, however. Only recently has it permitted landowners to charge their tenants market prices. In some cases, landowners have evicted tenants to make way for more modern, less labor-intensive farming techniques. This has made the subject of rent control one of the most potent political issues in this Middle Eastern nation.

For Critical Analysis

What market-based policies might the Egyptian government adopt to reduce the impact of the removal of rent controls on tenant farmers?

CONCEPTS IN BRIEF

- Rental prices perform three functions: (1) allocating existing scarce housing among competing claimants, (2) promoting efficient maintenance of existing houses and stimulating new housing construction, and (3) rationing the use of existing houses by current demanders.
- Effective rent controls reduce or alter the three functions of rental prices. Construction of new rental units is discouraged. Rent controls decrease spending on maintenance of existing ones and also lead to "housing gridlock."
- There are numerous ways to evade rent controls; key money is one.

PRICE FLOORS IN AGRICULTURE

Another way that government can affect markets is by imposing price floors or price supports. In the United States, price supports are most often associated with agricultural products.

Price Supports

During the Great Depression, the federal government swung into action to help farmers. In 1933, it established a system of price supports for many agricultural products. Until recently, there were price supports for wheat, feed grains, cotton, rice, soybeans, sorghum, and

FIGURE 4-4

Agricultural Price Supports

Free market equilibrium occurs at E, with an equilibrium price of P_e and an equilibrium quantity of Q_e. When the government set a support price at P_s, the quantity demanded was Q_d, and the quantity supplied was Q_s. The difference was the surplus, which the government bought. Note that farmers' total income was from consumers ($P_s \times Q_d$) plus taxpayers [$(Q_s - Q_d) \times P_s$].

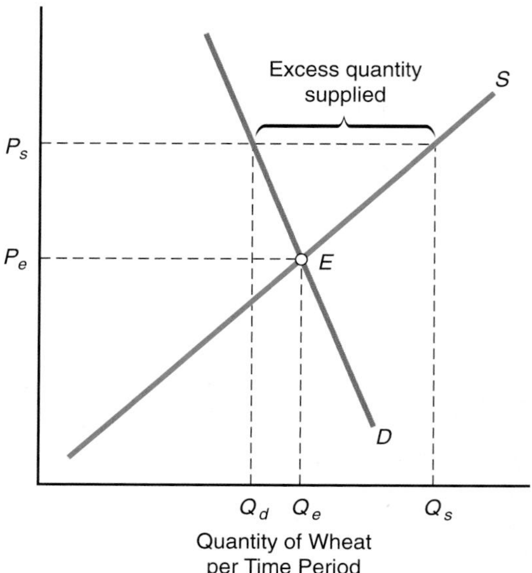

dairy products. The nature of the supports was quite simple: The government simply chose a *support price* for an agricultural product and then acted to ensure that the price of the product never fell below the support level. Figure 4-4 shows the market demand and supply of wheat. Without a price support program, competitive forces would yield an equilibrium price of P_e and an equilibrium quantity of Q_e. Clearly, if the government were to set the support price at P_e or below, the quantity of wheat demanded would equal the quantity of wheat supplied at point E because farmers can sell all they want at the market clearing price of P_e, above the price floor.

Until 1996, however, the government set the support price *above* P_e, at P_s. At a support price of P_s, the quantity demanded is only Q_d, but the quantity supplied is Q_s. The difference between them is called the *excess quantity supplied,* or *surplus.* As simple as this program seems, two questions arise: How did the government decide on the level of the support price P_s? And how did it prevent market forces from pushing the actual price down to P_e?

If production exceeded the amount consumers wanted to buy at the support price, what happened to the surplus? Quite simply, the government had to buy the surplus—the difference between Q_s and Q_d—if the price support program was to work. As a practical matter, the government acquired the quantity $Q_s - Q_d$ indirectly through a government agency. The government either stored the surplus or sold it to foreign countries at a greatly reduced price (or gave it away free of charge) under the Food for Peace program.

Who Benefited from Agricultural Price Supports?

Traditionally advocated as a way to guarantee a decent wage for low-income farmers, most of the benefits of agricultural price supports were skewed toward owners of very large farms. Price supports were made on a per-bushel basis, not on a per-farm basis. Thus traditionally, the larger the farm, the bigger the benefit from agricultural price supports. In addition, *all* of the benefits from price supports ultimately accrued to *landowners* on whose land price-supported crops could grow. Except for peanuts, tobacco, and sugar, the price support program was eliminated in 1996.

PRICE FLOORS IN THE LABOR MARKET 

Minimum wage 
A wage floor, legislated by government, setting the lowest hourly rate that firms may legally pay workers.

The **minimum wage** is the lowest hourly wage rate that firms may legally pay their workers. Proponents want higher minimum wages to ensure low-income workers a "decent" standard of living. Opponents claim that higher minimum wages cause increased unemployment, particularly among unskilled minority teenagers.

The federal minimum wage started in 1938 at 25 cents an hour, about 40 percent of the average manufacturing wage at the time. Typically, its level has stayed at about 40 to 50 percent of average manufacturing wages. It was increased to $5.15 in 1995 and may be higher by the time you read this. Many states and cities have their own minimum wage laws that sometimes exceed the federal minimum.

What happens when the government passes a floor on wages? The effects can be seen in Figure 4-5. We start off in equilibrium with the equilibrium wage rate of W_e and the equilibrium quantity of labor demanded and supplied equal to Q_e. A minimum wage, W_m, higher than W_e, is imposed. At W_m, the quantity demanded for labor is reduced to Q_d, and some workers now become unemployed. Note that the reduction in employment from Q_e to Q_d, or the distance from *B* to *A*, is less than the excess quantity of labor supplied at wage rate W_m. This excess quantity supplied is the distance between *A* and *C*, or the distance between Q_d and Q_s. The reason the reduction in employment is smaller than the excess supply of labor at the minimum wage is that the latter also includes a second component that consists of the additional workers who would like to work more hours at the new, higher minimum wage. Some workers may become

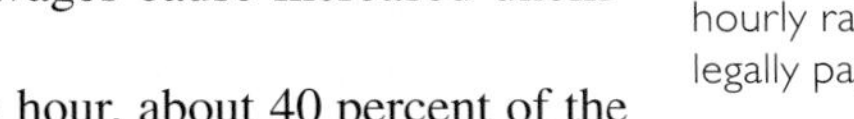

Can imposing price floors help keep industries from going out of business and worsening a nation's unemployment problem?

Yes, certain price floor arrangements can induce companies to keep producing unsold output, at least for a while. The social cost of such a policy can be very high, however. China's government, for instance, recently became concerned when a number of industries were unable to sell all their output at government-mandated price floors. The industries were threatening to downsize and lay off millions of Chinese workers. The government began purchasing unsold goods and storing them in warehouses. Of course, China's taxpayers must foot the bill for all this overproduction.

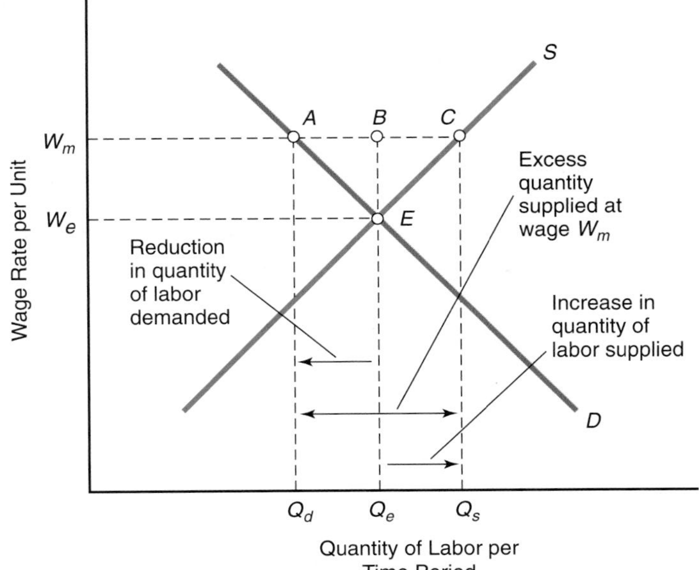

FIGURE 4-5
The Effect of Minimum Wages
The market clearing wage rate is W_e. The market clearing quantity of employment is Q_e, determined by the intersection of supply and demand at point *E*. A minimum wage equal to W_m is established. The quantity of labor demanded is reduced to Q_d; the reduction in employment from Q_e to Q_d is equal to the distance between *B* and *A*. That distance is smaller than the excess quantity of labor supplied at wage rate W_m. The distance between *B* and *C* is the increase in the quantity of labor supplied that results from the higher minimum wage rate.

Click here to keep up to date on recent federal and state developments concerning minimum wages.

unemployed as a result of the minimum wage, but others will move to sectors where minimum wage laws do not apply; wages will be pushed down in these uncovered sectors.

In the long run (a time period that is long enough to allow for adjustment by workers and firms), some of the reduction in labor demanded will result from a reduction in the number of firms, and some will result from changes in the number of workers employed by each firm. Economists estimate that a 10 percent increase in the real minimum wage decreases total employment of those affected by 1 to 2 percent.*

EIA

A Market for Low-Skilled Labor

Gain further understanding of the effects of the minimum wage.

QUANTITY RESTRICTIONS

Governments can impose quantity restrictions on a market. The most obvious restriction is an outright ban on the ownership or trading of a good. It is presently illegal to buy and sell human organs. It is also currently illegal to buy and sell certain psychoactive drugs such as cocaine, heroin, and marijuana. In some states, it is illegal to start a new hospital without obtaining a license for a particular number of beds to be offered to patients. This licensing requirement effectively limits the quantity of hospital beds in some states. From 1933 to 1973, it was illegal for U.S. citizens to own gold except for manufacturing, medicinal, or jewelry purposes.

POLICY EXAMPLE

Should the Legal Quantity of Cigarettes Supplied Be Set at Zero?

Nicotine has been used as a psychoactive drug by the native peoples of the Americas for approximately 8,000 years. Five hundred years ago, Christopher Columbus introduced tobacco to the Europeans, who discovered that once they overcame the nausea and dizziness produced by chewing, snorting, or smoking the tobacco, they simply could not get along without it. Nicotine quickly joined alcohol and caffeine as one of the world's most popular psychoactive drugs.

In the century after Columbus returned from the Americas with tobacco, consumption of and addiction to nicotine spread rapidly around the world. There followed numerous efforts to quash what had become known as the "evil weed." In 1603, the Japanese prohibited the use of tobacco and repeatedly increased the penalties for violating the ban, which wasn't lifted until 1625. By the middle of the seventeenth century, similar bans on tobacco were in place in Bavaria, Saxony, Zurich, Turkey, and Russia, with punishments ranging from confiscation of property to execution. Even in the early twentieth century, several state governments in the United States attempted to ban the use of tobacco.

A proposed quantity restriction—outright prohibition—was in the news again a few years ago when the head of the Food and Drug Administration announced that his agency had concluded that nicotine is addictive. He even argued that it should be classified with marijuana, heroin, and cocaine.

What can we predict if tobacco were ever completely prohibited today? Because tobacco is legal, the supply of illegal tobacco is zero. If the use of tobacco were restricted, the supply of illegal tobacco would not remain zero for long. Even if U.S. tobacco growers were forced out of business, the production of tobacco in other countries would increase to meet the demand. Consequently, the supply curve of illegal tobacco products would shift outward to the right as more foreign sources determined they wanted to enter the illegal U.S. tobacco market. The demand curve for illegal tobacco products would emerge almost immediately after the quantity restriction. The price people pay to satisfy their nicotine addiction would go up.

For Critical Analysis

What other goods or services follow the same analysis as the one presented here?

*Because we are referring to a long-run analysis here, the reduction in labor demanded would be demonstrated by an eventual shift inward to the left of the short-run demand curve, *D*, in Figure 4-5.

Some of the most common quantity restrictions exist in the area of international trade. The U.S. government, as well as many foreign governments, imposes import quotas on a variety of goods. An **import quota** is a supply restriction that prohibits the importation of more than a specified quantity of a particular good in a one-year period. The United States has had import quotas on tobacco, sugar, and immigrant labor. For many years, there were import quotas on oil coming into the United States. There are also "voluntary" import quotas on certain goods. Japanese automakers have agreed since 1981 "voluntarily" to restrict the amount of Japanese cars they send to the United States.

Import quota

A physical supply restriction on imports of a particular good, such as sugar. Foreign exporters are unable to sell in the United States more than the quantity specified in the import quota.

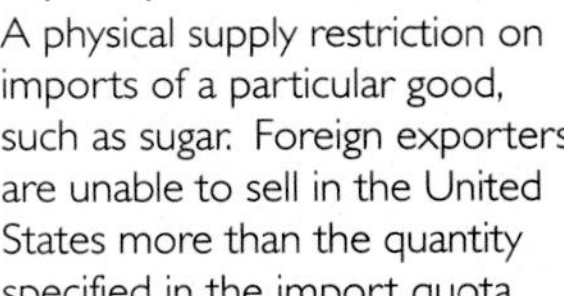

- With a price support system, the government sets a minimum price at which, say, qualifying farm products can be sold. Any farmers who cannot sell at that price can "sell" their surplus to the government. The only way a price support system can survive is for the government or some other entity to buy up the excess quantity supplied at the support price.
- When a floor is placed on wages at a rate that is above market equilibrium, the result is an excess quantity of labor supplied at that minimum wage.
- Quantity restrictions may take the form of import quotas, which are limits on the quantity of specific foreign goods that can be brought into the United States for resale purposes.

NETNOMICS

On-Line Ticket Scalpers Literally "Buy Out the House."

Recently, a large group of fans of a popular band from the 1970s, the Eagles, waited through the wee hours of the morning for the first tickets to go on sale for an upcoming concert at a Los Angeles arena. They had already waited so long that they were not overly concerned when the cashier opened the window to the ticket booth a couple of minutes late. They were a little more upset, however, when after making repeated attempts to place the ticket order of the first person in line, the cashier announced that only the highest-price seats to the show were still available—all the lower-priced seats had been completely sold out. It turned out that during the cashier's slight delay in opening the ticket booth, buyers on the Internet had, with a few clicks of a mouse, drained the pool of lower-priced tickets.

Although more people still buy tickets in person or over the phone, Internet buyers are purchasing tickets on-line in the largest permitted quantities. A number of buyers purchase additional lots using different names and credit cards. Once they have snapped up all the tickets they can, these on-line purchasers become scalpers, selling their tickets at on-line auctions. As noted in Chapter 3, scalping tickets is illegal in most states, but enforcement of these laws with respect to Internet sales is all but impossible. Auction sites such as eBay.com and Ubid.com provide forums that electronically bring together buyers and sellers of most anything, including tickets to entertainment and sporting events. For instance, when the movie *Star Wars: The Phantom Menace* was first released, tickets with a face value of $8.50 could be sold on eBay.com for as high as $40, a markup of 370 percent.

ISSUES & APPLICATIONS

Computer Science Students Respond to Incentives, Just Like Everyone Else

The past several years have witnessed an upsurge of interest in computer courses. Across the nation, enrollments in computer courses rose by more than 40 percent in just four years.

Concepts Applied

- Shift in Supply
- Shift in Demand
- Equilibrium

A Shrinkage of Computer Science Students: Does It Compute?

At the same time, however, fewer students who begin training for graduate degrees in computer science are finishing their studies. This trend has filtered down to undergraduates as well. Increasingly, computer science majors are following the example set by college dropout Bill Gates, the Microsoft co-founder.

What is luring these students from their studies is high entry-level wages. The starting salary for a promising computer specialist without a college degree can be as high as $60,000. For students who already have undergraduate degrees and have completed some graduate-level training, far higher salaries beckon.

Will Dropping Out Pay Off in the End?

Computer science professors and college officials think many of these students are making a big mistake. They point, for instance, to the boom-and-bust cycles that have been so common in information technology (IT) professions. As shown in panel (a) of Figure 4-6, employment growth for computer programmers and systems analysts has seesawed from year to year before leveling off somewhat recently. Academics in computer science warn students that as so many of them leave their studies to enter the marketplace, a rise in the market supply of IT specialists will ultimately drive salaries below today's levels.

It is of course in the best interest of professors and university officials to try to stem the tide of student defectors from academia to the private marketplace. Could they have a point nonetheless? Take a look at panel (b) of Figure 4-6, in which the initial demand for and supply of IT specialists are D_1 and S_1, respectively. Now suppose that there is a big jump in the demand for people with training in this area, as shown by the shift from D_1 to D_2. The result is a rise in the equilibrium wage. This encourages more people who currently possess IT skills to provide their services, resulting in an increase in the quantity of employed IT specialists. Now consider what happens when additional people—such as today's undergraduate and graduate students who leave school early—expect to receive higher wages in the near future and enter this market. Recall that when the sellers of any service, including labor services, anticipate earning a higher price, the result is a rise in market supply. The supply schedule therefore shifts from S_1 to S_2 in panel (b), pushing the equilibrium wage back down somewhat.

Thus academic naysayers are correct that other things being equal, the entry of students without degrees into the market for IT specialists should ultimately tend to depress wages. Nevertheless, this argument is based on the *ceteris paribus* assumption (see Chapter 1) that the demand schedule will not shift any farther to the right. As more and more consumers move on-line, the demand for IT specialists may in fact continue to increase. If so, the academic field of computer science may continue to shrink.

FOR CRITICAL ANALYSIS

1. As noted, a key factor determining what happens to future earnings of IT specialists will be changes in the demand for their services. What other factors will matter?
2. If wages for IT specialists do eventually fall back to or below their previous levels, what is likely to happen to college enrollments?

FIGURE 4-6

The Market for Computer Science Specialists

Employment opportunities for computer science specialists have experienced booms and busts over the past decade, as seen in panel (a). Leaving school before getting a degree may still make sense nonetheless. As panel (b) shows, demand has increased sufficiently that even with an increase in supply, wage rates will remain higher than they are today for information technology workers.

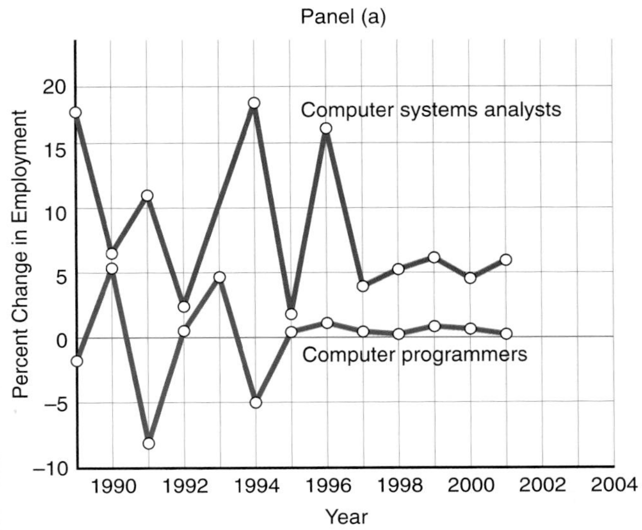

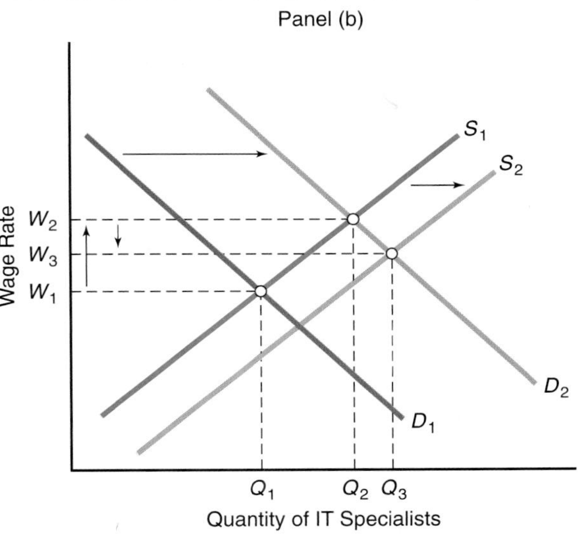

SUMMARY DISCUSSION OF LEARNING OBJECTIVES

1. **Essential Features of the Price System:** The price system, otherwise called the market system, allows prices to respond to changes in supply and demand for different commodities. Consumers' and business managers' decisions on resource use depend on what happens to prices. In the price system, exchange takes place in markets. The terms of exchange are communicated by prices in the marketplace, where individuals strive to minimize transaction costs, sometimes through the use of middlemen who bring buyers and sellers together.
2. **How Changes in Demand and Supply Affect the Market Price and Equilibrium Quantity:** With a stable supply curve, an increase in demand causes an increase in the market price and an increase in the equilibrium quantity, and a decrease in demand induces a fall in the market price and a decline in the equilibrium quantity. With a stable demand curve, an increase in supply causes a decrease in the market price and an increase in the equilibrium quantity, and a decrease in supply causes a rise in the market price and a decline in the equilibrium quantity. When both demand and supply shift at the same time, indeterminate results occur. We must know the direction and degree of each shift in order to predict the change in the market price and the equilibrium quantity.
3. **The Rationing Function of Prices:** In the market system, prices perform a rationing function—they ration scarce goods and services. Other ways of rationing include first come, first served; political power; physical force; lotteries; and coupons.
4. **The Effects of Price Ceilings:** Government-imposed price controls that require prices to be no

higher than a certain level are price ceilings. If a government sets a price ceiling below the market price, then at the ceiling price the quantity of the good demanded will exceed the quantity supplied. There will be a shortage of the good at the ceiling price. This can lead to nonprice rationing devices and black markets.

5. **The Effects of Price Floors:** Government-mandated price controls that require prices to be no lower than a certain level are price floors. If a government sets a price floor above the market price, then at the floor price the quantity of the good supplied will exceed the quantity demanded. There will be a surplus of the good at the floor price.
6. **Government-Imposed Restrictions on Market Quantities:** Quantity restrictions can take the form of outright government bans on the sale of certain goods, such as human organs or various psychoactive drugs. They can also arise from licensing requirements that limit the number of producers and thereby restrict the amount supplied of a good or service. Another example is an import quota, which limits the number of units of a foreign-produced good that can be legally sold domestically.

Key Terms and Concepts

Black market (82)
Import quota (89)
Minimum wage (87)
Nonprice rationing devices (82)
Price ceiling (82)
Price controls (82)
Price floor (82)
Price system (76)
Rent control (83)
Terms of exchange (76)
Transaction costs (77)
Voluntary exchange (76)

Problems

Answers to the odd-numbered problems appear at the back of the book.

4-1. Suppose that a rock band called the Raging Economists has released its first CD with Polyrock Records at a list price of $14.99. Explain how price serves as a purveyor of information to the band, the producer, and the consumer of rock CDs.

4-2. The pharmaceutical industry has benefited from advances in research and development that enable manufacturers to identify potential cures more quickly and therefore at lower cost. At the same time, our aging society has increased the demand for new drugs. Construct a supply and demand diagram of the market for pharmaceutical drugs. Illustrate the impact of these developments, and evaluate the effects on the market price and the equilibrium quantity.

4-3. The following table depicts the quantity demanded and quantity supplied of one-bedroom apartments in a small college town.

Monthly Rent	Quantity Demanded	Quantity Supplied
$400	3,000	1,600
$450	2,500	1,800
$500	2,000	2,000
$550	1,500	2,200
$600	1,000	2,400

What are the market price and equilibrium quantity of one-bedroom apartments in this town? Suppose that the mayor of this town decides to make housing more affordable for the local college students by imposing a rent control that holds the price of one-bedroom apartments to $450 a month. Explain the impact of this action on students desiring to live off campus and on owners of one-bedroom apartments. How many apartments are rented at the rate of $450 per month?

4-4. The United States provides considerable protection from foreign competition for its sugar industry. Suppose that one way it does this is by imposing a price floor that is above the market clearing price. Illustrate the U.S. sugar market with the price floor in place. Discuss the effects of the subsidy on conditions in the market for sugar in the United States.

4-5. The Canadian government and Canadian sugar industry have often complained that U.S. sugar manufacturers "dump" their sugar surpluses in the Canadian market. U.S. chocolate manufacturers and other U.S. businesses that use sugar as an input in their products have often complained that the high U.S. price of sugar hurts them in domestic and international markets. Explain how the imposition of a price floor for U.S. sugar, as described in Problem 4-4, affects these two markets. What are the changes in equilibrium quantities and market prices?

4-6. Suppose that the U.S. government places a ceiling on the price of Internet access. As a result, a black market for Internet providers arises, in which Internet service providers develop hidden means of connecting U.S. consumers. Illustrate the black market for Internet access, including the implicit supply schedule, the legal price, the black market supply and demand, and the black market equilibrium price and quantity. Also show why there is a shortage of Internet access at the legal price.

4-7. Airline routes are typically controlled by imposing a quota on the number of airline companies that may use the route and the number of flights on the route. Suppose that the following table illustrates the demand and supply schedules for seats on round-trip flights between Toronto and Chicago:

Price	Quantity Demanded	Quantity Supplied
$200	2,000	1,200
$300	1,800	1,400
$400	1,600	1,600
$500	1,400	1,800
$600	1,200	2,000

What are the market price and equilibrium quantity in this market? Now suppose that federal authorities limit the number of round-trip flights between the two cities to ensure that no more than 1,200 passengers can be flown. Explain the effects of this quota on the market price, quantity demanded, and quantity supplied.

4-8. The consequences of legalizing or decriminalizing illegal drugs have long been debated. Some individuals claim that legalization will lower the price of these drugs and therefore reduce related crime. Others claim that more people will use these drugs and the nation will face a health problem. Suppose that some of these drugs are legalized so that anyone may sell them and use them. Now consider the two claims—that price will fall and quantity will increase. Based on positive economic analysis, are these claims sound?

4-9. Look back at Figure 4-4. Suppose that the equilibrium price, P_e, is $1.00 per bushel of wheat and the support price is $1.25. In addition, suppose that the equilibrium quantity, Q_e, is 5 million bushels and the quantity supplied, Q_s, and quantity demanded, Q_d, with the price support are 8 million and 4 million, respectively. What was the total revenue of farmers before the price support program? What was the total revenue after the price support program? What is the cost of this program to taxpayers?

4-10. Using the information in Problem 4-9, calculate the total expenditures of wheat consumers before and after the price support program. Explain why these answers make sense.

Economics on the Net

The Floor on Milk Prices At various times the U.S. government has established price floors for milk. This application explains more about how governments implement floor prices and gives you an opportunity to apply what you have learned in this chapter to a real-world issue.

Title: Northeast Dairy Compact Commission

Navigation: Click here to visit the Web site of the Northeast Dairy Compact Commission.

Application Read the contents of the page, and answer the questions below.

1. Even though the federal government no longer formally sanctions the Northeast Dairy Compact, various states continue to coordinate their actions to regulate the price of milk. Based on the government-set price control concepts discussed in Chapter 4, explain the Northeast Dairy Compact that is in place in the Northeastern United States.

2. Draw a diagram illustrating the supply and demand of milk in the Northeast Dairy Compact and the supply and demand of milk outside of the Northeast Dairy Compact. Illustrate how the compact affects the quantities demanded and supplied for those participating in the compact. In addition, show how this affects the market for milk produced by those producers outside of the dairy compact.

3. In recent years, agricultural economists have found that Midwest dairy farmers are losing their dominance of milk production and sales. In light of your answer to question 2, explain how this occurred.

For Group Discussion and Analysis Discuss the impact of the Northeast Dairy Compact on farmers inside the compact and outside the compact. Discuss the impact of the Northeast Dairy Compact on consumers inside the compact and outside the compact. Debate the impact of eliminating the compact based on your earlier discussions. Identify in your debate arguments based on positive economic analysis and those based on normative arguments.

CHAPTER

5

THE PUBLIC SECTOR AND PUBLIC CHOICE

The average American reaches "tax freedom day" in early May. But the opportunity cost of filling out income tax forms is not considered in this calculation. On-line tax filing may reduce this cost but will never eliminate it.

In July 1776, John Adams wrote that Independence Day would be an occasion for "games, sports, guns, bells, bonfires, and illuminations, from one end of the continent to the other, from this time forevermore." For the average American, however, April 11 might also be a day to rejoice each year. This is touted as "tax freedom day"—the day when the average taxpayer has earned enough to pay all *federal* taxes for the current year. But don't overdo the celebrating. Almost another month's work will be required before the true tax freedom day arrives, on May 10. This is when the average American has earned enough to pay all federal, state, and local taxes *combined*. After nearly four and a half months of labor, U.S. taxpayers begin to earn income that they can keep for themselves.

Why does the U.S. government tax so much of its citizens' earnings for its own use? Before you can consider this question, you must learn some details about the public sector in America.

LEARNING OBJECTIVES

After reading this chapter, you should be able to:

1. **Explain how market failures such as externalities might justify economic functions of government**
2. **Distinguish between private goods and public goods and explain the nature of the free-rider problem**
3. **Describe political functions of government that entail its involvement in the economy**
4. **Distinguish between average tax rates and marginal tax rates**
5. **Explain the structure of the U.S. income tax system**
6. **Discuss the central elements of the theory of public choice**

Chapter Outline

Did You Know That... the U.S. government's total "take" from income taxes now exceeds $1 trillion each year? What is a trillion dollars? It is a million times a million. People earning an annual income of $200,000 or more typically pay just over 40 percent of these income taxes, and folks earning between $100,000 and $200,000 per year pay about 22 percent. Thus people earning more than $100,000 per year annually pay more than $620 billion in income taxes. People also pay miscellaneous other taxes, including sales and excise taxes. These also total to more than $1 trillion each year. So we cannot ignore the presence of government in our society. One of the reasons the government exists is to take care of what some people argue the price system does not do well.

WHAT A PRICE SYSTEM CAN AND CANNOT DO

Throughout the book so far, we have alluded to the benefits of a price system. High on the list is economic efficiency. In its most ideal form, a price system allows resources to move from lower-valued uses to higher-valued uses through voluntary exchange. The supreme point of economic efficiency occurs when all mutually advantageous trades have taken place. In a price system, consumers are sovereign; that is to say, they have the individual freedom to decide what they wish to purchase. Politicians and even business managers do not ultimately decide what is produced; consumers decide. Some proponents of the price system argue that this is its most important characteristic. A market organization of economic activity generally prevents one person from interfering with another in respect to most of his or her activities. Competition among sellers protects consumers from coercion by one seller, and sellers are protected from coercion by one consumer because other consumers are available.

Sometimes the price system does not generate these results, with too few or too many resources going to specific economic activities. Such situations are called **market failures.** Market failures prevent the price system from attaining economic efficiency and individual freedom, as well as other social goals. Market failures offer one of the strongest arguments in favor of certain economic functions of government, which we now examine.

Market failure 
A situation in which an unrestrained market economy leads to too few or too many resources going to a specific economic activity.

CORRECTING FOR EXTERNALITIES

In a pure market system, competition generates economic efficiency only when individuals know the true opportunity cost of their actions. In some circumstances, the price that someone actually pays for a resource, good, or service is higher or lower than the opportunity cost that all of society pays for that same resource, good, or service.

Consider a hypothetical world in which there is no government regulation against pollution. You are living in a town that until now has had clean air. A steel mill moves into town. It produces steel and has paid for the inputs—land, labor, capital, and entrepreneurship. The price it charges for the steel reflects, in this example, only the costs that the steel mill incurred. In the course of production, however, the mill gets one input—clean air—by simply taking it. This is indeed an input because in the making of steel, the furnaces emit smoke. The steel mill doesn't have to pay the cost of using the clean air; rather, it is the people in the community who pay that cost in the form of dirtier clothes, dirtier cars and houses, and more respiratory illnesses. The effect is similar to what would happen if the steel mill could take coal or oil or workers' services free. There has been an **externality,** an external cost. Some of the costs associated with the production of the steel have "spilled over" to affect **third parties,** parties other than the buyer and the seller of the steel.

Externality 
A consequence of an economic activity that spills over to affect third parties. Pollution is an externality.

Third parties 
Parties who are not directly involved in a given activity or transaction.

External Costs in Graphical Form

Look at panel (a) in Figure 5-1 on page 98. Here we show the demand curve for steel as D. The supply curve is S_1. The supply curve includes only the costs that the firms have to pay. The equilibrium, or market clearing, situation will occur at quantity Q_1. Let us take into account the fact that there are externalities—the external costs that you and your neighbors pay in the form of dirtier clothes, cars, and houses and increased respiratory disease due to the air pollution emitted from the steel mill; we also assume that all other suppliers of steel use clean air without having to pay for it. Let's include these external costs in our graph to find out what the full cost of steel production really is. This is equivalent to saying that the price of an input used in steel production increased. Recall from Chapter 3 that an increase in input prices shifts the supply curve. Thus in panel (a) of the figure, the supply curve shifts from S_1 to S_2; the external costs equal the vertical distance between A and E_1. If the external costs were somehow taken into account, the equilibrium quantity would fall to Q_2 and the price would rise to P_2. Equilibrium would shift from E to E_1. If the price does not account for external costs, third parties bear those costs—represented by the distance between A and E_1—in the form of dirtier clothes, houses, and cars and increased respiratory illnesses.

External Benefits in Graphical Form

Externalities and Public Goods
Practice thinking about external costs and external benefits.

Externalities can also be positive. To demonstrate external benefits in graphical form, we will use the example of inoculations against communicable disease. In panel (b) of Figure 5-1, we show the demand curve as D_1 (without taking account of any external benefits) and the supply curve as S. The equilibrium price is P_1, and the equilibrium quantity is Q_1. We assume, however, that inoculations against communicable diseases generate external benefits to individuals who may not be inoculated but will benefit nevertheless because epidemics will not break out. If such external benefits were taken into account, the demand curve would shift from D_1 to D_2. The new equilibrium quantity would be Q_2, and the new equilibrium price would be P_2. With no corrective action, this society is not devoting enough resources to inoculations against communicable diseases.

When there are external costs, the market will tend to *overallocate* resources to the production of the good or service in question, for those goods or services will be deceptively low-priced. With the example of steel, too much will be produced because the steel mill owners and managers are not required to take account of the external cost that steel production is imposing on the rest of society. In essence, the full cost of production is unknown to the owners and managers, so the price they charge the public for steel is lower than it would be otherwise. And of course, the lower price means that buyers are willing and able to buy more. More steel is produced and consumed than is socially optimal.

When there are external benefits, the market *underallocates* resources to the production of that good or service because the good or service is relatively too expensive (because the demand is relatively too low). In a market system, too many of the goods that generate external costs are produced and too few of the goods that generate external benefits are produced.

How the Government Corrects Negative Externalities

The government can in theory correct externality situations in a variety of ways in all cases that warrant such action. In the case of negative externalities, at least two avenues are open to the government: special taxes and legislative regulation or prohibition.

FIGURE 5-1

External Costs and Benefits

In panel (a), we show a situation in which the production of steel generates external costs. If the steel mills ignore pollution, at equilibrium the quantity of steel will be Q_1. If the mills had to pay for the additional cost borne by nearby residents that is caused by the steel mill's production, the supply curve would shift the vertical distance A–E_1, to S_2. If consumers were forced to pay a price that reflected the spillover costs, the quantity demanded would fall to Q_2. In panel (b), we show the situation in which inoculations against communicable diseases generate external benefits to those individuals who may not be inoculated but who will benefit because epidemics will not occur. If each individual ignores the external benefit of inoculations, the market clearing quantity will be Q_1. If external benefits are taken into account by purchasers of inoculations, however, the demand curve would shift to D_2. The new equilibrium quantity would be Q_2 and the price would be higher, P_2.

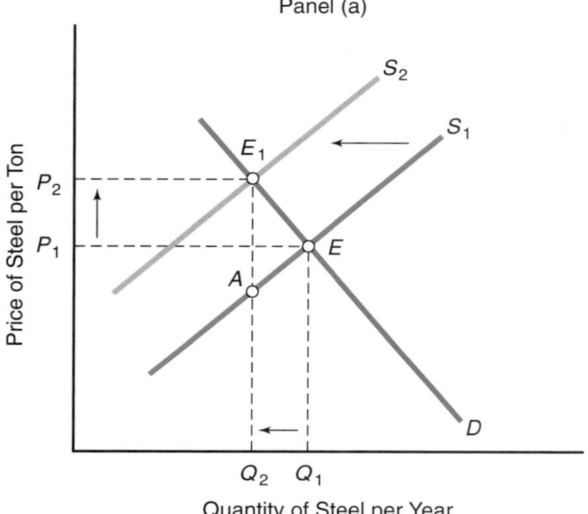

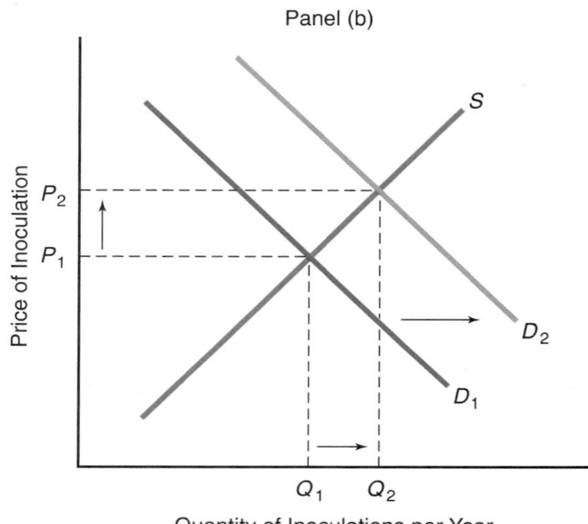

Special Taxes. In our example of the steel mill, the externality problem originates from the fact that the air as a waste disposal place is costless to the firm but not to society. The government could make the steel mill pay a tax for dumping its pollutants into the air. The government could attempt to tax the steel mill commensurate with the cost to third parties from smoke in the air. This, in effect, would be a pollution tax or an **effluent fee.** The ultimate effect would be to reduce the supply of steel and raise the price to consumers, ideally making the price equal to the full cost of production to society.

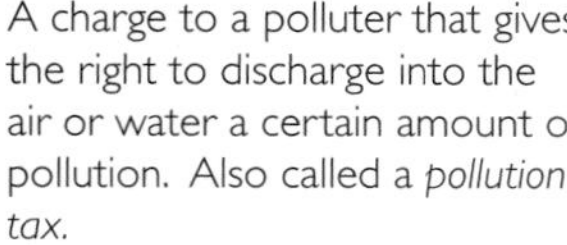

Effluent fee
A charge to a polluter that gives the right to discharge into the air or water a certain amount of pollution. Also called a *pollution tax.*

Regulation. To correct a negative externality arising from steel production, the government could specify a maximum allowable rate of pollution. This action would require that the steel mill install pollution abatement equipment at its facilities, that it reduce its rate of output, or some combination of the two. Note that the government's job would not be that simple, for it still would have to determine the level of pollution and then actually measure its output from steel production in order to enforce such regulation.

How the Government Corrects Positive Externalities

Click here to learn more about how the U.S. government uses regulations to try to protect the environment.

What can the government do when the production of one good spills *benefits* over to third parties? It has several policy options: financing the production of the good or producing the good itself, subsidies (negative taxes), and regulation.

Government Financing and Production. If the positive externalities seem extremely large, the government has the option of financing the desired additional production facilities so that the "right" amount of the good will be produced. Again consider inoculations against communicable diseases. The government could—and often does—finance campaigns to inoculate the population. It could (and does) even produce and operate centers for inoculation in which such inoculations would be given at no charge.

Subsidies. A subsidy is a negative tax; it is a payment made either to a business or to a consumer when the business produces or the consumer buys a good or a service. In the case of inoculations against communicable diseases, the government could subsidize everyone who obtains an inoculation by directly reimbursing those inoculated or by making payments to private firms that provide inoculations. If you are attending a state university, taxpayers are defraying part of the cost of providing your education; you are being subsidized by as much as 80 percent of the total cost. Subsidies reduce the net price to consumers, thereby causing a larger quantity to be demanded.

Regulation. In some cases involving positive externalities, the government can require by law that a certain action be undertaken by individuals in the society. For example, regulations require that all school-age children be inoculated before entering public and private schools. Some people believe that a basic school education itself generates positive externalities. Perhaps as a result of this belief, we have regulations—laws—that require all school-age children to be enrolled in a public or private school.

CONCEPTS IN BRIEF

- External costs lead to an overallocation of resources to the specific economic activity. Two possible ways of correcting these spillovers are taxation and regulation.
- External benefits result in an underallocation of resources to the specific activity. Three possible government corrections are financing the production of the activity, subsidizing private firms or consumers to engage in the activity, and regulation.

THE OTHER ECONOMIC FUNCTIONS OF GOVERNMENT

Besides correcting for externalities, the government performs many other economic functions that affect the way exchange is carried out. In contrast, the political functions of government have to do with deciding how income should be redistributed among households and selecting which goods and services have special merits and should therefore be treated differently. The economic and political functions of government can and do overlap.

Let's look at four more economic functions of government.

Providing a Legal System

The courts and the police may not at first seem like economic functions of government (although judges and police personnel must be paid). Their activities nonetheless have important consequences on economic activities in any country. You and I enter into contracts constantly, whether they be oral or written, expressed or implied. When we believe that we have been wronged, we seek redress of our grievances within our legal institutions. Moreover, consider the legal system that is necessary for the smooth functioning of our system. Our system has defined quite explicitly the legal status of businesses, the rights of private ownership, and a method for the enforcement of contracts. All relationships among consumers and businesses are governed by the legal rules of the game. We might consider the government in its judicial function, then, as the referee when there are disputes in the economic arena.

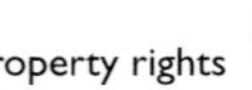

Property rights The rights of an owner to use and to exchange property.

Much of our legal system is involved with defining and protecting *property rights.* **Property rights** are the rights of an owner to use and to exchange his or her property. One might say that property rights are really the rules of our economic game. When property rights are well defined, owners of property have an incentive to use that property efficiently. Any mistakes in their decision about the use of property have negative consequences that the owners suffer. Furthermore, when property rights are well defined, owners of property have an incentive to maintain that property so that if those owners ever desire to sell it, it will fetch a better price.

Establishing and maintaining an independent constitutional judiciary, a familiar activity in the United States, is relatively new to Central and Eastern European countries.

INTERNATIONAL EXAMPLE

Post-Communist Rule of Law

Prior to the collapse of the Soviet empire, Central and Eastern European nations did not have an independent constitutional judiciary. Today that has changed. As a result, the institutional climate in these nations is more favorable for both domestic and foreign businesses.

The new constitutional frameworks in Central and Eastern European countries are based in large part on the U.S. Constitution. They emphasize the doctrines of separation of powers and checks and balances. They even give the courts the power of judicial review. (In the United States, this power allows the courts to declare laws unconstitutional.) A case in point is Hungary. There, legislators passed laws providing for restitution of nationalized land to pre-Communist owners. The court ruled that such laws were retroactive and thus invalid. The Hungarian court further stated that the only basis for returning land to former owners was through the transition to a market economy.

Bulgaria's constitutional court has consistently angered politicians. The court curbed government efforts to control radio and television. In Poland, the constitutional court voided a law passed by Parliament that would have lowered pensions of former state employees. This legal decision alone created a government obligation to pay almost $3 billion in compensation to almost 10 million Poles. This forced the government to sell bonds to pay for those pensions.

The trend toward highly independent court systems continues throughout Central and Eastern Europe.

For Critical Analysis

Why would an independent constitutional judiciary be important to someone who wished to invest in a new business in a Central or Eastern European country?

Promoting Competition

Antitrust legislation 
Laws that restrict the formation of monopolies and regulate certain anticompetitive business practices.

Monopoly 
A firm that has great control over the price of a good. In the extreme case, a monopoly is the only seller of a good or service.

Many people believe that the only way to attain economic efficiency is through competition. One of the roles of government is to serve as the protector of a competitive economic system. Congress and the various state governments have passed **antitrust legislation.** Such legislation makes illegal certain (but not all) economic activities that might restrain trade—that is, prevent free competition among actual and potential rival firms in the marketplace. The avowed aim of antitrust legislation is to reduce the power of **monopolies**—firms that have great control over the price of the goods they sell. A large number of antitrust laws have been passed that prohibit specific anticompetitive actions. Both the Antitrust Division of the Department of Justice and the Federal Trade Commission attempt to enforce these antitrust laws. Various state judicial agencies also expend efforts at maintaining competition.

Providing Public Goods 

The goods used in our examples up to this point have been **private goods.** When I eat a cheeseburger, you cannot eat the same one. So you and I are rivals for that cheeseburger, just as much as rivals for the title of world champion are. When I use a CD-ROM player, you cannot use the same player. When I use the services of an auto mechanic, that person cannot work at the same time for you. That is the distinguishing feature of private goods—their use is exclusive to the people who purchase or rent them. The **principle of rival consumption** applies to all private goods by definition. Rival consumption is easy to understand. With private goods, either you use them or I use them.

Private goods 
Goods that can be consumed by only one individual at a time. Private goods are subject to the principle of rival consumption.

Principle of rival consumption 
The recognition that individuals are rivals in consuming private goods because one person's consumption reduces the amount available for others to consume.

There is an entire class of goods that are not private goods. These are called **public goods.** The principle of rival consumption does not apply to them. That is, they can be consumed *jointly* by many individuals simultaneously. National defense, police protection, and the legal system, for example, are public goods. If you partake of them, you do not necessarily take away from anyone else's share of those goods.

Public goods 
Goods to which the principle of rival consumption does not apply; they can be jointly consumed by many individuals simultaneously at no additional cost and with no reduction in quality or quantity.

Characteristics of Public Goods. Several distinguishing characteristics of public goods set them apart from all other goods.*

1. *Public goods are often indivisible.* You can't buy or sell $5 worth of our ability to annihilate the world with bombs. Public goods cannot usually be produced or sold very easily in small units.
2. *Public goods can be used by more and more people at no additional cost.* Once money has been spent on national defense, the defense protection you receive does not reduce the amount of protection bestowed on anyone else. The opportunity cost of your receiving national defense once it is in place is zero.
3. *Additional users of public goods do not deprive others of any of the services of the goods.* If you turn on your television set, your neighbors don't get weaker reception because of your action.
4. *It is difficult to design a collection system for a public good on the basis of how much individuals use it.* It is nearly impossible to determine how much any person uses or values national defense. No one can be denied the benefits of national defense for failing to pay for that public good. This is often called the **exclusion principle.**

Exclusion principle 
The principle that no one can be excluded from the benefits of a public good, even if that person hasn't paid for it.

One of the problems of public goods is that the private sector has a difficult, if not impossible, time providing them. There is little or no incentive for individuals in the private sector to offer public goods because it is so difficult to make a profit so doing. Consequently, true public goods must necessarily be provided by government.

INTERNATIONAL EXAMPLE

Is a Lighthouse a Public Good?

One of the most common examples of a public good is asserted to be a lighthouse. Arguably, it satisfies all the criteria listed in points 1 through 4. One historical example suggests, however, that a lighthouse was not a public good, in that a collection system was devised and enforced on the basis of how much individuals used it.

(*cont.*)

---

*Sometimes the distinction is made between pure public goods, which have all the characteristics we have described here, and quasi- or near-public goods, which do not. The major feature of near-public goods is that they are jointly consumed, even though nonpaying customers can be, and often are, excluded—for example, movies, football games, and concerts.

In the thirteenth century, the city of Aigues-Mortes, a French southern port, erected a tower, called the King's Tower, designed to assert the will and power of Louis IX (Saint Louis). The 105-foot tower served as a lighthouse for ships. More important, it served as a lookout so that ships sailing on the open sea, but in its view, did not escape paying for use of the lighthouse. Those payments were then used for the construction of the city walls.

For Critical Analysis

Explain how a lighthouse satisfies the characteristics of public goods described in points 1, 2, and 3.

Free-rider problem 
A problem that arises when individuals presume that others will pay for public goods so that, individually, they can escape paying for their portion without causing a reduction in production.

Free Riders. The nature of public goods leads to the **free-rider problem,** a situation in which some individuals take advantage of the fact that others will take on the burden of paying for public goods such as national defense. Free riders will argue that they receive no value from such government services as national defense and therefore really should not pay for it. Suppose that citizens were taxed directly in proportion to how much they tell an interviewer that they value national defense. Some people will probably tell interviewers that they are unwilling to pay for national defense because they don't want any of it—it is of no value to them. We may all want to be free riders if we believe that someone else will provide the commodity in question that we actually value.

The free-rider problem arises with respect to the international burden of defense and how it should be shared. A country may choose to belong to a multilateral defense organization, such as the North Atlantic Treaty Organization (NATO), but then consistently attempt to avoid contributing funds to the organization. The nation knows it would be defended by others in NATO if it were attacked but would rather not pay for such defense. In short, it seeks a "free ride."

Ensuring Economywide Stability

The government attempts to stabilize the economy by smoothing out the ups and downs in overall business activity. Our economy sometimes faces the problems of unemployment and rising prices. The government, especially the federal government, has made an attempt to solve these problems by trying to stabilize the economy. The notion that the federal government should undertake actions to stabilize business activity is a relatively new idea in the United States, encouraged by high unemployment rates during the Great Depression of the 1930s and subsequent theories about possible ways by which government could reduce unemployment. In 1946, the government passed the Employment Act, a landmark law concerning government responsibility for economic performance. It established three goals for government accountability: full employment, price stability, and economic growth. These goals have provided the justification for many government economic programs during the post–World War II period.

CONCEPTS IN BRIEF

- The economic activities of government include (1) correcting for externalities, (2) providing a judicial system, (3) promoting competition, (4) producing public goods, and (5) ensuring economywide stability.
- Public goods can be consumed jointly. The principle of rival consumption does not apply as it does with private goods.
- Public goods have the following characteristics: (1) They are indivisible; (2) once they are produced, there is no opportunity cost when additional consumers use them; (3) your use of a public good does not deprive others of its simultaneous use; and (4) consumers cannot conveniently be charged on the basis of use.

THE POLITICAL FUNCTIONS OF GOVERNMENT

At least two areas of government are in the realm of political, or normative, functions rather than that of the economic ones discussed in the first part of this chapter. These two areas are (1) the regulation and provision of merit and demerit goods and (2) income redistribution.

Merit good 
A good that has been deemed socially desirable through the political process. Museums are an example.

Merit and Demerit Goods

Certain goods are considered to have special merit. A **merit good** is defined as any good that the political process has deemed socially desirable. (Note that nothing inherent in any particular good makes it a merit good. The designation is entirely subjective.) Some examples of merit goods in our society are sports stadiums, museums, ballets, plays, and concerts. In these areas, the government's role is the provision of merit goods to the people in society who would not otherwise purchase them at market clearing prices or who would not purchase an amount of them judged to be sufficient. This provision may take the form of government production and distribution of merit goods. It can also take the form of reimbursement for payment on merit goods or subsidies to producers or consumers for part of the cost of merit goods. Governments do indeed subsidize such merit goods as professional sports, concerts, ballets, museums, and plays. In most cases, such merit goods would rarely be so numerous without subsidization.

Demerit good 
A good that has been deemed socially undesirable through the political process. Heroin is an example.

FAQ ***Do government-funded sports stadiums have a positive effect on local economies?***

Probably not, even though in recent years many cities have decided that new football and baseball stadiums are merit goods worthy of public funding. Their rationale is that there is no collective mechanism besides government to ensure the construction of the stadiums that will draw big crowds. A local government, goes the argument, can regard a stadium as an investment because the crowds it draws benefit the local economy. Spending by the crowds can also generate tax revenues that help the government recoup its expenses. According to economist Andrew Zimbalist, however, "There has not been an independent study by an economist over the last 30 years that suggests you can anticipate a positive economic impact" from government investments in sports facilities.

Demerit goods are the opposite of merit goods. They are goods that, through the political process, are deemed socially undesirable. Heroin, cigarettes, gambling, and cocaine are examples. The government exercises its role in the area of demerit goods by taxing, regulating, or prohibiting their manufacture, sale, and use. Governments justify the relatively high taxes on alcohol and tobacco by declaring them demerit goods. The best-known example of governmental exercise of power in this area is the stance against certain psychoactive drugs. Most psychoactives (except nicotine, caffeine, and alcohol) are either expressly prohibited, as is the case for heroin, cocaine, and opium, or heavily regulated, as in the case of prescription psychoactives.

Transfer payments 
Money payments made by governments to individuals for which in return no services or goods are concurrently rendered. Examples are welfare, Social Security, and unemployment insurance benefits.

Income Redistribution

Another relatively recent political function of government has been the explicit redistribution of income. This redistribution uses two systems: the progressive income tax (described later in this chapter) and transfer payments. **Transfer payments** are payments made to individuals for which no services or goods are rendered in return. The three key money transfer payments in our system are welfare, Social Security, and unemployment insurance benefits. Income redistribution also includes a large amount of income **transfers in kind,** as opposed to money transfers. Some income transfers in kind are food stamps, Medicare and Medicaid, government health care services, and subsidized public housing.

Transfers in kind 
Payments that are in the form of actual goods and services, such as food stamps, subsidized public housing, and medical care, and for which in return no goods or services are rendered concurrently.

The government has also engaged in other activities as a form of redistribution of income. For example, the provision of public education is at least in part an attempt to redistribute income by making sure that the poor have access to education.

CONCEPTS IN BRIEF

- Political, or normative, activities of the government include the provision and regulation of merit and demerit goods and income redistribution.
- Merit and demerit goods do not have any inherent characteristics that qualify them as such; rather, collectively, through the political process, we make judgments about which goods and services are "good" for society and which are "bad."
- Income redistribution can be carried out by a system of progressive taxation, coupled with transfer payments, which can be made in money or in kind, such as food stamps and Medicare.

PAYING FOR THE PUBLIC SECTOR 

Jean-Baptiste Colbert, the seventeenth-century French finance minister, said the art of taxation was in "plucking the goose so as to obtain the largest amount of feathers with the least possible amount of hissing." In the United States, governments have designed a variety of methods of plucking the private-sector goose. To analyze any tax system, we must first understand the distinction between marginal tax rates and average tax rates.

Marginal and Average Tax Rates

If somebody says, "I pay 28 percent in taxes," you cannot really tell what that person means unless you know if he or she is referring to average taxes paid or the tax rate on the last dollars earned. The latter concept refers to the **marginal tax rate.***

Marginal tax rate 
The change in the tax payment divided by the change in income, or the percentage of additional dollars that must be paid in taxes. The marginal tax rate is applied to the highest tax bracket of taxable income reached.

The marginal tax rate is expressed as follows:

$$\text{Marginal tax rate} = \frac{\text{change in taxes due}}{\text{change in taxable income}}$$

It is important to understand that the marginal tax rate applies only to the income in the highest **tax bracket** reached, where a tax bracket is defined as a specified level of taxable income to which a specific and unique marginal tax rate is applied.

Tax bracket 
A specified interval of income to which a specific and unique marginal tax rate is applied.

The marginal tax rate is not the same thing as the **average tax rate,** which is defined as follows:

$$\text{Average tax rate} = \frac{\text{total taxes due}}{\text{total taxable income}}$$

Average tax rate 
The total tax payment divided by total income. It is the proportion of total income paid in taxes.

Taxation Systems

No matter how governments raise revenues—from income taxes, sales taxes, or other taxes—all of those taxes fit into one of three types of taxation systems: proportional, progressive, and regressive, according to the relationship between the percentage of tax, or tax rate, paid and income. To determine whether a tax system is proportional, progressive, or regressive, we simply ask, What is the relationship between the average tax rate and the marginal tax rate?

*The word *marginal* means "incremental" (or "decremental") here.

Proportional Taxation. **Proportional taxation** means that regardless of an individual's income, taxes comprise exactly the same proportion. In terms of marginal versus average tax rates, in a proportional taxation system, the marginal tax rate is always equal to the average tax rate. If every dollar is taxed at 20 percent, then the average tax rate is 20 percent, as is the marginal tax rate.

A proportional tax system is also called a *flat-rate tax.* Taxpayers at all income levels end up paying the same *percentage* of their income in taxes. If the proportional tax rate were 20 percent, an individual with an income of $10,000 would pay $2,000 in taxes, while an individual making $100,000 would pay $20,000, the identical 20 percent rate being levied on both.

Proportional taxation 
A tax system in which regardless of an individual's income, the tax bill comprises exactly the same proportion. Also called a *flat-rate tax.*

Progressive Taxation. Under **progressive taxation,** as a person's taxable income increases, the percentage of income paid in taxes increases. In terms of marginal versus average tax rates, in a progressive system, the marginal tax rate is above the average tax rate. If you are taxed 5 percent on the first $10,000 you make, 10 percent on the next $10,000 you make, and 30 percent on the last $10,000 you make, you face a progressive income tax system. Your marginal tax rate is always above your average tax rate.

Progressive taxation 
A tax system in which as income increases, a higher percentage of the additional income is taxed. The marginal tax rate exceeds the average tax rate as income rises.

Regressive Taxation. With **regressive taxation,** a smaller percentage of taxable income is taken in taxes as taxable income increases. The marginal rate is *below* the average rate. As income increases, the marginal tax rate falls, and so does the average tax rate. The U.S. Social Security tax is regressive. Once the legislative maximum taxable wage base is reached, no further Social Security taxes are paid. Consider a simplified hypothetical example: Every dollar up to $50,000 is taxed at 10 percent. After $50,000 there is no Social Security tax. Someone making $100,000 still pays only $5,000 in Social Security taxes. That person's average Social Security tax is 5 percent. The person making $50,000, by contrast, effectively pays 10 percent. The person making $1 million faces an average Social Security tax rate of only 0.5 percent in our simplified example.

Regressive taxation 
A tax system in which as more dollars are earned, the percentage of tax paid on them falls. The marginal tax rate is less than the average tax rate as income rises.

- Marginal tax rates are applied to marginal tax brackets, defined as spreads of income over which the tax rate is constant.
- Tax systems can be proportional, progressive, or regressive, depending on whether the marginal tax rate is the same as, greater than, or less than the average tax rate as income rises.

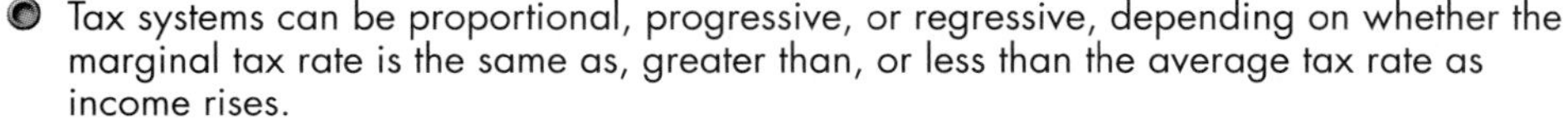

THE MOST IMPORTANT FEDERAL TAXES

The federal government imposes income taxes on both individuals and corporations and collects Social Security taxes and a variety of other taxes.

The Federal Personal Income Tax

The most important tax in the U.S. economy is the federal personal income tax, which accounts for about 49 percent of all federal revenues. All American citizens, resident aliens, and most others who earn income in the United States are required to pay federal income taxes on all taxable income. The rates that are paid rise as income increases, as can be seen in Table 5-1. Marginal income tax rates at the federal level have varied from as

Click here to learn about what distinguishes recent so-called "flat-tax" proposals from a truly proportional income tax system. Next, click on "Flat Tax Proposals."

TABLE 5-1
Federal Marginal Income Tax Rates
These rates became effective in 2000. The highest rate includes a 10 percent surcharge on taxable income above $283,150.

Single Persons		Married Couples	
Marginal Tax Bracket	Marginal Tax Rate	Marginal Tax Bracket	Marginal Tax Rate
$0–$25,750	15%	$0–$43,050	15%
$25,751–$62,450	28%	$43,051–$104,050	28%
$62,451–$130,250	31%	$104,051–$158,550	31%
$130,251–$283,150	36%	$158,551–$283,150	36%
$283,151 and up	39.6%	$283,151 and up	39.6%

Source: U.S. Department of the Treasury.

low as 1 percent after the passage of the Sixteenth Amendment to as high as 94 percent (reached in 1944). There were 14 separate tax brackets prior to the Tax Reform Act of 1986, which reduced the number to three. Advocates of a more progressive income tax system in the United States argue that such a system redistributes income from the rich to the poor, taxes people according to their ability to pay, and taxes people according to the benefits they receive from government. Although there is much controversy over the redistributional nature of our progressive tax system, there is no strong evidence that in fact the tax system has ever done much income redistribution in this country. Currently, about 85 percent of all Americans, rich or poor, pay roughly the same proportion of their total income in federal taxes.

POLICY EXAMPLE

The Federal Income Tax, Then and Now

The United States first used an income tax during the Civil War. Congress ended the federal income tax in 1872. Adoption of the Sixteenth Amendment to the U.S. Constitution in 1913 brought back the income tax, however. Debate over the constitutional amendment was heated. One lawmaker argued passionately that ultimately "a hand from Washington will stretch out to every man's house." Many proponents of the amendment ridiculed him. After all, exempted from paying any taxes were single people with incomes below $3,000 (about $46,300 today) and married couples with incomes less than $4,000 (about $61,800 today). Thus initially, only U.S. citizens with relatively high incomes would be assessed income taxes of any significance.

Take a look at Table 5-2. It shows the tax rates imposed on various income brackets in 1913 and those same brackets expressed in 2000 dollars. A 1 percent tax rate would be in effect on incomes up to around $309,000. The highest rate, 7 percent, would apply to incomes over $7.7 million measured in 2000 dollars. Obviously, that is not the present situation—take a look at Table 5-1. Clearly, the federal income tax system as initiated in 1913 was a quite different animal from our current system. Looking back at Table 5-1, you can see that current tax rates are considerably higher than rates in 1913, and they affect virtually all Americans. A hand from Washington may not have stretched out to every house in 1913, but it certainly does today.

For Critical Analysis

The first income tax form was the size of a postcard. Why are tax forms so much thicker and more complicated today?

TABLE 5-2
1913 U. S. Income Tax Rates and Brackets

Tax Rate	Income Level in 1913	Equivalent Income Level in 2000 Dollars
1%	Up to $20,000	Up to $308,955
2%	$20,000–$50,000	$308,956–$772,388
3%	$50,000–$75,000	$772,389–$1,158,582
4%	$75,000–$100,000	$1,158,583–$1,544,776
5%	$100,000–$250,000	$1,544,777–$3,861,940
6%	$250,000–$500,000	$3,861,941–$7,723,881
7%	Over $500,000	Over $7,723,881

Source: U.S. Department of the Treasury.

The Treatment of Capital Gains

The difference between the buying and selling price of an asset, such as a share of stock or a plot of land, is called a **capital gain** if it is a profit and a **capital loss** if it is not. As of 2000, there were several capital gains tax rates.

Capital gains are not always real. If you pay $100,000 for a house in one year and sell it for 50 percent more 10 years later, your nominal capital gain is $50,000. But what if, during those 10 years, there has been inflation such that average prices also went up by 50 percent? Your *real* capital gain would be zero. But you still have to pay taxes on that $50,000. To counter this problem, many economists have argued that capital gains should be indexed to the rate of inflation. This is exactly what is done with the marginal tax brackets in the federal income tax code. Tax brackets for the purposes of calculating marginal tax rates each year are expanded at the rate of inflation, or the rate at which the average of all prices is rising. So if the rate of inflation is 10 percent, each tax bracket is moved up by 10 percent. The same concept could be applied to capital gains. So far, Congress has refused to enact such a measure.

Capital gain 
The positive difference between the purchase price and the sale price of an asset. If a share of stock is bought for $5 and then sold for $15, the capital gain is $10.

Capital loss 
The negative difference between the purchase price and the sale price of an asset.

The Corporate Income Tax 

Corporate income taxes account for about 12 percent of all federal taxes collected and almost 8 percent of all state and local taxes collected. Corporations are generally taxed on the difference between their total revenues (or receipts) and their expenses. The federal corporate income tax structure is given in Table 5-3.

Double Taxation. Because individual stockholders must pay taxes on the dividends they receive, paid out of *after-tax* profits by the corporation, corporate profits are taxed twice.

TABLE 5-3
Federal Corporate Income Tax Schedule
The use rates were in effect through 2001.

Corporate Taxable Income	Corporate Tax Rate
$0–$50,000	15%
$50,001–$75,000	25%
$75,001–$10,000,000	34%
$10,000,000 and up	35%

Source: Internal Revenue Service.

Retained earnings 
Earnings that a corporation saves, or retains, for investment in other productive activities; earnings that are not distributed to stockholders.

If you receive $1,000 in dividends, you have to declare them as income, and you must pay taxes at your marginal tax rate. Before the corporation was able to pay you those dividends, it had to pay taxes on all its profits, including any that it put back into the company or did not distribute in the form of dividends. Eventually the new investment made possible by those **retained earnings**—profits not given out to stockholders—along with borrowed funds will be reflected in the increased value of the stock in that company. When you sell your stock in that company, you will have to pay taxes on the difference between what you paid for the stock and what you sold it for. In both cases, dividends and retained earnings (corporate profits) are taxed twice.

Tax incidence 
The distribution of tax burdens among various groups in society.

Who Really Pays the Corporate Income Tax? Corporations can exist only as long as consumers buy their products, employees make their goods, stockholders (owners) buy their shares, and bondholders buy their bonds. Corporations per se do not do anything. We must ask, then, who really pays the tax on corporate income. This is a question of **tax incidence.** (The question of tax incidence applies to all taxes, including sales taxes and Social Security taxes.) There remains considerable debate about the incidence of corporate taxation. Some economists say that corporations pass their tax burdens on to consumers by charging higher prices. Other economists believe that it is the stockholders who bear most of the tax. Still others believe that employees pay at least part of the tax by receiving lower wages than they would otherwise. Because the debate is not yet settled, we will not hazard a guess here as to what the correct conclusion may be. Suffice it to say that you should be cautious when you advocate increasing corporation income taxes. You may be the one who ultimately ends up paying the increase, at least in part, if you own shares in a corporation, buy its products, or work for it.

CONCEPTS IN BRIEF

- Because corporations must first pay an income tax on most earnings, the personal income tax shareholders pay on dividends received (or realized capital gains) constitutes double taxation.
- The corporate income tax is paid by one or more of the following groups: stockholder-owners, consumers of corporate-produced products, and employees in corporations.

Social Security and Unemployment Taxes

An increasing percentage of federal tax receipts is accounted for each year by taxes (other than income taxes) levied on payrolls. These taxes are for Social Security, retirement, survivors' disability, and old-age medical benefits (Medicare). As of 2000, the Social Security tax was imposed on earnings up to $72,600 at a rate of 6.2 percent on employers and 6.2 percent on employees. That is, the employer matches your "contribution" to Social Security. (The employer's contribution is really paid, at least in part, in the form of a reduced wage rate paid to employees.) A Medicare tax is imposed on all wage earnings at a combined rate of 2.9 percent. These taxes and the base on which they are levied are slated to rise in the next decade. Social Security taxes came into existence when the Federal Insurance Contributions Act (FICA) was passed in 1935. The future of Social Security is the subject of Chapter 6.

There is also a federal unemployment tax, which obviously has something to do with unemployment insurance. This tax rate is 0.8 percent on the first $7,000 of annual wages of each employee who earns more than $1,500. Only the employer makes the tax payment. This tax covers the costs of the unemployment insurance system and the costs of employment services. In addition to this federal tax, some states with an unemployment system impose an additional tax of up to about 3 percent, depending on the past record of the particular employer. An employer who frequently lays off workers will have a slightly higher state unemployment tax rate than an employer who never lays off workers.

SPENDING, GOVERNMENT SIZE, AND TAX RECEIPTS

The size of the public sector can be measured in many different ways. One way is to count the number of public employees. Another is to look at total government outlays. Government outlays include all government expenditures on employees, rent, electricity, and the like. In addition, total government outlays include transfer payments, such as welfare and Social Security. In Figure 5-2, you see that government outlays prior to World War I did not exceed 10 percent of annual national income. There was a spike during World War I, a general increase during the Great Depression, and then a huge spike during World War II. Contrary to previous postwar periods, after World War II government outlays as a percentage of total national income rose steadily before leveling off in the 1990s and 2000s.

Government Receipts

The main revenue raiser for all levels of government is taxes. We show in the two pie diagrams in Figure 5-3 on page 110 the percentage of receipts from various taxes obtained by the federal government and by state and local governments.

The Federal Government. The largest source of receipts for the federal government is the individual income tax. It accounts for 48.6 percent of all federal revenues. After that come social insurance taxes and contributions (Social Security), which account for 33.2 percent of total revenues. Next come corporate income taxes and then a number of other items, such as taxes on imported goods and excise taxes on such things as gasoline and alcoholic beverages.

State and Local Governments. As can be seen in Figure 5-3, there is quite a bit of difference in the origin of receipts for state and local governments and for the federal government. Personal and corporate income taxes account for only 20.4 percent of total state and

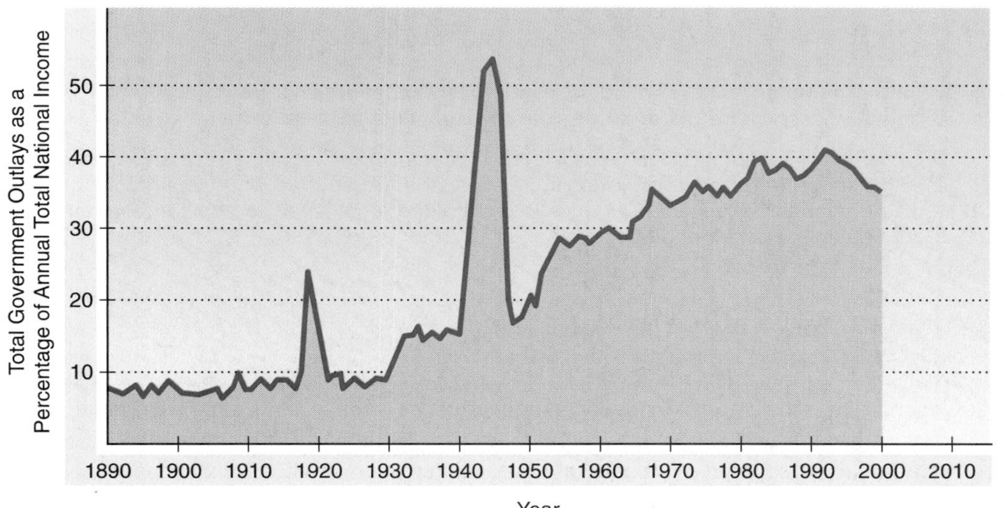

FIGURE 5-2
Total Government Outlays over Time
Here you see that total government outlays (federal, state, and local combined) remained small until the 1930s, except during World War I. Since World War II, government outlays have not fallen back to their historical average.

Sources: Facts and Figures on Government Finance and *Economic Indicators,* various issues.

FIGURE 5-3

Sources of Government Tax Receipts

Over 82 percent of federal revenues come from income and Social Security taxes (a), whereas state government revenues are spread more evenly across sources (b), with less emphasis on taxes based on individual income.

Source: U.S. Department of Commerce, Bureau of Economic Analysis.

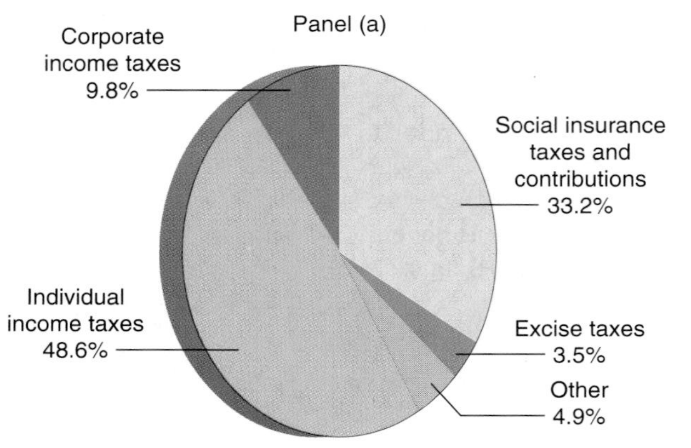

Federal Tax Receipts: Fiscal Year 2001 Estimate

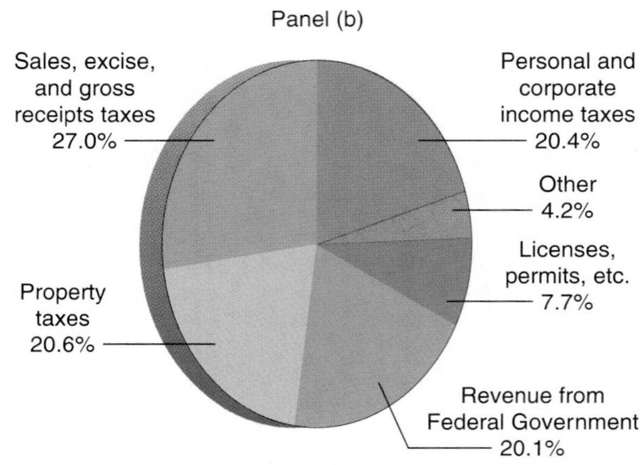

State and Local Tax Receipts: Fiscal Year 2001 Estimate

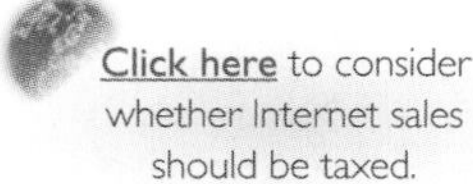

Click here to consider whether Internet sales should be taxed.

local revenues. There are even a number of states that collect no personal income tax. The largest sources of state and local receipts (other than from the federal government) are personal and corporate income taxes, sales taxes, and property taxes.

Comparing Federal with State and Local Spending. A typical federal government budget is given in panel (a) of Figure 5-4. The largest three categories are defense, income security, and Social Security, which together constitute 52.9 percent of the total federal budget.

The makeup of state and local expenditures is quite different. As panel (b) shows, education is the biggest category, accounting for 35.1 percent of all expenditures.

CONCEPTS IN BRIEF

- Total government outlays including transfers have continued to grow since World War II and now account for about 35 percent of yearly total national output.
- Government spending at the federal level is different from that at the state and local levels. At the federal level, defense, income security, and Social Security account for about 53 percent of the federal budget. At the state and local levels, education comprises 35 percent of all expenditures.

COLLECTIVE DECISION MAKING: THE THEORY OF PUBLIC CHOICE

Governments consist of individuals. No government actually thinks and acts; rather, government actions are the result of decision making by individuals in their roles as elected representatives, appointed officials, and salaried bureaucrats. Therefore, to understand how government works, we must examine the incentives for the people in government as well

FIGURE 5-4

Federal Government Spending Compared to State and Local Spending

The federal government's spending habits are quite different from those of the states and cities in panel (a), you can see that the categories of most importance in the federal budget are defense, income security, and Social Security, which make up 52.9 percent. In panel (b), the most important category at the state and local level is education, which makes up 35.1 percent. "Other" includes expenditures in such areas as waste treatment, garbage collection, mosquito abatement, and the judicial system.

Sources: Budget of the United States Government; Government Finances.

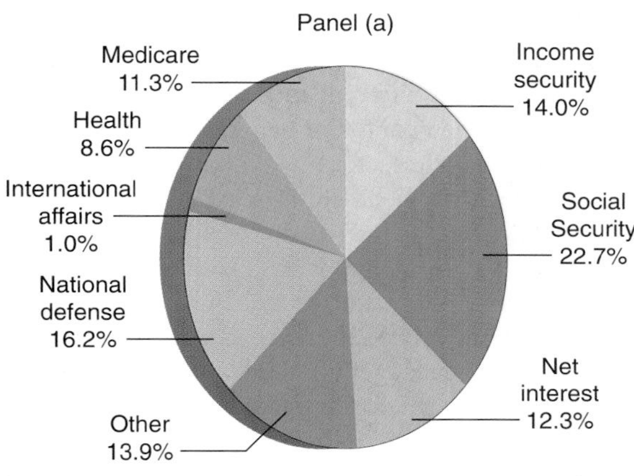

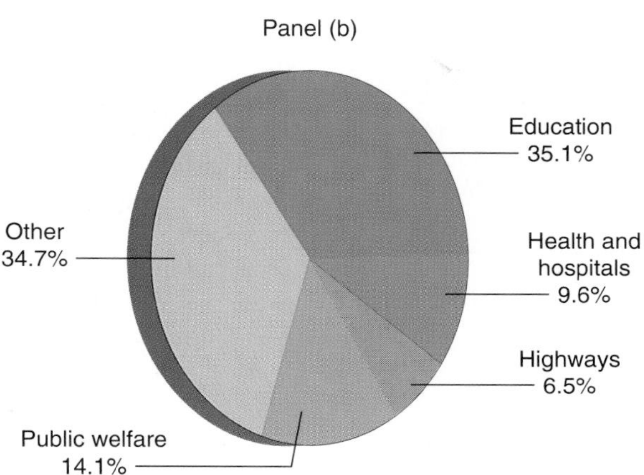

as those who would like to be in government—avowed or would-be candidates for elective or appointed positions—and special-interest lobbyists attempting to get government to do something. At issue is the analysis of **collective decision making.** Collective decision making involves the actions of voters, politicians, political parties, interest groups, and many other groups and individuals. The analysis of collective decision making is usually called the **theory of public choice.** It has been given this name because it involves hypotheses about how choices are made in the public sector, as opposed to the private sector. The foundation of public-choice theory is the assumption that individuals will act within the political process to maximize their *individual* (not collective) well-being. In that sense, the theory is similar to our analysis of the market economy, in which we also assume that individuals are motivated by self-interest.

Collective decision making 
How voters, politicians, and other interested parties act and how these actions influence nonmarket decisions.

Theory of public choice 
The study of collective decision making.

To understand public-choice theory, it is necessary to point out other similarities between the private market sector and the public, or government, sector; then we will look at the differences.

Similarities in Market and Public-Sector Decision Making

In addition to the similar assumption of self-interest being the motivating force in both sectors, there are other similarities.

Scarcity. At any given moment, the amount of resources is fixed. This means that for the private and the public sectors combined, there is a scarcity constraint. Everything that is spent by all levels of government, plus everything that is spent by the private sector, must add up to the total income available at any point in time. Hence every government action has an opportunity cost, just as in the market sector.

Competition. Although we typically think of competition as a private-market phenomenon, it is also present in collective action. Given the scarcity constraint government also faces, bureaucrats, appointed officials, and elected representatives will always be in competition for available government funds. Furthermore, the individuals within any government agency or institution will act as individuals do in the private sector: They will try to obtain higher wages, better working conditions, and higher job-level classifications. We assume that they will compete and act in their own, not society's, interest.

Similarity of Individuals. Contrary to popular belief, there are not two types of individuals, those who work in the private sector and those who work in the public sector; rather, individuals working in similar positions can be considered similar. The difference, as we shall see, is that the individuals in government face a different **incentive structure** than those in the private sector. For example, the costs and benefits of being efficient or inefficient differ when one goes from the private to the public sector.

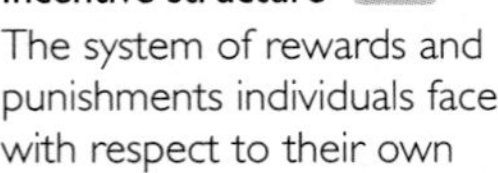

Incentive structure The system of rewards and punishments individuals face with respect to their own actions.

One approach to predicting government bureaucratic behavior is to ask what incentives bureaucrats face. Take the United States Postal Service (USPS) as an example. The bureaucrats running that government corporation are human beings with IQs not dissimilar to those possessed by workers in similar positions at Microsoft or American Airlines. Yet the USPS does not function like either of these companies. The difference can be explained, at least in part, in terms of the incentives provided for managers in the two types of institutions. When the bureaucratic managers and workers at Microsoft make incorrect decisions, work slowly, produce shoddy products, and are generally "inefficient," the profitability of the company declines. The owners—millions of shareholders—express their displeasure by selling some of their shares of company stock. The market value, as tracked on the stock exchange, falls. But what about the USPS? If a manager, a worker, or a bureaucrat in the USPS gives shoddy service, there is no straightforward mechanism by which the organization's owners—the taxpayers—can express their dissatisfaction. Despite the postal service's status as a "government corporation," taxpayers as shareholders do not really own shares of stock in the organization that they can sell.

The key, then, to understanding purported inefficiency in the government bureaucracy is not found in an examination of people and personalities but rather in an examination of incentives and institutional arrangements.

POLICY EXAMPLE

The U.S. Postal Service: Little Changed After More than Two Centuries

Like many private businesses, the federal government often desires to send urgent overnight mail. So to whom does it turn for delivery of the more than 8 million express letters and packages leaving federal offices for points around the nation and the world? Federal Express. Why not the U.S. Postal Service? The answer is that the USPS cannot legally reduce its prices to bid for competitive contracts. Even though the postal service now must make its own way without drawing on taxpayers, it still operates under a two-century-old mandate to serve every address, from backwoods farmhouses to crime-ridden urban apartments. It must do this while charging the same price to send a letter—whether regular first class or overnight delivery—from one point in New York City to another as it does from New York City to Anchorage, Alaska. This has made the postal service the provider of choice for transmitting items such as Pampers rebate coupons or proof-of-purchase seals from cereal boxes. But it has cost the USPS big revenues in the express-mail business. Its share of the overnight delivery pie is less than 10 percent. In recent years, supporters and critics of the postal service have both agreed that Congress must ultimately loosen the restraints that keep the USPS from competing with private firms in the marketplace. In the words of one member of Congress, if the postal service does not escape the bureaucratic shackles that bind it and compete in the private marketplace, it may "slowly strangle itself."

For Critical Analysis

If the U.S. Postal Service cannot reduce its prices, in what other ways can it try to compete for big overnight delivery contracts?

Differences Between Market and Collective Decision Making

There are probably more dissimilarities between the market sector and the public sector than there are similarities.

Government Goods at Zero Price. The majority of goods that governments produce are furnished to the ultimate consumers without direct money charge. **Government,** or **political, goods** can be either private or public goods. The fact that they are furnished to the ultimate consumer free of charge does *not* mean that the cost to society of those goods is zero, however; it only means that the price *charged* is zero. The full opportunity cost to society is the value of the resources used in the production of goods produced and provided by the government.

Government, or political, goods 
Goods (and services) provided by the public sector; they can be either private or public goods.

For example, none of us pays directly for each unit of consumption of defense or police protection. Rather, we pay for all these things indirectly through the taxes that support our governments—federal, state, and local. This special feature of government can be looked at in a different way. There is no longer a one-to-one relationship between consumption of a government-provided good and payment for that good. Consumers who pay taxes collectively pay for every political good, but the individual consumer may not be able to see the relationship between the taxes that he or she pays and the consumption of the good. Indeed, most taxpayers will find that their tax bill is the same whether or not they consume, or even like, government-provided goods.

Use of Force. All governments are able to engage in the legal use of force in their regulation of economic affairs. For example, governments can exercise the use of *expropriation,* which means that if you refuse to pay your taxes, your bank account and other assets may be seized by the Internal Revenue Service. In fact, you have no choice in the matter of paying taxes to governments. Collectively, we decide the total size of government through the political process, but individually, we cannot determine how much service we pay for just for ourselves during any one year.

Voting Versus Spending. In the private market sector, a dollar voting system is in effect. This dollar voting system is not equivalent to the voting system in the public sector. There are at least three differences:

1. In a political system, one person gets one vote, whereas in the market system, each dollar one spends counts separately.
2. The political system is run by **majority rule,** whereas the market system is run by **proportional rule.**
3. The spending of dollars can indicate intensity of want, whereas because of the all-or-nothing nature of political voting, a vote cannot.

Majority rule 
A collective decision-making system in which group decisions are made on the basis of more than 50 percent of the vote. In other words, whatever more than half of the electorate votes for, the entire electorate has to accept.

Proportional rule 
A decision-making system in which actions are based on the proportion of the "votes" cast and are in proportion to them. In a market system, if 10 percent of the "dollar votes" are cast for blue cars, 10 percent of the output will be blue cars.

Ultimately, the main distinction between political votes and dollar votes here is that political outcomes may differ from economic outcomes. Remember that economic efficiency is a situation in which, given the prevailing distribution of income, consumers get the economic goods they want. There is no corresponding situation using political voting. Thus we can never assume that a political voting process will lead to the same decisions that a dollar voting process will lead to in the marketplace.

Indeed, consider the dilemma every voter faces. Usually a voter is not asked to decide on a single issue (although this happens); rather, a voter is asked to choose among candidates who present a large number of issues and state a position on each of them. Just consider the average U.S. senator, who has to vote on several thousand different issues during a six-year term. When you vote for that senator, you are voting for a person who must make thousands of decisions during the next six years.

NETNOMICS

Protecting Private Property on the Internet: The Problem of Cyberpiracy

The U.S. Constitution grants Congress the power "to promote the Progress of Science and useful Arts, by securing for limited Times to Authors and Inventors the exclusive Rights to their respective Writings and Discoveries." Today, copyright laws are governed by the Copyright Act of 1976, as amended. This act has not been particularly effective, however, in preventing the theft of *intellectual property*. In contrast to physical property, intellectual property is any creation whose source is a person's mind or creativity.

Recent technological developments have greatly simplified the pirating of films, tapes, and CDs. Within days after the initial release of *Star Wars: The Phantom Menace*, people in China were selling tapes of the film that U.S. moviegoers had made by smuggling handheld videocassette recorders into theaters. The pirating of recorded music is also widespread. The International Federation of the Phonographic Industry (IFPI) estimates that one-fifth of all sales of recorded music are of pirated copies. The group estimates that one in three sales of CDs is pirated.

The IFPI's estimates are problematic, however. When estimating what legitimate CD sales would be in the absence of pirating, the IFPI assumes that pirated copies displace legitimate copies one for one, even though the pirated copies have much lower prices than legitimate copies. This assumption is a clear violation of the law of demand. In fact, there will be a larger quantity demanded at a lower price. Thus the lower-priced pirated copies of recorded music induce purchasers to buy more of them. If pirated copies did not exist, we could predict that legal sales of CDs would not simply replace them one for one.

This same analysis can apply to pirated copies of software. A person with a little computer background can develop relatively straightforward ways to transfer files from certain software programs for use by others who have not paid to use them. The Business Software Alliance estimates that a least half the global market for software is pirated products (remember the law of demand, however—this does not mean that if no pirating took place, legitimate sales of software would double).

There has been a significant change in pirating with the advent of the Internet: Not all pirates do so to profit. Some people, meaning to be kindhearted, offer downloadable copies of software and recorded music at no charge. Without ways to reduce this kind of unauthorized bootlegging, regardless of the motives of the bootleggers, people will reduce the time, effort, and creative energy they put into the development of software, recorded music, and other intellectual property.

This has led to calls from the film, recording, and software industries for stepped-up government efforts to protect their products under the copyright laws. Nonetheless, it is not clear how much the government can do when confronted with millions of Web sites to police. Many observers think that the solution will ultimately come from the private sector.

A Global Comparison of Income Tax Systems

Britain adopted the first national income tax in 1799 as a "temporary measure." Today residents of most developed nations pay income taxes every year. These nations typically strive to achieve progressivity of their tax structures.

Concepts Applied
- Income Tax
- Marginal Tax Rate
- Tax Freedom Day

Marginal Tax Rates in Other Nations

As you can see in panel (a) of Figure 5-5, Japan and several European nations have the highest marginal tax rates for the highest-income residents. By contrast, Hong Kong and Singapore stand out with much lower tax rates for the "rich." Residents with the lowest incomes also face lower marginal tax rates in these latter two nations.

FIGURE 5-5: Worldwide Income Tax Comparisons

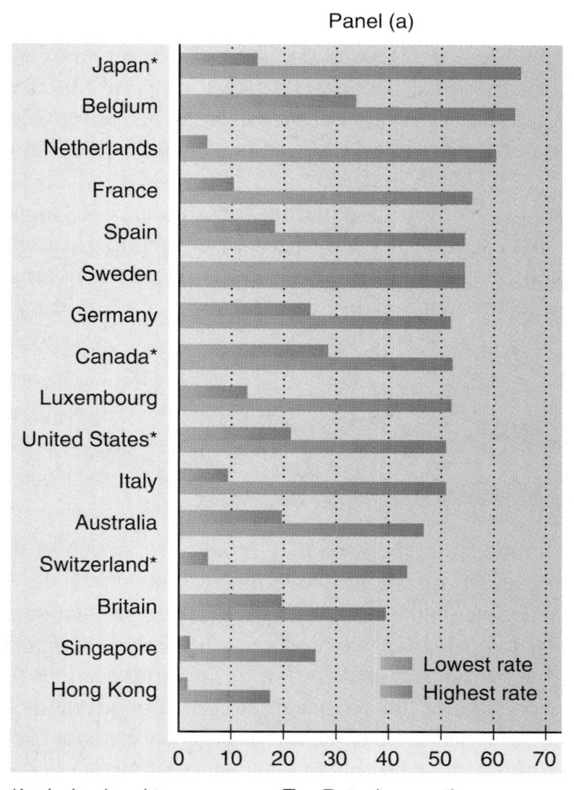

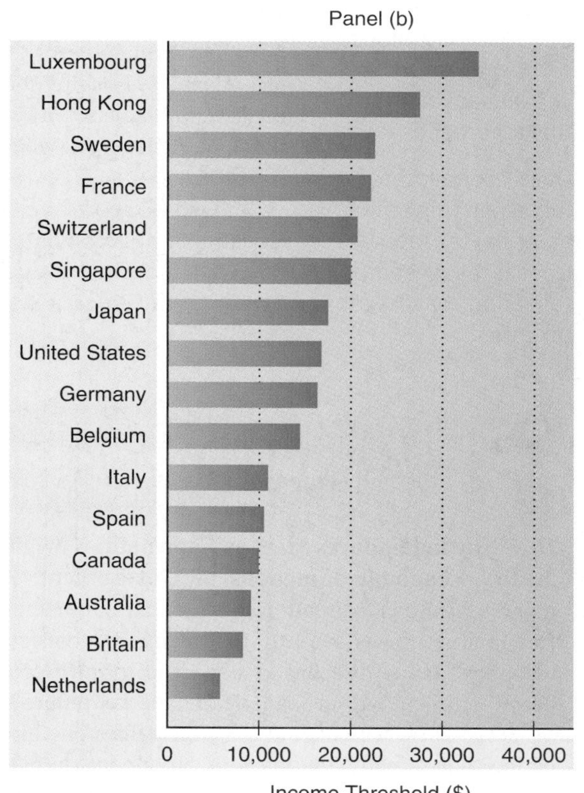

TABLE 5-4
Tax Freedom Day in Selected Nations
These figures exclude state, province, and local taxes.

Country	Date	Country	Date
Singapore	March 4	**Canada**	May 12
United States	April 11	**Germany**	May 23
Japan	April 12	**Italy**	June 2
Australia	April 25	**France**	June 12
Spain	May 5	**Netherlands**	June 12
Switzerland	May 6	**Belgium**	June 17
Britain	May 9	**Sweden**	July 3

Source: Organization for Economic Cooperation and Development.

FOR CRITICAL ANALYSIS

1. Some observers have attributed the strong employment and economic performance of Hong Kong and Singapore (despite the recession that affected Asian economies in 1997 and 1998) to the relatively small tax bite that they impose on income earners. Do you see any merit to this argument?
2. Does tax freedom day tell us anything about marginal tax rates? Does it tell us something about average tax rates?

Panel (b) of Figure 5-5 shows that some countries impose greater income tax burdens on lower-income residents than others do. A person can earn the equivalent of over $20,000 per year before owing any income taxes in Luxembourg, Hong Kong, Sweden, France, Switzerland, and Singapore. In contrast, in the United Kingdom and the Netherlands, a person earning less than the equivalent of $10,000 annually may owe income taxes to the government.

Tax Freedom Day—Anywhere Between March and July, Depending on Where You Live

Some governments rely more than others on the income tax as a significant source of tax revenues. For this reason, some international tax analysts like to look at a broader measure of tax assessments—the tax freedom day for a nation's average resident, which is the day each year when sufficient income has been earned to meet the nation's total tax bills.

Table 5-4 reports the "tax freedom day" for fourteen nations, based on tax payments to national governments. Based on this overall measure of tax assessments, residents of Sweden are the most tax-burdened people among developed nations: An average Swede begins to earn income on her or his own behalf only after the midpoint of each year!

SUMMARY DISCUSSION OF LEARNING OBJECTIVES

1. **How Market Failures Such as Externalities Might Justify Economic Functions of Government:** A market failure is a situation in which an unhindered free market gives rise to too many or too few resources' being directed to a specific form of economic activity. A good example of a market failure is an externality, which is a spillover effect on third parties not directly involved in producing or purchasing a good or service. In the case of a negative externality, firms do not pay for the costs arising from spillover effects that their production of a good imposes on others, so they produce too much of the good in question. Government may be able to improve on the situation by restricting production or by imposing fees on producers. In the case of a positive externality, buyers fail to take into account the benefits that their consumption of a good yields to others, so they purchase too little of the good. Government may be able to induce more consumption of the good by regulating the market or subsidizing consumption. It can also provide a legal system to adjudicate disagreements about property rights, con-

duct antitrust policies to discourage monopoly and promote competition, provide public goods, and engage in policies designed to promote economic stability.

2. **Private Goods Versus Public Goods and the Free-Rider Problem:** Private goods are subject to the principle of rival consumption, meaning that one person's consumption of such a good reduces the amount available for another person to consume. This is not so for public goods, which can be consumed by many people simultaneously at no additional cost and with no reduction in quality or quantity of the good. Indeed, public goods are subject to the exclusion principle: No individual can be excluded from the benefits of a public good even if that person fails to help pay for it. This leads to the free-rider problem, which is that a person who thinks that others will pay for a public good will seek to avoid contributing to financing production of the good.
3. **Political Functions of Government That Lead to Its Involvement in the Economy:** Through the political process, people may decide that certain goods are merit goods, which they deem socially desirable, or demerit goods, which they feel are socially undesirable. They may call on government to promote the production of merit goods but to restrict or even ban the production and sale of demerit goods. In addition, the political process may determine that income redistribution is socially desirable, and governments may become involved in supervising transfer payments or in-kind transfers in the form of nonmoney payments.
4. **Average Tax Rates Versus Marginal Tax Rates:** The average tax rate is the ratio of total tax payments to total income. By contrast, the marginal tax rate is the change in tax payments induced by a change in total taxable income. Thus the marginal tax rate applies to the last dollar that a person earns.
5. **The U.S. Income Tax System:** The United States' income tax system assesses taxes against both personal and business incomes. It is designed to be a progressive tax system, in which the marginal tax rate increases as income rises, so that the marginal tax rate exceeds the average tax rate. This contrasts with a regressive tax system, in which higher-income people pay lower marginal tax rates, resulting in a marginal tax rate that is less than the average tax rate. The marginal tax rate equals the average tax rate only under proportional taxation, in which the marginal tax rate does not vary with income.
6. **Central Elements of the Theory of Public Choice:** The theory of public choice is the study of collective decision making, or the process through which voters, politicians, and other interested parties interact to influence nonmarket choices. Public choice theory emphasizes the incentive structures, or system of rewards or punishments, that affect the provision of government goods by the public sector of the economy. This theory points out that certain aspects of public-sector decision making, such as scarcity and competition, are similar to those that affect private-sector choices. Others, however, such as legal coercion and majority-rule decision making, differ from those involved in the market system.

Key Terms and Concepts

Antitrust legislation (100)
Average tax rate (104)
Capital gain (107)
Capital loss (107)
Collective decision making (111)
Demerit good (103)
Effluent fee (98)
Exclusion principle (101)
Externality (96)
Free-rider problem (102)
Government, or political, goods (113)
Incentive structure (112)
Majority rule (113)
Marginal tax rate (104)
Market failure (96)
Merit good (103)
Monopoly (100)
Principle of rival consumption (101)
Private goods (101)
Progressive taxation (105)
Property rights (100)
Proportional rule (113)
Proportional taxation (105)
Public goods (101)
Regressive taxation (105)
Retained earnings (107)
Tax bracket (104)
Tax incidence (107)
Theory of public choice (111)
Third parties (96)
Transfer payments (103)
Transfers in kind (103)

Problems

Answers to the odd-numbered problems appear at the back of the book.

5-1. Suppose that studies reveal that repeated application of a particular type of pesticide used on orange trees eventually causes harmful contamination of groundwater. The pesticide is produced by a large number of chemical manufacturers and is applied annually in orange groves throughout the world. Most orange growers regard the pesticide as a key input in their production of oranges.

a. Use a diagram of the market for the pesticides to illustrate the essential implications of a failure of pesticide manufacturers' costs to reflect the social costs associated with groundwater contamination.

b. Use your diagram from part (a) to explain a government policy that might be effective in achieving the socially optimal amount of pesticide production.

5-2. Now draw a diagram of the market for oranges. Explain how the government policy you discussed in part (b) of Problem 5-1 is likely to affect the market price and equilibrium quantity in the orange market. In what sense do consumers of oranges "pay" for dealing with the spillover costs of pesticide production?

5-3. The government of a major city in the United States has determined that mass transit, such as bus lines, helps alleviate traffic congestion, thereby benefiting both individual auto commuters and companies who desire to move workers, products, and factors of production speedily along streets and highways. Nevertheless, even though several private bus lines are in service, commuters in the city are failing to take the social benefits of the use of mass transit into account.

a. Use a diagram of the market for the bus service to illustrate the essential implications of a failure of commuters to take into account the social benefits associated with bus ridership.

b. Use your diagram from part (a) to explain a government policy that might be effective in achieving the socially optimal use of bus services.

5-4. Draw a diagram of the market for automobiles, which are a substitute means of transit. Explain how the government policy you discussed in part (b) of Problem 5-3 is likely to affect the market price and equilibrium quantity in the auto market. How are auto consumers affected by this policy to attain the spillover benefits of bus transit?

5-5. To promote increased use of port facilities in a major coastal city, a state government has decided to construct a state-of-the-art lighthouse at a projected cost of $10 million. The state proposes to pay half this cost and asks the city to raise the additional funds. Rather than raise its $5 million in funds via an increase in city taxes and fees, however, the city's government asks major businesses in and near the port area to contribute voluntarily to the project. Discuss key problems that the city is likely to face in raising the funds.

5-6. A senior citizen gets a part-time job at a fast-food restaurant. She earns $8 per hour for each hour she works, and she works exactly 25 hours per week. Thus her total pretax weekly income is $200. Her total income tax assessment each week is $40, but she has determined that she is assessed $3 in taxes for the final hour she works each week.

a. What is this individual's average tax rate each week?

b. What is the marginal tax rate for the last hour she works each week?

5-7. For purposes of assessing income taxes, there are three official income levels for workers in a small country: high, medium, and low. For the last hour on the job during a 40-hour workweek, a high-income worker pays a marginal income tax rate of 15 percent, a medium-income worker pays a marginal tax rate of 20 percent, and a low-income worker is assessed a 25 percent marginal income tax rate. Based only on this information, does this nation's income tax system appear to be progressive, proportional, or regressive?

5-8. Governments of country A and country B spend the same amount each year. In country A, the government allocates 25 percent of its spending to functions relating to dealing with market externalities and public goods, and it allocates the rest of its expenditures to funding the provision of merit goods and efforts to restrict the production of demerit goods. In country B, however, these relative spending allocations are reversed. Given this information, which country's government is more heavily involved in the economy through economic functions of government as opposed to political functions of government? Explain.

5-9. A government agency is contemplating launching an effort to expand the scope of its activities. One rationale for doing so is that another government agency could make the same effort and, if successful, receive larger budget allocations in future years. Another rationale for expanding the agency's activities is that this will make the jobs of its workers more interesting, which may help the agency attract better-qualified employees. Nevertheless, to broaden its legal mandate, the agency will have to convince more than half of the House of Representatives and the Senate to approve a formal proposal to expand its activities. In addition, to expand its activities, the agency must have the authority to force private companies it does not currently regulate to be officially licensed by agency personnel. Identify which aspects of this problem are similar to those faced by firms that operate in private markets and which aspects are specific to the public sector.

Economics on the Net

Putting Tax Dollars to Work In this application, you will learn about how the U.S. government allocates its expenditures. This will enable you to conduct your own evaluation of the current functions of the federal government within the U.S. economy.

Title: Historical Tables: Budget of the United States Government

Navigation: Click here to visit home page of the U.S. Government Printing Office. Select the most recent budget available, then click on Historical tables.

Application After the document downloads, examine Section 3, Federal Government Outlays by Function, and in particular Table 3.1, Outlays by Superfunction and Function. Then answer the following questions:

1. What government functions have been capturing growing shares of government spending in recent years? Which of these do you believe to be related to the problem of addressing externalities, providing public goods, or dealing with other market failures? Which appear to be related to political functions instead of economic functions?

2. Which government functions are receiving declining shares of total spending? Are any of these related to the problem of addressing externalities, providing public goods, or dealing with other market failures? Are any related to political functions instead of economic functions?

For Group Study and Analysis Assign groups to the following overall categories of government functions: national defense, health, income security, and Social Security. Have each group prepare a brief report concerning long-term and recent trends in government spending on each category. Each group should take a stand on whether specific spending on items in its category are likely to relate to resolving market failures, public funding of merit goods, regulating the sale of demerit goods, and so on.

CHAPTER 6

YOUR FUTURE WITH SOCIAL SECURITY

Of the three generations of this American family hiking in Vermont, the oldest will benefit the most from the Social Security system. Does that mean that the youngest may not benefit at all?

You've probably heard of chain letters. The basic notion is this: If you send, say, a dollar to each of several people on a list and then add your name to the list and mail it to your friends, you'll supposedly soon receive thousands of dollars from other people all over the world. There is a government program that has at times operated very much like a chain letter. The name of this program? Social Security.

The government retirement system that started 65 years ago was a good deal for your grandparents and probably will be a break-even proposition for your parents. But Social Security and a related program, Medicare, pose an enormous challenge for the economy.

Why have Social Security and Medicare become such problems? To find out, you need to learn more about how Social Security operates and what it will look like in your future.

LEARNING OBJECTIVES

After reading this chapter, you should be able to:

1. **Identify the fundamental goals of Social Security and Medicare and the problems these programs pose for today's students**
2. **Analyze how Medicare affects the incentives to consume medical services**
3. **Explain why the Social Security Trust Fund is not a stock of savings we can draw on**
4. **Identify the key forces that caused the tremendous rise in Social Security spending**
5. **Explain how Social Security could be reformed**

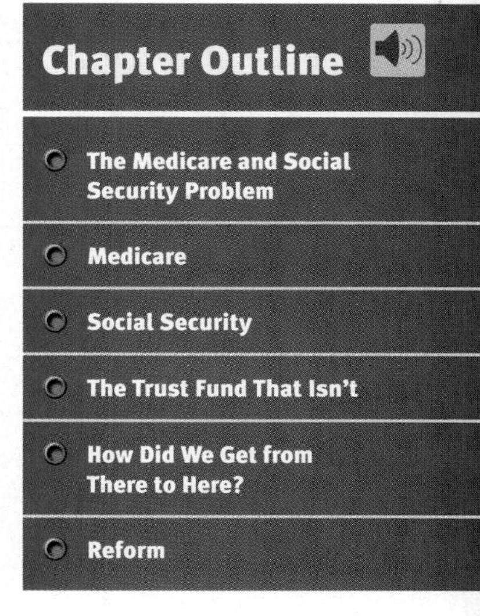

Chapter Outline
The Medicare and Social Security Problem
Medicare
Social Security
The Trust Fund That Isn't
How Did We Get from There to Here?
Reform

Did You Know That... America is getting old? The 78 million baby boomers born between 1946 and 1964 are entering middle age. Indeed, the future of America is now on display in Florida, where one person in five is over age 65. In 30 years, almost 20 percent of *all* Americans will be 65 or older.

Two principal forces are behind America's "senior boom." First, people are living longer. Average life expectancy in 1900 was 47. Today it is 77, and is likely to reach 80 within the next decade. Second, the birthrate is near record low levels. Today's mothers are having *half* the number of children that their mothers had. In short, the elderly are living longer, and the ranks of the young are growing too slowly to offset the added pressure of large numbers of retirees on the economy. Together, these forces are pushing the average age of the population higher and higher; in fact, the number of seniors is growing at *twice* the rate of the rest of the population. In 1970, the **median age** in the United States—the age that divides the older half of the population from the younger half—was 28; by 2000, the median age was over 35 and rising rapidly. Compounding these factors, the average age at retirement has been declining as well, from 65 in 1963 to 62 currently. Only 30 percent of the people age 55 and over hold jobs today, compared with 45 percent in 1930.

In this chapter, you will find out how the aging of America has caused an explosion of government spending, and you will learn about the potential impact of this increased spending on your future tax bills and retirement plans.

Median age 
The age that divides the older half of the population from the younger half.

THE MEDICARE AND SOCIAL SECURITY PROBLEM

Why should you be concerned with government programs designed to assist the elderly portion of the population? The main reason is that the elderly are expensive. In fact, people over 65 now consume over one-third of the federal government's budget. Social Security payments to retirees are the biggest item, now running over $300 billion a year. Medicare, the federal program that pays hospital and doctors' bills for the elderly, costs over $200 billion a year and is growing rapidly. Moreover, fully a third of the $150 billion-a-year budget for Medicaid, the government-sponsored program that helps pay medical bills for the poor of all ages, goes to people over the age of 65.

If current laws are maintained, the elderly will consume 40 percent of all federal spending within 10 years: Medicare's share of gross domestic product (GDP) will double, as will the number of "very old" people—those over 85, who are most in need of care. Within 25 years, probably *one-half* of the federal budget will go to caring for the elderly. In a nutshell, senior citizens are the beneficiaries of an expensive and rapidly growing share of all federal spending.

Click here for alternative perspectives on the problems of Social Security and Medicare.

Responsibility for paying the growing bills for Social Security and Medicare falls squarely on current and future workers, because both programs are financed by taxes on payrolls. Thirty years ago, these programs were adequately financed with a payroll levy of less than 10 percent of the typical worker's earnings. Today, the tax rate exceeds 15 percent of median wages, and it is expected to grow rapidly.

Consider what will happen if there is no change in the current structure of the Social Security system. By the year 2020, early baby boomers, born in the late 1940s and early 1950s, will have retired. Late baby boomers, born in the 1960s, will be nearing retirement. Both groups will leave today's college students, and their children, with a potentially staggering bill to pay. For Social Security and Medicare to be maintained, the payroll tax rate may have to rise to 25 percent of wages over the next 20 years. And a payroll tax rate of 40 percent is not unlikely by the middle of the twenty-first century.

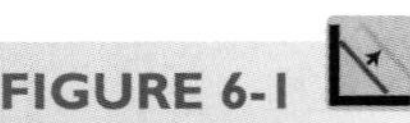

FIGURE 6-1

Workers Per Retiree

The average number of workers per Social Security retiree has declined dramatically since the program's inception.

Sources: Social Security Administration and author's estimates.

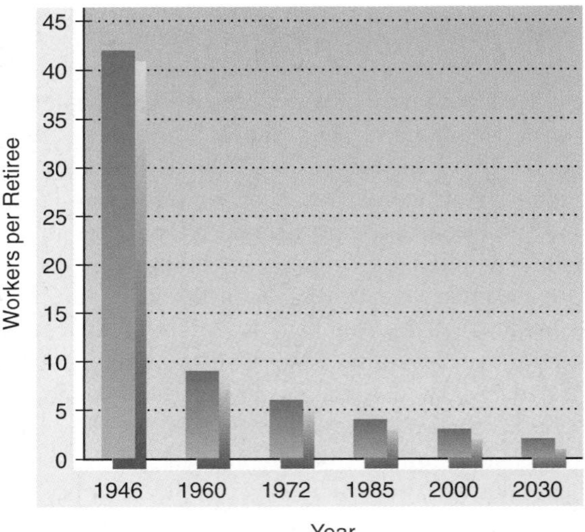

FAQ: *Why is the retirement age falling?*

Part of the exodus of the elderly from the workplace is due simply to their prosperity. Older people have higher disposable incomes than any other age group in the population, and they are using their wealth to consume more leisure. But early retirement is also being prompted by American businesses. Career advancement often slows after age 40; over 60 percent of American corporations offer early retirement plans, while only about 5 percent offer inducements to delay retirement. Even more important is the federal government's tax treatment of the elderly. Individuals age 70 and over, especially those in middle-income brackets, can be subject to a crushing array of taxes. They must pay taxes on up to 85 percent of their Social Security benefits, contribute payroll taxes if they keep working, and bear the loss of $1 in Social Security benefits for every $3 of wage income over about $10,000. Because these taxes can "piggyback" on each other, effective marginal tax rates can become astronomical for the elderly. In fact, for a fairly typical couple trying to supplement their retirement checks, income from work can be subject to a tax rate in excess of 80 percent, so little take-home pay remains after taxes. No wonder so many seniors are saying "no thanks" to seemingly attractive jobs.

One way to think about the future bill that could face today's college students and their successors in the absence of fundamental changes in Social Security is to consider the number of retirees each worker must support. In 1946, payroll taxes from 42 workers supported one Social Security recipient. By 1960, nine workers funded each retiree's Social Security benefits. Today, as shown in Figure 6-1, roughly three workers provide for each retiree's Social Security *and* Medicare benefits. Unless the current system is changed, by 2030 only two workers will be available to pay the Social Security and Medicare benefits due each recipient. In that event, a working couple would find itself responsible for supporting not only itself and its family but also someone outside the family who is receiving Social Security and Medicare benefits.

These figures illustrate why efforts to reform these programs have begun to dominate the nation's public agenda. Fortunately, the fact that Social Security and Medicare are your problems means that they are also your government's problems. What remains to be seen is how the government will ultimately resolve them.

CONCEPTS IN BRIEF

- Social Security and Medicare payments are using up a large and growing portion of the federal budget.

- Because of a shrinking number of workers available to support each retiree, the expense for future workers to fund these programs will grow rapidly unless reforms are implemented.

MEDICARE

Not surprisingly, medical expenses are a major concern for many elderly Americans. Since 1965, that concern has been reflected in the existence of the Medicare program, which heavily subsidizes the medical expenses of persons over the age of 65. In return for paying a tax on their earnings while in the workforce (currently set at 2.9 percent of wages and salaries), retirees are ensured that the majority of their hospital and doctor's bills will be paid for with public monies.

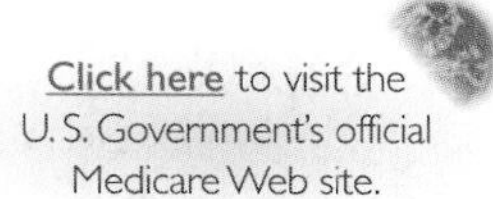

Click here to visit the U.S. Government's official Medicare Web site.

The United States Compared to Other Nations

As we shall see, the design of the Medicare system encourages the consumption of medical services and drives up total spending on such services—spending that is paid for out of current taxes. Reflecting those facts, each person under the age of 65 in America currently pays an average of around $1,500 *per year* in federal taxes to subsidize medical care for the elderly. Some 30 percent of Medicare's budget goes to patients in their last year of life. Coronary bypass operations—costing over $30,000 apiece—are routinely performed on Americans in their sixties and even seventies. And for those over 65, Medicare picks up the tab. Even heart transplants are now performed on people in their sixties, paid for by Medicare for those over 65. Britain's National Health Service generally will not provide kidney dialysis for people over 55. Yet Medicare subsidizes dialysis for more than 200,000 people, whose average age is 63. The cost: more than $8 billion a year. Overall, the elderly receive Medicare benefits worth 5 to 20 times the payroll taxes (plus interest) they paid for this program.

The Simple Economics of Medicare

To understand how, in only 35 years, Medicare became the second-biggest domestic spending program in existence, a bit of economics is in order. Consider Figure 6-2 on page 124, which shows the demand and supply of medical care.

The initial equilibrium price is P_0, and equilibrium quantity is Q_0. Perhaps because the government believes that Q_0 is not enough medical care for these consumers, suppose that the government begins paying a subsidy that eventually is set at M for each unit of medical care consumed. This will simultaneously tend to raise the price per unit of care received by providers (doctors, hospitals, and so on) and lower the perceived price per unit that consumers see when they make decisions about how much medical care to consume. As presented in the figure, the price received by providers rises to P_s, while the price paid by demanders falls to P_d. As a result, demanders of medical care want to consume Q_m units, and suppliers are quite happy to provide it for them.

Medicare Incentives at Work

We can now understand the problems that plague the Medicare system today. First, one of the things that people observed during the 20 years after the founding of Medicare was a huge upsurge in physicians' incomes and medical school applications, the spread of private

FIGURE 6-2

The Economic Effects of Medicare Subsidies

When the government pays a per-unit subsidy *M* for medical care, consumers pay the price P_d for the quantity of services Q_m. Providers receive the price P_s for supplying this quantity.

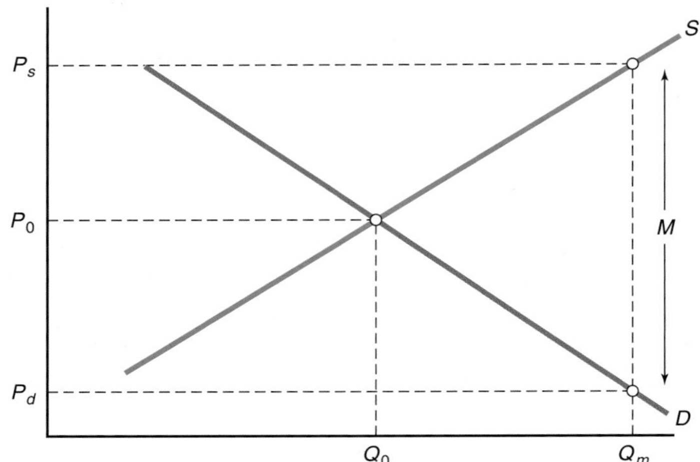

for-profit hospitals, and the rapid proliferation of new medical tests and procedures. All of this was being encouraged by the rise in the price of medical services from P_0 to P_s, which encouraged entry into this market.

Second, government expenditures on Medicare have routinely turned out to be far in excess of the expenditures forecast at the time the program was put in place or each time it was expanded. The reasons for this are easy to see. Bureaucratic planners often fail to recognize the incentive effects of government programs. On the demand side, they fail to account for the huge increase in consumption (from Q_0 to Q_m) that will result from a subsidy like Medicare. On the supply side, they fail to recognize that the larger amount of services can only be extracted from suppliers at a higher price, P_s. Consequently, original projected spending on Medicare was an area like $Q_0 \times (P_0 - P_d)$, because original plans for the program only allowed for consumption of Q_0 and assumed that the subsidy would have to be only $P_0 - P_d$ per unit. In fact, consumption rises to Q_m and marginal cost per unit of service rise to P_s, necessitating an increase in the per-unit subsidy to *M*. Hence actual expenditures turn out to be the far larger number $Q_m \times M$. The introduction of Medicare thus turned out to be more expensive than predicted, and every expansion of the program has followed the same pattern.

Third, total spending on medical services soars, consuming far more income than initially expected. Originally, total spending on medical services was $P_0 \times Q_0$. In the presence of Medicare, spending rises to $P_s \times Q_m$. This helps explain why current health care spending in the United States is 14 percent of GDP—the largest percentage spent anywhere in the world.

Finally, note that with the subsidy in place, consumers end up consuming many relatively low-value services that are nevertheless extremely costly to provide. For example, the value to consumers of the last few units of service consumed is only P_d per unit, but the cost of providing each of these units is P_s per unit. Hence the economic waste of having these last units provided—that is, the excess of cost over value received—is exactly equal to the subsidy per unit, *M*. This makes it clear why the United States spends so much money on high-cost procedures that have very low expected benefits for recipients: In America, the elderly are allowed to choose what they wish to consume at subsidized prices; in other countries, they often are not given the choice.

Spending and More Spending

Given these features of the Medicare system, it is little wonder that current health outlays per older person (over the age of 65) now average about $10,000 per year, a figure that has been rising at an inflation-adjusted rate of about 4 percent per year. At this sort of growth rate, real expenditures on each senior will average $25,000 per year by 2020. Moreover, the 65-and-older population will expand from 13 percent of the population today to 16.5 percent over that period. The combination of more elderly and more spending on each of them implies that medical spending is likely to rise to 20 percent of GDP over this period. As Victor Fuchs of Stanford University has observed, "Although people justifiably worry about Social Security, paying for old folks' health care is the real 800-pound gorilla facing the economy."

Public Versus Private Incentives

So far, the federal government's response to soaring Medicare costs has been to impose arbitrary reimbursement caps on specific procedures. Medicare's Prospective Payment System gives doctors and hospitals a flat fee for each of a wide variety of treatments and procedures. In principle, this should cap Medicare payments and give providers an incentive to cut costs by allowing them to pocket the difference. But as a practical matter, each of the caps is set in isolation from the others and without regard to the other incentives the caps give providers. Thus to avoid going over Medicare's reimbursement cap, hospitals often discharge patients too soon or in an unstable condition, making them more likely to end up back in the hospital or in a nursing home. For example, many hospitals fail to send elderly patients to rehabilitation centers after hip surgery. Six to 18 months later, the patients are back in the hospital with hip problems. Similarly, less than one-half of all Medicare heart patients receive anticlotting drugs after heart surgery, even though such drugs reduce the risk of a second heart attack by 50 percent. The result is elderly individuals who are sicker than they otherwise would be and Medicare costs that are actually higher *overall* because of the reimbursement caps on specific treatments and procedures.

Of course, even private health insurance companies and health maintenance organizations (HMOs)—organizations that are responsible for delivering, or arranging for the delivery of, and paying for their members' medical care—put limits on reimbursement levels. But they do so with a sharp eye to the reasonably predictable ways that physicians and patients are likely to respond to these caps. Hence insurers and HMOs go to great lengths to bundle services and reimbursement levels in ways that minimize the cost of achieving a given health outcome. Medicare administrators appear to pay far less attention to this issue.

- Medicare subsidizes the consumption of medical care by the elderly, thus increasing the amount of such care consumed.
- Expenditures on programs such as Medicare almost invariably turn out to be more than forecasted because of a rise in consumption and a rise in the per-unit cost of providing the services.
- People tend to purchase large amounts of low-value, high-cost services in programs like Medicare because they do not directly bear the full cost of their decisions.
- Medicare managers do a poorer job of accounting for the incentive effects of their decisions than private sector managers because they have fewer incentives to do so.

SOCIAL SECURITY

The Social Security system was founded in 1935, as America was beginning to recover from the Great Depression. The financial resources of many people had been demolished during the previous six years: Jobs had been lost, stock prices had tumbled, and thousands of banks had failed, wiping out the accounts of their depositors. It was widely feared that recent retirees and workers soon to retire faced destitution. Moreover, many people argued that the elderly should be protected from any similar disasters in the future. Hence the decision was made to establish Social Security as a means of guaranteeing a minimum level of pension benefits to all persons. Today, many people regard Social Security as a kind of "social compact"—a national promise to successive generations that they will receive support in their old age.

Social Security contributions
The mandatory taxes paid out of workers' wages and salaries. Although half are supposedly paid by employers, in fact the net wages of employees are lower by the full amount.

Rate of return
The interest rate necessary to make the present values of the costs and benefits of an action equal. For a situation in which a cost is incurred today and a benefit received one year from now, it is the percentage excess of the future benefit over the present cost.

Inflation-adjusted return
A rate of return that is measured in terms of real goods and services, that is, after the effects of inflation have been factored out.

Good Times for the First Retirees

The first Social Security taxes (called "contributions") were collected in 1937, but it was not until 1940 that retirement benefits were first paid. Ida May Fuller was the first person to receive a regular Social Security pension. She had paid a total of $25 in **Social Security contributions** before she retired. By the time she died in 1975 at age 100, she had received benefits totaling $23,000. Although Fuller did perhaps better than most, for the average retiree of 1940, the Social Security system was still more generous than any private investment plan anyone is likely to devise: After adjusting for inflation, the **rate of return** on their contributions was an astounding 135 percent. (Roughly speaking, every $100 of combined employer and employee contributions yielded $135 *per year* during each and every year of that person's retirement. This is also called the **inflation-adjusted return.**) Ever since then, however, the rate of return has decreased. Nonetheless, Social Security was an excellent deal for most retirees during the twentieth century. Figure 6-3 shows the rate of return for people retiring in different years.

Given that the inflation-adjusted long-term rate of return on the stock market is about 10 percent, it is clear that for retirees, Social Security was a good deal until at least 1970. In fact, because Social Security benefits are a lot less risky than stocks, Social Security actually remained a pretty good investment for many people until around 1990.

Social Security has managed to pay such high returns because at each point in time, current retirees are paid benefits out of the contributions of those who are currently working.

FIGURE 6-3
Private Rates of Return on Social Security Contributions, by Year of Retirement
The rate of return on Social Security contributions has steadily declined.
Sources: Social Security Administration and author's estimates.

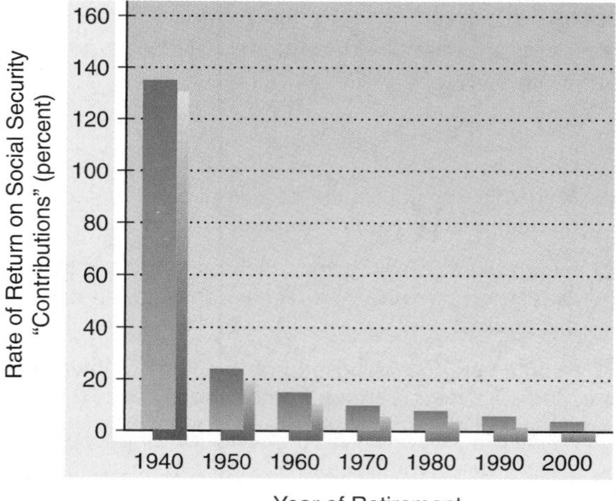

(The contributions of today's retirees were long ago used to pay the benefits of previous retirees.) As long as Social Security was pulling in growing numbers of workers, either through a burgeoning workforce or by expanding its coverage of individuals in the workforce, the impressive rates of return during the early years of the program were possible. But as membership growth slowed as the post–World War II baby boom generation began to reach retirement age, the rate of return fell. Moreover, because the early participants received more than they contributed, it follows that later participants must receive less—and that ultimately means a *negative* rate of return. And for today's college students—indeed, for most people now under the age of 30 or so—that negative rate of return is what lies ahead, unless reforms are implemented.

Lesser Benefits for Some

Another aspect of today's low Social Security rate of return is worth noting. The system was originally designed to assist those most likely to be in need of assistance in their retirement years, and even today, low-income individuals do earn a higher rate of return on their contributions than higher-income people. But blacks do much worse than whites under the current system, because their life expectancy is significantly lower: Many collect nothing because they die before becoming eligible for their pensions. In addition, although women were generally net beneficiaries of the system in its early years, mainly through their spouses' contributions, that pattern has been changing as women entered the workforce in greater numbers: They are paying more in contributions but will receive proportionately less in benefits. In fact, families with two income earners now receive a substantially lower rate of return on their contributions than families with only one earner.

CONCEPTS IN BRIEF

- During the early years of the Social Security system, taxes were low and benefits were relatively robust, resulting in a high rate of return for retirees.
- As taxes have risen relative to benefits, the rate of return has fallen steadily.
- Blacks have often fared poorly under Social Security, as have two-earner families in recent years.

THE TRUST FUND THAT ISN'T 

Click here to learn more about Social Security. Next, click on "Understanding Social Security and Aging."

During the early years of Social Security's existence, payroll taxes were collected, but no benefits were paid. The monies collected over this period were used to purchase bonds issued by the U.S. Treasury, and this accumulation of bonds was called the Social Security Trust Fund. (Medicare has a similar trust fund; because the basic principles apply to both funds, only Social Security's is discussed here in detail.) Even today, Social Security tax collections continue to exceed benefits, and so the trust fund has continued to grow. As the baby boomers move into retirement in a few years, benefit payments each year will exceed tax receipts, and the Social Security system will begin to sell the bonds in the trust fund to finance the difference. Eventually—current estimates are that in the absence of actions to alter the current system, it will be around the year 2030—all of the bonds in the trust fund will have been sold. Any further benefits will have to be explicitly financed out of current-day taxes.

The Prefunding Myth

Many supporters of the current system argue that the "prefunding" of Social Security that has taken place so far is advantageous, because it has enabled the system to build up assets. This, these supporters contend, is much like a private pension fund that builds up assets for its members during their working years or the process by which individuals build up assets in their own individual retirement accounts to draw on during their retirement years. According to this line of reasoning, the Social Security Trust Fund represents net assets that society can use to finance future benefit payments. Nothing could be further from the truth.

The obligations of the Social Security system consist of the benefits that the system promises to pay. It is equally true that the financing for those obligations consists of the taxes on the public that will be levied over time. The question is this: Given the promised level of benefits, does it matter whether the taxes it will take to pay those benefits are levied before, during, or after the benefits are paid? The answer is no. A given stream of benefits can be paid for with smaller taxes now or larger taxes later, but the economic value of those taxes now or later must be exactly equivalent, given the stream of benefits that has been promised.

Congressional Meddling

Whenever current Social Security taxes exceed current benefits (as they have for the past 60 years), Congress has been unable to resist the temptation to spend the difference on other programs. For instance, in 1999, President Clinton and Congress quibbled over who should receive credit for the government budget surplus of nearly $123 billion. In fact, $124 billion of this "budget surplus" was the Social Security Trust Fund, which the president and Congress had borrowed to fund current spending. Thus the federal government actually operated at a *deficit* of about $1 billion that year.

But to maintain the fiction that the Social Security system is an insurance plan, Congress gives Social Security IOUs for the money that it spends. These IOUs are simply Treasury bonds, which of course are redeemable only for future taxes to be levied on the American people. Thus the "assets" owned by Social Security are nothing more than promises of the Treasury to make payments based on taxes collected from Americans.

Essentially, by borrowing from the Social Security Trust Fund and issuing IOUs, Congress transforms what looks like a prefunded system into a pay-as-you-go operation. After all, when it is time for the trust fund to redeem those IOUs, Congress must increase taxes, cut other spending, or borrow more money to raise the cash. But this would be true even if there were *no* Treasury bonds in the trust fund: All benefits must ultimately be paid for out of taxes. So although the design of the system's funding may originally have been well intentioned, the accounting fiction of the trust fund is nothing more than that: a fiction designed to disguise the true system.

POLICY EXAMPLE

Smoothing Taxes over Time

If the trust fund is a fiction, why would prefunding ever be the preferred means of financing the system? Tax smoothing is one possible explanation.

Whenever the government imposes taxes, the people who are expected to pay those taxes have a natural incentive to try to avoid or evade them. These efforts to avoid taxes (and the corresponding effort by the government to prevent such avoidance) use up ("waste") scarce resources. Moreover, as taxes rise relative to income in any given period, the efforts devoted to avoiding (and collecting) taxes tend to rise disproportionately, implying that so do the resources that are wasted in such activities.

Hence for any given level of taxes to be collected over time, the amount of resources that are wasted in avoiding and collecting those taxes can be minimized by following this rule: Keep the ratio of taxes to income constant over time; that is, smooth taxes over time. Suppose (as has been true) that Social Security benefits rise over time faster than income, implying that the ratio of benefits to income is expected to rise. Ideally, we want to keep the ratio of taxes to income constant, which implies that taxes will initially have to be high relative to benefits, eventually becoming low relative to the more rapidly growing benefits. The result is "prefunding" of benefits, much as we had during the early years of the Social Security system.

For Critical Analysis

What incentive does prefunding give to members of Congress who might be looking for additional funds to be used to pay for other programs?

CONCEPTS IN BRIEF

- Social Security is paid for out of taxes, regardless of when those taxes are imposed. Prefunding does not create any additional wealth that can be used to pay benefits.
- Congress has consistently reappropriated much or all of the excess of Social Security taxes over benefits that have been collected.

HOW DID WE GET FROM THERE TO HERE?

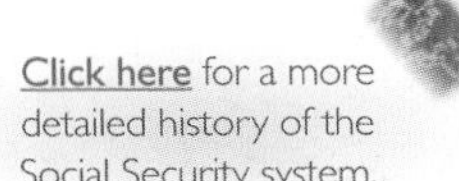
Click here for a more detailed history of the Social Security system.

If Social Security started as a system designed to relieve the misery of the destitute elderly in the aftermath of the Great Depression, it has certainly become something much different. There is no doubt that it has helped raise the standard of living of the 65-and-older age group to the highest of all the age groups. But it has also become the single largest drain on the U.S. taxpayer and the most important domestic policy problem facing politicians and public alike. What happened? There are many facets to the story, but we shall focus here on just two of them, both a mixture of economics and politics.

A Tale of Two Generations

The first of the forces that transformed Social Security is what we shall call the confluence of the generations. Until the 1960s, Social Security looked little different from when it had been founded three decades before. Tax collections still exceeded benefits, which had remained modest. And despite expansions of the system to cover industries and occupations not originally eligible, the political and economic scope of the system were relatively unobtrusive. Things began to change with the entry of the baby boom generation into the labor market: Taxes began flowing into the system at an unprecedented rate. And because the number of people then collecting benefits was small relative to the burgeoning labor force, and the boomers themselves were 40 years from collecting benefits themselves, the Social Security Trust Fund soon became a rich prize in the political arena.

In the early 1970s, the first members of the generation that had suffered through the Great Depression and then fought World War II began retiring. Most had private savings that were modest at best and strong memories of having endured much on behalf of their nation. Thus we had the confluence of a large source of cash (the taxes paid by the boomers) and a worthy cause on which to spend it (the retirement benefits of the generation that had fought to keep the world free in World War II). The result was enormous political pressure to expand Social Security benefits.

Inflation

At the same time, America was going through a period of inflation that was, by the standards of the day, quite significant, running as high as 4 percent per year. At the time, the dollar value of Social Security benefits was set by Congress and thus could be changed only by explicit congressional action. But a 4 percent rise in the price level in such circumstances meant a 4 percent decline in the real value of benefits that were fixed in dollar terms. This was not the sort of thing any member of Congress wanted to have happen to the deserving World War II generation who was collecting those benefits. And this was particularly true because the elderly were already well known for voting more regularly than any other age group. So Congress looked for a way to protect retirees from inflation, without at the same time having to vote on the level of Social Security benefits every year. With the aid of President Richard Nixon, who was himself facing reelection in 1972, Congress found what appeared to be the ideal answer: Benefits were indexed, or linked, to the Consumer Price Index (CPI), a measure of the dollar cost of consuming a fixed market basket of goods that we shall discuss in greater detail in Chapter 7. Once a year, the percentage increase in the CPI was computed, and nominal Social Security benefits were then automatically increased by the same percentage amount.

Bias in the CPI

There was one significant hitch in this process. The CPI is biased upward; that is, it tends to overstate the actual rate of inflation, by an amount estimated to be about 1.1 percent per year. Thus if the true inflation rate is 3 percent, the CPI will measure it at, say, 4.1 percent; if the true rate is 4.5 percent, the CPI will say 5.6 percent. What this meant was that every year, Social Security recipients were getting their benefits increased not just by enough to protect them from inflation but also by what amounted to an automatic raise in real benefits of about 1.1 percent per year. This may not sound like much, but over the next 30 years or so, the power of compounding translated this into a 50 percent increase in real benefits. Thus a simple device introduced to protect the elderly from the ravages of inflation became a powerful tool for increasing benefits well above the levels ever contemplated at the system's founding—and all without the necessity for any overt action by Congress.

CONCEPTS IN BRIEF

- The combination of a politically powerful older generation and a larger younger generation capable of paying payroll taxes into the system created the incentives for the huge increase in Social Security benefits over the past 30 years.
- The cost-of-living adjustment, calculated using the Consumer Price Index, was the means by which much of this increase in real benefits occurred because it did not compensate for the upward bias in the CPI.

REFORM

America now finds itself with a social compact—the Social Security system—that entails a flow of promised benefits that will exceed the inflow of taxes by about 2010. What, if anything, might be done about this? There have been several proposals, each of which will be discussed. But the point to keep in mind throughout is this: The entire burden of Social Security consists of the benefits that it promises to pay. Under the system currently in place, all of these benefits must be paid out of taxes levied on the American people. So unless we

Year	1935	1955	1975	2000
Payroll tax rate	2%	4%	11.7%	15.3%
Wage base to which tax is applied	$3,000	$4,200	$14,100	$72,600

Source: Social Security Administration and author's estimates.

TABLE 6-1
The Rise of Payroll Taxes
Both the payroll tax rate and the wage base are rising.

fundamentally alter the nature of the system, there are only four options—or combinations of these four options—for preserving the current social compact: (1) raise taxes, (2) reduce the number of people eligible for benefits, (3) cut the amount of benefits each person is eligible to receive, or (4) find a way to make the funding base of the system grow at a more robust rate.

Raising Taxes

The history of Social Security has been one of steadily increasing tax rates, applied to an ever-increasing wage base. Table 6-1 shows the tax rate (which includes Medicare taxes since 1965) for selected years, and the wage base to which that tax rate is applied.

The combination of a rising tax rate and a taxable base that in recent years has grown faster than the inflation rate means that payroll taxes are becoming an increasingly important source of revenue for the federal government. Indeed, as revealed in Figure 6-4, payroll taxes are now almost 40 times as important to the federal government as they were 65 years ago.

Given the steady rise in both the tax rate and the wage base to which it applies, it is perhaps not surprising that many of the proposals for "reforming" Social Security advocate more of the same: Raise the tax rate or increase the wage base. For example, one prominent proposal calls for increasing the payroll tax rate by 2.2 percentage points, lifting the overall rate to 17.5 percent. Such a move would generate additional tax collections of about $80 billion per year initially, an amount equivalent to a 10 percent increase in everyone's personal taxes. This is a huge tax hike, amounting to $880 per year for a worker earning $40,000; indeed, this would be the largest tax increase of any type in our nation's history. Even so, it will *at best* keep current taxes above current benefits until 2020, after which the system will again be in deficit. Although the long-run tax hike that it will take to keep

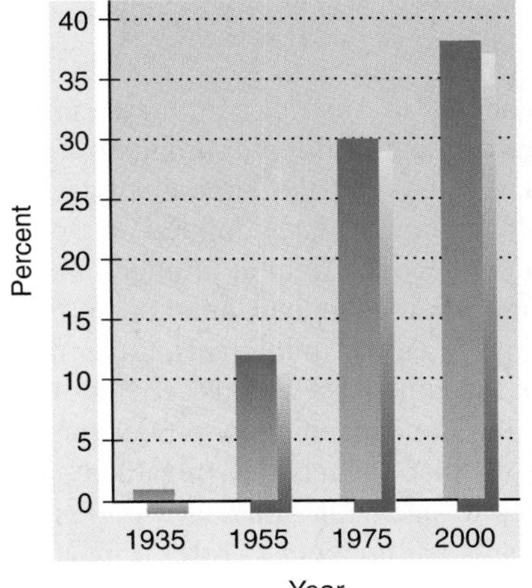

FIGURE 6-4
Payroll Taxes as a Share of Total Federal Tax Receipts, 1935–2000
Payroll taxes account for an increasing share of total federal tax revenues.
Sources: Social Security Administration, Council of Economic Advisers, and author's estimates.

Social Security solvent is subject to considerable uncertainty, best estimates now put that tax increase at around *seven* percentage points, not 2.2. Just to cover Social Security's projected deficits, the payroll tax will have to be increased to more than 22 percent.

Eliminating the Wage Cap

Another proposal is to eliminate the cap on the level of wages to which the payroll tax is applied. (This cap was lifted several years ago for the 2.9 percent Medicare component of payroll taxes.) All wage and salaries payments to workers would then be subject to the full brunt of payroll taxes. Although this proposal would not alter the tax obligations of workers earning less than $72,600 per year, it would result in a big hike in the marginal tax rate paid by millions of American workers. Indeed, the top rate paid would become 54.9 percent, the highest since the 1970s. Moreover, although this too would generate about $80 billion per year in additional tax revenues, it is not a long-term solution: Given projected benefit levels, the tax rate will eventually have to be increased. In fact, even the combination of eliminating the wage cap and a 2.2 percentage point tax increase is not enough to keep tax collections above benefit payments over the long run.

Cutting Benefits

The alternative to an increase in taxes is a cut in benefits. A small step in this direction has actually been taken, although not for the express purpose of reducing Social Security obligations. During the late 1990s, the Bureau of Labor Statistics revised the CPI to take better account of quality improvements in goods. One of the side effects of these revisions was to reduce slightly the upward bias in the CPI and thus reduce slightly the amount by which real benefits will be increased due to future cost-of-living adjustments.

No one has proposed cutting statutory benefits for existing retirees; future retirees are the target. One possibility is to raise the age of full eligibility. The eligibility age rose to 67 in 1999, but it could be increased further, perhaps to as high as 70. Another option is to cut benefits that are paid to nonworking spouses. A third proposal is to impose "means testing" on some or all Social Security benefits. As things stand now, all individuals covered by the system collect benefits when they retire, regardless of their assets or other sources of retirement income. Under a system of means testing, individuals with substantial alternative sources of retirement income would receive reduced Social Security benefits.

Immigration

Many experts believe that significant changes in America's immigration laws could offer the best hope for dealing with the tax burdens and workforce shrinkage of the future. About a million immigrants come to America each year, the largest number in our nation's history. Yet more than 90 percent of new immigrants are admitted on the basis of a selection system unchanged since 1952, under which the right of immigration is tied to family relationships. As a result, most people are admitted to the United States because they happen to be the spouses, children, or siblings of earlier immigrants, rather than because they have skills or training highly valued in the American workplace. Both Canada and Australia have modified their immigration laws to expand opportunities for immigrants who possess skills in short supply, with results that are generally regarded quite favorably in both nations. Unless Congress manages to overhaul America's immigration preference system, the taxes paid by new immigrants are unlikely to relieve much of the pressure building due to our aging population.

Investing in the Stock Market

Historically high returns were earned on most stock market investments during the 1990s. It is thus not surprising that some observers, including members of the Clinton administration, advocated that the Social Security system purchase stocks rather than Treasury bonds with the current excess of payroll taxes over current benefit payments. (Because this would necessitate that the Treasury borrow more from the public, this amounts to having the government borrow money from the public for the purpose of investing in the stock market.)

Although the added returns on stock investments could help stave off tax increases or benefit cuts, there are a few potential problems with this proposal. First, the rate of return on stocks during the 1990s was high by historical standards; we cannot expect such returns routinely in the future.

Second, the extra returns on stock market investments are not a sure thing; after all, during the early 1930s, the stock market dropped in value by nearly 90 percent. Despite the stock market's higher long-term returns, the inherent uncertainty of those returns is not entirely consistent with the function of Social Security as a source of *guaranteed* retirement income.

Finally, and most important, there is the issue of what stocks to invest in. There would surely be political pressure to invest in companies that happened to be politically popular and to refrain from investing in those that were unpopular, regardless of their returns. This sort of politically motivated investing would definitely reduce the expected returns from the government's stock portfolio—possibly even below the returns on Treasury bonds. This is exactly what has happened in Singapore: Workers there are required to pay 20 percent of their salary into the government-run Provident Fund, which has earned returns substantially below the market average.

INTERNATIONAL EXAMPLE

Privatizing Pensions in Chile

In 1981, Chile's state-run pension system was effectively bankrupt. So the government set up a mandatory system that was privately operated and funded. Workers were required to pay a minimum of 10 percent of their income each year into a private retirement account that the workers owned and controlled. To compensate workers for the public pensions they were giving up, the government issued "recognition bonds" that reflected the value of prior contributions to the old system. The government promised to redeem these bonds upon worker retirement, with the funding to come from a mixture of selling off state-owned enterprises and taxes on future workers and businesses.

The system is generally popular and well regarded by participants, perhaps in part because returns have averaged 13 percent per year. Annual retirement benefits are expected to be 50 percent to 70 percent above those payable under the old system. Nevertheless, the system is not flawless. Management charges on the retirement accounts have averaged nearly 3 percent per year, more than double the average charge on similar voluntary funds in the United States. Just as important, funds were initially restricted to investing only in Chile, a fact that depressed returns during the early years. Fund managers can now invest overseas, but 99 percent of fund assets remain invested in Chile, due to a peculiar incentive system imposed by the government. If a fund's return in any 12-month period is over two percentage points below the average for all funds, the firm managing that fund must make good the shortfall from its own capital. But there is no reward for outperforming the other funds. Not surprisingly, all of the funds have similar portfolios, and these portfolios are less risky—and yield lower average returns—than would be the case without this government-imposed reimbursement scheme.

For Critical Analysis

If the United States were to contemplate privatizing Social Security, what lessons might it learn from Chile's experience?

Growing the Economy

One way for the current Social Security problem to "go away" would be for the U.S. economy to grow at a faster pace. This would cause wages and salaries, which typically comprise more than 70 percent of total U.S. income, to increase, thereby expanding the tax base of the Social Security system. Additional funds would then flow into the Social Security system each year, thereby helping preserve the program's solvency.

As you learned in Chapter 2, expanding the economy's technological capabilities and producing more capital goods can help increase the nation's overall ability to produce and consume. Certainly, the U.S. economy has maintained steady growth in its productive capabilities. From the perspective of the Social Security system, however, the pace of growth has not been sufficient. As you will learn in Chapter 9, there are certain things that we could try to do to speed the pace of the nation's economic growth. Nevertheless, so far we have been unable to push the growth rate of national income much beyond 2 to 3 percent per year for more than a few years at a stretch. Saving the Social Security system without reforming it would require pushing long-term annual income growth up by at least 1 percentage point. In the absence of such a sustained increase in economic growth, the nation cannot postpone reforming its social compact.

CONCEPTS IN BRIEF

- One way or another, Social Security benefits will have to be cut, or taxes increased, or both.
- Although proposed tax increases will reduce the long-run Social Security deficit, no politicians have yet proposed raising them high enough to eliminate that deficit.
- Immigration would help the U.S. situation somewhat by increasing the workforce relative to the stock of retirees.
- Investing trust fund monies in the stock market might help, but there is a danger that political maneuvering with the funds would drastically reduce the returns.

ISSUES & APPLICATIONS

The Social Security Con Game

As we discussed in this chapter, Social Security offered retirees a rate of return in excess of 10 percent until around 1970. Given that the inflation-adjusted long-term rate of return on the stock market is about 10 percent, it is clear that for retirees, as noted, Social Security was an excellent deal for all beneficiaries until at least 1970 and for many until around 1990. But if investments on the stock market yielded only a 10 percent average real rate of return, how was Social Security able to offer such astonishingly high returns for so long? Moreover, why is it no longer able to do so?

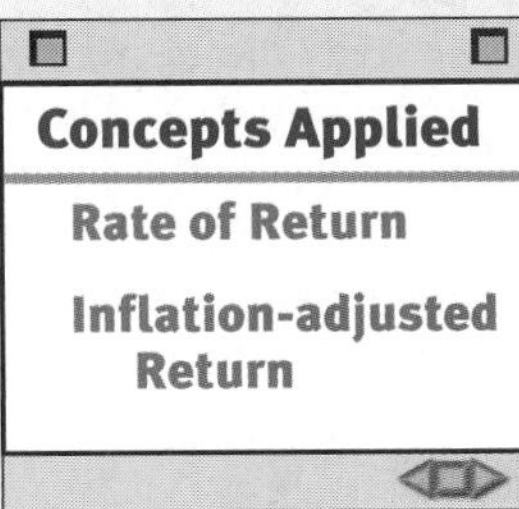

Concepts Applied
Rate of Return
Inflation-adjusted Return

The answer is that Social Security has been operated exactly like a Ponzi scheme, named after Charles Ponzi, a con artist operating in Boston during the early 1920s. Ponzi offered potential investors returns much like those paid to early Social Security retirees and actually managed to pay them for a while, in the same manner Social Security paid them—out of the funds contributed by new entrants into the plan. Because nothing was actually being invested or even produced in the plan, Ponzi's scheme, to stay afloat, required increasing numbers of participants to make ever-larger contributions, used to pay off the promises made to earlier contributors. As soon as people realized what was going on, the scheme collapsed, and Ponzi was prosecuted for fraud and sent to jail—but not before 10,000 investors had been bilked.

Ponzi's Scheme

It is arguable that Social Security has operated in much the same manner since its inception, although its operation is legally sanctioned and it is not in danger of immediate collapse. At each point in time, current retirees are paid benefits out of the contributions of people who are currently working and paying in. (The contributions of today's retirees were long ago used to pay the benefits of previous retirees.) As membership growth slows, the rate of return falls. And as noted, because the early participants received more than they contributed, later participants must necessarily receive less—and that ultimately means a *negative* rate of return.

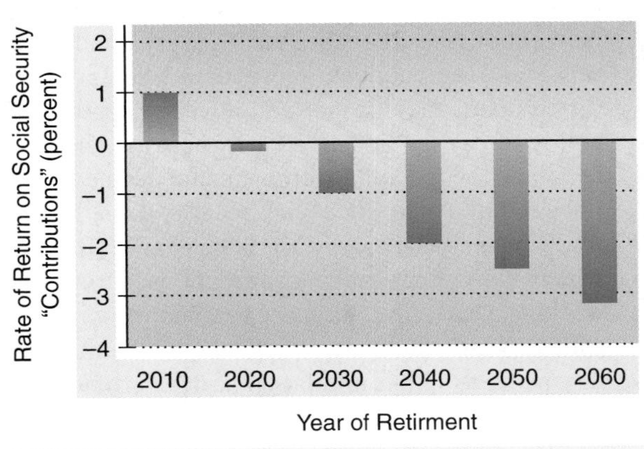

FIGURE 6-5
Projected Social Security Rates of Return for Future Retirees
While those who paid into Social Security in earlier years got a good deal, those who are now paying in and those who will pay in the future are facing low or negative rates of return.
Sources: Social Security Administration and author's estimates.

Parallels?

Indeed, as Figure 6-5 on the previous page shows, under any plausible assumptions about the future, unless the current Social Security system is changed, negative rates of returns will be the norm for retirees in the twenty-first century. In fact, for today's college students, who will begin retiring—if they can afford it—around 2040, in the absence of reform the situation looks particularly grim. As one economist has put it, "Today's students could get a better deal if they put their cash in a mattress—and then started smoking in bed." So unless you are not planning to retire, you'd better start saving now—or convincing your representatives in Congress to continue efforts to find a way to change the current system. Fortunately, there is every indication that the government is aware of the magnitude of the problem. It remains to be seen what proposed solution may ultimately be adopted.

FOR CRITICAL ANALYSIS

1. Based on what you have learned in this chapter, how might society find a way to avoid the negative projected rates of return displayed in Figure 6-5?
2. If the U.S. economy had grown at a much faster pace than it actually did between its inception and the present, would Social Security now look so much like a Ponzi scheme?

SUMMARY DISCUSSION OF LEARNING OBJECTIVES

1. **The Fundamental Problem That Social Security and Medicare Pose for Today's Students:** Both programs have promised (and paid) benefits far in excess of the amounts that can be sustained, given the taxes levied to finance the programs. In the future, taxes will have to be higher and benefits lower, and it is today's students who will suffer on both counts. In fact, the rate of return on both programs will almost surely be negative for anyone who is today under the age of 30. It is not surprising that Americans who are currently retired and those who are about to retire are very much in favor of keeping Social Security just the way it has always been. They have realized a very high rate of return on their "contributions" to the Social Security System.
2. **The Effect of Medicare on the Incentives to Consume Medical Services:** Medicare subsidizes the consumption of medical services by the elderly. As a result, the quantity consumed is higher, and so is the price per unit of those services. Thus Americans spend a larger proportion of GDP on medical care than any other nation in the world. Medicare also encourages people to consume medical services that are very low in value relative to the cost of providing them and places a substantial tax burden on other sectors of the economy. As Medicare has increasingly taken over the medical costs of the elderly, they have responded rationally by demanding more and better services. When the government foots the bill, decisions about what health services to purchase are not the same as in the private sector, where individuals pay the full opportunity cost of the products or services they use.
3. **The Myth That the Social Security Trust Fund Is a Stock of Savings:** Social Security benefits must be paid out of taxes. Because the Treasury bonds in the trust fund are nothing more than claims against future taxes, they do not add anything to society's ability to pay for Social Security benefits. Nonetheless, both the federal government and the media continue to talk about the Social Security Trust Fund as if it were the same as, say, a private pension fund into which individuals make contributions during their working years. The formal existence of something called a trust fund has allowed the government and the media to ignore the fact that our current Social Security system is a pay-as-you-go system.

4. **The Key Forces That Caused the Tremendous Rise in Social Security Spending:** The first force was the emergence of a politically powerful generation of elderly, who felt deserving of a retirement subsidized by younger persons. The second force was the entry of the huge baby boom generation into the workforce, which greatly increased the amount of money available to pay retirement benefits to the elderly. An important mechanism for creating higher real benefits has been the cost-of-living adjustment. Because of an upward bias in the index used to calculate this adjustment, real Social Security benefits have increased by 50 percent over the past several decades. This upward bias, however, is less today than in the past. The federal government has made some small corrections in how it calculates the price index in order to reduce the upward bias.

5. **How Social Security Could Be Reformed:** Because future benefits vastly exceed future scheduled taxes, some combination of higher taxes and lower benefits will have to be implemented. The situation could also be eased a bit if more immigration into the country were permitted. But an even better long-term reform would be to begin phasing out the current system and replacing it with one that is entirely privately run. Many possible replacement programs have been proposed by politicians and economists alike. Some have pointed to the apparent success of the privatization of the social security system in Chile. However, changing from a public system to a private system faces enormous political roadblocks in the United States.

Key Terms and Concepts

Inflation-adjusted return (126)
Rate of return (126)
Social Security contributions (126)
Median age (121)

Problems Test

Answers to the odd-numbered problems appear at the back of the book.

6-1. Suppose you invest \$100 today and receive in return \$150 exactly one year from now. What is the rate of return on this investment? (Hint: What is the percentage by which next year's benefit exceeds—or falls short of—this year's cost?)

6-2. Suppose you invest \$100 today and receive in return \$80 exactly one year from now. What is the rate of return on this investment? (Hint: What is the percentage by which next year's benefit exceeds—or falls short of—this year's cost?)

6-3. Suppose your employer is paying you a wage of \$10 per hour, and you are working 40 hours per week. Now the government imposes a \$2 per hour tax on your employment: \$1 is collected from your employer and \$1 is collected from you. The proceeds of the tax are used by the government to buy for you groceries that are valued by you at exactly \$80 per week. You are eligible for the grocery program only as long as you continue to work. Once the plan is in place, what hourly wage will the employer pay you?

6-4. Suppose that the current price of a CD-ROM drive is \$100 and that people are buying 1 million drives per year. In order to improve computer literacy, the government decides to begin subsidizing the purchase of new CD-ROM drives. The government believes that the appropriate price is \$60 per drive, so the program offers to send people cash for the difference between \$60 and whatever the people pay for each drive they buy.

a. If no one changes his or her drive-buying behavior, how much will this program cost the taxpayers?

b. Will the subsidy cause people to buy more, less, or the same number of drives? Explain.

c. Suppose people end up buying 1.5 million drives once the program is in place. If the market price of drives does not change, how much will this program cost the taxpayers?

d. Under the assumption that the program causes people to buy 1.5 million drives and also causes the market price of drives to rise to $120, how much will this program cost the taxpayers?

6-5. Scans of internal organs using magnetic resonance imaging (MRI) devices are often covered by subsidized health insurance programs such as Medicare. Consider the following table illustrating hypothetical quantities of individual MRI testing procedures demanded and supplied at various prices, and then answer the questions that follow.

Price	Quantity Demanded	Quantity Supplied
$100	100,000	40,000
$300	90,000	60,000
$500	80,000	80,000
$700	70,000	100,000
$900	60,000	120,000

a. In the absence of a government-subsidized health plan, what is the equilibrium price of a battery of MRI tests? What is the amount of society's total expense on MRI tests?

b. Suppose that the government establishes a health plan guaranteeing that all qualified participants can purchase MRI tests at an effective price (that is, out-of-pocket cost) to the individual of $100 per set of tests. How many batteries of MRI tests will people consume?

c. What is the per-unit cost incurred by producers to provide the amount of MRI tests demanded at the government-guaranteed price of $100? What is society's total expense on MRI tests?

d. Under the government's coverage of MRI tests, what is the per-unit subsidy it provides? What is the total subsidy that the government pays to support MRI testing at its guaranteed price?

6-6. Suppose that the following Social Security reform became law: All current Social Security recipients will continue to receive their benefits, but no increase will be made other than cost-of-living adjustments; Americans between age 40 and retirement not yet on Social Security can opt to continue with the current system; those who opt out can place what they would have "contributed" to Social Security into one or more government-approved mutual funds; and those under 40 must place their "contributions" into one or more government-approved mutual funds.

Now answer the following questions:

a. Who will be in favor of this reform and why?

b. Who will be against this reform and why?

c. What might happen to stock market indexes?

d. What additional risk is involved for those who end up in the private system?

e. What additional benefits are possible for the people in the private system?

f. Which firms in the mutual fund industry might not be approved by the federal government and why?

Economics on the Net

Social Security Privatization There are many proposals for reforming Social Security, but only one fundamentally alters the nature of the current system: privatization. The purpose of this exercise is to learn more about what would happen if Social Security were privatized.

Title: Social Security Privatization

Navigation: Click here to learn about Social Security Privatization. The entries you'll want to use are in the left-hand column.

Application For each of the entries noted, read the entry and answer the question.

1. Click on *African Americans and Social Security.* What are the likely consequences of Social Security privatization for African Americans? Why?

2. Click on *Women and Social Security.* What are the likely consequences of Social Security privatization for women? Why?

3. Click on *Low-Wage Workers and Social Security.* What are the likely consequences of Social Security privatization for low-wage workers? Why?

For Group Study and Analysis Taking into account the mix of gender, ethnic background, and other factors, is your group as a whole likely to be made better off or worse off if Social Security is privatized? Should your decision to support or oppose privatization be based solely on how it affects you personally? Or should your decision take into account how it might affect others in your group?

It will be worthwhile for those not nearing retirement age to examine what the "older" generation thinks about the idea of privatizing the Social Security system in the United States. So create two groups—one for and one against privatization. Each group will examine the following Web site and come up with arguments in favor or against the ideas expressed on it.

Click here to visit the Social Security Network homepage. Make sure that each side in this debate carefully reads the pages on the stance of the organization. Accept or rebut each statement, depending on the side to which you have been assigned. Be prepared to defend your reasons with more than just your feelings. At a minimum, be prepared to present arguments that are logical, if not entirely backed by facts.

TYING IT ALL TOGETHER

Part One Case Problem

Case Background

Cyber Dynamics International Corporation (CDI) is engaged in both business-to-consumer and business-to-business Internet applications as well as the production and distribution of new software programs. CDI is based in Singapore, but it sells its products and services throughout the world, including in the United States.

The management of CDI is well aware of the fact that in the Internet world everything happens at, well, Internet speed. New competitors are getting stronger every day. One of them appears to be Global Online Services. Indeed, in a recent planning meeting at CDI, the chief executive officer asked her management team to look into expanding into new areas on the Internet, new software applications, and new countries.

A week later the various officers and managers of the company have come forth with the following recommendations:

1. Lower the price of Internet access to compete more aggressively with Global Online Services and America Online.
2. Add numerous new features to the company's existing popular business accounting program and raise its price.
3. Break up the existing advertising and sales division into two separate divisions.
4. Open a major software manufacturing plant somewhere in the United States.
5. Enter into a partnership with a software company in the People's Republic of China.
6. Create a new employee's benefit in the form of a pension plan that will pay loyal workers a certain sum of money every month after they retire.

Points to Analyze

1. Do you think it matters that CDI's headquarters are in Singapore? To whom might it matter and why?
2. In recommendation number 1 above, a manager suggested that the company lower its price of Internet access. If it does, will the number of Internet access subscribers increase or decrease? Under what circumstances will total revenues increase? Decrease?
3. If the company's accounting program is enhanced, under what circumstances might it be able to raise the price and actually sell more copies?
4. Recommendation number 3 argues in favor of splitting up a division into two separate parts. What famous economist might applaud this action and why?
5. If you were in charge of deciding whether to support the recommendation that a software manufacturing plant be located in the United States, what are some of the factors that you

might want to analyze to reach your conclusion? One might be the going wage rate that would have to be paid to new workers. But there is another key cost for companies doing business in the United States. What is it?

6. While you might be convinced that entering the marketplace in the People's Republic of China is an exciting prospect ("everybody's doing it") there might be some problems with going into partnership with an existing Chinese company. Think about the economic functions of government that you learned in Chapter 5. Which function (or lack thereof) might create the biggest problem for your company's new partnership in China?

7. While the suggestion to create a new employee benefit involving a retirement system might seem appealing because it would attract more and better workers, would you want to offer the same retirement plan to your workers in all countries? What government-funded institution should you examine first in each country before you make such a decision?

Casing the Internet

1. **Click here to go to the Web site of Global Online Services. Once on this site, navigate through some of the sections.**
   a. **What part of the world is the main focus of the activities of this company?**
   b. **What various types of products does this company produce?**
   c. **Why do you suppose that there are so many informational Web pages located at this company's home page?**
   d. **The advertisements at this Web site relate to this company only. Could Global Online Services gain from allowing others to place advertisements at its site?**
   e. **Is it likely that other companies would want to place ads at this Web site? Why or why not?**
2. **Now click here to go to the Web site for Global Online Electronic Services.**
   a. **Do you think that this company competes directly with Global Online Services? Why or why not?**
   b. **To what audience is that Web site addressing itself?**
   c. **Under what circumstances would you want to purchase the services of Global Online Electronic Services?**
3. **Go to any popular search engine, such as Yahoo.com, Profusion.com, Google.com, or Lycos.com. Type in the word "global" and see what happens.**
   a. **Why do you think so many companies include the word global in their names today?**

   Do the same thing with typing the word "online" and see what happens.
   b. **Why do so many companies what to include the word online in their names today?**

Part 5
Dimensions of Microeconomics

CHAPTER

19

CONSUMER CHOICE

Internet access is offered by over 6,000 Internet service providers (ISPs) in the United States. What determines whether someone uses a high-priced service such as America Online at $21.95 per month or a lower-priced service such as VirtuallyFreeInternet.com at $15 per month?

Once you pay a connection fee to an Internet service provider such as America Online, you are "in." You incur no explicit fees for the time that you actually spend browsing the Internet. The only cost you incur is the opportunity cost of your time. Undoubtedly, the sweeping growth of the Internet owes much to this fact. A number of economists believe that the failure to price Internet use could also pose big problems for the system in the future. They claim that a very low price of Internet use induces people to spend too much time surfing the Web, thereby contributing to Internet congestion problems. To understand and evaluate this argument, you will need to understand the theory of consumer choice. This theory, it turns out, tells us how to value the last minute of time that a person spends on the Internet each day. It also permits us to speculate about whether the price of Internet usage is too low.

LEARNING OBJECTIVES

After reading this chapter, you should be able to:

1. Distinguish between total utility and marginal utility
2. Discuss why marginal utility at first rises but ultimately tends to decline as a person consumes more of a good or service
3. Explain why an individual's optimal choice of how much to consume of each good or service entails equalizing the marginal utility per dollar spent across all goods and services
4. Describe the substitution effect of a price change on quantity demanded of a good or service
5. Understand how the real-income effect of a price change affects the quantity demanded of a good or service
6. Evaluate why the price of diamonds is so much higher than the price of water even though people cannot survive long without water

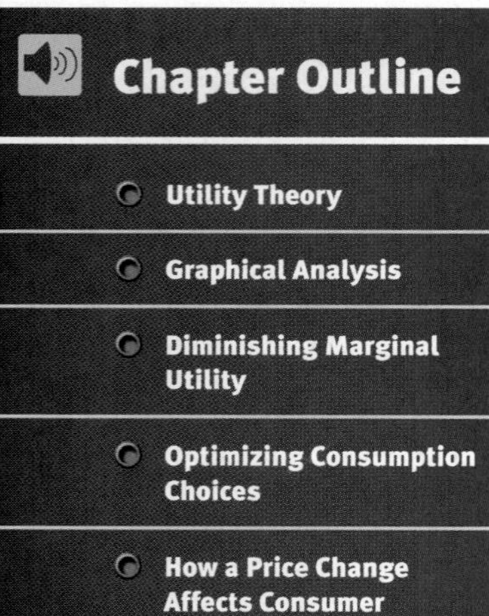

Did You Know That... more than 100 million people in the United States now have access to the Internet? Many of these people have decided to buy computers and to pay for regular access to the Internet at home. A significant portion of them own no computers, however. They choose to browse the Web at local schools or public libraries. What determines how much people spend on computers, Internet access, and other family budget items? One explanation is simply tastes—the values that family members place on different items on which they can spend their income. Different individuals have different preferences for how to allocate their limited incomes. Although there is no real theory of what determines people's tastes, we can examine some of the behavior that underlies how consumers react to changes in the prices of the goods and services that they purchase. Recall from Chapter 3 that people generally purchase less at higher prices than at lower prices. This is called the law of demand.

Understanding the derivation of the law of demand is useful because it allows us to arrange the relevant variables, such as price, income, and tastes, in such a way as to make better sense of the world and even perhaps generate predictions about it. One way of deriving the law of demand involves an analysis of the logic of consumer choice in a world of limited resources. In this chapter, therefore, we discuss what is called *utility analysis.*

UTILITY THEORY

Utility 
The want-satisfying power of a good or service.

When you buy something, you do so because of the satisfaction you expect to receive from having and using that good. For everything that you like to have, the more you have of it, the higher the level of satisfaction you receive. Another term that can be used for satisfaction is **utility,** or want-satisfying power. This property is common to all goods that are desired. The concept of utility is purely subjective, however. There is no way that you or I can measure the amount of utility that a consumer might be able to obtain from a particular good, for utility does not imply "useful" or "utilitarian" or "practical." For this reason, there can be no accurate scientific assessment of the utility that someone might receive by consuming a frozen dinner or a movie relative to the utility that another person might receive from that same good or service.

The utility that individuals receive from consuming a good depends on their tastes and preferences. These tastes and preferences are normally assumed to be given and stable for a given individual. An individual's tastes determine how much utility that individual derives from consuming a good, and this in turn determines how that individual allocates his or her income. People spend a greater proportion of their incomes on goods they like. But we cannot explain why tastes are different between individuals. For example, we cannot explain why some people like yogurt but others do not.

We can analyze in terms of utility the way consumers decide what to buy, just as physicists have analyzed some of their problems in terms of what they call force. No physicist has ever seen a unit of force, and no economist has ever seen a unit of utility. In both cases, however, these concepts have proved useful for analysis.

Utility analysis 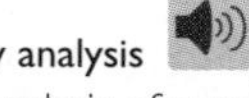
The analysis of consumer decision making based on utility maximization.

Throughout this chapter, we will be discussing **utility analysis,** which is the analysis of consumer decision making based on utility maximization.

Utility and Utils

Economists once believed that utility could be measured. In fact, there is a philosophical school of thought based on utility theory called *utilitarianism,* developed by the English philosopher Jeremy Bentham (1748–1832). Bentham held that society should seek the greatest happiness for the greatest number. He sought to apply an arithmetic formula for measuring happiness. He and his followers developed the notion of measurable utility and invented the **util** to measure it. For the moment, we will also assume that we can measure satisfaction using this representative unit. Our assumption will allow us to quantify the way we examine consumer behavior.* Thus the first chocolate bar that you eat might yield you 4 utils of satisfaction; the first peanut cluster, 6 utils; and so on. Today, no one really believes that we can actually measure utils, but the ideas forthcoming from such analysis will prove useful in our understanding of the way in which consumers choose among alternatives.

Util 
A representative unit by which utility is measured.

Total and Marginal Utility

Consider the satisfaction, or utility, that you receive each time that you rent and watch a video on your VCR. To make the example straightforward, let's say that there are hundreds of videos to choose from each year and that each of them is of the same quality. Let's say that you normally rent one video per week. You could, of course, rent two, or three, or four per week. Presumably, each time you rent another video per week, you will get additional satisfaction, or utility. The question, though, that we must ask is, given that you are already renting one per week, will the next one rented that week give you the same amount of additional utility?

That additional, or incremental, utility is called **marginal utility,** where *marginal,* as before, means "incremental" or "additional." (Marginal changes also refer to decreases, in which cases we talk about *decremental* changes.) The concept of marginality is important in economics because we make decisions at the margin. At any particular point, we compare additional (marginal) benefits with additional (marginal) costs.

Marginal utility 
The change in total utility due to a one-unit change in the quantity of a good or service consumed.

Applying Marginal Analysis to Utility

The specific example presented in Figure 19-1 (p. 458) will clarify the distinction between total utility and marginal utility. The table in panel (a) shows the total utility and the marginal utility of watching videos each week. Marginal utility is the difference between total utility derived from one level of consumption and total utility derived from another level of consumption within a given time interval. A simple formula for marginal utility is this:

$$\text{Marginal utility} = \frac{\text{change in total utility}}{\text{change in number of units consumed}}$$

In our example, when a person has already watched two videos in one week and then watches another, total utility increases from 16 utils to 19. Therefore, the marginal utility (of watching one more video after already having watched two in one week) is equal to 3 utils.

*What follows is typically called *cardinal utility analysis* because it requires cardinal measurement. Numbers such as 1, 2, and 3 are cardinals. We know that 2 is exactly twice as many as 1 and that 3 is exactly three times as many as 1. You will see in Appendix E at the end of this chapter a type of consumer behavior analysis that requires only *ordinal* (ranked or ordered) measurement of utility. *First, second,* and *third* are ordinal numbers; nothing can be said about their exact size relationships; we can only talk about their importance relative to each other. Temperature, for example, is an ordinal ranking. One hundred degrees Celsius is not twice as warm as 50 degrees Celsius. All we can say is that 100 degrees Celsius is warmer than 50 degrees Celsius.

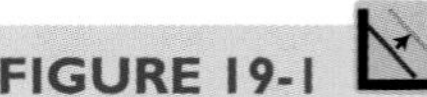

FIGURE 19-1

Total and Marginal Utility of Watching Videos

If we were able to assign specific values to the utility derived from watching videos each week, we could obtain a marginal utility schedule similar in pattern to the one shown in panel (a). In column 1 is the number of videos watched per week; in column 2, the total utility derived from each quantity; and in column 3, the marginal utility derived from each additional quantity, which is defined as the change in total utility due to a change of one unit of watching videos per week. Total utility from panel (a) is plotted in panel (b). Marginal utility is plotted in panel (c), where you see that it reaches zero where total utility hits its maximum at between 4 and 5 units.

Panel (a)

(1) Number of Videos Watched per Week	(2) Total Utility (utils per week)	(3) Marginal Utility (utils per week)
0	0	
		10 (10 – 0)
1	10	
		6 (16 – 10)
2	16	
		3 (19 – 16)
3	19	
		1 (20 – 19)
4	20	
		0 (20 – 20)
5	20	
		–2 (18 – 20)
6	18	

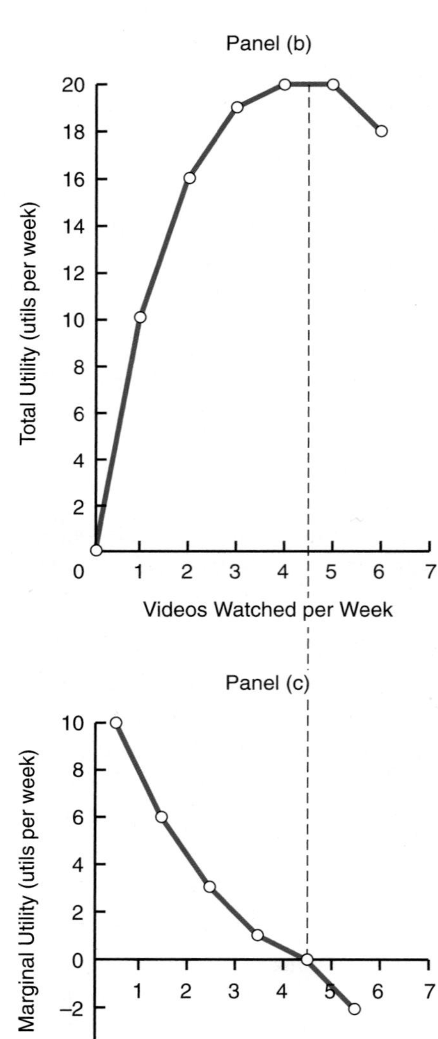

GRAPHICAL ANALYSIS

We can transfer the information in panel (a) onto a graph, as we do in panels (b) and (c) of Figure 19-1. Total utility, which is represented in column 2 of panel (a), is transferred to panel (b).

Total utility continues to rise until four videos are watched per week. This measure of utility remains at 20 utils through the fifth video, and at the sixth video per week it falls to 18 utils; we assume that at some quantity consumed per unit time period, boredom sets in. This is shown in panel (b).

Marginal Utility

If you look carefully at panels (b) and (c) of Figure 19-1, the notion of marginal utility becomes very clear. In economics, the term *marginal* always refers to a change in the total. The marginal utility of watching three videos per week instead of two videos per week is the increment in total utility and is equal to 3 utils per week. All of the points in panel (c) are taken from column 3 of the table in panel (a). Notice that marginal utility falls throughout the graph. A special point occurs after four videos are watched per week because the total utility curve in panel (b) is unchanged after the consumption of the fourth video. That means that the consumer receives no additional (marginal) utility from watching the fifth video. This is shown in panel (c) as *zero* marginal utility. After that point, marginal utility becomes negative.

Utility Theory
Get additional practice thinking about utility concepts.

In our example, when marginal utility becomes negative, it means that the consumer is fed up with watching videos and would require some form of compensation to watch any more. When marginal utility is negative, an additional unit consumed actually lowers total utility by becoming a nuisance. Rarely does a consumer face a situation of negative marginal utility. Whenever this point is reached, goods become in effect "bads." A rational consumer will stop consuming at the point at which marginal utility becomes negative, even if the good is available at a price of zero.

CONCEPTS IN BRIEF

- Utility is defined as want-satisfying power; it is a power common to all desired goods and services.
- We arbitrarily measure utility in units called utils.
- It is important to distinguish between total utility and marginal utility. Total utility is the total satisfaction derived from the consumption of a given quantity of a good or service. Marginal utility is the *change* in total utility due to a one-unit change in the consumption of the good or service.

DIMINISHING MARGINAL UTILITY

Notice that in panel (c) of Figure 19-1, marginal utility is continuously declining. This property has been named the principle of **diminishing marginal utility.** There is no way that we can prove diminishing marginal utility; nonetheless, economists and others have for years believed strongly in the notion. Diminishing marginal utility has even been called a law. This supposed law concerns a psychological, or subjective, utility that you receive as you consume more and more of a particular good. Stated formally, the law is as follows:

Diminishing marginal utility 
The principle that as more of any good or service is consumed, its extra benefit declines. Otherwise stated, increases in total utility from the consumption of a good or service become smaller and smaller as more is consumed during a given time period.

As an individual consumes more of a particular commodity, the total level of utility, or satisfaction, derived from that consumption usually increases. Eventually, however, the *rate* at which it increases diminishes as more is consumed.

Click here to see how diminishing marginal utility can complicate the task that wine tasters face when comparing different wines.

Take a hungry individual at a dinner table. The first serving is greatly appreciated, and the individual derives a substantial amount of utility from it. The second serving does not have quite as much pleasurable impact as the first one, and the third serving is likely to be even less satisfying. This individual experiences diminishing marginal utility of food until he or she stops eating, and this is true for most people. All-you-can-eat restaurants count on this fact; a second helping of ribs may provide some marginal utility, but the third helping would have only a little or even negative marginal utility. The fall in the marginal utility of other goods is even more dramatic.

Consider for a moment the opposite possibility—increasing marginal utility. Under such a situation, the marginal utility after consuming, say, one hamburger would increase. The second hamburger would be more valuable to you, and the third would be even more valuable yet. If increasing marginal utility existed, each of us would consume only one good or service! Rather than observing that "variety is the spice of life," we would see that monotony in consumption was preferred. We do not observe this, and therefore we have great confidence in the concept of diminishing marginal utility.

Consider an example. Your birthday is on December 25. Suppose that you derive utility from listening to new CDs each month. Even if you receive exactly the same number of CDs as presents on December 25 that you would have if your birthday were six months later, your total level of utility from these presents will be lower. Why? Because of diminishing marginal utility. Let's say that your relatives and friends all give you CDs as birthday and Christmas presents. The total utility you receive from, say, 20 CDs on December 25 is less than if you received 10 on December 25 and 10 on an alternative birthdate several months later.

EXAMPLE

Newspaper Vending Machines Versus Candy Vending Machines

Have you ever noticed that newspaper vending machines nearly everywhere in the United States allow you to put in the correct change, lift up the door, and take as many newspapers as you want? Contrast this type of vending machine with candy machines. They are completely locked at all times. You must designate the candy that you wish, normally by using some type of keypad. The candy then drops down to a place where you reach to retrieve it but from which you cannot grab any other candy.

The difference between these two types of vending machines is explained by diminishing marginal utility. Newspaper companies dispense newspapers from coin-operated boxes that allow dishonest people to take more copies than they pay for. What would a dishonest person do with more than one copy of a newspaper, however? The marginal utility of a second newspaper is normally zero. The benefit of storing excessive newspapers is usually nil because yesterday's news has no value. But the same analysis does not hold for candy. The marginal utility of a second candy bar is certainly less than the first, but it is normally not zero. Moreover, one can store candy for relatively long periods of time at relatively low cost. Consequently, food vending machine companies have to worry about dishonest users of their machines and must make their machines much more theftproof than newspaper companies do.

For Critical Analysis

Can you think of a circumstance under which a substantial number of newspaper purchasers might be inclined to take more than one newspaper out of a vending machine?

OPTIMIZING CONSUMPTION CHOICES 

Every consumer has a limited income. Choices must be made. When a consumer has made all of his or her choices about what to buy and in what quantities, and when the total level of satisfaction, or utility, from that set of choices is as great as it can be, we say that the consumer has *optimized.* When the consumer has attained an optimum consumption set of goods and services, we say that he or she has reached **consumer optimum.***

Consumer optimum 
A choice of a set of goods and services that maximizes the level of satisfaction for each consumer, subject to limited income.

Consider a simple two-good example. The consumer has to choose between spending income on the rental of videos at $5 each and on purchasing deluxe hamburgers at $3 each. Let's say that when the consumer has spent all income on videos and hamburgers, the last dollar spent on hamburgers yields 3 utils of utility but the last dollar spent on video rentals yields 10 utils. Wouldn't this consumer increase total utility if some dollars were taken away from hamburger consumption and allocated to video rentals? The answer is yes. Given diminishing marginal utility, more dollars spent on video rentals will reduce marginal utility per last dollar spent, whereas fewer dollars spent on hamburger consumption will increase marginal utility per last dollar spent. The optimum—where total utility is maximized—might occur when the satisfaction per last dollar spent on both hamburgers and video rentals per week is equal for the two goods. Thus the amount of goods consumed depends on the prices of the goods, the income of the consumers, and the marginal utility derived from each good.

Table 19-1 presents information on utility derived from consuming various quantities of videos and hamburgers. Columns 4 and 8 show the marginal utility per dollar spent on videos and hamburgers, respectively. If the prices of both goods are zero, individuals will consume each as long as their respective marginal utility is positive (at least five units of

TABLE 19-1
Total and Marginal Utility from Consuming Videos and Hamburgers on an Income of $26

(1) Videos per Period	(2) Total Utility of Videos per Period (utils)	(3) Marginal Utility (utils) MU_v	(4) Marginal Utility per Dollar Spent (MU_v/P_v) (price = $5)	(5) Hamburgers per Period	(6) Total Utility of Hamburgers per Period (utils)	(7) Marginal Utility (utils) MU_h	(8) Marginal Utility per Dollar Spent (MU_h/P_h) (price = $3)
0	0.0	—	—	0	0	—	—
1	50.0	50.0	10.0	1	25	25	8.3
2	95.0	45.0	9.0	2	47	22	7.3
3	135.0	40.0	8.0	3	65	18	6.0
4	171.5	36.5	7.3	4	80	15	5.0
5	200.0	28.5	5.7	5	89	9	3.0

*Optimization typically refers to individual decision-making processes. When we deal with many individuals interacting in the marketplace, we talk in terms of an equilibrium in the marketplace. Generally speaking, equilibrium is a property of markets rather than of individual decision making.

each and probably much more). It is also true that a consumer with infinite income will continue consuming goods until the marginal utility of each is equal to zero. When the price is zero or the consumer's income is infinite, there is no effective constraint on consumption.

Consumer optimum is attained when the marginal utility of the last dollar spent on each good yields the same utility and income is completely exhausted. The individual's income is $26. From columns 4 and 8 of Table 19-1, equal marginal utilities per dollar spent occur at the consumption level of four videos and two hamburgers (the marginal utility per dollar spent equals 7.3). Notice that the marginal utility per dollar spent for both goods is also (approximately) equal at the consumption level of three videos and one hamburger, but here total income is not completely exhausted. Likewise, the marginal utility per dollar spent is (approximately) equal at five videos and three hamburgers, but the expenditures necessary for that level of consumption ($28) exceed the individual's income.

Table 19-2 shows the steps taken to arrive at consumer optimum. The first video would yield a marginal utility per dollar of 10 (50 units of utility divided by $5 per video), while the first hamburger would yield a marginal utility of only 8.3 per dollar (25 units of utility divided by $3 per hamburger). Because it yields the higher marginal utility per dollar, the video is purchased. This leaves $21 of income. The second video yields a higher marginal utility per dollar (9, versus 8.3 for hamburgers), so it is also purchased, leaving an unspent income of $16. At the third purchase, the first hamburger now yields a higher marginal utility per dollar than the next video (8.3 versus 8), so the first hamburger is purchased. This leaves income of $13 to spend. The process continues until all income is exhausted and the marginal utility per dollar spent is equal for both goods.

To restate, consumer optimum requires the following:

> A consumer's money income should be allocated so that the last dollar spent on each good purchased yields the same amount of marginal utility (when all income is spent).

TABLE 19-2

Steps to Consumer Optimum

In each purchase situation described here, the consumer always purchases the good with the higher marginal utility per dollar spent (*MU/P*). For example, at the time of the third purchase, the marginal utility per last dollar spent on videos is 8, but it is 8.3 for hamburgers, and $16 of income remains, so the next purchase will be a hamburger. Here $P_v = \$5$, $P_h = \$3$, MU_v is the marginal utility of video consumption, and MU_h is the marginal utility of hamburger consumption.

	Choices					
	Videos		Hamburgers			
Purchase	Unit	(MU_v/P_v)	Unit	$(MU_h/(P_h)$	Buying Decision	Remaining Income
1	First	10.0	First	8.3	First video	$26 – $5 = $21
2	Second	9.0	First	8.3	Second video	$21 – $5 = $16
3	Third	8.0	First	8.3	First hamburger	$16 – $3 = $13
4	Third	8.0	Second	7.3	Third video	$13 – $5 = $ 8
5	Fourth	7.3	Second	7.3	Fourth video and second hamburger	$ 8 – $5 = $ 3 $ 3 – $3 = $ 0

A Little Math

We can state the rule of consumer optimum in algebraic terms by examining the ratio of marginal utilities and prices of individual products. This is sometimes called the *rule of equal marginal utilities per dollar spent* on a basket of goods. The rule simply states that a consumer maximizes personal satisfaction when allocating money income in such a way that the last dollars spent on good A, good B, good C, and so on, yield equal amounts of marginal utility. Marginal utility (*MU*) from good A is indicated by "*MU* of good A." For good B, it is "*MU* of good B." Our algebraic formulation of this rule, therefore, becomes

$$\frac{MU \text{ of good A}}{\text{Price of good A}} = \frac{MU \text{ of good B}}{\text{price of good B}} = \cdots = \frac{MU \text{ of good Z}}{\text{price of good Z}}$$

The letters A, B, . . . , Z indicate the various goods and services that the consumer might purchase.

We know, then, that the marginal utility of good A divided by the price of good A must equal the marginal utility of any other good divided by its price in order for the consumer to maximize utility. Note, though, that the application of the rule of equal marginal utility per dollar spent is not an explicit or conscious act on the part of consumers. Rather, this is a model of consumer optimum.

HOW A PRICE CHANGE AFFECTS CONSUMER OPTIMUM

Consumption decisions are summarized in the law of demand, which states that the amount purchased is inversely related to price. We can now see why by using the law of diminishing marginal utility.

When a consumer has optimally allocated all her income to purchases, the marginal utility per dollar spent at current prices of goods and services is the same for each good or service she buys. No consumer will, when optimizing, buy 10 units of a good per unit time period when the marginal utility per dollar spent on the tenth unit of that good is less than the marginal utility per dollar spent on some other item.

If we start out at a consumer optimum and then observe a good's price decrease, we can predict that consumers will respond to the price decrease by consuming more of that good. This is because before the price change, the marginal utility per dollar spent on each good or service consumed was the same. Now, when a specific good's price is lower, it is possible to consume more of that good while continuing to equalize the marginal utility per dollar spent on that good with the marginal utility per dollar spent on other goods and services. If the law of diminishing marginal utility holds, then the purchase and consumption of additional units of the lower-priced good will cause the marginal utility from consuming the good to fall. Eventually it will fall to the point at which the marginal utility per dollar spent on the good is once again equalized with the marginal utility per dollar spent on other goods and services. At this point, the consumer will stop buying additional units of the lower-priced good.

A hypothetical demand curve for video rentals per week for a typical consumer is presented in Figure 19-2. At a rental price of $5 per video, the marginal utility of the last video rented per week is MU_1. At a rental price of $4 per video per week, the marginal utility is represented by MU_2. Because of the law of diminishing marginal utility—with the consumption of more videos, the marginal utility of the last unit of these additional videos is lower—MU_2 must be less than MU_1. What has happened is that at a lower price, the number of video rentals per week increased from two to three; marginal utility must

FIGURE 19-2
Video Rental Prices and Marginal Utility
The rate of video rentals per week will increase as long as the marginal utility per last video rental per week exceeds the cost of that rental. A reduction in price from $5 to $4 per video rental causes consumers to increase consumption until marginal utility falls from MU_1 to MU_2 (because of the law of diminishing marginal utility).

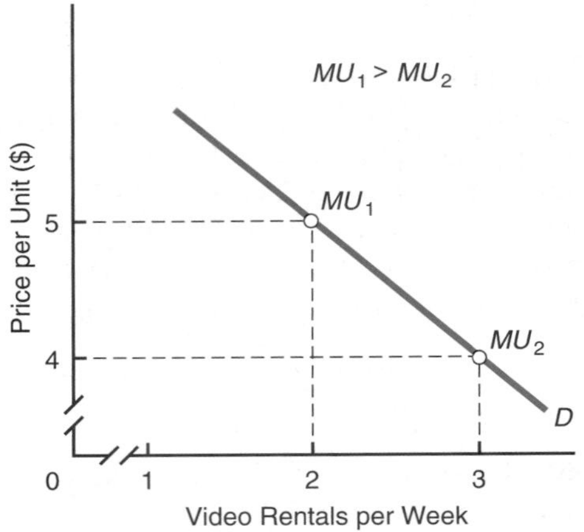

have fallen. At a higher consumption rate, the marginal utility falls in response to the rise in video consumption so that the marginal utility per dollar spent is equalized across purchases.

The Substitution Effect 

Substitution effect 
The tendency of people to substitute cheaper commodities for more expensive commodities.

Principle of substitution 
The principle that consumers and producers shift away from goods and resources that become priced relatively higher in favor of goods and resources that are now priced relatively lower.

What is happening as the price of video rental falls is that consumers are substituting the now relatively cheaper video rentals for other goods and services, such as restaurant meals and live concerts. We call this the **substitution effect** of a change in price of a good because it occurs when consumers substitute relatively cheaper goods for relatively more expensive ones.

We assume that people desire a variety of goods and pursue a variety of goals. That means that few, if any, goods are irreplaceable in meeting demand. We are generally able to substitute one product for another to satisfy demand. This is commonly referred to as the **principle of substitution.**

Let's assume now that there are several goods, not exactly the same, and perhaps even very different from one another, but all serving basically the same purpose. If the relative price of one particular good falls, we will most likely substitute in favor of the lower-priced good and against the other similar goods that we might have been purchasing. Conversely, if the price of that good rises relative to the price of the other similar goods, we will substitute in favor of them and not buy as much of the now higher-priced good. An example is the growth in purchases of personal computers since the late 1980s. As the relative price of computers has plummeted, people have substituted away from other, now relatively more expensive goods in favor of purchasing additional computers to use in their homes.

If the price of some item that you purchase goes down while your money income and all other prices stay the same, your ability to

Is there a racial "digital divide" in home computer use and Internet access?

Yes. A study by Donna Hoffman and Thomas Novak of Vanderbilt University found that more than 40 percent of all white Americans now own a personal computer, whereas only about 25 percent of African Americans and Hispanic Americans have a computer at home. A key factor explaining different rates of computer ownership was income differences among the groups. There are smaller differences among Internet access rates for these groups, however. The reason is that many people who do not own personal computers can still get connected to the Internet at work or school.

purchase goods goes up. That is to say that your effective **purchasing power** is increased, even though your money income has stayed the same. If you purchase 20 gallons of gas a week at $1.60 per gallon, your total outlay for gas is $32. If the price goes down by 50 percent, to 80 cents a gallon, you would have to spend only $16 a week to purchase the same number of gallons of gas. If your money income and the prices of other goods remain the same, it would be possible for you to continue purchasing 20 gallons of gas a week *and* to purchase more of other goods. You will feel richer and will indeed probably purchase more of a number of goods, including perhaps even more gasoline.

Purchasing power
The value of money for buying goods and services. If your money income stays the same but the price of one good that you are buying goes up, your effective purchasing power falls, and vice versa.

The converse will also be true. When the price of one good you are purchasing goes up, without any other change in prices or income, the purchasing power of your income will drop. You will have to reduce your purchases of either the now higher-priced good or other goods (or a combination).

In general, this **real-income effect** is usually quite small. After all, unless we consider broad categories, such as housing or food, a change in the price of one particular item that we purchase will have a relatively small effect on our total purchasing power. Thus we expect the substitution effect usually to be more important than the real-income effect in causing us to purchase more of goods that have become cheaper and less of goods that have become more expensive.

Real-income effect 
The change in people's purchasing power that occurs when, other things being constant, the price of one good that they purchase changes. When that price goes up, real income, or purchasing power, falls, and when that price goes down, real income increases.

THE DEMAND CURVE REVISITED

Linking the "law" of diminishing marginal utility and the rule of equal marginal utilities per dollar gives us a negative relationship between the quantity demanded of a good or service and its price. As the relative price of video rentals goes up, for example, the quantity demanded will fall; and as the relative price of video rentals goes down, the quantity demanded will rise. Figure 19-2 shows this demand curve for video rentals. As the price of video rentals falls, the consumer can maximize total utility only by renting more videos, and vice versa. In other words, the relationship between price and quantity desired is simply a downward-sloping demand curve. Note, though, that this downward-sloping demand curve (the law of demand) is derived under the assumption of constant tastes and incomes. You must remember that we are keeping these important determining variables constant when we look at the relationship between price and quantity demanded.

Marginal Utility, Total Utility, and the Diamond-Water Paradox

Even though water is essential to life and diamonds are not, water is cheap and diamonds are dear. The economist Adam Smith in 1776 called this the "diamond-water paradox." The paradox is easily understood when we make the distinction between total utility and marginal utility. The total utility of water greatly exceeds the total utility derived from diamonds. What determines the price, though, is what happens on the margin. We have relatively few diamonds, so the marginal utility of the last diamond consumed is relatively high. The opposite is true for water. Total utility does not determine what people are willing to pay for a unit of a particular commodity; marginal utility does. Look at the situation graphically in Figure 19-3 on page 466. We show the demand curve for diamonds, labeled D_{diamonds}. The demand curve for water is labeled D_{water}. We plot quantity in terms of kilograms per unit time period on the horizontal axis. On the vertical axis we plot price in dollars per kilogram. We use kilograms as our common unit of measurement for water and for diamonds. We could just as well have used gallons, acre-feet, or liters.

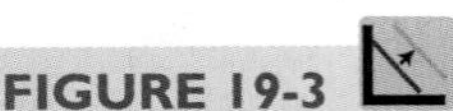

FIGURE 19-3

The Diamond-Water Paradox

We pick kilograms as a common unit of measurement for both water and diamonds. To demonstrate that the demand and supply of water is immense, we have put a break in the horizontal quantity axis. Although the demand for water is much greater than the demand for diamonds, the marginal valuation of water is given by the marginal value placed on the last unit of water consumed. To find that, we must know the supply of water, which is given as S_1. At that supply, the price of water is P_{water}. But the supply for diamonds is given by S_2. At that supply, the price of diamonds is $P_{diamonds}$. The total valuation that consumers place on water is tremendous relative to the total valuation consumers place on diamonds. What is important for price determination, however, is the marginal valuation, or the marginal utility received.

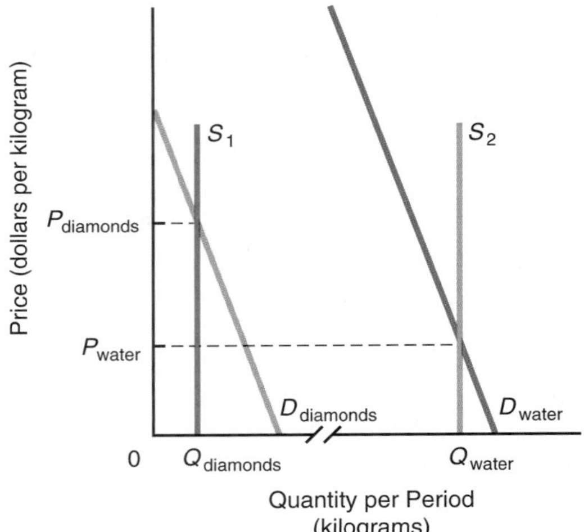

Notice that the demand for water is many, many times the demand for diamonds (even though we really don't show this in the diagram). We draw the supply curve of water as S_1 at a quantity of Q_{water}. The supply curve for diamonds is given as S_2 at quantity $Q_{diamonds}$. At the intersection of the supply curve of water with the demand curve of water, the price per kilogram is P_{water}. The intersection of the supply curve of diamonds with the demand curve of diamonds is at $P_{diamonds}$. Notice that $P_{diamonds}$ exceeds P_{water}. Diamonds sell at a higher price than water.

INTERNATIONAL EXAMPLE

Water in Saudi Arabia

The diamond-water paradox deals with the situation in which water, although necessary for life, may be much cheaper than some luxury item. In Saudi Arabia, as you might expect, the contrary can be true. A liter of water costs five times as much as a liter of gasoline, whereas a pair of custom-made British wool dress pants costs only \$20. These relative prices are quite different from what we are used to seeing in America. Water costs next to nothing, a liter of gas about 40 cents, and custom-made wool pants at least \$200. To understand what has happened in Saudi Arabia, simply substitute gasoline for water and water for diamonds in Figure 19-3.

For Critical Analysis

List some of the effects on human behavior that such a high relative price of water would cause.

CONCEPTS IN BRIEF

- The law of diminishing marginal utility tells us that each successive marginal unit of a good consumed adds less extra utility.
- Each consumer with a limited income must make a choice about the basket of commodities to purchase; economic theory assumes that the consumer chooses the basket of commodities that yields optimum consumption. The consumer maximizes total utility by equating the marginal utility of the last dollar spent on one good with the marginal utility per last dollar spent on all other goods. That is the state of consumer optimum.
- To remain in consumer optimum, a price decrease requires an increase in consumption; a price increase requires a decrease in consumption.

- Each change in price has a substitution effect and a real-income effect. When price falls, the consumer substitutes in favor of the relatively cheaper good. When price falls, the consumer's real purchasing power increases, causing the consumer to purchase more of most goods. The opposite would occur when price increases. Assuming that the law of diminishing marginal utility holds, the demand curve must slope downward.

NETNOMICS

The Meat and Potatoes of On-Line Shopping

In their quest to avoid time-consuming phone calls to travel agents or trips to shopping malls, millions of American consumers now routinely order airline tickets, books, and videos over the Internet. Nevertheless, even though the typical household goes to the grocery store two to three times per week, grocery shopping over the Internet has been slow to take off. Sales of groceries are small potatoes in comparison with the Internet sales of products offered by companies such as Amazon.com or Ticketmaster.

Consider the experience of NetGrocer Inc., a New York company that had worked out special promotional arrangements with America Online and Yahoo! Within a year after setting up a Web site modeled on that of Amazon.com—but designed for placing orders for items such as canned goods, toilet paper, and toothpaste instead of books—NetGrocer had laid off more than half of its staff and fired its chief executive officer. The company's problem was simple, provided that you think like an economist who understands consumer choice. The big advantage of Internet shopping is that it can save an individual the time and trouble of shopping in person. That is, Internet shopping reduces the opportunity cost of shopping, which reduces the *total* price that a person must pay for an airline ticket, a book, or a basket of groceries.

Like other Internet-grocery startups, NetGrocer shipped only dry goods and bottled beverages. It did not ship perishable goods that must be refrigerated, such as milk, butter, and eggs. Consequently, people who made Web purchases from NetGrocer still had to shop at their local grocery store. As long as shoppers had to go to the store anyway, few could see a big cost advantage in buying their nonrefrigerated grocery items over the Net.

Thus the grocery business has been a tough market for new Internet companies to crack. Indeed, some observers of the industry think that the biggest opportunities to earn profits by selling groceries on the Internet are available to existing grocers. Many of these companies already have chains of grocery stores spread across large regions. To start competing via the Internet, all these companies have to do is post Web pages, lease delivery trucks, and hire clerks to stock orders and drivers to make home deliveries. Indeed, a number of existing grocers are entering the Internet-shopping business, which some in the industry project could ultimately account for between 5 and 10 percent of total grocery sales within the next five years.

Issues & Applications

Should You Be Charged to Use the Internet?

Many Internet users continue to experience intermittent problems with delays in data transmission. System failures occur from time to time. A few years ago, Internet traffic in Scandanavia became so congested that network administrators temporarily shut down all Internet transmissions throughout much of northern Europe. It turned out that a single user had tried to download a huge multimedia file and had overloaded the system. Network administrators were able to restore access to other users once they located and disconnected the computer belonging to the individual who had tried to download the file. He said that he didn't mean to cause a problem; he was just bored and was spending some free time "playing around" on the Internet.

Concepts Applied

Marginal Utility

Consumer Optimum

Consumer Choice with a Nearly Zero Price of Usage

Some economists believe that the Internet congestion problem will get worse before it gets better. The problem, they argue, is that for many users, the price of using the Internet is much too low. Recall that as a result of the choices a consumer makes, for the last dollar spent on each good or service, the ratio of marginal utility to price will be the same.

For example, suppose that for a typical individual, a consumer optimum is attained when the ratio of marginal utility to price for each good or service consumed is a relatively small positive number, such as 1 unit of utility per dollar spent. Now suppose that another good that a typical individual consumes is Internet access time, which has an explicit price very close to zero. At a consumer optimum in which the marginal utility per dollar is not a huge number (such as 1), this will require spending sufficient time on the Internet to push the marginal utility of surfing the Net very close to zero as well. Compared to the units of utility from consuming other goods, how could a consumer derive such little additional utility from an hour's worth of time on the Internet? The law of diminishing marginal utility tells us that utility ultimately declines with greater consumption of a good. Thus pushing the marginal utility from surfing the Net close to zero likely entails spending *many* hours surfing the Web. Because spending time on the Internet is such a low-cost activity, the individual ends up spending a large number of hours on the Internet, thereby contributing to the potential for Internet congestion.

Good News for the Internet: People Value Their Time

The *effective* price of Internet usage is probably much higher than "nearly zero," however. Most people place a value on their time that is well above zero. After all, an hour spent surfing the Net could otherwise be allocated to earning income at a market wage. Even for a person possessing very few skills, this opportunity cost of time is likely to be at least a couple of dollars per hour. For the average person, the effective price of using the Internet—inclusive of both explicit and implicit costs—is probably several dollars per hour. In the context of our numerical example, suppose that this effective price is $10 per hour. At this price, attaining a ratio of 1 unit of utility per dollar spent on the last hour of Internet access entails a marginal utility of 10 units per hour. The law of diminishing marginal utility thereby implies that a person who places a relatively high value on his time will likely spend much less time surfing the Net.

Explicit pricing of Internet usage would undoubtedly reduce Internet congestion problems. Nonetheless, a big check on "overuse" of the Net is that many people value their time at more than $0 per hour.

FOR CRITICAL ANALYSIS

1. How could time-based fees for Internet usage be assessed?
2. Who could assess fees for using the Internet? What might they do with the funds?

SUMMARY DISCUSSION OF LEARNING OBJECTIVES

1. **Total Utility Versus Marginal Utility:** Total utility is the total satisfaction that an individual derives from consuming a given amount of a good or service during a given period. By way of contrast, marginal utility is the additional satisfaction that a person gains by consuming an additional unit of the good or service.
2. **The Law of Diminishing Marginal Utility:** For at least the first unit of consumption of a good or service, a person's marginal utility increases with increased consumption. Eventually, however, the rate at which an individual's utility rises with greater consumption tends to fall. Thus marginal utility ultimately declines as the person consumes more and more of the good or service.
3. **The Consumer Optimum:** An individual optimally allocates available income to consumption of all goods and services when the marginal utility per dollar spent on the last unit consumed of each good is equalized. Thus a consumer optimum occurs when the ratio of the marginal utility derived from consuming a good or service to the price of that good or service is equal across all goods and services that the person consumes and when the person spends all available income.
4. **The Substitution Effect of a Price Change:** One effect of a change in the price of a good or service is that the price change induces people to substitute among goods. For example, if the price of a good rises, the individual will tend to consume some other good that has become relatively less expensive as a result. In addition, the individual will tend to reduce consumption of the good whose price increased.
5. **The Real-Income Effect of a Price Change:** Another effect of a price change is that it affects the purchasing power of an individual's available income. For instance, if there is an increase in the price of a good, a person must reduce purchases of either the now higher-priced good or other goods (or a combination of both of these responses). Normally, we anticipate that the real-income effect is smaller than the substitution effect, so that when the price of a good or service increases, people will purchase more of goods or services that have lower relative prices as a result.
6. **Why the Price of Diamonds Exceeds the Price of Water Even Though People Cannot Long Survive Without Water:** The reason for this price difference is that marginal utility, not total utility, determines how much people are willing to pay for any particular good. Because there are relatively few diamonds, the number of diamonds consumed by a typical individual is relatively small, which means that the marginal utility derived from consuming a diamond is relatively high. By contrast, water is abundant, so people consume relatively large volumes of water, and the marginal utility for the last unit of water consumed is relatively low. It follows that at a consumer optimum, in which the marginal utility per dollar spent is equalized for diamonds and water, people are willing to pay a much higher price for diamonds.

Key Terms and Concepts

Consumer optimum (461)
Diminishing marginal utility (459)
Marginal utility (457)
Principle of substitution (464)
Purchasing power (465)
Real-income effect (465)
Substitution effect (464)
Util (457)
Utility (456)
Utility analysis (456)

Problems

Answers to the odd-numbered problems appear at the back of the book.

19-1. The campus pizzeria sells a single pizza for $12. If you order a second pizza, however, its price is only $5. Explain how this relates to marginal utility.

19-2. As an individual consumes more units of an item, the person eventually experiences diminishing marginal utility. This means that in order to increase marginal utility, the person must often consume less of an item. This seems paradoxical. Explain the logic of this using the example in Problem 19-1.

19-3. Complete the missing cells in the table.

Number of Cheese-burgers	Total Utility of Cheese-burgers	Marginal Utility of Cheese-burgers	Bags of French Fries	Total Utility of French Fries	Marginal Utility of French Fries
0	0	—	0	0	—
1	20	—	1	—	8
2	36	—	2	—	6
3	—	12	3	—	4
4	—	8	4	20	—
5	—	4	5	20	—

19-4. If the price of a cheeseburger is $2 and the price of a bag of french fries is $1 and you have $6 to spend (and you spend all of it), what is the utility-maximizing combination of cheeseburgers and french fries?

19-5. Suppose that you observe that total utility rises as more of an item is consumed. What can you say for certain about marginal utility? Can you say for sure that it is rising or falling or that it is positive or negative?

19-6. After monitoring your daily consumption patterns, you determine that your daily consumption of soft drinks is 3 and your daily consumption of tacos is 4 when the prices per unit are 50 cents and $1, respectively. Explain what happens to your consumption bundle, the marginal utility of soft drinks, and the marginal utility of tacos when the price of soft drinks rises to 75 cents.

19-7. At a consumer optimum, for all goods purchased, marginal utility per dollar spent is equalized. A high school student is deciding between attending Western State University and Eastern State University. The student cannot attend both universities simultaneously. Both are fine universities, but the reputation of Western is slightly higher, as is the tuition. Use the rule of consumer optimum to explain how the student will go about deciding which university to attend.

19-8. Suppose that 5 apples and 6 bananas generate a total utility of 50 for you. In addition, 4 apples and 8 bananas generate a total utility of 50. Given this information, what can you say about the marginal utility of apples relative to the marginal utility of bananas?

19-9. Return to Problem 19-4. Suppose that the price of cheeseburgers falls to $1. Determine the new utility-maximizing combination of cheeseburgers and french fries. Use this new combination of goods to explain the income and substitution effects.

19-10. Using your answers to Problems 19-4 and 19-9, illustrate a simple demand curve for cheeseburgers.

Economics on the Net

Book Prices and Consumer Optimum This application helps you see how a consumer optimum can be attained when one engages in Internet shopping.

Title: Amazon.com Web Site

Navigation: Click here to start at Amazon.com's homepage. Click on the Books tab.

Application

1. On the right-hand side of the page, find the list of the top books in the Amazon.com 100 section. Click on the number 1 book. Record the price of the book. Then, locate the Search window. Type in Roger LeRoy Miller. Scroll down until you find your class text listed. Record the price.
2. Suppose you are an individual who has purchased both the number 1 book and your class text through Amazon.com. Describe how economic analysis would explain this choice.
3. Using the prices you recorded for the two books, write an equation that relates the prices and your marginal utilities of the two books. Use this equation to explain verbally how you might quantify the magnitude of your marginal utility for the number 1 book relative to your marginal utility for your class text.

For Group Study and Analysis Discuss what changes might occur if the price of the number 1 book were lowered but the student remains enrolled in this course. Discuss what changes might take place regarding the consumer optimum if the student was not enrolled in this course.

APPENDIX E

MORE ADVANCED CONSUMER CHOICE THEORY

It is possible to analyze consumer choice verbally, as we did for the most part in Chapter 19. The theory of diminishing marginal utility can be fairly well accepted on intuitive grounds and by introspection. If we want to be more formal and perhaps more elegant in our theorizing, however, we can translate our discussion into a graphical analysis with what we call *indifference curves* and the *budget constraint.* Here we discuss these terms and their relationship and demonstrate consumer equilibrium in geometric form.

ON BEING INDIFFERENT

What does it mean to be indifferent? It usually means that you don't care one way or the other about something—you are equally disposed to either of two alternatives. With this interpretation in mind, we will turn to two choices, video rentals and restaurant meals. In panel (a) of Figure E-1, we show several combinations of video rentals and restaurant meals per week that a representative consumer considers equally satisfactory. That is to say, for each combination, *A, B, C,* and *D,* this consumer will have exactly the same level of total utility.

The simple numerical example that we have used happens to concern video rentals and restaurant meals per week. This example is used to illustrate general features of indifference curves and related analytical tools that are necessary for deriving the demand curve. Obviously, we could have used any two commodities. Just remember that we are using a *specific* example to illustrate a *general* analysis.

We can plot these combinations graphically in panel (b) of Figure E-1, with restaurant meals per week on the horizontal axis and video rentals per week on the vertical axis. These are our consumer's indifference combinations—the consumer finds each combination as acceptable as the others. When we connect these combinations with a smooth curve, we obtain

FIGURE E-1
Combinations That Yield Equal Levels of Satisfaction
A, B, C, and *D* represent combinations of video rentals and restaurant meals per week that give an equal level of satisfaction to this consumer. In other words, the consumer is indifferent among these four combinations.

Panel (a)

Combination	Video Rentals per Week	Restaurant Meals per Week
A	1	7
B	2	4
C	3	2
D	4	1

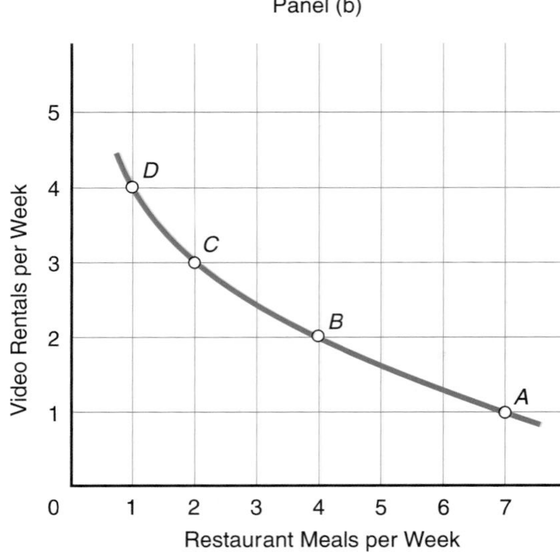

what is called the consumer's **indifference curve.** Along the indifference curve, every combination of the two goods in question yields the same level of satisfaction. Every point along the indifference curve is equally desirable to the consumer. For example, four video rentals per week and one restaurant meal per week will give our representative consumer exactly the same total satisfaction as two video rentals per week and four restaurant meals per week.

Indifference curve 
A curve composed of a set of consumption alternatives, each of which yields the same total amount of satisfaction.

PROPERTIES OF INDIFFERENCE CURVES

Indifference curves have special properties relating to their slope and shape.

Downward Slope

The indifference curve shown in panel (b) of Figure E-1 slopes downward; that is, it has a negative slope. Now consider Figure E-2. Here we show two points, *A* and *B*. Point *A* represents four video rentals per week and two restaurant meals per week. Point *B* represents five video rentals per week and six restaurant meals per week. Clearly, *B* is always preferred to *A* because *B* represents more of everything. If *B* is always preferred to *A,* it is impossible for points *A* and *B* to be on the same indifference curve because the definition of the indifference curve is a set of combinations of two goods that are preferred equally.

Curvature

The indifference curve that we have drawn in panel (b) of Figure E-1 is special. Notice that it is curved. Why didn't we just draw a straight line, as we have usually done for a demand curve? To find out why we don't posit straight-line indifference curves, consider the implications. We show such a straight-line indifference curve in Figure E-3 (p. 474). Start at point *A.* The consumer has no restaurant meals and five video rentals per week. Now the consumer wishes to go to point *B.* He or she is willing to give up only one video rental in order to get one restaurant meal. Now let's assume that the consumer is at point *C,* consuming one video rental and four restaurant meals per week. If the consumer wants to go to point *D,* he or she is again willing to give up one video rental in order to get one more restaurant meal per week.

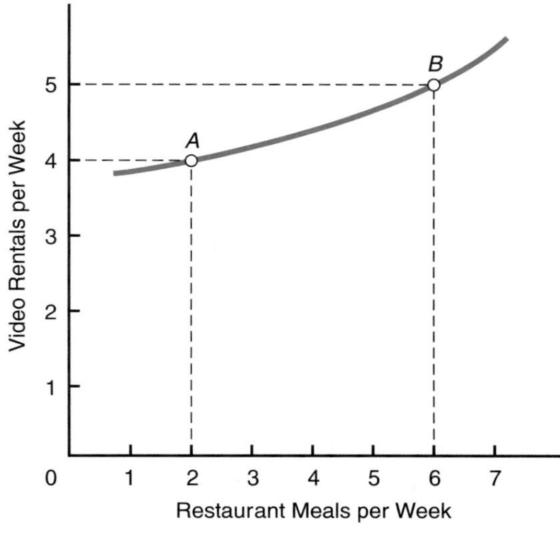

FIGURE E-2
Indifference Curves: Impossibility of an Upward Slope
Point *B* represents a consumption of more video rentals per week and more restaurant meals per week than point *A. B* is always preferred to *A*. Therefore, *A* and *B* cannot be on the same indifference curve, which is positively sloped, because an indifference curve shows *equally preferred* combinations of the two goods.

FIGURE E-3

Implications of a Straight-Line Indifference Curve

If the indifference curve is a straight line, the consumer will be willing to give up the same number of video rentals (one for one in this simple example) to get one more restaurant meal per week, whether the consumer has no restaurant meals or a lot of restaurant meals per week. For example, the consumer at point *A* has five video rentals and no restaurant meals per week. He or she is willing to give up one video rental in order to get one restaurant meal per week. At point *C*, however, the consumer has only one video rental and four restaurant meals per week. Because of the straight-line indifference curve, this consumer is willing to give up the last video rental in order to get one more restaurant meal per week, even though he or she already has four.

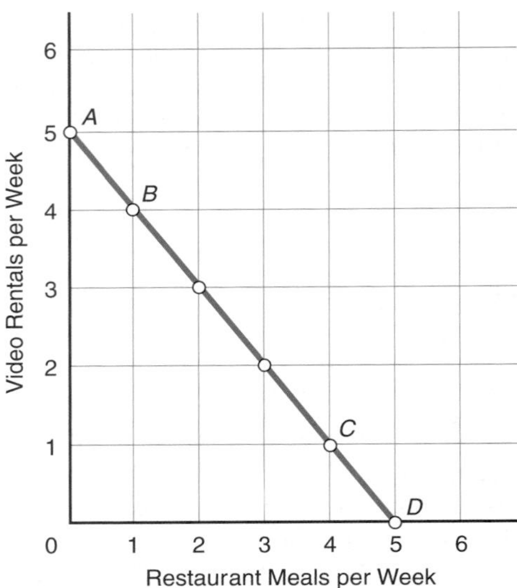

In other words, no matter how many videos the consumer rents, he or she is willing to give up one video rental to get one restaurant meal per week—which does not seem plausible. Doesn't it make sense to hypothesize that the more videos the consumer rents per week, the less he or she will value an *additional* video rental? Presumably, when the consumer has five video rentals and no restaurant meals per week, he or she should be willing to give up more than one video rental in order to get one restaurant meal. Therefore, a straight-line indifference curve as shown in Figure E-3 no longer seems plausible.

In mathematical jargon, an indifference curve is convex with respect to the origin. Let's look at this in panel (a) of Figure E-1 on page 472. Starting with combination *A,* the consumer has one video rental but seven restaurant meals per week. To remain indifferent, the consumer would have to be willing to give up three restaurant meals to obtain one more video rental (as shown in combination *B*). However, to go from combination *C* to combination *D,* notice that the consumer would have to be willing to give up only one restaurant meal for an additional video rental per week. The quantity of the substitute considered acceptable changes as the rate of consumption of the original item changes.

Consequently, the indifference curve in panel (b) of Figure E-1 will be convex when viewed from the origin.

THE MARGINAL RATE OF SUBSTITUTION

Instead of using marginal utility, we can talk in terms of the *marginal rate of substitution* between restaurant meals and video rentals per week. We can formally define the consumer's marginal rate of substitution as follows:

> The marginal rate of substitution is equal to the change in the quantity of one good that just offsets a one-unit change in the consumption of another good, such that total satisfaction remains constant.

We can see numerically what happens to the marginal rate of substitution in our example if we rearrange panel (a) of Figure E-1 into Table E-1. Here we show restaurant meals in the second column and video rentals in the third. Now we ask the question, what change

(1) Combination	(2) Restaurant Meals Per Week	(3) Video Rentals Per Week	(4) Marginal Rate of Substitution of Restaurant Meals for Video Rentals
A	7	1	
			3:1
B	4	2	
			2:1
C	2	3	
			1:1
D	1	4	

TABLE E-1

Calculating the Marginal Rate of Substitution

As we move from combination *A* to combination *B*, we are still on the same indifference curve. To stay on that curve, the number of restaurant meals decreases by three and the number of video rentals increases by one. The marginal rate of substitution is 3:1. A three-unit decrease in restaurant meals requires an increase in one video rental to leave the consumer's total utility unaltered.

in the consumption of video rentals per week will just compensate for a three-unit change in the consumption of restaurant meals per week and leave the consumer's total utility constant? The movement from *A* to *B* increases video rental consumption by one. Here the marginal rate of substitution is 3:1—a three-unit decrease in restaurant meals requires an increase of one video rental to leave the consumer's total utility unaltered. Thus the consumer values the three restaurant meals as the equivalent of one video rental. We do this for the rest of the table and find that as restaurant meals decrease further, the marginal rate of substitution goes from 3:1 to 2:1 to 1:1. The marginal rate of substitution of restaurant meals for video rentals per week falls as the consumer obtains more video rentals. That is, the consumer values successive units of video rentals less and less in terms of restaurant meals. The first video rental is valued at three restaurant meals; the last (fourth) video rental is valued at only one restaurant meal. The fact that the marginal rate of substitution falls is sometimes called the *law of substitution.*

In geometric language, the slope of the consumer's indifference curve (actually, the negative of the slope) measures the consumer's marginal rate of substitution. Notice that this marginal rate of substitution is purely subjective or psychological.

THE INDIFFERENCE MAP

Let's now consider the possibility of having both more video rentals *and* more restaurant meals per week. When we do this, we can no longer stay on the same indifference curve that we drew in Figure E-1. That indifference curve was drawn for equally satisfying combinations of video rentals and restaurant meals per week. If the individual can now obtain more of both, a new indifference curve will have to be drawn, above and to the right of the one shown in panel (b) of Figure E-1. Alternatively, if the individual faces the possibility of having less of both video rentals and restaurant meals per week, an indifference curve will have to be drawn below and to the left of the one in panel (b) of Figure E-1. We can map out a whole set of indifference curves corresponding to these possibilities.

Figure E-4 on page 476 shows three possible indifference curves. Indifference curves that are higher than others necessarily imply that for every given quantity of one good, more of the other good can be obtained on a higher indifference curve. Looked at another way, if one goes from curve I_1 to I_2, it is possible to consume the same number of restaurant meals *and* be able to rent more videos per week. This is shown as a movement from point *A* to point *B* in Figure E-4. We could do it the other way. When we move from a lower to a higher indifference

FIGURE E-4
A Set of Indifference Curves
An infinite number of indifference curves can be drawn. We show three possible ones. Realize that a higher indifference curve represents the possibility of higher rates of consumption of both goods. Hence a higher indifference curve is preferred to a lower one because more is preferred to less. Look at points *A* and *B*. Point *B* represents more video rentals than point *A;* therefore, bundles on indifference curve I_2 have to be preferred over bundles on I_1 because the number of restaurant meals per week is the same at points *A* and *B*.

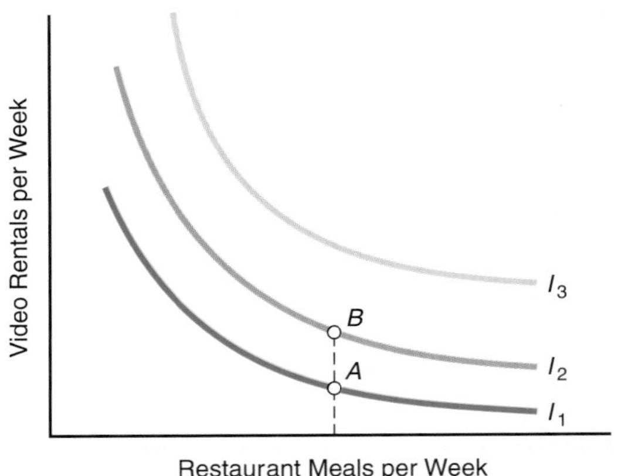

curve, it is possible to rent the same number of videos *and* to consume more restaurant meals per week. Thus the higher a consumer is on the indifference map, the greater that consumer's total level of satisfaction.

THE BUDGET CONSTRAINT

Budget constraint 
All of the possible combinations of goods that can be purchased (at fixed prices) with a specific budget.

Our problem here is to find out how to maximize consumer satisfaction. To do so, we must consult not only our *preferences*—given by indifference curves—but also our *market opportunities*—given by our available income and prices, called our **budget constraint.** We might want more of everything, but for any given budget constraint, we have to make choices, or trade-offs, among possible goods. Everyone has a budget constraint; that is, everyone faces a limited consumption potential. How do we show this graphically? We must find the prices of the goods in question and determine the maximum consumption of each allowed by our budget. For example, let's assume that videos rent for \$10 apiece and restaurant meals cost \$20. Let's also assume that our representative consumer has a total budget of \$60 per week. What is the maximum number of videos the consumer can rent? Six. And the maximum number of restaurant meals per week he or she can consume? Three. So now, as shown in Figure E-5, we have two points on our budget line, which is sometimes called the *consumption possibilities curve.* These anchor points of the budget line are obtained by dividing money income by the price of each product. The first point is at *b* on the vertical axis; the second, at *b′* on the horizontal axis. The budget line is linear because prices are given.

Any combination along line *bb′* is possible; in fact, any combination in the colored area is possible. We will assume, however, that the individual consumer completely uses up the available budget, and we will consider as possible only those points along *bb′*.

Slope of the Budget Constraint

The budget constraint is a line that slopes downward from left to right. The slope of that line has a special meaning. Look carefully at the budget line in Figure E-5. Remember from our discussion of graphs in Appendix A that we measure a negative slope by the ratio of the fall in *Y* over the run in *X*. In this case, *Y* is video rentals per week and *X* is restaurant meals per week. In Figure E-5, the fall in *Y* is − 2 video rentals per week (a drop from 4 to 2) for

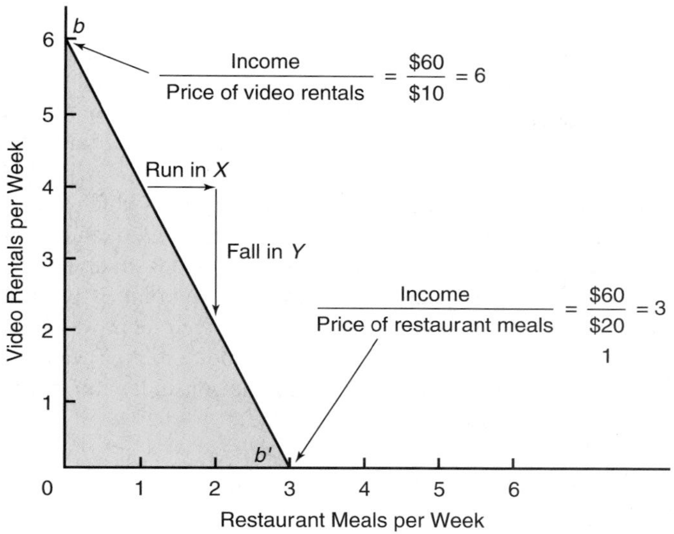

FIGURE E-5
The Budget Constraint
The line bb' represents this individual's budget constraint. Assuming that video rentals cost $10 each, restaurant meals cost $20 each, and the individual has a budget of $60 per week, a maximum of six video rentals or three restaurant meals can be bought each week. These two extreme points are connected to form the budget constraint. All combinations within the colored area and on the budget constraint line are feasible.

a run in X of one restaurant meal per week (an increase from 1 to 2); therefore, the slope of the budget constraint is $-2/1$, or -2. This slope of the budget constraint represents the rate of exchange between video rentals and restaurant meals.

Now we are ready to determine how the consumer achieves the optimum consumption rate.

CONSUMER OPTIMUM REVISITED

Consumers will try to attain the highest level of total utility possible, given their budget constraints. How can this be shown graphically? We draw a set of indifference curves similar to those in Figure E-4, and we bring in reality—the budget constraint bb'. Both are drawn in Figure E-6. Because a higher level of total satisfaction is represented by a higher indifference curve, we know that the consumer will strive to be on the highest indifference

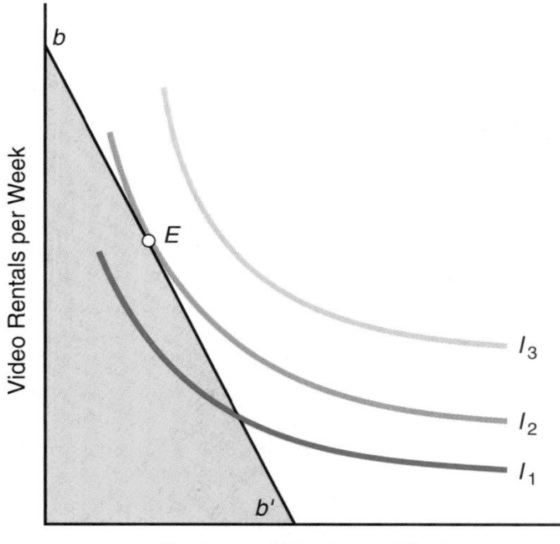

FIGURE E-6
Consumer Optimum
A consumer reaches an optimum when he or she ends up on the highest indifference curve possible, given a limited budget. This occurs at the tangency between an indifference curve and the budget constraint. In this diagram, the tangency is at *E*.

Click here for a numerical example illustrating the consumer optimum.

curve possible. However, the consumer cannot get to indifference curve I_3 because the budget will be exhausted before any combination of video rentals and restaurant meals represented on indifference curve I_3 is attained. This consumer can maximize total utility, subject to the budget constraint, only by being at point E on indifference curve I_2 because here the consumer's income is just being exhausted. Mathematically, point E is called the *tangency point* of the curve I_2 to the straight line bb'.

Consumer optimum is achieved when the marginal rate of substitution (which is subjective) is just equal to the feasible, or realistic, rate of exchange between video rentals and restaurant meals. This realistic rate is the ratio of the two prices of the goods involved. It is represented by the absolute value of the slope of the budget constraint. At point E, the point of tangency between indifference curve I_2 and budget constraint bb', the rate at which the consumer wishes to substitute video rentals for restaurant meals (the numerical value of slope of the indifference curve) is just equal to the rate at which the consumer *can* substitute video rentals for restaurant meals (the slope of the budget line).

EFFECTS OF CHANGES IN INCOME

A change in income will shift the budget constraint bb' in Figure E-6. Consider only increases in income and no changes in price. The budget constraint will shift outward. Each new budget line will be parallel to the original one because we are not allowing a change in the relative prices of video rentals and restaurant meals. We would now like to find out how an individual consumer responds to successive increases in income when relative prices remain constant. We do this in Figure E-7. We start out with an income that is represented by a budget line bb'. Consumer optimum is at point E, where the consumer attains the highest indifference curve I_1, given the budget constraint bb'. Now we let income increase. This is shown by a shift outward in the budget line to cc'. The consumer attains a new optimum at point E'. That is where a higher indifference curve, I_2, is reached. Again, the consumer's income is increased so that the new budget line is dd'. The new optimum now moves to E''. This is where indifference curve I_3 is reached. If we connect the three consumer optimum points, E, E', and E'', we have what is called an income-consumption curve. The **income-consumption curve** shows the optimum consumption points that

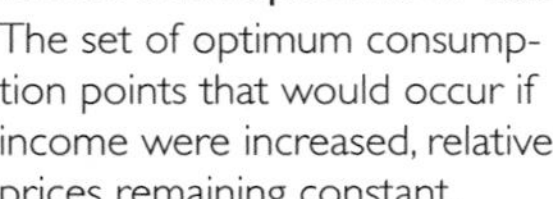

Income-consumption curve
The set of optimum consumption points that would occur if income were increased, relative prices remaining constant.

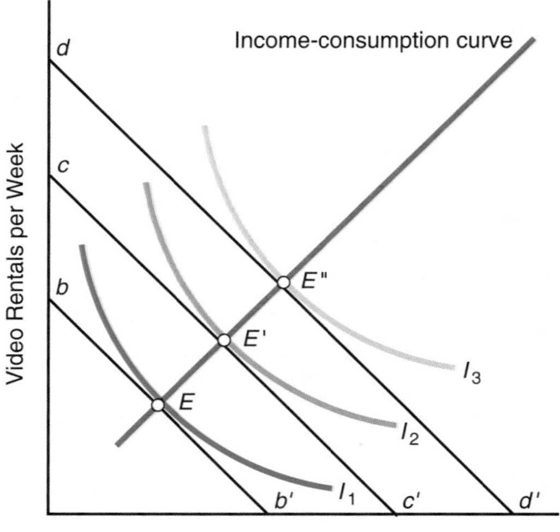

FIGURE E-7
Income-Consumption Curve
We start off with income sufficient to yield budget constraint bb'. The highest attainable indifference curve is I_1, which is just tangent to bb' at E. Next we increase income. The budget line moves outward to cc', which is parallel to bb'. The new highest indifference curve is I_2, which is just tangent to cc' at E'. We increase income again, which is represented by a shift in the budget line to dd'. The new tangency point of the highest indifference curve, I_3, with dd', is at point E''. When we connect these three points, we obtain the income-consumption curve.

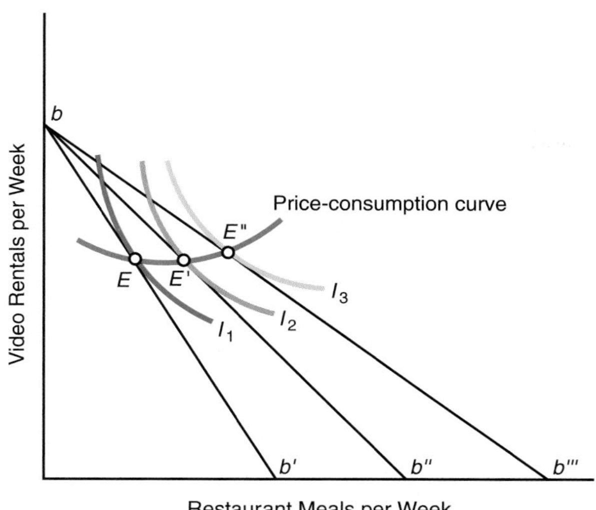

FIGURE E-8
Price-Consumption Curve
As we lower the price of restaurant meals, income measured in terms of restaurant meals per week increases. We show this by rotating the budget constraint from *bb′* to *bb″* and finally to *bb‴*. We then find the highest indifference curve that is attainable for each successive budget constraint. For budget constraint *bb′*, the highest indifference curve is I_1, which is tangent to *bb′* at point *E*. We do this for the next two budget constraints. When we connect the optimum points, *E*, *E′*, and *E″*, we derive the price-consumption curve, which shows the combinations of the two commodities that a consumer will purchase when money income and the price of one commodity remain constant while the other commodity's price changes.

would occur if income for that consumer were increased continuously, holding the prices of video rentals and restaurant meals constant.

THE PRICE-CONSUMPTION CURVE

In Figure E-8, we hold money income and the price of video rentals constant while we lower the price of restaurant meals. As we keep lowering the price of restaurant meals, the quantity of meals that could be purchased if all income were spent on restaurant meals increases; thus the extreme points for the budget constraint keep moving outward to the right as the price of restaurant meals falls. In other words, the budget line rotates outward from *bb′* to *bb″* and *bb‴*. Each time the price of restaurant meals falls, a new budget line is formed. There has to be a new optimum point. We find it by locating on each new budget line the highest attainable indifference curve. This is shown at points *E*, *E′*, and *E″*. We see that as price decreases for restaurant meals, the consumer purchases more restaurant meals per week. We call the line connecting points *E*, *E′*, and *E″* the **price-consumption curve.** It connects the tangency points of the budget constraints and indifference curves, thus showing the amounts of two goods that a consumer will buy when money income and the price of one commodity are held constant while the price of the remaining good changes.

Price-consumption curve
The set of consumer optimum combinations of two goods that the consumer would choose as the price of one good changes, while money income and the price of the other good remain constant.

DERIVING THE DEMAND CURVE

We are now in a position to derive the demand curve using indifference curve analysis. In panel (a) of Figure E-9 on page 480, we show what happens when the price of restaurant meals decreases, holding both the price of video rentals and income constant. If the price of restaurant meals decreases, the budget line rotates from *bb′* to *bb″*. The two optimum points are given by the tangency at the highest indifference curve that just touches those two budget lines. This is at *E* and *E′*. But those two points give us two price-quantity pairs. At point *E*, the price of restaurant meals is $20; the quantity demanded is 2. Thus we have one point that we can transfer to panel (b) of Figure E-9. At point *E′*, we have another price-quantity pair. The price has fallen to $10; the quantity demanded has increased to 5. We therefore transfer this other point to panel (b). When we connect these two points (and all the others in between), we derive the demand curve for restaurant meals; it slopes downward.

FIGURE E-9

Deriving the Demand Curve

In panel (a), we show the effects of a decrease in the price of restaurant meals from \$20 to \$10. At \$20, the highest indifference curve touches the budget line *bb′* at point *E*. The quantity of restaurant meals consumed is two. We transfer this combination—price, \$20; quantity demanded, 2—down to panel (b). Next we decrease the price of restaurant meals to \$10. This generates a new budget line, or constraint, which is *bb″*. Consumer optimum is now at *E′*. The optimum quantity of restaurant meals demanded at a price of \$10 is five. We transfer this point—price, \$10; quantity demanded, 5—down to panel (b). When we connect these two points, we have a demand curve, *D*, for restaurant meals.

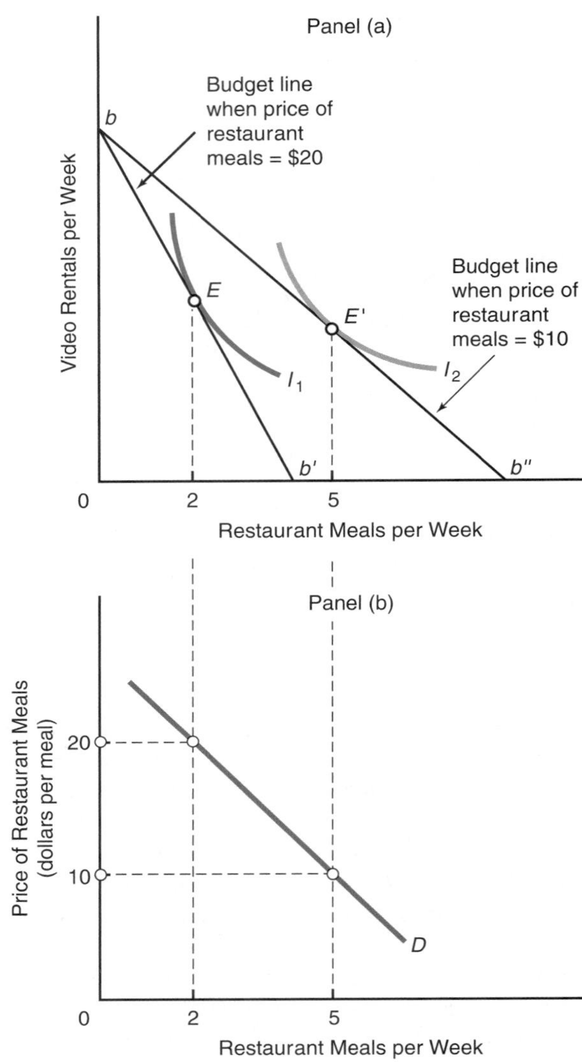

Appendix Summary

1. Along an indifference curve, the consumer experiences equal levels of satisfaction. That is to say, along any indifference curve, every combination of the two goods in question yields exactly the same level of satisfaction.
2. Indifference curves usually slope downward and are usually convex to the origin.
3. To measure the marginal rate of substitution, we find out how much of one good has to be given up in order to allow the consumer to consume one more unit of the other good while still remaining on the same indifference curve. The marginal rate of substitution falls as one moves down an indifference curve.
4. Indifference curves represent preferences. A budget constraint represents opportunities—how much can be purchased with a given level of income. Consumer optimum is obtained when the highest indifference curve is just tangent to the budget constraint line; at that point, the consumer reaches the highest feasible indifference curve.
5. When income increases, the budget constraint shifts outward to the right, parallel to the previous budget constraint line.

6. As income increases, the consumer optimum moves up to higher and higher indifference curves. When we connect those points with a line, we derive the income-consumption curve.

7. As the price of one good decreases, the budget line rotates. When we connect the tangency points of the highest indifference curves to these new budget lines, we derive the price-consumption curve.

Problems

Answers to the odd-numbered problems appear at the back of the book.

E-1. Consider the indifference curve illustrated in Figure E-1. Explain, in economic terms, why the curve is convex to the origin.

E-2. Your classmate tells you that he is indifferent between three soft drinks and two hamburgers or two soft drinks and three hamburgers. He is also indifferent between two soft drinks and three hamburgers and one soft drink and four hamburgers. However, he prefers three soft drinks and two hamburgers to one soft drink and four hamburgers. Illustrate your friend's preferences as described. How many indifference curves are in your illustration? Explain why he can have these preferences.

E-3. The following table represents Sue's preferences for bottled water and soft drinks, which yield the same level of utility.

Combination of Bottled Water and Soft Drinks	Bottled Water per Month	Soft Drinks per Month
A	5	11
B	10	7
C	15	4
D	20	2
E	25	1

Calculate Sue's marginal rate of substitution of soft drinks for bottled water. Relate the marginal rate of substitution to marginal utility.

E-4. Using the information provided in Problem E-3, illustrate Sue's indifference curve, with water on the horizontal axis and soft drinks on the vertical axis.

E-5. Sue's monthly budget for bottled water and soft drinks is $23. Bottled water costs $1 per bottle, and soft drinks cost $2 per bottle. Calculate the slope of Sue's budget constraint. Given this information and the information provided in Problem E-3, find the combination of goods that satisfies Sue's utility maximization problem in light of her budget constraint.

E-6. Using the indifference curve diagram you constructed in Problem E-4, add in Sue's budget constraint given the information in Problem E-5. Illustrate the utility-maximizing combination of bottled water and soft drinks.

E-7. Using the information provided in Problem E-5, suppose now that the price of a soft drink falls to $1. Now Sue's constant-utility preferences are as follows:

Combination of Bottled Water and Soft Drinks	Bottled Water per Month	Soft Drinks per Month
A	5	22
B	10	14
C	15	8
D	20	4
E	25	2

Calculate the slope of Sue's new budget constraint. Next, find the combination of goods that satisfies Sue's utility maximization problem in light of her budget constraint.

E-8. Illustrate Sue's new budget constraint and indifference curve in the diagram you constructed for Problem E-6. Illustrate also the utility-maximizing combination of goods. Finally, draw the price-consumption curve.

E-9. Given your answers to Problems E-5 and E-7, are Sue's preferences for soft drinks consistent with the law of demand?

E-10. Using your answer to Problem E-8, draw Sue's demand curve for soft drinks.

CHAPTER 20

DEMAND AND SUPPLY ELASTICITY

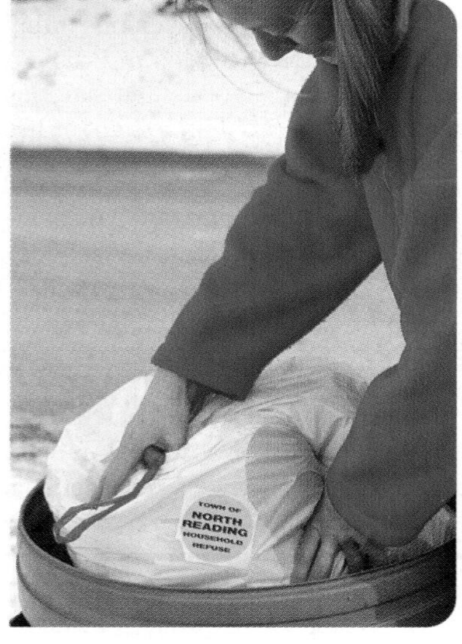

This resident of North Reading, Massachusetts, must place a "paid for" sticker on each trash bag that is to be picked up. Can charging explicit prices for hauling away trash reduce the flow of garbage? Can people vary the amount of garbage they generate?

For some American cities, the crisis began in the 1980s. It spread to other municipalities during the 1990s, and today most villages, towns, counties, and cities throughout the nation are affected. The affliction they share is an overabundance of trash. Even though landfill prices have declined in many areas, municipalities foresee a time when local landfills will be full, requiring big expenses to transport trash to more remote areas. Municipal sanitation department managers everywhere are searching for places to send future trash and affordable ways to get it there. Some municipalities, however, have discovered that charging explicit prices to haul away trash can help stem the flow of garbage. Experiments are under way to determine how high prices must go to induce people to cut back significantly on how much they throw away. To understand how successful a trash-pricing policy may turn out to be, you must learn more about how people respond to changing prices.

LEARNING OBJECTIVES

After reading this chapter, you should be able to:

1. **Express and calculate price elasticity of demand**
2. **Understand the relationship between the price elasticity of demand and total revenues**
3. **Discuss the factors that determine the price elasticity of demand**
4. **Describe the cross price elasticity of demand and how it may be used to indicate whether two goods are substitutes or complements**
5. **Explain the income elasticity of demand**
6. **Classify supply elasticities and explain how the length of time for adjustment affects the price elasticity of supply**

Did You Know That... the government predicted it would raise $6 million per year in new revenues from a new 10 percent luxury tax on private airplane and yacht sales a few years ago, but it actually collected only $53,000? How can that be? The answer lies in understanding the relationship between the quantities that people demand at lower prices relative to the quantities that people demand at higher prices. The year during which the 10 percent luxury tax was imposed also saw expensive new yacht sales fall to almost nothing. Clearly, even rich people respond to rising prices, which in this case were caused by the new tax.

The government isn't alone in having to worry about how individuals respond to rising prices; it is perhaps even more important that businesses take into account consumer response to changing prices. If McDonald's lowers its prices by 10 percent, will fast-food consumers respond by buying so many more Big Macs that the company's revenues will rise? At the other end of the spectrum, can Rolls Royce dealers "get away" with a 2 percent increase in prices? Otherwise stated, will Rolls Royce purchasers respond so little to the relatively small increase in price that the total revenues received for Rolls Royce sales will not fall and may actually rise? The only way to answer these questions is to know how responsive people in the real world will be to changes in prices. Economists have a special name for price responsiveness—*elasticity,* which is the subject of this chapter.

Chapter Outline

PRICE ELASTICITY

To begin to understand what elasticity is all about, just keep in mind that it means "responsiveness." Here we are concerned with the price elasticity of demand. We wish to know the extent to which a change in the price of, say, petroleum products will cause the quantity demanded to change, other things held constant. We want to determine the percentage change in quantity demanded in response to a percentage change in price.

Price Elasticity of Demand

We will formally define the **price elasticity of demand,** which we will label E_p, as follows:

$$E_p = \frac{\text{percentage change in quantity demanded}}{\text{percentage change in price}}$$

Price elasticity of demand (E_p) 
The responsiveness of the quantity demanded of a commodity to changes in its price; defined as the percentage change in quantity demanded divided by the percentage change in price.

What will price elasticity of demand tell us? It will tell us the relative amount by which the quantity demanded will change in response to a change in the price of a particular good.

Consider an example in which a 10 percent rise in the price of oil leads to a reduction in quantity demanded of only 1 percent. Putting these numbers into the formula, we find that the price elasticity of demand for oil in this case equals the percentage change in quantity demanded divided by the percentage change in price, or

$$E_p = \frac{-1\%}{+10\%} = -.1$$

An elasticity of $-.1$ means that a 1 percent *increase* in the price would lead to a mere .1 percent *decrease* in the quantity demanded. If you were now told, in contrast, that the price elasticity of demand for oil was -1, you would know that a 1 percent increase in the price of oil would lead to a 1 percent decrease in the quantity demanded.

Relative Quantities Only. Notice that in our elasticity formula, we talk about *percentage* changes in quantity demanded divided by *percentage* changes in price. We are therefore

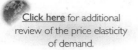

Click here for additional review of the price elasticity of demand.

not interested in the absolute changes, only in relative amounts. This means that it doesn't matter if we measure price changes in terms of cents, dollars, or hundreds of dollars. It also doesn't matter whether we measure quantity changes in ounces, grams, or pounds. The percentage change will be independent of the units chosen.

Always Negative. The law of demand states that quantity demanded is *inversely* related to the relative price. An *increase* in the price of a good leads to a *decrease* in the quantity demanded. If a *decrease* in the relative price of a good should occur, the quantity demanded would *increase* by a certain percentage. The point is that price elasticity of demand will always be negative. By convention, however, *we will ignore the minus sign in our discussion from this point on.*

Basically, the greater the *absolute* price elasticity of demand (disregarding sign), the greater the demand responsiveness to relative price changes—a small change in price has a great impact on quantity demanded. The smaller the absolute price elasticity of demand, the smaller the demand responsiveness to relative price changes—a large change in price has little effect on quantity demanded.

EXAMPLE

To Cut Teen Drug Use, Make the Price of a "High" Higher

Recently, John Tauras of the University of Illinois at Chicago and Michael Grossman of the City University of New York conducted a study of teen use of cocaine. They found that compared with adults, youthful drug abusers are three times more sensitive to price changes. Whereas adult cocaine demand is inelastic, teen cocaine demand is nearly unit-elastic over the range of market prices tabulated by the Drug Enforcement Administration. In other words, a 33 percent increase in the market price of cocaine likely would reduce the teen purchases and consumption of cocaine by a third. Undoubtedly, some teens would substitute other drugs. Nonetheless, cocaine and a derivative drug, crack cocaine, are considered addictive substances. Inducing teens to reduce cocaine use might therefore take a significant bite out of the nation's longer-term problems with drug abuse. An implication of this study is that legal crackdowns on cocaine dealers that restrict the supply of the drug and push up its price might be an appropriate strategy in the war against drugs.

For Critical Analysis

If teen price elasticity of demand for cocaine equals 1, what will happen to drug dealers' revenues from sales to teens if cocaine prices rise?

CONCEPTS IN BRIEF

- Elasticity is a measure of the price responsiveness of the quantity demanded and quantity supplied.
- The price elasticity of demand is equal to the percentage change in quantity demanded divided by the percentage change in price.
- Price elasticity of demand is calculated in terms of percentage changes in quantity demanded and in price. Thus it is expressed as a unitless, dimensionless number.
- The law of demand states that quantity demanded and price are inversely related. Therefore, the price elasticity of demand is always negative, because an increase in price will lead to a decrease in quantity demanded and a decrease in price will lead to an increase in quantity demanded. By convention, we ignore the negative sign in discussions of the price elasticity of demand.

Calculating Elasticity

To calculate the price elasticity of demand, we have to compute percentage changes in quantity demanded and in relative price. To obtain the percentage change in quantity demanded, we divide the change in the quantity demanded by the original quantity demanded:

$$\frac{\text{Change in quantity demand}}{\text{Original quantity demand}}$$

To find the percentage change in price, we divide the change in price by the original price:

$$\frac{\text{Change in price}}{\text{Original price}}$$

There is an arithmetic problem, though, when we calculate percentage changes in this manner. The percentage change, say, from 2 to 3—50 percent—is not the same as the percentage change from 3 to 2—$33\frac{1}{3}$ percent. In other words, it makes a difference where you start. One way out of this dilemma is simply to use average values.

To compute the price elasticity of demand, we need to deal with the average change in quantity demanded caused by the average change in price. That means that we take the average of the two prices and the two quantities over the range we are considering and compare the change with these averages. For relatively small changes in price, the formula for computing the price elasticity of demand then becomes

$$E_p = \frac{\text{change in quantity}}{\text{sum of quantities/2}} \div \frac{\text{change in price}}{\text{sum of prices/2}}$$

We can rewrite this more simply if we do two things: (1) We can let Q_1 and Q_2 equal the two different quantities demanded before and after the price change and let P_1 and P_2 equal the two different prices. (2) Because we will be dividing a percentage by a percentage, we simply use the ratio, or the decimal form, of the percentages. Therefore,

$$E_p = \frac{\Delta Q}{(Q_1 + Q_2)/2} \div \frac{\Delta P}{(P_1 + P_2)/2}$$

where the Greek letter Δ stands for "change in."

INTERNATIONAL EXAMPLE

The Price Elasticity of Demand for Newspapers

Newspaper owners are always seeking to increase their paper's circulation, not because they want the revenue generated from the sales of the paper, but because the larger the circulation, the more the newspaper can charge for its advertising space. The source of most of a paper's revenues—and profits—comes from its advertisers.

One newspaper owner, Rupert Murdoch, ran an experiment to see how high he could boost sales of a particular newspaper by lowering its price. For one day, he lowered the price of the British daily paper *Today* from 25 pence to 10 pence. According to London's *Financial Times,* sales of *Today* almost doubled that day, increasing the circulation from 590,000 to 1,050,000 copies. We can estimate the price elasticity of demand for *Today* by using the formula presented earlier (under the assumption, of course, that all other things were held constant):

$$E_p = \frac{\Delta Q}{(Q_1 + Q_2)/2} \div \frac{\Delta P}{(P_1 + P_2)/2}$$

$$= \frac{1{,}050{,}000 - 590{,}000}{(590{,}000 + 1{,}050{,}000)/2} \div \frac{25 \text{ pence} - 10 \text{ pence}}{(10 \text{ pence} + 25 \text{ pence})/2}$$

$$= \frac{460{,}000}{820{,}000} \div \frac{15 \text{ pence}}{17.5 \text{ pence}} = .66$$

The price elasticity of demand of .66 means that a 1 percent decrease in price will lead to a .66 percent increase in quantity demanded.

For Critical Analysis

Would the estimated price elasticity of the *Today* newspaper have been different if we had *not* used the average-values formula? How?

Elastic demand 

A demand relationship in which a given percentage change in price will result in a larger percentage change in quantity demanded. Total expenditures and price changes are inversely related in the elastic region of the demand curve.

Unit elasticity of demand 

A demand relationship in which the quantity demanded changes exactly in proportion to the change in price. Total expenditures are invariant to price changes in the unit-elastic region of the demand curve.

Inelastic demand 

A demand relationship in which a given percentage change in price will result in a less than proportionate percentage change in the quantity demanded. Total expenditures and price are directly related in the inelastic region of the demand curve.

Perfectly inelastic demand 

A demand that exhibits zero responsiveness to price changes; no matter what the price is, the quantity demanded remains the same.

Perfectly elastic demand 

A demand that has the characteristic that even the slightest increase in price will lead to zero quantity demanded.

PRICE ELASTICITY RANGES

We have names for the varying ranges of price elasticities, depending on whether a 1 percent change in price elicits more or less than a 1 percent change in the quantity demanded.

- We say that a good has an **elastic demand** whenever the price elasticity of demand is greater than 1. A 1 percent change in price causes a greater than 1 percent change in the quantity demanded.
- In a situation of **unit elasticity of demand,** a 1 percent change in price causes exactly a 1 percent change in the quantity demanded.
- In a situation of **inelastic demand,** a 1 percent change in price causes a change of less than 1 percent in the quantity demanded.

When we say that a commodity's demand is elastic, we are indicating that consumers are relatively responsive to changes in price. When we say that a commodity's demand is inelastic, we are indicating that its consumers are relatively unresponsive to price changes. When economists say that demand is inelastic, it does not mean that quantity demanded is totally unresponsive to price changes. Remember, the law of demand suggests that there will be some responsiveness in quantity demanded to a price change. The question is how much. That's what elasticity attempts to determine.

Extreme Elasticities

There are two extremes in price elasticities of demand. One extreme represents total unresponsiveness of quantity demanded to price changes, which is referred to as **perfectly inelastic demand,** or zero elasticity. The other represents total responsiveness, which is referred to as infinitely or **perfectly elastic demand.**

We show perfect inelasticity in panel (a) of Figure 20-1. Notice that the quantity demanded per year is 8 million units, no matter what the price. Hence for any percentage price change, the quantity demanded will remain the same, and thus the change in the quantity demanded will be zero. Look back at our formula for computing elasticity. If the change in the quantity demanded is zero, the numerator is also zero, and a nonzero number divided into zero results in an answer of zero too. This is true at any point along the demand curve. Hence there is perfect inelasticity. At the opposite extreme is the situation depicted in panel (b) of Figure 20-1. Here we show that at a price of 30 cents, an unlimited quantity will be demanded. At a price that is only slightly above 30 cents, no quantity will be demanded. There is complete, or infinite, responsiveness at each point along this curve, and hence we call the demand schedule in panel (b) infinitely elastic.

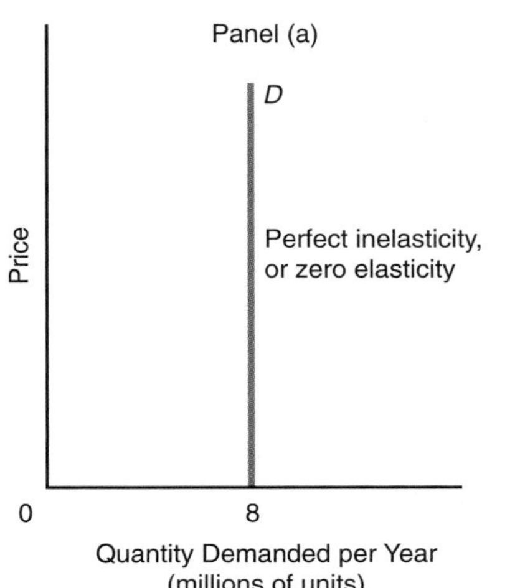

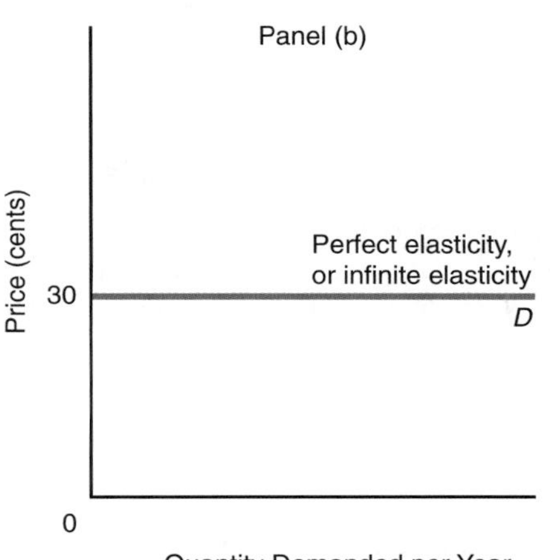

FIGURE 20-1

Extreme Price Elasticities

In panel (a), we show complete price unresponsiveness. The demand curve is vertical at the quantity of 8 million units per year. This means that the price elasticity of demand is zero. In panel (b), we show complete price responsiveness. At a price of 30 cents, in this example, consumers will demand an unlimited quantity of the particular good in question. This is a case of infinite price elasticity of demand.

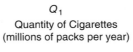

POLICY EXAMPLE

Who Pays Higher Cigarette Taxes?

In recent years, Congress and state legislatures have steadily pushed up taxes on cigarettes, which are assessed as a flat amount per physical unit of sales (that is, per standard pack of cigarettes). These taxes are paid by sellers of cigarettes from the revenues they earn from their total sales. Thus to receive the same effective price for selling a given quantity, a cigarette seller must charge an actual price that is higher by exactly the amount of the tax. As shown in panel (a) of Figure 20-2, this means that imposing a cigarette tax shifts the supply

FIGURE 20-2

Price Elasticity and a Cigarette Tax

Placing a per-pack tax on cigarettes causes the supply curve to shift upward by the amount of the tax, as illustrated in panel (a), in order for sellers to earn the same effective price for any given quantity of cigarettes they sell. If the demand for cigarettes were perfectly inelastic, as depicted in panel (b), imposing the tax causes the market price of cigarettes to rise by the amount of the tax, so that cigarette consumers would effectively pay all the tax. Conversely, if the demand for cigarettes were perfectly elastic, as shown in panel (c), the market price would not change, and sellers would pay all the tax. The quantity demanded would fall to Q_2.

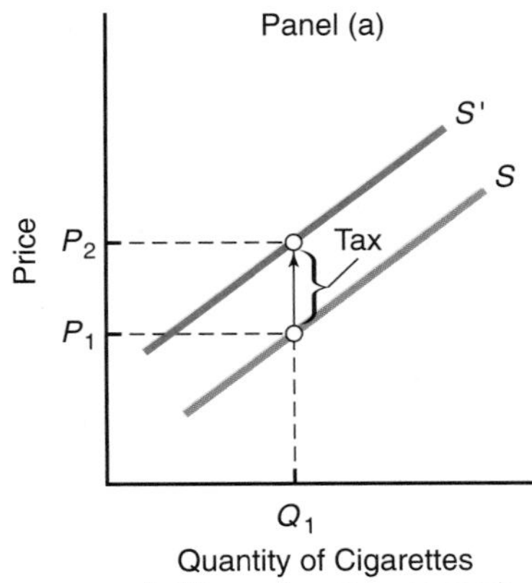

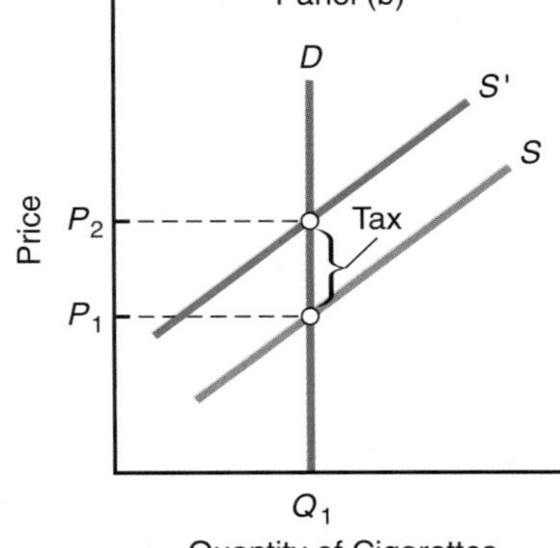

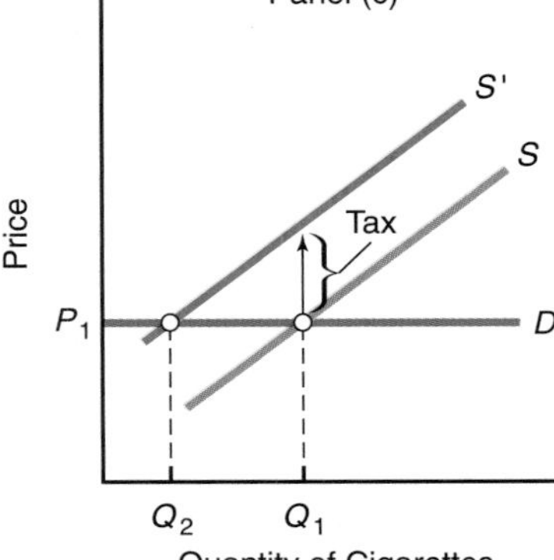

curve upward by the amount of the tax. At any given quantity of cigarettes sold, sellers supply the same quantity of cigarettes, but at a price that is higher by the amount of the tax that they will have to pass along to the government.

Who *truly* pays the tax depends on the price elasticity of demand, however. Take a look at panel (b) of Figure 20-2, which illustrates what happens to the market price in the case of perfectly inelastic demand for cigarettes. In this instance, the market price rises by the full amount that the supply curve shifts upward. This amount, of course, is the amount of the tax. Consequently, if cigarette consumers have a perfectly inelastic demand for cigarettes, they effectively pay the entire tax in the form of higher prices. Panel (c) illustrates the opposite case, in which the demand for cigarettes is perfectly elastic. In this situation, the market price is unresponsive to a tax-induced shift in the supply curve, so sellers must pay all the tax.

Realistically, many cigarette smokers are "addicted" and have a very low price elasticity of demand for cigarettes. Most studies indicate that these people are also often of lower socioeconimic status. But some consumers are "recreational smokers" who cut back on their consumption when they face higher prices. These people tend to fall into higher-income categories. Thus as the federal and state governments continue to ratchet up cigarette taxes, the burden of those taxes, in the form of higher prices for consumers, increasingly tends to fall on lower-income smokers.

For Critical Analysis

Do cigarette taxes appear to be progressive or regressive?

- One extreme elasticity occurs when a demand curve is vertical. It has zero price elasticity of demand; it is completely inelastic.
- Another extreme elasticity occurs when a demand curve is horizontal. It has completely elastic demand; its price elasticity of demand is infinite.

Who Pays the Sales Tax?
Gain further understanding of how the price elasticity of demand influences the burden of taxation.

ELASTICITY AND TOTAL REVENUES

Suppose that you are in charge of the pricing decision for a cellular telephone service company. How would you know when it is best to raise or not to raise prices? The answer depends in part on the effect of your pricing decision on total revenues, or the total receipts of your company. (The rest of the equation is, of course, your cost structure, a subject we examine in Chapter 22.) It is commonly thought that the way to increase total receipts is to increase price per unit. But is this always the case? Is it possible that a rise in price per unit could lead to a decrease in total revenues? The answers to these questions depend on the price elasticity of demand.

Let's look at Figure 20-3. In panel (a), column 1 shows the price of cellular telephone service in dollars per minute, and column 2 represents billions of minutes per year. In column 3, we multiply column 1 times column 2 to derive total revenue because total revenue is always equal to the number of units (quantity) sold times the price per unit, and in column 4, we calculate values of elasticity. Notice what happens to total revenues throughout the schedule. They rise steadily as the price rises from 10 cents to 50 cents per minute; but when the price rises further to 60 cents per minute, total revenues remain constant at $3 billion. At prices per minute higher than 60 cents, total revenues fall as price increases. Indeed, if prices are above 60 cents per minute, total revenues can be increased only by *cutting* prices, not by raising them.

FIGURE 20-3

The Relationship Between Price Elasticity of Demand and Total Revenues for Cellular Phone Service

In panel (a), we show the elastic, unit-elastic, and inelastic sections of the demand schedule according to whether a reduction in price increases total revenues, causes them to remain constant, or causes them to decrease, respectively. In panel (b), we show these regions graphically on the demand curve. In panel (c), we show them on the total revenue curve.

Panel (a)

(1) Price, *P*, per Minute of cellular phone service	(2) Quantity Demanded, *D* (billions of minutes)	(3) Total Revenue ($ billions) = (1) X (2)	(4) Elasticity, $E_p = \frac{\text{Change in } Q}{(Q_1 + Q_2)/2} \div \frac{\text{Change in } P}{(P_1 + P_2)/2}$	
$1.10	0	0		
			21.000	Elastic
1.00	1	1.0		
			6.330	Elastic
.90	2	1.8		
			3.400	Elastic
.80	3	2.4		
			2.143	Elastic
.70	4	2.8		
			1.144	Elastic
.60	5	3.0		
			1.000	Unit-elastic
.50	6	3.0		
			.692	Inelastic
.40	7	2.8		
			.467	Inelastic
.30	8	2.4		
			.294	Inelastic
.20	9	1.8		
			.158	Inelastic
.10	10	1.0		

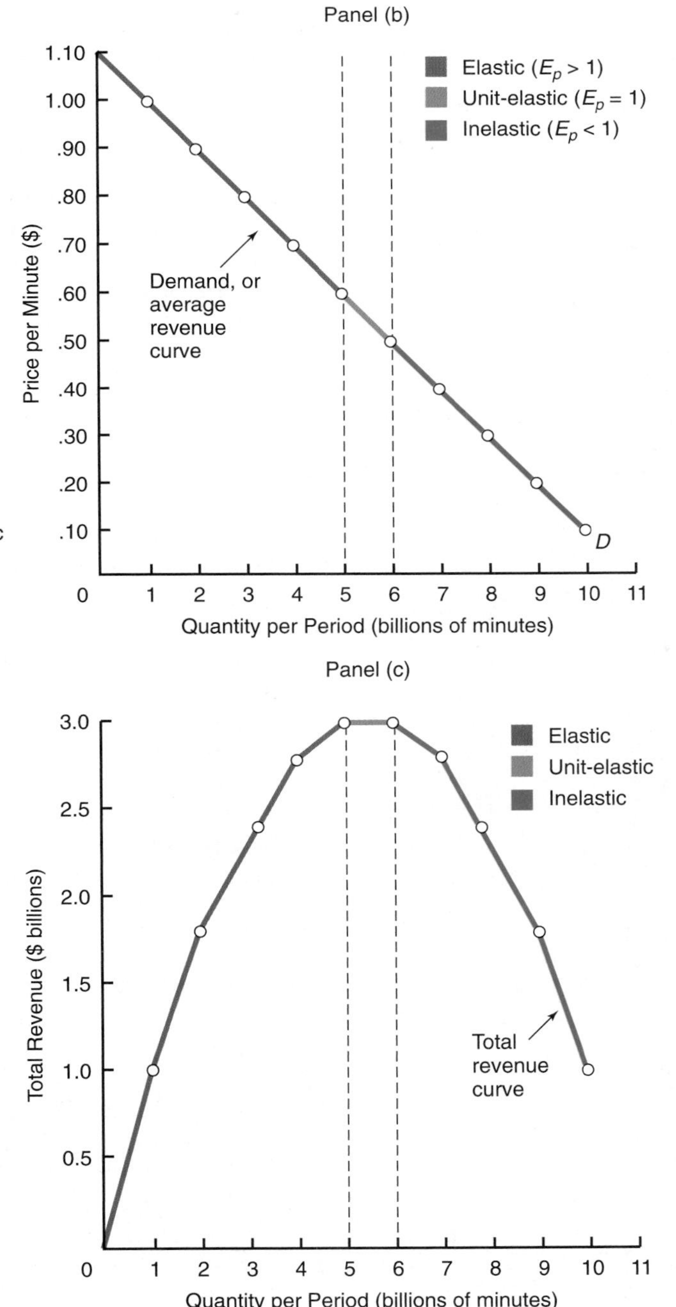

Labeling Elasticity

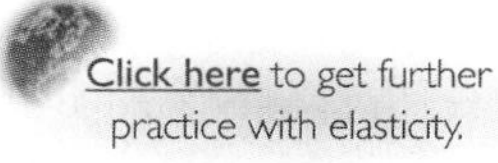

Click here to get further practice with elasticity.

The relationship between price and quantity on the demand schedule is given in columns 1 and 2 of panel (a) in Figure 20-3. In panel (b), the demand curve, *D,* representing that schedule is drawn. In panel (c), the total revenue curve representing the data in column 3 is drawn. Notice first the level of these curves at small quantities. The demand curve is at a maximum height, but total revenue is zero, which makes sense according to this demand schedule—at a price of $1.10 and above, no units will be purchased, and therefore total revenue will be zero. As price is lowered, we travel down the demand curve, and total revenues increase until price is 60 cents per minute, remain constant from 60 cents to 50 cents per minute, and then fall at lower unit prices. Corresponding to those three sections, demand is elastic, unit-elastic, and inelastic. Hence we have three relationships among the three types of price elasticity and total revenues.

- *Elastic demand.* A negative relationship exists between small changes in price and changes in total revenues. That is to say, if price is lowered, total revenues will rise when the firm faces demand that is elastic, and if it raises price, total revenues will fall. Consider another example. If the price of Diet Coke were raised by 25 percent and the price of all other soft drinks remained constant, the quantity demanded of Diet Coke would probably fall dramatically. The decrease in quantity demanded due to the increase in the price of Diet Coke would lead in this example to a reduction in the total revenues of the Coca-Cola Company. Therefore, if demand is elastic, price and total revenues will move in *opposite* directions.
- *Unit-elastic demand.* Changes in price do not change total revenues. When the firm is facing demand that is unit-elastic, if it increases price, total revenues will not change; if it decreases price, total revenues will not change either.
- *Inelastic demand.* A positive relationship exists between changes in price and total revenues. When the firm is facing demand that is inelastic, if it raises price, total revenues will go up; if it lowers price, total revenues will fall. Consider another example. You have just invented a cure for the common cold that has been approved by the Food and Drug Administration for sale to the public. You are not sure what price you should charge, so you start out with a price of $1 per pill. You sell 20 million pills at that price over a year. The next year, you decide to raise the price by 25 percent, to $1.25. The number of pills you sell drops to 18 million per year. The price increase of 25 percent has led to a 10 percent decrease in quantity demanded. Your total revenues, however, will rise to $22.5 million because of the price increase. We therefore conclude that if demand is inelastic, price and total revenues move in the *same* direction.

The elastic, unit-elastic, and inelastic areas of the demand curve are shown in Figure 20-3. For prices from $1.10 per minute of cellular phone time to 60 cents per minute, as price decreases, total revenues rise from zero to $3 billion. Demand is price-elastic. When price changes from 60 cents to 50 cents, however, total revenues remain constant at $3 billion; demand is unit-elastic. Finally, when price falls from 50 cents to 10 cents, total revenues decrease from $3 billion to $1 billion; demand is inelastic. In panels (b) and (c) of Figure 20-3, we have labeled the sections of the demand curve accordingly, and we have also shown how total revenues first rise, then remain constant, and finally fall.

The relationship between price elasticity of demand and total revenues brings together some important microeconomic concepts. Total revenues, as we have noted, are the product of price per unit times number of units sold. The law of demand states that along a given demand curve, price and quantity changes will move in opposite directions: One increases as the other decreases. Consequently, what happens to the product of price times quantity

TABLE 20-1
Relationship Between Price Elasticity of Demand and Total Revenues

Price Elasticity of Demand		Effect of Price Change on Total Revenues (TR)	
		Price Decrease	Price Increase
Inelastic	($E_p < 1$)	TR ↓	TR ↑
Unit-elastic	($E_p = 1$)	No change in TR	No change in TR
Elastic	($E_p > 1$)	TR ↑	TR ↓

depends on which of the opposing changes exerts a greater force on total revenues. But this is just what price elasticity of demand is designed to measure—responsiveness of quantity demanded to a change in price. The relationship between price elasticity of demand and total revenues is summarized in Table 20-1.

INTERNATIONAL EXAMPLE

A Pricing Decision at Disneyland Paris

Several years after it opened with great fanfare, the $4 billion investment in Disneyland Paris (formerly called EuroDisney) was in trouble. In an attempt to improve profits (actually, decrease losses), Disney management decided to lower prices. Entrance fees during peak periods (April 1 to October 1) dropped from 250 francs (about $50) to 195 francs (about $40). Was this 22 percent reduction in ticket prices a good management strategy for Disney officials? That depends in part on what happened to total revenues. As it turned out, park attendance increased by 700,000 visitors, and total revenues increased by more than 22 percent. This indicates that the demand for Disneyland Paris was elastic in the price range of $40 to $50.

For Critical Analysis

What other factors may have affected attendance at Disneyland Paris?

CONCEPTS IN BRIEF

- Price elasticity of demand is related to total revenues (and total consumer expenditures).
- When demand is *elastic,* the change in price elicits a change in total revenues (and total consumer expenditures) in the direction opposite that of the price change.
- When demand is *unit-elastic,* a change in price elicits no change in total revenues (or in total consumer expenditures).
- When demand is *inelastic,* a change in price elicits a change in total revenues (and in consumer expenditures) in the same direction as the price change.

DETERMINANTS OF THE PRICE ELASTICITY OF DEMAND 

We have learned how to calculate the price elasticity of demand. We know that theoretically it ranges numerically from zero, completely inelastic, to infinity, completely elastic. What we would like to do now is come up with a list of the determinants of the price elasticity of demand. The price elasticity of demand for a particular commodity at any price depends, at a minimum, on the following:

- The existence, number, and quality of substitutes
- The percentage of a consumer's total budget devoted to purchases of that commodity
- The length of time allowed for adjustment to changes in the price of the commodity

Existence of Substitutes

The closer the substitutes for a particular commodity and the more substitutes there are, the greater will be its price elasticity of demand. At the limit, if there is a perfect substitute, the elasticity of demand for the commodity will be infinity. Thus even the slightest increase in the commodity's price will cause an enormous reduction in the quantity demanded: Quantity demanded will fall to zero. We are really talking about two goods that the consumer believes are exactly alike and equally desirable, like dollar bills whose only difference is serial numbers. When we talk about less extreme examples, we can speak only in terms of the number and the similarity of substitutes that are available. Thus we will find that the more narrowly we define a good, the closer and greater will be the number of substitutes available. For example, the demand for a Diet Coke may be highly elastic because consumers can switch to Diet Pepsi. The demand for diet drinks in general, however, is relatively less elastic because there are fewer substitutes.

Share of Budget

We know that the greater the percentage of a total budget spent on the commodity, the greater the person's price elasticity of demand for that commodity. The demand for pepper is thought to be very inelastic merely because individuals spend so little on it relative to their total budgets. In contrast, the demand for things such as transportation and housing is thought to be far more elastic because they occupy a large part of people's budgets—changes in their prices cannot be ignored so easily without sacrificing a lot of other alternative goods that could be purchased.

Consider a numerical example. A household earns $40,000 a year. It purchases $4 of pepper per year and $4,000 of transportation services. Now consider the spending power of this family when the price of pepper and the price of transportation both double. If the household buys the same amount of pepper, it will now spend $8. It will thus have to reduce other expenditures by $4. This $4 represents only .01 percent of the entire household budget. By contrast, a doubling of transportation costs requires that the family spend $8,000, or $4,000 more on transportation, if it is to purchase the same quantity. That increased expenditure on transportation of $4,000 represents 10 percent of total expenditures that must be switched from other purchases. We would therefore predict that the household will react differently to the doubling of prices for pepper than it will for transportation. It will buy almost the same amount of pepper but will buy significantly less transportation.

Time for Adjustment

When the price of a commodity changes and that price change persists, more people will learn about it. Further, consumers will be better able to revise their consumption patterns the longer the time period they have to do so. And in fact, the longer the time they do take, the less costly it will be for them to engage in this revision of consumption patterns. Consider a price decrease. The longer the price decrease persists, the greater will be the number of new uses that consumers will discover for the particular commodity, and the greater will be the number of new users of that particular commodity.

It is possible to make a very strong statement about the relationship between the price elasticity of demand and the time allowed for adjustment:

> The longer any price change persists, the greater the elasticity of demand, other things held constant. Elasticity of demand is greater in the long run than in the short run.

Let's take an example. Suppose that the price of electricity goes up 50 percent. How do you adjust in the short run? You can turn the lights off more often, you can stop using the stereo as much as you do, and so on. Otherwise it's very difficult to cut back on your consumption of electricity. In the long run, though, you can devise methods to reduce your consumption. Instead of using electric heaters, the next time you have a house built you will install gas heaters. Instead of using an electric stove, the next time you move you will have a gas stove installed. You will purchase fluorescent bulbs because they use less electricity. The more time you have to think about it, the more ways you will find to cut your electricity consumption. We would expect, therefore, that the short-run demand curve for electricity would be relatively less elastic (in the price range around P_e), as demonstrated by D_1 in Figure 20-4. However, the long-run demand curve may exhibit much more elasticity (in the neighborhood of P_e), as demonstrated by D_3. Indeed, we can think of an entire family of demand curves such as those depicted in the figure. The short-run demand curve is for the period when there is no time for adjustment. As more time is allowed, the demand curve goes first to D_2 and then all the way to D_3. Thus in the neighborhood of P_e, elasticity differs for each of these curves. It is greater for the less steep curves (but slope alone does not measure elasticity for the entire curve).

How to Define the Short Run and the Long Run. We've mentioned the short run and the long run. Is the short run one week, two weeks, one month, two months? Is the long run three years, four years, five years? The answer is that there is no single answer. What we mean by the long run is the period of time necessary for consumers to make a full adjustment to a given price change, all other things held constant. In the case of the demand for electricity, the long run will be however long it takes consumers to switch over to cheaper sources of heating, to buy houses that are more energy-efficient, to purchase

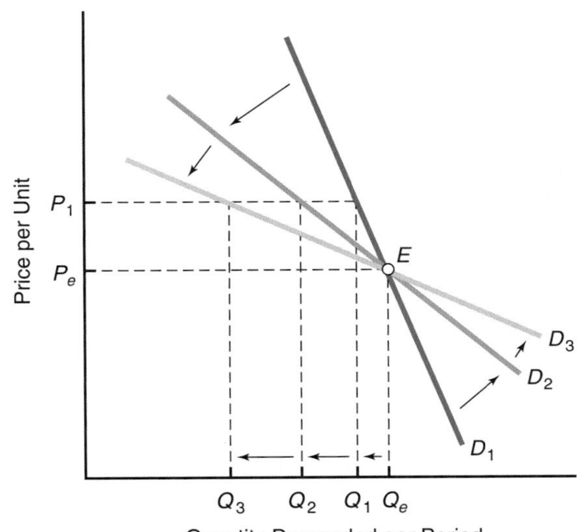

FIGURE 20-4

Short-Run and Long-Run Price Elasticity of Demand

Consider an equilibrium situation in which the market price is P_e and the quantity demanded is Q_e. Then there is a price increase to P_1. In the short run, as evidenced by the demand curve D_1, we move from equilibrium quantity demanded, Q_e, to Q_1. After more time is allowed for adjustment, the demand curve rotates at original price P_e to D_2. Quantity demanded falls again, now to Q_2. After even more time is allowed for adjustment, the demand curve rotates at price P_e to D_3. At the higher price P_1, in the long run, the quantity demanded falls all the way to Q_3.

appliances that are more energy-efficient, and so on. The long-run elasticity of demand for electricity therefore relates to a period of at least several years. The short run—by default—is any period less than the long run.

EXAMPLE

What Do Real-World Price Elasticities of Demand Look Like?

In Table 20-2, we present demand elasticities for selected goods. None of them is zero, and the largest is 3.8—a far cry from infinity. Remember that even though we are leaving off the negative sign, there is an inverse relationship between price and quantity demanded, and the minus sign is understood. Also remember that these elasticities represent averages over given price ranges. Choosing different price ranges would yield different elasticity estimates for these goods.

Economists have consistently found that estimated price elasticities of demand are greater in the long run than in the short run, as seen in Table 20-2. There you see, for example, in the far-right column that the long-run price elasticity of demand for tires and related items is 1.2, whereas the estimate for the short run is .8. Throughout the table, you see that all estimates of long-run price elasticities of demand exceed their short-run counterparts.

For Critical Analysis

Explain the intuitive reasoning behind the difference between long-run and short-run price elasticity of demand.

TABLE 20-2

Demand Elasticity for Selected Goods

Here are estimated demand elasticities for selected goods. All of them are negative, although we omit the minus sign. We have given some estimates of the long-run price elasticities of demand. The long run is associated with the time necessary for consumers to adjust fully to any given price change.

	Estimated Elasticity	
Category	Short Run	Long Run
Lamb	2.7	—
Bread	.2	—
Tires and related items	.8	1.2
Auto repair and related services	1.4	2.4
Radio and television repair	.5	3.8
Legitimate theater and opera	.2	.3
Motion pictures	.9	3.7
Foreign travel by U.S. residents	.1	1.8
Taxicabs	.6	—
Local public transportation	.6	1.2
Intercity bus	.6	2.2
Electricity	.1	1.8
Jewelry and watches	.4	.6

CROSS PRICE ELASTICITY OF DEMAND 

In Chapter 3, we discussed the effect of a change in the price of one good on the demand for a related good. We defined substitutes and complements in terms of whether a reduction in the price of one caused a decrease or an increase, respectively, in the demand for the other. If the price of compact disks is held constant, the amount of CDs demanded (at any price) will certainly be influenced by the price of a close substitute such as audiocassettes. If the price of stereo speakers is held constant, the amount of stereo speakers demanded (at any price) will certainly be affected by changes in the price of stereo amplifiers.

What we now need to do is come up with a numerical measure of the price responsiveness of demand to the prices of related goods. This is called the **cross price elasticity of demand (E_{xy})**, which is defined as the percentage change in the demand for one good (a shift in the demand curve) divided by the percentage change in the price of the related good. In equation form, the cross price elasticity of demand for good X with good Y is

Cross price elasticity of demand (E_{xy}) 
The percentage change in the demand for one good (holding its price constant) divided by the percentage change in the price of a related good.

$$E_{xy} = \frac{\text{percentage change in demand for good X}}{\text{percentage change in price of good Y}}$$

Alternatively, the cross price elasticity of demand for good Y with good X would use the percentage change in the demand for good Y as the numerator and the percentage change in the price of good X as the denominator.

When two goods are substitutes, the cross price elasticity of demand will be positive. For example, when the price of margarine goes up, the demand for butter will rise too as consumers shift away from the now relatively more expensive margarine to butter. A producer of margarine could benefit from a numerical estimate of the cross price elasticity of demand between butter and margarine. For example, if the price of butter went up by 10 percent and the margarine producer knew that the cross price elasticity of demand was 1, the margarine producer could estimate that the demand for margarine would also go up by 10 percent at any given price. Plans for increasing margarine production could then be made.

FAQ *Are people substituting away from public libraries to the Internet as their main source of information?*

Yes. Although careful studies have not yet been done, there is considerable anecdotal evidence that the relatively inexpensive accessibility of the Internet together with the availability of Internet search engines has reduced the price of on-line information services. This has induced a decline in the demand for traditional public library services. No one has yet explicitly computed the cross price elasticity of demand for traditional library services. One key indicator that extensive substitution is taking place, however, is that libraries are hiring fewer librarians. Today, they mainly wish to hire people skilled in information technologies—people who can assist visitors who mainly desire to use the libraries' computers to search the Internet.

When two related goods are complements, the cross price elasticity of demand will be negative (and we will not disregard the minus sign). For example, when the price of stereo amplifiers goes up, the demand for stereo speakers will fall. This is because as prices of amplifiers increase, the quantity of amplifiers demanded will naturally decrease. Because amplifiers and stereo speakers are often used together, the demand for speakers is likely to fall. Any manufacturer of stereo speakers must take this into account in making production plans.

If goods are completely unrelated, their cross price elasticity of demand will be zero.

INCOME ELASTICITY OF DEMAND

Income elasticity of demand (E_i)

The percentage change in demand for any good, holding its price constant, divided by the percentage change in income; the responsiveness of demand to changes in income, holding the good's relative price constant.

In Chapter 3, we discussed the determinants of demand. One of those determinants was income. Briefly, we can apply our understanding of elasticity to the relationship between changes in income and changes in demand. We measure the responsiveness of quantity demanded to income changes by the **income elasticity of demand (E_i):**

$$E_i = \frac{\text{percentage change in demand}}{\text{percentage change in income}}$$

holding relative price constant.

Income elasticity of demand refers to a *horizontal shift* in the demand curve in response to changes in income, whereas price elasticity of demand refers to a *movement along* the curve in response to price changes. Thus income elasticity of demand is calculated at a given price, and price elasticity of demand is calculated at a given income.

A simple example will demonstrate how income elasticity of demand can be computed. Table 20-3 gives the relevant data. The product in question is compact disks. We assume that the price of CDs remains constant relative to other prices. In period 1, six CDs per month are purchased. Income per month is \$400. In period 2, monthly income increases to \$600, and the quantity of CDs demanded per month is increased to eight. We can apply the following calculation:

$$E_i = \frac{(8-6)/6}{(600-400)/400} = \frac{1/3}{1/2} = \frac{2}{3} = .667$$

Hence measured income elasticity of demand for CDs for the individual represented in this example is .667. Note that this holds only for the move from six CDs to eight CDs purchased per month. If the situation were reversed, with income decreasing from \$600 to \$400 per month and CDs purchased dropping from eight to six CDs per month, the calculation becomes

$$E_i = \frac{(6-8)/8}{(400-600)/600} = \frac{-2/8}{-1/3} = \frac{-1/4}{-1/3} = \frac{3}{4} = .75$$

In this case, the measured income elasticity of demand is equal to .75.

To get the same income elasticity of demand over the same range of values regardless of direction of change (increase or decrease), we can use the same formula that we used in computing the price elasticity of demand. When doing so, we have

$$E_i = \frac{\text{change in quantity}}{\text{sum of quantities}/2} \div \frac{\text{change in income}}{\text{sum of incomes}/2}$$

Elasticities and Applications
Review additional elasticity concepts and choose the type of elasticity you wish to study.

You have just been introduced to three types of elasticities. All three elasticities are important in influencing the quantity demanded for most goods. Reasonably accurate estimates of these can go a long way toward making accurate forecasts of demand for goods or services.

TABLE 20-3
How Income Affects Quantity of CDs Demanded

Period	Number of CDs Demanded per Month	Income per Month
1	6	\$400
2	8	600

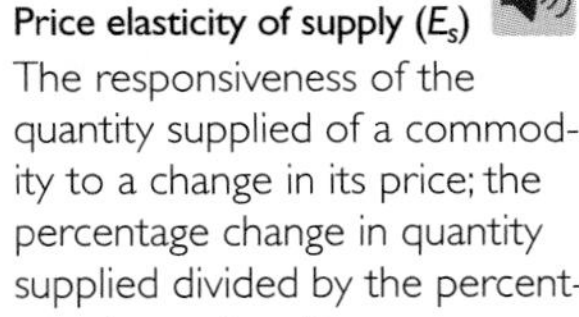

- Some determinants of price elasticity of demand are (1) the existence, number, and quality of substitutes; (2) the share of the total budget spent on the good in question; and (3) the length of time allowed for adjustment to a change in prices.
- Cross price elasticity of demand measures one good's demand responsiveness to another's price changes. For substitutes, it is positive; for complements, it is negative.
- Income elasticity of demand tells you by what percentage demand will change for a particular percentage change in income.

ELASTICITY OF SUPPLY

The **price elasticity of supply (E_s)** is defined similarly to the price elasticity of demand. Supply elasticities are generally positive; this is because at higher prices, larger quantities will generally be forthcoming from suppliers. The definition of the price elasticity of supply is as follows:

$$E_s = \frac{\text{percentage change in quantity supplied}}{\text{percentage change in price}}$$

Price elasticity of supply (E_s) The responsiveness of the quantity supplied of a commodity to a change in its price; the percentage change in quantity supplied divided by the percentage change in price.

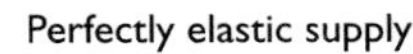

Classifying Supply Elasticities

Just as with demand, there are different ranges of supply elasticities. They are similar in definition to the ranges of demand elasticities.

If a 1 percent increase in price elicits a greater than 1 percent increase in the quantity supplied, we say that at the particular price in question on the supply schedule, *supply is elastic.* The most extreme elastic supply is called **perfectly elastic supply**—the slightest reduction in price will cause quantity supplied to fall to zero.

If, conversely, a 1 percent increase in price elicits a less than 1 percent increase in the quantity supplied, we refer to that as an *inelastic supply.* The most extreme inelastic supply is called **perfectly inelastic supply**—no matter what the price, the quantity supplied remains the same.

If the percentage change in the quantity supplied is just equal to the percentage change in the price, we call this *unit-elastic supply.*

We show in Figure 20-5 two supply schedules, S and S'. You can tell at a glance, without reading the labels, which one is infinitely elastic and which one is perfectly inelastic.

Perfectly elastic supply A supply characterized by a reduction in quantity supplied to zero when there is the slightest decrease in price.

Perfectly inelastic supply A supply for which quantity supplied remains constant, no matter what happens to price.

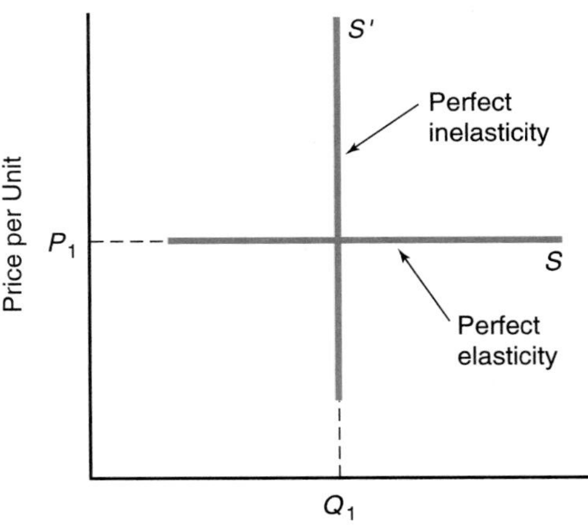

FIGURE 20-5
The Extremes in Supply Curves
Here we have drawn two extremes of supply schedules; S is a perfectly elastic supply curve; S' is a perfectly inelastic one. In the former, an unlimited quantity will be supplied at price P_1. In the latter, no matter what the price, the quantity supplied will be Q_1. An example of S' might be the supply curve for fresh fish on the morning the boats come in.

As you might expect, most supply schedules exhibit elasticities that are somewhere between zero and infinity.

Price Elasticity of Supply and Length of Time for Adjustment

We pointed out earlier that the longer the time period allowed for adjustment, the greater the price elasticity of demand. It turns out that the same proposition applies to supply. The longer the time for adjustment, the more elastic the supply curve. Consider why this is true:

1. The longer the time allowed for adjustment, the more resources can flow into (or out of) an industry through expansion (or contraction) of existing firms.
2. The longer the time allowed for adjustment, the more firms are able to figure out ways to increase (or decrease) production in an industry.

We therefore talk about short-run and long-run price elasticities of supply. The short run is defined as the time period during which full adjustment has not yet taken place. The long run is the time period during which firms have been able to adjust fully to the change in price.

Consider an increase in the price of housing. In the immediate run, when there is no time allowed for any adjustment, the amount of housing offered for rent or for sale is perfectly inelastic. However, as more time is allowed for adjustment, current owners of the housing stock can find ways to increase the amount of housing they will offer for rent from given buildings. The owner of a large house can decide, for example, to have two children move into one room so that a "new" extra bedroom can be rented out. This can also be done by the owner of a large house who decides to move into an apartment and rent each floor of the house to a separate family. Thus the quantity of housing supplied will increase. With more time, landlords will find it profitable to build new rental units.

We can show a whole set of supply curves similar to the ones we generated for demand. As Figure 20-6 shows, when nothing can be done in the immediate run, the supply curve is vertical, S_1. As more time is allowed for adjustment, the supply curve rotates to S_2 and then to S_3, becoming more elastic as it rotates.

FIGURE 20-6 

Short-Run and Long-Run Price Elasticity of Supply

Consider a situation in which the price is P_e and the quantity supplied is Q_e. In the immediate run, we hypothesize a vertical supply curve, S_1. With the price increase to P_1, therefore, there will be no change in the short run in quantity supplied; it will remain at Q_e. Given some time for adjustment, the supply curve will rotate to S_2. The new amount supplied will increase to Q_1. The long-run supply curve is shown by S_3. The amount supplied again increases to Q_2.

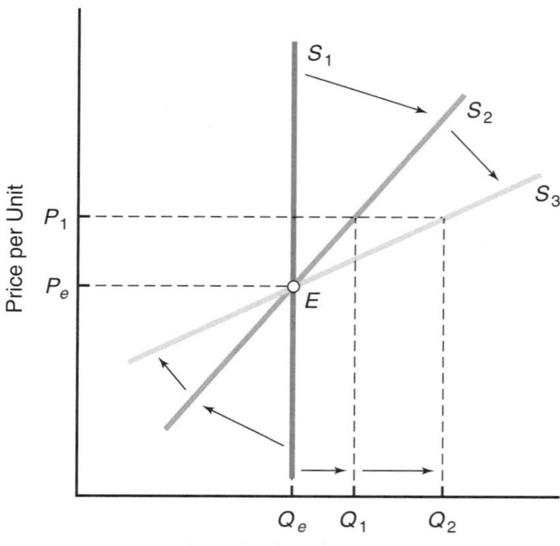

INTERNATIONAL EXAMPLE

French Truffle Production Takes a Nosedive

Some of the best truffles in the world come from the seven *départements* (counties) in the middle of France that make up the Périgord region. Black truffles are often called "black diamonds" because they are so expensive and also because they have a faceted skin. Their official name is *Tuber melanosporum.* Ranging in size from that of a hazelnut to that of a baseball, truffles are sliced fine and used in cooking as a pungent addition to many refined dishes. Their prices range from $250 to $500 a pound wholesale to as much as $1,000 a pound retail. Yet things are not well in the French truffle industry. The Chinese have started exporting their version of truffles, considered inferior by the French but popular nonetheless in the open market. By 1996, the average price for French-grown truffles had dropped by 30 percent. Many French farmers, fed up with lower prices, simply gave up on truffles. French production subsequently decreased by 25 percent. Hence the estimated short-run price elasticity of supply of French truffles was .83. (Why?)

For Critical Analysis

There is a company in the United States that will sell you trees inoculated with the truffle organism so that you can "grow your own." How will this affect the price of truffles and thus French production?

CONCEPTS IN BRIEF

- Price elasticity of supply is calculated by dividing the percentage change in quantity supplied by the percentage change in price.
- Usually, price elasticities of supply are positive—higher prices yield larger quantities supplied.
- Long-run supply curves are more elastic than short-run supply curves because the longer the time allowed, the more resources can flow into or out of an industry when price changes.

NETNOMICS

How Clever Internet Companies Infer Their Customers' Price Elasticity of Demand

As you learned in this chapter, a company that wishes to increase its revenues should raise the price it charges customers with an inelastic demand for the goods it sells. By contrast, a firm can bring about an increase in its revenues by reducing the price it charges customers whose demand is elastic.

Increasingly, companies are using the Internet to try to have it both ways. One California software firm has developed a program that allows Internet sellers to track the shopping patterns of customers who visit their Web sites. The software studies a Web surfer's "clickstream"—the manner in which the customer navigates through the site. For example, if the customer quickly zeroes in on a specific item and makes little effort to shop around for better prices, the software program tags the customer as one whose demand for that item is likely to be relatively inelastic. The program then automatically quotes a relatively high price. If another Web surfer who visits the site behaves like a price-sensitive shopper—perhaps by comparing many different products without jumping to buy—the program concludes that the customer's demand is more likely to be relatively elastic. It then automatically quotes a lower price to this customer.

Thus new technologies are making it easier for Net-based firms to increase their revenues, and thus their profits, by charging higher prices to customers whose price elasticity of demand is less than 1 and lower prices to customers whose price elasticity of demand is greater than 1. (Charging different prices for the same product, as you will learn in Chapter 27, is known as *price discrimination.*) Of course, this is an old idea extended to a high-tech age. After all, makers of breakfast cereals, disposable diapers, and other retail products have done the same sort of thing for years by offering rebates to people who save boxtops or proof-of-purchase seals. These rebates effectively amount to lower prices for penny-pinchers, whose demand is relatively elastic. Busy people with less elastic demands end up paying the full, undiscounted, and effectively higher retail price.

What remains to be seen is whether Internet customers will respond to the new pricing strategies of Internet sellers. Will spendthrifts with a low price elasticity of demand try to masquerade as skinflints with a high price elasticity of demand by displaying artificially cautious clickstreams? Probably not. People with a low price elasticity of demand are typically in a hurry to get what they want. They will not wish to waste precious time trying to fool Internet sellers' pricing programs.

ISSUES & APPLICATIONS

Discovering the Value of Garbage

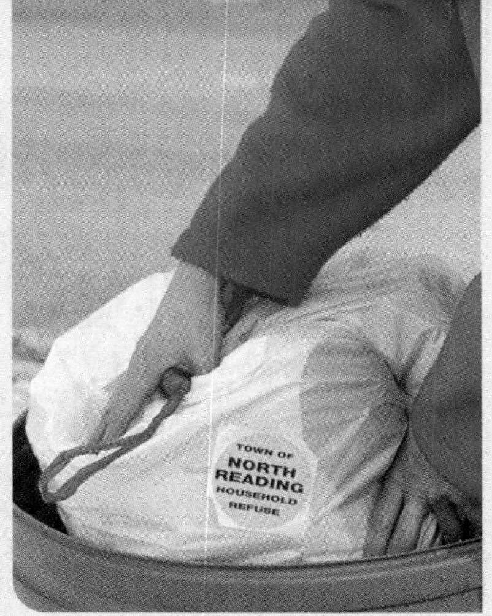

Each day, a massive volume of garbage flows away from the driveways and doorsteps of American homes. It has to go somewhere. Although some trash is incinerated, today most goes into landfills. Increasing land values, however, have put landfill space at a premium for municipalities that collect and dump their residents' trash.

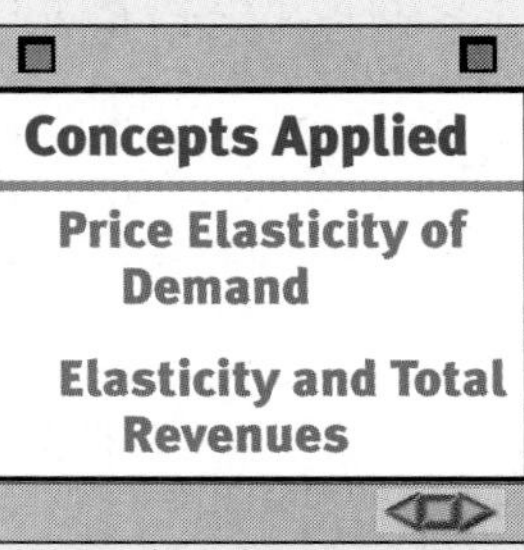

Concepts Applied
Price Elasticity of Demand
Elasticity and Total Revenues

Trying to Make the Market Work

The town of Charlottesville, Virginia, recently experimented with charging a per-unit price for trash collection. Previously, like most municipalities, Charlottesville had financed its trash collection from property taxes. Of course, this meant that the effective price to a household of putting each additional bag of trash out for curbside collection was zero. Once they had paid their taxes, Charlottesville residents could set out as many bags of garbage as they wished on trash pickup day.

In light of the high cost of finding a place to put all the town's trash, Charlottesville decided to try to let market forces work by charging a fee of 80 cents per 32-gallon bag or can of residential garbage collected at the curb. Just as predicted by the law of demand, the amount of trash that Charlottesville's residents wished to dump declined following the imposition of this fee. The percentage reduction in quantity of trash collection services demanded was 37 percent, which translated into about 1,500 fewer tons of trash for the town to handle each year. Thus charging a fee to haul trash from people's homes significantly reduced the volume of trash collected in Charlottesville by over one-third. Because the initial explicit price of dumping trash was zero, the change in price to 80 cents per bag occurred along the inelastic range of the demand curve for trash collection services. Thus raising the per-bag collection fee increased the town's revenues from trash collection—from zero to positive revenues.

Some Unintended Consequences

What did Charlottesville residents do with all the garbage they withheld from collection following the imposition of the per-bag fee? Residents found that they could recycle about a third of it, and they were able to compost roughly another third of the garbage. Unfortunately, some residents apparently illegally engaged in "midnight dumping": To avoid paying the fee, they dumped trash along roadsides and in vacant lots. Trying to increase enforcement of antilittering laws was a costly activity for the town. So was the cost of administering the pricing program. Printing tags for all the trash bags the town collected and keeping track of residents' payments turned out to be a high-cost activity also.

On net, it turned out that the costs of enforcing and administering the pricing program were so high that trash collection revenues failed to cover the costs of the program. Thus Charlottesville suffered an economic loss on its trash collection business. In light of Charlottesville's experience, other municipalities are currently contemplating ways to implement similar pricing programs while containing administrative costs.

FOR CRITICAL ANALYSIS

1. If the demand for trash collection services is inelastic over a relatively large range of prices above 80 cents per bag, how might Charlottesville try to push up its trash collection revenues to earn a profit from hauling trash?
2. Critics of city trash collection pricing programs contend that they are unlikely to be profitable whenever governments administer the programs and argue that trash collection should be done by private firms. Do you agree with this perspective? Why or why not?

SUMMARY DISCUSSION OF LEARNING OBJECTIVES

1. **Expressing and Calculating the Price Elasticity of Demand:** The price elasticity of demand is the responsiveness of the quantity demanded of a good to a change in the price of the good. It is the percentage change in quantity demanded divided by the percentage change in price. To calculate the price elasticity of demand for relatively small changes in price, the percentage change in quantity demanded is equal to the change in the quantity resulting from a price change divided by the average of the initial and final quantities, and the percentage change in price is equal to the price change divided by the average of the initial and final prices.
2. **The Relationship Between the Price Elasticity of Demand and Total Revenues:** Demand is elastic when the price elasticity of demand exceeds 1, and over the elastic range of a demand curve, an increase in price reduces total revenues. Demand is inelastic when the price elasticity of demand is less than 1, and over this range of a demand curve, an increase in price raises total revenues. Finally, demand is unit-elastic when the price elasticity of demand equals 1, and over this range of a demand curve, an increase in price does not affect total revenues.
3. **Factors That Determine the Price Elasticity of Demand:** Three factors affect the price elasticity of demand. If there are more close substitutes for a good, the price elasticity of demand increases. The price elasticity of demand for a good also tends to be higher when a larger portion of a person's budget is spent on the good. In addition, if people have a longer period of time to adjust to a price change and change their consumption patterns, the price elasticity of demand tends to be higher.
4. **The Cross Price Elasticity of Demand and Using It to Determine Whether Two Goods Are Substitutes or Complements:** The cross price elasticity of demand for a good is the percentage change in the demand for that good divided by the percentage change in the price of a related good. If two goods are substitutes in consumption, a percentage increase in the price of one of the goods induces a percentage increase in the demand for the other good, so that the cross price elasticity of demand is positive. By contrast, if two goods are complements in consumption, a percentage increase in the price of one of the goods brings about a percentage decrease in the demand for the other good, so that the cross price elasticity of demand is negative.
5. **The Income Elasticity of Demand:** The income elasticity of demand for any good is the responsiveness of the demand for the good to a change in income, holding the good's relative price un changed. It is equal to the percentage change in demand for the good divided by the percentage change in income.
6. **Classifying Supply Elasticities and How the Length of Time for Adjustment Affects the Price Elasticity of Supply:** The price elasticity of supply is equal to the percentage change in quantity supplied divided by the percentage change in price. If the price elasticity of supply is greater than 1, supply is elastic, and if the price elasticity of supply is less than 1, supply is inelastic. Supply is unit-elastic if the price elasticity of supply equals 1. Supply is more likely to be elastic when sellers have more time to adjust to price changes. One reason for this is that the more time sellers have to adjust, the more resources can flow into (or out of) an industry via expansion (or contraction) of firms. Another reason is that the longer the time allowed for adjustment, the more firms are able to find ways to increase (or decrease) production in response to a price increase (or decrease).

Key Terms and Concepts

Cross price elasticity of demand (E_{xy}) (495)

Elastic demand (486)

Income elasticity of demand (E_i) (496)

Inelastic demand (486)

Perfectly elastic demand (497)

Perfectly elastic supply (486)

Perfectly inelastic demand (486)

Perfectly inelastic supply (497)

Price elasticity of demand (E_p) (483)

Price elasticity of supply (E_s) (497)

Unit elasticity of demand (486)

Problems

Answers to the odd-numbered problems appear at the back of the book.

20-1. A student organization finds that when it prices shirts emblazoned with the college logo at $10, the organization sells 150 per week. When the price is reduced to $9, the organization sells 200 per week. Based on this information, calculate the price elasticity of demand for logo-emblazoned shirts.

20-2. Table 20-2 indicates that the price elasticity of demand for motion picture tickets is 0.9. If a theater raises the price of a movie ticket from $5 to $6, by what percentage should it expect the quantity of tickets sold to change?

20-3. When Joe's Campus Grill priced its famous hamburgers at $1, it sold 200 a week. When the price was $2, Joe's sold only 100 a week. Based on this information, calculate the price elasticity of demand for Joe's hamburgers.

20-4. Using the information in Problem 20-3, calculate the price elasticity of demand. Is demand elastic, unit-elastic, or inelastic?

20-5. It is difficult, if not impossible, to find commodities with perfectly elastic or perfectly inelastic demand. We can, however, find commodities that lie near these extremes. Characterize the following goods as being near perfectly elastic or near perfectly inelastic.

a. Corn grown and harvested by a small farmer in Iowa
b. Heroin for a drug addict
c. The services of the only dentist in town
d. The required text for the only section of a required economics course

20-6. A craftsman who makes guitars by hand finds that when he prices his guitars at $800, his annual revenue is $64,000. When he prices his guitars at $700, his annual revenue is $63,000. Over this range of guitar prices, does the craftsman face elastic, unit-elastic, or inelastic demand?

20-7. Suppose that over a range of prices, the price elasticity of demand varies from 15.0 to 2.5. Over another range of prices, price elasticity of demand varies from 1.5 to .75. What can you say about total revenue and the total revenue curve over these two ranges of the demand curve as price falls?

20-8. Based on the information provided alone, characterize the following goods as being more elastic or more inelastic.

a. A 45-cent box of kosher salt that you buy once a year
b. A type of high-powered ski boat that you can rent from any one of a number of rental agencies
c. A specific brand of bottled water
d. Automobile insurance in a state that requires autos to be insured but has few insurance companies
e. A 75-cent guitar pick for the lead guitarist of a major rock band

20-9. The value of cross price elasticity of demand between goods X and Y is 1.25, while the cross price elasticity of demand between goods X and Z is 2.0. Characterize X and Y, X and Z, and Y and Z as substitutes or complements.

20-10. Suppose that the cross price elasticity of demand between eggs and bacon is $-.5$. What would you expect to happen to the sales of bacon if the price of eggs rises by 10 percent?

20-11. Assume that the income elasticity of demand for hot dogs is -1.25 and that the income elasticity of demand for lobster is 1.25. Explain why the measure for hot dogs is negative while that for lobster is positive. Based on this information alone, are these normal or inferior goods? (Hint: You may want to refer to the discussion of normal and inferior goods in Chapter 3.)

20-12. The price elasticity of supply of a basic commodity that a nation produces domestically and that it also imports is 2. What would you expect to happen to the volume of imports if the price of this commodity rises by 10 percent?

Economics on the Net

Cigarettes, Elasticity, and Government Policy In recent years, state and federal governments have focused considerable attention on cigarettes. This application helps you understand the role that elasticity plays in this issue.

Title: Measures to Reduce the Demand for Tobacco

Navigation: Click here to go directly to the Web page provided by UICC GLOBALink: The International Tobacco Control Network.

Application Read the article and answer the following questions.

1. In general, is the elasticity of demand for cigarettes elastic, unit-elastic, or inelastic? Explain why.
2. Would a tax hike on cigarettes have much of an impact on cigarette smoking?
3. Based on the forecasts provided in the article, is cigarette consumption perfectly elastic?

For Group Study and Analysis Explore the impact of the government subsidies to tobacco growers and of taxes on the consumption of cigarettes. Illustrate the effects of these two programs in a supply and demand diagram for cigarettes. Discuss the logic of the government's approaches to cigarette consumption. Attempt to reach a consensus on the "right" approach for the government to take.

CHAPTER 21

THE GLOBAL FINANCIAL ENVIRONMENT OF BUSINESS

This scene from the floor of a stock exchange used to be of little interest to most Americans. Today, in contrast, at least 40 percent of American families own stocks. How might changes in the stock market affect consumer spending?

Someone in your family probably owns stock in at least one American corporation. And you undoubtedly know plenty of other people who own corporate stock. Stock ownership has become much more widespread in America over the past half century. In 1952, for example, only 4 percent of Americans owned stock. But the proportion has risen more than 10-fold. The economic consequences of this wider ownership of American corporations are considerable. For example, upturns and downturns in the stock market now have a much stronger impact on consumer spending than they used to. But the fact that all parts of the income distribution now have a stake in Wall Street also has political implications, ranging from opposition to particular tax policies to support for certain types of foreign policy. Before you can grasp the full importance of America's love affair with the stock market, however, you need to know more about the global financial environment of business.

LEARNING OBJECTIVES

After reading this chapter, you should be able to:

1. Distinguish among the main organizational forms of business and explain the chief advantages and disadvantages of each
2. Explain the three main sources of corporate funds
3. Discuss the difference between stocks and bonds
4. Evaluate the economic impact of on-line trading of stocks and bonds
5. Explain the global nature of capital markets
6. Understand the problems of corporate control

Chapter Outline

- The Legal Organization of Firms
- Methods of Corporate Financing
- The Markets for Stocks and Bonds
- Global Capital Markets
- Electronic Securities Trading
- Problems in Corporate Governance

Did You Know That... at the start of the twenty-first century, nearly one-half of all retail purchases of corporate stock in the United States were made over the Internet? Moreover, corporate bonds and many other financial assets could also be purchased over the Internet with just the click of a mouse. In fact, some corporations seeking **financial capital** had begun to make initial public offerings (IPOs)—their initial start-up sales of stocks—over the Internet. Just five years before, none of this was possible. As it is doing to so much of life, the Internet is changing the nature of global financial markets.

You were introduced to the term *physical capital* as one of the five factors of production. In that context, capital consists of the goods that do not directly satisfy human wants but are used to make other goods. *Financial capital* is the money that is made available to purchase capital goods.

Different types of businesses are able to raise financial capital in different ways. And because of the Internet, raising capital is becoming easier and less costly. The first step in understanding the firm's financial environment is to understand the way firms are organized.

Financial capital 
Money used to purchase capital goods such as buildings and equipment.

THE LEGAL ORGANIZATION OF FIRMS

We all know that firms differ from one another. Some sell frozen yogurt, others make automobiles; some advertise, some do not; some have annual sales of a few thousand dollars, others have sales in the billions of dollars. The list of differences is probably endless. Yet for all this diversity, the basic organization of *all* firms can be thought of in terms of a few simple structures, the most important of which are the proprietorship, the partnership, and the corporation.

Proprietorships

Proprietorship 
A business owned by one individual who makes the business decisions, receives all the profits, and is legally responsible for all the debts of the firm.

The most common form of business organization is the **proprietorship;** as shown in Table 21-1, more than 73 percent of all firms in the United States are proprietorships. Each is owned by a single individual who makes the business decisions, receives all the profits, and is legally responsible for all the debts of the firm. Although proprietorships are numerous, they are generally rather small businesses, with annual sales typically under $50,000. For this reason, even though there are more than 10 million proprietorships in the United States, they account for only about 5 percent of all business revenues.

TABLE 21-1
Forms of Business Organization

Type of Firm	Percentage of U.S. Firms	Average Size (annual sales in dollars)	Percentage of Total Business Revenues
Proprietorship	73.1	49,000	5.1
Partnership	7.0	540,000	5.5
Corporation	19.9	3,122,000	89.4

Sources: U.S. Bureau of the Census; *2000 Statistical Abstract.*

Advantages of Proprietorships. Proprietorships offer several advantages as a form of business organization. First, they are *easy to form and to dissolve.* In the simplest case, all one must do to start a business is to start working; to dissolve the firm, one simply stops working. Second, *all decision-making power resides with the sole proprietor.* No partners, shareholders, or board of directors need be consulted. The third advantage is that its *profit is taxed only once.* All profit is treated by law as the net income of the proprietor and as such is subject only to personal income taxation.

Disadvantages of Proprietorships. The most important disadvantage of a proprietorship is that the proprietor faces **unlimited liability** *for the debts of the firm.* This means that the owner is personally responsible for all of the firm's debts. The second disadvantage is that it has *limited ability to raise funds,* to expand the business or even simply to help it survive bad times. Because of this, many lenders are reluctant to lend large sums to a proprietorship. The third disadvantage of proprietorships is that they normally *end with the death of the proprietor,* which creates added uncertainty for prospective lenders or employees.

Unlimited liability 
A legal concept whereby the personal assets of the owner of a firm can be seized to pay off the firm's debts.

Partnerships

The second important form of business organization is the **partnership.** As shown in Table 21-1, partnerships are far less numerous than proprietorships but tend to be significantly larger, with average sales about 10 times greater. A partnership differs from a proprietorship chiefly in that there are two or more co-owners, called partners. They share the responsibilities of operating the firm and its profits, and they are *each* legally responsible for *all* of the debts incurred by the firm. In this sense, a partnership may be viewed as a proprietorship with more than one owner.

Partnership 
A business owned by two or more joint owners, or partners, who share the responsibilities and the profits of the firm and are individually liable for all of the debts of the partnership.

Advantages of Partnerships. The first advantage of a partnership is that it is *easy to form.* In fact, it is almost as easy as forming a proprietorship. Second, partnerships, like proprietorships, often help *reduce the costs of monitoring job performance.* This is particularly true when interpersonal skills are important for successful performance and in lines of business where, even after the fact, it is difficult to measure performance objectively. Thus attorneys and physicians often organize themselves as partnerships. A third advantage of the partnership is that it *permits more effective specialization* in occupations in which, for legal or other reasons, the multiple talents required for success are unlikely to be uniform across individuals. Finally, the income of the partnership is treated as personal income and thus is *subject only to personal taxation.*

Disadvantages of Partnerships. Partnerships also have their disadvantages. First, the *partners each have unlimited liability.* Thus the personal assets of *each* partner are at risk due to debts incurred on behalf of the partnership by *any* of the partners. Second, *decision making is generally more costly* in a partnership than in a proprietorship; there are more people involved in making decisions, and they may have differences of opinion that must be resolved before action is possible. Finally, *dissolution of the partnership is generally necessary* when a partner dies or voluntarily withdraws or when one or more partners wish to remove someone from the partnership. This creates potential uncertainty for creditors and employees.

Corporations

Corporation 
A legal entity that may conduct business in its own name just as an individual does; the owners of a corporation, called shareholders, own shares of the firm's profits and enjoy the protection of limited liability.

A **corporation** is a legal entity that may conduct business in its own name just as an individual does. The owners of a corporation are called *shareholders* because they own shares of the profits earned by the firm. By law, shareholders enjoy **limited liability,** so that if the corporation incurs debts that it cannot pay, the shareholders' personal property is shielded from claims by the firm's creditors. As shown in Table 21-1, corporations are far less numerous than proprietorships, but because of their large size, they are responsible for about 90 percent of all business revenues in the United States.

Limited liability 
A legal concept whereby the responsibility, or liability, of the owners of a corporation is limited to the value of the shares in the firm that they own.

Advantages of Corporations. Perhaps the greatest advantage of corporations is that their owners (the shareholders) enjoy *limited liability.* The liability of shareholders is limited to the value of their shares. The second advantage arises because legally, the corporation *continues to exist* even if one or more owners cease to be owners. A third advantage of the corporation stems from the first two: Corporations are well positioned to *raise large sums of financial capital.* People are able to buy ownership shares or lend money to the corporation knowing that their liability is limited to the amount of money they invest and confident that the corporation's existence does not depend on the life of any one of the firm's owners.

Dividends 
Portion of a corporation's profits paid to its owners (shareholders).

Disadvantages of Corporations. The chief disadvantage of the corporation is that corporate income is subject to *double taxation.* The profits of the corporation are subject first to corporate taxation. Then, if any of the after-tax profits are distributed to shareholders as **dividends,** such payments are treated as personal income to the shareholders and subject to personal taxation. Owners of corporations pay about twice as much in taxes on corporate income as they do on other forms of income.

A second disadvantage of the corporation is that corporations are potentially subject to problems associated with the *separation of ownership and control.* The owners and managers of a corporation are typically different persons and may have different incentives. The problems that can result are discussed later in the chapter.

CONCEPTS IN BRIEF

- Proprietorships are the most common form of business organization, comprising 73 percent of all firms. Each is owned by a single individual who makes all business decisions, receives all the profits, and has unlimited liability for the firm's debts.
- Partnerships are much like proprietorships, except that two or more individuals, or partners, share the decisions and the profits of the firm. In addition, each partner has unlimited liability for the debts of the firm.
- Corporations are responsible for the largest share of business revenues. The owners, called shareholders, share in the firm's profits but normally have little responsibility for the firm's day-to-day operations. They enjoy limited liability for the debts of the firm.

METHODS OF CORPORATE FINANCING

When the Dutch East India Company was founded in 1602, it raised financial capital by selling shares of its expected future profits to investors. The investors thus became the owners of the company, and their ownership shares eventually became known as "shares of stock," or simply *stocks.* The company also issued notes of indebtedness, which involved borrowing money in return for interest on the funds, plus eventual repayment of the principal amount borrowed. In modern parlance, these notes of indebtedness are called *bonds.* As the company prospered over time, some of its revenues were used to pay lenders the interest and principal owed them; of the profits that remained, some were paid to shareholders in the form of dividends, and some were retained by the company for reinvestment in further enterprises. The methods of financing used by the Dutch East India Company four centuries ago—stocks, bonds, and reinvestment—remain the principal methods of financing for today's corporations.

Share of stock 
A legal claim to a share of a corporation's future profits; if it is *common stock*, it incorporates certain voting rights regarding major policy decisions of the corporation; if it is *preferred stock*, its owners are accorded preferential treatment in the payment of dividends.

A **share of stock** in a corporation is simply a legal claim to a share of the corporation's future profits. If there are 100,000 shares of stock in a company and you own 1,000 of them, you own the right to 1 percent of that company's future profits. If the stock you own is *common stock,* you also have the right to vote on major policy decisions affecting the company, such as the selection of the corporation's board of directors. Your 1,000 shares would entitle you to cast 1 percent of the votes on such issues. If the stock you own is *preferred stock,* you also own a share of the future profits of the corporation, but you do *not* have regular voting rights. You do, however, get something in return for giving up your voting rights: preferential treatment in the payment of dividends. Specifically, the owners of preferred stock generally must receive at least a certain amount of dividends in each period before the owners of common stock can receive *any* dividends.

Bond 
A legal claim against a firm, usually entitling the owner of the bond to receive a fixed annual coupon payment, plus a lump-sum payment at the bond's maturity date. Bonds are issued in return for funds lent to the firm.

A **bond** is a legal claim against a firm, entitling the owner of the bond to receive a fixed annual *coupon* payment, plus a lump-sum payment at the maturity date of the bond.* Bonds are issued in return for funds lent to the firm; the coupon payments represent interest on the amount borrowed by the firm, and the lump-sum payment at maturity of the bond generally equals the amount originally borrowed by the firm. Bonds are *not* claims on the future profits of the firm; legally, bondholders must be paid whether the firm prospers or not. To help ensure this, bondholders generally receive their coupon payments each year, along with any principal that is due, before *any* shareholders can receive dividend payments.

Reinvestment 
Profits (or depreciation reserves) used to purchase new capital equipment.

Reinvestment takes place when the firm uses some of its profits to purchase new capital equipment rather than paying the money out as dividends to shareholders. Although sales of stock are an important source of financing for new firms, reinvestment and borrowing are the primary means of financing for existing firms. Indeed, reinvestment by established firms is such an important source of financing that it dominates the other two sources of corporate finance, amounting to roughly 75 percent of new financial capital for corporations in recent years. Also, small businesses, which are the source of much current growth, often cannot rely on the stock market to raise investment funds.

THE MARKETS FOR STOCKS AND BONDS

Securities 
Stocks and bonds.

Economists often refer to the "market for wheat" or the "market for labor," but these are concepts rather than actual places. For **securities** (stocks and bonds), however, there really are markets—centralized, physical locations where exchange takes place. The most prestigious of these are the New York Stock Exchange (NYSE) and the New York Bond Exchange, both located in New York City. Numerous other stock and bond markets, or exchanges, exist throughout the United States and in various financial capitals of the world, such as London and Tokyo. Although the exact process by which exchanges are conducted

*Coupon payments on bonds get their name from the fact that bonds once had coupons attached to them when they were issued. Each year, the owner would clip a coupon off the bond and send it to the issuing firm in return for that year's interest on the bond.

in these markets varies slightly from one to another, the process used on the NYSE is representative of the principles involved.*

What is the Dow Jones Industrial Average?

The Dow Jones Industrial Average—"the Dow" for short—is an index that measures the average price of the stocks of 30 major American corporations, including McDonald's (fast food), Hewlett-Packard (computers and printers), and Wal-Mart (retail sales). The Dow was set up in 1896 (with just 12 stocks) by publisher Charles Dow and has been expanded and revised ever since by the editors of the *Wall Street Journal*. In principle, changes in the Dow mirror changes in the average price of the thousands of American stocks. But in reality, the Dow reflects only the average price of the specific stocks that comprise it: A $1 per share change in the price of a component stock causes a 4-point change in the Dow. Because the Dow comprises so few stocks, many observers think its usefulness as a measure of the overall stock market is limited. Still, it remains the most widely watched stock index in the world, and when it broke 10,000 for the first time in 1999, every major newspaper and newscast in America covered the story.

More than 2,500 stocks are traded on the NYSE, which is sometimes called the "Big Board." Leading brokerage firms—about 600 of them—own seats on the NYSE. These seats, which are actually rights to buy and sell stocks on the floor of the Big Board, are themselves regularly exchanged. In recent years, their value has fluctuated between $350,000 and $2 million each. These prices reflect the fact that stock trades on the NYSE are ultimately handled by the firms owning these seats, and the firms earn commissions on each trade.

The Theory of Efficient Markets

At any point in time, there are tens of thousands, even millions of persons looking for any bit of information that will enable them to forecast correctly the future prices of stocks. Responding to any information that seems useful, these people try to buy low and sell high. The result is that all publicly available information that might be used to forecast stock prices gets taken into account by those with access to the information and the knowledge and ability to learn from it, leaving no forecastable profit opportunities. And because so many people are involved in this process, it occurs quite swiftly. Indeed, there is some evidence that *all* information entering the market is fully incorporated into stock prices within less than a minute of its arrival. One view is that any information about specific stocks will prove to have little value by the time it reaches you.

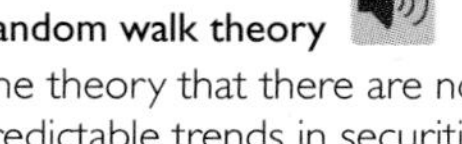

Random walk theory
The theory that there are no predictable trends in securities prices that can be used to "get rich quick."

Consequently, stock prices tend to follow a *random walk,* which is to say that the best forecast of tomorrow's price is today's price. This is called the **random walk theory.** Although large values of the random component of stock price changes are less likely than small values, nothing else about the magnitude or direction of a stock price change can be predicted. Indeed, the random component of stock prices exhibits behavior much like what would occur if you rolled two dice and subtracted 7 from the resulting total. On average, the dice will show a total of 7, so after you subtract 7, the average result will be zero. It is true that rolling a 12 or a 2 (resulting in a total of +5 or −5) is less likely than rolling an 8 or a 6 (yielding a total of +1 or −1). Nevertheless, positive and negative totals are equally likely, and the expected total is zero.

Inside Information

Inside information 
Information that is not available to the general public about what is happening in a corporation.

Isn't there any way to "beat the market"? The answer is yes—but normally only if you have **inside information** that is not available to the public. Suppose that your best friend is in charge of new product development at the country's largest software firm, Microsoft Corporation.

*A number of stocks and bonds are traded in so-called over-the-counter (OTC) markets, which, although not physically centralized, otherwise operate in much the same way as the NYSE and so are not treated separately in this text.

Your friend tells you that the company's smartest programmer has just come up with major new software that millions of computer users will want to buy. No one but your friend and the programmer—and now you—is aware of this. You could indeed make money using this information by purchasing shares of Microsoft and then selling them (at a higher price) as soon as the new product is publicly announced. There is one problem: Stock trading based on inside information such as this is illegal, punishable by substantial fines and even imprisonment. So unless you happen to have a stronger than average desire for a long vacation in a federal prison, you might be better off investing in Microsoft after the new program is publicly announced.

Click here to explore how the U.S. Securities and Exchange Commission seeks to prevent the use of inside information.

EXAMPLE

How to Read the Financial Press: Stock Prices

Table 21-2, reproduced from the *Wall Street Journal,* contains information about the stocks of four companies. Across the top of the financial page are a series of column headings. Under the heading "Stock" we find the name of the company—in the second row, for example, is Eastman Kodak, the photographic materials firm. The two columns to the left of the company's name show the highest and lowest prices at which

TABLE 21-2
Reading Stock Quotes

52 Weeks											
Hi	Low	Stock	Sym	Div.	Yld %	PE	Vol 100s	Hi	Lo	Close	Net Chg
$69\frac{9}{16}$	$40\frac{3}{16}$	Eastman Chm	EMN	1.76	3.4	21	2838	52	51	51	$+\frac{3}{4}$
$88\frac{15}{16}$	$60\frac{13}{16}$	EKodak	EK	1.76	2.4	18	17286	74	$72\frac{3}{8}$	73	$-2\frac{9}{16}$
$92\frac{7}{16}$	57	Eaton	ETN	1.76	2.1	19	4198	$89\frac{1}{8}$	84	85	$-4\frac{9}{16}$
$29\frac{5}{8}$	$17\frac{5}{8}$	Eaton/Vance	EV	.30	1.0	na	710	$30\frac{5}{8}$	$29\frac{9}{16}$	30	$+\frac{7}{16}$

The summary of stock market information presented on the financial pages of many newspapers reveals the following:

52 Weeks Hi/Lo: The highest and lowest prices, in dollars per share, of the stock during the previous 52 weeks

Stock: The name of the company (frequently abbreviated)

Sym: Highly abbreviated name of the company, as it appears on the stock exchange ticker tape

Div: Dividend paid, in dollars per share

Yld %: Yield in percent per year; the dividend divided by the price of the stock

PE: Price-earnings ratio; the price of the stock divided by the earnings (profits) per share of the company

Vol 100s: Number of shares traded during the day, in hundreds of shares

Hi: Highest price at which the stock traded that day

Lo: Lowest price at which the stock traded that day

Close: Last price at which the stock traded that day

Net Chg: Net change in the stock's price from the previous day's closing price shares of that company's stock traded during the past 52 weeks. These prices are typically quoted in dollars and fractions of dollars.

Immediately to the right of the company's name you will find the company's *symbol* on the NYSE. This symbol (omitted by some newspapers) is simply the unique identifier used by the exchange when it reports information about the stock. For example, the designation EK is used by the exchange as the unique identifier for the firm Eastman Kodak.

The last four columns of information for each firm summarize the behavior of the firm's stock price on the latest trading day. On this particular day, the highest price at which Kodak stock traded was $74.50, the lowest price was $72.375, and the last (or closing) price at which it traded was $73.00 per share. The *net change* in the price of Kodak stock was −$2.5625, which means that it *closed* the day at a price about $2.56 per share below the price at which it closed the day before.

The dividend column, headed "Div," shows the annual dividend (in dollars and cents) that the company has paid over the preceding year on each share of its stock. In Kodak's case, this amounts to $1.76 a share. If the dividend is divided by the closing price of the stock ($1.76 ÷ $73.00), the result is 2.4 percent, which is shown in the yield percentage ("Yld %") column for Kodak. In a sense, the company is paying interest on the stock at a rate of about 2.4 percent. At first glance, this seems like an absurdly low amount; after all, at the time this issue of the *Wall Street Journal* was printed, ordinary checking accounts were paying about this much. The reason people tolerate this seemingly low yield on Kodak (or any other stock) is that they expect that the price of the stock will rise over time, yielding capital gains.

The column heading "PE" stands for *price-earnings ratio*. To obtain the entries for this column, the firm's total earnings (profits) for the year are divided by the number of the firm's shares in existence to give the earnings per share. When the price of the stock is divided by the earnings per share, the result is the price-earnings ratio.

The column to the right of the PE ratio shows the total *volume* of the shares of the stock traded that day, measured in hundreds of shares.

For Critical Analysis

Is there necessarily any relationship between the net change in a stock's price and how many shares have been sold on a particular day?

CONCEPTS IN BRIEF

- Many economists believe that asset markets, especially the stock market, are efficient, meaning that one cannot make a higher than normal rate of return without having inside information (information that the general public does not possess).
- Stock prices normally follow a random walk, meaning that you cannot predict changes in future stock prices based on information about stock price behavior in the past.

GLOBAL CAPITAL MARKETS

Financial institutions in the United States are tied to the rest of the world via their lending capacities. In addition, integration of all financial markets is increasing. Indeed, recent changes in world finance have been nothing short of remarkable. Distinctions among financial institutions and between financial institutions and nonfinancial institutions have blurred. As the legal barriers that have preserved such distinctions are dismantled, multinational corporations offering a wide array of financial services are becoming dominant worldwide.

The globalization of financial markets is not entirely new. U.S. banks developed worldwide branch networks in the 1960s and 1970s for loans, check clearing, and foreign exchange (currency) trading. Also in the 1970s, firms dealing in U.S. securities expanded their operations in London (on the Eurobond market) and then into other financial centers, including Tokyo. Similarly, foreign firms invaded U.S. shores: first the banks, then securities firms. The "big four" Japanese securities firms now have offices in New York and London.

Money and capital markets today are truly international. Markets for U.S. government securities, interbank lending and borrowing, foreign exchange trading, and common stocks are now trading continuously, in vast quantities, around the clock and around the world.

Trading for U.S. government securities has been described as "the world's fastest-growing 24-hour market." This market was made possible by (1) sophisticated communications and computer technology, (2) deregulation of financial markets in foreign countries to permit such trading, (3) U.S. legislation in 1984 to enable foreign investors to buy U.S. government securities tax-free, and (4) huge annual U.S. government budget deficits, which have poured a steady stream of tradable debt into the world markets.

Foreign exchange—the buying and selling of foreign currencies—became a 24-hour, worldwide market in the 1970s. Instruments tied to government bonds, foreign exchange, stock market indexes, and commodities (grains, metals, oil) are now traded increasingly in financial futures markets in all the world's major centers of commerce. Most financial firms are coming to the conclusion that to survive as a force in any one of the world's leading financial markets, a firm must have a significant presence in all of them. As we enter the twenty-first century, between 30 and 50 financial institutions are at the centers of world finance—New York, London, Tokyo, and Frankfurt—and they are competing in all those markets to do business with the world's major corporations and portfolio managers. Today, major corporate borrowers throughout the world can choose to borrow from a wide variety of lenders, also located throughout the world. Moreover, as discussed in the next section, on-line securities trading is transforming finanical markets into a unified whole.

EXAMPLE

Going Global Without Knowing It

Although it seems much easier to buy and sell stocks of American companies than stocks of foreign companies, it is in fact quite easy to invest globally, even without realizing it. Consider recent retirees Mary Jo and George Paoni, residents of Illinois. Part of their savings are in a money market fund with ties to J. P. Morgan, the investment banker. Morgan has in turn engaged in $1 billion in high-risk trades in the baht, the national currency of Thailand. The Paonis' money market fund also had assets tied up with Bangkok Land, a real estate development company. Bangkok Land currently owns a modern—and largely worthless—ghost town near Bangkok airport that was supposed to be a city of 700,000. Mrs. Paoni's stake in the Illinois State Pension Fund turns out to have connections even more farflung. For example, the pension fund owns a piece of Aracruz Cellulose S.A., a Brazilian pulp and paper company hit by a sharp drop in commodity prices in the late 1990s. The drop in pulp prices from $850 a ton to $420 a ton drove the value of the pension fund's investment in the same direction. The fund also indirectly owns a stake in the Russian department store GUM (doing as poorly as the Russian economy) and in Peregrine Investments, a Hong Kong investment bank. Peregrine collapsed in 1998 with more than 2,000 creditors owed more than $4 billion. Although Mrs. Paoni's retirement check is as yet in no danger, the Illinois Pension Fund's investment in Peregrine is currently worthless.

For Critical Analysis

Should pension funds be limited by law in the nature of the investments they are allowed to make?

CONCEPTS IN BRIEF

- Financial markets throughout the world have become increasingly integrated, leading to a global financial market. Interbank lending and borrowing, foreign exchange trading, and stock sales now occur virtually 24 hours a day throughout the world.
- Many U.S. government or government-guaranteed securities trade 24 hours a day.

ELECTRONIC SECURITIES TRADING

On-line trading of shares of corporate stock is transforming the market for these securities. It all began in the mid-1990s with the establishment of just a few Internet addresses, such as www.etrade.com, www.schwab.com, and www.lombard.com. These Web sites offered something never before available: the capability to buy shares of stock on-line.

Benefits of On-Line Trading

What these Internet sites also offered were low brokerage fees. To buy 100 shares of stock in AOL–Time Warner from a traditional brokerage firm entailed fees in the neighborhood of $100; on-line brokers typically charged about $10 to make the same transaction. The result was predictable: On-line securities trading took off. By 2000, more than 2 million on-line trading accounts had been established. Total on-line stock trading had grown to about $200 billion. Observers expect that by 2003, the number of on-line stock-trading accounts will increase to as many as 11 million, with at least $700 billion traded via those accounts.

These estimates could prove to be low. They take into account only "hard-wired" trading via desktop and laptop computers. Recently, some high-tech firms have begun to introduce on-line securities trading systems that use cellular telephones, two-way pagers, and handheld computers connected to wireless modems. Today, there are more than 200 million mobile telephone subscribers, and that figure is expected to exceed 500 million worldwide by 2003. Thus there is a significant potential for even more growth in on-line securities trading.

Trading Speed

On-line trading does not just entail lower explicit expenses. It is faster, too. Anyone can reach Internet-based brokerage accounts from any computer with a secure Web browser. Today, literally at one's fingertips are hundreds of sites offering investment research sources and trading capabilities—all of which help make the Web a logical fit with the fast-paced, high-tech world of Wall Street.

To connect to an on-line trading site, an Internet trader punches in an ID and account password. Typically, she then has access to a package of services that might otherwise be quite costly if purchased separately. These include portfolio-tracking software and databases containing information about the market capitalization and earnings growth of listed companies. After conducting market research, an Internet trader can scan her portfolio of holdings, search for key information on companies whose stock she owns, and send an order to buy or sell more stock.

Moreover, she can do all this in a few minutes. That saves time, and time is valuable. Any time that she spends trading securities is time that she could have allocated to other endeavors. Thus the speed of on-line trading reduces the opportunity cost of trading.

EXAMPLE

Funding a Start-Up Company on the Internet

Getting a business off the ground requires more than lots of hard work. It requires raising hard cash. Many small businesses have trouble raising seed money to get started. But those that succeed in raising the initial funds can seek out venture capital firms for additional financing. Eventually they can "go public" by floating a stock issue.

Today, a business can to go public on the Net—it can sell shares of stock to the public directly. Spring Street Brewing Company made history in 1995 when it became the first company to conduct an initial public offering (IPO) over the Internet. It made history again in March 1996 when the Securities and Exchange Commission (SEC) allowed Spring Street to trade its shares via its Web site without registering as a broker-dealer. The SEC only required Spring Street to use an independent agent, such as a bank or an escrow agent, to process the funds it raised on the Net.

The SEC estimates that going public via the traditional, non-Internet route takes about 900 hours of work. Most of this time is devoted to preparing a prospectus prior to the sale of stock. Companies also have to hire specialized lawyers and use an underwriter, who normally charges a fee equal to about 10 percent of the value of the IPO. The cyber-based alternative is to buy a computer program called CapScape. This program automates the process of compiling the offer documents, permitting a company to sell shares directly to investors over the Internet.

Who will ultimately benefit from Internet IPOs? Small businesses.

For Critical Analysis

Who stands to lose if Internet IPOs become commonplace?

Can Brokerage Firms Keep Up?

Internet trading benefits the brokerage firms that offer it. Most Wall Street discount brokers now accept on-line orders. Internet-based brokerage firms can get by with less printed marketing material to send to clients, smaller customer service staffs, and fewer physical branches.

On July 16, 1996, U.S. stock prices suddenly dropped. Home computer screens flickered as stock prices then recovered somewhat while thousands of people followed the events on-line. For many brand-new Internet brokers, that day turned out to be a supreme test of the capacities of their systems.

Some brokerage firms almost failed the test, however. People across the nation reacted to the sudden fluctuation in stock prices by turning on their home computers to conduct a speedy on-line reshuffling of their portfolios. Many, however, discovered after a few clicks of their mouse buttons that they were frozen out of their Internet trading accounts. One New Jersey trader, for instance, indicated that found himself "stuck in Never-Never Land" for two hours that day. During that time, he was unable to log on to his account, check his account status, obtain stock price quotes, or even check the values of market indexes such as the Dow Jones Industrial Average. He was finally able to get connected later in the day, but even then the system reported incorrect stock prices. Ultimately, his on-line broker sent him a negotiated payment to try to compensate for its inability to handle the unexpectedly large volume of Internet traffic it experienced that day.

Nowadays, Internet brokers are much better equipped to handle huge trading volumes. Nevertheless, the July 1996 experience showed that Internet traders cannot rule out the possibility of a new kind of stock market crash: the crash of an on-line system along with the market itself. When Internet traders crowd on-line at once, computer systems can fail to handle the overflow. As a result, active traders who like the minute-to-minute control offered by on-line trading might actually find themselves completely frozen out of the market.

A Lower Return to "Day Trading"?

Click here to see one way that day traders keep up with scheduled initial public offerings and news of mergers and acquisitions.

Not everyone possesses the savvy to be a successful stock trader. The average customer of a traditional stockbroker makes just four or five transactions a year. By contrast, the typical Internet trader makes more than 20 transactions per year, and some, known as "day traders," spend significant portions of each day buying and selling stocks on-line in pursuit of quick profits.

Unfortunately for some of these day traders, researchers Terrance Odean and Brad Barber of the University of California, Davis, have found evidence that people who engage in more stock purchases and sales tend to earn lower overall returns on their portfolios. One possible reason for this is that many people who trade less often may think more carefully about the trades they make. Some people who trade more frequently may be more inclined to act on impulse. Such hasty decision making can result in lower earnings.

According to some observers—particularly traditional brokers facing growing competition from on-line brokers—the spontaneity of Internet trading could actually make some people worse off. Many of us know otherwise reasonable people who sometimes act as impulsive consumers, wasting hard-earned income on goods or services they realize later they did not really desire. Likewise, some Internet stock traders can end up losing hard-earned savings by impulsively buying stocks that perform worse than they expected.

Currently, around one person in 10 who trade stocks does so on-line. Furthermore, the $1.5 trillion in retail on-line trading predicted for 2003 would account for less than 10 percent of the total volume of securities trading likely to take place. This indicates that people have not given up on traditional stockbrokers. So in fact, a two-tiered stock market seems to be emerging. One group of savers will trade on their own accounts on-line. The other will continue to rely on brokers, both to offer advice and to execute transactions.

Policy Issues of Globalized On-Line Trading

For the myriad financial firms setting up shop on the Internet, the promise of avoiding the costs of physical offices has been perceived as a key advantage. Nevertheless, the on-line broker E*Trade ran into a snag in the late 1990s when it attempted to offer its services in Australia, Canada, New Zealand, and the United Kingdom. It found that securities regulators required the company to open bricks-and-mortar offices in those countries before having the legal right to do any business there. The United Kingdom's Securities and Investments Board (SIB) even threatened to require E*Trade to locate some of its computers within Britain as well. The SIB was unconvinced by E*Trade's argument that cyberspace is both everywhere and anywhere. The British agency noted that the United Kingdom has laws forbidding solicitation by unauthorized foreign securities firms. It ruled that merely setting up a Web site constitutes solicitation. It held that whenever a British-based computer was used to make offers to buy or sell securities over the Internet, those offers were legally made in Britain. The SIB therefore concluded that anyone establishing financial trading Web sites must comply with Britain's laws or else face penalties of prison or a fine.

Should national securities trading regulators cooperate by enforcing the rules of all other nations? For instance, should the U.S. Securities and Exchange Commission compel companies such as E*Trade to abide by the rules of the British SIB and all other national regulators? Alternatively, should all countries follow the example set by the European Union and automatically authorize companies in other nations to sell their services across borders under the rules of the nations in which the companies themselves are based? For example, should the SIB concentrate only on regulating British Internet trading firms, thereby risking a flight of business away from the United Kingdom? These are the kinds of questions that public policymakers are struggling to answer as Internet trading continues to spread.

CONCEPTS IN BRIEF

- On-line securities trading has grown rapidly in recent years, largely because on-line brokers' fees are much lower than those of full-service brokers and because people can execute on-line trades more quickly.
- On-line brokerage firms have struggled to keep up with the growing volumes of Internet stock trading, particularly during periods of rapid stock price swings that have generated big increases in trading activity. This has exposed some on-line traders to problems when on-line systems have crashed.
- In principle, on-line trading can span national borders, but securities regulators have offered different legal interpretations about the extent to which on-line brokers are subject to national regulations.

PROBLEMS IN CORPORATE GOVERNANCE

Many corporations issue stock to raise financial capital that they will use to fund expansion or modernization. The decision to raise capital in this way is ordinarily made not by the owners of the corporation—the holders of its stock—but by the company's managers. This **separation of ownership and control** in corporations leads to incentive problems. Managers may not act in the best interest of shareholders. Further incentive problems arise when corporations borrow money in financial markets. These corporate governance problems have to do with information that is not the same for everyone.

Separation of ownership and control 
The situation that exists in corporations in which the owners (shareholders) are not the people who control the operation of the corporation (managers). The goals of these two groups are often different.

Asymmetric Information: The Perils of Adverse Selection and Moral Hazard

If you invest in a corporation, you give purchasing power to the managers of that corporation. Those managers have much more information about what is happening to the corporation and its future than you do. As you learned in Chapter 14 the inequality of knowledge between the two parties is called *asymmetric information.* If asymmetric information exists before a transaction takes place, we have a circumstance of *adverse selection.* In financial markets, adverse selection occurs because borrowers who are the worst credit risks (and thus likely to yield the most adverse outcomes) are the ones most likely to seek, and perhaps to receive, loans.

Consider two firms seeking to borrow funds by selling bonds. Suppose that one of the firms, the Dynamic Corporation, is pursuing a project with a small chance of yielding large profits and a large chance of bankruptcy. The other firm, the Reliable Company, intends to invest in a project that is guaranteed to yield the competitive rate of return, thereby ensuring repayment of its debts. Because Dynamic knows the chance is high that it will go bankrupt and never have to pay its debts, it can offer a high interest rate on the bonds it issues. Unless prospective bond purchasers can distinguish perfectly between the two firms' projects, they will select the high-yielding bonds offered by Dynamic and refuse to buy the low-yielding bonds offered by Reliable. Firms like Reliable will be unable to get funding, yet lenders will lose money on firms like Dynamic. Adverse selection thus makes investors less likely to lend to anyone and more inclined to charge higher interest rates when they do lend.

Moral hazard occurs as a result of asymmetric information *after* a transaction has occurred. To continue with our example of the Dynamic Corporation, once the firm has sold the bonds, it must choose among alternative strategies in executing its project. Lenders face the hazard that Dynamic may choose strategies contrary to the lenders' well-being and thus "immoral" from their perspective. Because bondholders are entitled to a fixed amount regardless of the firm's profits, Dynamic has an incentive to select strategies offering a small chance of high profits, thereby enabling the owners to keep the largest amount after paying bondholders. Such strategies are also the riskiest—ones that make it more likely that lenders will not be repaid—so the presence of moral hazard makes lenders less likely to lend to anyone and more inclined to charge higher interest rates when they do lend.

The Principal-Agent Problem 

Principal-agent problem The conflict of interest that occurs when agents—managers of firms—pursue their own objectives to the detriment of the goals of the firms' principals, or owners.

A type of moral hazard problem that occurs within firms is called the **principal-agent problem.** The shareholders who own a firm are referred to as *principals,* and the managers who operate the firm are the *agents* of the owners. When the managers do not own all of a firm (as is usually the case), a separation of ownership and control exists, and if the stockholders have less information about the firm's opportunities and risks than the managers do (as is also usually the case), the managers may act in their own self-interest rather than in the interest of the shareholders.

Consider, for example, the choice between two investment projects, one of which involves an enormous amount of work but also promises high profits, while the other requires little effort and promises small returns. Because the managers must do all the work while the shareholders receive all the profits, the managers' incentives are different from those of the shareholders. In this case, the presence of moral hazard will induce the managers to choose the "good life," the easy but low-yielding project—an outcome that fails to maximize the economic value of the firm.

Solving Principal-Agent and Moral Hazard Problems

Collateral An asset pledged to guarantee the repayment of a loan.

Incentive-compatible contract  A loan contract under which a significant amount of the borrower's assets are at risk, providing an incentive for the borrower to look after the lender's interests.

The dangers associated with asymmetric information are well known to participants in financial markets, who regularly undertake vigorous steps to minimize its costly consequences. For example, research companies such as Standard & Poor's gather financial data and other information about corporations and sell the information to their subscribers. When even this is insufficient to eliminate the dangers of adverse selection, lenders often require that borrowers post **collateral**—assets that the borrower will forfeit in the event that repayment of a debt is not made. A variant of this strategy, designed to reduce moral hazard problems, is called the **incentive-compatible contract:** Lenders make sure that borrowers have a large amount of their own assets at risk so that the incentives of the borrower are compatible with the interests of the lender. Although measures such as these cannot eliminate the losses caused by asymmetric information, they reduce them below what would otherwise be the case.

- When two parties to a transaction have different amounts of information, we call this asymmetric information. Asymmetric information before a transaction can result in adverse selection. Adverse selection causes borrowers who are the worst credit risks to be the ones most likely to seek loans.

- Asymmetric information after a transaction can cause moral hazard. Lenders often face the hazard that borrowers will choose riskier actions after borrowers have taken out loans.
- The separation of ownership and control in today's large corporations can give rise to the principal-agent problem, whereby the agents (managers) may have interests that differ from those of the principals (shareholders).
- Several methods exist for solving the principal-agent and moral hazard problems. They include requiring lenders to post collateral and devising incentive-compatible contracts in which borrowers have a large amount of their own assets at risk.

NETNOMICS

The Economic Effects of On-Line Trading

The biggest appeal of on-line trading for many investors is the low cost per trade—often one-half to one-tenth the cost of dealing with a human being at a full-service stock brokerage. Quite apart the potential for putting money into the pocket of investors, the advent of on-line trading helps make the stock and bond markets more efficient in two ways.

First, on every trade that takes place, fewer resources are used when an investor chooses to make the trade on-line rather than otherwise. But note that one can't merely subtract the difference between the conventional broker's fee and the on-line fee and conclude that the difference is all savings. After all, on-line traders typically have to spend some added amount of their own time and computer resources to make those on-line trades. Suppose, for example, that on a trade of 1,000 shares of stock, the conventional fee would be $250 and the on-line fee is $50. If the investor devotes, say, an additional $35 of her time on research and computer time in making the on-line trade, the net resource savings on the trade are $165 (= $250 − $50 − $35). When added up over thousands of trades that on-line traders across the country are making each day, these savings for the economy can be significant.

The lower costs of on-line trading also improve the efficiency of the securities markets by making more trades possible. When trading costs are high, some people refrain from buying stocks or bonds they believe have upside potential, while others refrain from selling stocks or bonds they feel are headed downward. With lower costs due to on-line trading, both types of investors will be able to do more of what they want to do, thereby making both better off.

Interestingly, the fact that costs per trade are lower on-line has the potential to *raise* the total amount that investors are spending on stock and bond trades! How is this possible? Well, the lower costs per trade encourage more trades, and the total amount spent on trading is the product of price (the fee per trade) times quantity (the number of trades). If the number of trades increases enough—which it will, if the demand for trading services is elastic—the net effect of the lower cost per trade will be more money spent on trading. But note that even if traders end up spending more on trading, this does not wipe out their gains from using on-line services: Indeed, they will continue to use those services only if they accrue net benefits from doing so. What it does mean is that the simple arithmetic of on-line trading doesn't always add up to the correct economics of on-line trading.

Issues & Applications

The Spread of Corporate Stock Ownership

Shortly after World War II ended, only one out of 25 Americans owned corporate stock. By 1981, one out of 16 Americans owned stock. At the beginning of the 1990s, the number was one out of four, and by the year 2000, almost one of every two Americans owned stock. Why has this growth in stock ownership taken place, and what does it mean—for the economy and for politics?

No single factor can account for the growing popularity of stock ownership over the past 50 years, although several factors have clearly played a role. The low incidence of stock ownership after World War II was due in part to memories of the Great Depression, heralded by a spectacular drop in stock prices in 1929. As memories of hard times faded, however, more Americans became willing to trust in the stock market.

Concepts Applied

- On-line Stock Trading
- Capital Gains
- Taxation and Regulatory Policies
- Recession

The advent of the Individual Retirement Account (IRA) more than 20 years ago also gave stock ownership a boost. Because the taxes on profits from successful stock trades could be deferred if the stocks were in IRA accounts, stock ownership became much more attractive. The strong economy and booming stock market of the 1980s and 1990s also spurred interest in stock ownership as more and more people realized that unlike objects bound by gravity, stock prices that went up did not have to go down. And when low-cost stock trading over the Internet became possible, interest in stocks became a passion. By the end of the twentieth century, Americans were holding some $12 trillion worth of corporate stocks—more than $40,000 for each person in the country.

How Growing Stock Ownership Matters

Of course, as stock holding in America became more widespread, the consequences of changes in the value of those stocks became broader too. During much of the 1980s and 1990s, rising stock prices helped fuel consumer spending, leading to record-breaking economic expansions. But there can be a downside as well. For example, when stock prices plunged 20 percent in late 1987, it sparked a slowdown in consumer spending. And when stocks dropped sharply again in 1997, consumer spending faltered in several sectors of the economy until stock prices bounced back. Some economists think that with the huge amount of wealth now in the form of corporate stocks, a sudden and sustained 20 percent drop in stock prices might be enough to trigger a recession.

It is on the political front, however, that the implications of America's interest in the stock market can be the most surprising. Once upon a time, stock holding in America was confined to the wealthy and the elderly. This set up a natural sort of "us versus them" rivalry when it came to tax and regulatory policies affecting the bottom line of American corporations. Low-income individuals and young people tended to favor higher corporate and capital gains taxes and heavier regulatory intervention by the government. (Capital gains taxes are levied on the positive difference between the sale and purchase price of an asset, such as corporate stock.) In contrast, the wealthy and the over-40 crowd were more likely to push for policies that enhanced corporate profits and let investors keep more of their gains from higher stock prices. All of this is changing in the new era of stock ownership.

The Role of Internet Trading

More than half of all families with incomes between $25,000 and $50,000 own stock, and although stock ownership is less prevalent among families with incomes below $25,000, stock ownership is increasing faster in this low-income segment than in any other. Moreover, Internet-savvy young people are becoming a growing force in the on-line trading of stocks—and are therefore well aware of which government policies are likely to earn them profits or yield losses. The result is a changing dynamic in American politics.

For example, among individuals with more than $5,000 in stocks or bonds, one poll found nearly two-thirds support lower capital gains taxes, compared to 46 percent among noninvestors. Moreover, support for capital gains tax cuts rises with stock ownership. Perhaps this helps explain the turnaround on this issue in Washington. In the 1980s, Democrats attacked Republicans as being elitists for proposing cuts in the capital gains tax. In the late 1990s, a Democratic president cheerfully signed legislation that cut the rate sharply—and left much more of the profits from the rising stock market in the hands of voters.

The spread of stock ownership is affecting other political areas as well. For example, the growing investor class is expressing increasing support for expanded IRAs (especially the Roth IRA, which allows tax-free withdrawals) and the initiation of personal Social Security accounts under the control of the beneficiary rather than a government bureaucrat. There is even evidence that today's knowledgeable investors are starting to pay attention to the effects of new government regulations on their personal bottom line. And the fact that the investor class is growing will boost support for market-oriented economic policies. The challenge for our political leaders is to turn this support into sensible economic policies.

FOR CRITICAL ANALYSIS

1. Could a drop in the value of U.S. stocks cause a recession in other countries?
2. How does a reduction in the capital gains tax affect the incentives to own corporate stocks and to buy and sell them on a regular basis?

SUMMARY DISCUSSION OF LEARNING OBJECTIVES

1. **The Main Organizational Forms of Business and the Chief Advantages and Disadvantages of Each:** The primary organizational forms businesses take are the proprietorship, the partnership, and the corporation. The proprietorship is owned by a single person, the proprietor, who makes the business decisions, is entitled to all the profits, and is subject to unlimited liability—that is, is personally responsible for all debts incurred by the firm. The partnership differs from the proprietorship chiefly in that there are two or more owners, called partners. They share the responsibility for decision making, share the firm's profits, and individually bear unlimited liability for the firm's debts. The net income, or profits, of both proprietorships and partnerships is subject only to personal income taxes. Both types of firms legally cease to exist when the proprietor or a partner gives up ownership or dies. The corporation differs from proprietorships and partnerships in three important dimensions. Owners of corporations enjoy limited liability; that is, their responsibility for the debts of the corporation is limited to the value of their ownership shares. In addition, the income from corporations is subject to double taxation—corporate taxation when income is earned by the corporation and personal taxation when after-tax profits are paid as dividends to the owners. Finally, corporations do not legally cease to exist due to a change of ownership or the death of an owner.
2. **The Three Main Sources of Corporate Funds:** The main sources of financial capital for corporations are stocks, bonds, and reinvestment of profits. Stocks are ownership shares, promising a share of profits, sold to investors. Common stocks also embody voting rights regarding the major decisions of the firm; preferred stocks typically have no voting rights but enjoy priority status in the

payment of dividends. Bonds are notes of indebtedness, issued in return for the loan of money. They typically promise to pay interest in the form of annual coupon payments, plus repayment of the original principal amount upon maturity. Bondholders are generally promised payment before any payment of dividends to shareholders, and for this reason bonds are less risky than stocks. Reinvestment involves the purchase of assets by the firm, using retained profits or depreciation reserves it has set aside for this purpose. No new stocks or bonds are issued in the course of reinvestment, although its value is fully reflected in the price of existing shares of stock.

3. **The Differences Between Stocks and Bonds:** Stocks represent ownership in a corporation. They are called equity capital. Bonds represent the debt of a corporation. They are part of the debt capital of a corporation. Bond owners normally receive a fixed interest payment on a regular basis, whereas owners of stock are not normally guaranteed any dividends. If a corporation goes out of business, bondholders have first priority on whatever value still exists in the entity. Owners of stock get whatever is left over. Finally, if the corporation is very successful, owners of stock can reap the increases in the market value of their shares of stock. In contrast, the market value of corporate bonds is not so closely tied to the profits of a corporation but is rather influenced by how interest rates are changing in the economy in general.
4. **The Economic Impact of On-Line Trading of Stocks and Bonds:** On-line trading helps make stock and bond markets more efficient in two ways. First, fewer resources are used when an investor trades on-line rather than through a broker. To calculate the cost savings, one has to add the value of one's time and personal computer costs to the on-line fees and compare that total to what a conventional broker would charge. Added up over thousands of trades that on-line traders make each day, the net savings for the economy can be significant. Second, the lower costs of on-line trading improve the efficiency of the stock market by making more trades possible. When trading costs are high, some people refrain from buying or selling stocks or bonds. Thanks to the lower costs of on-line trading, investors will be able to do more of what they want to do. The fact that costs per trade are lower on-line has the potential to *increase* the total amount that investors are spending on stock and bond trades because lower costs per trade encourage more trades.
5. **The Global Nature of Capital Markets:** Trading in U.S. government securities is one of the fastest-growing 24-hour markets in the world, thanks to sophisticated communications and computer technology. The deregulation of financial markets in foreign countries now permits much more of such trading. Also, since 1984, the United States has allowed foreign investors to buy U.S. government securities tax-free. Moreover, the rapid growth of on-line securities trading has the potential to turn the world's financial markets into one unified market that responds instantly to events, whenever and wherever they occur.
6. **The Problems of Corporate Control:** When two parties to a transaction have different amounts of information, we call this asymmetric information. Asymmetric information before a transaction can result in adverse selection. Adverse selection causes borrowers who are the worst credit risks to be the ones most likely to seek loans. Asymmetric information after a transaction can cause moral hazard. Lenders often face the hazard that borrowers will choose riskier actions after having been granted loans. The separation of ownership and control in today's large corporation has led to the principal-agent problem, whereby the agents (managers) may have interests that differ from those of the principals (shareholders). Several methods exist for solving the principal-agent and moral hazard problems, including requiring lenders to post collateral and devising incentive-compatible contracts in which borrowers have a large amount of their own assets at risk.

Key Terms and Concepts

Bond (509)
Collateral (518)
Corporation (508)
Dividends (508)
Financial capital (506)
Incentive-compatible contract (518)
Inside information (510)
Limited liability (508)
Partnership (507)

Principal-agent problem (518)
Proprietorship (506)
Random walk theory (510)
Reinvestment (509)
Securities (509)
Separation of ownership and control (517)
Shares of stock (509)
Unlimited liability (507)

Problems

Answers to the odd-numbered problems appear at the back of the book.

21-1. Classify the following items as either financial capital or physical capital.
- **a.** A drill press owned by a manufacturing company
- **b.** $100,000 set aside in an account to purchase a drill press
- **c.** Funds raised through a bond offer to expand plant and equipment
- **d.** A warehouse owned by a shipping company

21-2. Write a brief explanation of the difference between a sole proprietorship, a partnership, and a corporation. In addition, list one advantage and one disadvantage of a sole proprietorship, a partnership, and a corporation.

21-3. Explain the difference between the dividends of a corporation and the profits of a sole proprietorship or partnership, particularly in their tax treatment.

21-4. Outline the differences between common stock and preferred stock.

21-5. The owner of WebCity is trying to decide whether to remain a proprietorship or to incorporate. Suppose that the corporate tax rate on profits is 20 percent and the personal income tax rate is 30 percent. For simplicity, assume that all corporate profits (after corporate taxes are paid) are distributed as dividends in the year they are earned and that such dividends are subject to the personal income tax.
- **a.** If the owner of WebCity expects to earn $100,000 in before-tax profits this year, regardless of whether the firm is a proprietorship or a corporation, which method of organization should be chosen?
- **b.** What is the dollar value of the after-tax advantage of that form of organization?
- **c.** Suppose that the corporate form of organization has cost advantages that will raise before-tax profits by $50,000. Should the owner of WebCity incorporate?
- **d.** By how much will after-tax profits change due to incorporation?
- **e.** Suppose that tax policy is changed to exempt from personal taxation the first $40,000 per year in dividends. Would this change in policy affect the decision made in part (a)?
- **f.** How can you explain the fact that even though corporate profits are subject to double taxation, most business in America is conducted by corporations rather than by proprietorships or partnerships?

21-6. Suppose that you are trying to decide whether to spend $1,000 on stocks issued by WildWeb or on bonds issued by the same company. There is a 50 percent chance that the value of the stock will rise to $2,200 at the end of the year and a 50 percent chance that the stock will be worthless at the end of the year. The bonds promise an interest rate of 20 percent per year, and it is certain that the bonds and interest will be repaid at the end of the year.
- **a.** Assuming that your time horizon is exactly one year, will you choose the stocks or the bonds?
- **b.** By how much is your expected end-of-year wealth reduced if you make the wrong choice?
- **c.** Suppose the odds of success improve for WildWeb: Now there is a 60 percent chance that the value of the stock will be $2,200 at year's end and only a 40 percent chance that it will be worthless. Should you now choose the stocks or the bonds?
- **d.** By how much did your expected end-of-year wealth rise as a result of the improved outlook for WildWeb?

21-7. Lucinda is a financial consultant whose time is worth \$120 per hour. Ralph is an accountant whose time is worth \$40 per hour. FSB, a full-service brokerage, offers to make stock trades for its clients on the following basis: For each trade there is a fee of \$25, plus 10 cents per share for each share traded. WebTrader offers to make trades for a flat rate of \$50 per trade, regardless of how many shares are traded. Because of the design of the WebTrader Web site, it takes people 30 minutes more to execute a trade with WebTrader than to execute with FSB.

a. If Lucinda and Ralph are each separately considering a trade involving 100 shares, with whom will each person execute the trade?

b. If Lucinda and Ralph are each separately considering a trade involving 500 shares, with whom will each person execute the trade?

c. If Lucinda and Ralph are each separately considering a trade involving 1,000 shares, with whom will each person execute the trade?

d. In general, will larger or smaller trades be executed with WebTrader or with FSB? Explain your answer.

e. In general, how will the value of a person's time affect the choice of using WebTrader or FSB? Explain.

21-8. After graduating from college with an economics major, Sally Smith started her own consulting firm. After her first year of operation, Sally is contemplating whether to remain a sole proprietorship or to incorporate. Based on her first year's experience, Sally expects to generate \$250,000 in pretax profits for the upcoming year. If she remains a sole proprietorship, her profits will be subject to a personal income tax rate of 35 percent. If she incorporates, the corporation faces a 25 percent corporate tax rate. All profits of the corporation will be paid as dividends to Sally as personal income.

a. How do after-tax profits differ under the two types of organizational structure?

b. Based on income considerations alone, which organizational structure should Sally choose?

21-9. Classify each event as an example of asymmetric information, moral hazard, or adverse selection.

a. The Wired Corporation is contemplating starting a string of Internet cafés. Market research shows this to be a very risky venture that will either ensure the success of the company or drive it into bankruptcy. The finance department therefore suggests offering bonds at a rate higher than the market average.

b. Based on your limited knowledge of Internet cafés, you believe that this is a "sure thing" and therefore buy the bonds issued by the Wired Corporation.

c. Instead of setting up a string of Internet cafés as it had promised, the Wired Corporation buys a bankrupt fast-food chain and takes the chance that it can turn the chain around, resell it, and make more profit, albeit at a higher risk.

21-10. Explain the basic differences between a share of stock and a bond.

21-11. Suppose that one of your classmates informs you that he has developed a method of forecasting stock market returns based on past trends. With a monetary investment by you, the two of you could profit handsomely from this forecasting method. How should you respond to your classmate?

Economics on the Net

How the New York Stock Exchange Operates This application gives you the chance to learn about how the New York Stock Exchange functions.

Title: The New York Stock Exchange: How the NYSE Operates

Navigation: Click here to visit the New York Stock Exchange. In the left margin, click Education. Along the top, select the tab named Educational Publications. Then, click on You and the Investment World. Next, click on Chapter 3: How the NYSE Operates.

Application Read the chapter, and answer the following questions.

1. According to the article, the price of a seat on the NYSE can sell for more than $1 million. Why do you suppose that someone would be willing to pay this much for a seat? (Hint: Think about the potential ways that someone could generate earnings from holding an NYSE seat.)
2. List the key functions of a stock exchange specialist. Why is the "Point-of-Sale Display Book" likely to be particularly useful for a specialist?

For Group Study and Analysis Divide the class into groups, and have each group examine and discuss the description of how NYSE trades are executed. Ask each group to compose a listing of the various points at which Internet trading may be a more efficient way to execute a trade, as compared with trading via a traditional brokerage firm. Then go through these as a class, and discuss the following issue: In the New York Stock Exchange, which people cannot be replaced by new information technologies?

TYING IT ALL TOGETHER Part 5 Case Problem

Case Background

Top executives for Southern Cola, a privately owned manufacturer and distributor of soft drinks marketed under the names of various grocery store chains throughout the Southwest and Southeast, have decided that the company will enter the vending business in these same U.S. regions. Their next decision is what type of vending machines to purchase. They must balance their desire to purchase high-tech vending machines with the constraints they will face in financing this major investment.

Management Issues in the Emerging High-Tech Vending Business Southern Cola's executives can choose among several lines of vending machines, ranging from the standard, no-frills coin- and bill-operated model to a top-of-the-line, Internet-connected model. One increasingly common feature is to include a card slot that can read credit cards and debit cards. Another new and relatively high-tech feature, which has been available since Coca-Cola's first experiments in 1999, is a device that automatically increases the soft-drink prices in hot weather. This feature requires only a temperature sensor and a computer chip, both of which are now relatively inexpensive "old technologies."

If Southern Cola chooses machines with the latter option, the company can also upgrade to vending machines with a higher-quality microprocessor that enables the machines to perform several other functions. One is keeping track of the time of day and adjusting prices upward during periods of the day when people are most likely to be in buildings or near kiosks where the machines are located.

Another option, which also requires access to a fiber-optic cable or other telecommunications connection, is to automatically keep tabs on the machine's inventories of various soft drinks. In real time, therefore, the machine's microprocessor could inform Southern Cola's central office when the machine is running low on popular soft drinks. Then the company can dispatch employees for just-in-time inventory restocking of the machines, which would keep employees from making unnecessary trips to well-stocked vending machines—thereby reducing the company's employee expenses. Furthermore, the company's central office could readily compile the streams of data obtained from its vending machines to help its marketing force determine which drinks are selling best in which locations. This could help not only in short-term marketing efforts but also in longer-term planning for the introduction of new products in the future.

Real-time inventory management could also allow for pricing adjustments. If one brand is clearly more popular than another, the microprocessor could be programmed to charge a slightly higher price for the more popular brand. In addition, if some brands are temporarily out of stock, Southern Cola could program the vending machine to automatically raise the prices of remaining items somewhat.

Vending is a brand-new business for Southern Cola, however. To finance its entry into this business, the executives realize that they will have to convince the owners of the company to "take it public" via an initial public offering (IPO).

The executives realize that they face an interlocking set of decisions. They must determine if high-tech vending machines are a necessary part of their long-term strategy for succeeding in this new business. If so, a successful IPO would go a long way toward making the new venture a success. A merely adequate IPO, however, might force the company to face the prospect of either scaling back the scope of its market entry or taking on additional debt to finance the grand leapfrogging effort that its executives wish to achieve.

Points to Analyze

1. Which of the vending machine features that Southern Cola's executives are considering would adjust prices to take into account changes in the position of the demand curve at each of the company's vending machines?
2. What vending machine features would adjust soft-drink prices in light of variations in the price elasticity of demand at each vending machine?
3. What are the advantages and disadvantages of making Southern Cola a publicly owned company?
4. Why do the company's executives believe that developing a business plan that demonstrates a significant potential for revenue enhancements and cost efficiencies is crucial to the success of the IPO?

Casing the Internet

1. **Click here to go to Coca-Cola's home page.**
   a. **Click on "Our Company" and then click on "Citizenship." Click on "Environment." Why do you suppose that Coca-Cola is so interested in convincing visitors to its site that it is an environment-friendly corporation? Do you think that this discussion is aimed at consumers, investors, or both? Why?**
   b. **Click here to go to the homepage of PepsiCo, the maker and distributor of Pepsi-Cola and related soft-drink products. In what ways does this homepage differ from the homepage of Coca-Cola? Do you see any similarities between the objectives of the two companies' Web sites? Differences?**
2. **Click here to go to the homepage of Mars Electronics International (MEI). Select a region and language. Then click on "Register Later."**
   a. **Click on "Product Applications," then click on "Soft Drink," and read the description of this business. How many types of vending machines does this company market? Why do you think there are so many models to choose from?**

Part 6

Market Structure, Resource Allocation, and Regulation

CHAPTER

22

THE FIRM: COST AND OUTPUT DETERMINATION

This bank was originally called First Chicago but was acquired by Bank One. There have been over 4,000 bank mergers in the past 10 years. Why do banks want to get bigger by merger?

Since 1989, nearly 4,000 mergers have occurred among U.S. commercial banks—financial firms that issue checking accounts and use the funds they raise from this activity to earn interest returns from loans and holdings of government securities. More than two-thirds of the nation's banking resources have been involved in these mergers. Bank consolidation has also produced some very large banking firms, at least relative to historical standards for the United States. Presumably, bank owners and managers have had good reasons to conclude that bigger is better. The most common rationale that bank owners and managers offer is that large banks are more cost-efficient than small banks. Before you can evaluate this contention, however, you must understand the nature of cost curves that individual businesses face.

LEARNING OBJECTIVES

After reading this chapter, you should be able to:

1. **Distinguish between accounting profits and economic profits**
2. **Discuss the difference between the short run and the long run from the perspective of a firm**
3. **Understand why the marginal physical product of labor eventually declines as more units of labor are employed**
4. **Explain the short-run cost curves a typical firm faces**
5. **Describe the long-run cost curves a typical firm faces**
6. **Identify situations of economies and diseconomies of scale and define a firm's minimum efficient scale**

Chapter Outline

Did You Know That... there are more than 25 steps in the process of manufacturing a simple lead pencil? In the production of an automobile, there are literally thousands. At each step, the manufacturer can have the job done by workers or machines or some combination of the two. The manufacturer must also figure out how much to produce each month. Should a new machine be bought that can replace 10 workers? Should more workers be hired, or should the existing workers be paid overtime? If the price of aluminum is rising, should the company try to make do with plastic? What you will learn about in this chapter is how producers can select the best combination of inputs for any given output that is desired.

Before we look at the firm's costs, we need to define a firm.

THE FIRM

We define a business, or **firm,** as follows:

> A firm is an organization that brings together factors of production—labor, land, physical capital, human capital, and entrepreneurial skill—to produce a product or service that it hopes can be sold at a profit.

Firm 
A business organization that employs resources to produce goods or services for profit. A firm normally owns and operates at least one plant in order to produce.

A typical firm will have an organizational structure consisting of an entrepreneur, managers, and workers. The entrepreneur is the person who takes the risks, mainly of losing his or her personal wealth. In compensation, the entrepreneur will get any profits that are made. Recall from Chapter 2 that entrepreneurs take the initiative in combining land, labor, and capital to produce a good or a service. Entrepreneurs are the ones who innovate in the form of new production and new products. The entrepreneur also decides whom to hire to manage the firm. Some economists maintain that the true quality of an entrepreneur becomes evident with his or her selection of managers. Managers, in turn, decide who should be hired and fired and how the business generally should be set up. The workers ultimately use the other inputs to produce the products or services that are being sold by the firm. Workers and managers are paid contractual wages. They receive a specified amount of income for a specified time period. Entrepreneurs are not paid contractual wages. They receive no reward specified in advance. The entrepreneurs make profits if there are any, for profits accrue to those who are willing to take risks. (Because the entrepreneur gets only what is left over after all expenses are paid, he or she is often referred to as a *residual claimant.* The entrepreneur lays claim to the residual—whatever is left.)

Profit and Costs

Most people think of profit as the difference between the amount of revenues a business takes in and the amount it spends for wages, materials, and so on. In a bookkeeping sense, the following formula could be used:

$$\text{Accounting profits} = \text{total revenues} - \text{explicit costs}$$

Explicit costs 
Costs that business managers must take account of because they must be paid; examples are wages, taxes, and rent.

Accounting profit 
Total revenues minus total explicit costs.

where **explicit costs** are expenses that the business managers must take account of because they must actually be paid out by the firm. This definition of profit is known as **accounting profit.** It is appropriate when used by accountants to determine a firm's taxable income. Economists are more interested in how firm managers react not just to changes in explicit costs but also to changes in **implicit costs,** defined as expenses that business managers do not have to pay out of pocket but are costs to the firm nonetheless because they represent an opportunity cost. These are noncash costs—they do not involve any direct cash outlay by the firm and must therefore be measured by the alternative cost principle. That is to say, they are measured by what the resources (land, capital) currently used in producing a particular good or service could earn in other uses. Economists use the full opportunity cost of all resources (including both explicit and implicit costs) as the figure to subtract from revenues to obtain a definition of profit. Another definition of implicit cost is therefore the opportunity cost of using factors that a producer does not buy or hire but already owns.

Implicit costs 
Expenses that managers do not have to pay out of pocket and hence do not normally explicitly calculate, such as the opportunity cost of factors of production that are owned; examples are owner-provided capital and owner-provided labor.

Opportunity Cost of Capital

Firms enter or remain in an industry if they earn, at minimum, a **normal rate of return.** People will not invest their wealth in a business unless they obtain a positive normal (competitive) rate of return—that is, unless their invested wealth pays off. Any business wishing to attract capital must expect to pay at least the same rate of return on that capital as all other businesses (of similar risk) are willing to pay. Put another way, when a firm requires the use of a resource in producing a particular product, it must bid against alternative users of that resource. Thus the firm must offer a price that is at least as much as other potential users are offering to pay. For example, if individuals can invest their wealth in almost any publishing firm and get a rate of return of 10 percent per year, each firm in the publishing industry must *expect* to pay 10 percent as the normal rate of return to present and future investors. This 10 percent is a *cost to the firm,* the **opportunity cost of capital.** The opportunity cost of capital is the amount of income, or yield, that could have been earned by investing in the next-best alternative. Capital will not stay in firms or industries in which the expected rate of return falls below its opportunity cost, that is, what could be earned elsewhere. If a firm owns some capital equipment, it can either use it or lease it and earn a return. If the firm uses the equipment for production, part of the cost of using that equipment is the forgone revenue that the firm could have earned had it leased out that equipment.

Normal rate of return 
The amount that must be paid to an investor to induce investment in a business; also known as the *opportunity cost of capital.*

Opportunity cost of capital 
The normal rate of return, or the available return on the next-best alternative investment. Economists consider this a cost of production, and it is included in our cost examples.

Opportunity Cost of Owner-Provided Labor and Capital

Single-owner proprietorships often grossly exaggerate their profit rates because they understate the opportunity cost of the labor that the proprietor provides to the business. Here we are referring to the opportunity cost of labor. For example, you may know people who run a small grocery store. These people will sit down at the end of the year and figure out what their "profits" are. They will add up all their sales and subtract what they had to pay to other workers, what they had to pay to their suppliers, what they had to pay in taxes, and so on. The end result they will call "profit." They normally will not, however, have figured into their costs the salary that they could have made if they had worked for somebody else in a similar type of job. By working for themselves, they become residual claimants—they receive what is left after all explicit costs have been accounted for. However, part of the costs should include the salary the owner-operator could have received working for someone else.

Consider a simple example of a skilled auto mechanic working 14 hours a day at his own service station, six days a week. Compare this situation to how much he could earn as a trucking company mechanic 84 hours a week. This self-employed auto mechanic might have an opportunity cost of about $20 an hour. For his 84-hour week in his own service station, he is forfeiting $1,680. Unless his service station shows accounting profits of more than that per week, he is losing money in an economic sense.

Click here to obtain the most recent estimates of U.S. firms' annual revenues and payroll expenses.

Another way of looking at the opportunity cost of running a business is that opportunity cost consists of all explicit and implicit costs. Accountants only take account of explicit costs. Therefore, accounting profit ends up being the residual after only explicit costs are subtracted from total revenues.

This same analysis can apply to owner-provided capital, such as land or buildings. The fact that the owner owns the building or the land with which he or she operates a business does not mean that it is "free." Rather, use of the building and land still has an opportunity cost—the value of the next-best alternative use for those assets.

Accounting Profits Versus Economic Profits

Economic profits Total revenues minus total opportunity costs of all inputs used, or the total of all implicit and explicit costs.

The term *profits* in economics means the income that entrepreneurs earn, over and above all costs including their own opportunity cost of time, plus the opportunity cost of the capital they have invested in their business. Profits can be regarded as total revenues minus total costs—which is how accountants think of them—but we must now include *all* costs. Our definition of **economic profits** will be the following:

$$\text{Economic profits} = \text{total revenues} - \text{total opportunity cost of all inputs used}$$

or

$$\text{Economic profits} = \text{total revenues} - (\text{explicit} + \text{implicit costs})$$

Remember that implicit costs include a normal rate of return on invested capital. We show this relationship in Figure 22-1.

The Goal of the Firm: Profit Maximization 

When we examined the theory of consumer demand, utility (or satisfaction) maximization by the individual provided the basis for the analysis. In the theory of the firm and production, *profit maximization* is the underlying hypothesis of our predictive theory. The goal of

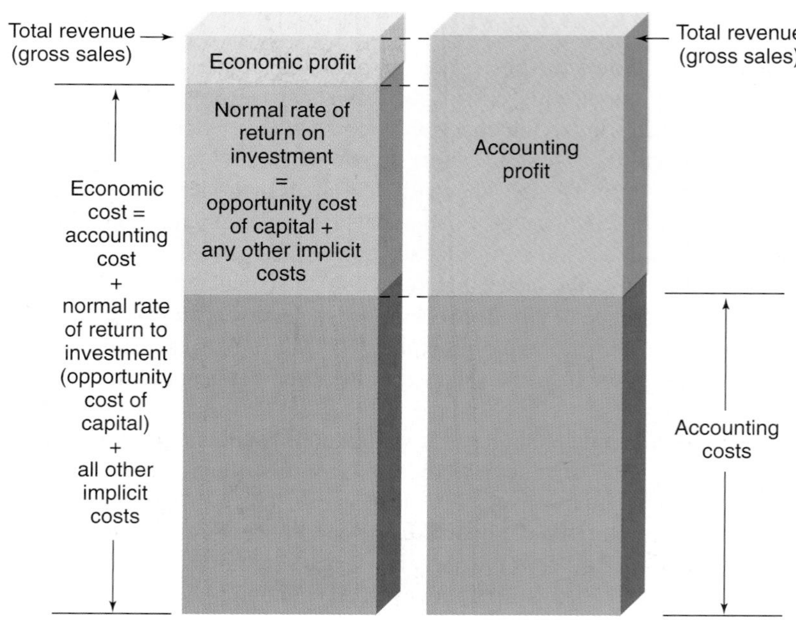

FIGURE 22-1
Simplified View of Economic and Accounting Profit
We see on the right column that accounting profit is the difference between total revenues and total explicit accounting costs. Conversely, we see on the left column that economic profit is equal to total revenues minus economic costs. Economic costs equal explicit accounting costs plus all implicit costs, including a normal rate of return on invested capital.

the firm is to maximize economic profits, and the firm is expected to try to make the positive difference between total revenues and total costs as large as it can.

Our justification for assuming profit maximization by firms is similar to our belief in utility maximization by individuals. To obtain labor, capital, and other resources required to produce commodities, firms must first obtain financing from investors. In general, investors are indifferent about the details of how a firm uses the money they provide. They are most interested in the earnings on this money and the risk of obtaining lower returns or losing the money they have invested. Firms that can provide relatively higher risk-corrected returns will therefore have an advantage in obtaining the financing needed to continue or expand production. Over time we would expect a policy of profit maximization to become the dominant mode of behavior for firms that survive.

FAQ

Haven't the profit rates of American corporations been growing?

No, after accounting for year-to-year variations arising from cyclical factors, pretax U.S. corporate profit rates have generally declined since the 1970s. Between 1950 and the mid-1970s, pretax corporate profits averaged about 11 percent of GDP. Over the period since the mid-1970s, pretax profits have averaged slightly less than 8 percent of GDP. The rate of *after*-tax profits relative to GDP has remained relatively stable, within a range of about 4 to 6 percent.

CONCEPTS IN BRIEF

- Accounting profits differ from economic profits. Economic profits are defined as total revenues minus total costs, where costs include the full opportunity cost of all of the factors of production plus all other implicit costs.
- Single-owner proprietorships often fail to consider the opportunity cost of the labor services provided by the owner.
- The full opportunity cost of capital invested in a business is generally not included as a cost when accounting profits are calculated. Thus accounting profits often overstate economic profits.
- We assume throughout these chapters that the goal of the firm is to maximize economic profits.

SHORT RUN VERSUS LONG RUN

In Chapter 20, we discussed short-run and long-run price elasticities of supply and demand. For consumers, the long run meant the time period during which all adjustments to a change in price could be made, and anything shorter than that was considered the short run. For suppliers, the long run was the time in which all adjustments could be made, and anything shorter than that was the short run.

Now that we are discussing firms only, we will maintain a similar distinction between the short and the long run, but we will be more specific. In the theory of the firm, the **short run** is defined as any time period that is so short that there is at least one input, such as current **plant size,** that the firm cannot alter.* In other words, during the short run, a firm makes do with whatever big machines and factory size it already has, no matter how much more it wants to produce because of increased demand for its product. We consider the plant and heavy equipment, the size or amount of which cannot be varied in the short run,

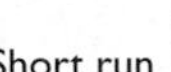

Short run The time period when at least one input, such as plant size, cannot be changed.

Plant size The physical size of the factories that a firm owns and operates to produce its output. Plant size can be defined by square footage, maximum physical capacity, and other physical measures.

*There can be many short runs but only one long run. For ease of analysis, in this section we simplify the case to one short run and talk about short-run costs.

as fixed resources. In agriculture and in some other businesses, land may be a fixed resource.

There are, of course, variable resources that the firm can alter when it wants to change its rate of production. These are called *variable inputs* or *variable factors of production.* Typically, the variable inputs of a firm are its labor and its purchases of raw materials. In the short run, in response to changes in demand, the firm can, by definition, change only the amounts of its variable inputs.

Long run
The time period in which all factors of production can be varied.

The **long run** can now be considered the period of time in which *all* inputs can be varied. Specifically, in the long run, the firm can alter its plant size. How long is the long run? That depends on each individual industry. For Wendy's or McDonald's, the long run may be four or five months, because that is the time it takes to add new franchises. For a steel company, the long run may be several years, because that's how long it takes to plan and build a new plant. An electric utility might need over a decade to build a new plant, as another example.

Short run and *long run* in our discussion are in fact management planning terms that apply to decisions made by managers. The firm can operate only in the short run in the sense that decisions must be made in the present. The same analysis applies to your own behavior. You may have many long-run plans about graduate school, vacations, and the like, but you always operate in the short run—you make decisions every day about what you do every day.

THE RELATIONSHIP BETWEEN OUTPUT AND INPUTS

A firm takes numerous inputs, combines them using a technological production process, and ends up with an output. There are, of course, a great many factors of production, or inputs. We classify production inputs into two broad categories (ignoring land)—labor and capital. The relationship between output and these two inputs is as follows:

Output per time period = some function of capital and labor inputs

In simple math, the production relationship can be written $Q = f(K, L)$, where Q = output per time period, K = capital, and L = labor.

Production 
Any activity that results in the conversion of resources into products that can be used in consumption.

We have used the word *production* but have not defined it. **Production** is any process by which resources are transformed into goods or services. Production includes not only making things but also transporting them, retailing, repackaging them, and so on. Notice that if we know that production occurs, we do not necessarily know the value of the output. The production relationship tells nothing about the worth or value of the inputs or the output.

INTERNATIONAL EXAMPLE

Europeans Use More Capital

Since 1970, the 15 nations of the European Union (EU) have increased their total annual output of goods and services relatively steadily. But over this same time period, the EU has dramatically increased the amount of capital relative to the amount of labor it uses in its production processes. Business managers in the EU have substituted capital for labor much more than in the United States because the cost of labor (wages corrected for inflation) has increased by almost 60 percent in the EU but by only 15 percent in the United States.

For Critical Analysis

How does a firm decide when to buy more machines?

The Production Function: A Numerical Example

The relationship between maximum physical output and the quantity of capital and labor used in the production process is sometimes called a **production function.** The production function is a technological relationship between inputs and output. Firms that are inefficient or wasteful in their use of capital and labor will obtain less output than the production function in theory will show. No firm can obtain more output than the production function shows, however. The production function specifies the maximum possible output that can be produced with a given amount of inputs. It also specifies the minimum amount of inputs necessary to produce a given level of output. The production function depends on the technology available to the firm. It follows that an improvement in technology that allows the firm to produce more output with the same amount of inputs (or the same output with fewer inputs) results in a new production function.

Production function 
The relationship between inputs and maximum physical output. A production function is a technological, not an economic, relationship.

Look at panel (a) of Figure 22-2 on page 538. It shows a production function relating total output in column 2 to the quantity of labor measured in workers per week in column 1. When there are zero workers per week of input, there is no output. When there are 5 workers per week of input (given the capital stock), there is a total output of 50 bushels per week. (Ignore for the moment the rest of that panel.) Panel (b) of Figure 22-2 shows this particular hypothetical production function graphically. Note again that it relates to the short run and that it is for an individual firm.

The Theory of Firm Production
Gain further understanding of the production function for a firm.

Panel (b) shows a total physical product curve, or the maximum amount of physical output that is possible when we add successive equal-sized units of labor while holding all other inputs constant. The graph of the production function in panel (b) is not a straight line. In fact, it peaks at 7 workers per week and starts to go down. To understand why it starts to go down with an individual firm in the short run, we have to analyze in detail the **law of diminishing (marginal) returns.**

Law of diminishing (marginal) returns 
The observation that after some point, successive equal-sized increases in a variable factor of production, such as labor, added to fixed factors of production, will result in smaller increases in output.

But before that, let's examine the meaning of columns 3 and 4 of panel (a) of Figure 22-2—that is, average and marginal physical product.

Average and Physical Marginal Product

The definition of **average physical product** is straightforward: It is the total product divided by the number of worker weeks. You can see in column 3 of panel (a) of Figure 22-2 that the average physical product of labor first rises and then steadily falls after two workers are hired.

Average physical product 
Total product divided by the variable input.

Remember that *marginal* means "additional." Hence the **marginal physical product** of labor is the change in total product that occurs when a worker joins an existing production process. (The term *physical* here emphasizes the fact that we are measuring in terms of physical units of production, not in dollar terms.) It is also the *change* in total product that occurs when that worker quits or is laid off an existing production process. The marginal physical product of labor therefore refers to the *change in output caused by a one-unit change in the labor input.* (Marginal physical product is also referred to as *marginal product* and *marginal return.*)

Marginal physical product 
The physical output that is due to the addition of one more unit of a variable factor of production; the change in total product occurring when a variable input is increased and all other inputs are held constant; also called *marginal product* or *marginal return.*

DIMINISHING MARGINAL RETURNS

The concept of diminishing marginal returns—also known as diminishing marginal product—applies to many situations. If you put a seat belt across your lap, a certain amount of safety is obtained. If you add another seat belt over your shoulder, some additional safety

FIGURE 22-2

Diminishing Returns, the Production Function, and Marginal Product: A Hypothetical Case

Marginal product is the addition to the total product that results when one additional worker is hired. Thus the marginal product of the fourth worker is eight bushels of wheat. With four workers, 44 bushels are produced, but with three workers, only 36 are produced; the difference is 8. In panel (b), we plot the numbers from columns 1 and 2 of panel (a). In panel (c), we plot the numbers from columns 1 and 4 of panel (a). When we go from 0 to 1, marginal product is 10. When we go from one worker to two workers, marginal product increases to 16. After two workers, marginal product declines, but it is still positive. Total product (output) reaches its peak at seven workers, so after seven workers marginal product is negative. When we move from seven to eight workers, marginal product becomes −1 bushel.

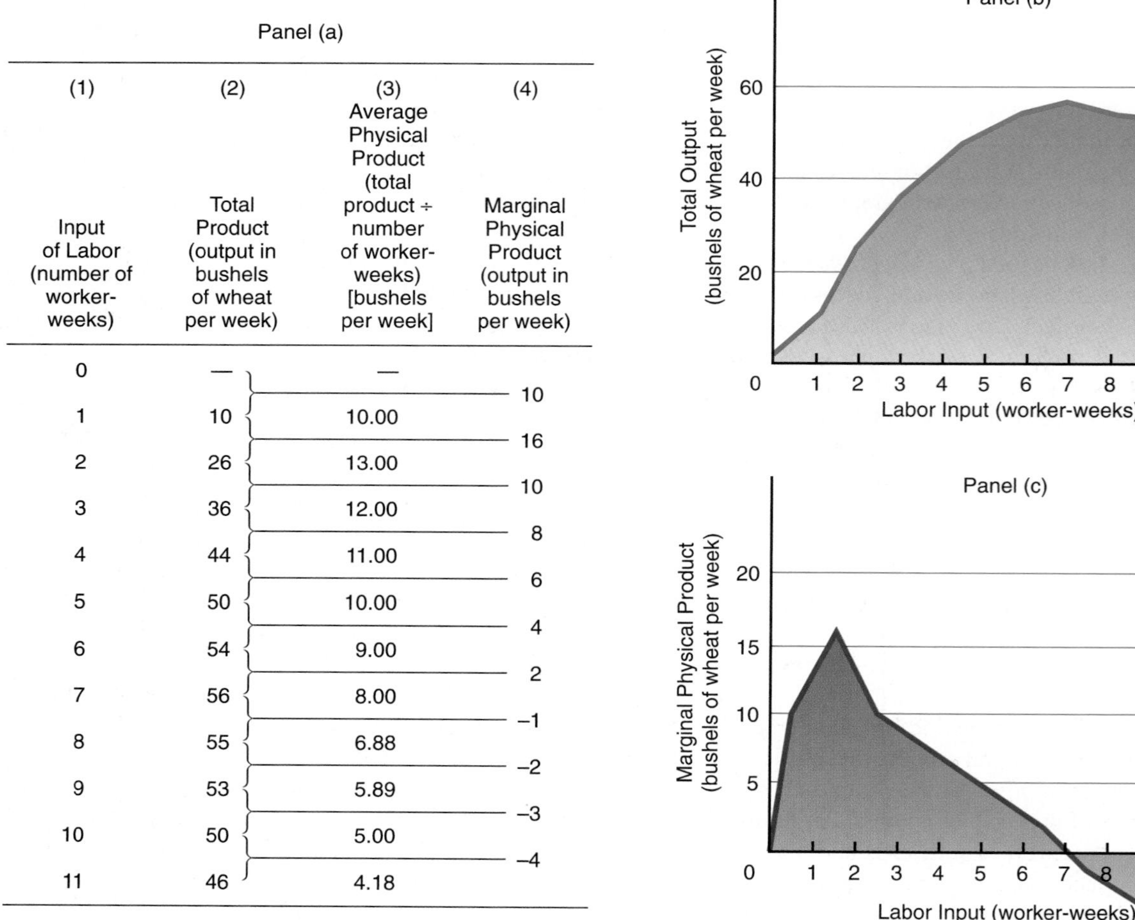

Panel (a)

(1) Input of Labor (number of worker-weeks)	(2) Total Product (output in bushels of wheat per week)	(3) Average Physical Product (total product ÷ number of worker-weeks) [bushels per week]	(4) Marginal Physical Product (output in bushels per week)
0	—	—	
			10
1	10	10.00	
			16
2	26	13.00	
			10
3	36	12.00	
			8
4	44	11.00	
			6
5	50	10.00	
			4
6	54	9.00	
			2
7	56	8.00	
			−1
8	55	6.88	
			−2
9	53	5.89	
			−3
10	50	5.00	
			−4
11	46	4.18	

is obtained, but less than when the first belt was secured. When you add a third seat belt over the other shoulder, the amount of *additional* safety obtained is even smaller.

The same analysis holds for firms in their use of productive inputs. When the returns from hiring more workers are diminishing, it does not necessarily mean that more workers won't be hired. In fact, workers will be hired until the returns, in terms of the *value* of the *extra* output produced, are equal to the additional wages that have to be paid for those workers to produce the extra output. Before we get into that decision-making process, let's demonstrate that diminishing returns can be represented graphically and can be used in our analysis of the firm.

Measuring Diminishing Returns

How do we measure diminishing returns? First, we limit the analysis to only one variable factor of production (or input)—let's say the factor is labor. Every other factor of production, such as machines, must be held constant. Only in this way can we calculate the marginal returns from using more workers and know when we reach the point of diminishing marginal returns.

Click here to consider an additional numerical illustration of a production function and diminishing returns.

The marginal productivity of labor may increase rapidly at the very beginning. A firm starts with no workers, only machines. The firm then hires one worker, who finds it difficult to get the work started. But when the firm hires more workers, each is able to *specialize,* and the marginal product of those additional workers may actually be greater than the marginal product of the previous few workers. Beyond some point, however, diminishing returns must set in—*not* because new workers are less qualified but because each worker has, on average, fewer machines with which to work (remember, all other inputs are fixed). In fact, eventually the firm will become so crowded that workers will start to get in each other's way. At that point, marginal physical product becomes negative, and total production declines.

Using these ideas, we can define the law of diminishing returns as follows:

> As successive equal increases in a variable factor of production are added to fixed factors of production, there will be a point beyond which the extra, or marginal, product that can be attributed to each additional unit of the variable factor of production will decline.

Note that the law of diminishing returns is a statement about the *physical* relationships between inputs and outputs that we have observed in many firms. If the law of diminishing returns were not a fairly accurate statement about the world, what would stop firms from hiring additional workers forever?

An Example of the Law of Diminishing Returns

Agriculture provides an example of the law of diminishing returns. With a fixed amount of land, fertilizer, and tractors, the addition of more farm workers eventually yields decreasing increases in output. After a while, when all the tractors are being used, additional farm workers will have to start farming manually. They obviously won't be as productive as the first farm workers who manned the tractors. The marginal physical product of an additional farm worker, given a specified amount of capital, must eventually be less than that for the previous workers.

A hypothetical set of numbers illustrating the law of diminishing marginal returns is presented in panel (a) of Figure 22-2. The numbers are presented graphically in panel (c). Marginal productivity (returns from adding more workers) first increases, then decreases, and finally becomes negative.

When one worker is hired, total output goes from 0 to 10. Thus marginal physical product is 10 bushels of wheat per week. When the second worker is hired, total product goes from 10 to 26 bushels of wheat per week. Marginal physical product therefore increases to 16 bushels of wheat per week. When a third worker is hired, total product again increases, from 26 to 36 bushels of wheat per week. This represents a marginal physical product of only 10 bushels of wheat per week. Therefore, the point of diminishing marginal returns occurs after two workers are hired.

Notice that after 7 workers per week, marginal physical product becomes negative. That means that the hiring of an eighth worker would create a situation that reduces total product. Sometimes this is called the *point of saturation,* indicating that given the amount of fixed inputs, there is no further positive use for more of the variable input. We have entered the region of negative marginal returns.

EXAMPLE

Microsoft Confronts the Law of Diminishing Marginal Returns

One of the great success stories of the computer age has been Microsoft's Windows, which for some time has been the dominant operating system for personal computers. Many businesses and households have also come to rely on another Microsoft desktop software package called Office, a "suite" of programs, including Word, Excel, PowerPoint, and Access. In 1999, Microsoft released Office 2000, which incorporated Internet-friendly features. The scheduled 2002 release of Office 2003 promises speech-recognition programs that may make certain keyboard and mouse functions redundant.

In spite of these features, Microsoft has had to work harder at promoting each new version of the software package. The reason is that many users of Office increasingly find that its programs are so crammed with features that they cannot begin to exhaust the possibilities. According to some estimates, even enterprising users with lots of time on their hands are unlikely to use more than a quarter of the features of the Word 2000 word processing program. Consequently, a large number of computer users are concluding that upgrading to bigger, more sophisticated versions of the Office suite does little to enhance their productivity.

Because so many users of Office are confronting diminishing marginal returns from adding further to the already extensive software code stored on their hard drives, Microsoft is working hard on the suite's new speech-recognition features. Presumably, the company is hoping that if nothing else, people will appreciate having their computers do what they tell them to do.

For Critical Analysis

Under what circumstances could adding computer software yield a *negative* marginal product, at least within a period following installation of the software?

CONCEPTS IN BRIEF

- The technological relationship between output and input is called the production function. It relates output per time period to the several inputs, such as capital and labor.
- After some rate of output, the firm generally experiences diminishing marginal returns.
- The law of diminishing returns states that if all factors of production are held constant except one, equal increments in that one variable factor will eventually yield decreasing increments in output.

SHORT-RUN COSTS TO THE FIRM 

You will see that costs are the extension of the production ideas just presented. Let's consider the costs the firm faces in the short run. To make this example simple, assume that there are only two factors of production, capital and labor. Our definition of the short run will be the time during which capital is fixed but labor is variable.

In the short run, a firm incurs certain types of costs. We label all costs incurred **total costs.** Then we break total costs down into total fixed costs and total variable costs, which we will explain shortly. Therefore,

Total costs (TC) = total fixed costs (TFC) + total variable costs (TVC)

Total costs
The sum of total fixed costs and total variable costs.

Remember that these total costs include both explicit and implicit costs, including the normal rate of return on investment.

After we have looked at the elements of total costs, we will find out how to compute average and marginal costs.

Total Fixed Costs

Let's look at an ongoing business such as Dell Computer. The decision makers in that corporate giant can look around and see big machines, thousands of parts, huge buildings, and a multitude of other components of plant and equipment that have already been bought and are in place. Dell has to take account of the technological obsolescence of this equipment, no matter how many computers it produces. The payments on the loans taken out to buy the equipment will all be exactly the same. The opportunity costs of any land that Dell owns will all be exactly the same. These costs are more or less the same for Dell no matter how many computers it produces.

We also have to point out that the opportunity cost (or normal rate of return) of capital must be included along with other costs. Remember that we are dealing in the short run, during which capital is fixed. If investors in Dell have already put $100 million into a new factory addition, the opportunity cost of that capital invested is now, in essence, a *fixed cost.* Why? Because in the short run, nothing can be done about that cost; the investment has already been made. This leads us to a very straightforward definition of fixed costs: All costs that do not vary—that is, all costs that do not depend on the rate of production—are called **fixed costs.**

Fixed costs 
Costs that do not vary with output. Fixed costs include such things as rent on a building. These costs are fixed for a certain period of time; in the long run, they are variable.

Let's now take as an example the fixed costs incurred by an assembler of pocket calculators. This firm's total fixed costs will equal the cost of the rent on its equipment and the insurance it has to pay. We see in panel (a) of Figure 22-3 on page 542 that total fixed costs per day are $10. In panel (b), these total fixed costs are represented by the horizontal line at $10 per day. They are invariant to changes in the output of calculators per day—no matter how many are produced, fixed costs will remain at $10 per day.

Total Variable Costs

Variable costs 
Costs that vary with the rate of production. They include wages paid to workers and purchases of materials.

Total **variable costs** are costs whose magnitude varies with the rate of production. One obvious variable cost is wages. The more the firm produces, the more labor it has to hire; therefore, the more wages it has to pay. Another variable cost is parts. In the assembly of calculators, for example, microchips must be bought. The more calculators that are made, the more chips must be bought. Part of the rate of depreciation (the rate of wear and tear) on machines that are used in the assembly process can also be considered a variable cost if depreciation depends partly on how long and how intensively the machines are used. Total variable costs are given in column 3 in panel (a) of Figure 22-3. These are translated into the total variable cost curve in panel (b). Notice that the total variable cost curve lies below the total cost curve by the vertical distance of $10. This vertical distance represents, of course, total fixed costs.

FIGURE 22-3

Cost of Production: An Example

In panel (a), the derivation of columns 4 through 9 are given in parentheses in each column heading. For example, column 6, average variable costs, is derived by dividing column 3, total variable costs, by column 1, total output per day. Note that marginal cost (MC) in panel (c) intersects average variable costs (AVC) at the latter's minimum point. Also, MC intersects average total costs (ATC) at that latter's minimum point. It is a little more difficult to see that MC equals AVC and ATC at their respective minimum points in panel (a) because we are using discrete one-unit changes. You can see, though, that the marginal cost of going from 4 units per day to 5 units per day is $2 and increases to $3 when we move to 6 units per day. Somewhere in the middle it equals AVC of $2.60, which is in fact the minimum average variable cost. The same analysis holds for ATC, which hits minimum at 7 units per day at $4.28 per unit. MC goes from $4 to $5 and just equals ATC somewhere in between.

Panel (a)

(1) Total Output (*Q*/day)	(2) Total Fixed Costs (TFC)	(3) Total Variable Costs (TVC)	(4) Total Costs (TC) (4) = (2) + (3)	(5) Average Fixed Costs (AFC) (5) = (2) ÷ (1)	(6) Average Variable Costs (AVC) (6) = (3) ÷ (1)	(7) Average Total Costs (ATC) (7) = (4) ÷ (1)	(8) Total Costs (TC) (4)	(9) Marginal Cost (MC) (9) = change in (8) / change in (1)
0	$10	$ 0	$10	—	—	—	$10	
1	10	5	15	$10.00	$5.00	$15.00	15	$5
2	10	8	18	5.00	4.00	9.00	18	3
3	10	10	20	3.33	3.33	6.67	20	2
4	10	11	21	2.50	2.75	5.25	21	1
5	10	13	23	2.00	2.60	4.60	23	2
6	10	16	26	1.67	2.67	4.33	26	3
7	10	20	30	1.43	2.86	4.28	30	4
8	10	25	35	1.25	3.13	4.38	35	5
9	10	31	41	1.11	3.44	4.56	41	6
10	10	38	48	1.00	3.80	4.80	48	7
11	10	46	56	.91	4.18	5.09	56	8

Panel (b)

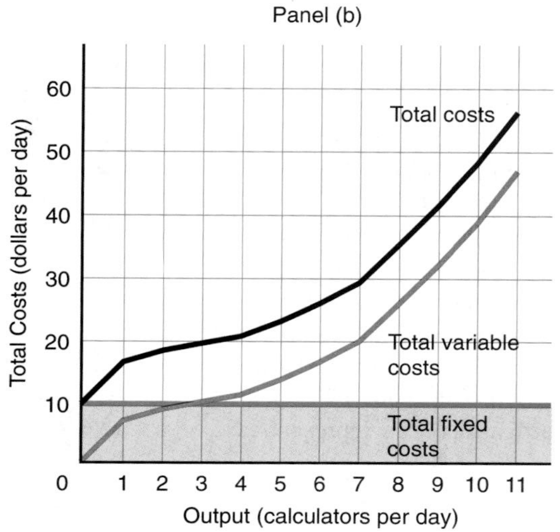

Panel (c)

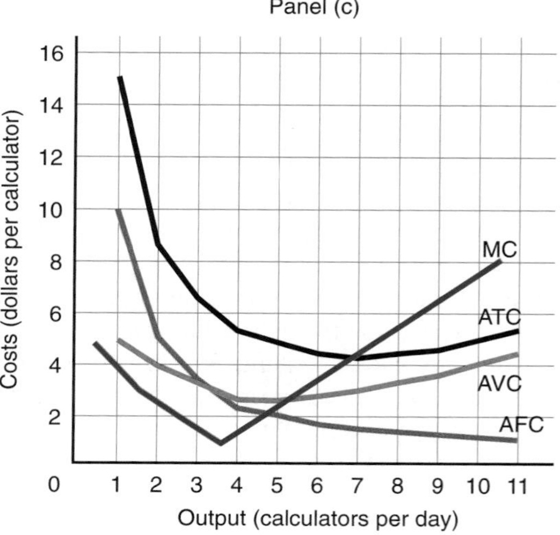

Short-Run Average Cost Curves

In panel (b) of Figure 22-3, we see total costs, total variable costs, and total fixed costs. Now we want to look at average cost. The average cost concept is one in which we are measuring cost per unit of output. It is a matter of simple arithmetic to figure the averages of these three cost concepts. We can define them as follows:

$$\text{Average total costs (ATC)} = \frac{\text{total costs (TC)}}{\text{output } (Q)}$$

$$\text{Average variable costs (AVC)} = \frac{\text{total variable costs (TVC)}}{\text{output } (Q)}$$

$$\text{Average fixed costs (AFC)} = \frac{\text{total fixed costs (TFC)}}{\text{output } (Q)}$$

The arithmetic is done in columns 5, 6, and 7 in panel (a) of Figure 22-3. The numerical results are translated into a graphical format in panel (c). Because total costs (TC) equal variable costs (TVC) plus fixed costs (TFC), the difference between average total costs (ATC) and average variable costs (AVC) will always be identical to average fixed costs (AFC). That means that average total costs and average variable costs move together as output expands.

Now let's see what we can observe about the three average cost curves in Figure 22-3.

Average Fixed Costs (AFC). **Average fixed costs** continue to fall throughout the output range. In fact, if we were to continue panel (c) (see diagram) farther to the right, we would find that average fixed costs would get closer and closer to the horizontal axis. That is because total fixed costs remain constant. As we divide this fixed number by a larger and larger number of units of output, the resulting AFC has to become smaller and smaller. In business, this is called "spreading the overhead."

Average fixed costs
Total fixed costs divided by the number of units produced.

Average Variable Costs (AVC). We assume a particular form of the curve for **average variable costs.** The form that it takes is U-shaped: First it falls; then it starts to rise. It is possible for the AVC curve to take other shapes in the long run.

Average variable costs
Total variable costs divided by the number of units produced.

Average Total Costs (ATC). This curve has a shape similar to that of the AVC curve. However, it falls even more dramatically in the beginning and rises more slowly after it has reached a minimum point. It falls and then rises because **average total costs** are the summation of the AFC curve and the AVC curve. Thus when AFC and AVC are both falling, ATC must fall too. At some point, however, AVC starts to increase while AFC continues to fall. Once the increase in the AVC curve outweighs the decrease in the AFC curve, the ATC curve will start to increase and will develop its familiar U shape.

Average total costs
Total costs divided by the number of units produced; sometimes called *average per-unit total costs.*

Marginal Cost

We have stated repeatedly that the basis of decisions is always on the margin—movement in economics is always determined at the margin. This dictum also holds true within the firm. Firms, according to the analysis we use to predict their behavior, are very interested in their **marginal costs.** Because the term *marginal* means "additional" or "incremental" (or "decremental," too) here, marginal costs refer to costs that result from a one-unit

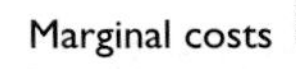

Marginal costs
The change in total costs due to a one-unit change in production rate.

change in the production rate. For example, if the production of 10 calculators per day costs a firm $48 and the production of 11 calculators costs it $56 per day, the marginal cost of producing 11 rather than 10 calculators per day is $8.

Marginal costs can be measured by using the formula

$$\text{Marginal cost} = \frac{\text{change in total cost}}{\text{change in output}}$$

We show the marginal costs of calculator production per day in column 9 of panel (a) in Figure 22-3, calculated according to the formula just given. In our example, we have changed output by one unit every time, so we can ignore variations in the denominator in that particular formula.

This marginal cost schedule is shown graphically in panel (c) of Figure 22-3. Just like average variable costs and average total costs, marginal costs first fall and then rise. The U shape of the marginal cost curve is a result of increasing and then diminishing marginal returns. At lower levels of output, the marginal cost curve declines. The reasoning is that as marginal physical product increases with each addition of output, the marginal cost of this last unit of output must fall. Conversely, when diminishing marginal returns set in, marginal physical product decreases (and eventually becomes negative); it follows that the marginal cost must rise when the marginal product begins its decline. These relationships are clearly reflected in the geometry of panels (b) and (c) of Figure 22-3.

In summary:

As long as marginal physical product rises, marginal cost will fall, and when marginal physical product starts to fall (after reaching the point of diminishing marginal returns), marginal cost will begin to rise.

POLICY EXAMPLE

Can "Three Strikes" Laws Reduce Crime?

Crime and violence have been the top concern of Americans for at least a decade. At both the federal and the state level, politicians have responded with a variety of policies aimed at reducing crime. One popular new law has been labeled "three strikes and you're out." A defendant with a prior conviction for two serious or violent offenses faces mandatory life imprisonment for a third offense.

Such legislation has dramatically affected the marginal cost of violence and murder to potential criminal defendants who have already been convicted of two felonies. Here is what one career criminal, Frank Schweickert, said in a *New York Times* interview: "Before, if I was doing a robbery and getting chased by cops, I'd lay my gun down. . . . But now you are talking about a life sentence. Why isn't it worth doing whatever it takes to get away? If that meant shooting a cop, if that meant shooting a store clerk, if that meant shooting someone innocent in my way, well, they'd have gotten shot. Because what is the worst thing that could happen to me: life imprisonment? If I'm getting a murder sentence anyway, I might as well do whatever it takes to maybe get away." In other words, the "three strikes" legislation has reduced to zero the marginal cost of murder (in non-capital-punishment states) committed while engaging in a criminal activity after two prior felony convictions.

For Critical Analysis

Do criminals subject to the new legislation have to understand the concept of marginal cost in order for our theory to predict well? Explain.

The Relationship Between Average and Marginal Costs

Let us now examine the relationship between average costs and marginal costs. There is always a definite relationship between averages and marginals. Consider the example of 10 football players with an average weight of 200 pounds. An eleventh player is added. His weight is 250 pounds. That represents the marginal weight. What happens now to the average weight of the team? It must increase. Thus when the marginal player weighs more than the average, the average must increase. Likewise, if the marginal player weighs less than 200 pounds, the average weight will decrease.

The Short-Run Costs of the Firm
Get extra practice applying average and marginal costs.

There is a similar relationship between average variable costs and marginal costs. When marginal costs are less than average costs, the latter must fall. Conversely, when marginal costs are greater than average costs, the latter must rise. When you think about it, the relationship makes sense. The only way for average variable costs to fall is for the extra cost of the marginal unit produced to be less than the average variable cost of all the preceding units. For example, if the average variable cost for two units of production is $4.00 a unit, the only way for the average variable cost of three units to be less than that of two units is for the variable costs attributable to the last unit—the marginal cost—to be less than the average of the past units. In this particular case, if average variable cost falls to $3.33 a unit, total variable cost for the three units would be three times $3.33, or almost exactly $10.00. Total variable cost for two units is two times $4.00, or $8.00. The marginal cost is therefore $10.00 minus $8.00, or $2.00, which is less than the average variable cost of $3.33.

A similar type of computation can be carried out for rising average variable costs. The only way for average variable costs to rise is for the average variable cost of additional units to be more than that for units already produced. But the incremental cost is the marginal cost. In this particular case, the marginal costs have to be higher than the average variable costs.

There is also a relationship between marginal costs and average total costs. Remember that average total cost is equal to total cost divided by the number of units produced. Remember also that marginal cost does not include any fixed costs. Fixed costs are, by definition, fixed and cannot influence marginal costs. Our example can therefore be repeated substituting *average total cost* for *average variable cost.*

These rising and falling relationships can be seen in Figure 22-3, where MC intersects AVC and ATC at their respective minimum points.

Minimum Cost Points

At what rate of output of calculators per day does our representative firm experience the minimum average total costs? Column 7 in panel (a) of Figure 22-3 shows that the minimum average total cost is $4.28, which occurs at an output rate of seven calculators per day. We can also find this minimum cost by finding the point in panel (c) of Figure 22-3 at which the marginal cost curve intersects the average total cost curve. This should not be surprising. When marginal cost is below average total cost, average total cost falls. When marginal cost is above average total cost, average total cost rises. At the point where average total cost is neither falling nor rising, marginal cost must then be equal to average total cost. When we represent this graphically, the marginal cost curve will intersect the average total cost curve at the latter's minimum.

The same analysis applies to the intersection of the marginal cost curve and the average variable cost curve. When are average variable costs at a minimum? According to panel (a) of Figure 22-3, average variable costs are at a minimum of $2.60 at an output rate of five calculators per day. This is where the marginal cost curve intersects the average variable cost curve in panel (c) of Figure 22-3.

CONCEPTS IN BRIEF

- Total costs equal total fixed costs plus total variable costs.
- Fixed costs are those that do not vary with the rate of production; variable costs are those that do vary with the rate of production.
- Average total costs equal total costs divided by output ($ATC=TC/Q$).
- Average variable costs equal total variable costs divided by output ($AVC=TVC/Q$).
- Average fixed costs equal total fixed costs divided by output ($AFC=TFC/Q$).
- Marginal cost equals the change in total cost divided by the change in output ($MC=\Delta TC/\Delta Q$, where Δ means "change in").
- The marginal cost curve intersects the minimum point of the average total cost curve and the minimum point of the average variable cost curve.

THE RELATIONSHIP BETWEEN DIMINISHING MARGINAL RETURNS AND COST CURVES

There is a unique relationship between output and the shape of the various cost curves we have drawn. Let's consider specifically the relationship between marginal cost and the example of diminishing marginal physical returns in panel (a) of Figure 22-4. It turns out that if wage rates are constant, the shape of the marginal cost curve in panel (d) of Figure 22-4 is both a reflection of and a consequence of the law of diminishing returns. Let's assume that each unit of labor can be purchased at a constant price. Further assume that labor is the only variable input. We see that as more workers are hired, marginal physical product first rises and then falls after the point at which diminishing returns are encountered. Thus the marginal cost of each extra unit of output will first fall as long as marginal physical product is rising, and then it will rise as long as marginal physical product is falling. Recall that marginal cost is defined as

$$MC = \frac{\text{change in total cost}}{\text{change in output}}$$

Because the price of labor is assumed to be constant, the change in total cost depends solely on the constant price of labor, *W*. The change in output is simply the marginal physical product (MPP) of the one-unit increase in labor. Therefore, we see that

$$\text{Marginal cost} = \frac{W}{\text{MPP}}$$

This means that initially, when there are increasing returns, marginal cost falls (we are dividing *W* by increasingly larger numbers), and later, when diminishing returns set in and marginal physical product is falling, marginal cost must increase (we are dividing *W* by smaller numbers). As marginal physical product increases, marginal cost decreases, and as marginal physical product decreases, marginal cost must increase. Thus when marginal physical product reaches its maximum, marginal cost necessarily reaches its minimum. To illustrate this, let's return to Figure 22-2 and consider specifically panel (a). Assume that a worker is paid $100 a week. When we go from zero labor input to one unit, output increases by 10 bushels of wheat. Each of those 10 bushels of wheat has a marginal cost of $10. Now the second unit of labor is hired, and it too costs $100 per week. Output increases by 16. Thus the marginal cost is $\$100 \div 16 = \$6.25$. We continue the experiment. We see that the next unit of labor yields only 10 additional bushels of wheat, so marginal cost starts to rise again back to $10. The following unit of labor increases marginal physical product by only 8, so marginal cost becomes $\$100 \div 8 = \$12.50$.

Panel (a)

(1) Labor Input	(2) Total Product (number of pairs sold)	(3) Average Physical Product (pairs per salesperson) (3) = (2) ÷ (1)	(4) Marginal Physical Product	(5) Average Variable Cost (5) = *W* ($100) ÷ (3)	(6) Marginal Cost (6) = *W* ($100) ÷ (4)
0	0	—	—	—	—
1	50	50	50	$2.00	$2.00
2	110	55	60	1.82	1.67
3	180	60	70	1.67	1.43
4	240	60	60	1.67	1.67
5	290	58	50	1.72	2.00
6	330	55	40	1.82	2.50
7	360	51	30	1.96	3.33

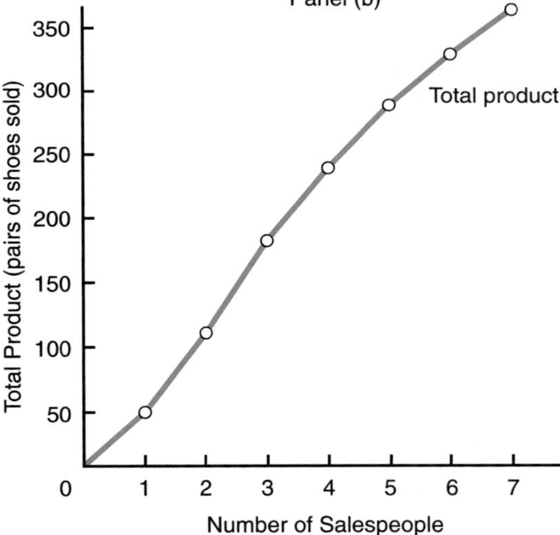

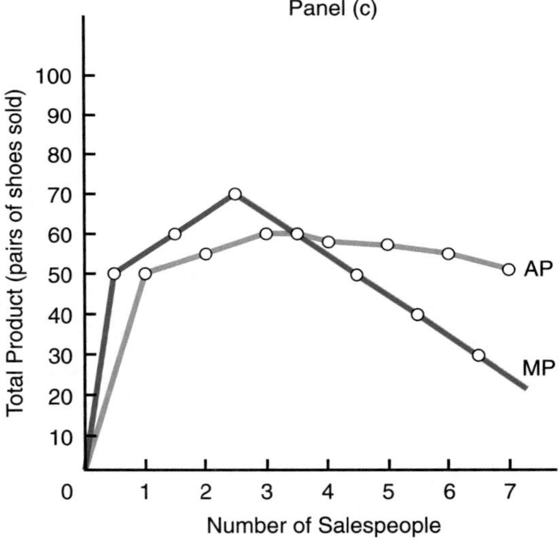

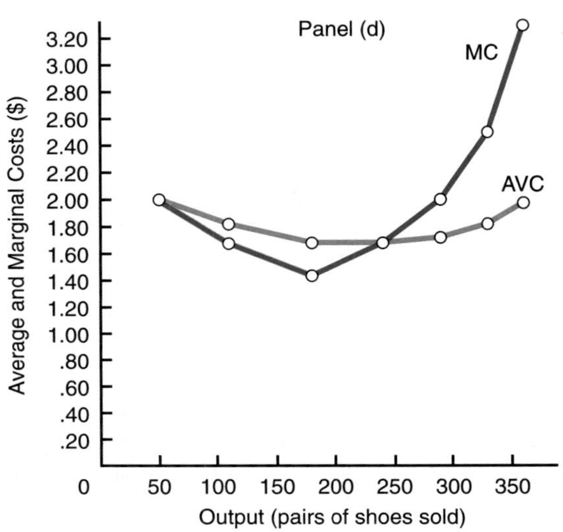

FIGURE 22-4

The Relationship Between Physical Output and Costs

As the number of salespeople increases, the total number of pairs of shoes sold rises, as shown in panels (a) and (b). In panel (c), marginal physical product (MPP) first rises and then falls. Average physical product (APP) follows. The mirror image of panel (c) is shown in panel (d), in which MC and AVC first fall and then rise.

All of the foregoing can be restated in relatively straightforward terms:

> Firms' short-run cost curves are a reflection of the law of diminishing marginal returns. Given any constant price of the variable input, marginal costs decline as long as the marginal product of the variable resource is rising. At the point at which diminishing marginal returns begin, marginal costs begin to rise as the marginal product of the variable input begins to decline.

The result is a marginal cost curve that slopes down, hits a minimum, and then slopes up. The average total cost curve and average variable cost curve are of course affected. They will have their familiar U shape in the short run. Again, to see this, recall that

$$\text{AVC} = \frac{\text{total variable costs}}{\text{total output}}$$

As we move from zero labor input to one unit in panel (a) of Figure 22-2, output increases from zero to 10 bushels. The total variable costs are the price per worker, *W* ($100), times the number of workers (1). Because the average product of one worker (column 3) is 10, we can write the total product, 10, as the average product, 10, times the number of workers, 1. Thus we see that

$$\text{AVC} = \frac{\$100 \times 1}{10 \times 1} = \frac{\$100}{10} = \frac{W}{\text{AP}}$$

From column 3 in panel (a) of Figure 22-2 we see that the average product increases, reaches a maximum, and then declines. Because AVC = *W*/AP, average variable cost decreases as average product increases and increases as average product decreases. AVC reaches its minimum when average product reaches its maximum. Furthermore, because ATC = AVC+AFC, the average total cost curve inherits the relationship between the average variable cost and diminishing returns.

To illustrate, consider a shoe store that employs salespeople to sell shoes. Panel (a) of Figure 22-4 presents in column 2 the total number of pairs of shoes sold as the number of salespeople increases. Notice that the total product first increases at an increasing rate and later increases at a decreasing rate. This is reflected in column 4, which shows that the marginal physical product increases at first and then falls. The average physical product too first rises and then falls. The marginal and average physical products are graphed in panel (c) of Figure 22-4. Our immediate interest here is the average variable and marginal costs. Because we can define average variable cost as $100/AP (assuming that the wage paid is constant at $100), as the average product rises from 50 to 55 to 60 pairs of shoes sold, the average variable cost falls from $2.00 to $1.82 to $1.67. Conversely, as average product falls from 60 to 50, average variable cost rises from $1.67 to $2.00. Likewise, because marginal cost can also be defined as *W*/MPP, we see that as marginal physical product rises from 50 to 70, marginal cost falls from $2.00 to $1.43. As marginal physical product falls to 30, marginal cost rises to $3.33. These relationships are also expressed in panels (b), (c), and (d) of Figure 22-4.

LONG-RUN COST CURVES

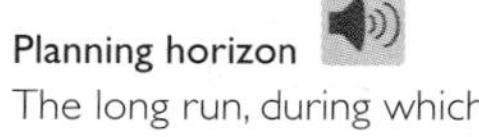

Planning horizon
The long run, during which all inputs are variable.

The long run is defined as a time period during which full adjustment can be made to any change in the economic environment. Thus in the long run, *all* factors of production are variable. Long-run curves are sometimes called *planning curves,* and the long run is sometimes called the **planning horizon.** We start out our analysis of long-run cost curves by

FIGURE 22-5
Preferable Plant Size and the Long-Run Average Cost Curve
If the anticipated permanent rate of output per unit time period is Q_1, the optimal plant to build would be the one corresponding to SAC_1 in panel (a) because average costs are lower. However, if the permanent rate of output increases to Q_2, it will be more profitable to have a plant size corresponding to SAC_2. Unit costs fall to C_3.

If we draw all the possible short-run average cost curves that correspond to different plant sizes and then draw the envelope (a curve tangent to each member of a set of curves) to these various curves, SAC_1–SAC_8, we obtain the long-run average cost curve, or the planning curve, as shown in panel (b).

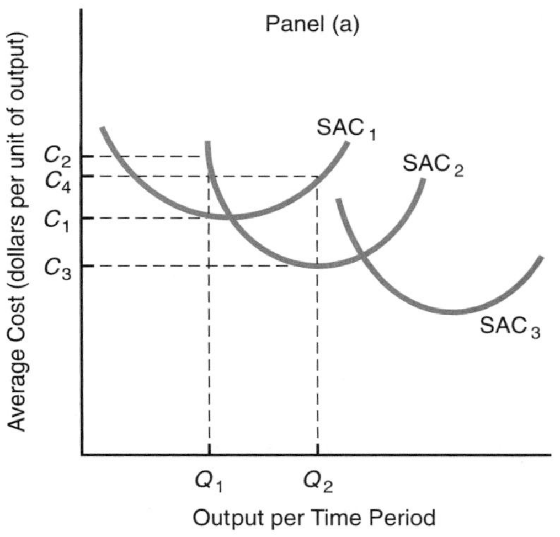

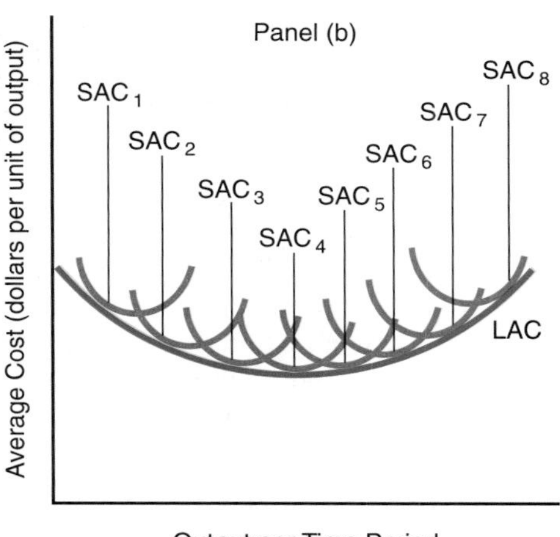

considering a single firm contemplating the construction of a single plant. The firm has three alternative plant sizes from which to choose on the planning horizon. Each particular plant size generates its own short-run average total cost curve. Now that we are talking about the difference between long-run and short-run cost curves, we will label all short-run curves with an *S* and long-run curves with an *L;* short-run average (total) costs will be labeled SAC; and long-run average cost curves will be labeled LAC.

Panel (a) of Figure 22-5 shows three short-run average cost curves for three successively larger plants. Which is the optimal size to build? That depends on the anticipated normal, sustained (permanent) rate of output per time period. Assume for a moment that the anticipated normal, sustained rate is Q_1. If a plant of size 1 is built, the average costs will be C_1. If a plant of size 2 is built, we see on SAC_2 that the average costs will be C_2, which is greater than C_1. Thus if the anticipated rate of output is Q_1, the appropriate plant size is the one from which SAC_1 was derived.

However, if the anticipated permanent rate of output per time period goes from Q_1 to Q_2 and a plant of size 1 had been decided on, average costs would be C_4. If a plant of size 2 had been decided on, average costs would be C_3, which is clearly less than C_4.

In choosing the appropriate plant size for a single-plant firm during the planning horizon, the firm will pick the size whose short-run average cost curve generates an average cost that is lowest for the expected rate of output.

Long-Run Average Cost Curve

If we now assume that the entrepreneur faces an infinite number of choices of plant sizes in the long run, we can conceive of an infinite number of SAC curves similar to the three in panel (a) of Figure 22-5. We are not able, of course, to draw an infinite number; we have drawn quite a few, however, in panel (b) of Figure 22-5. We then draw the "envelope" to all these various short-run average cost curves. The resulting envelope is the **long-run average cost curve.** This long-run average cost curve is sometimes called the **planning curve,** for it represents the various average costs attainable at the planning stage of the firm's decision making. It represents the locus (path) of points giving the least unit cost of producing any given rate of output. Note that the LAC curve is *not* tangent to each individual SAC curve at the latter's minimum points. This is true only at the minimum point of the LAC curve. Then and only then are minimum long-run average costs equal to minimum short-run average costs.

Long-run average cost curve 
The locus of points representing the minimum unit cost of producing any given rate of output, given current technology and resource prices.

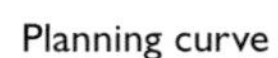 
Planning curve
The long-run average cost curve.

WHY THE LONG-RUN AVERAGE COST CURVE IS U-SHAPED

Notice that the long-run average cost curve, LAC, in panel (b) of Figure 22-5 is U-shaped, similar to the U shape of the short-run average cost curve developed earlier in this chapter. The reason behind the U shape of the two curves is not the same, however. The short-run average cost curve is U-shaped because of the law of diminishing marginal returns. But the law cannot apply to the long run, because in the long run, all factors of production are variable; there is no point of diminishing marginal returns because there is no fixed factor of production.

Why, then, do we see the U shape in the long-run average cost curve? The reasoning has to do with economies of scale, constant returns to scale, and diseconomies of scale. When the firm is experiencing **economies of scale,** the long-run average cost curve slopes downward—an increase in scale and production leads to a fall in unit costs. When the firm is experiencing **constant returns to scale,** the long-run average cost curve is at its minimum point, such that an increase in scale and production does not change unit costs. When the firm is experiencing **diseconomies of scale,** the long-run average cost curve slopes upward—an increase in scale and production increases unit costs. These three sections of the long-run average cost curves are broken up into panels (a), (b), and (c) in Figure 22-6.

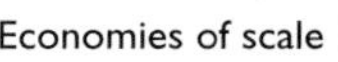 
Economies of scale
Decreases in long-run average costs resulting from increases in output.

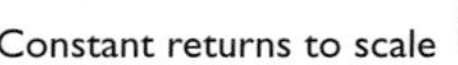 
Constant returns to scale
No change in long-run average costs when output increases.

Diseconomies of scale 
Increases in long-run average costs that occur as output increases.

Reasons for Economies of Scale

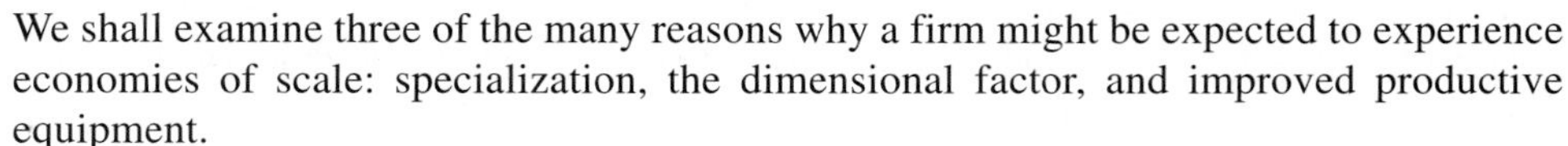

We shall examine three of the many reasons why a firm might be expected to experience economies of scale: specialization, the dimensional factor, and improved productive equipment.

Specialization. As a firm's scale of operation increases, the opportunities for specialization in the use of resource inputs also increase. This is sometimes called *increased division of tasks* or *operations.* Gains from such division of labor or increased specialization are well known. When we consider managerial staffs, we also find that larger enterprises may be able to put together more highly specialized staffs.

Dimensional Factor. Large-scale firms often require proportionately less input per unit of output simply because certain inputs do not have to be physically doubled in order to double

FIGURE 22-6

Economies of Scale, Constant Returns to Scale, and Diseconomies of Scale Shown with the Long-Run Average Cost Curve

Long-run average cost curves will fall when there are economies of scale, as shown in panel (a). They will be constant (flat) when the firm is experiencing constant returns to scale, as shown in panel (b). They will rise when the firm is experiencing diseconomies of scale, as shown in panel (c).

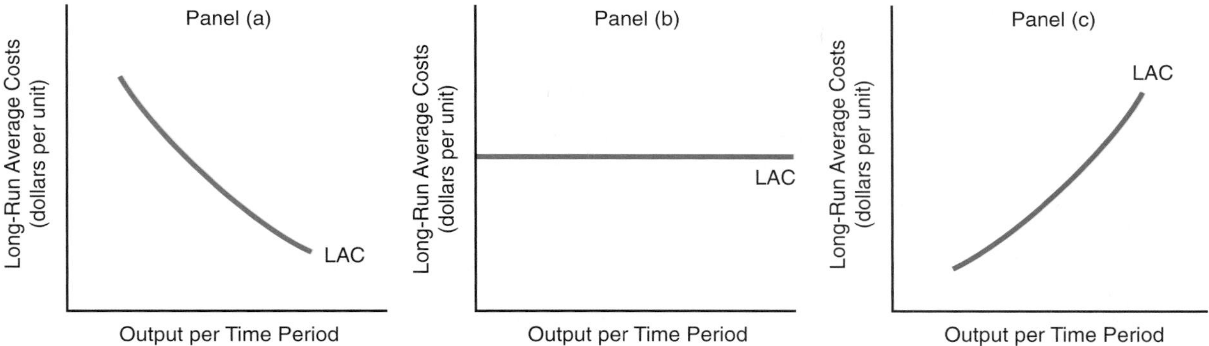

the output. Consider the cost of storage of oil. The cost of storage is basically related to the cost of steel that goes into building the storage container; however, the amount of steel required goes up less than in proportion to the volume (storage capacity) of the container (because the volume of a container increases more than proportionately with its surface area).

Improved Productive Equipment. The larger the scale of the enterprise, the more the firm is able to take advantage of larger-volume (output capacity) types of machinery. Small-scale operations may not be able profitably to use large-volume machines that can be more efficient per unit of output. Also, smaller firms often cannot use technologically more advanced machinery because they are unable to spread out the high cost of such sophisticated equipment over a large output.

For any of these reasons, the firm may experience economies of scale, which means that equal percentage increases in output result in a decrease in average cost. Thus output can double, but total costs will less than double; hence average cost falls. Note that the factors listed for causing economies of scale are all *internal* to the firm; they do not depend on what other firms are doing or what is happening in the economy.

EXAMPLE

Measuring the Value of Ideas

When contemplating the appropriate scale for production, it is relatively straightforward for a business to evaluate the amount of machines and buildings available for the production of the goods or services it produces. Another fundamental internal factor that a firm must take into account is assessing the scale of its operations, however, is its internal base of knowledge and ideas. Today more than ever, the physical aspects of a business's plants and equipment are supplemented and even overshadowed by more intangible factors, such as patents, computer software, research and development programs, and the expertise—the ideas—of managers and employees.

A reflection of problems in measuring these intangible factors is the fact that since the 1970s, the median ratio of the stock market values of public U.S. companies relative to their book values (values as measured by accountants) has more than doubled. The gap between market values and book values has increased particularly among companies for which intangible factors such as ideas are most crucial—software developers and manufacturers, Internet marketers, and the like.

To improve their ability to measure ideas and other intangible factors of production, some companies have begun to develop "intellectual capital reports" that take into account the educational attainments of staff, the age profile of employees, and investments in research and development. These companies hope to be able to use these reports alongside traditional measures of capital resources when determining the current scale of their enterprises. For instance, after taking into account the value of ideas and knowledge, Baruch Lev of New York University estimates that Merck, a pharmaceutical company, has "knowledge capital" worth about $50 billion and that DuPont, a manufacturer of chemicals and plastics, has knowledge capital in excess of $25 billion.

In the past, companies have regarded the wages they pay their employees solely as short-run costs. Nevertheless, every time an employee leaves a company, the company loses a bit of the intangible knowledge capital locked up in that employee's mind. Recognition of this fact has induced more companies to consider the information contained in intellectual capital reports so that they can better gauge the long-run implications of their staffing decisions.

For Critical Analysis

What problems are companies likely to encounter when they attempt to measure the value of knowledge and ideas?

Why a Firm Might Experience Diseconomies of Scale

One of the basic reasons that a firm can expect to run into diseconomies of scale is that there are limits to the efficient functioning of management. Moreover, as more workers are hired, a more than proportionate increase in managers and staff people may be needed, and this could cause increased costs per unit. This is so because larger levels of output imply successively larger *plant* size, which in turn implies successively larger *firm* size. Thus, as the level of output increases, more people must be hired, and the firm gets bigger. As this happens, however, the support, supervisory, and administrative staff and the general paperwork of the firm all increase. As the layers of supervision grow, the costs of information and communication grow more than proportionately; hence the average unit cost will start to increase.

The Long-Run Costs of the Firm
Gain additional experience with the concepts of long-run costs and scale economies.

Some observers of corporate giants claim that many of them have been experiencing some diseconomies of scale. Witness the problems that General Motors and IBM had in the early 1990s. Some analysts say that the financial problems they encountered were at least partly a function of their size relative to their smaller, more flexible competitors, who could make decisions more quickly and then take advantage of changing market conditions more rapidly. This was particularly true for IBM. Initially, the company adapted very slowly to the fact that the large mainframe computer business was declining as micro- and mini-computers became more and more powerful. Finally, by the end of the 1990s, IBM had adjusted to a more appropriate scale.

MINIMUM EFFICIENT SCALE

Economists and statisticians have obtained actual data on the relationship between changes in all inputs and changes in average cost. It turns out that for many industries, the long-run average cost curve does not resemble that shown in panel (b) of Figure 22-5. Rather, it

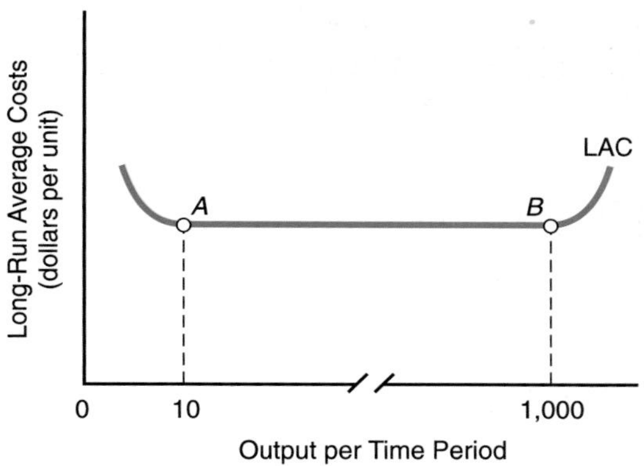

FIGURE 22-7

Minimum Efficient Scale

This long-run average cost curve reaches a minimum point at *A*. After that point, long-run average costs remain horizontal, or constant, and then rise at some later rate of output. Point *A* is called the minimum efficient scale for the firm because that is the point at which it reaches minimum costs. It is the lowest rate of output at which the average long-run costs are minimized.

more closely resembles Figure 22-7. What you can observe there is a small portion of declining long-run average costs (economies of scale) and then a wide range of outputs over which the firm experiences relatively constant economies of scale. At the output rate when economies of scale end and constant economies of scale start, the **minimum efficient scale (MES)** for the firm is encountered. It occurs at point *A*. (The point is, of course, approximate. The more smoothly the curve declines into its flat portion, the more approximate will be our estimate of the MES.) The minimum efficient scale will always be the lowest rate of output at which long-run average costs are minimized. In any industry with a long-run average cost curve similar to the one in Figure 22-7, larger firms will have no cost-saving advantage over smaller firms as long as the smaller firms have at least obtained the minimum efficient scale at point *A*.

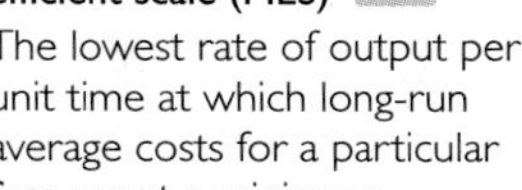

Minimum efficient scale (MES)
The lowest rate of output per unit time at which long-run average costs for a particular firm are at a minimum.

Among its uses, the minimum efficient scale gives us a rough measure of the degree of competition in an industry. If the MES is small relative to industry demand, the degree of competition in that industry is likely to be high because there is room for many efficiently sized plants. Conversely, when the MES is large relative to industry demand, the degree of competition is likely to be small because there is room for a relatively small number of efficiently sized plants or firms. Looked at another way, if it takes a very large scale of plant to obtain minimum long-run average cost, the output of just a few of these very large firms can fully satisfy total market demand. This means that there isn't room for a large number of smaller plants if maximum efficiency is to be obtained in the industry.

CONCEPTS IN BRIEF

- The long run is often called the planning horizon. The long-run average cost curve is the planning curve. It is found by drawing a line tangent to one point on a series of short-run average cost curves, each corresponding to a different plant size.
- The firm can experience economies of scale, diseconomies of scale, and constant returns to scale, all according to whether the long-run average cost curve slopes downward, slopes upward, or is horizontal (flat). Economies of scale refer to what happens to average cost when all factors of production are increased.
- We observe economies of scale for a number of reasons, among which are specialization, improved productive equipment, and the dimensional factor, because large-scale firms require proportionately less input per unit of output. The firm may experience diseconomies of scale primarily because of limits to the efficient functioning of management.
- The minimum efficient scale occurs at the lowest rate of output at which long-run average costs are minimized.

Classified Ads That Fido Can't Chew Up

The typical American consumer makes 80 percent of all purchases within 20 miles of home. A traditional "local purchase" is the hometown newspaper. After all, that is where one can find local movie and concert listings, classified ads, and news. Never mind that getting a newspaper printed and delivered is a complicated task involving lots of paper and ink, subscription clerks, and home delivery personnel. Where else can you go to find out what is going on in your neighborhood?

Microsoft Corporation came up with a possible answer. It is called Sidewalk. In mid-1997, Microsoft set up Sidewalk Web sites for three cities: Boston, New York, and Seattle. The company geared these sites toward local residents rather than tourists, offering listings of concerts, movies, and restaurants, information about planned civic events, and so on. Today, you can find a Sidewalk Web site for Birmingham, Alabama; Flint, Michigan; Winston-Salem, North Carolina; and about 100 other cities.

Why was Microsoft interested in providing people with hometown information? The reason was that the company wanted a share of the revenues earned by local newspapers and other local media—an estimated $70 billion is spent on such advertisements. Sidewalk sells space on its site to local advertisers, just as newspapers sell portions of their pages for print ads.

Why was Microsoft convinced that Sidewalk could compete? In its view, it has a big cost advantage over newspapers. Instead of running the presses each day and churning out a lot of paper that people throw out or recycle the next day, Sidewalk employees simply change the data for Sidewalk Web sites electronically. It is as if your local newspaper could get by with just a staff of reporters armed with word processors but no presses, paper, or delivery people. A potential result may be a big efficiency advantage in the form of much lower average variable costs for providing the same basic services that local newspapers have traditionally provided.

Some media experts believe that local newspapers will lose at least $2 billion in local ad revenues to on-line services such as Sidewalk over the next few years. And if heightened competition from Internet services also pushes down the market price of ads, local papers stand to lose even more.

Are Bigger Banks Necessarily More Efficient?

Since the late 1980s, U.S. commercial banking has experienced a wave of mergers (combinations of existing banks) and acquisitions (purchases of banks by other banks). As you can see in Table 22-1, thousands of banks have been involved in mergers and acquisitions since 1989. Hundreds of millions of dollars in bank assets—loans, securities, and cash—are being consolidated within a smaller number of banks. The average bank is getting bigger. Most banking experts anticipate that this trend will persist for several more years.

Concepts Applied

Long-Run Average Cost

Economies of Scale

Minimum Efficient Scale

Bank Managers' Claim: Cost Savings in Mergers and Acquisitions

Combining banks into a single financial services company is a time-consuming and expensive task. Nevertheless, bank managers promote mergers and acquisitions as a means of achieving reductions in the long-run costs of operating new, enlarged institutions. Combining banks, they argue, permits banks to pool more loans under the management of fewer lending officers, to apply computer technologies to managing financial risks for a bigger set of assets, and to handle check clearing for more customers using equipment housed within a single bank.

According to this rationale, therefore, merged banks can reduce labor expenses by shedding employees and can slash other operating expenses by using fewer computers and

Year	New Bank Startups Less Bank Failures	Reduction Due to Mergers and Acquisitions	Total Number of U.S. Banks at Year End
1990	25	−393	12,329
1991	26	−446	11,909
1992	−32	−428	11,449
1993	−25	−480	10,944
1994	34	−547	10,431
1995	99	−609	9,921
1996	142	−553	9,510
1997	213	−599	9,124
1998	195	−563	8,756
1999	241	−417	8,580
2000	212	−404	8,388
Total Change, 1990–2000	1,130	−5,439	−4,309

Source: Federal Deposit Insurance Corporation *Historical Banking Statistics*, 2000.
*Author's estimates based on first-quarter data.

TABLE 22-1
Bank Mergers and the Declining Number of U.S. Banks
About 1,130 more new banks have opened than those that have failed since 1990. Nevertheless, an estimated 5,439 ceased to exist because of mergers. On net, therefore, the total number of U.S. commercial banks has declined by more than one-third since 1989.

other capital goods. In short, by expanding to a larger size, consolidated banks can lower their long-run average cost. They can take advantage of economies of scale.

Does the Reality of Bank Mergers and Acquisitions Support the Claim?

Nevertheless, many economists have had trouble finding evidence of economies of scale in banking. Banking output is notoriously hard to measure, but no matter what output gauge economists have used—total assets, total deposits, index measures of banking services—studies have typically found that the minimum efficient scale in banking is no greater than about $50 million. To explain the existence of multibillion-dollar behemoths such as Citibank or Bank of America, economists often relied on the idea that there might be "economies of scope" in banking: Banks might achieve lower long-run average costs by pooling all kinds of financial services in a single big company.

Studies of bank mergers that occurred during the late 1980s and early 1990s seemed to provide a more cynical rationale for bank mergers. They typically found that one of the few unambiguous effects of a merger or acquisition was a big increase in the salaries of the managers who survived staffing cuts. Although studies of these early mergers and acquisitions found glimmers of evidence of cost savings, the efficiency gains were generally insignificant. Managers seemed to benefit the most.

More recent studies, however, have given new life to bank managers' claims that bigger banks really are more efficient. Consolidations that have taken place since the mid-1990s appear to have reduced long-run average costs for merged banks by as much as 20 percent. In addition, some banks created by earlier consolidations have found ways to reduce their costs, albeit more slowly than originally promised.

Why are consolidated banks more cost-efficient now than in earlier years? One possible reason is that recent regulatory changes allowing banks to expand the scope of their activities—notably, permitting them to sell insurance and mutual funds—have helped them realize cost savings from greater size. Another is that bigger banks may have a cost advantage in operating on-line banking services and using other financial services technologies that were not available when the banking consolidation wave began. If new technologies are responsible for the reduction in costs, then the managers of banks that merged earlier were either quite prophetic, or, more likely, just plain lucky.

FOR CRITICAL ANALYSIS

1. If big banks are more efficient, why are there thousands of small banks in the United States?
2. Why would difficulties in measuring a bank's output make determining its minimum efficient scale more complicated?

SUMMARY DISCUSSION OF LEARNING OBJECTIVES

1. **Accounting Profits Versus Economic Profits:** A firm's accounting profits equal its total revenues minus its total explicit costs, which are expenses directly paid out by the firm. Economic profits equal accounting profits minus implicit costs, which are expenses that managers do not have pay out of pocket, such as the opportunity cost of factors of production dedicated to the firm's production process. Owners of a firm seek to maximize the firm's economic profits to ensure that they earn at least a normal rate of return, meaning that the firm's total revenues at least cover explicit costs and implicit opportunity costs.
2. **The Short Run Versus the Long Run from a Firm's Perspective:** The short run for a firm is a period during which at least one input, such as plant size, cannot be altered. Inputs that cannot be changed in the short run are fixed inputs, whereas factors of production that may be adjusted in the short run are variable inputs. The long run is a period in which a firm may vary all factors of production.
3. **The Law of Diminishing Marginal Returns:** The production function is the relationship between inputs and the maximum physical output, or total product, that a firm can produce. Typically, a firm's marginal physi-

cal product—the physical output resulting from the addition of one more unit of a variable factor of production—increases with the first few units of the variable factor of production that it employs. Eventually, however, as the firm adds more and more units of the variable input, the marginal physical product begins to decline. This is the law of diminishing returns.

4. **A Firm's Short-Run Cost Curves:** The expenses for a firm's fixed inputs are its fixed costs, and the expenses for its variable inputs are variable costs. The total costs of a firm are the sum of its fixed costs and variable costs. Dividing fixed costs by various possible output levels traces out the firm's average fixed cost curve, which slopes downward because dividing fixed costs by a larger total product yields a lower average fixed cost. Average variable cost equals total variable cost divided by total product, and average total cost equals total cost divided by total product; doing these computations at various possible output levels yields U-shaped curves. Finally, marginal cost is the change in total cost resulting from a one-unit change in production. A firm's marginal cost curve typically declines as the firm produces the first few units of output, but at the point of diminishing marginal returns, the marginal cost curve begins to slope upward. The marginal cost curve also intersects the minimum points of the average variable cost curve and average total cost curve.
5. **A Firm's Long-Run Cost Curves:** Over a firm's long-run, or planning, horizon, it can choose all factors of production, including plant size. Thus it can choose a long-run scale of production along a long-run average cost curve. The long-run average cost curve, which for most firms is U-shaped, is traced out by the short-run average cost curves corresponding to various plant sizes.
6. **Economies and Diseconomies of Scale and a Firm's Minimum Efficient Scale:** Along the downward-sloping range of a firm's long-run average cost curve, the firm experiences economies of scale, meaning that its long-run production costs decline as it increases its plant size and thereby raises its output scale. By contrast, along the upward-sloping portion of the long-run average cost curve, the firm encounters diseconomies of scale, so that its long-run costs of production rises as it increases its output scale. The minimum point of the long-run average cost curve occurs at the firm's minimum efficient scale, which is the lowest rate of output at which the firm can achieve minimum long-run average cost.

Key Terms and Concepts

Accounting profit (532)
Average fixed costs (543)
Average physical product (537)
Average total costs (543)
Average variable costs (543)
Constant returns to scale (550)
Diseconomies of scale (550)
Economic profits (534)
Economies of scale (550)
Explicit costs (532)
Firm (532)
Fixed costs (541)
Implicit costs (532)
Law of diminishing (marginal) returns (537)
Long run (536)
Long-run average cost curve (550)
Marginal costs (543)
Marginal physical product (537)
Minimum efficient scale (MES) (553)
Normal rate of return (533)
Opportunity cost of capital (533)
Planning curve (550)
Planning horizon (548)
Plant size (535)
Production (536)
Production function (537)
Short run (535)
Total costs (541)
Variable costs (541)

Problems Test

Answers to the odd-numbered problems appear at the back of the book.

22-1. After graduation, you face a choice. One option is to work for a multinational consulting firm and earn a starting salary (benefits included) of $40,000. The other option is to use $5,000 in savings to start your own consulting firm. You could have earned an interest return of 5 percent on your savings. You choose to start your own consulting firm. At the end of the first year, you add up all of your expenses and revenues. Your total includes $12,000 in rent, $1,000 in office supplies, $20,000 for office staff, and $4,000 in telephone expenses. What are your total explicit costs and total implicit costs?

22-2. Suppose, as in Problem 22-1, that you choose to start your own consulting firm upon graduation. At the end of the first year, your total revenues are $77,250. Based on the information in Problem 22-1, what is your accounting profit and what is your economic profit?

22-3. The academic calendar for a university is August 15 through May 15. A professor commits to a contract that binds her to a teaching position at this university for this period. Based on this information, explain the short run and long run that the professor faces.

22-4. The short-run production function for a manufacturer of DVD drives is as follows:

Input of Labor (workers per week)	Total Output of DVD Drives
0	0
1	25
2	60
3	85
4	105
5	115
6	120

Based on this information, calculate the average physical product at each quantity of labor.

22-5. Using the information provided in Problem 22-4, calculate the marginal physical product labor at each quantity of labor.

22-6. For the manufacturer of DVD drives in Problems 22-4 and 22-5, at what point do diminishing marginal returns set in?

22-7. At the end of the year, a firm produced 10,000 laptop computers. Its total costs were $5 million, and its fixed costs were $2 million. What are the average variable costs of this firm?

22-8. The cost structure of a manufacturer of cable modems is described in the following table. The firm's fixed costs equal $30 per day.

Output (cable modems per day)	Total Cost of Output ($ thousands)
0	10
25	60
50	95
75	150
100	220
125	325
150	465

Calculate the average variable cost, average fixed cost, and average total cost at each output level.

22-9. Calculate the marginal cost that the manufacturer of cable modems in Problem 22-8 faces at each daily output rate, including the first cable modem it produces. At what production rate do diminishing marginal returns set in?

22-10. A watch manufacturer finds that at 1,000 units of output, its marginal costs are below average total costs. If it produces an additional watch, will its average total costs rise, fall, or stay the same?

22-11. A manufacturing firm with a single plant is contemplating changing its plant size. It must choose from among seven alternative plant sizes. In the table below, plant size A is the smallest it might build, and size G is the largest. Currently, the firm's plant size is B.

Plant Size	Average Total Cost ($)
A (smallest)	5,000
B	4,000
C	3,500
D	3,100
E	3,000
F	3,250
G (largest)	4,100

a. Is this firm currently experiencing economies of scale or diseconomies of scale?

b. What is the firm's minimum efficient scale?

Economics on the Net

Industry-Level Corporate Profits In this chapter, you learned how to measure profits. This Internet application provides you with an opportunity to take a look at the rates of profitability of various industries in the United States.

Title: Corporate Profits by Industry

Navigation: Click here to view the Bureau of Economic Analysis page about Corporate Profits. Select Table 11, Corporate Profits by Industry.

Application Consider the categories under Durable Goods.

1. Is the BEA reporting economic profits or accounting profits?
2. Which industry generates the greatest amount of profit in the United States? Which industry generates the least amount of profit in the United States?
3. Which industry experienced the greatest growth in profits over the past year? Which industry experienced the greatest decline in profit over the past year?

For Group Discussion and Analysis Which industries generated the greatest increase in their rate of return on investment over the past year? Discuss why you believe these industries do so well. Which industries generated the greatest decline in their rate of return on investment over the past year? Discuss why you believe these industries do so poorly. (Hint: Think of some companies that serve as examples for these industries.)

CHAPTER 23

PERFECT COMPETITION

Today, there are more brands and styles of sports footwear than ever before. Does this mean that the American marketplace is more competitive today than in the past? If so, should the profits of large corporations be falling or rising?

Few Americans today would say that competition does not exist in the United States. After all, since the early 1990s, a multitude of new firms, ranging from corner bakeries to Internet booksellers to software developers, have jumped into the marketplace. But has all this activity really produced a more competitive American economy? In the world of perfect competition, which you will read about in this chapter, consumers can choose among virtually identical baked goods, books, and software produced by a host of suppliers. Within each industry, therefore, there is widespread substitutability among goods or services produced by rival firms. Is the American marketplace truly more competitive today than in years past? To answer this question, you need to learn about the model of perfect competition and its assumptions.

LEARNING OBJECTIVES

After reading this chapter, you should be able to:

1. Identify the characteristics of a perfectly competitive market structure
2. Discuss the process by which a perfectly competitive firm decides how much output to produce
3. Understand how the short-run supply curve for a perfectly competitive firm is determined
4. Explain how the equilibirum price is determined in perfectly competitive market
5. Describe what factors induce firms to enter or exit a perfectly competitive industry
6. Distinguish among constant-, increasing-, and decreasing-cost industries based on the shape of the long-run industry supply curve

Did You Know That... in the United States, there are tens of thousands of copy shops? There are also several thousand desktop publishing companies offering their services. The number of companies wanting to sell only Web site development is much smaller but growing. The number of companies offering to write software applications is somewhere in between, but that is only in the United States. Today, because of the cheapness and rapidity of modern telecommunications, much of the software code that goes in today's computer applications programs produced by American companies is written in India and elsewhere.

Competition is the word that applies to all of these situations. As used in common speech, *competition* simply means "rivalry." In perfectly competitive situations, individual buyers and sellers cannot affect the market price—it is determined by the market forces of demand and supply. In this chapter, we examine what has become known as perfect competition.

Chapter Outline 

CHARACTERISTICS OF A PERFECTLY COMPETITIVE MARKET STRUCTURE

We are interested in studying how a firm acting within a perfectly competitive market structure makes decisions about how much to produce. In a situation of **perfect competition,** each firm is such a small part that it cannot affect the price of the product in question. That means that each **perfectly competitive firm** in the industry is a **price taker**—the firm takes price as a given, something determined *outside* the individual firm.

This definition of a competitive firm is obviously idealized, for in one sense the individual firm *has* to set prices. How can we ever have a situation in which firms regard prices as set by forces outside their control? The answer is that even though every firm sets its own prices, a firm in a perfectly competitive situation will find that it will eventually have no customers at all if it sets its price above the competitive price. The best example is in agriculture. Although the individual farmer can set any price for a bushel of wheat, if that price doesn't coincide with the market price of a bushel of similar-quality wheat, no one will purchase the wheat at a higher price; nor would the farmer be inclined to reduce revenues by selling below the market price.

Let's examine the reasons why a firm in a perfectly competitive industry ends up being a price taker.

1. *There must be a large number of buyers and sellers.* When this is the case, the quantity demanded by an individual buyer or the quantity supplied by the seller is negligible relative to the market quantity. No one buyer or one seller has any influence on price.
2. *The product sold by the firms in the industry must be homogeneous.* The product sold by each firm in the industry must be a perfect substitute for the product sold by each other firm. Buyers must be able to choose from a large number of sellers of a product that the buyers believe to be the same.
3. *Any firm can enter or leave the industry without serious impediments.* Firms in a competitive industry cannot be hampered in their ability to get resources or relocate resources. They move labor and capital in pursuit of profit-making opportunities to whatever business venture gives them their highest expected rate of return on their investment.
4. *Both buyers and sellers have equal access to information.* Consumers have to be able to find out about lower prices charged by competing firms. Firms have to be able to

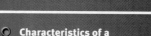

Perfect competition 
A market structure in which the decisions of individual buyers and sellers have no effect on market price.

Perfectly competitive firm 
A firm that is such a small part of the total industry that it cannot affect the price of the product it sells.

Price taker 
A competitive firm that must take the price of its product as given because the firm cannot influence its price.

find out about cost-saving innovations in order to lower production costs and prices, and they have to be able to learn about profitable opportunities in other industries.

INTERNATIONAL EXAMPLE

A Common Pricing Denominator in Europe

Perfect competition is more likely to thrive in an environment in which buyers and sellers have more nearly complete and equal access to information. Historically, a factor hindering the development of European-wide competitive markets has been that a consumer in a country such as Portugal who was contemplating whether to buy substitute goods manufactured by a German, Italian, or Belgian firm had to compare prices quoted in German marks, Italian lire, and Belgian francs.

Making accurate price comparisons of this sort required that every consumer stay abreast of the latest currency conversion rates, making it harder for consumers to shop around for the best buys. This contributed to great variability in the prices of the same goods from nation to nation within Europe. Figure 23-1 shows average price variations for several products for nine European nations: Austria, Belgium, France, Germany, Ireland, Italy, the Netherlands, Portugal, and Spain. Across these countries, the average price of a Big Mac varied by more than 10 percent. The typical fee for a bank account varied by well over 50 percent from one country to the next.

Beginning in 2002, European price differentials should start to narrow, thanks to a coordinated policy decision on the part of the governments of these nine European nations, plus Finland and Luxembourg. At the beginning of that year, the euro, a unit of account created in 1999, will replace national currencies. When

FIGURE 23-1
Variability in the Domestic Prices of Selected Products in Nine European Nations
In advance of the adoption of the euro as a single currency, the prices of products sold in European nations varied from just under 5 percent for the Volkswagen Golf to more than 50 percent for financial products such as insurance and bank accounts.

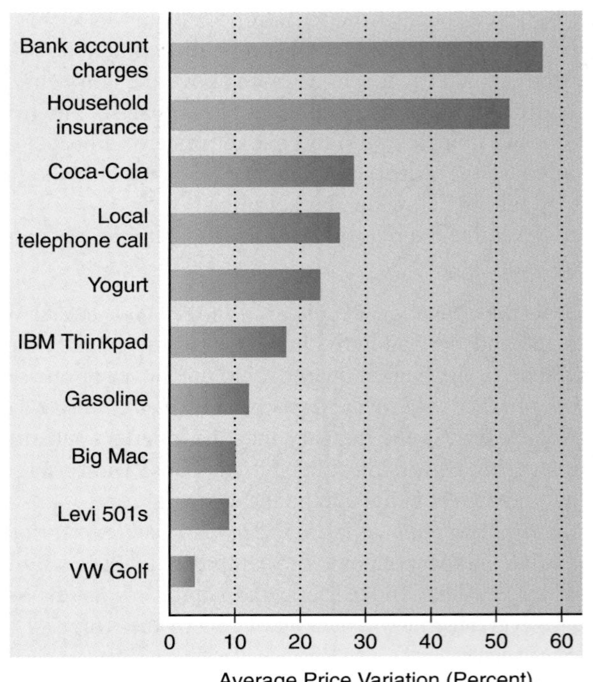

all prices are quoted in euros, the nearly 300 million consumers residing in these 11 countries will have an easier time spotting the best buys. This change should go long way toward promoting more competitive markets in Europe.

For Critical Analysis

Are regional price differences likely to disappear completely following full adoption of the euro as a hand-to-hand currency? (Hint: Are there regional dollar price differences for the same goods in the United States?)

THE DEMAND CURVE OF THE PERFECT COMPETITOR

When we discussed substitutes in Chapter 20, we pointed out that the more substitutes there were and the more similar they were to the commodity in question, the greater was the price elasticity of demand. Here we assume for the perfectly competitive firm that it is producing a homogeneous commodity that has perfect substitutes. That means that if the individual firm raises its price one penny, it will lose all of its business. This, then, is how we characterize the demand schedule for a perfectly competitive firm: It is the going market price as determined by the forces of market supply and market demand—that is, where the market demand curve intersects the market supply curve. The demand curve for the product of an individual firm in a perfectly competitive industry is perfectly elastic at the going market price. Remember that with a perfectly elastic demand curve, any increase in price leads to zero quantity demanded.

We show the market demand and supply curves in panel (a) of Figure 23-2. Their intersection occurs at the price of $5. The commodity in question is computer minidisks. Assume for the purposes of this exposition that all minidisks are perfect substitutes for all others. At the going market price of $5 apiece, a hypothetical individual demand curve for a minidisk producer who sells a very, very small part of total industry production is shown in panel (b). At the market price, this firm can sell all the output it wants. At the market price of $5 each, which is where the demand curve for the individual producer lies, consumer demand for the minidisks of that one producer is perfectly elastic. This can be seen by noting that if the firm raises its price, consumers, who are assumed to know that this supplier is charging more than other producers, will buy elsewhere, and the producer in

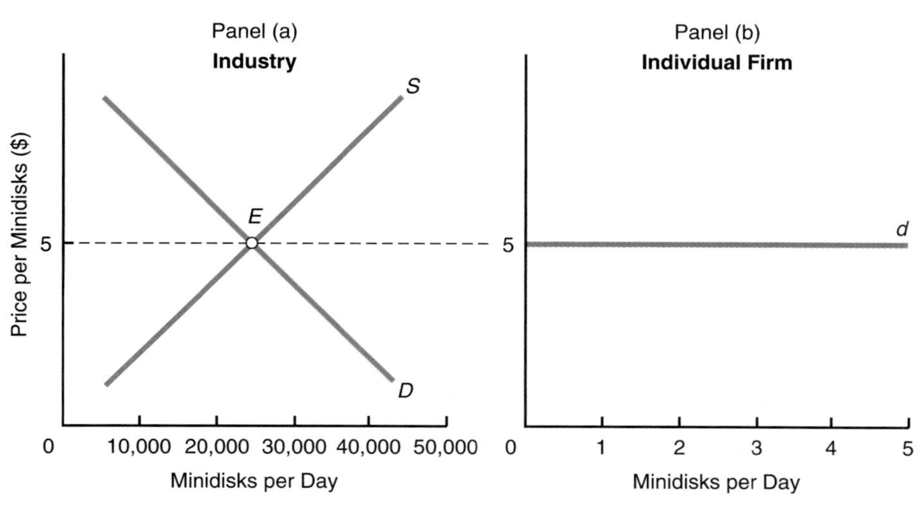

FIGURE 23-2

The Demand Curve for a Minidisk Producer

At $5—where market demand, *D*, and market supply, *S*, intersect—the individual firm faces a perfectly elastic demand curve, *d*. If it raises its price even one penny, it will sell no minidisks at all. Notice the difference in the quantities of minidisks represented on the horizontal axis of panels (a) and (b).

question will have no sales at all. Thus the demand curve for that producer is perfectly elastic. We label the individual producer's demand curve *d,* whereas the *market* demand curve is always labeled *D.*

HOW MUCH SHOULD THE PERFECT COMPETITOR PRODUCE?

As we have shown, a perfect competitor has to accept the price of the product as a given. If the firm raises its price, it sells nothing; if it lowers its price, it earns lower revenues per unit sold than it otherwise could. The firm has one decision left: How much should it produce? We will apply our model of the firm to this question to come up with an answer. We'll use the *profit-maximization model,* which assumes that firms attempt to maximize their total profits—the positive difference between total revenues and total costs. This also means that firms seek to minimize any losses that arise in times when total revenues may be less than total costs.

Total Revenues

Total revenues The price per unit times the total quantity sold.

Every firm has to consider its *total revenues,* or TR. **Total revenues** are defined as the quantity sold multiplied by the price. (They are the same as total receipts from the sale of output.) The perfect competitor must take the price as a given.

Look at Figure 23-3. Much of the information in panel (a) comes from panel (a) of Figure 22-3, but we have added some essential columns for our analysis. Column 3 is the market price, *P,* of $5 per minidisk. Column 4 shows the total revenues, or TR, as equal to the market price, *P,* times the total output per day, or *Q*. Thus TR = *PQ*.

For the perfect competitor, price is also equal to average revenue (AR) because

$$\text{AR} = \frac{\text{TR}}{Q} = \frac{PQ}{Q} = P$$

where *Q* stands for quantity. If we assume that all units sell for the same price, it becomes apparent that another name for the demand curve is the *average revenue curve* (this is true regardless of the type of market structure under consideration).

We are assuming that the market supply and demand schedules intersect at a price of $5 and that this price holds for all the firm's production. We are also assuming that because our minidisk maker is a small part of the market, it can sell all that it produces at that price. Thus panel (b) of Figure 23-3 shows the total revenue curve as a straight green line. For every unit of sales, total revenue is increased by $5.

Comparing Total Costs with Total Revenues

Total costs are given in column 2 of panel (a) of Figure 23-3 and plotted in panel (b). Remember, the firm's costs always include a normal rate of return on investment. So whenever we refer to total costs, we are talking not about accounting costs but about economic costs. When the total cost curve is above the total revenue curve, the firm is experiencing losses. When it is below the total revenue curve, the firm is making profits.

By comparing total costs with total revenues, we can figure out the number of minidisks the individual competitive firm should produce per day. Our analysis rests on the assumption that the firm will attempt to maximize total profits. In panel (a) of Figure 23-3, we see that total profits reach a maximum at a production rate of either seven or eight minidisks per

Panel (a)

(1) Total Output and Sales per Day (*Q*)	(2) Total Costs (TC)	(3) Market Price (*P*)	(4) Total Revenue (TR) (4) = (3) x (1)	(5) Total Profit (TR – TC) (5) = (4) – (2)	(6) Average Total Cost (ATC) (6) = (2) ÷ (1)	(7) Average Variable Cost (AVC)	(8) Marginal Cost (MC) (8) = Change in (2) / Change in (1)	(9) Marginal Revenue (MR) (9) = Change in (4) / Change in (1)
0	$10	$5	$ 0	–$10	—	—		
1	15	5	5	– 10	$15.00	$5.00	$5	$5
2	18	5	10	– 8	9.00	4.00	3	5
3	20	5	15	– 5	6.67	3.33	2	5
4	21	5	20	– 1	5.25	2.75	1	5
5	23	5	25	2	4.60	2.60	2	5
6	26	5	30	4	4.33	2.67	3	5
7	30	5	35	**5**	4.28	2.86	4	5
8	35	5	40	**5**	4.38	3.12	5	5
9	41	5	45	4	4.56	3.44	6	5
10	48	5	50	2	4.80	3.80	7	5
11	56	5	55	– 1	5.09	4.18	8	5

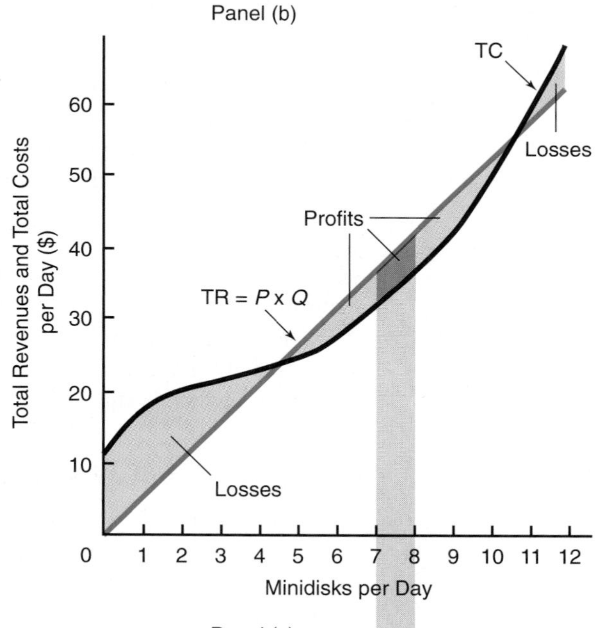

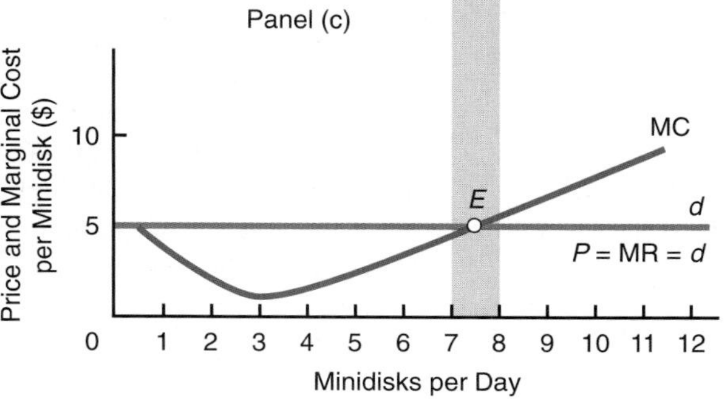

FIGURE 23-3

Profit Maximization

Profit maximization occurs where marginal revenue equals marginal cost. Panel (a) indicates that this point occurs at a rate of sales of between seven and eight minidisks per day. In panel (b), we find maximum profits where total revenues exceed total costs by the largest amount. This occurs at a rate of production and sales per day of seven or eight minidisks. In panel (c), the marginal cost curve, MC, intersects the marginal revenue curve at a rate of output and sales of somewhere between seven and eight minidisks per day.

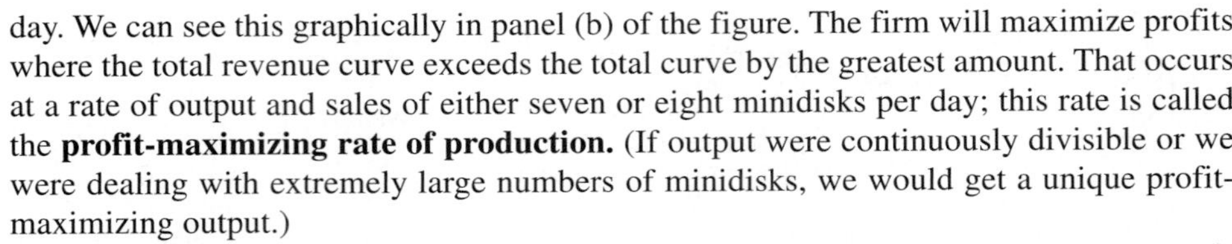

day. We can see this graphically in panel (b) of the figure. The firm will maximize profits where the total revenue curve exceeds the total curve by the greatest amount. That occurs at a rate of output and sales of either seven or eight minidisks per day; this rate is called the **profit-maximizing rate of production.** (If output were continuously divisible or we were dealing with extremely large numbers of minidisks, we would get a unique profit-maximizing output.)

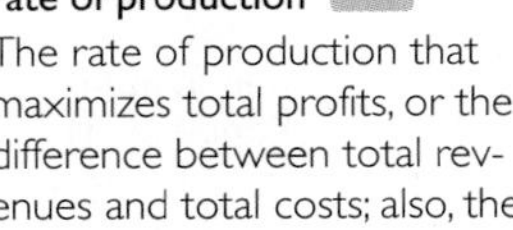

Profit-maximizing rate of production
The rate of production that maximizes total profits, or the difference between total revenues and total costs; also, the rate of production at which marginal revenue equals marginal cost.

We can also find this profit-maximizing rate of production for the individual competitive firm by looking at marginal revenues and marginal costs.

USING MARGINAL ANALYSIS TO DETERMINE THE PROFIT-MAXIMIZING RATE OF PRODUCTION

It is possible—indeed, preferred—to use marginal analysis to determine the profit-maximizing rate of production. We end up with the same results derived in a different manner, one that focuses more on where decisions are really made—on the margin. Managers examine changes in costs and relate them to changes in revenues. In fact, we almost always compare changes in cost with changes in benefits, where change is occurring at the margin, whether it be with respect to how much more or less to produce, how many more workers to hire or fire, or how much more to study or not study.

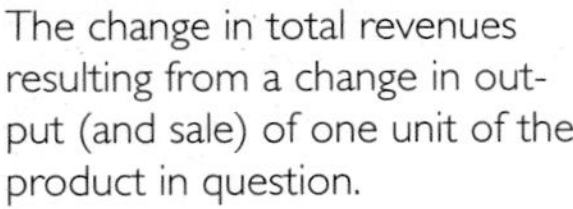

Marginal revenue
The change in total revenues resulting from a change in output (and sale) of one unit of the product in question.

Marginal revenue represents the change in total revenues attributable to changing production by one unit of the product in question. Hence a more formal definition of marginal revenue is

$$\text{Marginal revenue} = \frac{\text{change in total revenues}}{\text{change in output}}$$

In a perfectly competitive market, the marginal revenue curve is exactly equivalent to the price line or the individual firm's demand curve. Each time the firm produces and sells one more unit, total revenues rise by an amount equal to the (constant) market price of the good. Thus in Figure 23-2 on page 563, the demand curve, *d,* for the individual producer is at a price of $5—the price line is coincident with the demand curve. But so is the marginal revenue curve, for marginal revenue in this case also equals $5.

The marginal revenue curve for our competitive minidisk producer is shown as a line at $5 in panel (c) of Figure 23-3. Notice again that the marginal revenue curve is equal to the price line, which is equal to the individual firm's demand, or average revenue, curve, *d.*

When Are Profits Maximized?

Now we add the marginal cost curve, MC, taken from column 8 in panel (a) of Figure 23-3. As shown in panel (c) of that figure, the marginal cost curve first falls and then starts to rise because of the law of diminishing returns, eventually intersecting the marginal revenue curve and then rising above it. Notice that the numbers for both the marginal cost schedule, column 8 in panel (a), and the marginal revenue schedule, column 9 in panel (a), are printed *between* the rows on which the quantities appear. This indicates that we are looking at a *change* between one rate of output and the next.

In panel (c), the marginal cost curve intersects the marginal revenue curve somewhere between seven and eight minidisks per day. The firm has an incentive to produce and sell until the amount of the additional revenue received from selling one more mindisk just equals the additional costs incurred for producing and selling that minidisk. This is how the firm maximizes profit. Whenever marginal cost is less than marginal revenue, the firm will always make more profit by increasing production.

Now consider the possibility of producing at an output rate of 10 minidisks per day. The marginal cost curve at that output rate is higher than the marginal revenue (or *d*) curve. The firm would be spending more to produce that additional output than it would be receiving in revenues; it would be foolish to continue producing at this rate.

But how much should it produce? It should produce at point *E*, where the marginal cost curve intersects the marginal revenue curve from below.* The firm should continue production until the cost of increasing output by one more unit is just equal to the revenues obtainable from that extra unit. This is a fundamental rule in economics:

> Profit maximization normally occurs at the rate of output at which marginal revenue equals marginal cost.

Output and Price Determination Under Perfect Competition
Get more practice thinking through how perfectly competitive firms determine how much to produce.

For a perfectly competitive firm, this is at the intersection of the demand schedule, *d*, and the marginal cost curve, MC. When MR exceeds MC, each additional unit of output adds more to total revenues than to total costs, causing losses to decrease or profits to increase. When MC is greater than MR, each unit produced adds more to total cost than to total revenues, causing profits to decrease or losses to increase. Therefore, profit maximization occurs when MC equals MR. In our particular example, our profit-maximizing, perfectly competitive minidisk producer will produce at a rate of either seven or eight minidisks a day. (If we were dealing with a very large rate of output, we would come up with an exact profit-maximizing rate.)

CONCEPTS IN BRIEF

- Four fundamental characteristics of the market in perfect competition are (1) a large number of buyers and sellers, (2) a homogeneous product, (3) unrestrained exit from and entry into the industry by other firms, and (4) good information in the hands of both buyers and sellers.
- A perfectly competitive firm is a price taker. It has no control over price and consequently has to take price as a given, but it can sell all that it wants at the going market price.
- The demand curve for a perfect competitor is a line at the going market price. The demand curve is also the perfect competitor's marginal revenue curve because marginal revenue is defined as the change in total revenue due to a one-unit change in output.
- Profit is maximized at the rate of output where the positive difference between total revenues and total costs is the greatest. This is the same level of output at which marginal revenue equals marginal cost. The perfectly competitive firm produces at an output rate at which marginal cost equals the price per unit of output, because $MR \equiv P$.

SHORT-RUN PROFITS

To find what our competitive individual minidisk producer is making in terms of profits in the short run, we have to add the average total cost curve to panel (c) of Figure 23-3. We take the information from column 6 in panel (a) and add it to panel (c) to get Figure 23-4 on page 568. Again the profit-maximizing rate of output is between seven and eight mini-

*The marginal cost curve, MC, also cuts the marginal revenue curve, *d*, from above at an output rate of less than 1 in this example. This intersection should be ignored because it is irrelevant to the firm's decisions.

FIGURE 23-4

Measuring Total Profits

Profits are represented by the shaded area. The height of the profit rectangle is given by the difference between average total costs and price ($5), where price is also equal to average revenue. This is found by the vertical difference between the ATC curve and the price, or average revenue, line *d,* at the profit-maximizing rate of output of between seven and eight minidisks per day.

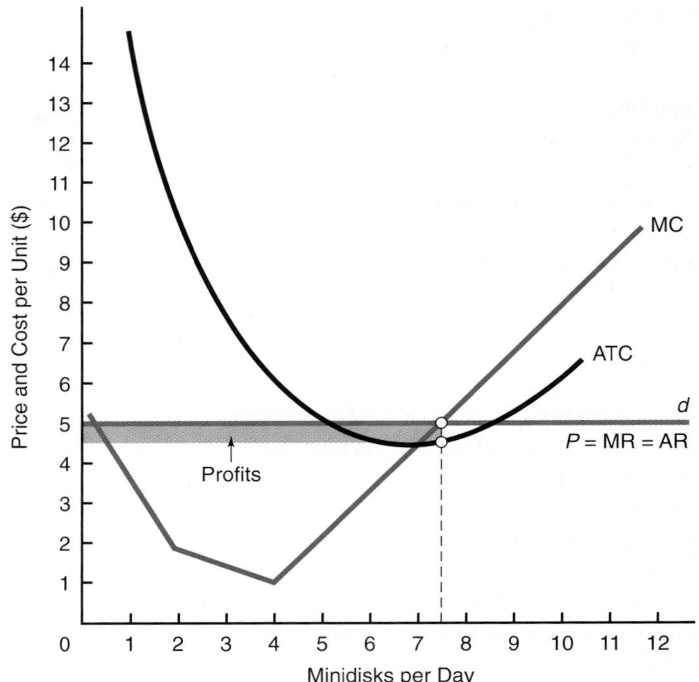

disks per day. If we have production and sales of seven minidisks per day, total revenues will be $35 a day. Total costs will be $30 a day, leaving a profit of $5 a day. If the rate of output in sales is eight minidisks per day, total revenues will be $40 and total costs will be $35, again leaving a profit of $5 a day. In Figure 23-4, the lower boundary of the rectangle labeled "Profits" is determined by the intersection of the profit-maximizing quantity line represented by vertical dashes and the average total cost curve. Why? Because the ATC curve gives us the cost per unit, whereas the price ($5), represented by *d,* gives us the revenue per unit, or average revenue. The difference is profit per unit. So the height of the rectangular box representing profits equals profit per unit, and the length equals the amount of units produced. When we multiply these two quantities, we get total profits. Note, as pointed out earlier, that we are talking about *economic profits* because a normal rate of return on investment is included in the average total cost curve, ATC.

It is certainly possible, also, for the competitive firm to make short-run losses. We give an example in Figure 23-5, where we show the firm's demand curve shifting from d_1 to d_2. The going market price has fallen from $5 to $3 per minidisk because of changes in market supply or demand conditions (or both). The firm will do the best it can by producing where marginal revenue equals marginal cost. We see in Figure 23-5 that the marginal revenue (d_2) curve is intersected (from below) by the marginal cost curve at an output rate of about $5\frac{1}{2}$ minidisks per day. The firm is clearly not making profits because average total costs at that output rate are greater than the price of $3 per minidisk. The losses are shown in the shaded area. By producing where marginal revenue equals marginal cost, however, the firm is minimizing its losses; that is, losses would be greater at any other output.

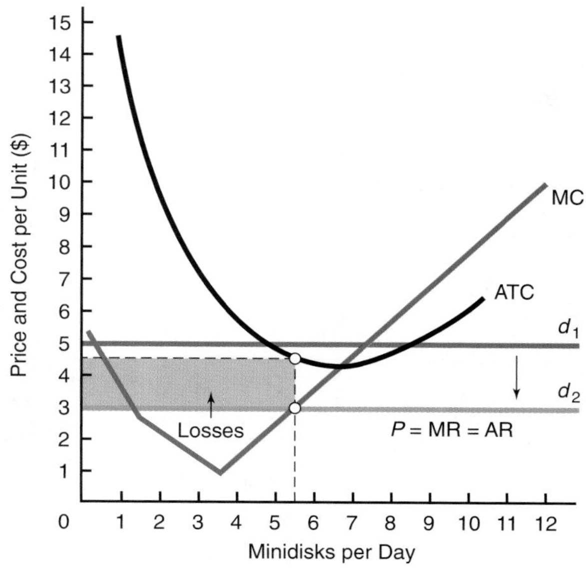

FIGURE 23-5

Minimization of Short-Run Losses

In cases in which average total costs exceed the average revenue, or price (and price is greater than or equal to average variable cost), profit maximization is equivalent to loss minimization. This again occurs where marginal cost equals marginal revenue. Losses are shown in the shaded area.

THE SHORT-RUN SHUTDOWN PRICE 

In Figure 23-5, the firm is sustaining economic losses. Will it go out of business? In the long run it will, but in the short run the firm will not necessarily go out of business. As long as the loss from staying in business is less than the loss from shutting down, the firm will continue to produce. A firm *goes out of business* when the owners sell its assets to someone else. A firm temporarily *shuts down* when it stops producing, but it still is in business.

Now how can we tell when the firm is sustaining economic losses in the short run and it is still worthwhile not to shut down? The firm must compare the cost of producing (while incurring losses) with the cost of closing down. The cost of staying in production in the short run is given by the total *variable* cost. Looking at the problem on a per-unit basis, as long as average variable cost (AVC) is covered by average revenues (price), the firm is better off continuing to produce. If average variable costs are exceeded even a little bit by the price of the product, staying in production produces some revenues in excess of variable costs that can be applied toward covering fixed costs.

A simple example will demonstrate this situation. The price of a product is $8, and average total costs equal $9 at an output of 100. In this example, average total costs are broken up into average variable costs of $7 and average fixed costs of $2. Total revenues, then, equal $8 × 100, or $800, and total costs equal $9 × 100, or $900. Total losses therefore equal $100. However, this does not mean that the firm will shut down. After all, if it does shut down, it still has fixed costs to pay. And in this case, because average fixed costs equal $2 at an output of 100, the fixed costs are $200. Thus the firm has losses of $100 if it continues to produce, but it has losses of $200 (the fixed costs) if it shuts down. The logic is fairly straightforward:

> As long as the price per unit sold exceeds the average *variable* cost per unit produced, the firm will be covering at least part of the opportunity cost of the investment in the business—that is, part of its fixed costs.

FIGURE 23-6

Short-Run Shutdown and Break-Even Prices

We can find the short-run break-even price and the short-run shutdown price by comparing price with average total costs and average variable costs. If the demand curve is d_1, profit maximization occurs at output E_1, where MC equals marginal revenue (the *d* curve). Because the ATC curve includes all relevant opportunity costs, point E_1 is the break-even point, and zero economic profits are being made. The firm is earning a normal rate of return. If the demand curve falls to d_2, profit maximization (loss minimization) occurs at the intersection of MC and MR (the d_2 curve), or E_2. Below this price, it does not pay for the firm to continue in operation because its average variable costs are not covered by the price of the product.

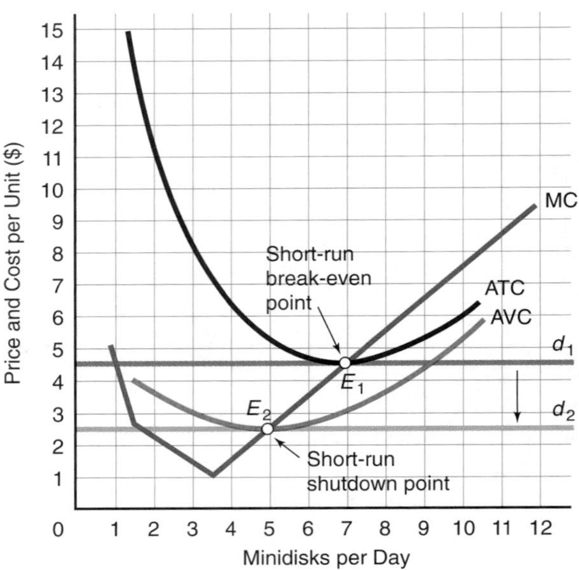

Calculating the Short-Run Break-Even Price

Look at demand curve d_1 in Figure 23-6. It just touches the minimum point of the average total cost curve, which, as you will remember, is exactly where the marginal cost curve intersects the average total cost curve. At that price, which is about $4.30, the firm will be making exactly zero short-run economic profits. That price is called the **short-run break-even price,** and point E_1 therefore occurs at the short-run break-even price for a competitive firm. It is the point at which marginal revenue, marginal cost, and average total cost are all equal (that is, at which P = MC and P = ATC). The break-even price is the one that yields zero short-run economic profits or losses.

Short-run break-even price 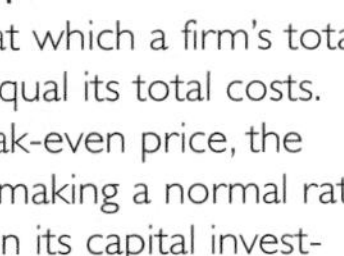

The price at which a firm's total revenues equal its total costs. At the break-even price, the firm is just making a normal rate of return on its capital investment. (It is covering its explicit and implicit costs.)

Calculating the Short-Run Shutdown Price

To calculate the firm's shutdown price, we must introduce the average variable cost (AVC) to our graph. In Figure 23-6, we have plotted the AVC values from column 7 in panel (a) of Figure 23-3. For the moment, consider two possible demand curves, d_1 and d_2, which are also the firm's respective marginal revenue curves. Therefore, if demand is d_1, the firm will produce at E_1, where that curve intersects the marginal cost curve. If demand falls to d_2, the firm will produce at E_2. The special feature of the hypothetical demand curve, d_2, is that it just touches the average variable cost curve at the latter's minimum point, which is also where the marginal cost curve intersects it. This price is the **short-run shutdown price.** Why? Below this price, the firm would be paying out more in variable costs than it is receiving in revenues from the sale of its product. Each unit it sold would add to its losses. Clearly, the way to avoid incurring these additional losses, if price falls below the shutdown point, is in fact to shut down operations.

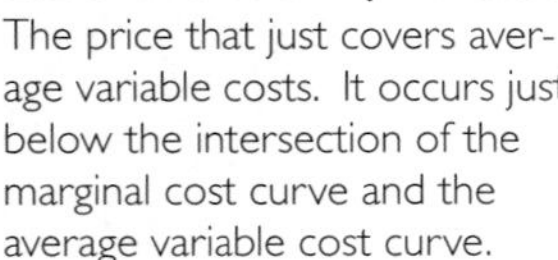
Short-run shutdown price

The price that just covers average variable costs. It occurs just below the intersection of the marginal cost curve and the average variable cost curve.

The intersection of the price line, the marginal cost curve, and the average variable cost curve is labeled E_2. The resulting short-run shutdown price is valid only for the short run because, of course, in the long run the firm will not stay in business at a yield less than a normal rate of return and hence at least zero economic profits.

THE MEANING OF ZERO ECONOMIC PROFITS 

The fact that we labeled point E_1 in Figure 23-6 the break-even point may have disturbed you. At point E_1, price is just equal to average total cost. If this is the case, why would a firm continue to produce if it were making no profits whatsoever? If we again make the distinction between accounting profits and economic profits, then at that price the firm has zero economic profits but positive accounting profits. Recall that accounting profits are total revenues minus total explicit costs. What is ignored in such accounting is the reward offered to investors—the opportunity cost of capital—plus all other implicit costs.

In economic analysis, the average total cost curve includes the full opportunity cost of capital. Indeed, the average total cost curve includes the opportunity cost of *all* factors of production used in the production process. At the short-run break-even price, economic profits are, by definition, zero. Accounting profits at that price are not, however, equal to zero; they are positive. Consider an example. A baseball bat manufacturer sells bats at some price. The owners of the firm have supplied all the funds in the business. They have borrowed no money from anyone else, and they explicitly pay the full opportunity cost to all factors of production, including any managerial labor that they themselves contribute to the business. Their salaries show up as a cost in the books and are equal to what they could have earned in the next-best alternative occupation. At the end of the year, the owners find that after they subtract all explicit costs from total revenues, they have earned \$100,000. Let's say that their investment was \$1 million. Thus the rate of return on that investment is 10 percent per year. We will assume that this turns out to be equal to the rate of return that, on average, all other baseball bat manufacturers make in the industry.

Click here for an analysis of whether the drug market fits the model of perfect competition.

This \$100,000, or 10 percent rate of return, is actually, then, a competitive, or normal, rate of return on invested capital in that industry or in other industries with similar risks. If the owners had made only \$50,000, or 5 percent on their investment, they would have been able to make higher profits by leaving the industry. The 10 percent rate of return is the opportunity cost of capital. Accountants show it as a profit; economists call it a cost. We include that cost in the average total cost curve, similar to the one shown in Figure 23-6. At the short-run break-even price, average total cost, including this opportunity cost of capital, will just equal that price. The firm will be making zero economic profits but a 10 percent *accounting* rate of return.

Now we are ready to derive the firm's supply curve.

The Perfect Competitor's Short-Run Supply Curve

What does the supply curve for the individual firm look like? Actually, we have been looking at it all along. We know that when the price of minidisks is \$5, the firm will supply seven or eight of them per day. If the price falls to \$3, the firm will supply five or six minidisks per day. And if the price falls below \$3, the firm will shut down in the short run. Hence in Figure 23-7, the firm's supply curve is the marginal cost curve above the short-run shutdown point. This is shown as the solid part of the marginal cost curve. ***The definition, then, of the individual firm's short-run supply curve in a competitive industry is its marginal cost curve equal to and above the point of intersection with the average variable cost curve.***

The Short-Run Industry Supply Curve

In Chapter 3, we indicated that the market supply curve was the summation of individual supply curves. At the beginning of this chapter, we drew a market supply curve in Figure 23-2. Now we want to derive more precisely a market, or industry, supply curve to reflect individual

FIGURE 23-7

The Individual Firm's Short-Run Supply Curve

The individual firm's short-run supply curve is the portion of its marginal cost curve above the minimum point on the average variable cost curve.

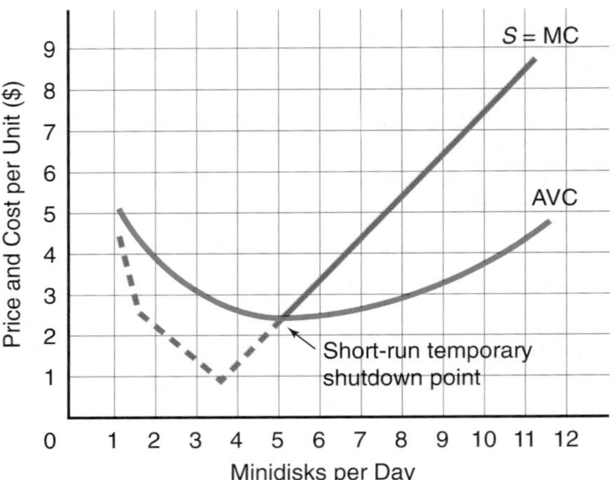

producer behavior in that industry. First we must ask, What is an industry? It is merely a collection of firms producing a particular product. Therefore, we have a way to figure out the total supply curve of any industry: We add the quantities that each firm will supply at every possible price. In other words, we sum the individual supply curves of all the competitive firms *horizontally.* The individual supply curves, as we just saw, are simply the marginal cost curves of each firm.

Consider doing this for a hypothetical world in which there are only two minidisk producers in the industry, firm A and firm B. These two firms' marginal cost curves are given in panels (a) and (b) of Figure 23-8. The marginal cost curves for the two separate firms are presented as MC_A in panel (a) and MC_B in panel (b). Those two marginal cost curves are

FIGURE 23-8

Deriving the Industry Supply Curve

Marginal cost curves above average minimum variable cost are presented in panels (a) and (b) for firms A and B. We horizontally sum the two quantities supplied, q_{A1} and q_{B1}, at price P_1. This gives us point *F* in panel (c). We do the same thing for the quantities at price P_2. This gives us point *G*. When we connect those points, we have the industry supply curve, *S*, which is the horizontal summation [represented by the Greek letter sigma (Σ)] of the firms' marginal cost curves above their respective average minimum costs.

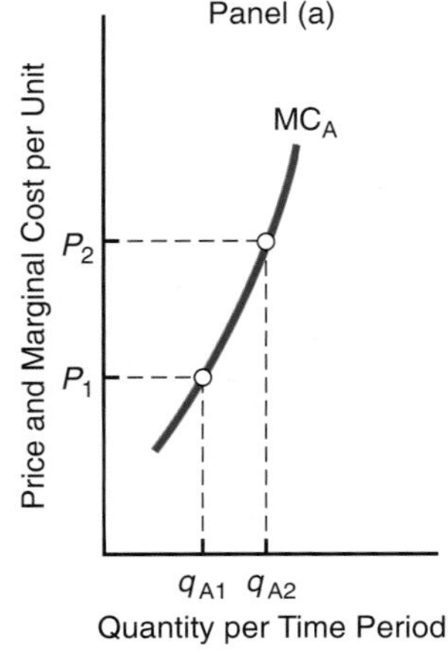

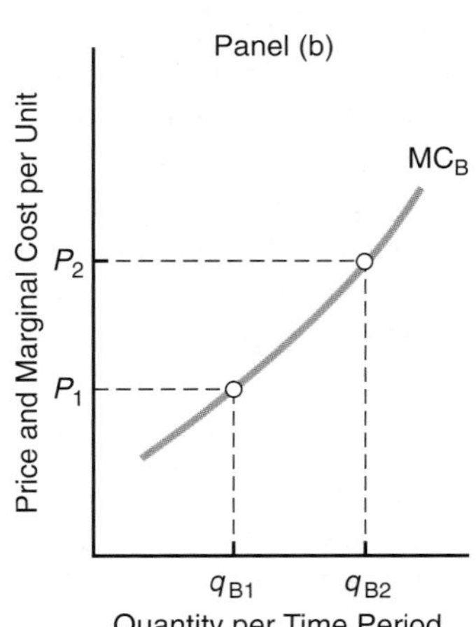

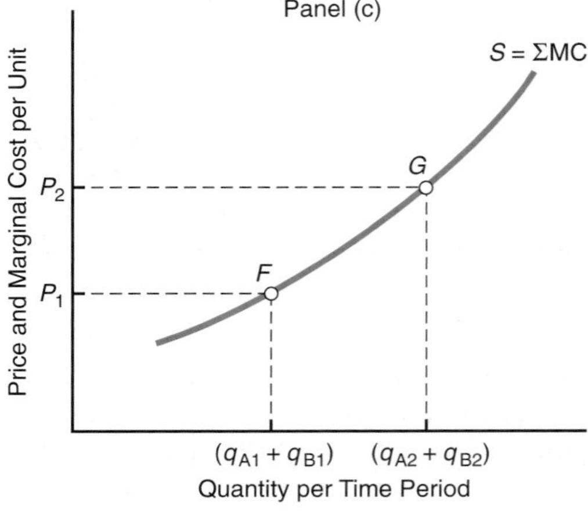

drawn only for prices above the minimum average variable cost for each respective firm. Hence we are not including any of the marginal cost curves below minimum average variable cost. In panel (a), for firm A, at price P_1, the quantity supplied would be q_{A1}. At price P_2, the quantity supplied would be q_{A2}. In panel (b), we see the two different quantities that would be supplied by firm B corresponding to those two prices. Now for price P_1 we add horizontally the quantity of q_{A1} and q_{B1}. This gives us one point, *F*, for our short-run **industry supply curve,** *S.* We obtain the other point, *G,* by doing the same horizontal adding of quantities at P_2. When we connect points *F* and *G,* we obtain industry supply curve *S,* which is also marked ΣMC, indicating that it is the horizontal summation of the marginal cost curves (above the respective minimum average variable cost of each firm).* Because the law of diminishing returns makes marginal cost curves rise, the short-run supply curve of a perfectly competitive industry must be upward-sloping.

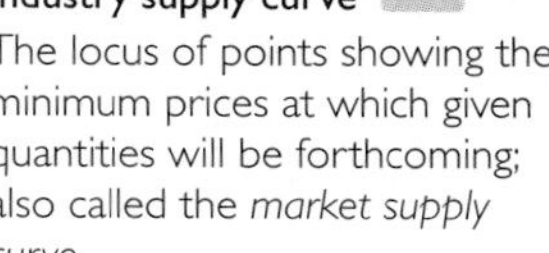
Industry supply curve
The locus of points showing the minimum prices at which given quantities will be forthcoming; also called the *market supply curve.*

Factors That Influence the Industry Supply Curve

As you have just seen, the industry supply curve is the horizontal summation of all of the individual firms' marginal cost curves above their respective minimum average variable cost points. This means that anything that affects the marginal cost curves of the firm will influence the industry supply curve. Therefore, the individual factors that will influence the supply schedule in a competitive industry can be summarized as the factors that cause the variable costs of production to change. These are factors that affect the individual marginal cost curves, such as changes in the individual firm's productivity, in factor costs (wages paid to labor, prices of raw materials, etc.), in taxes, and in anything else that would influence the individual firm's marginal cost curve.

All of these are *ceteris paribus* conditions of supply. Because they affect the position of the marginal cost curve for the individual firm, they affect the position of the industry supply curve. A change in any of these will shift the market supply curve.

CONCEPTS IN BRIEF

- Short-run average profits or average losses are determined by comparing average total costs with price (average revenue) at the profit-maximizing rate of output. In the short run, the perfectly competitive firm can make economic profits or economic losses.
- The competitive firm's short-run break-even output occurs at the minimum point on its average total cost curve, which is where the marginal cost curve intersects the average total cost curve.
- The competitive firm's short-run shutdown output is at the minimum point on its average variable cost curve, which is also where the marginal cost curve intersects the average variable cost curve. Shutdown will occur if price falls below average variable cost.
- The firm will continue production at a price that exceeds average variable costs even though the full opportunity cost of capital is not being met; at least some revenues are going toward paying fixed costs.
- At the short-run break-even price, the firm is making zero economic profits, which means that it is just making a normal rate of return in that industry.
- The firm's short-run supply curve is the portion of its marginal cost curve equal to or above minimum average variable costs. The industry short-run supply curve is a horizontal summation of the individual firms' marginal cost curves above their respective minimum average variable costs.

*The capital Greek sigma, Σ, is the symbol for summation.

FIGURE 23-9

Industry Demand and Supply Curves and the Individual Firm Demand Curve

The industry demand curve is represented by D in panel (a). The short-run industry supply curve is S and equal to ΣMC. The intersection of the demand and supply curves at E determines the equilibrium or market clearing price at P_e. The individual firm demand curve in panel (b) is set at the market clearing price determined in panel (a). If the producer has a marginal cost curve MC, this producer's individual profit-maximizing output level is at q_e. For AC_1, economic profits are zero; for AC_2, profits are negative; and for AC_3, profits are positive.

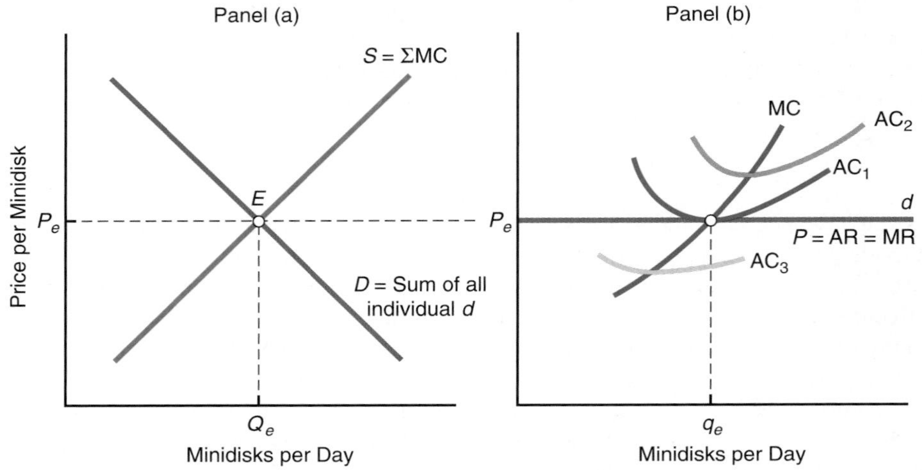

COMPETITIVE PRICE DETERMINATION

How is the market, or "going," price established in a competitive market? This price is established by the interaction of all the suppliers (firms) and all the demanders. The market demand schedule, D, in panel (a) of Figure 23-9 represents the demand schedule for the entire industry, and the supply schedule, S, represents the supply schedule for the entire industry. Price P_e is established by the forces of supply and demand at the intersection of D and the short-run industry supply curve, S. Even though each individual firm has no control or effect on the price of its product in a competitive industry, the interaction of *all* the producers and buyers determines the price at which the product will be sold. We say that the price P_e and the quantity Q_e in panel (a) of Figure 23-9 constitute the competitive solution to the pricing-quantity problem in that particular industry. It is the equilibrium where quantity demanded equals quantity supplied, and both suppliers and demanders are maximizing. The resulting individual firm demand curve, d, is shown in panel (b) of Figure 23-9 at the price P_e.

In a purely competitive industry, the individual producer takes price as a given and chooses the output level that maximizes profits. (This is also the equilibrium level of output from the producer's standpoint.) We see in panel (b) of Figure 23-9 that this is at q_e. If the producer's average costs are given by AC_1, q_e is also the short-run break-even output (see Figure 23-6); if its average costs are given by AC_2, at q_e, AC exceeds price (average revenue), and the firm is incurring losses. Alternatively, if average costs are given by AC_3, the firm will be making economic profits at q_e. In the former case, we would expect, over time, that firms will cease production (exit the industry), causing supply to shift inward, whereas in the latter case, we would expect new firms to enter the industry to take advantage of the economic profits, thereby causing supply to shift outward. We now turn to these long-run considerations.

EXAMPLE

Even Harvard Can't Charge an Above-Market Price

How things have changed since 1991. In that year, the U.S. Department of Justice filed suit against Ivy League universities. It claimed that they had conspired in their financial aid decisions, thereby forestalling the competitive determination of tuition rates for their students. Recently, however, Princeton University began to offer full scholarships to academically qualified students with family incomes below $40,000, and it increased its aid offers for students from middle-income families. Not long afterward, Yale also announced more financial aid for middle-income students, as did Brown and Cornell. Then Stanford and MIT (outside the Ivy League, but close competitors nonetheless) established similar aid plans.

Finally, the nation's oldest and most distinguished university, Harvard, sent a letter to each newly admitted student. In part, it said, "We expect that some of our students will have particularly attractive offers from the institutions with new aid programs, and those students should not assume that we will not respond." Translation: We'll meet the market price. Even Harvard is a perfect competitor in the market for top-notch higher education.

For Critical Analysis

According to the perfect competition model, all sellers charge the market price. But if sellers conspire to fix prices, they also charge the same price. How might one discern if sellers are charging competitive or noncompetitive prices for their products?

THE LONG-RUN INDUSTRY SITUATION: EXIT AND ENTRY

In the long run in a competitive situation, firms will be making zero economic profits. In the long run, we surmise that perfectly competitive firms will tend to have average total cost curves that just touch the price (marginal revenue) curve, or individual demand curve *d*. How does this occur? It is through an adjustment process that depends on economic profits and losses.

Exit and Entry of Firms

Go back and look at Figures 23-4 (p. 568) and 23-5 (p. 569). The existence of either profits or losses is a signal to owners of capital both within and outside the industry. If the industry is characterized by firms showing economic profits as represented in Figure 23-4, this will signal owners of capital elsewhere in the economy that they, too, should enter this industry. If, by contrast, there are firms in the industry like the ones suffering economic losses represented in Figure 23-5, this signals resource owners outside the industry to stay out. It also signals resource owners within the industry not to reinvest and if possible to leave the industry. It is in this sense that we say that profits direct resources to their highest-valued use. In the long run, capital will flow into industries in which profitability is highest and will flow out of industries in which profitability is lowest.

Long-Run Adjustments
Gain more experience thinking about long-run equilibrium under perfect competition.

The price system therefore allocates capital according to the relative expected rates of return on alternative investments. Entry restrictions will thereby hinder economic efficiency, and thus welfare, by not allowing resources to flow to their highest-valued use. Similarly, exit restrictions (such as laws that require firms to give advance notice of closings) will act to trap resources (temporarily) in sectors in which their value is below that in alternative uses. Such laws will also inhibit the ability of firms to respond to changes in the domestic and international marketplace.

Not every industry presents an immediate source of opportunity for every firm. In a brief period of time, it may be impossible for a firm that produces tractors to switch to the production of computers, even if there are very large profits to be made. Over the long run, however, we would expect to see such a change, whether or not the tractor producers want to change over to another product. In a market economy, investors supply firms in the more profitable industry with more investment funds, which they take from firms in less profitable industries. (Also, profits give existing firms internal investment funds for expansion.) Consequently, resources useful in the production of more profitable goods, such as labor, will be bid away from lower-valued opportunities. Investors and other suppliers of resources respond to market **signals** about their highest-valued opportunities.

Signals
Compact ways of conveying to economic decision makers information needed to make decisions. A true signal not only conveys information but also provides the incentive to react appropriately. Economic profits and economic losses are such signals.

Market adjustment to changes in demand will occur regardless of the wishes of the managers of firms in less profitable markets. They can either attempt to adjust their product line to respond to the new demands, be replaced by managers who are more responsive to new conditions, or see their firms go bankrupt as they find themselves unable to replace worn-out plant and equipment.

In addition, when we say that in a competitive long-run equilibrium situation firms will be making zero economic profits, we must realize that at a particular point in time it would be pure coincidence for a firm to be making *exactly* zero economic profits. Real-world information is not as precise as the curves we use to simplify our analysis. Things change all the time in a dynamic world, and firms, even in a very competitive situation, may for many reasons not be making exactly zero economic profits. We say that there is a *tendency* toward that equilibrium position, but firms are adjusting all the time to changes in their cost curves and in their individual demand curves.

EXAMPLE

Who Really Shops at Club Warehouses?

One of the most pervasive competitive innovations in retailing in the United States has been the club warehouse phenomenon. These now ubiquitous retail outlets were first developed by San Diego's Sol Price. He started the Price Club chain in 1976. Since then, entry into the club warehouse business has been aggressive. It is dominated today by Wal-Mart-owned Sam's Club and Costco, the successor to the original Price Club. Smaller club warehouse chains, such as B.J.'s (a subsidiary of Waban, Inc.), dominate regional markets.

One interesting aspect of club warehouses involves who shops there and their reasons for doing so. One might assume at first glance that poorer American families would patronize club warehouses more heavily because of the their lower prices. The reality is just the opposite—the average family shopping at a club warehouse has above-average income. What accounts for that? A club warehouse stocks only a few branded goods in each product category. In essence, the club warehouse has done each customer's comparison shopping and obtained the best terms from the vendors. Individuals who have a relatively higher opportunity cost of time (usually those who make higher incomes) find this a value-added service.

For Critical Analysis

Why do you think the club warehouse market is dominated by a few large firms?

Long-Run Industry Supply Curves

In panel (a) of Figure 23-9 on page 574, we drew the summation of all of the portions of the individual firms' marginal cost curve above each firm's respective minimum average variable costs as the upward-sloping supply curve of the entire industry. We should be aware, however, that a relatively steep upward-sloping supply curve may be appropriate only in the short run. After all, one of the prerequisites of a competitive industry is free entry.

Remember that our definition of the long run is a period of time in which all adjustments can be made. The **long-run industry supply curve** is a supply curve showing the relationship between quantities supplied by the entire industry at different prices after firms have been allowed to either enter or leave the industry, depending on whether there have been positive or negative economic profits. Also, the long-run industry supply curve is drawn under the assumption that entry and exit have been completed. Thus along the long-run industry supply curve, firms in the industry earn zero economic profits.

Long-run industry supply curve 
A market supply curve showing the relationship between prices and quantities forthcoming after firms have been allowed the time to enter into or exit from an industry, depending on whether there have been positive or negative economic profits.

The long-run industry supply curve can take one of three shapes, depending on whether input costs stay constant, increase, or decrease as the number of firms in the industry changes. In Chapter 22, we assumed that input prices remained constant to the firm regardless of the firm's rate of output. When we look at the entire industry, when all firms are expanding and new firms are entering, they may simultaneously bid up input prices.

Constant-Cost Industries. In principle, there are industries that use such a small percentage of the total supply of inputs required for industrywide production that firms can enter the industry without bidding up input prices. In such a situation, we are dealing with a **constant-cost industry.** Its long-run industry supply curve is therefore horizontal and is represented by S_L in panel (a) of Figure 23-10.

Constant-cost industry 
An industry whose total output can be increased without an increase in long-run per-unit costs; an industry whose long-run supply curve is horizontal.

We can work through the case in which constant costs prevail. We start out in panel (a) with demand curve D_1 and supply curve S_1. The equilibrium price is P_1. Market demand shifts rightward to D_2. In the short run, the equilibrium price rises to P_2. This generates positive economic profits for existing firms in the industry. Such economic profits induce capital to flow into the industry. The existing firms expand or new firms enter (or both). The short-run supply curve shifts outward to S_2. The new intersection with the new demand

FIGURE 23-10
Constant-Cost, Increasing-Cost, and Decreasing-Cost Industries
In panel (a), we show a situation in which the demand curve shifts from D_1 to D_2. Price increases from P_1 to P_2; however, in time the short-run supply curve shifts outward because positive profits are being earned, and the equilibrium shifts from E_2 to E_3. The market clearing price is again P_1. If we connect points such as E_1 and E_3, we come up with the long-run supply curve S_L. This is a constant-cost industry. In panel (b), costs are increasing for the industry, and therefore the long-run supply curve slopes upward and long-run prices rise from P_1 to P_2. In panel (c), costs are decreasing for the industry as it expands, and therefore the long-run supply curve slopes downward such that long-run prices decline from P_1 to P_2.

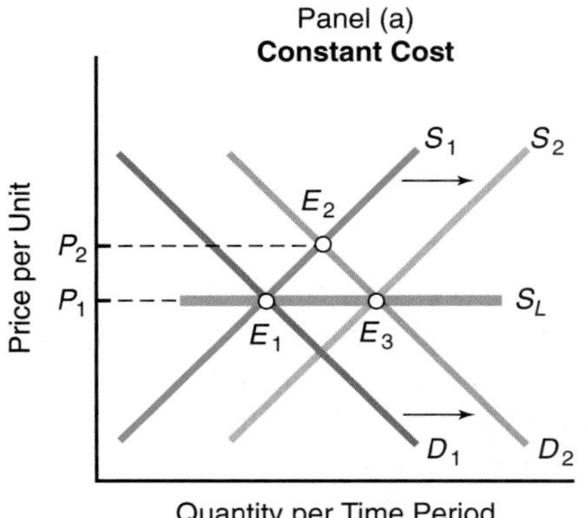

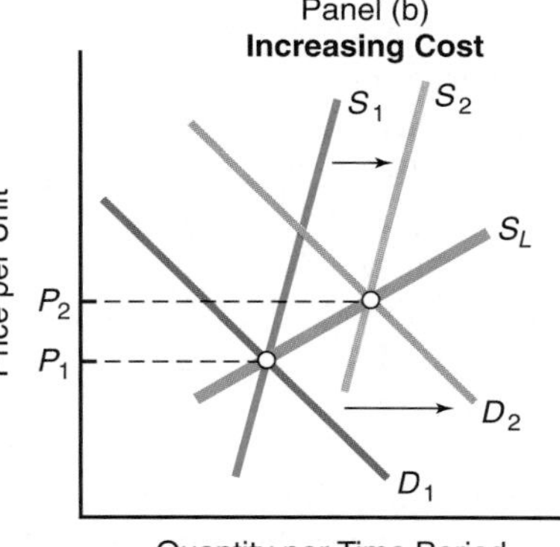

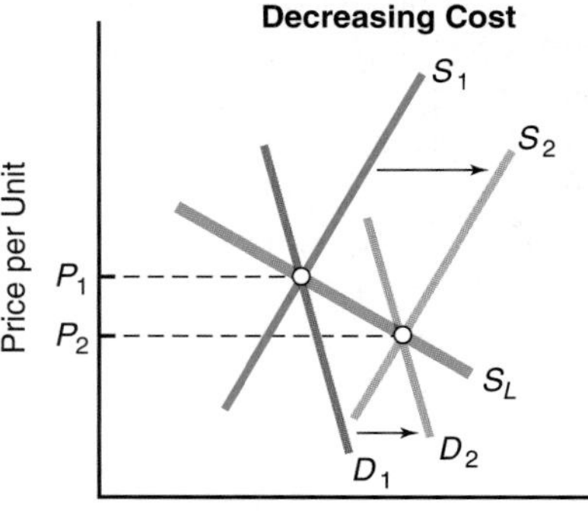

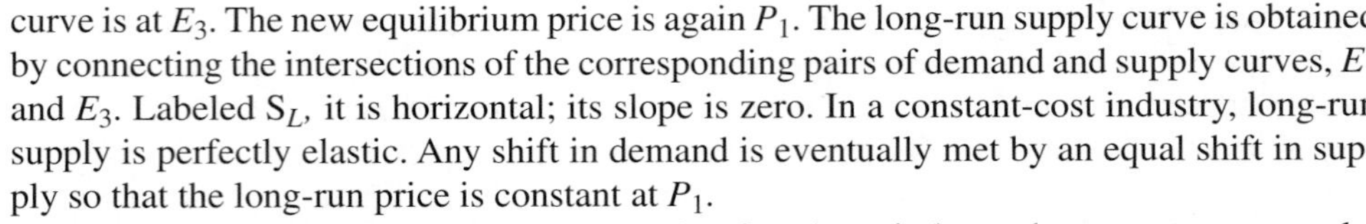

curve is at E_3. The new equilibrium price is again P_1. The long-run supply curve is obtained by connecting the intersections of the corresponding pairs of demand and supply curves, E_1 and E_3. Labeled S_L, it is horizontal; its slope is zero. In a constant-cost industry, long-run supply is perfectly elastic. Any shift in demand is eventually met by an equal shift in supply so that the long-run price is constant at P_1.

Retail trade is often given as an example of such an industry because output can be expanded or contracted without affecting input prices. Banking is another example.

Increasing-cost industry
An industry in which an increase in industry output is accompanied by an increase in long-run per-unit costs, such that the long-run industry supply curve slopes upward.

Increasing-Cost Industries. In an **increasing-cost industry,** expansion by existing firms and the addition of new firms cause the price of inputs specialized within that industry to be bid up. As costs of production rise, the ATC curve and the firms' MC curves shift upward, causing short-run supply curves (each firm's marginal cost curve) to shift upward. The result is a long-run industry supply curve that slopes upward, as represented by S_L in panel (b) of Figure 23-10. Examples are residential construction and coal mining—both use specialized inputs that cannot be obtained in ever-increasing quantities without causing their prices to rise.

Decreasing-Cost Industries. An expansion in the number of firms in an industry can lead to a reduction in input costs and a downward shift in the ATC and MC curves. When this occurs, the long-run industry supply curve will slope downward. An example is given in panel (c) of Figure 23-10. This is a **decreasing-cost industry.**

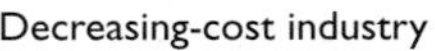

Decreasing-cost industry
An industry in which an increase in output leads to a reduction in long-run per-unit costs, such that the long-run industry supply curve slopes downward.

LONG-RUN EQUILIBRIUM

In the long run, the firm can change the scale of its plant, adjusting its plant size in such a way that it has no further incentive to change. It will do so until profits are maximized. Figure 23-11 shows the long-run equilibrium of the perfectly competitive firm. Given a price of P and a marginal cost curve, MC, the firm produces at output Q_e. Because profits must be zero in the long run, the firm's short-run average costs (SAC) must equal P at Q_e, which occurs at minimum SAC. In addition, because we are in long-run equilibrium, any economies of scale must be exhausted so that we are on the minimum point of the long-run average cost curve (LAC). In other words, the long-run equilibrium position is where "everything is equal," which is at point E in Figure 23-11. There, *price* equals *marginal revenue* equals *marginal cost* equals *average cost* (minimum, short-run, and long-run).

In the long run, don't national boundaries limit the extent to which firms can compete?

National borders can restrain competition only to the extent that governments are successful in erecting enforceable barriers to foreign competition. Emerging information technologies are doing an end run around many of these barriers. Anyone can shop on the Internet, as long as there are relatively few restraints on their ability to receive goods from delivery services. Even in markets for traditional goods such as agricultural products, artificial restraints on trade have ultimately given way to the forces of competition. Today, U.S. consumers buy fruit grown in South America, and African consumers purchase grains harvested in the American Midwest. Furthermore, agricultural businesses around the world enter and exit in response to price changes that occur in a global marketplace.

Perfect Competition and Minimum Average Total Cost

Look again at Figure 23-11. In long-run equilibrium, the perfectly competitive firm finds itself producing at output rate Q_e. At that rate of output, the price is just equal to the minimum long-run average cost as well as the minimum short-run average cost. In this sense, perfect competition results in the production of goods and services using the least costly combination of resources. This is an important attribute of a perfectly competitive long-run equilibrium, particularly when we wish to compare the

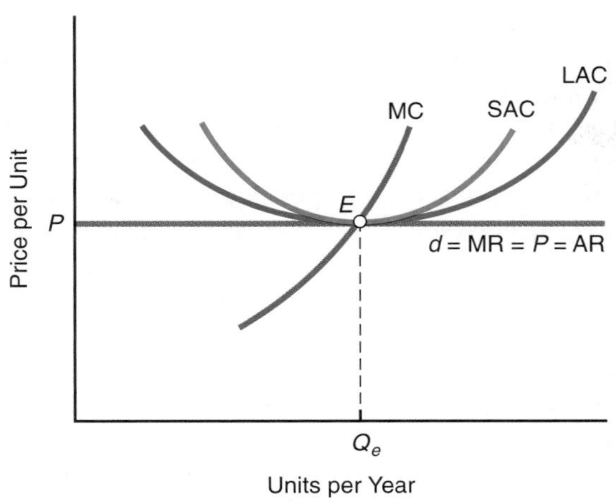

FIGURE 23-11
Long-Run Firm Competitive Equilibrium
In the long run, the firm operates where price, marginal revenue, marginal cost, short-run minimum average cost, and long-run minimum average cost are all equal. This occurs at point *E*.

market structure of perfect competition with other market structures that are less than perfectly competitive. We will examine these other market structures in later chapters.

COMPETITIVE PRICING: MARGINAL COST PRICING

In a perfectly competitive industry, each firm produces where its marginal cost curve intersects its marginal revenue curve from below. Thus perfectly competitive firms always sell their goods at a price that just equals marginal cost. This represents an optimal pricing situation because the price that consumers pay reflects the opportunity cost to society of producing the good. Recall that marginal cost is the amount that a firm must spend to purchase the additional resources needed to expand output by one unit. Given competitive markets, the amount paid for a resource will be the same in all of its alternative uses. Thus MC reflects relative resource input use; that is, if the MC of good 1 is twice the MC of good 2, one more unit of good 1 requires twice the resource input of one more unit of good 2. Because price equals marginal cost under perfect competition, the consumer, in determining allocation of income on purchases on the basis of relative prices, is actually allocating income on the basis of relative resource input use.

Click here to find out how the Congressional Budget Office tries to judge whether banks engage in marginal cost pricing with automated teller machines.

Marginal Cost Pricing

The competitive firm produces up to the point at which the market price just equals the marginal cost. Herein lies the element of the optimal nature of a competitive solution. It is called **marginal cost pricing.** The competitive firm sells its product at a price that just equals the cost to society—the opportunity cost—for that is what the marginal cost curve represents. (But note here that it is the self-interest of firm owners that causes price to equal the additional cost to society.) In other words, the marginal benefit to consumers, given by the price that they are willing to pay for the last unit of the good purchased, just equals the marginal cost to society of producing the last unit. [If the marginal benefit exceeds the marginal cost ($P > \text{MC}$), too little is being produced in that people value additional units more than the cost to society of producing them; if $P < \text{MC}$, the opposite is true.]

Marginal cost pricing A system of pricing in which the price charged is equal to the opportunity cost to society of producing one more unit of the good or service in question. The opportunity cost is the marginal cost to society.

When an individual pays a price equal to the marginal cost of production, the cost to the user of that product is equal to the sacrifice or cost to society of producing that quantity of that good as opposed to more of some other good. (We are assuming that all marginal social costs are accounted for.) The competitive solution, then, is called *efficient,* in the economic sense of the word. Economic efficiency means that it is impossible to increase the output of any good without lowering the *value* of the total output produced in the economy. No juggling of resources, such as labor and capital, will result in an output that is higher in total value than the value of all of the goods and services already being produced. In an efficient situation, it is impossible to make one person better off without making someone else worse off. All resources are used in the most advantageous way possible, and society therefore enjoys an efficient allocation of productive resources. All goods and services are sold at their opportunity cost, and marginal cost pricing prevails throughout.

Market failure 
A situation in which an unrestrained market operation leads to either too few or too many resources going to a specific economic activity.

Market Failure

Although perfect competition does offer many desirable results, situations arise when perfectly competitive markets cannot efficiently allocate resources. Either too many or too few resources are used in the production of a good or service. These situations are instances of **market failure.** Externalities and public goods are examples. For reasons discussed in later chapters, perfectly competitive markets cannot efficiently allocate resources in these situations, and alternative allocation mechanisms are called for. In some cases, alternative market structures, or government intervention, *may* improve the economic outcome.

Lemons problem 
The situation in which consumers, who do not know details about the quality of a product, are willing to pay no more than the price of a low-quality product, even if a higher-quality product at a higher price exists.

The competitive price is determined by the intersection of the market demand curve and the market supply curve; the market supply curve is equal to the horizontal summation of

POLICY EXAMPLE

Can the Government Cure Market Failure Due to Asymmetric Information, or Are Lemons Here to Stay?

One kind of market failure may occur when assumption 4 (p. 561) with respect to perfect competition is violated. Specifically, if information is not the same for buyers and sellers, markets may be dominated by low-quality products. This is a situation of asymmetric information. It has been called the **lemons problem** because cars, particularly used cars, that turn out to be "bad deals" are called lemons. The potential buyer of a used car has relatively little information about the true quality of the car—its motor, transmission, brakes, and so on. The only way the buyer can find out is to purchase the car and use it for a time. In contrast, the seller usually has much greater information about the quality of the car, for the seller has been using it for some time. The owner of the used car knows whether or not it is a lemon. In situations like this, with asymmetric information between buyer and seller, buyers tend to want to pay only a price that reflects the lower quality of the typical used car in the market, not a price that reflects the higher value of a truly good used car.

From the car seller's point of view, given that the price of used cars will tend to reflect average qualities, all of the owners of known lemons will want to put their cars up for sale. The owners of high-quality used cars will be more reluctant to do so. The logical result of this adverse selection is a disproportionate number of lemons on the used car market and consequently relatively fewer sales than would exist if information were symmetric.

So lemons will be overpriced and great-running used cars will be underpriced. Is there room for government policy to improve this market? Because the government has no better information than used-car buyers, it cannot provide any improved information. What the government has done, though, is require mileage certificates on all used cars and the disclosure of major defects and work that has been performed on them. What the market has done is use brand names both for cars and for firms that sell used cars. Used-car retailers also offer extended warranties.

For Critical Analysis

If used-car dealers depend on repeat customers, is the lemons problem reduced or eliminated?

the portions of the individual marginal cost curves above their respective minimum average variable costs.

CONCEPTS IN BRIEF

- In the long run, competitive firms make zero economic profits because of entry and exit of firms into and out of the industry whenever there are industrywide economic profits or economic losses.
- A constant-cost industry will have a horizontal long-run supply curve. An increasing-cost industry will have a upward-sloping long-run supply curve. A decreasing-cost industry will have a downward-sloping long-run supply curve.
- In the long run, a competitive firm produces where price, marginal revenue, marginal cost, short-run minimum average cost, and long-run minimum average cost are all equal.
- Competitive pricing is essentially marginal cost pricing, and therefore the competitive solution is called efficient because marginal cost represents the social opportunity cost of producing one more unit of the good; when consumers face a price equal to the full opportunity cost of the product they are buying, their purchasing decisions will lead to an efficient use of available resources.

NETNOMICS

Emerging Competitive Market for International Communications Services

Ask your parents about the "bad old days" of telecommunications, during which the typical American house contained a single telephone. Families had no choice but to lease that telephone from a single licensed company, and they were stuck with that company's rates on local calls. For long-distance service, the "choice" was either to pay the rates established by a single company or not to make long-distance calls at all. Of course, deregulation changed all that. Today, many families have four or more wired telephones and at least one cellular phone. They can choose among long-distance phone services, and a growing number of people can even choose which local phone company will get their business.

The international telephone business has been slower to experience heightened competition. Various restraints on competition among national phone companies have led to profit margins on international phone calls in excess of 60 percent. As a result, national phone companies earn more than $25 billion in annual global revenues from international calls.

This state of affairs may not last much longer, however. It is now possible to use the Internet to send not only e-mail but also relatively inexpensive fax, verbal, and video transmissions. The technology has existed for several years, but until recently, Internet-based calls have suffered from lags and inferior voice quality compared to traditional phone calls. But now that the technology of Internet-based communications promises to improve over the next few years, a number of Internet-based companies are likely to begin offering communications services, directly competing with traditional phone companies. This heralds a more competitive market in international communications services.

Such a development could pose particular problems for the world's biggest provider of international calling services, AT&T. U.S. callers tend to spend more time on the phone during international calls, which helps explain why AT&T earns about a third of world revenues from international calls. But U.S. residents also spend more time on-line than others around the world. Consequently, they may be the quickest to defect to AT&T's emerging Internet rivals. Some experts on the international telecommunications industry estimate that e-mail and Internet communications technologies have already siphoned away as much as $350 million in revenues that AT&T once earned from international phone calls. AT&T and other traditional providers of international telephone services are now considering whether they should get into the Internet telephony business.

ISSUES & APPLICATIONS

Has the U.S. Economy Become More Competitive?

It is commonplace to read, see, and hear media accounts of "how much more competitive" the U.S. economy has become. Consumers report enjoying a greater range of substitution when they shop for goods and services. Businesspeople complain about the "pricing pressures" they face in today's marketplace. According to General Electric CEO John Welch, "There's no pricing power at all" in U.S. markets; that is, firms are price takers. Perception is one thing, but reality is another. Is the overall U.S. economy really more competitive than it used to be?

Concepts Applied

Perfect Competition

Competitive Price Determination

Groundwork for Greater Competition: Deregulation in the 1970s and 1980s

There is good reason to think that many American industries ought to be more competitive than they once were. Table 23-1 lists key regulatory changes enacted in the 1970s and 1980s. As you can see, common descriptors for regulatory initiatives adopted for various

TABLE 23-1
Significant Deregulation Since the 1970s

Industry	Major Initiatives
Airlines	CAB Liberalization of Entry and Discount Fare Experiments (mid 1970s)
	Airline Deregulation Act (1978)
Trucking	ICC Liberalization of Truck Rates (late 1970s)
	Motor Carrier Reform Act (1980)
Railroads	ICC Liberalization of Rail Rates and Contracting (late 1970s)
	Staggers Rail Act (1980)
Telecommunications	Federal Communications Commission (FCC) Court Decisions (late 1960s–mid 1970s)
	Execunet Decision (1977)
	AT&T Settlement (1982)
Cable television	FCC Rulemakings and other Regulatory Proceedings (late 1970s)
	Cable Television Deregulation Act (1984)
Brokerage	Securities Acts Amendments (1975)
Banking	Depository Institution Deregulation and Monetary Control Act (1980)
	Garn–St. Germain Depository Institutions Act (1982)
Petroleum	Decontrol of crude oil and refined petroleum products (executive orders beginning in 1979)
Natural gas	Natural Gas Policy Act (1978)

major industries for were "liberalization" and "deregulation." The U.S. government clearly sought to lay the groundwork for more competition a generation ago.

Some Evidence: Trying to Measure Overall Competition

If the American economy has truly become more competitive, firm profits should be closer to normal levels, indicating heightened rivalry among firms. With more scope for consumers to substitute among competing products, firms should be unable to set prices in excess of average production costs. One way to evaluate whether the entire U.S. economy is more competitive might be to examine each and every American industry in search of evidence that these predictions are better satisfied today than before. If this were true for most industries, we might feel comfortable saying that competition really has increased in the United States.

Another approach, however, is to take a "big picture" perspective. Economists have sought to do this by examining aggregate profit data for all U.S. firms. This is the approach taken by John Duca of the Federal Reserve Bank of Dallas and David VanHoose of the University of Alabama. They use data on aggregate U.S. business profits since the early 1950s to develop year-to-year estimates of the extent to which companies have been able to "mark up" their prices over and above their average costs of production. Naturally, the

FIGURE 23-12

Aggregate Competition in the United States

Aggregate year-to-year markups of prices over average production costs implied by data on the total profits of American companies yield an index measure of U.S. competition. This competition index has trended upward.

Source: John Duca and David VanHoose, "Has Greater Competition Restrained Inflation?" *Southern Economic Journal*, January 2000.

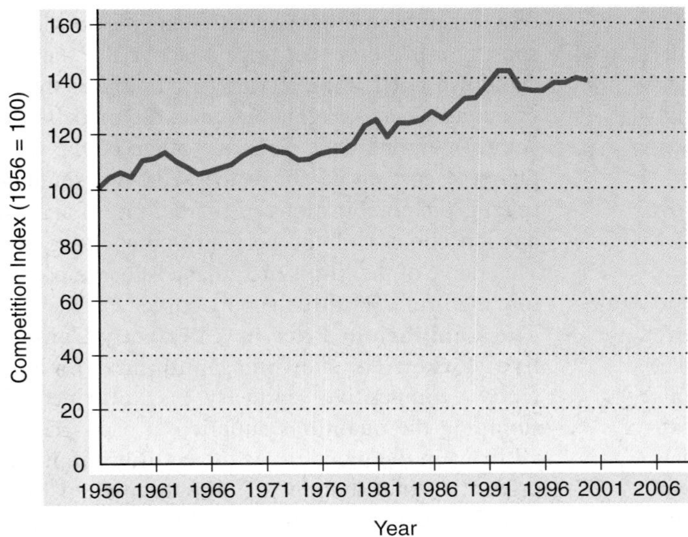

perfect competition model indicates that a greater range of substitution among goods that firms produce should restrain the size of price markups over average cost. Consequently, Duca and VanHoose's estimates of aggregate year-to-year price markups implied by total profit data essentially yield an aggregate measure of how substitutable the products of American firms have been over time. In short, they yield an index measure of "overall competition" in the U.S. economy.

Annual estimates of this index measure are plotted in Figure 23-12. Although there is some year-to-year variability in this aggregate competition index, it exhibits a definite upward trend. This is particularly notable since the 1970s, when widespread deregulation of a number U.S. industries began to reduce many barriers to entry and exit. The index has continued to increase as the information technology revolution has further enhanced the ability of consumers to shop for the best price among the products of rival firms. Aggregate profit data, therefore, indicate that the U.S. economy is indeed more competitive than it used to be.

FOR CRITICAL ANALYSIS

1. Based on the evidence in Figure 23-12, was the average U.S. company more or less likely to earn above-zero economic profits in the 1960s, compared with today?
2. Does a higher degree of overall U.S. competition today necessarily mean that every U.S. industry conforms more closely with the perfect competition model relative to earlier years?

SG

SUMMARY DISCUSSION OF LEARNING OBJECTIVES

1. **The Characteristics of a Perfectly Competitive Market Structure:** There are four fundamental characteristics of a perfectly competitive industry: (1) there are a large number of buyers and sellers, (2) firms in the industry produce and sell a homogeneous product, (3) there are insignificant barriers to industry entry or exit, and (4) information is equally accessible to both buyers and sellers. These characteristics imply that each firm in a perfectly competitive industry is a price taker, meaning that the firm takes the market price as given and outside its control.
2. **How a Perfectly Competitive Firm Decides How Much to Produce:** Because a perfectly competitive firm sells the amount that it wishes at the market price, the additional revenue it earns from selling an additional unit of output is the market price. Thus the firm's marginal revenue curve is horizontal at the market price, and this marginal revenue curve is the firm's own perfectly elastic demand curve. The firm maximizes economic profits when marginal cost equals marginal revenue, as long as the market price is not below the short-run shutdown price, where the marginal cost curve crosses the average variable cost curve.
3. **The Short-Run Supply Curve of a Perfectly Competitive Firm:** If the market price is below the short-run shutdown price, the firm's total revenues fail to cover its variable costs. Then the firm would be better off halting production and incurring only its fixed costs, thereby minimizing its economic loss in the short run. If the market price is above the short-run shutdown price, however, the firm produces the rate of output where marginal revenue, the market price, equals marginal cost. Thus the range of the firm's marginal cost curve above the short-run shutdown price gives combinations of market prices and production choices of the perfectly competitive firm. This range of the firm's marginal cost curve is therefore the firm's short-run supply curve.
4. **The Equilibrium Price in a Perfectly Competitive Market:** The short-run supply curve for a perfectly competitive industry is obtained by summing the quantities supplied at each price by all firms in the industry. At the equilibrium market price, the total amount of output supplied by all firms is equal to the total amount of output demanded by all buyers.

5. **Incentives to Enter or Exit a Perfectly Competitive Industry:** In the short run, a perfectly firm will continue to produce output as long as the market price exceeds the short-run shutdown price. This is so even if the market price is below the short-run break-even point where the marginal cost curve crosses the firm's average total cost curve. Even though the firm earns an economic loss, it minimizes the amount of the loss by continuing to produce in the short run. In the long run, however, an economic loss is a signal that the firm is not engaged in the highest-value activity available to its owners, and continued economic losses in the long run will induce the firm to exit the industry. Conversely, persistent economic profits induce new firms to enter a perfectly competitive industry. In long-run equilibrium, the market price is equal to the minimum average total cost of production for the firms in the industry, because at this point firms earn zero economic profits.
6. **The Long-Run Industry Supply Curve and Constant-, Increasing-, and Decreasing-Cost Industries:** The long-run industry supply curve in a perfectly competitive industry shows the relationship between prices and quantities after firms have the opportunity to enter or leave the industry in response to economic profits or losses. In a constant-cost industry, total output can increase without a rise in long-run per-unit production costs, so the long-run industry supply curve is horizontal. In an increasing-cost industry, however, per-unit costs increase with a rise in industry output, so that the long-run industry supply curve slopes upward. By contrast, per-unit costs decline as industry output increases, and the long-run industry supply curve slopes downward.

Key Terms and Concepts

Constant-cost industry (577)
Decreasing-cost industry (578)
Increasing-cost industry (578)
Industry supply curve (573)
Lemons problem (580)
Long-run industry supply curve (577)
Marginal cost pricing (579)
Marginal revenue (566)
Market failure (580)
Perfect competition (561)
Perfectly competitive firm (561)
Price taker (562)
Profit-maximizing rate of production (566)
Short-run break-even price (570)
Short-run shutdown price (570)
Signals (576)
Total revenues (564)

Problems

Answers to the odd-numbered problems appear at the back of the book.

23-1. Explain why each of the following examples is not a competitive industry.

a. Even though one firm produces a large portion of the industry's total output, there are many firms in the industry, and their products are indistinguishable. Firms can easily exit and enter the industry.

b. There are many buyers and sellers in the industry. Consumers have equal information about the prices of firms' products, which differ slightly in quality from firm to firm.

c. There are many taxicabs that compete in a city. The city's government requires all taxicabs to provide identical service. Taxicabs are virtually identical, and all drivers must wear a designated uniform. The government also controls the number of taxicab companies that can operate within the city's boundaries.

23-2. Illustrate the following situation in the market for video rentals, which is perfectly competitive: The supply curve slopes upward, the demand curve slopes downward, and the equilibrium rental price equals $3.50. Next, illustrate the demand curve that a single independent video rental store faces. Finally, illustrate how an increase in the market demand for video rentals affects the market price and the demand curve faced by the individual rental store.

23-3. The campus barber faces stiff competition from the large number of shops that surround the campus area. For all practical purposes, therefore, this is a competitive market. He charges $6 for a haircut and cuts hair for 15 people a day. His shop is open five days a week. Calculate his weekly total revenue, average revenue, and marginal revenue.

23-4. The following table represents the hourly output and cost structure for a local pizza shop. The market is perfectly competitive, and the market price of a pizza in the area is $10. Total costs include all implicit opportunity costs.

Total Output and Sales of Pizzas	Total Cost ($)
0	5
1	9
2	11
3	12
4	14
5	18
6	24
7	32
8	42
9	54
10	68

a. Calculate the total revenue and total economic profit for this pizza shop at each rate of output.

b. Assuming that the pizza shop always produces and sells at least one pizza per hour, does this appear to be a situation of short-run or long-run equilibrium?

23-5. Using the information provided in Problem 23-4, calculate the pizza shop's marginal cost and marginal revenue at each rate of output. Based on marginal analysis, what is the profit-maximizing rate of output for the pizza shop?

23-6. Based on the information in Problems 23-4 and 23-5 and your answers to them, draw a diagram depicting the short-run marginal revenue and marginal cost curves for this pizza shop, and illustrate the determination of its profit-maximizing output rate.

23-7. Consider the information provided in Problem 23-4. Suppose the market price drops to only $5 per pizza. In the short run, should this pizza shop continue to make pizzas, or will it maximize its economic profits (that is, minimize its economic loss) by shutting down?

23-8. Suppose that a firm in a competitive industry finds that at its current output rate, marginal revenue exceeds the minimum average total cost of producing any feasible rate of output. Furthermore, the firm is producing an output rate for which marginal cost at that output rate is less than the average total cost of that rate of output. Is the firm maximizing its economic profits? Why or why not?

23-9. A perfectly competitive industry is initially in a short-run equilibrium in which all firms are earning zero economic profits but in which firms are operating below their minimum efficient scale. Explain the long-run adjustments that will take place for the industry to attain long-run equilibrium with firms operating at their minimum efficient scale.

23-10. A perfectly competitive industry is initially in a long-run equilibrium at which the market price of its output is $40 per unit and total industry output is 500,000 units. Then there is a decline in demand for the product that the industry produces. Some firms exit in response to declining profits, and eventually the industry reattains a long-run equilibrium at a market price of $35 per unit and total industry output of 450,000 units.

a. Draw the long-run supply curve for this industry.

b. Is this a decreasing-, constant-, or increasing-cost industry?

Economics on the Net

The Cost Structure of the Movie Theater Business A key idea in this chapter is that competition among firms in an industry can influence the long-run cost structure within the industry. Here you get a chance to apply this concept to a multinational company that owns movie theaters.

Title: AMC International

Navigation: Click here to visit American Multi-Cinema's homepage.

Application Answer the following questions.

1. Click on Investor Relations. What is the average number of screens in an AMC theater? How many theaters does it own and manage?
2. Click on AMC International and select Locations. Select the theater in Toyohashi City, Japan. This is the largest megaplex theater in Japan. How many screens does the megaplex have?
3. Based on the average number of screens at an AMC theater and the number of screens at the new Japanese facility, what can you conclude about the cost structure of this industry? Illustrate the long-run average cost curve for this industry.

For Group Discussion and Analysis Is the Japanese facility the largest multiplex? What do you think constrains the size of a multiplex in Japan? Given the location of AMC's headquarters, how does that affect the cost structure of the firm? Is it easier for AMC to have fewer facilities that are larger in size?

CHAPTER

24

MONOPOLY

An extremely high percentage of all jewelry-quality diamonds are marketed through the De Beers company's selling organization. Has this monopoly guaranteed De Beers perpetually high diamond prices?

"Diamonds are forever." For decades, the expression has applied not just to diamonds but also to South Africa's De Beers diamond cartel. In any given year, its marketing arm, the London-based Central Selling Organization (CSO), sells about 70 percent of the world's rough-cut diamonds. The CSO's annual revenues range from $3 billion to $5 billion, approximately 10 percent of which is typically profit. Each year, however, the company withholds from the marketplace a stockpile of $4 billion to $5 billion in uncut diamonds. Why would the CSO choose to forgo additional revenues that it could earn if it were to sell these additional diamonds? To understand the CSO's motivation, you need to know about the theory of monopoly.

LEARNING OBJECTIVES

After reading this chapter, you should be able to:

1. **Identify situations that can give rise to monopoly**
2. **Describe the demand and marginal revenue conditions a monopolist faces**
3. **Discuss how a monopolist determines how much output to produce and what price to charge**
4. **Evaluate the profits earned by a monopolist**
5. **Understand price discrimination**
6. **Explain the social cost of monopolies**

Did You Know That... from the Great Depression of the 1930s until 1996, New York City kept the number of taxicab licenses (called "medallions") fixed at 11,787? The owner of a medallion can use or lease the medallion by the day or the week, and the owner can require a taxi driver to supply a car and provide insurance. In 1996, bidders for 53 new medallions paid an average of $177,000 for the right to sell taxi services. Today, the medallions are valued at more than $300,000. Why has there been such a big price increase? The reason is that there are so few taxis relative to the population in New York City. The absolute limit on the number of sellers of taxi services permits those sellers to extract the maximum amount of profit possible.

In some instances, there is only one seller of a good or service. Single sellers of goods and services exist all around you. The company that sells food in your school cafeteria has most probably been granted the exclusive right to do so by your college or university. The ski resort that offers you food at the top of the mountain does not allow anyone else to open a restaurant next to it. When you run a business that is the only one of its type in a particular location, you can usually charge a higher price per constant-quality unit than when there is intense competition. In this chapter, you will read more about situations in which competition is restricted. We call these situations *monopoly.*

Chapter Outline 

DEFINITION OF A MONOPOLIST

The word *monopoly* probably brings to mind notions of a business that gouges the consumer, sells faulty products, and gets unconscionably rich in the process. But if we are to succeed in analyzing and predicting the behavior of noncompetitive firms, we will have to be more objective in our definition. Although most monopolies in the United States are relatively large, our definition will be equally applicable to small businesses: A **monopolist** is the *single supplier* of a good or service for which there is no close substitute.

Monopolist 
A single supplier that comprises its entire industry for a good or service for which there is no close substitute.

In a monopoly market structure, the firm (the monopolist) and the industry are one and the same. Occasionally there may be a problem in identifying an industry and therefore determining if a monopoly exists. For example, should we think of aluminum and steel as separate industries, or should we define the industry in terms of basic metals? Our answer depends on the extent to which aluminum and steel can be substituted in the production of a wide range of products.

As we shall see in this chapter, a seller prefers to have a monopoly than to face competitors. In general, we think of monopoly prices as being higher than prices under perfect competition and of monopoly profits as being higher than profits under perfect competition (which are, in the long run, merely equivalent to a normal rate of return). How does a firm obtain a monopoly in an industry? Basically, there must be *barriers to entry* that enable firms to receive monopoly profits in the long run. Barriers to entry are restrictions on who can start a business or who can stay in a business.

BARRIERS TO ENTRY 

For any amount of monopoly power to continue to exist in the long run, the market must be closed to entry in some way. Either legal means or certain aspects of the industry's technical or cost structure may prevent entry. We will discuss several of the barriers to entry that have allowed firms to reap monopoly profits in the long run (even if they are not pure monopolists in the technical sense).

Ownership of Resources Without Close Substitutes

Preventing a newcomer from entering an industry is often difficult. Indeed, some economists contend that no monopoly acting without government support has been able to prevent entry into the industry unless that monopoly has had the control of some essential natural resource. Consider the possibility of one firm's owning the entire supply of a raw material input that is essential to the production of a particular commodity. The exclusive ownership of such a vital resource serves as a barrier to entry until an alternative source of the raw material input is found or an alternative technology not requiring the raw material in question is developed. A good example of control over a vital input is the Aluminum Company of America (Alcoa), a firm that prior to World War II controlled the world's bauxite, the essential raw material in the production of aluminum. Such a situation is rare, though, and is ordinarily temporary.

Problems in Raising Adequate Capital

Certain industries require a large initial capital investment. The firms already in the industry can, according to some economists, obtain monopoly profits in the long run because no competitors can raise the large amount of capital needed to enter the industry. This is called the "imperfect" capital market argument employed to explain long-run, relatively high rates of return in certain industries. These industries are generally ones in which large fixed costs must be incurred merely to start production. Their fixed costs are generally for expensive machines necessary to the production process.

EXAMPLE

"Intel Inside"

Many observers of today's high-stakes high-technology world argue that the world's largest manufacturer of microprocessors, Intel, is a monopoly. They point out that to compete effectively with Intel, a potential adversary would have to invest billions of dollars. Intel provides the critical microprocessor chip that goes into the majority of the world's personal computers. Each new generation of microprocessor quickly becomes the industry standard for all IBM-compatible personal computers. Apple computers for years used a Motorola-made chip. In an attempt to fight back against Intel, Apple, Motorola, and IBM formed an alliance that did develop the Power PC microprocessor. So far, though, it has not made serious inroads into Intel's market. A few companies have attempted to clone Intel's chips, but they have not been very successful for both legal and technical reasons.

For Critical Analysis

Intel spends billions of dollars developing each new generation of microprocessor. Would it spend more or less if it had a smaller share of the microprocessor market?

Economies of Scale

Sometimes it is not profitable for more than one firm to exist in an industry. This is so if one firm would have to produce such a large quantity in order to realize lower unit costs that there would not be sufficient demand to warrant a second producer of the same product. Such a situation may arise because of a phenomenon we discussed in Chapter 22, economies of scale. When economies of scale exist, total costs increase less than proportionately to the increase in output. That is, proportional increases in output yield proportionately smaller increases in total costs, and per-unit costs drop. The advantage in

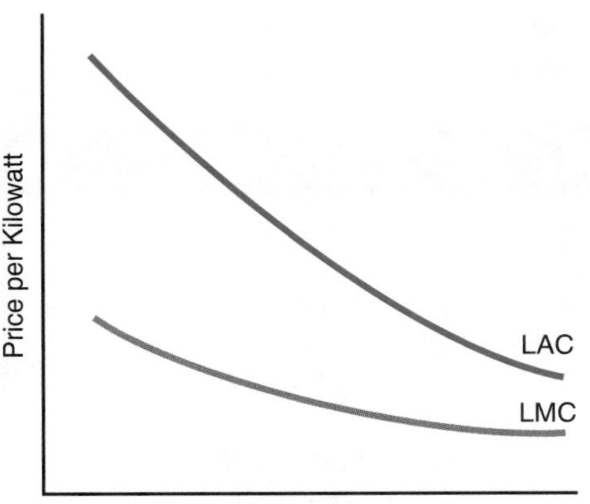

FIGURE 24-1
The Cost Curves That Might Lead to a Natural Monopoly: The Case of Electricity
Whenever long-run average costs are falling, so, too, will be long-run marginal costs. Also, long-run marginal costs (LMC) will always be below long-run average costs (LAC). A natural monopoly might arise in such a situation. The first firm to establish the low-unit-cost capacity would be able to take advantage of the lower average total cost curve. This firm would drive out all rivals by charging a lower price than the others could sustain at their higher average costs.

economies of scale lies in the fact that larger firms (with larger output) have lower costs that enable them to charge lower prices, and that drives smaller firms out of business.

When economies of scale occur over a wide range of outputs, a **natural monopoly** may develop. The natural monopoly is the firm that first takes advantage of persistent declining long-run average costs as scale increases. The natural monopolist is able to underprice its competitors and eventually force all of them out of the market.

Natural monopoly 
A monopoly that arises from the peculiar production characteristics in an industry. It usually arises when there are large economies of scale relative to the industry's demand such that one firm can produce at a lower average cost than can be achieved by multiple firms.

In Figure 24-1, we have drawn a downward-sloping long-run average cost curve (LAC). Recall that when average costs are falling, marginal costs are less than average costs. We can apply the same analysis in the long run. When the long-run average cost curve (LAC) is falling, the long-run marginal cost curve (LMC) will be below the LAC.

In our example, long-run average costs are falling over such a large range of production rates that we would expect only one firm to survive in such an industry. That firm would be the natural monopolist. It would be the first one to take advantage of the decreasing average costs; that is, it would construct the large-scale facilities first. As its average costs fell, it would lower prices and get an increasingly larger share of the market. Once that firm had driven all other firms out of the industry, it would set its price to maximize profits.

Legal or Governmental Restrictions

Governments and legislatures can also erect barriers to entry. These include licenses, franchises, patents, tariffs, and specific regulations that tend to limit entry.

Licenses, Franchises, and Certificates of Convenience. In many industries, it is illegal to enter without a government license, or a "certificate of convenience and public necessity." For example, in some states you still cannot form an electrical utility to compete with the electrical utility already operating in your area. You would first have to obtain a certificate of convenience and public necessity from the appropriate authority, which is usually the state's public utility commission. Yet public utility commissions in these states rarely, if ever, issue a certificate to a group of investors who want to compete directly in the same geographic area with an existing electrical utility; hence entry into the industry in a particular geographic area is prohibited, and long-run monopoly profits could conceivably be earned by the electrical utility already serving the area.

To enter interstate (and also many intrastate) markets for pipelines, television and radio broadcasting, and transmission of natural gas, to cite a few such industries, it is often necessary to obtain similar permits. Because these franchises or licenses are restricted, long-run monopoly profits might be earned by the firms already in the industry.

INTERNATIONAL EXAMPLE

Will Mexico Ever Hang Up on Its Telephone Monopoly?

Suppose that two businesspeople are competing to close a deal with a firm based in London. One is from the United States, and the other is from Mexico. Each person makes five four-minute calls. The American will typically pay $5 or $6 for the calls. The Mexican will pay $25 to $30. The reason for this big price disparity is simple: There are numerous competing long-distance providers in the United States, but there is one national phone company in Mexico.

Under the terms of a 1995 Mexican telecommunications law, this company, Telmex, is a regulated monopoly. A government agency is charged with regulating the company's rate of return. Telmex is the second-largest corporation in Mexico, and it is the largest company listed on the Mexican Stock Exchange. In recent years, the Mexican government has aimed for high and stable Mexican stock prices. Instead of taking the interests of consumers into account, the Mexican government has encouraged Telmex to maximize its profits to keep the prices of its shares high in the stock market.

As the monopoly model suggests, the result has been hefty telephone rates for consumers. In one year alone, Telmex raised the prices of local phone services throughout Mexico by 67 percent. Many Mexican residents have responded by forgoing phone service altogether. On average, there are only 10 telephones per 100 residents in Mexico.

For Critical Analysis

How would telephone rates and usage change if the Mexican government allowed other firms to compete with Telemex?

Click here to learn more about patents and trademarks; Click here to learn all about copyrights.

Patents. A patent is issued to an inventor to provide protection from having the invention copied or stolen for a period of 20 years. Suppose that engineers working for Ford Motor Company discover a way to build an engine that requires half the parts of a regular engine and weighs only half as much. If Ford is successful in obtaining a patent on this discovery, it can (in principle) prevent others from copying it. The patent holder has a monopoly. It is the patent holder's responsibility to defend the patent, however. That means that Ford—like other patent owners—must expend resources to prevent others from imitating its invention. If in fact the costs of enforcing a particular patent are greater than the benefits, the patent may not bestow any monopoly profits on its owner. The policing costs would be just too high.

EXAMPLE

Patents as Intellectual Property

A patent may bestow on its owner a monopoly for a given time period. So, too, may copyrights. Trademarks don't actually bestow monopoly power, but they do in certain cases have extreme value. Coca-Cola can exploit its trademark by licensing it for clothes and paraphernalia. So, too, can Harley-Davidson. Both of those companies have done so. Copyrights, trademarks, patents, and the like are all part of what is known as intellectual property. Songs, music, computer programs, and designs are all intellectual property. Indeed, some economists believe that the world value of intellectual property now exceeds the value of physical property, such as real estate, buildings, and equipment. Not surprisingly, in the corporate world, when a business buys another business, the acquiring company's lawyers have to worry a great deal about the acquired company's intellectual property portfolio. What intellectual property rights in terms of patents, trademarks, and copyrights does the soon-to-be-acquired company actually own?

For Critical Analysis

Why doesn't the ownership of a well-known trademark bestow true monopoly power on its owner?

Tariffs. **Tariffs** are special taxes that are imposed on certain imported goods. Tariffs have the effect of making imports relatively more expensive than their domestic counterparts, so that consumers switch to the relatively cheaper domestically made products. If the tariffs are high enough, domestic producers gain monopoly advantage as the sole suppliers. Many countries have tried this protectionist strategy by using high tariffs to shut out foreign competitors.

Tariffs 
Taxes on imported goods.

Regulations. During much of the twentieth century, government regulation of the American economy has increased, especially along the dimensions of safety and quality. For example, pharmaceutical quality-control regulations enforced by the Food and Drug Administration may require that each pharmaceutical company install a $2 million computerized testing machine that requires elaborate monitoring and maintenance. Presumably, this large fixed cost can be spread over a larger number of units of output by larger firms than by smaller firms, thereby putting the smaller firms at a competitive disadvantage. It will also deter entry to the extent that the scale of operation of a potential entrant must be sufficiently large to cover the average fixed costs of the required equipment. We examine regulation in more detail in Chapter 26.

Cartels

"Being the only game in town" is preferable because such a monopoly position normally allows the monopolist to charge higher prices and make greater profits. Not surprisingly, manufacturers and sellers have often attempted to form an organization (which often is international) that acts as one. This is called a **cartel.** Cartels are an attempt by their members to earn higher than competitive profits. They set common prices and output quotas for their members. The key to the success of a cartel is keeping one member from competing against other members by expanding production and thereby lowering price. Apparently, one of the most successful international cartels ever was the Organization of Petroleum Exporting Countries (OPEC), an association of the world's largest oil-producing countries, including Saudi Arabia, which at times has accounted for a significant percentage of the world's crude oil output. OPEC effectively organized a significant cutback on the production of crude oil in the wake of the so-called Yom Kippur War in the Middle East in 1973. Within one year, the spot price of crude oil jumped from $2.12 to $7.61 per barrel on the world market. By the early 1980s, the price had risen to over $30.

Cartel 
An association of producers in an industry that agree to set common prices and output quotas to prevent competition.

Most cartels have not had as much success.

INTERNATIONAL EXAMPLE

"We're Just Trying to Keep the Market Stable"

The stated goal of most international cartels is keeping markets "stable." In reality, cartel members are seeking higher prices (and profits) for their product. But to achieve their aims, the producing countries have to be willing to withhold some of their production from the world market.

Nowhere are international cartels as prevalent as in the market for commodities. The International Coffee Organization lasted 30 years until the United States pulled out; it was succeeded by the Association of Coffee Producing Countries. Cocoa has the International Cocoa Organization. There is even an ostrich cartel called the Little Karoo Agricultural Cooperative.

The U.S. government has at times sanctioned the equivalent of a cartel. A meeting in Washington, D.C., involving executives from a dozen global aluminum producers and government officials representing the United States, the European Union, and four other nations ultimately resulted in an agreement by all those attending to reduce aluminum production. All such reductions were voluntary except by Russia. In exchange for cutting primary aluminum production by 500,000 tons over a two-year period, Russia received the promise of $250 million of U.S. taxpayers' money for equity investments. U.S. government officials claim that "the markets are still open" nonetheless.

For Critical Analysis

The price of gasoline today (corrected for inflation) is less than what it was in 1984. What does that tell you about the long-run effectiveness of global cartels?

CONCEPTS IN BRIEF

- A monopolist is defined as a single seller of a product or a good for which there is no good close substitute.
- To maintain a monopoly, there must be barriers to entry. Barriers to entry include ownership of resources without close substitutes; large capital requirements in order to enter the industry; economies of scale; legally required licenses, franchises, and certificates of convenience; patents; tariffs; and safety and quality regulations.

THE DEMAND CURVE A MONOPOLIST FACES

A *pure monopolist* is the sole supplier of *one* product, good, or service. A pure monopolist faces a demand curve that is the demand curve for the entire market for that good.

The monopolist faces the industry demand curve because the monopolist is the entire industry.

Because the monopolist faces the industry demand curve, which is by definition downward-sloping, its decision-making process with respect to how much to produce is not the same as for a perfect competitor. When a monopolist changes output, it does not automatically receive the same price per unit that it did before the change.

Profits to Be Made from Increasing Production

How do firms benefit from changing production rates? What happens to price in each case? Let's first review the situation among perfect competitors.

Marginal Revenue for the Perfect Competitor. Recall that a competitive firm has a perfectly elastic demand curve. That is because the competitive firm is such a small part of the market that it cannot influence the price of its product. It is a *price taker.* If the forces of supply and demand establish that the price per constant-quality pair of shoes is $50, the individual firm can sell all the pairs of shoes it wants to produce at $50 per pair. The average revenue is $50, the price is $50, and the marginal revenue is also $50.

Let us again define marginal revenue:

Marginal revenue equals the change in total revenue due to a one-unit change in the quantity produced and sold.

In the case of a competitive industry, each time a single firm changes production by one unit, total revenue changes by the going price, and price is always the same. Marginal revenue never changes; it always equals price, or average revenue. Average revenue was defined as total revenue divided by quantity demanded, or

$$\text{Average revenue} = \frac{\text{TR}}{Q} = \frac{PQ}{Q} = P$$

Hence marginal revenue, average revenue, and price are all the same for the price-taking firm.

Marginal Revenue for the Monopolist. What about a monopoly firm? Because a monopoly is the entire industry, the monopoly firm's demand curve is the market demand curve. The market demand curve slopes downward, just like the other demand curves that we have seen. Therefore, to sell more of a particular product, given the industry demand curve, the monopoly firm must lower the price. Thus the monopoly firm moves *down* the demand curve. If all buyers are to be charged the same price, the monopoly must lower the price on all units sold in order to sell more. It cannot just lower the price on the *last* unit sold in any given time period in order to sell a larger quantity.

Put yourself in the shoes of a monopoly ferryboat owner. You have a government-bestowed franchise, and no one can compete with you. Your ferryboat goes between two islands. If you are charging $1 per crossing, a certain quantity of your services will be demanded. Let's say that you are ferrying 100 people a day each way at that price. If you decide that you would like to ferry more individuals, you must lower your price to all individuals—you must move *down* the existing demand curve for ferrying services. To calculate the marginal revenue of your change in price, you must first calculate the total revenues you received at $1 per passenger per crossing and then calculate the total revenues you would receive at, say, 90 cents per passenger per crossing.

It is sometimes useful to compare monopoly markets with perfectly competitive markets. The only way the monopolist can increase its total revenues is by getting consumers to spend more of their incomes on the monopolist's product and less on all other products combined. Thus the monopolist is constrained by the entire market demand curve for its product. We see this in Figure 24-2, which compares the demand curves of the perfect competitor and the monopolist.

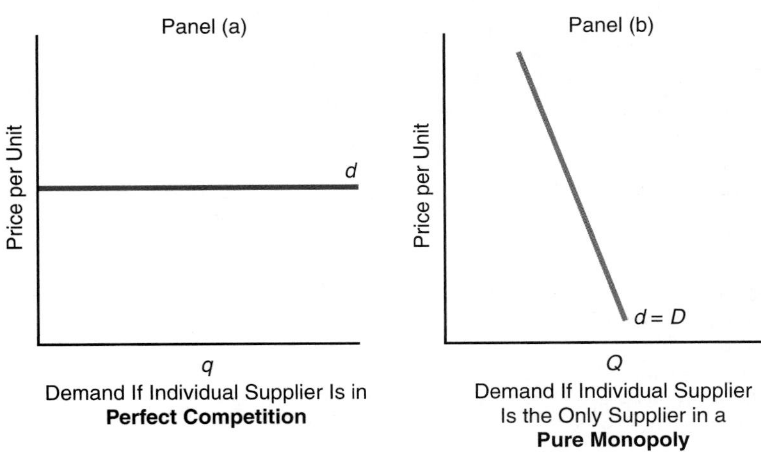

FIGURE 24-2

Demand Curves for the Perfect Competitor and the Monopolist

The perfect competitor in panel (a) faces a perfectly elastic demand curve, *d*. The monopolist in panel (b) faces the entire industry demand curve, which slopes downward.

Here we see the fundamental difference between the monopolist and the competitor. The competitor doesn't have to worry about lowering price to sell more. In a purely competitive situation, the competitive firm accounts for such a small part of the market that it can sell its entire output, whatever that may be, at the same price. The monopolist cannot. The more the monopolist wants to sell, the lower the price it has to charge on the last unit (and on *all* units put on the market for sale). Obviously, the extra revenues the monopolist receives from selling one more unit are going to be smaller than the extra revenues received from selling the next-to-last unit. The monopolist has to lower the price on the last unit to sell it because it is facing a downward-sloping demand curve and the only way to move down the demand curve is to lower the price on all units.

The Monopolist's Marginal Revenue: Less than Price

An essential point is that for the monopolist, marginal revenue is always less than price. To understand why, look at Figure 24-3, which shows a unit increase in output sold due to a reduction in the price of a commodity from P_1 to P_2. After all, the only way that the firm can sell more output, given a downward-sloping demand curve, is for the price to fall. Price P_2 is the price received for the last unit. Thus price P_2 times the last unit sold represents revenues received from the last unit sold. That is equal to the vertical column (area A). Area A is one unit wide by P_2 high.

But price times the last unit sold is *not* the addition to *total* revenues received from selling that last unit. Why? Because price had to be reduced on all previous units sold (Q) in order to sell the larger quantity $Q + 1$. The reduction in price is represented by the vertical distance from P_1 to P_2 on the vertical axis. We must therefore subtract area B from area A to come up with the *change* in total revenues due to a one-unit increase in sales. Clearly, the change in total revenues—that is, marginal revenue—must be less than price because marginal revenue is always the difference between areas A and B in Figure 24-3. For example, if the initial price is \$8 and quantity demanded is 3, to increase quantity to 4 units, it is necessary to decrease price to \$7, not just for the fourth unit, but on all three previous units as well. Thus at a price of \$7, marginal revenue is \$7 − \$3 = \$4 because there is a \$1 per unit price reduction on three previous units. Hence marginal revenue, \$4, is less than price, \$7.

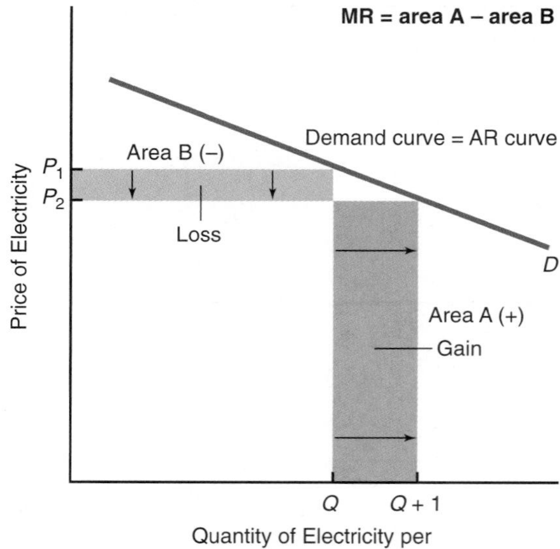

FIGURE 24-3

Marginal Revenue: Always Less than Price

The price received for the last unit sold is equal to P_2. The revenues received from selling this last unit are equal to P_2 times one unit, or the area of the vertical column. However, if a single price is being charged for all units, total revenues do not go up by the amount of the area represented by that column. The price had to be reduced on all the previous Q units that were being sold at price P_1. Thus we must subtract area B—the rectangle between P_1 and P_2 from the origin to Q—from area A in order to derive marginal revenue. Marginal revenue is therefore always less than price.

ELASTICITY AND MONOPOLY 

The monopolist faces a downward-sloping demand curve (its average revenue curve). That means that it cannot charge just *any* price with no changes in quantity (a common misconception) because, depending on the price charged, a different quantity will be demanded.

Earlier we defined a monopolist as the single seller of a well-defined good or service with no *close* substitute. This does not mean, however, that the demand curve for a monopoly is vertical or exhibits zero price elasticity of demand. (Indeed, as we shall see, the profit-maximizing monopolist will never operate in a price range in which demand is inelastic.) After all, consumers have limited incomes and alternative wants. The downward slope of a monopolist's demand curve occurs because individuals compare the marginal satisfaction they will receive to the cost of the commodity to be purchased. Take the example of telephone service. Even if miraculously there were absolutely no substitute whatsoever for telephone service, the market demand curve would still slope downward. At lower prices, people will add more phones and separate lines for different family members.

Furthermore, the demand curve for telephone service slopes downward because there are at least several *imperfect* substitutes, such as letters, e-mails, in-person conversations, and Internet telephony. Thus even though we defined a monopolist as a single seller of a commodity with no *close* substitute, we can talk about the range of *imperfect* substitutes. The more such imperfect substitutes there are, and the better these substitutes are, the more elastic will be the monopolist's demand curve, all other things held constant.

CONCEPTS IN BRIEF

- The monopolist estimates its marginal revenue curve, where marginal revenue is defined as the change in total revenues due to a one-unit change in quantity sold.
- For the perfect competitor, price equals marginal revenue equals average revenue. For the monopolist, price is always greater than marginal revenue. For the monopolist, marginal revenue is always less than price because price must be reduced on all units to sell more.
- The price elasticity of demand for the monopolist depends on the number and similarity of substitutes. The more numerous and more similar the substitutes, the greater the price elasticity of demand of the monopolist's demand curve.

COSTS AND MONOPOLY PROFIT MAXIMIZATION

To find out the rate of output at which the perfect competitor would maximize profits, we had to add cost data. We will do the same thing now for the monopolist. We assume that profit maximization is the goal of the pure monopolist, just as for the perfect competitor. The perfect competitor, however, has only to decide on the profit-maximizing rate of output because price is given. The competitor is a price taker. For the pure monopolist, we must seek a profit-maximizing *price-output combination* because the monopolist is a **price searcher.** We can determine this profit-maximizing price-output combination with either of two equivalent approaches—by looking at total revenues and total costs or by looking at marginal revenues and marginal costs. We shall examine both approaches.

Price searcher 
A firm that must determine the price-output combination that maximizes profit because it faces a downward-sloping demand curve.

The Total Revenues–Total Costs Approach

We show hypothetical demand (rate of output and price per unit), revenues, costs, and other data in panel (a) of Figure 24-4. In column 3, we see total revenues for our hypothetical monopolist, and in column 4, we see total costs. We can transfer these two columns to

FIGURE 24-4

Monopoly Costs, Revenues, and Profits

In panel (a), we give hypothetical demand (rate of output and price per unit), revenues, costs, and other relevant data. As shown in panel (b), the monopolist maximizes profits where the positive difference between TR and TC is greatest. This is at an output rate of between 9 and 10. Put another way, profit maximization occurs where marginal revenue equals marginal cost, as shown in panel (c). This is at the same output rate of between 9 and 10. (The MC curve must cut the MR curve from below.)

Panel (a)

(1) Output (units)	(2) Price per Unit	(3) Total Revenues (TR) (3) = (2) x (1)	(4) Total Costs (TC)	(5) Total Profit (5) = (3) – (4)	(6) Marginal Cost (MC)	(7) Marginal Revenue (MR)
0	$8.00	$ .00	$10.00	–$10.00		
					$4.00	$7.80
1	7.80	7.80	14.00	– 6.20		
					3.50	7.40
2	7.60	15.20	17.50	– 2.30		
					3.25	7.00
3	7.40	22.20	20.75	1.45		
					3.05	6.60
4	7.20	28.80	23.80	5.00		
					2.90	6.20
5	7.00	35.00	26.70	8.30		
					2.80	5.80
6	6.80	40.80	29.50	11.30		
					2.75	5.40
7	6.60	46.20	32.25	13.95		
					2.85	5.00
8	6.40	51.20	35.10	16.10		
					3.20	4.60
9	6.20	55.80	38.30	17.50		
					4.00	4.20
10	6.00	60.00	42.30	17.70		
					6.00	3.80
11	5.80	63.80	48.30	15.50		
					9.00	3.40
12	5.60	67.20	57.30	9.90		

Panel (b)

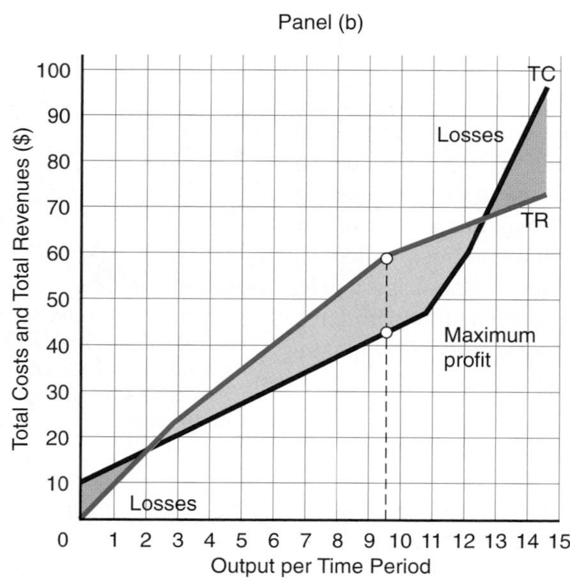

Panel (c)

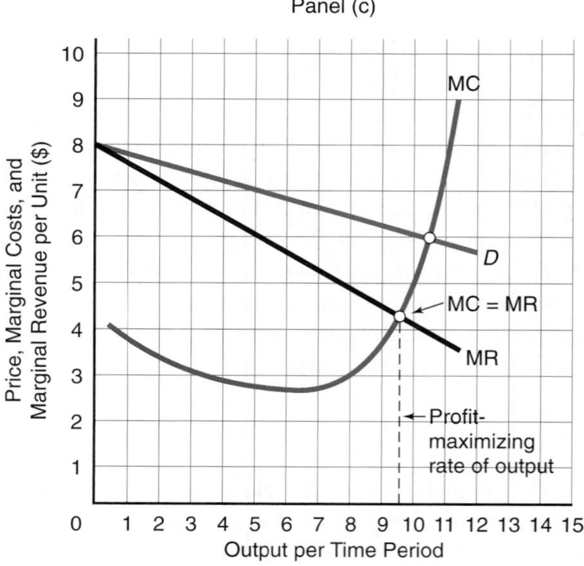

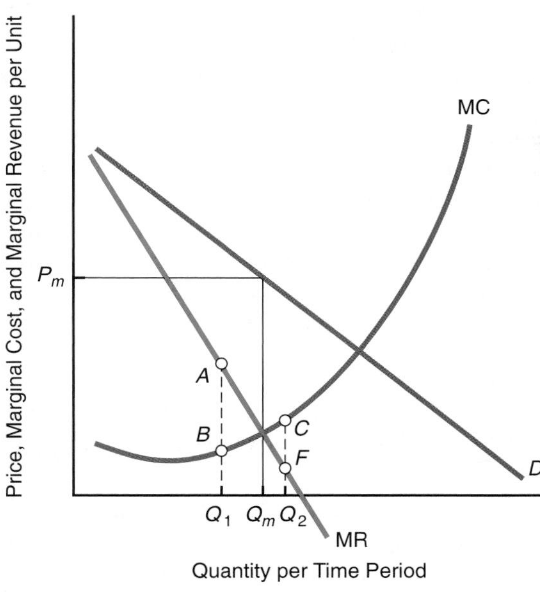

FIGURE 24-5
Maximizing Profits
The profit-maximizing production rate is Q_m, and the profit-maximizing price is P_m. The monopolist would be unwise to produce at the rate Q_1 because here marginal revenue would be Q_1A and marginal costs would be Q_1B. Marginal revenue exceeds marginal cost. The firm will keep producing until the point Q_m, where marginal revenue just equals marginal cost. It would be foolish to produce at the rate Q_2, for here marginal cost exceeds marginal revenue. It behooves the monopolist to cut production back to Q_m.

panel (b). The only difference between the total revenue and total cost diagram in panel (b) and the one we showed for a perfect competitor in Chapter 23 is that the total revenue line is no longer straight. Rather, it curves. For any given demand curve, in order to sell more, the monopolist must lower the price. Thus, the basic difference between a monopolist and a perfect competitor has to do with the demand curve for the two types of firms. Monopoly market power is derived from facing a downward-sloping demand curve.

Click here to see how effective OPEC has been in trying to act as an oil market monopolist.

Profit maximization involves maximizing the positive difference between total revenues and total costs. This occurs at an output rate of between 9 and 10 units.

The Marginal Revenue–Marginal Cost Approach

Profit maximization will also occur where marginal revenue equals marginal cost. This is as true for a monopolist as it is for a perfect competitor (but the monopolist will charge a higher price). When we transfer marginal cost and marginal revenue information from columns 6 and 7 in panel (a) of Figure 24-4 to panel (c), we see that marginal revenue equals marginal cost at an output rate of between 9 and 10 units. Profit maximization occurs at the same output as in panel (b).

Is the Organization of Petroleum Exporting Countries (OPEC) an effective oil monopoly?

Not any more. In the 1970s, OPEC succeeded in restraining world oil production and driving up prices for several years. Today, however, there are so many oil producers that it is hard to induce them all to withhold oil from the market. For instance, in the summer of 1998, OPEC's biggest producers, Saudi Arabia, Mexico, and Venezuela, agreed to cut back on output in an effort to stem a big decline in oil prices. This simply opened up sales opportunities for smaller producers, however. Within four months, Venezuelan companies had broken the terms of the OPEC agreement.

Why Produce Where Marginal Revenue Equals Marginal Cost? If the monopolist goes past the point where marginal revenue equals marginal cost, marginal cost will exceed marginal revenue. That is, the incremental cost of producing any more units will exceed the incremental revenue. It just would not be worthwhile, as was true also in perfect competition. But if the monopolist produces less than that, it is also not making maximum profits. Look at output rate Q_1 in Figure 24-5. Here the monopolist's marginal revenue is at A, but marginal cost is at B. Marginal revenue exceeds marginal cost on the last unit sold; the profit for that *particular* unit, Q_1, is equal to the vertical difference between A and B, or the difference between marginal revenue and marginal cost. The monopolist would be foolish to stop at output rate Q_1 because if output is expanded, marginal revenue will still exceed marginal cost, and therefore total profits will rise. In fact, the profit-maximizing monopolist will continue to expand output and sales until marginal revenue equals marginal cost, which is at output rate Q_m. The monopolist won't produce at rate Q_2 because here, as we see, marginal costs are C and marginal revenues are F. The difference between C and F represents the *reduction* in total profits from producing that additional unit. Total profits will rise as the monopolist reduces its rate of output back toward Q_m.

Monopoly Output and Price Determination
Gain further understanding of how a monopolist sets its output rate and product price.

POLICY EXAMPLE

Limiting Limos in Las Vegas

Las Vegas, Nevada, is one of the leading convention centers on the planet. It welcomes 25 million visitors per year. When they reach the city's airport, these visitors typically hire taxicabs and limousines. The city has not allowed a single new taxi in over 25 years, so enterprising limo operators began to offer their services.

In 1997, however, the Nevada legislature passed a law creating the state Transportation Services Authority. Its main source of funds is money it raises from application fees and fines it assesses on violators of limitations on limousine services. The law requires an applicant for a limo license to prove that a new limo in the market will "not unreasonably and adversely affect other carriers." A recent applicant submitted more than 1,000 pages of documentation and incurred \$15,000 in application fees and expenses. His application was rejected. So was an application by a quadriplegic who wanted to provide specialized limo services to wheelchair-bound people. The rationale for both rejections was that additional limos would cut into the profits currently earned by existing operators. Keeping those profits up requires restricting the quantity of limo services available for use by visitors.

For Critical Analysis

Some cities, such as Denver and Indianapolis, have opened their markets for taxi and limo services to increased competition. How do you predict that the quantity and prices of these transportation services changed in these cities?

What Price to Charge for Output?

How does the monopolist set prices? We know the quantity is set at the point at which marginal revenue equals marginal cost. The monopolist then finds out how much can be charged—how much the market will bear—for that particular quantity, Q_m, in Figure 24-5. We know that the demand curve is defined as showing the *maximum* price for which a given quantity can be sold. That means that our monopolist knows that to sell Q_m, it can charge only P_m because that is the price at which that specific quantity, Q_m, is demanded. This price is found by drawing a vertical line from the quantity, Q_m, to the market demand curve. Where that line hits the market demand curve, the price is determined. We find that price by drawing a horizontal line from the demand curve over to the price axis; that gives us the profit-maximizing price, P_m.

In our detailed numerical example, at a profit-maximizing rate of output of a little less than 10 in Figure 24-4, the firm can charge a maximum price of about \$6 and still sell all the goods produced, all at the same price.

The basic procedure for finding the profit-maximizing short-run price-quantity combination for the monopolist is first to determine the profit-maximizing rate of output, by either the total revenue-total cost method or the marginal revenue-marginal cost method, and then to determine by use of the demand curve, *D*, the maximum price that can be charged to sell that output.

Don't get the impression that just because we are able to draw an exact demand curve in Figure 24-4 and Figure 24-5, real-world monopolists have such perfect information. The process of price searching by a less than perfect competitor is just that—a process. A monopolist can only estimate the actual demand curve and therefore can only make an educated guess when it sets its profit-maximizing price. This is not a problem for the perfect competitor because price is given already by the intersection of market demand and market supply. The monopolist, in contrast, reaches the profit-maximizing output-price combination by trial and error.

CALCULATING MONOPOLY PROFIT

We have talked about the monopolist's profit, but we have yet to indicate how much profit the monopolist makes. We have actually shown total profits in column 5 of panel (a) in Figure 24-4. We can also find total profits by adding an average total cost curve to panel (c) of that figure. We do that in Figure 24-6. When we add the average total cost curve, we find that the profit that a monopolist makes is equal to the shaded area [or total revenues minus total costs (ATC × *Q*)]. Given the demand curve and a uniform pricing system (i.e., all units sold at the same price), there is no way for a monopolist to make greater profits than those shown by the shaded area. The monopolist is maximizing profits where marginal cost equals marginal revenue. If the monopolist produces less than that, it will be forfeiting some profits. If the monopolist produces more than that, it will be forfeiting some profits.

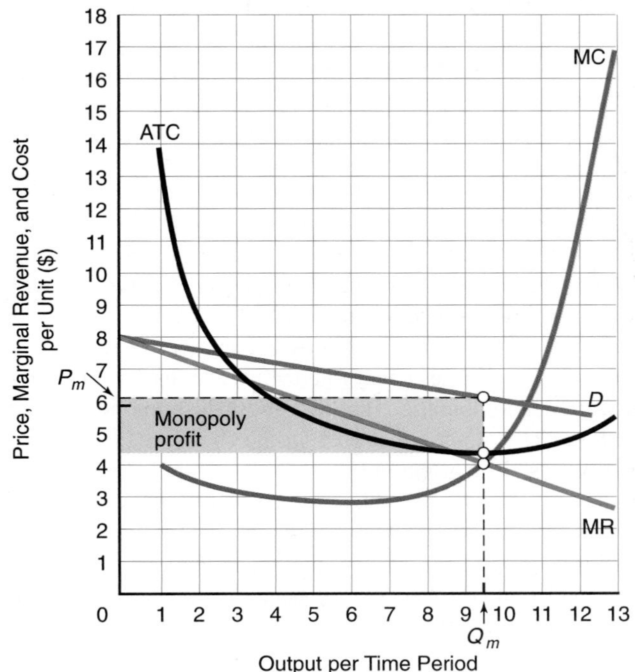

FIGURE 24-6
Monopoly Profit
We find monopoly profit by subtracting total costs from total revenues at an output rate of almost 10, labeled Q_m, which is the profit-maximizing rate of output for the monopolist. The profit-maximizing price is therefore about $6 and is labeled P_m. Monopoly profit is given by the shaded area, which is equal to total revenues (P × Q) minus total costs (ATC × Q). This diagram is similar to panel (c) of Figure 24-4, with the short-run average total cost curve (ATC) added.

FIGURE 24-7

Monopolies: Not Always Profitable

Some monopolists face the situation shown here. The average total cost curve, ATC, is everywhere above the average revenue, or demand, curve, D. In the short run, the monopolist will produce where MC = MR at point E. Output Q_m will be sold at price P_m, but average total cost per unit is C_1. Losses are the shaded rectangle. Eventually, the monopolist will go out of business.

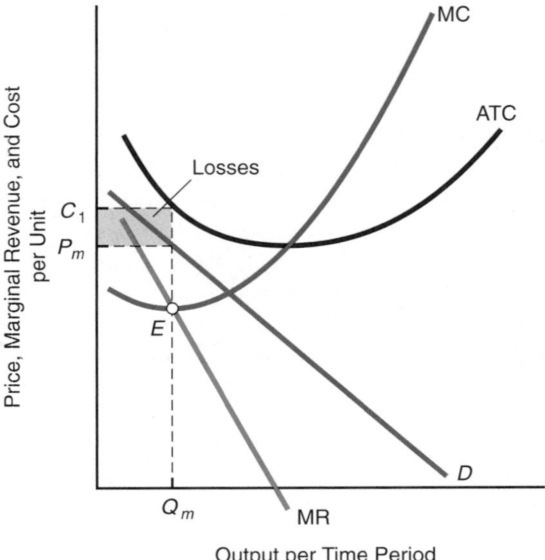

The same is true of a perfect competitor. The competitor produces where marginal revenues equal marginal costs because it produces at the point where the marginal cost curve intersects the perfectly elastic firm demand curve. The perfectly elastic firm demand curve represents the marginal revenue curve for the pure competitor, for the same average revenues are obtained on all the units sold. Perfect competitors maximize profits at MR = MC, as do pure monopolists. But the perfect competitor makes no true economic profits in the long run; rather, all it makes is a normal, competitive rate of return.

In Chapter 23, we talked about companies experiencing short-run economic profits because they had, for example, invented something new. Competition, though, gradually eroded those higher than normal profits. The fact that a firm experiences higher than normal profits today does not mean that it has a monopoly forever. Try as companies may, keeping competitors away is never easy.

No Guarantee of Profits

The term *monopoly* conjures up the notion of a greedy firm ripping off the public and making exorbitant profits. However, the mere existence of a monopoly does not guarantee high profits. Numerous monopolies have gone bankrupt. Figure 24-7 shows the monopolist's demand curve as D and the resultant marginal revenue curve as MR. It does not matter at what rate of output this particular monopolist operates; total costs cannot be covered. Look at the position of the average total cost curve. It lies everywhere above D (the average revenue curve). Thus there is no price-output combination that will allow the monopolist even to cover costs, much less earn profits. This monopolist will, in the short run, suffer economic losses as shown by the shaded area. The graph in Figure 24-7 depicts a situation for millions of typical monopolies that exist; they are called inventions. The owner of a patented invention or discovery has a pure legal monopoly, but the demand and cost curves may be such that production is not profitable. Every year at inventors' conventions, one can see many inventions that have never been put into production because they were deemed "uneconomic" by potential producers and users.

CONCEPTS IN BRIEF

- The basic difference between a monopolist and a perfect competitor is that a monopolist faces a downward-sloping demand curve, and therefore marginal revenue is less than price.
- The monopolist must choose the profit-maximizing price-output combination—the output at which marginal revenue equals marginal cost and the highest price possible as given by the demand curve for that particular output rate.
- Monopoly short-run profits are found by looking at average total costs compared to price per unit. This difference multiplied by quantity sold at that price determines monopoly profit.
- A monopolist does not necessarily earn a profit. If the average total cost curve lies entirely above the demand curve for a monopoly, production will not be profitable.

ON MAKING HIGHER PROFITS: PRICE DISCRIMINATION 

In a perfectly competitive market, each buyer is charged the same price for every unit of the particular commodity (corrected for differential transportation charges). Because the product is homogeneous and we also assume full knowledge on the part of the buyers, a difference in price cannot exist. Any seller of the product who tried to charge a price higher than the going market price would find that no one would purchase it from that seller.

In this chapter we have assumed until now that the monopolist charged all consumers the same price for all units. A monopolist, however, may be able to charge different people different prices or different unit prices for successive units sought by a given buyer. When there is no cost difference, either one or a combination of these strategies is called **price discrimination.** A firm will engage in price discrimination whenever feasible to increase profits. A price-discriminating firm is able to charge some customers more than other customers.

Price discrimination 
Selling a given product at more than one price, with the price difference being unrelated to differences in cost.

It must be made clear at the outset that charging different prices to different people or for different units that reflect differences in the cost of service to those particular people does not amount to price discrimination. This is **price differentiation:** differences in price that reflect differences in marginal cost.

Price differentiation 
Establishing different prices for similar products to reflect differences in marginal cost in providing those commodities to different groups of buyers.

We can also say that a uniform price does not necessarily indicate an absence of price discrimination. Charging all customers the same price when production costs vary by customer is actually a case of price discrimination.

Necessary Conditions for Price Discrimination

Four conditions are necessary for price discrimination to exist:

1. The firm must face a downward-sloping demand curve.
2. The firm must be able to separate markets at a reasonable cost.
3. The buyers in the various markets must have different price elasticities of demand.
4. The firm must be able to prevent resale of the product or service.

Monopolistic Price Discrimination
See how a monopolist can segment a market for its product to allow it to engage in price discrimination.

For example, charging students a lower price than nonstudents for a movie can be done relatively easily. The cost of checking student IDs is apparently not significant. Also, it is fairly easy to make sure that students do not resell their tickets to nonstudents.

EXAMPLE

Cheaper Airfares for Some, Exorbitant Fares for Others

First-class airfares are often stunningly higher than coach class—far higher than any additional marginal cost warrants. This is a good example of price discrimination. And even in coach class, there may be fare differences of 800 percent. All coach passengers are packed in like sardines, so why the difference in price among them? The answer is again price discrimination, but this time it is based on how badly a person wants to fly. If you are a businessperson who is called to a meeting for the next day, you want to fly very badly. The fact that your company will not allow you to fly first class will not save you from having to pay, say, $2,000 to fly round-trip from Cincinnati to Los Angeles, particularly if you do not stay over on a Saturday. The Saturday stay-over requirement for low fares neatly differentiates individuals who must travel from those who have the time to stay over—people on business trips versus people on leisure trips. If you have a relatively high price elasticity of demand, you will also want to take advantage of low fares that require 7 days', 14 days', or longer advance purchase. The more price-sensitive you are, the more you will pay attention to such cheap-fare requirements, and the lower will be the fare you are likely to pay.

Airlines, with sophisticated computer programs performing what is known as yield management, are also able to change prices constantly. Such programs allow them to project relatively precisely how many last-minute business travelers are going to pay full fare to get on a flight. Computerized yield management works so well because of a mathematical formula that Bell Laboratories patented in 1988. It allows rapid calculations on fare problems with thousands of variables. The airlines compare historical databases on ridership with what is happening in terms of bookings right now. A typical flight will be divided into seven fare "buckets" that may have a differential of as much as 800 percent. The yield management computers constantly adjust the number of seats available in each bucket. When advance bookings are few, more seats are added to the low-fare buckets. When advance bookings are above normal, more seats are added to the highest-fare buckets. The result is lower fares for many and much higher fares for a few. In essence, the airlines are attempting to hit every "price point" on the demand curve for airline travel, as is shown in Figure 24-8.

For Critical Analysis

Assuming that the Bell Laboratories mathematical formula had been available 25 years ago, why couldn't airlines have used it then?

FIGURE 24-8

Toward Perfect Price Discrimination

What the airlines attempt to do by dividing any particular round-trip fare into "buckets" is to price-discriminate as finely as possible. Here we show the airlines setting seven different prices for the same round trip. Those who pay price P_7 are the ones who are the last to ask for a reservation. Those who pay price P_1 are the ones who planned furthest in advance or happened to hit it lucky when seats were added to the low-fare bucket.

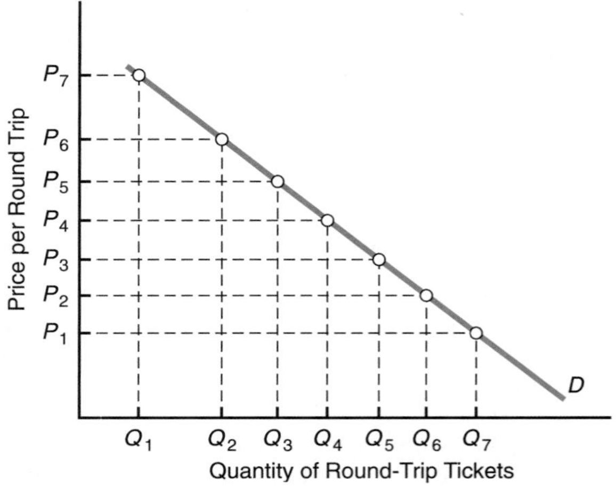

THE SOCIAL COST OF MONOPOLIES

Let's run a little experiment. We will start with a purely competitive industry with numerous firms, each one unable to affect the price of its product. The supply curve of the industry is equal to the horizontal sum of the marginal cost curves of the individual producers above their respective minimum average variable costs. In panel (a) of Figure 24-9, we show the market demand curve and the market supply curve in a perfectly competitive situation. The competitive price in equilibrium is equal to P_e, and the equilibrium quantity at that price is equal to Q_e. Each individual competitor faces a demand curve (not shown) that is coincident with the price line P_e. No individual supplier faces the market demand curve, *D*.

Now let's assume that a monopolist comes in and buys up every single competitor in the industry. In so doing, we'll assume that the monopolist does not affect any of the marginal cost curves or demand. We can therefore redraw *D* and *S* in panel (b) of Figure 24-9, exactly the same as in panel (a).

How does this monopolist decide how much to charge and how much to produce? If the monopolist is profit-maximizing, it is going to look at the marginal revenue curve and produce at the output where marginal revenue equals marginal cost. But what is the marginal cost curve in panel (b) of Figure 24-9? It is merely *S,* because we said that *S* was equal to

FIGURE 24-9

The Effects of Monopolizing an Industry

In panel (a), we show a competitive situation in which equilibrium is established at the intersection of *D* and *S* at point *E*. The equilibrium price would be P_e, and the equilibrium quantity would be Q_e. Each individual competitive producer faces a demand curve that is a horizontal line at the market clearing price, P_e. What happens if the industry is suddenly monopolized? We assume that the costs stay the same; the only thing that changes is that the monopolist now faces the entire downward-sloping demand curve. In panel (b), we draw the marginal revenue curve. Marginal cost is *S* because that is the horizontal summation of all the individual marginal cost curves. The monopolist therefore produces at Q_m and charges price P_m. This price P_m in panel (b) is higher than P_e in panel (a), and Q_m is less than Q_e. We see, then, that a monopolist charges a higher price and produces less than an industry in a competitive situation.

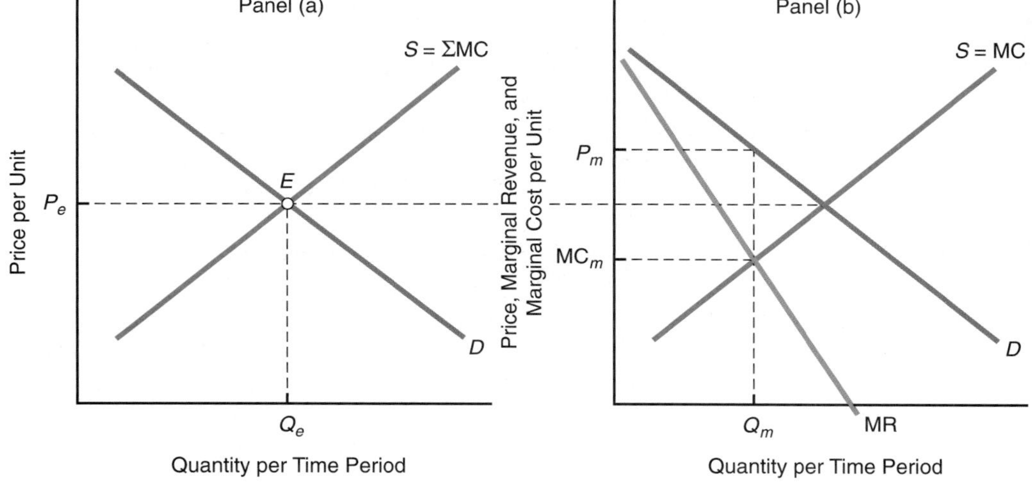

the horizontal summation of the portions of the individual marginal cost curves above each firm's respective minimum average variable cost. The monopolist therefore produces quantity Q_m and sells it at price P_m. Notice that Q_m is less than Q_e and that P_m is greater than P_e. A monopolist therefore produces a smaller quantity and sells it at a higher price. This is the reason usually given when economists criticize monopolists. Monopolists raise the price and restrict production, compared to a competitive situation. For a monopolist's product, consumers are forced to pay a price that exceeds the marginal cost of production. Resources are misallocated in such a situation—too few resources are being used in the monopolist's industry, and too many are used elsewhere.

Notice from Figure 24-9 that by setting MR = MC, the monopolist produces at a rate of output where $P > \text{MC}$ (compare P_m to MC_m). The marginal cost of a commodity (MC) represents what society had to give up in order to obtain the last unit produced. Price, by contrast, represents what buyers are willing to pay to acquire that last unit. Thus the price of a good represents society's valuation of the last unit produced. The monopoly outcome of $P > \text{MC}$ means that the value to society of the last unit produced is greater than its cost (MC); hence not enough of the good is being produced. As we have pointed out before, these differences between monopoly and competition arise not because of differences in costs but rather because of differences in the demand curves the individual firms face. The monopolist has monopoly power because it faces a downward-sloping demand curve. The individual perfect competitor faces a perfectly elastic demand curve.

Before we leave the topic of the cost to society of monopolies, we must repeat that our analysis is based on a heroic assumption. That assumption is that the monopolization of the perfectly competitive industry does not change the cost structure. If monopolization results in higher marginal cost, the cost to society is even greater. Conversely, if monopolization results in cost savings, the cost, if any, to society is less than we infer from our analysis. Indeed, we could have presented a hypothetical example in which monopolization led to such a dramatic reduction in average cost that society actually benefited. Such a situation is a possibility in industries in which economies of scale exist for a very great range of outputs.

CONCEPTS IN BRIEF

- Four conditions are necessary for price discrimination: (1) The firm must face a downward-sloping demand curve, (2) the firm must be able to distinguish markets, (3) buyers in different markets must have different price elasticities of demand, and (4) resale of the product or service must be preventable.
- A monopolist can make higher profits if it can price-discriminate. Price discrimination requires that two or more identifiable classes of buyers exist whose price elasticities of demand for the product or service are different and that these two classes of buyers can be distinguished at little cost.
- Price differentiation should not be confused with price discrimination. The former occurs when differences in price reflect differences in marginal cost.
- Monopoly results in a lower quantity being sold, because the price is higher than it would be in an ideal perfectly competitive industry in which the cost curves were essentially the same as the monopolist's.

NETNOMICS

Arrest That Software! It's Practicing Law Without a License!

Not long ago, a U.S. district court judge in Texas ruled that Internet downloads and computer shop purchases of Quicken Family Lawyer, a software program, are illegal activities in that state. Why? The program was too good. It went beyond allowing users to print out prepackaged versions of wills and other legal documents. It permitted users to *customize* legal documents by asking questions such as how many children they had or where they lived—in other words, soliciting the kind of information for which people lavishly pay lawyers to incorporate into customized wills.

Arguments in favor of making the software available to Texas consumers fell on deaf ears. The judge ruled that the software enabled the "unauthorized practice of law," and only lawyers, he decided, can customize legal documents. In other words, lawyers have the legal right to be free of competition from computer software.

Critics of the decision questioned the state's capability to enforce the decision. They wondered if Texas police will search people for minidisks at the Oklahoma border or if all Internet traffic will have to be routed through state offices. A more basic question was whether it is legal, under the judge's ruling, to purchase a legal textbook. After all, a textbook can teach a person to do everything the software program does, thereby permitting anyone to compete with lawyers and reduce their market power.

ISSUES & APPLICATIONS

Trying to Open a Crack in the Diamond Cartel

The De Beers diamond cartel is so named because the De Beers diamond-mining company of South Africa coordinates its actions. At the center of the cartel's operations is the De Beers marketing subsidiary, the Central Selling Organization (CSO). By restricting diamond sales each year, the CSO aims to maximize profits earned by De Beers and other members of a global cartel of diamond producers.

Concepts Applied

- Market Power
- Monopoly
- Entry
- Competition

Tough Times in the Diamond Cartel

A key to the cartel's profit-maximizing effort has been a coordinated attempt to restrict world diamond sales. To ensure that only a carefully regulated quantity of diamonds makes its way into the marketplace, the CSO regularly purchases diamonds from companies that are not part of the cartel. Between 1986 and 1998, the result was a 50 percent increase in diamond prices.

Since 1998, however, things have not gone so smoothly for the cartel. On the one hand, there was a 5 percent drop in the world demand for diamonds. On the other hand, Russian producers, squeezed by a weakening national economy, violated their contract with the CSO and began selling large volumes of low-quality, so-called near-gem diamonds. When the CSO retaliated by sharply reducing the price it would pay to buy low-quality diamonds, British and Australian companies that also sold near-gem diamonds responded by breaking with the CSO's restraints on diamond sales. Both of these events combined to push down diamond prices by as much as 20 percent. Overall, De Beers's 1998 revenues from diamond sales dropped by more than one-fourth, the second-biggest one-year drop in the company's sales since the end of the Great Depression.

Segmenting the Diamond Market

The De Beers cartel has not given up on keeping its market power, however. Because it produces so many of the world's high-quality diamonds, De Beers has sought to distinguish its diamonds from those produced by others. The demand for these "true-gem" diamonds tends to be less elastic, and that permits De Beers to earn more profits if it can maintain a higher price. To emphasize the higher quality of the diamonds it produces—and hence reinforce the demand for "true gems"—De Beers has begun etching serial numbers on the diamonds it sells. These numbers, plus a De Beers logo also etched into the gems, are invisible to the human eye but can be viewed with special instruments. In the meantime, the CSO continues to restrict the supply of high-quality gems to the world's market. Its stockpile of unsold diamonds has continued to grow.

Simultaneously, the CSO let the world price of low-quality diamonds drop so low that Russian producers found themselves losing money. In the end, most Russian diamond firms rejoined the De Beers cartel and stopped "leaking" low-quality gems into the market. Nevertheless, some experts predict that open competition in diamonds will emerge eventually—at least in the low-quality market. In the market for high-quality diamonds, however, the De Beers cartel still has a firm grip on production and pricing. Indeed, De Beers has been trying to bolster the CSO's market share by seeking joint ventures with other miners of high-quality gems. A key feature of these ventures, of course, is an agreement by the parties to sell only a fraction of the diamonds that are mined.

FOR CRITICAL ANALYSIS

1. Why is withholding a large stockpile of diamonds from the marketplace in the interests of De Beers?
2. Why can other individual mining companies gain, at least in the short term, from violating CSO contracts to restrict their production and sales of diamonds?

SUMMARY DISCUSSION OF LEARNING OBJECTIVES

1. **Why Monopoly Can Occur:** Monopoly, a situation in which a single firm produces and sells a good or service, can occur when there are significant barriers to market entry by other firms. Examples of barriers to entry include (1) ownership of important resources for which there are no close substitutes, (2) problems in raising adequate capital to begin production, (3) economies of scale for even large ranges of output, or natural monopoly conditions, (4) legal or governmental restrictions, and (5) associations of productions called cartels that work together to stifle competition.
2. **Demand and Marginal Revenue Conditions a Monopolist Faces:** Because a monopolist constitutes the entire industry, it faces the entire market demand curve. When it reduces the price of its product, it is able to sell more units at the new price, which pushes up its revenues, but it also sells other units at this lower price, which pushes its revenues down somewhat. For this reason, the monopolist's marginal revenue at any given quantity of production is less than the price at which it sells that quantity of output. Hence the monopolist's marginal revenue curve slopes downward and lies below the demand curve it faces.
3. **How a Monopolist Determines How Much Output to Produce and What Price to Charge:** A monopolist is a price searcher, meaning that it seeks to charge the price consistent with the production level that maximizes its economic profits. It maximizes its profits by producing to the point at which marginal revenue equals marginal cost. The monopolist then charges the maximum price for this amount of output, which is the price that consumers are willing to pay for that quantity of output.
4. **A Monopolist's Profits:** The amount of profit earned by a monopolist is equal to the difference between the price it charges and its average production cost times the amount of output it produces and sells. At the profit-maximizing output rate, the monopolist's price is at the point on the demand curve corresponding to this output rate, and its average total cost of producing this output rate is at the corresponding point on the monopolist's average total cost curve. Typically, a monopolist earns positive economic profits, but situations can arise in which average total cost exceeds the profit-maximizing price. In this case, the maximum profit is negative, and the monopolist earns an economic loss.
5. **Price Discrimination:** If a monopolist engages in price discrimination, it sells its product at more than one price, with the price difference being unrelated to differences in production costs. To be able to engage successfully in price discrimination, a monopolist must be able to identify and separate buyers with different price elasticities of demand. This allows the monopolist to sell some of its output at higher prices to consumers with less elastic demand. Even then, however, the monopolist must be able to prevent resale of its product by those with less elastic demand who can buy it at a lower price.
6. **Social Cost of Monopolies:** Because a monopoly is a price searcher, it is able to charge the highest price that people are willing to pay for the amount of output it produces. This price exceeds the marginal cost of producing the output. In addition, if the monopolist's marginal cost curve corresponds to the sum of the marginal cost curves for a number of firms that would exist if the industry were perfectly competitive instead, then the monopolist produces and sells less output than perfectly competitive firms would have produced and sold. Consequently, a monopolist sells output at a higher price and produces less output than would be produced under perfect competition.

Key Terms and Concepts

Problems

Answers to the odd-numbered problems appear at the back of the book.

24-1. An international coffee cartel exists to smooth market supply and price fluctuations over the growing seasons. Since the 1960s, the number of coffee-exporting countries has grown dramatically. Explain the likely effect of this trend on the prospects for maintaining a successful coffee cartel.

24-2. Discuss the difference in the price elasticity of demand for an individual firm in a perfectly competitive industry as compared with a monopolist. Explain, in economic terms, why the price elasticities are different.

24-3. The following table depicts the daily output, price, and costs of the only dry cleaner located near the campus of a small college town in a remote location. The dry cleaner is effectively a monopolist.

Output (suits cleaned)	Price per Suit ($)	Total Costs ($)
0	8.00	3.00
1	7.50	6.00
2	7.00	8.50
3	6.50	10.50
4	6.00	11.50
5	5.50	13.50
6	5.00	16.00
7	4.50	19.00
8	4.00	24.00

a. Calculate the dry cleaner's total revenue and total profit at each output level.

b. What is the profit-maximizing level of output?

24-4. Given the information in Problem 24-3, calculate the dry cleaner's marginal revenue and marginal cost at each output level. Based on marginal analysis, what is the profit-maximizing level of output?

24-5. A manager of a monopoly firm notices that the firm is producing output at a rate at which average total cost is falling but is not at its minimum feasible point. The manager argues that surely the firm must not be maximizing its economic profits. Is this argument correct? Explain.

24-6. Referring to the accompanying diagram, answer the following questions.

a. What is monopolist's profit-maximizing rate of output?

b. At the profit-maximizing output rate, what are the monopolist's average total cost and average revenue?

c. At the profit-maximizing output rate, what are the monopolist's total cost and total revenue?

d. What is the maximum profit?

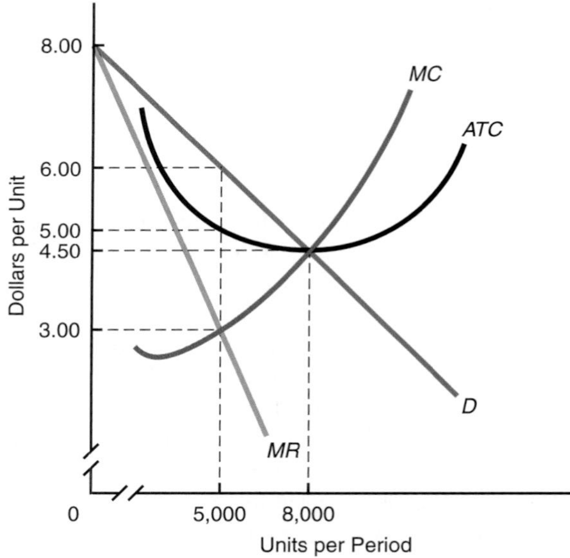

24-7. Using the diagram for Problem 24-6, suppose that the marginal cost and average total cost curves also illustrate the horizontal summation of the individual firms in a competitive industry in the long run. Based on this, what would the market price and equilibrium output be if the market were competitive? Explain the economic cost to society of allowing a monopoly to exist in this industry.

24-8. For each of the following examples, explain how and why a firm with monopoly power would attempt to price-discriminate.

a. Providing air travel for business people and tourists

b. A fastfood restaurant that serves business people and retired people

c. A theater that shows the same movie to large families and to individuals and couples

24-9. A monopolist finds that it is currently producing output at a rate at which the total revenue it earns varies directly with the price it charges. Is the monopolist maximizing its economic profits? Why or why not?

24-10. A new competitor enters the industry and competes with a second firm, which up to this point had been a monopolist. The second firm finds that although demand is not perfectly elastic, it is now relatively more elastic. What will happen to the marginal revenue curve and to the profit-maximizing price that the monopolist charges?

24-11. Because of an increase in the price of resources that are inputs in its production process, a monopolist finds that its marginal cost curve has shifted upward. What is likely to happen to the monopolist's price, output rate, and economic profits?

Economics on the Net

Patents, Trademarks, and Intellectual Property Governments often grant legal protections against efforts to copy new products. This Internet application gives you the opportunity to explore one company's view on the advantages of alternative forms of protection.

Title: Intellectual Property

Navigation: Click here to visit the GlaxoSmithKline Web site. Select Investor Relations, then Financial Reports. View the GlaxoWellcome Annual Report 1999. Scroll down to Intellectual Property (Page 18.)

Application Read the statement on intellectual property and the accompanying table.

1. What does intellectual property include? What are the differences between patents, trademarks, and registered designs and copyrights?
2. What are GlaxoWellcome's objectives regarding intellectual property? What seems to be more important, patents or trademarks? In what areas of medical research does GlaxoWellcome excel?

For Group Discussion and Analysis In 1969, GlaxoWellcome developed Ventolin, a treatment for asthma symptoms. Though the patent and trademark have long expired, the company still retains over a third of the market in this treatment. Explain, in economic terms, the source of GlaxoWellcome's strength in this area. Discuss whether patents and trademarks are beneficial for the development and discovery of new treatments.

CHAPTER

25

MONOPOLISTIC COMPETITION, OLIGOPOLY, AND STRATEGIC BEHAVIOR

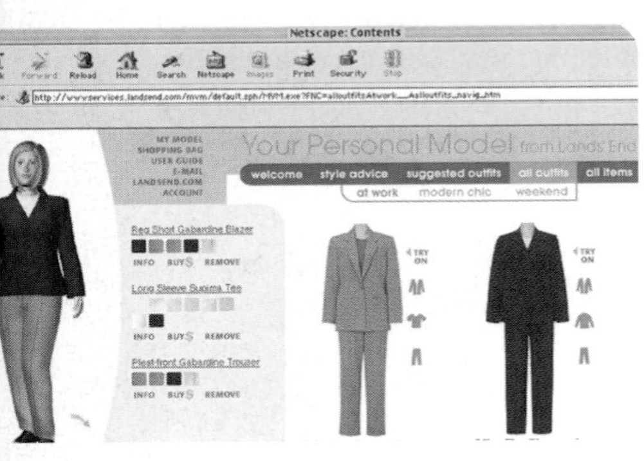

Here is a Web page from the Lands' End site, where Internet shoppers can "try on" different styles and combinations of clothes. Will on-line customization of clothing affect traditional retailers?

If you shop at the Web site of direct retailer Lands' End, you can create a "3-D, personalized shopping model" with your exact measurements. Do you want to see how a blue, nine-button blouse will look with plaid pants? Just click and drag the clothes together for a look. The company's Web site has other features, including a personalized e-mail service alerting customers to sales on the latest in their favorite fashions. By making its Web site interesting and useful, Lands' End seeks to differentiate its brand name from those of its many rivals. The company wants to grab customers away from other apparel sellers, and it wants to keep those customers. To understand the actions of firms that sell similar but differentiated goods, you must learn about monopolistic competition, one subject of this chapter.

LEARNING OBJECTIVES

After reading this chapter, you should be able to:

1. Discuss the key characteristics of a monopolistically competitive industry
2. Contrast the output and pricing decisions of monopolistically competitive firms with those of perfectly competitive firms
3. Outline the fundamental characteristics of oligopoly
4. Understand how to apply game theory to evaluate the pricing strategies of oligopolistic firms
5. Explain the kinked demand theory of oligopolistic price rigidity
6. Describe theories of how firms may deter market entry by potential rivals

Did You Know That... 80 percent of initial customer contacts for General Motors' Saturn division now originate on the Internet? GM's first Saturn Web site offered lots of car specifications and dealer referrals, but few people visited the site. Then the company added more useful features, such as an auto lease pricing calculator, an interactive design shop for experimenting with the looks of alternative car options, and on-line order forms for Saturns. GM vigorously promoted these on-line features in a television commercial showing a college student buying a Saturn over the Internet. Within weeks, the number of Web surfers visiting the Saturn site tripled to as many as 7,000 per day.

In their quest to let people know of their existence and products, American businesses will leave no stone unturned—and no corner of cyberspace unexplored. Companies pull out all the stops to inform people about what they sell, where people can buy it, and at what price.

Advertising did not show up in our analysis of perfect competition. Nevertheless, it plays a large role in industries that cannot be described as perfectly competitive but cannot be described as pure monopolies either. A combination of consumers' preferences for variety and competition among producers has led to similar but *differentiated* products in the marketplace. This situation has been described as *monopolistic competition,* the subject of the first part of this chapter. In the second part of the chapter, we look at firms that are neither perfect competitors nor pure monopolists that do not have to worry about actual competitors. And clearly, perfect competitors cannot make any strategic decisions, for they must take the market price as given. We call firms that have the ability to make strategic decisions *oligopolies,* which we will define more formally later in this chapter.

Chapter Outline 

MONOPOLISTIC COMPETITION 

In the 1920s and 1930s, economists became increasingly aware that there were many industries for which both the perfectly competitive model and the pure monopoly model did not apply and did not seem to yield very accurate predictions. Theoretical and empirical research was instituted to develop some sort of middle ground. Two separately developed models of **monopolistic competition** resulted. At Harvard, Edward Chamberlin published *Theory of Monopolistic Competition* in 1933. The same year, Britain's Joan Robinson published *The Economics of Imperfect Competition.* In this chapter, we will outline the theory as presented by Chamberlin.

Monopolistic competition 
A market situation in which a large number of firms produce similar but not identical products. Entry into the industry is relatively easy.

Chamberlin defined monopolistic competition as a market structure in which there is a relatively large number of producers offering similar but differentiated products. Monopolistic competition therefore has the following features:

1. Significant numbers of sellers in a highly competitive market
2. Differentiated products
3. Sales promotion and advertising
4. Easy entry of new firms in the long run

Even a cursory look at the American economy leads to the conclusion that monopolistic competition is an important form of market structure in the United States. Indeed, that is true of all developed economies.

Number of Firms

In a perfectly competitive situation, there is an extremely large number of firms; in pure monopoly, there is only one. In monopolistic competition, there is a large number of firms, but not as many as in perfect competition. This fact has several important implications for a monopolistically competitive industry.

1. *Small share of market.* With so many firms, each firm has a relatively small share of the total market.
2. *Lack of collusion.* With so many firms, it is very difficult for all of them to get together to collude—to cooperate in setting a pure monopoly price (and output). Price rigging in a monopolistically competitive industry is virtually impossible. Also, barriers to entry are minor, and the flow of new firms into the industry makes collusive agreements less likely. The large number of firms makes the monitoring and detection of cheating very costly and extremely difficult. This difficulty is compounded by differentiated products and high rates of innovation; collusive agreements are easier for a homogeneous product than for heterogeneous ones.
3. *Independence.* Because there are so many firms, each one acts independently of the others. No firm attempts to take into account the reaction of all of its rival firms—that would be impossible with so many rivals. Rivals' reactions to output and price changes are largely ignored.

Product Differentiation

Product differentiation

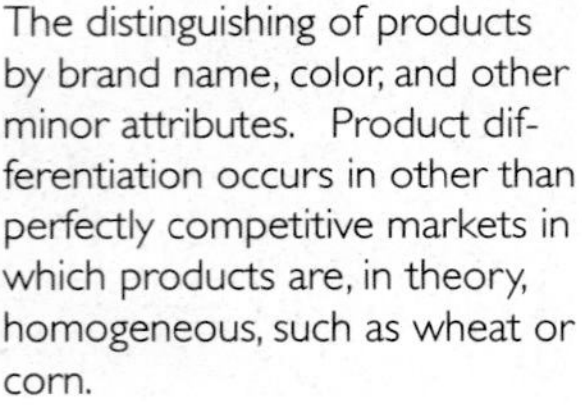

The distinguishing of products by brand name, color, and other minor attributes. Product differentiation occurs in other than perfectly competitive markets in which products are, in theory, homogeneous, such as wheat or corn.

Perhaps the most important feature of the monopolistically competitive market is **product differentiation.** We can say that each individual manufacturer of a product has an absolute monopoly over its own product, which is slightly differentiated from other similar products. This means that the firm has some control over the price it charges. Unlike the perfectly competitive firm, it faces a downward-sloping demand curve.

Consider the abundance of brand names for toothpaste, soap, gasoline, vitamins, shampoo, and most other consumer goods and a great many services. We are not obliged to buy just one type of television set, just one type of jeans, or just one type of footwear. There are usually a number of similar but differentiated products from which to choose. One reason is that the greater a firm's success at product differentiation, the greater the firm's pricing options.

Each separate differentiated product has numerous similar substitutes. This clearly has an impact on the price elasticity of demand for the individual firm. Recall that one determinant of price elasticity of demand is the availability of substitutes: The greater the number and closeness of substitutes available, other things being equal, the greater the price elasticity of demand. If the consumer has a vast array of alternatives that are just about as good as the product under study, a relatively small increase in the price of that product will lead many consumers to switch to one of the many close substitutes. Thus the ability of a firm to raise the price above the price of *close* substitutes is very small. The result of this is that even though the demand curve slopes downward, it does so only slightly. In other words, it is relatively elastic (over that price range) compared to a monopolist's demand curve. In the extreme case, with perfect competition, the substitutes are perfect because we are dealing with only one particular undifferentiated product. In that case, the individual firm has a perfectly elastic demand curve.

Ease of Entry

For any current monopolistic competitor, potential competition is always lurking in the background. The easier—that is, the less costly—entry is, the more a current monopolistic competitor must worry about losing business.

A good example of a monopolistic competitive industry is the computer software industry. Many small firms provide different programs for many applications. The fixed capital costs required to enter this industry are small; all you need are skilled programmers. In addition, there are few legal restrictions. The firms in this industry also engage in extensive advertising in over 150 computer publications.

Sales Promotion and Advertising

Monopolistic competition differs from perfect competition in that no individual firm in a perfectly competitive market will advertise. A perfectly competitive firm, by definition, can sell all that it wants to sell at the going market price anyway. Why, then, would it spend even one penny on advertising? Furthermore, by definition, the perfect competitor is selling a product that is identical to the product that all other firms in the industry are selling. Any advertisement that induces consumers to buy more of that product will, in effect, be helping all the competitors, too. A perfect competitor therefore cannot be expected to incur any advertising costs (except for all firms in an industry collectively agreeing to advertise to urge the public to buy more beef or drink more milk).

But because the monopolistic competitor has at least *some* monopoly power, advertising may result in increased profits. Advertising is used to increase demand and to differentiate one's product. How much advertising should be undertaken? It should be carried to the point at which the additional revenue from one more dollar of advertising just equals that one dollar of marginal cost.

Advertising as Signaling Behavior. Recall from Chapter 23 that signals are compact gestures or actions that convey information. For example, high profits in an industry are signals that resources should flow to that industry. Individual companies can explicitly engage in signaling behavior. They do so by establishing brand names or trademarks, and then promoting them heavily. This is a signal to prospective consumers that this is a company that plans to stay in business. Before the modern age of advertising, banks in America faced a problem of signaling their soundness. They chose to make the bank building large, imposing, and constructed out of marble and granite. Stone communicated permanence. The effect was to give the bank's customers confidence that they were not doing business with a fly-by-night operation.

When Dell Computer advertises its brand name heavily, it incurs substantial costs. The only way it can recoup those costs is by selling lots of Dell computers over a long period of time. Thus heavy advertising of its brand name is a signal to personal computer buyers that Dell is interested in each customer's repeat business.

But what about advertising that does not seem to convey any information, not even about price? What good is an advertisement for, say, Wal-Mart that simply states, "We give you value that you can count on"?

EXAMPLE

Can Advertising Lead to Efficiency?

Advertising budgets by major retailers may just seem like an added expense, not a step on the road to economic efficiency. According to research by economists Kyle Bagwell of Northwestern University and Garey Ramey of the University of California at San Diego, just the opposite is true. When retailers advertise heavily, they increase the number of shoppers that come to their store. Such increased traffic allows retailers to offer a wider selection of goods, to invest in cost-reduction technology (such as computerized inventory and satellite communications), and to exploit manufacturers' quantity discounts. Such cost reductions can help explain the success of Wal-Mart, Circuit City, and Home Depot. Consequently, Bagwell and Ramey conclude that advertising can help promote efficiency even if it provides no "hard" information. Advertising signals to consumers where they can find big-company, low-priced, high-variety stores.

For Critical Analysis

Which is true, then: "We are bigger because we are better" or "We are better because we are bigger"?

CONCEPTS IN BRIEF

- Monopolistic competition is a market structure that lies between pure monopoly and perfect competition.
- A monopolistically competitive market structure has (1) a large number of sellers, (2) differentiated products, (3) advertising, and (4) easy entry of firms in the long run.
- Because of the large number of firms, each has a small share of the market, making collusion difficult; the firms are independent.

PRICE AND OUTPUT FOR THE MONOPOLISTIC COMPETITOR

Now that we are aware of the assumptions underlying the monopolistic competition model, we can analyze the price and output behavior of each firm in a monopolistically competitive industry. We assume in the analysis that follows that the desired product type and quality have been chosen. We further assume that the budget and the type of promotional activity have already been chosen and do not change.

The Individual Firm's Demand and Cost Curves

Because the individual firm is not a perfect competitor, its demand curve slopes downward, as is shown in all three panels of Figure 25-1. Hence it faces a marginal revenue curve that is also downward-sloping and below the demand curve. To find the profit-maximizing rate of output and the profit-maximizing price, we go to the output where the marginal cost curve intersects the marginal revenue curve from below. That gives us the profit-maximizing output rate. Then we draw a vertical line up to the demand curve. That gives us the price that can be charged to sell exactly that quantity produced. This is what we have done in Figure 25-1. In each panel, a marginal cost curve intersects the marginal revenue curve at *E*. The profit-maximizing rate of output is q_e, and the profit-maximizing price is *P*.

Short-Run Equilibrium

In the short run, it is possible for a monopolistic competitor to make economic profits—profits over and above the normal rate of return or beyond what is necessary to keep that firm in that industry. We show such a situation in panel (a) of Figure 25-1. The average total cost curve is drawn in below the demand curve, *d*, at the profit-maximizing rate of output, q_e. Economic profits are shown by the shaded rectangle in that panel.

Losses in the short run are clearly also possible. They are presented in panel (b) of Figure 25-1. Here the average total cost curve lies everywhere above the individual firm's demand curve, *d*. The losses are marked as the shaded rectangle.

FIGURE 25-1

Short-Run and Long-Run Equilibrium with Monopolistic Competition

In panel (a), the typical monopolistic competitor is shown making economic profits. If that were the situation, there would be entry into the industry, forcing the demand curve for the individual monopolistic competitor leftward. Eventually, firms would find themselves in the situation depicted in panel (c), where zero economic profits are being made. In panel (b), the typical firm is in a monopolistically competitive industry making economic losses. If that were the case, firms would leave the industry. Each remaining firm's demand curve would shift outward to the right. Eventually, the typical firm would find itself in the situation depicted in panel (c).

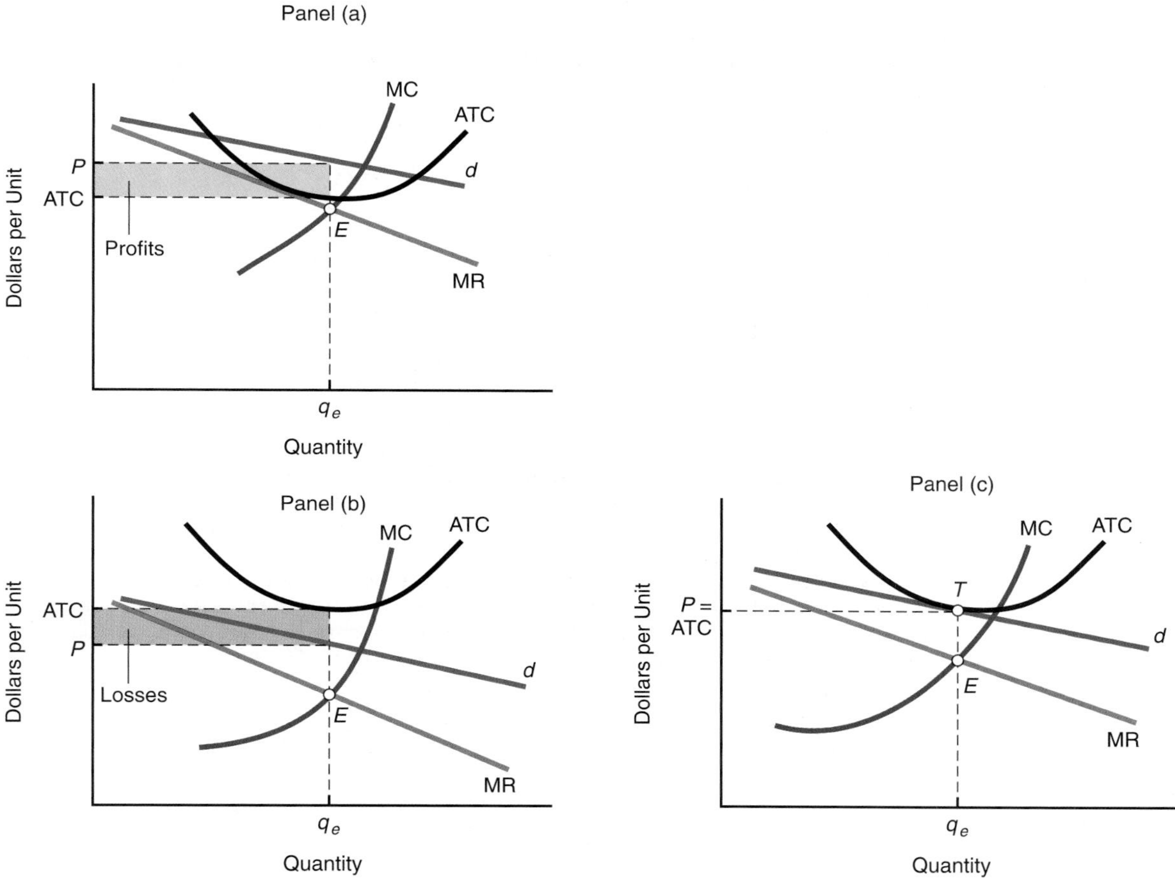

Just as with any market structure or any firm, in the short run it is possible to observe either economic profits or economic losses. (In the long run such is not the case with monopolistic competition, however.) In either case, the price does not equal marginal cost but rather is above it. Therefore, there is some misallocation of resources, a topic that we will discuss later in this chapter.

The Long Run: Zero Economic Profits

The long run is where the similarity between perfect competition and monopolistic competition becomes more obvious. In the long run, because so many firms produce substitutes for the product in question, any economic profits will disappear with competition. They

Monopolistic Competition
Further study monopolistic competition.

will be reduced to zero either through entry by new firms seeing a chance to make a higher rate of return than elsewhere or by changes in product quality and advertising outlays by existing firms in the industry. (Profitable products will be imitated by other firms.) As for economic losses in the short run, they will disappear in the long run because the firms that suffer them will leave the industry. They will go into another business where the expected rate of return is at least normal. Panels (a) and (b) of Figure 25-1 therefore represent only short-run situations for a monopolistically competitive firm. In the long run, the individual firm's demand curve *d* will just touch the average total cost curve at the particular price that is profit-maximizing for that particular firm. This is shown in panel (c) of Figure 25-1.

A word of warning: This is an idealized, long-run equilibrium situation for each firm in the industry. It does not mean that even in the long run we will observe every single firm in a monopolistically competitive industry making *exactly* zero economic profits or *just* a normal rate of return. We live in a dynamic world. All we are saying is that if this model is correct, the rate of return will *tend toward* normal—economic profits will *tend toward* zero.

COMPARING PERFECT COMPETITION WITH MONOPOLISTIC COMPETITION

If both the monopolistic competitor and the perfect competitor make zero economic profits in the long run, how are they different? The answer lies in the fact that the demand curve for the individual perfect competitor is perfectly elastic. Such is not the case for the individual

FIGURE 25-2

Comparison of the Perfect Competitor with the Monopolistic Competitor

In panel (a), the perfectly competitive firm has zero economic profits in the long run. The price is set equal to marginal cost, and the price is P_1. The firm's demand curve is just tangent to the minimum point on its average total cost curve, which means that the firm is operating at an optimum rate of production. With the monopolistically competitive firm in panel (b), there are also zero economic profits in the long run. The price is greater than marginal cost; the monopolistically competitive firm does not find itself at the minimum point on its average total cost curve. It is operating at a rate of output to the left of the minimum point on the ATC curve.

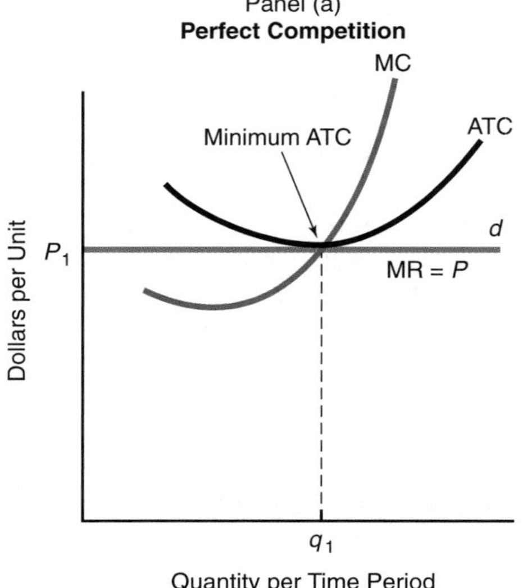

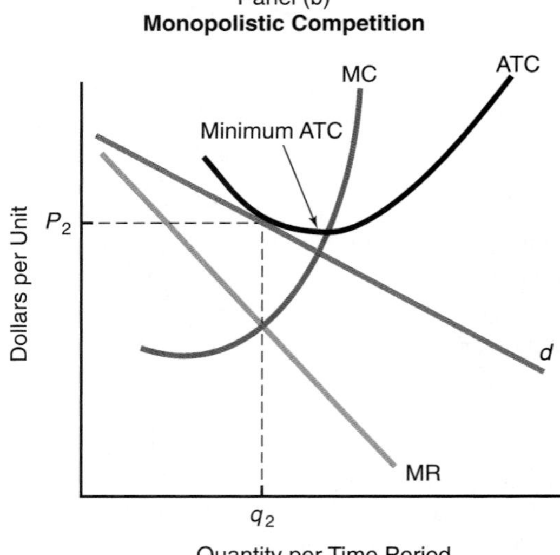

monopolistic competitor; its demand curve is less than perfectly elastic. This firm has some control over price. Price elasticity of demand is not infinite.

We see the two situations in Figure 25-2. Both panels show average total costs just touching the respective demand curves at the particular price at which the firm is selling the product. Notice, however, that the perfect competitor's average total costs are at a minimum. This is not the case with the monopolistic competitor. The equilibrium rate of output is to the left of the minimum point on the average total cost curve where price is greater than marginal cost. The monopolistic competitor cannot expand output to the point of minimum costs without lowering price, and then marginal cost would exceed marginal revenue. A monopolistic competitor at profit maximization charges a price that exceeds marginal cost. In this respect it is similar to the monopolist.

It has consequently been argued that monopolistic competition involves waste because minimum average total costs are not achieved and price exceeds marginal cost. There are too many firms, each with excess capacity, producing too little output. According to critics of monopolistic competition, society's resources are being wasted.

Chamberlin had an answer to this criticism. He contended that the difference between the average cost of production for a monopolistically competitive firm in an open market and the minimum average total cost represented what he called the cost of producing "differentness." Chamberlin did not consider this difference in cost between perfect competition and monopolistic competition a waste. In fact, he argued that it is rational for consumers to have a taste for differentiation; consumers willingly accept the resultant increased production costs in return for choice and variety of output.

CONCEPTS IN BRIEF

- In the short run, it is possible for monopolistically competitive firms to make economic profits or economic losses.
- In the long run, monopolistically competitive firms will make zero economic profits—that is, they will make a normal rate of return.
- Because the monopolistic competitor faces a downward-sloping demand curve, it does not produce at the minimum point on its average total cost curve. Hence we say that a monopolistic competitor has higher average total costs per unit than a perfect competitor would have.
- Chamberlin argued that the difference between the average cost of production for a monopolistically competitive firm and the minimum average total cost at which a competitive firm would produce is the cost of producing "differentness."

OLIGOPOLY

There is another market structure that we have yet to discuss, and it is an important one indeed. It involves a situation in which a few large firms dominate an entire industry. They are not competitive in the sense that we have used the term; they are not even monopolistically competitive. And because there are several of them, a pure monopoly does not exist. We call such a situation an **oligopoly,** which consists of a small number of interdependent sellers. Each firm in the industry knows that other firms will react to its changes in prices, quantities, and qualities. An oligopoly market structure can exist for either a homogeneous or a differentiated product.

Oligopoly 
A market situation in which there are very few sellers. Each seller knows that the other sellers will react to its changes in prices and quantities.

Characteristics of Oligopoly

Oligopoly is characterized by the small number of interdependent firms that constitute the entire market.

Small Number of Firms. How many is "a small number of firms"? More than two but less than 100? The question is not easy to answer. Basically, though, oligopoly exists when a handful of firms dominate the industry enough to set prices. The top few firms in the industry account for an overwhelming percentage of total industry output.

Oligopolies usually involve three to five big companies that produce the bulk of industry output. Between World War II and the 1970s, three firms—General Motors, Chrysler, and Ford—sold nearly all the output of the U.S. automobile industry. Among manufacturers of chewing gum and coin-operated amusement games, four large firms sell essentially the entire output of each industry.

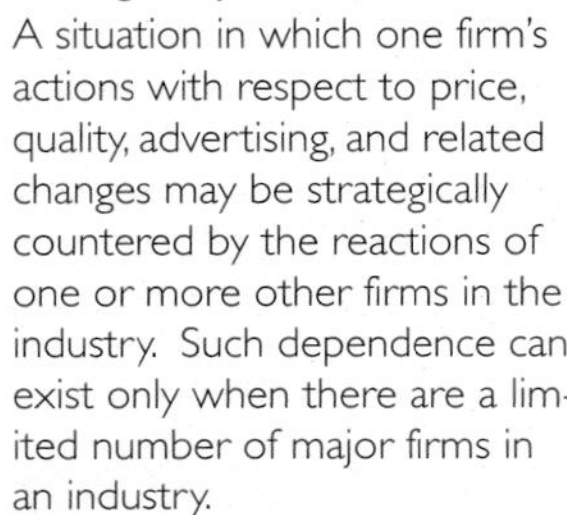

Strategic dependence
A situation in which one firm's actions with respect to price, quality, advertising, and related changes may be strategically countered by the reactions of one or more other firms in the industry. Such dependence can exist only when there are a limited number of major firms in an industry.

Interdependence. All markets and all firms are, in a sense, interdependent. But only when a few large firms dominate an industry does the question of **strategic dependence** of one on the others' actions arise. The firms must recognize that they are interdependent. Any action on the part of one firm with respect to output, price, quality, or product differentiation will cause a reaction on the part of other firms. A model of such mutual interdependence is difficult to build, but examples of such behavior are not hard to find in the real world. Oligopolists in the cigarette industry, for example, are constantly reacting to each other.

Recall that in the model of perfect competition, each firm ignores the behavior of other firms because each firm is able to sell all that it wants at the going market price. At the other extreme, the pure monopolist does not have to worry about the reaction of current rivals because there are none. In an oligopolistic market structure, the managers of firms are like generals in a war: *They must attempt to predict the reaction of rival firms.* It is a strategic game.

Why Oligopoly Occurs

Why are some industries dominated by a few large firms? What causes an industry that might otherwise be competitive to tend toward oligopoly? We can provide some partial answers here.

Economies of Scale. Perhaps the strongest reason that has been offered for the existence of oligopoly is economies of scale. Recall that economies of scale are defined as a situation in which a doubling of output results in less than a doubling of total costs. When economies of scale exist, the firm's average total cost curve will slope downward as the firm produces more and more output. Average total cost can be reduced by continuing to expand the scale of operation. Smaller firms in such a situation will have a tendency to be inefficient. Their average total costs will be greater than those incurred by a large firm. Little by little, they will go out of business or be absorbed into the larger firm.

Barriers to Entry. It is possible that certain barriers to entry have prevented more competition in oligopolistic industries. They include legal barriers, such as patents, and control and ownership over critical supplies. Indeed, we can find periods in the past when firms maintained market power because they were able not only to erect a barrier to entry but also to keep it in place year after year. In principle, the chemical, electronics, and aluminum industries have been at one time or another either monopolistic or oligopolistic because of the ownership of patents and the control of strategic inputs by specific firms.

Oligopoly by Merger. Another reason that oligopolistic market structures may sometimes develop is that firms merge. A merger is the joining of two or more firms under single ownership or control. The merged firm naturally becomes larger, enjoys greater economies of scale as output increases, and may ultimately have a greater ability to influence the market price for the industry's output.

There are two types of mergers, horizontal and vertical. A **horizontal merger** involves firms selling a similar product. If two shoe manufacturing firms merge, that is a horizontal merger. If a group of firms, all producing steel, merge into one, that is also a horizontal merger. A **vertical merger** occurs when one firm merges with either a firm from which it purchases an input or a firm to which it sells its output. Vertical mergers occur, for example, when a coal-using electrical utility purchases a coal-mining firm or when a shoe manufacturer purchases retail shoe outlets. (Obviously, vertical mergers cannot create oligopoly as we have defined it.)

We have been talking about oligopoly in a theoretical manner until now. It is time to look at the actual picture of oligopolies in the United States.

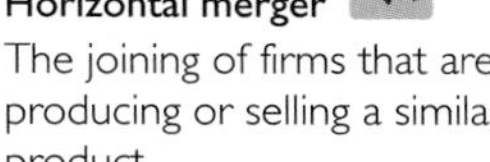

Horizontal merger
The joining of firms that are producing or selling a similar product.

Vertical merger
The joining of a firm with another to which it sells an output or from which it buys an input.

Click here to simulate the effects of an industry merger.

Measuring Industry Concentration

As we have stated, oligopoly is a situation in which a few interdependent firms produce a large part of total output in an industry. This has been called *industry concentration.* Before we show the concentration statistics in the United States, let's determine how industry concentration can be measured.

Concentration Ratio. The most popular way to compute industry concentration is to determine the percentage of total sales or production accounted for by the top four or top eight firms in an industry. This gives the four-or eight-firm **concentration ratio.** An example of an industry with 25 firms is given in Table 25-1. We can see in that table that the four largest firms account for almost 90 percent of total output in the hypothetical industry. That is an example of an oligopoly.

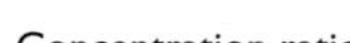

Concentration ratio
The percentage of all sales contributed by the leading four or leading eight firms in an industry; sometimes called the *industry concentration ratio.*

TABLE 25-1
Computing the Four-Firm Concentration Ratio

Firm	Annual Sales ($ millions)		
1	150	= 400 (firms 1–4)	Total number of firms in industry = 25
2	100		
3	80		
4	70		
5 through 25	50		
Total	450		

$$\text{Four-firm concentration ratio} = \frac{400}{450} = 88.9\%$$

TABLE 25-2
Four-Firm Domestic Concentration Ratios for Selected U.S. Industries

Industry	Share of Value of Total Domestic Shipments Accounted for by the Top Four Firms (%)
Tobacco products	93
Breakfast cereals	85
Domestic motor vehicles	84
Soft drinks	69
Primary aluminum	59
Household vacuum cleaners	59
Electronic computers	45
Printing and publishing	23

Source: U.S. Bureau of the Census.

U.S. Concentration Ratios. Table 25-2 shows the four-firm *domestic* concentration ratios for various industries. Is there any way that we can show or determine which industries to classify as oligopolistic? There is no definite answer. If we arbitrarily picked a four-firm concentration ratio of 75 percent, we could indicate that tobacco products, breakfast cereals, and domestic motor vehicles were oligopolistic. But we would always be dealing with an arbitrary definition.

Oligopoly, Efficiency, and Resource Allocation

Although oligopoly is not the dominant form of market structure in the United States, oligopolistic industries do exist. To the extent that oligopolists have *market power*—an ability to *individually* affect the *market* price for the industry's output—they lead to resource misallocations, just as monopolies do. Oligopolists charge prices that exceed marginal cost. But what about oligopolies that occur because of economies of scale? One could argue that consumers end up paying lower prices than if the industry were composed of numerous smaller firms.

Reaction function 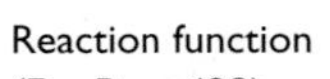
(For Page 623)
The manner in which one oligopolist reacts to a change in price, output, or quality made by another oligopolist in the industry.

All in all, there is no definite evidence of serious resource misallocation in the United States because of oligopolies. In any event, the more U.S. firms face competition from the rest of the world, the less any current oligopoly will be able to exercise market power.

- An oligopoly is a market situation in which there are a small number of interdependent sellers.
- Oligopoly may result from (1) economies of scale, (2) barriers to entry, and (3) mergers.
- Horizontal mergers involve the joining of firms selling a similar product.
- Vertical mergers involve the merging of one firm either with the supplier of an input or the purchaser of its output.
- Industry concentration can be measured by the percentage of total sales accounted for by the top four or top eight firms.

Game theory
A way of describing the various possible outcomes in any situation involving two or more interacting individuals when those individuals are aware of the interactive nature of their situation and plan accordingly. The plans made by these individuals are known as *game strategies.*

STRATEGIC BEHAVIOR AND GAME THEORY

At this point, we should be able to show oligopoly price and output determination in the way we showed it for perfect competition, pure monopoly, and monopolistic competition, but we cannot. Whenever there are relatively few firms competing in an industry, each can and does react to the price, quantity, quality, and product innovations that the others undertake. In other words, each oligopolist has a **reaction function.** Oligopolistic competitors are interdependent. Consequently, the decision makers in such firms must employ strategies. And we must be able to model their strategic behavior if we wish to predict how prices and outputs are determined in oligopolistic market structures. In general, we can think of reactions of other firms to one firm's actions as part of a *game* that is played by all firms in the industry. Not surprisingly, economists have developed **game theory** models to describe firms' rational interactions. Game theory is the analytical framework in which two or more individuals, companies, or nations compete for certain payoffs that depend on the strategy that the others employ. Poker is such a game situation because it involves a strategy of reacting to the actions of others.

Cooperative game 
A game in which the players explicity cooperate to make themselves better off. As applied to firms, it involves companies colluding in order to make higher than competitive rates of return.

Noncooperative game 
A game in which the players neither negotiate nor cooperate in any way. As applied to firms in an industry, this is the common situation in which there are relatively few firms and each has some ability to change price.

Some Basic Notions About Game Theory

Games can be either cooperative or noncooperative. If firms get together to collude or form a cartel, that is considered a **cooperative game.** Whenever it is too costly for firms to negotiate such collusive agreements and to enforce them, they are in a **noncooperative game** situation. Most strategic behavior in the marketplace would be described as a noncooperative game.

Games can be classified by whether the payoffs are negative, zero, or positive. A **zero-sum game** is one in which one player's losses are offset by another player's gains; at any time, sum totals are zero. If two retailers have an absolutely fixed total number of customers, the customers that one retailer wins over are exactly equal to the customers that the other retailer loses. A **negative-sum game** is one in which players as a group lose at the end of the game (although one perhaps by more than the other, and it's possible for one or more players to win). A **positive-sum game** is one in which players as a group end up better off. Some economists describe all voluntary exchanges as positive-sum games. After an exchange, both the buyer and the seller are better off than they were prior to the exchange.

Zero-sum game 
A game in which any gains within the group are exactly offset by equal losses by the end of the game.

Negative-sum game 
A game in which players as a group lose at the end of the game.

Positive-sum game 
A game in which players as a group are better off at the end of the game.

Strategies in Noncooperative Games. Players, such as decision makers in oligopolistic firms, have to devise a **strategy,** which is defined as a rule used to make a choice. The goal of the decision maker is to devise a strategy that is more successful than alternative strategies. Whenever a firm's decision makers can come up with certain strategies that are generally successful no matter what actions competitors take, these are called **dominant strategies.** The dominant strategy always yields the unique best action for the decision maker no matter what action the other "players" undertake. Relatively few business decision makers over a long period of time have successfully devised dominant strategies. We know this by observation: Few firms in oligopolistic industries have maintained relatively high profits consistently over time.

Strategy 
Any rule that is used to make a choice, such as "Always pick heads"; any potential choice that can be made by players in a game.

Dominant strategies 
Strategies that always yield the highest benefit. Regardless of what other players do, a dominant strategy will yield the most benefit for the player using it.

EXAMPLE

The Prisoners' Dilemma

One real-world example of game theory occurs when two people involved in a bank robbery are caught. What should they do when questioned by police? The result has been called the **prisoners' dilemma.** The two suspects, Sam and Carol, are interrogated separately (they cannot communicate with each other) and are given various alternatives. The interrogator indicates to Sam and Carol the following:

1. If both confess to the bank robbery, they will both go to jail for five years.
2. If neither confesses, they will each be given a sentence of two years on a lesser charge.
3. If one prisoner turns state's evidence and confesses, that prisoner goes free and the other one, who did not confess, will serve 10 years on bank robbery charges.

You can see the prisoners' alternatives in the **payoff matrix** in Figure 25-3. The two possibilities for each prisoner are "confess" and "don't confess." There are four possibilities:

1. Both confess.
2. Neither confesses.
3. Sam confesses (turns state's evidence) but Carol doesn't.
4. Carol confesses (turns state's evidence) but Sam doesn't.

In Figure 25-3, all of Sam's possible outcomes are shown on the upper half of each rectangle, and all of Carol's possible outcomes are shown on the lower half.

By looking at the payoff matrix, you can see that if Carol confesses, Sam's best strategy is to confess also—he'll get only 5 years instead of 10. Conversely, if Sam confesses, Carol's best strategy is also to confess—she'll get 5 years instead of 10. Now let's say that Sam is being interrogated and Carol doesn't confess. Sam's best strategy is still to confess, because then he goes free instead of serving two years. Conversely, if Carol is being interrogated, her best strategy is still to confess even if Sam hasn't. She'll go free instead of serving 10 years. To confess is a dominant strategy for Sam. To confess is also a dominant strategy for Carol. The situation is exactly symmetrical. So this is the prisoners' dilemma. The prisoners know that both of them will be better off if neither confesses. Yet it is in each individual prisoner's interest to confess, even though the *collective* outcome of each prisoner's pursuing his or her own interest is inferior for both.

For Critical Analysis

Can you apply the prisoners' dilemma to the firms in a two-firm industry that agree to share market sales equally? (Hint: Think about the payoff to cheating on the market-sharing agreement.)

FIGURE 25-3

The Prisoners' Dilemma Payoff Matrix

Regardless of what the other prisoner does, each person is better off if he or she confesses. So confessing is the dominant strategy and each ends up behind bars for five years.

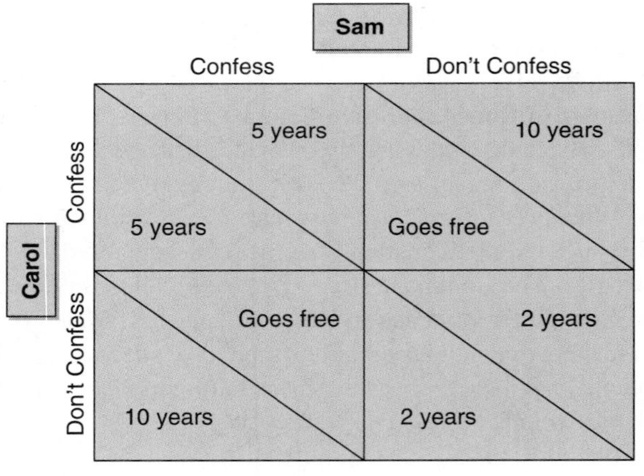

Prisoners' dilemma

A famous strategic game in which two prisoners have a choice between confessing and not confessing to a crime. If neither confesses, they serve a minimum sentence. If both confess, they serve a maximum sentence. If one confesses and the other doesn't, the one who confesses goes free. The dominant strategy is always to confess.

Payoff matrix 

A matrix of outcomes, or consequences, of the strategies available to the players in a game.

Applying Game Theory to Pricing Strategies

We can apply game strategy to two firms—oligopolists—that have to decide on their pricing strategy. Each can choose either a high or a low price. Their payoff matrix is shown in Figure 25-4. If they each choose high prices, they can each make $6 million, but if they each choose low prices, they will only make $4 million each. If one sets a high price and the other a low one, the low-priced firm will make $8 million, but the high-priced firm will only make $2 million. As in the prisoners' dilemma, in the absence of collusion, they will end up choosing low prices.

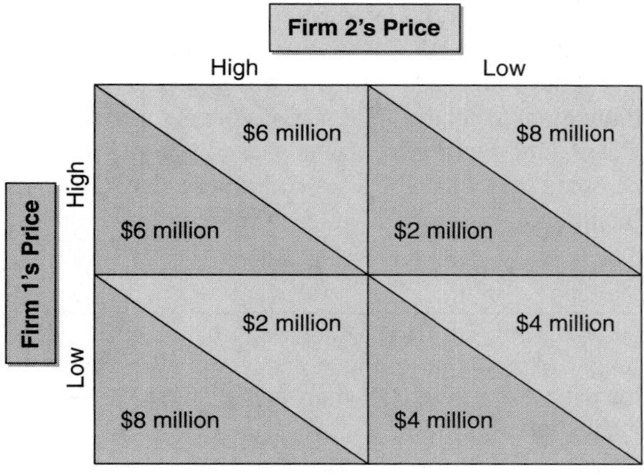

FIGURE 25-4
Game Theory and Pricing Strategies
This payoff matrix shows that if both oligopolists choose a high price, each makes $6 million. If they both choose a low price, each makes $4 million. If one chooses a low price and the other doesn't, the low-priced firm will make $8 million. Unless they collude, however, they will end up at the low-priced solution.

Opportunistic Behavior 

In the prisoners' dilemma, it was clear that cooperative behavior—both parties standing firm without admitting to anything—leads to the best outcome for both players. But each prisoner (player) stands to gain by cheating. Such action is called **opportunistic behavior.** Our daily economic activities involve the equivalent of the prisoners' dilemma all the time. We could engage in opportunistic behavior. You could write a check for a purchase knowing that it is going to bounce because you have just closed that bank account. When you agree to perform a specific task for pay, you could perform your work in a substandard way. When you go to buy an item, the seller might be able to cheat you by selling you a defective item.

Opportunistic behavior 
Actions that ignore the possible long-run benefits of cooperation and focus solely on short-run gains.

In short, if all of us—sellers and buyers—engaged in opportunistic behavior all of the time, we would always end up in the upper left-hand box of the prisoners' dilemma payoff matrix in Figure 25-3. We would constantly be acting in a world of noncooperative behavior. That is not the world in which most of us live, however. Why not? Because most of us engage in *repeat transactions.* Manufacturers would like us to keep purchasing their products. Sellers would like us to keep coming back to their stores. As a seller of labor services, each of us would like to keep our jobs, get promotions, or be hired away by another firm at a higher wage rate. We engage in a **tit-for-tat strategic behavior.** In tit-for-tat strategy, manufacturers and sellers continue to guarantee their merchandise, in spite of cheating by a small percentage of consumers.

Strategic Behavior
Practice applying game theory.

Tit-for-tat strategic behavior 
In game theory, cooperation that continues so long as the other players continue to cooperate.

INTERNATIONAL EXAMPLE

Strategically Relating Loan Subsidies to Nuclear Weapons

Companies are not the only entities that can engage in opportunistic behavior. Nations can do so, too, particularly in their interactions with international agencies such as the International Monetary Fund (IMF). The IMF routinely offers loans to developing countries and to nations that suffer foreign exchange crises. Typically, the IMF grants loans only after receiving promises of "economic self-discipline." The IMF might require, for instance, that a nation reduce its inflation rate, cut its fiscal deficit, improve its legal system, and so on. That is the tack the IMF took when it loaned Pakistan $1.6 billion in the latter part of the 1990s. In 1999, the IMF discovered that in 1998 and 1999 the Pakistani government fudged its budget deficit figures to hide

$2 billion in government spending. Much of this spending was directed toward Pakistan's military budget, including development of nuclear weapons.

From July 1999 to the spring of 2000, the IMF withheld loan installments from the Pakistani government. Soon the government of Pakistan found itself facing default on its debt. The country's military government was already struggling to deal with declines in national saving, investment, exports, and output, and the nation only had sufficient foreign exchange reserves to cover six weeks of imports. Faced with a weakening economy, Pakistan's military leaders began to hint that they might forgo more nuclear tests if Western governments, which fund the IMF, encouraged the international agency to back a debt-rescheduling plan for Pakistan. The IMF gave Pakistan a reprieve until 2001, which gave its leaders some breathing room to get the government's budget in order.

Pakistani government officials acted opportunistically toward the IMF. They did so because they knew they could get away with it, at least for a while.

For Critical Analysis

Why might a foreign government engage in more opportunistic behavior with the IMF than it would with a private lending institution?

PRICE RIGIDITY AND THE KINKED DEMAND CURVE

Let's hypothesize that the decision makers in an oligopolistic firm assume that rivals will react in the following way: They will match all price decreases (in order not to be undersold) but not price increases (because they want to capture more business). There is no collusion. The implications of this reaction function are rigid prices and a kinked demand curve.

Nature of the Kinked Demand Curve

In Figure 25-5, we draw a kinked demand curve, which is implicit in the assumption that oligopolists match price decreases but not price increases. We start off at a given price of P_0 and assume that the quantity demanded at the price for this individual oligopolist is q_0. The starting price of P_0 is usually the stable market price. If the oligopolist assumes that rivals will not react, it faces demand curve d_1d_1 with marginal revenue curve MR_1. Conversely, if it assumes that rivals will react, it faces demand curve d_2d_2 with marginal revenue curve MR_2. More than likely, the oligopoly firm will assume that if it lowers price, rivals will react by matching that reduction to avoid losing their respective shares of the market. The oligopolist that initially lowers its price will not greatly increase its quantity demanded. So when it lowers its price, it believes that it will face demand curve d_2d_2. But if it increases price above P_0, rivals will probably not follow suit. Thus a higher price than P_0 will cause quantity demanded to decrease rapidly. The demand schedule to the left of and above point E will be relatively elastic, as represented by d_1d_1. At prices above P_0, the relevant demand curve is d_1d_1, whereas below price P_0, the relevant demand curve will be d_2d_2. Consequently, at point E there will be a *kink* in the resulting demand curve. This is shown in panel (b) of Figure 25-5, where the demand curve is labeled d_1d_2. The resulting marginal revenue curve is labeled MR_1MR_2. It has a discontinuous portion, or gap, represented by the boldfaced dashed vertical lines in both panels.

Price Rigidity

The kinked demand curve analysis may help explain why price changes might be infrequent in an oligopolistic industry without collusion. Each oligopolist can see only harm in a price change: If price is increased, the oligopolist will lose many of its customers to rivals

FIGURE 25-5

The Kinked Demand Curve

If the oligopolist firm assumes that rivals will not match price changes, it faces demand curve d_1d_1 and marginal revenue curve MR_1. If it assumes that rivals will match price changes, it faces demand curve d_2d_2 and marginal revenue curve MR_2. If the oligopolist believes that rivals will not react to price increases but will react to price decreases, at prices above P_0 it faces demand curve d_1d_1 and at prices below P_0 it faces the other demand curve, d_2d_2. The overall demand curve will therefore have a kink, as is seen in panel (b) at price P_0. The marginal revenue curve will have a vertical break, as shown by the dashed line in panel (b).

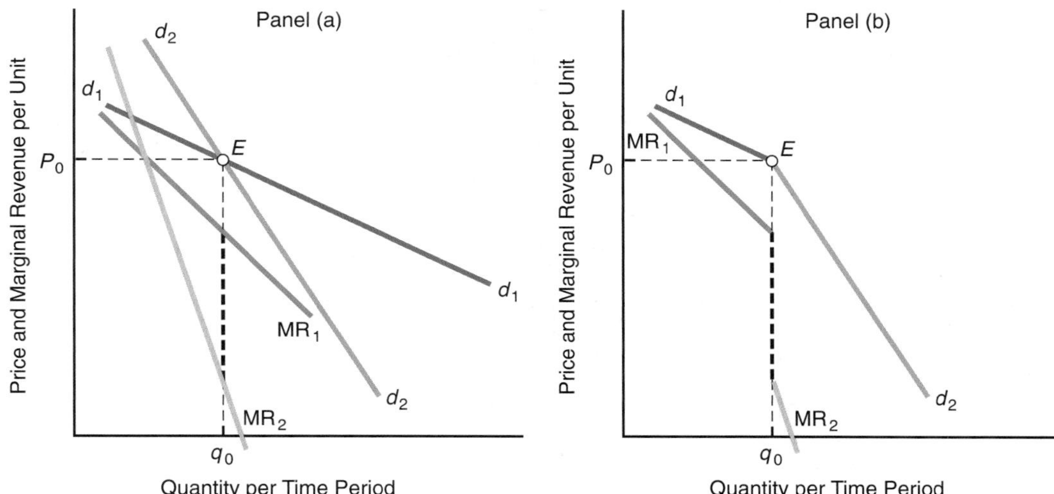

who do not raise their prices. That is to say, the oligopolist moves up from point *E* along demand curve d_1 in panel (b) of Figure 25-5. However, if an oligopolist lowers its price, given that rivals will lower their prices too, its sales will not increase very much. Moving down from point *E* in panel (b) of Figure 25-5, we see that the demand curve is relatively inelastic. If the elasticity is less than 1, total revenues will fall rather than rise with the lowering of price. Given that the production of a larger output will increase total costs, the oligopolist's profits will fall. The lowering of price by the oligopolist might start a *price war* in which its rival firms will charge an even lower price.

The theoretical reason for price inflexibility under the kinked demand curve model has to do with the discontinuous portion of the marginal revenue curve shown in panel (b) of Figure 25-5, which we reproduce in Figure 25-6. Assume that marginal cost is represented by MC. The profit-maximizing rate of output is q_0, which can be sold at a price of P_0. Now assume that the marginal cost curve rises to MC′. What will happen to the profit-maximizing rate of output? Nothing. Both quantity and price will remain the same for this oligopolist.

Remember that the profit-maximizing rate of output is where marginal revenue equals marginal cost. The shift in the marginal cost curve to MC′ does not change the profit-maximizing rate of output in Figure 25-6 because MC′ still cuts the marginal revenue curve in the latter's discontinuous portion. Thus the equality between marginal revenue and marginal cost still holds at output rate q_0 even when the marginal cost curve shifts upward. What will happen when marginal costs fall to MC″? Nothing. This oligopolist will continue to produce at a rate of output q_0 and charge a price of P_0. Whenever the marginal cost curve cuts the discontinuous portion of the marginal revenue curve, fluctuations (within limits) in marginal cost will not affect output or price because the profit-maximizing condition MR = MC will hold. The result

FIGURE 25-6

Changes in Cost May Not Alter the Profit-Maximizing Price and Output

As long as the marginal cost curve intersects the marginal revenue curve in the latter's discontinuous portion, the profit-maximizing price P_0 (and output q_0) will remain unchanged even with changes in MC. (However, the firm's rate of profit will change.)

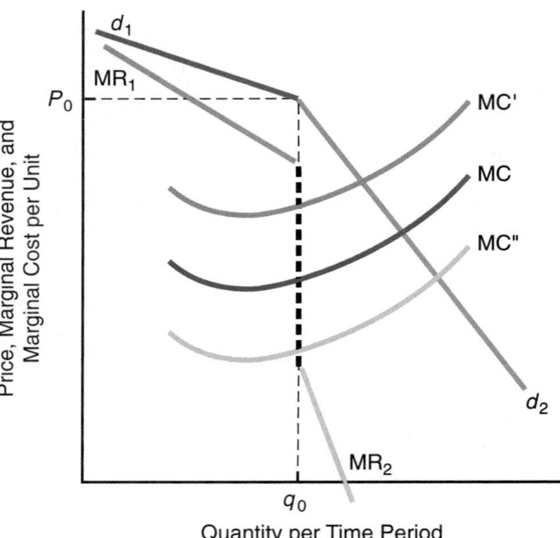

is that even when firms in an oligopolistic industry such as this experience increases or decreases in costs, their prices do not change as long as MC cuts MR in the discontinuous portion. Hence prices are seen to be rigid in oligopolistic industries if oligopolists react the way we assume they do in this model.

Criticisms of the Kinked Demand Curve

One of the criticisms directed against the kinked demand curve is that we have no idea how the existing price, P_0, came to be. If every oligopolistic firm faced a kinked demand curve, it would not pay for it to change prices. The problem is that the kinked demand curve does not show us how demand and supply originally determine the going price of an oligopolist's product.

As far as the evidence goes, it is not encouraging. Oligopoly prices do not appear to be as rigid, particularly in the upward direction, as the kinked demand curve theory implies. During the 1970s and early 1980s, when prices in the economy were rising overall, oligopolistic producers increased their prices frequently. Evidence of price changes during the Great Depression showed that oligopolies changed prices much more frequently than monopolies.

EXAMPLE

Do Pet Products Have Nine Lives?

H. J. Heinz's Pet Products Company knows all about the kinked demand curve. It makes 9-Lives cat food. To meet increased competition (at lower prices) from Nestlé, Quaker, Grand Metropolitan, and Mars, Heinz dropped prices by over 22 percent on the wholesale price of a case of 9-Lives. Finally, it had "had enough." It decided to buck the trend by *raising* prices. The result? A disaster, because none of Heinz's four major competitors increased their prices. Heinz's market share dropped from 23 percent to 15 percent almost overnight.

For Critical Analysis

What does Heinz's experience with 9-Lives perhaps suggest about the price elasticity of demand for its product?

CONCEPTS IN BRIEF

- Each oligopolist has a reaction function because oligopolistic competitors are interdependent. They must therefore engage in strategic behavior. One way to model this behavior is to use game theory.
- Games can be either cooperative or noncooperative. A cartel is cooperative. When a cartel breaks down and its members start cheating, the industry becomes a noncooperative game. In a zero-sum game, one player's losses are exactly offset by another player's gains. In a negative-sum game, all players collectively lose, perhaps one more than the others. In a positive-sum game, the players as a group end up better off.
- Decision makers in oligopolistic firms must devise a strategy. A dominant strategy is one that is generally successful no matter what actions competitors take.
- The kinked demand curve oligopoly model predicts that major shifts in marginal cost will cause any change in industry price.

STRATEGIC BEHAVIOR WITH IMPLICIT COLLUSION: A MODEL OF PRICE LEADERSHIP

What if oligopolists do not actually collude to raise prices and share markets but do so implicitly? There are no formal cartel arrangements and no formal meetings. Nonetheless, there is *tacit collusion.* One example of this is the model of **price leadership.**

Price leadership 
A practice in many oligopolistic industries in which the largest firm publishes its price list ahead of its competitors, who then match those announced prices. Also called *parallel pricing.*

In this model, the basic assumption is that the dominant firm, usually the biggest, sets the price and allows other firms to sell all they can at that price. The dominant firm then sells the rest. The dominant firm always makes the first move in a price leadership model. By definition, price leadership requires that one firm be the leader. Because of laws against collusion, firms in an industry cannot communicate this directly. That is why it is often natural for the largest firm to become the price leader. In the automobile industry during the period of General Motors' dominance (until the 1980s), that company was traditionally the price leader. At various times in the breakfast food industry, Kellogg was the price leader. Some observers have argued that Harvard University was once the price leader among Ivy League schools. In the banking industry, various dominant banks have been price leaders in announcing changes in the prime rate, the interest rate charged on loans offered to the best credit risks. One day a large New York–based bank, such as Chase Manhattan, would announce an increase or decrease in its prime rate. Five or six hours later, all other banks would announce the same change in their prime rate.

Price Wars

Price leadership may not always work. If the price leader ends up much better off than the firms that follow, the followers may in fact not set prices according to those set by the dominant firm. The result may be a **price war.** The dominant firm lowers its prices a little bit, but the other firms lower theirs even more. Price wars have occurred in many industries. Supermarkets within a given locale often engage in price wars, especially during holiday periods. One may offer turkeys at so much per pound on Wednesday; competing stores cut their price on turkeys on Thursday, so the first store cuts its price even more on Friday. We see price wars virtually every year in the airline industry.

Price war 
A pricing campaign designed to capture additional market share by repeatedly cutting prices.

EXAMPLE

Cigarette Price Wars

Price wars occur commonly between long-distance telephone companies, between airlines, and between the makers of cigarettes, soft drinks, computer disc drives, diapers, frozen dinners, and personal computer hardware and software. They do not always lead to the desired result for the company that started the price war. Consider the case of Philip Morris, which cut the price of Marlboro cigarettes by 40 cents a pack to about $1.80. Its main competitor, RJR Nabisco, matched the price cut for Camels. Philip Morris claimed victory because Marlboro's market share increased from 22.1 percent to 27.3 percent. But the domestic operating profits for both companies plummeted in the process; so, too, did the trading value of their stocks. According to business consultants Mike Marn and Robert Garda of McKinsey & Company, the reason is that most companies are unable to offset lower prices with higher volume because variable costs do not start falling until sales increase by about 20 percent. When Philip Morris cut its prices by 18 percent, unit sales increased by only 12.5 percent and profits fell by 25 percent.

For Critical Analysis

How do price wars fit into the tit-for-tat strategic behavior of game theory?

DETERRING ENTRY INTO AN INDUSTRY

Some economists believe that all decision making by existing firms in a stable industry involves some type of game playing. An important part of game playing does not have to do with how existing competitors might react to a decision by others. Rather, it has to do with how *potential* competitors might react. Strategic decision making requires that existing firms in an industry come up with strategies to deter entrance into that industry. One important way is, of course, to get a local, state, or federal government to restrict entry. Adopting certain pricing and investment strategies may also deter entry.

Increasing Entry Costs

Entry deterrence strategy
Any strategy undertaken by firms in an industry, either individually or together, with the intent or effect of raising the cost of entry into the industry by a new firm.

One **entry deterrence strategy** is to raise the cost of entry by a new firm. The threat of a price war is one technique. To sustain a long price war, existing firms might invest in excess capacity so that they can expand output if necessary. When existing firms invest in excess capacity, they are signaling potential competitors that they will engage in a price war.

Another way that existing domestic firms can raise the entry cost of foreign firms is by getting the U.S. government to pass stringent environmental or health and safety standards. These typically raise costs more for foreign producers, often in developing countries, than for domestic producers.

EXAMPLE

Should Hair Braiders Be Licensed?

Many service industries have raised entry costs by getting legislation passed that requires extensive training and licensing before someone can enter the industry. Physicians and lawyers are good examples. Less well known are the high entry costs imposed on individuals who wish to give therapeutic massages or trim and style hair. For example, in California, a license to style hair requires the expenditure of about $6,000 for 1,600 hours of cosmetology classes. Hairstylists in California spend about $600 million a year on classes and test administration fees.

Enter hair braiders, who are hairstylists for the African-American community. Individuals entering this business long assumed that because they use no chemicals, they would not be required to take extensive classes in the use of chemicals. But the California Barbering and Cosmetology Board has recently ruled otherwise. Given that there are about 10,000 hair braiders in America, this issue affects more than California. Currently, there are several lawsuits challenging the licensing requirement for hair braiders. Hair braiders offer a lower-cost alternative to regular beauty salons, and the latter are fighting to prevent this new competition.

For Critical Analysis

Besides currently licensed hairstylists, who else might favor required cosmetology licensing for hair braiders?

Limit-Pricing Strategies

Sometimes existing firms will make it clear to potential competitors that the existing firms would not change their output rate if new firms were to enter the industry. Instead, the existing firms would simply lower the market price (moving down their demand curves) enough to sell the same quantity as they currently do. This new price would be below the level at which an entering firm could earn a normal profit, and that prospect effectively discourages entry. This is called the **limit-pricing model.**

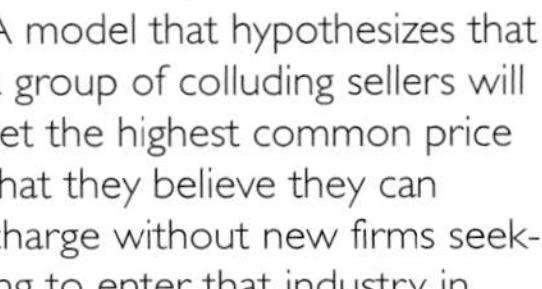

Limit-pricing model
A model that hypothesizes that a group of colluding sellers will set the highest common price that they believe they can charge without new firms seeking to enter that industry in search of relatively high profits.

EXAMPLE

Giving Away Services on the Web: Thwarting an Emerging Rival, Limit Pricing, or Both?

eBay, the Internet auctioneer, earns revenues by assessing commissions based on sales prices. It is a popular site for selling anything from concert tickets to computers to antiques. It is so popular, in fact, that some businesses began to run ads on eBay's Web site because they knew so many people were visiting it. That is how eBay got into the Web advertisement business.

This development alarmed Yahoo! and other Internet search engines because it constituted a threat to a core part of their business. People who use Yahoo!, for example, are exposed to the ads on its site, ads that generate significant revenues for Yahoo!. Yahoo! felt it had to make a strategic response. So it began to offer free auction services. Although Yahoo! leaves it to buyers and sellers to finalize agreements, its service performs the basic auctioneer function of matching the two. Launching this free service allowed Yahoo! to establish an initial presence in the market for on-line auctions. At the same time, however, it established a limit price of zero for other firms that might contemplate becoming auctioneers as a means of horning in on its bread-and-butter on-line advertising business.

In spite of Yahoo!'s action and competition from other Internet sellers such as Onsale.com and Amazon.com, eBay remains the most popular auction site on the Internet. Most observers agree that its popularity is the key to its success, because when sellers list items in auctions, they want to be certain that there will be lots of potential buyers. In addition, eBay continues to provide a wider range of auctioneering services.

For Critical Analysis

How can eBay continue to charge auction commissions while Yahoo! offers its auction services at no charge?

Doesn't a company like Amazon.com have to be really big before it can sell books on the Net at discounted prices?

No, as demonstrated by Lyle Bowlin of the University of Northern Iowa. He is a book lover who decided to contact the same wholesalers from whom Amazon buys the books that it markets. Bowlin learned that to get essentially the same volume discounts that Amazon gets, he had to buy only five copies of each book he ordered. He calculated that if he maintained a Web site, his daughter did his accounting, and his wife handled the shipping, he could beat Amazon's prices. Soon he had gotten into the Internet bookselling business himself, with customers in half the U.S. states and Canada.

Raising Customers' Switching Costs

If an existing firm can make it more costly for customers to switch from its product or service to a competitor's, the existing firm can deter entry. There are a host of ways in which existing firms can raise customers' switching costs. Makers of computer equipment have in the past produced operating systems and software that would not run on competitors' computers. Any customer wanting to change from one computer system to another faced a high switching cost.

CONCEPTS IN BRIEF

- One type of strategic behavior involving implicit collusion is price leadership. The dominant firm is assumed to set the price and then allows other firms to sell all that they want to sell at that price. Whatever is left over is sold by the dominant firm. The dominant firm always makes the first move in a price leadership model. If the nondominant firms decide to compete, they may start a price war.
- One strategic decision may be to attempt to raise the cost of entry of new firms into an industry. The threat of a price war is one technique. Another is to lobby the federal government to pass stringent environmental or health and safety standards in an attempt to keep out foreign competition.
- If existing firms limit prices to a level above competitive prices before entry but are willing to reduce it, this is called a limit-pricing model.
- Another way to raise the cost to new firms is to make it more costly for customers to switch from one product or service to a competitor's.

COMPARING MARKET STRUCTURES

Now that we have looked at perfect competition, pure monopoly, monopolistic competition, and oligopoly, we are in a position to compare the attributes of these four different market structures. We do this in summary form in Table 25-3, in which we compare the number of sellers, their ability to set price, and whether product differentiation exists, and we give some examples of each of the four market structures.

TABLE 25-3
Comparing Market Structures

Market Structure	Number of Sellers	Unrestricted Entry and Exit	Ability to Set Price	Long-Run Economic Profits Possible	Product Differentiation	Nonprice Competition	Examples
Perfect competition	Numerous	Yes	None	No	None	None	Agriculture, coal
Monopolistic competition	Many	Yes	Some	No	Considerable	Yes	Toothpaste, toilet paper, soap, retail trade
Oligopoly	Few	Partial	Some	Yes	Frequent	Yes	Cigarettes, steel
Pure monopoly	One	No (for entry)	Consider-able	Yes	None (product is unique)	Yes	Some electric companies, some local telephone companies

NETNOMICS

Will Shopbots Make Internet Sellers More Competitive, or Will They Make the Kinked Demand Curve More Relevant?

Shopbots are software programs that consumers can use to search the Net for the best prices. Most observers have argued that they will be a boon for consumers. Enthusiasts contend that by enabling consumers to flock to Web sites that post the lowest prices, shopbots encourage firms to keep their prices at the marginal cost of production. Any Internet seller that tries to raise its price above this level would lose customers rapidly, they argue.

Hal Varian, an economist at the University of California at Berkeley, thinks that the story isn't quite so simple. He points out that there is nothing to stop Internet sellers from using shopbot programs, too. Indeed, some firms are already programming shopbots to keep tabs on the Web sites of rival sellers, permitting them to respond almost instantaneously to price cuts by competitors. If all rivals in the marketplace follow the same strategy—and know that they do—then the price rigidity predicted by the kinked demand curve can arise. Price can then exceed marginal and average cost, and Internet-based oligopolists will be able to earn economic profits.

Varian argues that which outcome eventually prevails depends on whether consumers or producers move faster in spotting and responding to price differences. In his view, there is good reason to think that consumers will be at a disadvantage in this regard. They will unleash their shopbots only when they happen to be shopping for a specific item. But producers will keep their shopbots busy checking out rivals' prices. A number of Internet sellers, for instance, engage in real-time monitoring of the Web sites of their competitors and automatically match any price cut.

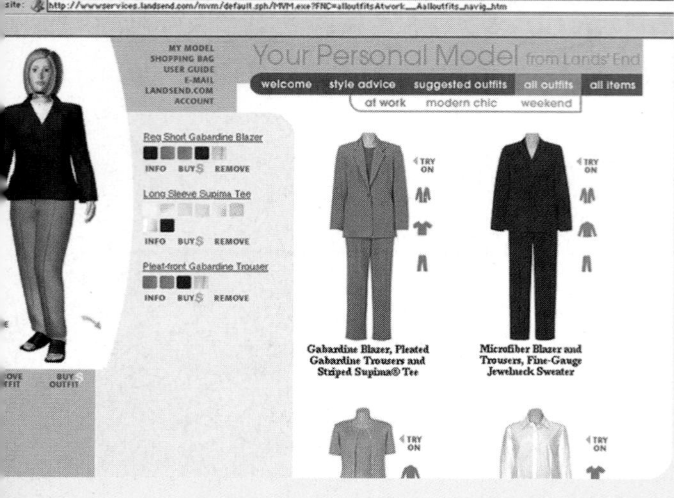

ISSUES & APPLICATIONS

Product Differentiation on the Web

"To do it well is worth millions." This is one marketing specialist's evaluation of the gain from making a big splash on the Internet. As the older mass media of print, radio, and television have become more fragmented, building brands via these advertising vehicles is difficult. For companies whose product lines "grew up" with television, solving the puzzle of marketing on the Net may be the key to continued success or ultimate failure amid an array of competing brand names.

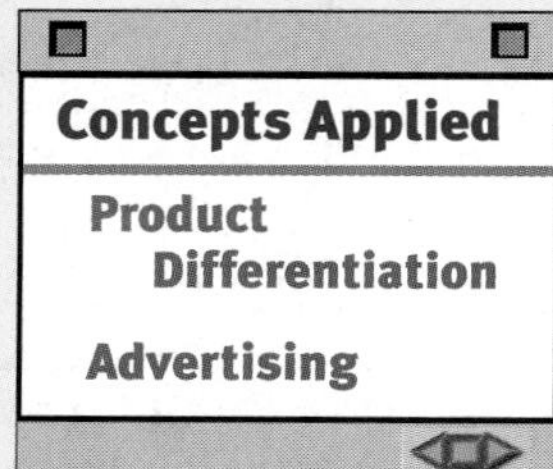

Learning from Current and Past Successes

Some Internet-based companies have scored huge successes. Notable examples are America Online and Yahoo!, which within a few years catapulted into the top echelons of American business. For these companies, forging a recognized brand name has been crucial. Because their actual and potential customers evaluate their products by viewing images in small spaces on flat computer screens, these firms have spent fortunes—and gained even greater fortunes in return—finding ways to make themselves into household names.

One lesson from these successes is that in cyberspace, anybody with sufficient resources to purchase space on a server and build some brand recognition is a potentially threatening rival. Both old companies trying to develop an Internet presence and new Internet start-ups have found that one route to success is to emulate successful firms on the Net. It is no accident, for instance, that the Web site of Barnes & Noble, a traditional bookseller, and Books.com, the Net-based rival Barnes & Noble gobbled up, looked so much like the Amazon.com site. The people at Amazon.com discovered a successful way to sell books on the Net, and its rivals copied that proven strategy.

Another lesson learned by companies hoping to market their brands on the Net is that just posting a Web site full of colorful banners does not necessarily attract customers. Cyberspace can be a lonely place when there are only a few routes to a Web site. Taking out ad space on search engines is one way to attract attention to a company's Web site. Another, however, is to use the old-fashioned communications media. Amazon.com, for instance, advertises heavily in print and on television.

The Key to Internet Selling: Give People Something to Do

Some old approaches have not panned out, however. For instance, Bell Atlantic Corporation tried running a weekly soap opera on its Web site. It couldn't find much evidence that anyone tuned in, and within weeks the soap opera was history.

What Bell Atlantic and other companies have discovered is that potential customers watch television to be passively entertained, but they surf the Internet to *do* something. This is why Lands' End provides on-line birthday reminder services, Macy's offers personal shopping assistance via e-mail, and Toys 'Я' Us provides a Web gift registry for kids with upcoming birthdays. The importance of activity-based selling on the Internet may be bad news for makers of packaged and bottled goods. Consider the example of Coca-Cola, which developed a Cherrycoke.com Web site as an entertainment gateway to interesting Web sites. The company discovered that the average visitor to the site spent no more than 90 seconds there before surfing away. For sellers of soda pop, finding something useful for Web surfers to do while they learn about a brand may prove to be a real challenge.

FOR CRITICAL ANALYSIS

1. McDonald's has a Web site with financial data, kids' games, and maps displaying locations of its stores. In what ways is this a potentially successful way to market hamburgers?
2. How might a breakfast cereal manufacturer effectively promote its brands on the Internet?

SUMMARY DISCUSSION OF LEARNING OBJECTIVES

1. **The Key Characteristics of a Monopolistically Competitive Industry:** A monopolistically competitive industry consists of a large number of firms that sell differentiated products that are close substitutes. Firms can easily enter or exit a monopolistically competitive industry. Because monopolistically competitive firms can increase their profits if they can successfully distinguish their products from those of their rivals, they have an incentive to engage in sales promotions and advertising.
2. **Contrasting the Output and Pricing Decisions of Monopolistically Competitive Firms with Those of Perfectly Competitive Firms:** In the short run, a monopolistically competitive firm produces output to the point where marginal revenue equals marginal cost. The price it charges for this output, which is the maximum price that people are willing to pay as determined by the demand for its product, can exceed both marginal cost and average total cost in the short run, and the resulting economic profits can induce new firms to enter the industry. As they do, existing firms in the industry experience declines in the demand for their products and reduce their prices to the point at which price equals average total cost. In the long run, therefore, monopolistically competitive firms, like perfectly competitive firms, earn zero economic profits. In contrast to perfectly competitive firms, however, price still exceeds marginal cost in the long-run equilibrium for monopolistically competitive firms.
3. **The Fundamental Characteristics of Oligopoly:** Economies of scale, certain barriers to entry, and horizontal mergers among firms that sell similar products can result in a few firms' producing the bulk of an industry's total output, which is a situation of oligopoly. To measure the extent to which a few firms account for an industry's production and sales, economists calculate concentration ratios, which are the percentages of total sales or total production by the top handful of firms in an industry. Strategic dependence is an important characteristic of oligopoly. One firm's decisions concerning price, product quality, or advertising can bring about responses by other firms. Thus one firm's choices can affect the prices charged by other firms in the industry.
4. **Applying Game Theory to Evaluate the Pricing Strategies of Oligopolistic Firms:** Game theory is the analytical framework that economists apply to evaluate how two or more individuals, companies, or nations compete for payoffs that depend on the strategies that others employ. When firms get together to collude or form a cartel, they participate in cooperative games, but when they cannot work together, they engage in noncooperative games. One important type of game often applied to oligopoly situations is the prisoners' dilemma, in which inability to cooperate in determining prices of their products can cause firms to choose lower prices than they otherwise would prefer.
5. **The Kinked Demand Theory of Oligopolistic Price Rigidity:** If an oligopolistic firm believes that no other firms selling similar products will raise their prices in response to an increase in the price of its product, it perceives the demand curve for its product to be relatively elastic at prices above the price it currently charges. At the same time, if the firm believes that all other firms would respond to a cut in the price of its product by reducing the prices of their products, it views the demand for its product as relatively inelastic at prices below the current price. Hence in this situation, the firm perceives the demand for its product to be kinked, which means that its marginal revenue curve has a break at the current price. Changes in the firm's marginal cost will therefore not necessarily induce the firm to change its production and pricing decisions, so price rigidity may result.
6. **How Firms May Deter Market Entry by Potential Rivals:** To strategically deter market entry by potential competitors, firms in an industry may seek to raise the entry costs that such potential rivals would face. For example, existing firms may invest in excess productive capacity to signal that they could outlast other firms in sustained price wars, or they might engage in lobbying efforts to forestall competition from potential foreign entrants into domestic markets. Existing firms may also engage in limit pricing, signaling to potential entrants that the entry of new rivals would cause them to reduce prices so low that entering the market is no longer economically attractive. Existing firms may also develop ways to make it difficult for current customers to switch to products produced by new entrants.

Key Terms and Concepts

Concentration ratio (621)
Cooperative game (623)
Dominant strategies (623)
Entry deterrence strategy (630)
Game theory (622)
Horizontal merger (621)
Limit-pricing model (631)
Monopolistic competition (613)
Negative-sum game (623)
Noncooperative game (623)
Oligopoly (619)
Opportunistic behavior (625)
Payoff matrix (624)
Positive-sum game (623)
Price leadership (629)
Price war (629)
Prisoners' dilemma (625)
Product differentiation (614)
Reaction function (623)
Strategic dependence (620)
Strategy (623)
Tit-for-tat strategic behavior (625)
Vertical merger (621)
Zero-sum game (623)

Problems

Answers to the odd-numbered problems appear at the back of the book.

25-1. Explain why the following are examples of monopolistic competition.

a. There are a number of fast-food restaurants in town, and they compete fiercely. Some restaurants cook their hamburgers over open flames. Others fry their hamburgers. In addition, some serve broiled fish sandwiches, while others serve fried fish sandwiches. A few serve ice-cream cones for dessert, while others offer frozen ice-cream pies.

b. There is a vast number of colleges and universities across the country. Each competes for top students. All offer similar courses and programs, but some have better programs in business, while others have stronger programs in the arts and humanities. Still others are academically stronger in the sciences.

25-2. A father goes to the pharmacy late at night for cold medicine for a sick child. There are many liquid cold medicines, each of which has almost exactly the same ingredients. Yet medicines with brand names that the man recognizes from television commercials sell for more than the generic versions. Explain, in economic terms, this perplexing situation to the father.

25-3. The following table depicts the prices and total costs a local used bookstore faces. The bookstore competes with a number of similar stores, but it capitalizes on its location and the word-of-mouth reputation of the coffee it serves to its customers.

Output	Price per Book ($)	Total Costs ($)
0	6.00	2.00
1	5.75	5.00
2	5.50	7.50
3	5.25	9.50
4	5.00	10.50
5	4.75	12.50
6	4.50	15.00
7	4.00	18.00

Calculate the store's total revenue, total profit, marginal revenue, and marginal cost. Based on marginal analysis, what is the profit-maximizing level of output for this business?

25-4. Calculate average total costs for the bookstore in Problem 25-3. Illustrate the store's short-run situation by plotting demand, marginal revenue, average total costs, and marginal costs. What is its total profit?

25-5. Suppose that after long-run adjustments take place in the used book market, the business in Problem 25-3 ends up producing 4 units of output. What are the market price and economic profits of this monopolistic competitor in the long run?

25-6. The soft drink market is dominated by a very small number of firms that produce a wide spectrum of drinks and spend vast amounts on advertising. There is very little variation in the prices charged by the leading companies. What is likely to happen if the number one company runs a major new ad campaign and reduces its prices by 5 percent?

25-7. Characterize the followwing examples as a positive-sum game, zero-sum game, or negative-sum game.

a. You play a card game in your dorm room with three other students. Each player brings $5 to the game.

b. Two nations exchange goods in a mutually beneficial transaction.

c. A thousand people buy $1 lottery tickets with a single payoff of $800.

25-8. Last weekend, Bob attended the university football game. At the opening kickoff, the crowd stood up. Bob, therefore, had to stand up as well in order to see the game. For the crowd, not the football team, explain the outcomes of a cooperative game and a noncooperative game. Explain what Bob's "tit-for-tat strategic behavior" would be.

25-9. One of the three shops on campus that sell university logo clothing has found that if it sells a sweatshirt for $30 or more, the other two shops keep their prices constant and the store loses money. If, however, the shop reduces its price below $30, the other stores react by lowering their prices. What kind of market structure does this store face? If the store's marginal costs fluctuate up and down very slightly, how should the store adjust its prices?

25-10. At the beginning of each semester, the university cafeteria posts the prices of its sandwiches. Business students note that as soon as the university posts these prices, the area delis adjust their prices accordingly. The business students argue that this is price collusion and that the university should be held liable. Are the students correct?

Economics on the Net

Current Concentration Ratios in U.S. Manufacturing Industries As you learned in this chapter, economists typically use concentration ratios to evaluate whether industries are oligopolies. In this application, you will make your own determination using the most recent data available.

Title: Concentration Ratios in Manufacturing

Navigation: Click here to start at the U.S. Census Department's homepage. Click on the letter C in the subject area on the left-hand side of the page. Scroll down to and click on Concentration Ratios. Click on Concentration Ratios in Manufacturing.

Application

1. Find the four-firm concentration ratios for the following industries: milk (2026), women's dresses (2335), greeting cards (2771), plumbing fixtures (3261).
2. Which industries are characterized by a high level of competition? Which industries are characterized by a low level of competition? Which industries qualify as oligopolies?
3. Name some of the firms that operate in the industries that qualify as oligopolies.

For Group Discussion and Analysis Discuss whether the four-industry concentration ratio is a good measure of competition. Consider some of the firms you named in item 3. Do you consider these firms to be "competitive" in their pricing and output decisions? Consider the four-firm concentration ratio for ready-mix concrete (3273). Do you think that on a local basis, this industry is competitive? Why or why not?

CHAPTER

26

REGULATION AND ANTITRUST POLICY IN A WORLD OF MULTINATIONAL FIRMS

This crowd waiting to be checked in is typical at most airports today. Might such increasing numbers of air travelers be related to the deregulation of airfares? How?

The U.S. government has long regulated the airline industry. A key feature of airline regulation is enforcement of safety rules under the auspices of the Federal Aviation Administration. Today, there are no more than 20 to 30 accidents by any aircraft for every 100,000 hours of flight by all U.S. planes.

Passenger safety is not the only motivation for government regulation of airlines. Traditionally, the federal government has also done everything from regulating flight schedules to defining permissible in-flight passenger services. In the late 1970s, the government took a more hands-off approach to such regulation. Recently, however, the Justice Department and the Transportation Department have begun to study whether to regulate airline pricing. Would this be a sensible area for government regulatory involvement? Before you answer this question, you need to know about regulation and antitrust policy.

LEARNING OBJECTIVES

After reading this chapter, you should be able to:

1. **Recognize practical difficulties that arise when regulating the prices charged by natural monopolies**
2. **Explain the main rationales for government regulation of business**
3. **Identify alternative theories aimed at explaining the behavior of regulators**
4. **Describe short-run and long-run economic effects of deregulation**
5. **Understand the foundations of antitrust laws and regulations**
6. **Discuss basic issues that arise in efforts to enforce antitrust laws**

Did You Know That... each year about 75,000 pages of new or modified federal regulations are published? These regulations, found in the *Federal Register,* cover virtually every aspect of the way business can be conducted, products can be built, and services can be offered. In addition, every state and municipality publishes regulations relating to worker safety, restaurant cleanliness, and the number of lights needed in each room in a day-care center. There is no question about it, American business activities are highly regulated. Consequently, how regulators should act to increase economic efficiency and how they actually act are important topics for understanding our economy today. In addition to regulation, the government has one additional weapon to use in its attempts to prevent restraints of trade. It is called antitrust law, and it is the subject of the later part of this chapter.

Let's look first at how government might best regulate a single firm that has obtained a monopoly because of constantly falling long-run average costs, a situation known as a natural monopoly.

Chapter Outline

NATURAL MONOPOLIES REVISITED

You will recall from our discussion of natural monopolies in Chapter 24 that whenever a single firm has the ability to produce all of the industry's output at a lower per-unit cost than other firms attempting to produce less than total industry output, a natural monopoly arises. Natural gas and electric utilities are examples. Long-run average costs for those firms typically fall as output increases. In a natural monopoly, economies of large-scale production dominate, leading to a single-firm industry.

The Pricing and Output Decision of the Natural Monopolist

A monopolist (like any other firm) will set the output rate where marginal revenue is equal to marginal cost. We draw the market demand curve, *D,* and the revenue curve, MR, in panel (a) of Figure 26-1 on page 640. The intersection of the marginal revenue curve and the marginal cost curve is at point *A*. The monopolist would therefore produce quantity Q_m and charge a price of P_m.

What do we know about a monopolist's solution to the price-quantity question? When compared to a competitive situation, we know that consumers end up paying a higher price for the product, and consequently they purchase less of it than they would purchase under competition. The monopoly solution is economically inefficient from society's point of view; the price charged for the product is higher than the opportunity cost to society, and consequently there is a misallocation of resources. That is, the price does not equal the true marginal cost of producing the good because the true marginal cost is at the intersection *A,* not at price P_m.

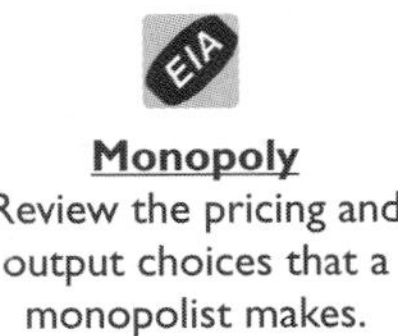

Monopoly
Review the pricing and output choices that a monopolist makes.

Regulating the Natural Monopolist

Assume that the government wants the natural monopolist to produce at an output at which price equals marginal cost, so that the value of the satisfaction that individuals receive from the marginal unit purchased is just equal to the marginal cost to society. Where is that solution in panel (b) of Figure 26-1? It is at the intersection of the marginal cost curve and the demand curve, point *B*. Recall how we derived the competitive industry supply curve. We

FIGURE 26-1

Profit Maximization and Regulation Through Marginal Cost Pricing

The profit-maximizing natural monopolist here would produce at the point in panel (a) where marginal costs equal marginal revenue—that is, at point *A*, which gives the quantity of production Q_m. The price charged would be P_m. If a regulatory commission attempted to regulate natural monopolies so that price equaled long-run marginal cost, the commission would make the monopolist set production at the point where the marginal cost curve intersects the demand schedule. This is shown in panel (b). The quantity produced would be Q_1, and the price would be P_1. However, average costs at Q_1 are equal to AC_1. Losses would ensue, equal to the shaded area. It would be self-defeating for a regulatory commission to force a natural monopolist to produce at an output rate at which MC = *P* without subsidizing some of its costs because losses would eventually drive the natural monopolist out of business.

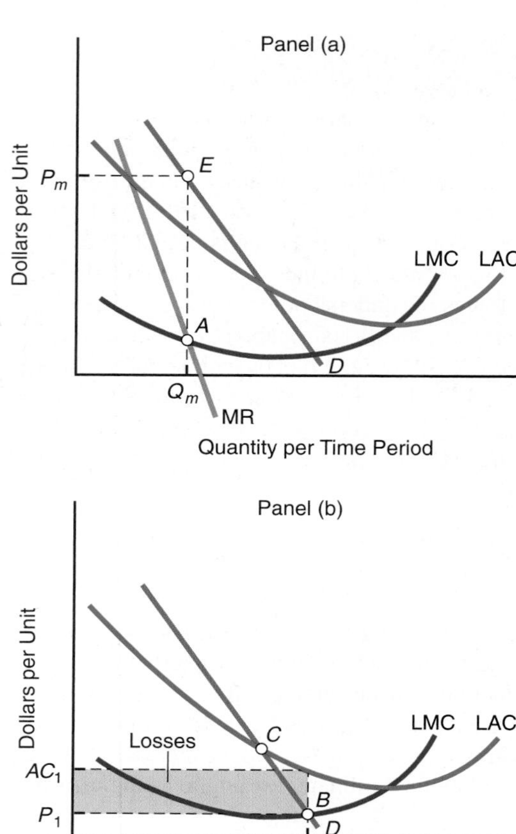

looked at all of the upward-sloping portions of actual and potential firms' marginal cost curves above their respective average variable costs. We then summed all of these portions of the firms' supply curves; that gave us the industry supply curve. We assume that a regulatory commission forces the natural monopolist to engage in marginal cost pricing and hence to produce at quantity Q_1 and to sell the product at price P_1. How large will the monopolist's profits be? Profits, of course, are the *positive* difference between total revenues and total costs. In this case, total revenues equal P_1 times Q_1, and total costs equal average costs times the number of units produced. At Q_1, average cost is equal to AC_1. Average costs are higher than the price that the regulatory commission forces our natural monopolist to charge. Profits turn out to be losses and are equal to the shaded area in panel (b) of Figure 26-1. Thus regulation that forces a natural monopolist to produce and price as if it were in a competitive situation would also force that monopolist into negative profits, or losses. Obviously, the monopolist would rather go out of business than be subject to such regulation.

As a practical matter, then, regulators can't force a natural monopolist to engage in marginal cost pricing. Consequently, regulation of natural monopolies has often taken the form of allowing the regulated natural monopolist to set price where LAC intersects the demand curve *D* at point *C* in panel (b) of Figure 26-1. This is called *average cost pricing*. Average cost includes what the regulators deem a "fair" rate of return on investment.

POLICY EXAMPLE

Power Surges at Electric Utilities: Shocking?

When we discussed natural monopolies, we used a few examples. Panel (a) of Figure 26-1 seems to apply to electric utilities. Technology is changing in that situation, however. Efficient high-voltage transmission lines now exist. This means that the market for electricity generation can transcend local and even national boundaries. This led governments to remove most restrictions on the sale of electric power, thereby permitting competition in the electric utility market. The Department of Energy forecast that by 2010, greater competition in electricity generation could cause the average retail price of electricity to fall to three-fourths of its 1997 level.

Shortly after deregulation began, however, a Midwest heatwave induced two energy-trading companies to default on contracts to deliver electric power to Chicago-based Commonwealth Edison Company. It then had to pay up to $5,000 per megawatt-hour to buy electricity on the spot market—more than 100 times the price that had prevailed during preceding weeks. Commonwealth Edison cut power to manufacturers, and the utility sent out emergency notices prevailing on households to conserve electricity. A number of congressional representatives immediately called for rolling back recent legislation authorizing the new competition in electricity generation.

An interesting thing happened, however. The incident helped convince an independent power producer to invest in a $100 million gas turbine power-generating plant near Chicago. That is, higher electricity prices induced market entry. This reduced the likelihood of a similar problem arising in Chicago in the future. Just as the competition model predicts, price boosts induce new firms to enter the market, which ultimately helps push market prices down toward competitive levels.

For Critical Analysis

Is there really any true natural monopoly left in the world?

CONCEPTS IN BRIEF

- A natural monopoly arises when one firm can produce all of an industry's output at a lower per-unit cost than other firms.
- The first firm to take advantage of the declining long-run average cost curve can undercut the prices of all other sellers, forcing them out of business, thereby obtaining a natural monopoly.
- A natural monopolist allowed to maximize profit will set quantity where marginal revenue equals long-run marginal cost. Price is determined from the demand curve at that quantity.
- A natural monopolist that is forced to set price equal to long-run marginal cost will sustain losses.

REGULATION

The U.S. government began regulating social and economic activity early in the nation's history, but the amount of government regulation has increased in the twentieth century. There are three types of government regulation: regulation of natural monopolies; regulation of inherently competitive industries; and regulation for public welfare across all industries, or so-called social regulation. For example, various state commissions regulate the rates and quality of service of electric power companies, which are considered natural monopolies. Trucking and interstate moving companies are inherently competitive industries but have nonetheless been made subject to government regulation in the past. And federal and state governments impose occupational, health, and safety rules on a wide variety of employers.

Objectives of Economic Regulation

Economic regulation is typically intended to control the prices that regulated enterprises are allowed to charge. Various public utility commissions throughout the United States regulate the rates (prices) of electrical utility companies and some telephone operating companies. This has usually been called rate regulation. The goal of rate regulation has, in principle, been the prevention of both monopoly profits and predatory competition.

Cost-of-service regulation Regulation based on allowing prices to reflect only the actual cost of production and no monopoly profits.

Rate-of-return regulation Regulation that seeks to keep the rate of return in the industry at a competitive level by not allowing excessive prices to be charged.

Two traditional methods of rate regulation have involved cost-of-service regulation and rate-of-return regulation. A regulatory commission using **cost-of-service regulation** allows the regulated companies to charge only prices that reflect the actual average cost of providing the services to the customer. In a somewhat similar vein, regulatory commissions using the **rate-of-return regulation** method allow regulated companies to set prices that ensure a normal, or competitive, rate of return on the investment in the business. We implicitly analyzed these two types of regulation when discussing panel (b) of Figure 26-1. If the long-run average cost curve in that figure includes a competitive rate of return on investment, regulating the price at AC_1 is an example of rate-of-return regulation.

A major problem with regulating monopolies concerns the quality of the service or product involved. Consider the many facets of telephone service: getting a dial tone, hearing other voices clearly, getting the operator to answer quickly, having out-of-order telephone lines repaired rapidly, putting through a long-distance call quickly and efficiently—the list goes on and on. But regulation of a telephone company usually dealt with the prices charged for telephone service. Of course, regulators were concerned with the quality of service, but how could that be measured? Indeed, it cannot be measured very easily. Therefore, it is extremely difficult for any type of regulation to be successful in regulating the *price per constant-quality unit.* Certainly, it is possible to regulate the price per unit, but we don't really know that the quality remains unchanged when the price is not allowed to rise "enough." Thus if regulation doesn't allow prices to rise, quality of service may be lowered, thereby raising the price per constant-quality unit.

Social Regulation

Click here to see how yet another regulatory agency, the Federal Trade Commission, imposes regulations intended to protect consumers.

As mentioned, social regulation reflects concern for public welfare across all industries. In other words, regulation is focused on the impact of production on the environment and society, the working conditions under which goods and services are produced, and sometimes the physical attributes of goods. The aim is a better quality of life for all through a less polluted environment, better working conditions, and safer and better products. For example, the Food and Drug Administration (FDA) attempts to protect against impure and unsafe foods, drugs, cosmetics, and other potentially hazardous products; the Consumer Product Safety Commission (CPSC) specifies minimum standards for consumer products in an attempt to reduce "unreasonable" risks of injury; the Environmental Protection Agency (EPA) watches over the amount of pollutants released into the environment; the Occupational Safety and Health Administration (OSHA) attempts to protect workers against work-related injuries and illnesses; and the Equal Employment Opportunity Commission (EEOC) seeks to provide fair access to jobs.

Table 26-1 lists some major federal regulatory agencies and their areas of concern. Although most people agree with the idea behind such social regulation, many disagree on whether we have too much regulation—whether it costs us more than the benefits we receive. Some contend that the costs that firms incur in abiding by regulations run into the hundreds of billions of dollars per year. The result is higher production costs, which are then passed on

TABLE 26-1
Some Federal Regulatory Agencies

Agency	Jurisdiction	Date Formed	Major Regulatory Functions
Federal Communications Commission (FCC)	Product markets	1934	Regulates broadcasting, telephone, and other communication services.
Federal Trade Commission (FTC)	Product markets	1914	Responsible for preventing businesses from engaging in unfair trade practices and in monopolistic actions, as well as protecting consumer rights.
Equal Employment Opportunity Commission (EEOC)	Labor markets	1964	Investigates complaints of discrimination based on race, religion, sex, or age in hiring, promotion, firing, wages, testing, and all other conditions of employment.
Securities and Exchange Commission (SEC)	Financial markets	1934	Regulates all public securities markets to promote full disclosure.
Environmental Protection Agency (EPA)	Environment	1970	Develops and enforces environmental standards for air, water, toxic waste, and noise.
Occupational Safety and Health Administration (OSHA)	Health and safety	1970	Regulates workplace safety and health conditions.

to consumers. Also, the resources invested in complying with regulatory measures could be invested in other uses. Furthermore, extensive regulation may have an anticompetitive effect because it may represent a relatively greater burden for smaller firms than for larger ones.

But the *potential* benefits of more social regulation are many. For example, the water we drink in some cities is known to be contaminated with cancer-causing chemicals; air pollution from emissions and toxic wastes from production processes cause many illnesses. Some contaminated areas have been cleaned up, but many other problem areas remain.

The benefits of social regulation may not be easy to measure and may accrue to society for a long time. Furthermore, it is difficult to put a dollar value on safer working conditions and a cleaner environment. In any case, the debate goes on. However, it should be pointed out that the controversy is generally not about whether we should have social regulation but about when and how it is being done and whether we take *all* of the costs and benefits into account. For example, is regulation best carried out by federal, state, or local authorities? Is a specific regulation economically justified through a complete cost-benefit analysis?

INTERNATIONAL POLICY EXAMPLE

Conflicting Social Regulations in a World of Multinational Firms

The Data Protection Directive recently took effect in all nations of the European Union. This law governs how firms collect and export personal data about European citizens. Under the rule, any company doing business within the European Union must obtain consumers' permission to collect information about them, disclose how they will use the information, and reveal why it is being collected.

European backers of the law argue that it protects consumers against Big Brother–style corporate intrusion. For U.S. multinational firms, however, the law is a headache. The European requirements run counter to standard business practice in the United States, where it is relatively common to gather information about customers and corporate rivals without their knowledge. Some American business leaders have argued that because information on U.S. firms and consumers is so readily available, the directive gives European firms an unfair advantage in compiling information about competitors and potential business partners in the United States. Indeed, the law will severely limit the ability of U.S. firms to do the same in Europe. In this regard, the directive effectively acts as a protectionist mechanism to hinder U.S. and other foreign companies from competing in Europe.

The law is particularly burdensome for multinational financial firms. Major U.S. banks have had to set up separate systems for American and European customers. In addition, U.S. bankers and government officials worry that criminals will use the directive as a way to learn about investigations of their activities. The directive requires all firms to give customers unlimited access to the information held on them, including files opened as part of investigations into money laundering. Such investigative records are closed in the United States. Some law enforcement officials are already forecasting that money laundering will soon become a big business in Europe.

For Critical Analysis

Critics of the gathering and sale of information about consumers argue that many firms do it to earn higher profits. Why are companies willing to buy this information from other firms?

Creative Response and Feedback Effects: Results of Regulation 

Creative response Behavior on the part of a firm that allows it to comply with the letter of the law but violate the spirit, significantly lessening the law's effects.

Regulated firms commonly try to avoid the effects of regulation whenever they can. In other words, the firms engage in **creative response,** which is a response to a regulation that conforms to the letter of the law but undermines its spirit. Take state laws requiring male-female pay-equity: The wages of women must be on a par with those paid to males who are performing the same tasks. Employers that pay the same wages to both males and females are clearly not in violation of the law. Yet wages are only one component of total employee compensation. Another component is fringe benefits, such as on-the-job training. Because on-the-job training is difficult to observe from outside the firm, employers could offer less on-the-job training to women and still not be in technical violation of pay-equity laws. This unobservable difference would mean that males were able to acquire skills that could raise their future income even though current wages among males and females were equal, in compliance with the law.

Individuals have a type of creative response that has been labeled a *feedback effect.* Regulation may alter individuals' behavior after the regulation has been put into effect. If regulation requires fluoridated water, then parents know that their children's teeth have significant protection against tooth decay. Consequently, the feedback effect on parents' behavior is that they may be less concerned about how many sweets their children eat.

EXAMPLE

The Effectiveness of Auto Safety Regulation

A good example of the feedback effect has to do with automotive safety regulation. Since the 1960s, the federal government has required automobile manufacturers to make cars increasingly safer. Some of the earlier requirements involved nonprotruding door handles, collapsible steering columns, and shatterproof glass. More recent requirements involve I-beams in the doors, better seat belts, and airbags. The desired result was fewer injuries and deaths for drivers involved in accidents. According to economist Sam Peltzman, however, due to the feedback effect, drivers have gradually started driving more recklessly. Automobiles with more safety features have been involved in a disproportionate number of accidents.

For Critical Analysis

The feedback effect has also been called the law of unintended consequences. Why?

EXPLAINING REGULATORS' BEHAVIOR

Regulation has usually been defended by contending that government regulatory agencies are needed to correct market imperfections. We are dealing with a nonmarket situation because regulators are paid by the government and their decisions are not determined or constrained by the market. A number of theories have been put forward to describe the behavior of regulators. These theories can help us understand how regulation has often harmed consumers through higher prices and less choice and benefited producers through higher profits and fewer competitive forces. Two of the best-known theories of regulatory behavior are the *capture hypothesis* and the *share-the-gains, share-the-pains theory.*

The Capture Hypothesis

It has been observed that with the passage of time, regulators often end up adopting the views of the regulated. According to the **capture hypothesis,*** no matter what the reason for a regulatory agency's having been set up, it will eventually be captured by the special interests of the industry that is being regulated. Consider the reasons.

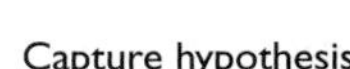

A theory of regulatory behavior that predicts that the regulators will eventually be captured by the special interests of the industry being regulated.

Who knows best about the industry that is being regulated? The people already in the industry. Who, then, will be asked to regulate the industry? Again, people who have been in the industry. And people who used to be in the industry have allegiances and friendships with others in the industry.

Also consider that whenever regulatory hearings are held, the affected consumer groups will have much less information about the industry than the people already in the industry, the producers. Furthermore, the cost to any one consumer to show up at a regulatory hearing to express concern about a change in the rate structure will certainly exceed any perceived benefit that that consumer could obtain from going to the rate-making hearing.

Because they have little incentive to do so, consumers and taxpayers will not be well organized, nor will they be greatly concerned with regulatory actions. But the special interests of the industry are going to be well organized and well defined. Political entrepreneurs within the regulatory agency see little payoff in supporting the views of consumers and taxpayers anyway. After all, few consumers understand the benefits deriving from regulatory agency actions. Moreover, how much could a consumer directly benefit someone who works in an agency? Regulators have the most incentive to support the position of a well-organized special-interest group within the industry that is being regulated.

*See George Stigler, *The Citizen and the State: Essays on Regulation* (Chicago: University of Chicago Press, 1975).

"Share the Gains, Share the Pains"

Share-the-gains, share-the-pains theory 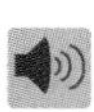
A theory of regulatory behavior in which the regulators must take account of the demands of three groups: legislators, who established and who oversee the regulatory agency; members of the regulated industry; and consumers of the regulated industry's products or services.

A somewhat different view of regulators' behavior is given in the **share-the-gains, share-the-pains theory.*** This theory looks at the specific aims of the regulators. It posits that a regulator simply wants to continue in the job. To do so, the regulator must obtain the approval of both the legislators who established and oversee the regulatory agency and the industry that is being regulated. A third group that must be taken into account is, of course, the customers of the industry.

Under the capture hypothesis, only the special interests of the industry being regulated had to be taken into account by the regulators. The share-the-gains, share-the-pains model contends that such a position is too risky because customers who are really hurt by improper regulation will complain to legislators, who might fire the regulators. Thus each regulator has to attach some weight to these three separate groups. What happens if there is an abrupt increase in fuel costs for electrical utilities? The capture theory would predict that regulators would relatively quickly allow for a rate increase in order to maintain the profits of the industry. The share-the-gains, share-the-pains theory, however, would predict that there will be an adjustment in rates, but not as quickly or as completely as the capture theory would predict. The regulatory agency is not completely captured by the industry; it has to take account of legislators and consumers.

POLICY EXAMPLE

"The Toys Are Safe, But Would You Please Halt Production Anyway?"

A couple of years ago, the Consumer Product Safety Commission (CPSC) did what it does every year around Christmastime: It released a list of toys that can scratch, cut, trap, or choke a child. The CPSC also did something new. It released a study evaluating whether a certain plastic (diisononyl phthalate) used in squeezable children's toys could cause kidney and liver damage, including cancer. The study concluded that "few, if any, children are at risk from liver or other organ toxicity . . . from these products. This is because the amount they might ingest does not reach a level that would be harmful." At the same time the CPSC released these conclusions, however, it told parents of infants to throw away toys containing the plastic. The CPSC also suggested to toy manufacturers and retailers that they should "voluntarily remove" toys containing the plastic from the marketplace. Of course, the companies did. After all, the CPSC's warning to parents and request of manufacturers and retailers could be used in court by a lawyer representing any child who had ever chewed a rattle containing the plastic and then happened to come down with a liver or kidney disease. The risk of future litigation was simply too high for the toymakers and sellers. For the CPSC, however, all turned out well. It had satisfied consumer activists, and at the same time it hadn't issued any mandates for companies to stop selling the squeeze toys.

For Critical Analysis

Does the CPSC appear to have applied cost-benefit analysis in releasing its conflicting statements concerning the use of diisononyl phthalate in squeezable toys?

THE COSTS OF REGULATION

There is no truly accurate way to measure the costs of regulation. Panel (a) of Figure 26-2 shows regulatory spending in 1998 dollars. Except in the years 1981–1985, regulatory spending by federal agencies has increased. This is consistent with what has happened to the number of pages in the *Federal Register,* which publishes all the new federal regulatory

*See Sam Peltzman, "Towards a More General Theory of Regulation," *Journal of Law and Economics,* 19 (1976), pp. 211–240.

FIGURE 26-2
Regulation on the Rise
In panel (a), federal government regulatory spending is shown to exceed $16 billion per year today. State and local spending is not shown. In panel (b), the number of pages in the *Federal Register* per year has been rising since about 1990.
Sources: Institute for University Studies; *Federal Register,* various issues.

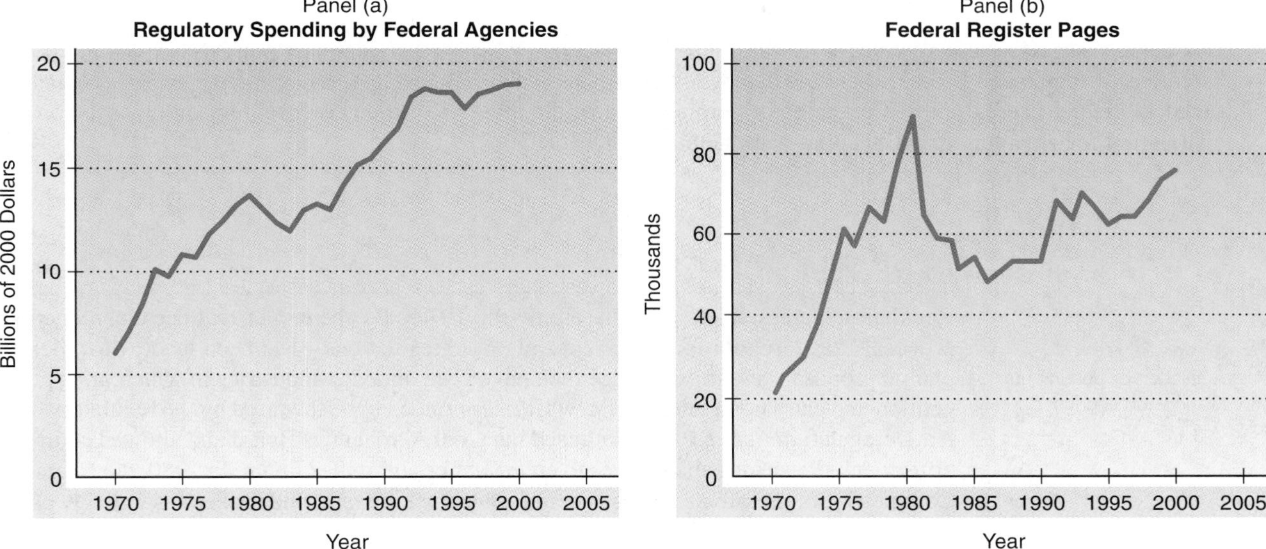

rules; you can see that in panel (b). But actual direct costs to taxpayers are only a small part of the overall cost of regulation. Pharmaceutical-manufacturing safety standards raise the price of drugs. Automobile safety standards raise the price of cars. Environmental controls on manufacturing raise the price of manufactured goods. All of these increased prices add to the cost of regulation. According to economist Thomas Hopkins at the Rochester Institute of Technology, the economic cost of environmental and safety regulation exceeds $200 billion a year. When he adds the cost of all other kinds of regulations, he comes up with a grand total of over $700 billion a year, or about 8 percent of each year's total income in this country. Not surprisingly, the increasing cost of regulation on occasion has brought about cries for deregulation.

POLICY EXAMPLE

Dueling Regulators: What's a Bank to Do?

Recently, the Securities and Exchange Commission (SEC) announced a major enforcement action against a bank known as one of the most conservatively managed in the country, SunTrust Bank of Florida. SunTrust, the SEC claimed, had intentionally manipulated year-to-year changes in its "loan loss reserves," which are anticipated liabilities of the bank resulting from future defaults by a bank's borrowers. According to the SEC, SunTrust had overstated its likely loan losses during a long stretch of good economic times when borrower defaults were unlikely to occur. A possible aim of adding "too much" to loan loss reserves, the SEC concluded, was to intentionally understate the bank's net income, thereby deceiving its shareholders, to whom it distributed dividends that were based on its reported earnings.

The problem was that the bank was following a long-standing practice favored by the Federal Reserve, the Comptroller of the Currency, and the Federal Deposit Insurance Corporation, which are charged with regulating banks to limit failures. Traditionally, these banking regulators have encouraged banks to add to their loan loss reserves in good times so that they will be better prepared when bad times hit and squeeze bank balance sheets. Suddenly SunTrust—and, shortly thereafter, a number of other banks—found itself forced to defend itself from SEC charges of earnings falsification for engaging in actions that were helping generate high ratings from banking regulators. This regulatory squeeze kept the bank's accounting and legal staffs tied up in knots for months, at least until the SEC and banking regulators reached "tentative agreement" on the issue.

For Critical Analysis

Time devoted to dealing with the SEC's complaint was time that SunTrust's accountants could have spent developing expense-reducing systems for the bank. In what way did the SEC action impose regulatory costs on SunTrust?

DEREGULATION

Deregulation
The elimination or phasing out of regulations on economic activity.

Regulation increased substantially during the 1970s. By the end of that decade, numerous proposals for **deregulation**—the removal of old regulations—had been made. Most deregulation proposals and actions since then have been aimed at industries in which price competition and entry competition by new firms continued to be thwarted by the regulators. The Air Deregulation Act of 1978 eliminated the Civil Aeronautics Board and allowed competition among the airlines themselves to control fares and routes flown. In 1980, the Interstate Commerce Commission's power over interstate trucking rates and routes was virtually eliminated, and the same occurred for buses in 1982. Savings account interest rates were deregulated in 1980. Railroad pricing was made more flexible during the same year.

Even prior to this spate of deregulatory acts by Congress, the Federal Communications Commission (FCC) had started in 1972 to deregulate the television broadcast industry. The result has been an increased number of channels, more direct satellite broadcasting, and more cable television transmissions. (Further deregulation occurred in 1996.) In 1975, the Securities and Exchange Commission (SEC) deregulated brokerage fees charged by brokers on the New York Stock Exchange.

Short-Run Versus Long-Run Effects of Deregulation

The short-run effects of deregulation are not the same as the long-run effects. In the short run, a regulated industry that becomes deregulated may experience numerous temporary adjustments. One is the inevitable shakeout of higher-cost producers with the concomitant removal of excess monopoly profits. Another is the sometimes dramatic displacement of workers who have labored long and hard in the formerly regulated industry. The level of service for some consumers may fall; for example, after the deregulation of the telephone industry, some aspects of telephone service decreased in quality. When airlines were deregulated, service to some small cities was eliminated or became more expensive. The power of unions in the formerly regulated industry may decrease. And bankruptcies may cause disruptions, particularly in the local economy where the headquarters of the formerly regulated firm are located.

Proponents of deregulation, or at least of less regulation, contend that there are long-run, permanent benefits. These include lower prices that are closer to marginal cost. Furthermore, fewer monopoly profits are made in the deregulated industry. Such proponents argue that deregulation has had positive *net* benefits.

Deregulation and Contestable Markets 

A major argument in favor of deregulation is that when government-imposed barriers to entry are removed, competition will cause firms to enter markets that previously had only a few firms due to those entry barriers. Potential competitors will become actual competitors, and prices will fall toward a competitive level. This argument has been bolstered by a model of efficient firm behavior that predicts competitive prices in spite of a lack of a large number of firms. This model is called the **theory of contestable markets.** Under the theory of contestable markets, most of the outcomes predicted by the theory of perfect competition will occur in certain industries with relatively few firms. Specifically, where the theory of contestable markets is applicable, the few firms may still produce the output at which price equals marginal cost in both the short run and the long run. These firms will receive zero economic profits in the long run.

Theory of contestable markets 
A hypothesis concerning pricing behavior that holds that even though there are only a few firms in an industry, they are forced to price their products more or less competitively because of the ease of entry by outsiders. The key aspect of a contestable market is relatively costless entry into and exit from the industry.

Unconstrained and Relatively Costless Entry and Exit. For a market to be perfectly contestable, firms must be able to enter and leave the industry easily. Freedom of entry and exit implies an absence of nonprice constraints and of serious fixed costs associated with a potential competitor's decision to enter a contestable market. Such an absence of important fixed costs results if the firm need buy no specific durable inputs in order to enter, if it uses up all such inputs it does purchase, or if all of its specific durable inputs are salable upon exit without any losses beyond those normally incurred from depreciation. The important issue is whether or not a potential entrant can easily get his or her investment out at any time in the future.

The mathematical model of perfect contestability is complex, but the underlying logic is straightforward. As long as conditions for free entry prevail, any excess profits, or any inefficiencies on the part of incumbent firms, will serve as an inducement for potential entrants to enter. By entering, new firms can temporarily profit at no risk to themselves from the less than competitive situation in the industry. Once competitive conditions are again restored, these firms will leave the industry just as quickly.

Benefits of Contestable Markets. Contestable markets have several desirable characteristics. One has to do with profits. Profits that exceed the opportunity cost of capital will not exist in the long run because of freedom of entry, just as in a perfectly competitive industry. The elimination of "excess" profits can occur even with only a couple of firms in an industry. The threat of entry will cause them to expand output to eliminate excess profit.

Also, firms that have cost curves that are higher than those of the most efficient firms will find that they cannot compete. These firms will be replaced by entrants whose cost curves are consistent with the most efficient technology. In other words, in contestable markets, there will be no cost inefficiencies in the long run.

Rethinking Regulation Using Cost-Benefit Analysis

Rather than considering deregulation as the only solution to "too much" regulation, some economists argue that regulation should simply be put to a cost-benefit test. Specifically, the cost of existing and proposed regulations should be compared to the benefits. Unless it can be demonstrated that regulations generate net positive benefits (benefits greater than costs), such regulations should not be in effect.

CONCEPTS IN BRIEF

- It is difficult to regulate the price per constant-quality unit because it is difficult to measure all dimensions of quality.
- The capture hypothesis holds that regulatory agencies will eventually be captured by special interests of the industry. This is because consumers are a diffuse group who individually are not affected greatly by regulation, whereas industry groups are well focused and know that large amounts of potential profits are at stake and depend on the outcome of regulatory proceedings.
- In the share-the-gains, share-the-pains theory of regulation, regulators must take account of the interests of three groups: the industry, legislators, and consumers.
- The 1970s and 1980s were periods of deregulation during which formerly regulated industries became much more competitive. The short-run effects of deregulation in some industries were numerous bankruptcies and disrupted service. The long-run results in many deregulated industries included better service, more variety, and lower costs. One argument in favor of deregulation involves the theory of contestable markets—if entry and exit are relatively costless, the number of firms in an industry is irrelevant in terms of determining whether consumers pay competitive prices.

ANTITRUST POLICY

It is the expressed aim of our government to foster competition in the economy. To this end, numerous attempts have been made to legislate against business practices that seemingly destroy the competitive nature of the system. This is the general idea behind antitrust legislation: If the courts can prevent collusion among sellers of a product, monopoly prices will not result; there will be no restriction of output if the members of an industry are not allowed to join together in restraint of trade. Remember that the competitive solution to the price-quantity problem is one in which the price of the item produced is equal to its marginal social opportunity cost. Also, no *economic* profits are made in the long run.

The Sherman Antitrust Act of 1890

The Sherman Antitrust Act was passed in 1890. It was the first attempt by the federal government to control the growth of monopoly in the United States. The most important provisions of that act are as follows:

Click here to for more details on the history of antitrust regulation.

Section 1: Every contract, combination in the form of trust or otherwise, or conspiracy, in restraint of trade or commerce among the several states, or with foreign nations, is hereby declared to be illegal.

Section 2: Every person who shall monopolize, or attempt to monopolize, or combine or conspire with any other person or persons to monopolize any part of the trade or commerce . . .shall be guilty of a misdemeanor.*

Notice how vague this act really is. No definition is given for the terms *restraint of trade* or *monopolization.* Despite this vagueness, however, the act was used to prosecute the infamous Standard Oil trust of New Jersey. Standard Oil of New Jersey was charged with violations of Sections 1 and 2 of the Sherman Antitrust Act. This was in 1906, when Standard Oil controlled over 80 percent of the nation's oil-refining capacity. Among other things, Standard Oil was accused of both predatory price cutting to drive rivals out of business and obtaining preferential price treatment from the railroads for transporting Standard Oil products, thus allowing Standard to sell at lower prices.

*This is now a felony.

Standard Oil was convicted in a district court. The company then appealed to the Supreme Court, which ruled that Standard's control of and power over the oil market created "a *prima facie* presumption of intent and purpose to maintain dominancy . . . not as a result from normal methods of industrial development, but by means of combination." Here the word *combination* meant taking over other businesses and obtaining preferential price treatment from railroads. The Supreme Court forced Standard Oil of New Jersey to break up into many smaller companies.

POLICY EXAMPLE

Microsoft: Gentle Giant or Big Bad Wolf?

A few years back, Netscape was the dominant seller of Web browser software. Its product was called Navigator. Microsoft developed similar features for its Internet Explorer browser. For a while, the two systems competed side by side. But when Microsoft decided to include a new version of Internet Explorer as part of its Windows software, Netscape raised a ruckus—and understandably so: 80 percent of the world's personal computers use the Windows operating system. If Microsoft started "bundling" browser software with Windows, few PC users would need Navigator, and that would quickly drive Netscape out of business. In May 1998, the U.S. Department of Justice took Netscape's side, arguing that "Microsoft possesses (and for several years has possessed) monopoly power in the market for personal computer operating systems." By bundling Internet Explorer within Windows, Justice alleged, "Microsoft is unlawfully taking advantage of its Windows monopoly to protect and extend that monopoly." A federal judge's findings of fact in November 1999 generally supported the Justice Department's interpretation, and thereafter Justice pressed its case for a legal remedy that will entail splitting Microsoft into two different companies.

Monopolies charge prices that are higher than they would be if competition prevailed. Nevertheless, in the software markets, prices have been falling, and the prices of Microsoft's products have not been immune to this downward drift. When someone pointed this out to a Justice Department official, he stated that Justice had to look to the future. In other words, the Justice Department believed that it could predict what will happen in the computer industry, and that was why it was trying to prevent Microsoft from bundling Internet Explorer with Windows.

Of course, none of us can be sure our future predictions will be borne out by events. In fact, in the midst of the Microsoft antitrust action, everyone, including the Justice Department, was taken by surprise when America Online acquired Netscape. Then in 2000 America Online aquired Time Warner in a deal valued at nearly $200 billion, creating a corporate giant rivaling Microsoft. Indeed, some economists began to wonder if Microsoft would be able to compete with America Online's new multimedia empire. Nevertheless, the antitrust action against Microsoft continued.

For Critical Analysis

Why do you suppose that the Justice Department did not drop its antitrust action against Microsoft after America Online purchased Netscape and Time Warner?

The Clayton Act of 1914

The Sherman Act was so vague that in 1914 a new law was passed to sharpen its antitrust provisions. This law was called the Clayton Act. It prohibited or limited a number of very specific business practices, which again were said to be "unreasonable" attempts at restraining trade or commerce. Section 2 of that act made it illegal to "discriminate in price between different purchasers" except in cases in which the differences are due to actual differences in selling or transportation costs. Section 3 stated that producers cannot sell goods "on the condition, agreement or understanding that the . . . purchaser thereof shall not use

Click here to learn more about antitrust policy.

or deal in the goods . . . of a competitor or competitors of the seller." And Section 7 provided that corporations cannot hold stock in another company if the effect "may be to substantially lessen competition."

The Federal Trade Commission Act of 1914 and Its 1938 Amendment

The Federal Trade Commission Act was designed to stipulate acceptable competitive behavior. In particular, it was supposed to prevent cutthroat pricing—so-called excessively aggressive competition which would tend to eliminate too many competitors. One of the basic features of the act was the creation of the Federal Trade Commission (FTC), charged with the power to investigate unfair competitive practices. The FTC can do this on its own or at the request of firms that feel they have been wronged. It can issue cease and desist orders where "unfair methods of competition in commerce" are discovered. In 1938, the Wheeler-Lea Act amended the 1914 act. The amendment expressly prohibits "unfair or deceptive acts or practices in commerce." Pursuant to that act, the FTC engages in what it sees as a battle against false or misleading advertising, as well as the misrepresentation of goods and services for sale in the marketplace.

The Robinson-Patman Act of 1936

In 1936, Section 2 of the Clayton Act was amended by the Robinson-Patman Act. The Robinson-Patman Act was aimed at preventing producers from driving out smaller competitors by means of selected discriminatory price cuts. The act has often been referred to as the "Chain Store Act" because it was meant to protect *independent* retailers and wholesalers from "unfair discrimination" by chain stores.

The act was the natural outgrowth of increasing competition that independents faced when chain stores and mass distributors started to develop after World War I. The essential provisions of the act are as follows:

1. It was made illegal to pay brokerage fees unless an independent broker was employed.
2. It was made illegal to offer concessions, such as discounts, free advertising, or promotional allowances, to one buyer of a firm's product if the firm did not offer the same concessions to all buyers of that product.
3. Other forms of discrimination, such as quantity discounts, were also made illegal whenever they "substantially" lessened competition.
4. It was made illegal to charge lower prices in one location than in another or to sell at "unreasonably low prices" if such marketing techniques were designed to "destroy competition or eliminate a competitor."

Exemptions from Antitrust Laws

Numerous laws exempt the following industries and business practices from antitrust legislation:

1. Labor unions
2. Public utilities—electric, gas, and telephone companies
3. Professional baseball
4. Cooperative activities among American exporters
5. Hospitals
6. Public transit and water systems

7. Suppliers of military equipment
8. Joint publishing arrangement in a single city by two or more newspapers

Doesn't an antitrust exemption for major league baseball benefit team owners at the expense of all professional baseball players?

Yes and no. Certainly, the antitrust exemption makes it easier for team owners to work together to restrict the ability of players to negotiate the best possible contract with the team of their choice. Nevertheless, if Congress did away with the antitrust exemption, it might also make it illegal for major league players to have union representation. This might have the effect of pushing down the average salaries of players who are not stars. In addition, without antitrust protection, teams would be unable to bind minor league players to a major league team under the "reserve clause" of major league baseball. This would remove a key incentive for major league teams to support minor league teams, thereby depressing the salaries of minor league players.

THE ENFORCEMENT OF ANTITRUST LAWS 

Most antitrust enforcement today is based on the Sherman Act. The Supreme Court has defined the offense of **monopolization** as involving the following elements: "(1) the possession of monopoly power in the relevant market and (2) the willful acquisition or maintenance of that power, as distinguished from growth or development as a consequence of a superior product, business acumen, or historical accident."

Monopoly Power and the Relevant Market

The Sherman Act does not define monopoly. Monopoly clearly is not a single entity. Also, monopoly is not a function of size alone. For example, a "mom and pop" grocery store located in an isolated desert town is a monopolist in at least one sense.

It is difficult to define and measure market power precisely. As a workable proxy, courts often look to the firm's percentage share of the "relevant market." This is the so-called **market share test.** A firm is generally considered to have monopoly power if its share of the relevant market is 70 percent or more. This is not an absolute dictum, however. It is only a loose rule of thumb; in some cases, a smaller share may be held to constitute monopoly power.

Monopolization 
The possession of monopoly power in the relevant market and the willful acquisition or maintenance of that power, as distinguished from growth or development as a consequence of a superior product, business acumen, or historical accident.

Market share test 
The percentage of a market that a particular firm supplies, used as the primary measure of monopoly power.

The relevant market consists of two elements: a relevant product market and a relevant geographic market. What should the relevant product market include? It must include all products produced by different firms that have identical attributes, such as sugar. Yet products that are not identical may sometimes be substituted for one another. Coffee may be substituted for tea, for example. In defining the relevant product market, the key issue is the degree of interchangeability between products. If one product is a sufficient substitute for another, the two products are considered to be part of the same product market.

The second component of the relevant market is the geographic boundaries of the market. For products that are sold nationwide, the geographic boundaries of the market encompass the entire United States. If a producer and its competitors sell in only a limited area (one in which customers have no access to other sources of the product), the geographic market is limited to that area. A national firm may thus compete in several distinct areas and have monopoly power in one area but not in another.

Concentration Ratios
See how to calculate market shares.

Cross-Border Mergers and the Relevant Market

An emerging challenge to the application of antitrust laws is cross-border mergers. How should antitrust authorities define the "relevant market" when Daimler-Benz of Germany desires to merge with Chrysler Corporation or when Deutsche Bank, also of Germany, wishes to purchase one of the nation's largest banks, Banker's Trust? U.S. authorities

Click here to keep up with the latest stances toward mergers by antitrust authorities.

approved both of these mergers. Their conclusion was that the automotive and banking markets have become global in scope, thereby justifying these cross-border combinations. It remains to be seen whether U.S. antitrust authorities will be so open-minded if the cross-national merger wave continues in these industries or spreads to others in future years. Undoubtedly, internal pressures will emerge to restrain merger activity intended to make home industries more competitive internationally.

Consider the recent experience of the Canadian banking industry. For all its massive geographic size, Canada's population is slightly smaller than California's. The nation has four dominant Toronto-based banking institutions—the Royal Bank of Canada, the Bank of Montreal, the Toronto-Dominion Bank, and the Canadian Imperial Bank of Commerce—which serve as depositories for two-thirds of all funds in Canadian banks. In 1998, the four institutions proposed merging into two, with Royal Bank of Canada set to merge with the Bank of Montreal and the Toronto-Dominion Bank poised to merge with the Canadian Imperial Bank of Commerce. The four institutions wanted to consolidate to assist in fending off competition from big U.S. banks. They also wanted to embark on an effort to compete more successfully in the United States, thereby diversifying their operations geographically. Canadian authorities disallowed both merger requests, however, ruling that the "relevant banking market" was Canada alone. For the banks that had proposed to merge, however, this was a serious blow to their long-range plans regarding their ability to compete effectively in the *international* banking markets that *they* felt were most relevant.

CONCEPTS IN BRIEF

- The first national antitrust law was the Sherman Antitrust Act, passed in 1890, which made illegal every contract and combination in the form of a trust in restraint of trade.
- The Clayton Act made price discrimination and interlocking directorates illegal.
- The Federal Trade Commission Act of 1914 established the Federal Trade Commission. The Wheeler-Lea Act of 1938 amended the 1914 act to prohibit "unfair or deceptive acts or practices in commerce."
- The Robinson-Patman Act of 1936 was aimed at preventing large producers from driving out small competitors by means of selective discriminatory price cuts.

NETNOMICS

Is the Internet Destined to Be Regulated?

According to J. Bradford De Long of the University of California at Berkeley and law professor A. Michael Froomkin of the University of Miami, some of the very characteristics that have driven the rapid adoption of information technology could prove to be its undoing. Recall from Chapter 5 that only one person at a time can consume a *private good.* For instance, when a computer repairperson is working on someone else's hard drive, that individual cannot work at the same time to repair your DVD drive. On the Internet, however, the situation is not quite as clear-cut. If one person is using a Web site, a thousand can. If a thousand are, ten thousand might as well. Indeed, in the network economy, if more people are consuming a good, it becomes more valuable. A dozen people trying to share the same phone booth have a problem, but tens of millions who have access to e-mail may have a distinct advantage over those who don't, because this makes it easier for each one to communicate with the others. Among economists who specialize in Internet economics, the expression "network externalities" is commonly used to describe this situation.

According to De Long and Froomkin, network externalities may yield significant economies of scale that pave the way for domination of portions of cyberspace by individual Internet firms. They suggest that in coming years, this could induce many consumers to clamor for regulating these companies' activities. In addition, De Long and Froomkin note that because digital data are so easy to copy, getting users to pay could become increasingly difficult. As a result, the *excludability principle* discussed in Chapter 5 may not always apply. Sellers may have difficulty inducing consumers to pay for all that they use on their Web sites, so sellers themselves may also perceive advantages in government intervention.

Thus De Long and Froomkin envision a future ablaze with disagreements about whether Internet commerce should be subjected to the same kinds of governmental interventions that traditional firms have experienced. If they are correct, the virtual world of the Web could end up looking a lot like the nonvirtual reality we inhabited before the advent of the Internet.

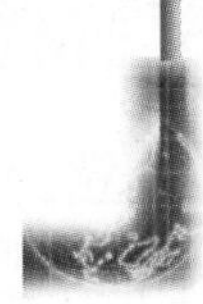

ISSUES & APPLICATIONS

Putting Government Behind the Airline Ticket Counter: Should Airlines Be Forced to Raise Their Fares?

If you have ever shopped around for an airline ticket, you may have been surprised to learn that a round-trip flight from, say, Nashville, Tennessee, to the Raleigh-Durham airport in neighboring North Carolina might cost $600 on one airline but only $200 on another. The second fare looks, comparatively, like a great deal for consumers. To the Department of Justice and the Department of Transportation, however, it is a possible indication of "predatory pricing," a common epithet applied to discriminatory price cuts that are illegal under the Robinson-Patman Act.

Concepts Applied

- Regulation
- Capture Hypothesis
- Share-the-Gain, Share-the-Pain Theory

Fair or Foul?

Some government officials contend that big airlines have entrenched themselves at "fortress hubs"—for instance, the United hub in Denver, the Delta hub in Atlanta, and the Northwest hub in Minneapolis—where their planes often account for more than three-fourths of all flights. Using these hubs, government critics argue, the big carriers can undercut any rival that dares to enter "their" airports.

What is their alleged weapon? According to some officials, it is rock-bottom fares that please consumers for a time but remain in effect only long enough to prevent rivals from establishing a market niche.

Mixed Weather for Airline Markets

There are a number of contrary signals about airline competition. Since 1978, when Congress lifted many economic restrictions on airlines, average airfares have dropped by 40 percent in real terms. The number of flights has risen by 50 percent, and annual passenger boardings have jumped from 275 million to about 600 million. Air travel used to be the domain of businesspeople and the well-off. Now it has become accessible to many ordinary people. Firms in service industries where market power is prevalent tend to charge higher prices and restrict sales of their services. There is little evidence this has been happening in the airline industry.

In addition, the government has since 1969 reserved a number of landings and takeoffs at Chicago's O'Hare airport, Washington's Reagan National Airport, and New York's La Guardia and Kennedy airports. These landing and takeoff "slots," as they are known, are by government edict the "property" of a handful of carriers. There were only two minor expansions in the numbers of government-awarded slots at these airports since 1969. Not until 1998 did the government grant slot exemptions at O'Hare and La Guardia for previously excluded minor carriers trying to break into those markets. Thus the government itself has made it difficult to establish a market niche at four of the nation's busiest airports.

So far there is no sign of any consideration of reducing the competition-stifling regulation of landing slots at major airports. In the meantime, however, the Justice Department has launched an antitrust investigation of possible predatory pricing by major airlines, and the Transportation Department has proposed rules establishing steep fines for airlines that set their fares "too low." Essentially, the government seems intent on establishing price floors in the airline industry. What remains to be seen is how this action would benefit consumers.

FOR CRITICAL ANALYSIS

1. Why do you suppose that the government restricts landing and takeoff slots at big airports?
2. If the government were to establish a "floor airfare" that is above the equilibrium fare that would prevail in a free market, what can you predict would be the likely result?

SUMMARY DISCUSSION OF LEARNING OBJECTIVES

1. **Practical Difficulties in Regulating the Prices Charged by Natural Monopolies:** To try to ensure that a monopolist charges a price consistent with the marginal cost to it and to society of producing the good or service that it produces, a government regulator might contemplate requiring the firm to set price equal to marginal cost. This is the point where the demand curve the monopolist faces crosses its marginal cost curve. A problem arises, however, in the case of a natural monopoly, for which the long-run average total cost curve and the long-run marginal cost curve slope downward as a firm's output rate increases. In this situation, long-run marginal cost is typically less than long-run average total cost, so requiring marginal cost pricing forces the natural monopoly to earn an economic loss. As a practical matter, therefore, regulators normally aim for a natural monopoly to charge a price equal to average total cost so that the firm earns zero economic profits.
2. **Rationales for Government Regulation of Business:** There are three types of government regulation of business: regulation of natural monopolies, regulation of inherently competitive industries, and social regulation aimed at ensuring public welfare. Regulation of natural monopolies often takes the form of cost-of-service regulation that seeks to achieve average-cost pricing and rate-of-return regulation aimed at attaining a competitive, zero-profit rate of return. Regulation of otherwise competitive industries is typically designed to address perceived market failures. Social regulations, however, encompass a broad set of objectives concerning such issues as the quality of products, product safety, and conditions under which employees work.
3. **Alternative Theories of Regulator Behavior:** The capture theory of regulator behavior predicts that because people with expertise about a regulated industry are most likely to be selected to regulate the industry, these regulators eventually find themselves supporting the positions of the firms that they regulate. An alternative view, called the share-the-gains, share-the pains theory, predicts that a regulator takes into account the preferences of legislators and consumers as well as the regulated firms themselves. Thus a regulator tries to satisfy all constituencies, at least in part.
4. **Short- and Long-Run Economic Effects of Deregulation:** A number of industries have been deregulated since the late 1970s. The short-run effects of deregulation are typically a number of temporary adjustments, such as failures of high-cost producers, some cutbacks in products or services to some consumers, and the loss of jobs by some workers in the industry. As these adjustments are completed, profits fall toward competitive levels, and prices drop closer to marginal cost. The key issue in assessing deregulation is whether these long-term benefits for society outweigh the short-term adjustment costs.
5. **Foundations of Antitrust:** There are four key antitrust laws. The Sherman Act of 1890 forbids attempts to monopolize an industry. The Clayton Act of 1914 clarified antitrust law by prohibiting specific types of business practices that Congress determined were aimed at restraining trade. In addition, the Federal Trade Commission Act of 1914, as amended in 1938, seeks to prohibit deceptive business practices and to prevent "cutthroat pricing," which Congress felt could unfairly eliminate too many competitors. Finally, the Robinson-Patman Act of 1936 outlawed price cuts that Congress determined to be discriminatory and predatory.
6. **Issues in Enforcing Antitrust Laws:** Because antitrust laws are relatively vague, enforcement of the laws is based on Supreme Court interpretations of their meaning. The Supreme Court has defined monopolization as possessing monopoly pricing power in the "relevant market" or engaging in willful efforts to obtain such power. Authoities charged with enforcing antitrust laws typically use a market share test in which they examine the percentage of market production or sales by the firm under investigation. A key issue in applying the market share test is defining the relevant market. Recent increases in international competition have complicated efforts to do this.

Key Terms and Concepts

Capture hypothesis (645)
Cost-of-service regulation (642)
Creative response (644)
Deregulation (648)
Market share test (653)
Monopolization (653)
Rate-of-return regulation (642)
Share-the-gains, share-the-pains theory (646)
Theory of contestable markets (649)

Problems

Answers to the odd-numbered problems appear at the back of the book.

26-1. Local cable companies are usually granted monopoly rights to service a particular territory of a metropolitan area. The companies typically pay special taxes and license fees to local municipalities. Why might a municipality give monopoly rights to a cable company?

26-2. "A local cable company, the sole provider of cable television service, is regulated by the municipal government. The owner of the company claims that she is opposed to regulation by government but asserts that regulation is necessary because local residents would not want a large number of different cables spanning the skies of the city. Why do you think the owner is defending regulation by the city?

26-3. The following table depicts the cost and demand structure a natural monopoly faces.

Quantity	Price($)	Long-Run Total Cost ($)
0	100	0
1	95	90
2	90	175
3	85	255
4	80	330
5	75	405
6	70	485

If this firm were allowed to operate as a monopolist, what would be the quantity produced and price charged by the firm? What is the amount of monopoly profit?

26-4. If regulators required the firm in Problem 26-3 to practice marginal cost pricing, what quantity would it produce, and what price would it charge? What is the firm's profit under this regulatory framework?

26-5. If regulators required the firm in Problem 26-3 to practice average cost pricing, what quantity would it produce, and what price would it charge? What is the firm's profit under this regulatory framework?

26-6. Discuss the major strength and weakness of the two traditional approaches to economic regulation.

26-7. Contrast the major objectives of economic regulation and social regulation.

26-8. Research into genetically modified crops has led to significant productivity gains for countries such as the United States that employ these techniques. Countries such as the European Union member nations, however, have imposed controls on the import of these products, citing concern for public health. Is the European Union's regulation of genetically modified crops social regulation or economic regulation?

26-9. Using the example in Problem 26-8, do you think this is most likely an example of the capture hypothesis or the share-the-gains, share-the-pains theory? Why?

26-10. In spite of a number of available sites to establish a business, few regulations, and minimum zoning problems, there is only one fast-food restaurant bordering campus. Given the significant potential for entry by other competitors, will this monopoly necessarily maximize its potential monopoly profits?

Economics on the Net

Guidelines for U.S. Antitrust Merger Enforcement How does the U.S. government apply anitrust laws to mergers? This application gives you the opportunity to learn about the standards applied by the Antitrust Division of the U.S. Department of Justice when it evaluates a proposed merger.

Title: U.S. Department of Justice Antitrust Merger Enforcement Guidelines

Navigation: Click here to start at the homepage of the Antitrust Division of the U.S. Department of Justice. Click on Public Documents and then on Merger Enforcement.

Application

1. Click on Horizontal Merger Guidelines. In section 1, click on Overview, and read this section. What factors do U.S. antitrust authorities consider when evaluating the potential for a horizontal merger to "enhance market power"—that is, to place the combination in a monopoly situation?
2. Back up to the page titled Merger Enforcement Guidelines, and click on Non-Horizontal Merger Guidelines. Read the guidelines. In what situations will the antitrust authorities most likely question a nonhorizontal merger?

For Group Study and Analysis Have three groups of students from the class examine sections 1, 2, and 3 of the Horizontal Merger Guidelines discussed in item 1. After each group reports on the all the factors that the antitrust authorities consider when evaluating a horizontal merger, discuss why it is that large teams of lawyers and many economic consultants are typically involved when the Antitrust Division of the Department of Justice alleges that a proposed merger would be "anticompetitive."

TYING IT ALL TOGETHER

Part 6 Case Problem

Case Background

Readme.com is a new company created by two book lovers who wish to emulate the success of Amazon.com and other Internet-based booksellers. These entrepreneurs, who have raised considerable funds from investors, believe that they have developed systems for processing book orders and shipping that are superior than those used by other booksellers on the Web. The problem they face, however, is that they must find a way to establish a presence in an already crowded bookselling market in cyberspace.

Lessons from the Battle Between Amazon.com and Barnes & Noble
Amazon.com first cracked the bookselling market by opening up shop on the Internet in 1995. Between December 1995 and late 1997, the average number of daily visits to Amazon.com's Web site increased from 2,000 to 1 million. It transformed its online catalog into a virtual index of book titles and detailed information about those titles, including outside reviews and even reviews by its own customers. The company also attracted customers by advertising in traditional print publications. It also developed an "associates program" that allowed other Internet sellers to display hot links to Amazon.com and offer books of interest to their customers, and Amazon.com paid other companies referral fees for revenues generated by such orders.

The day in 1997 that Barnes & Noble launched its Web-based bookselling system, Amazon.com expanded its list of discounted books and nearly doubled the fees it paid to Internet sellers in its associates program. Amazon.com also continued to advertise heavily in traditional media, and it built a new warehouse near the East Coast to speed deliveries in the eastern part of the nation.

Assessing the Market for Books on the Web The owners and managers of Readme.com wish to evaluate how Amazon.com, Barnes & Noble, and other firms already in the Internet-bookselling market may respond to the entry of their firm. They are wrestling with the following questions:

1. Will other Internet booksellers respond to the market entry of Readme.com with noticeable price cuts on a wide range of books?
2. If so, will these price cuts be so steep that if Readme.com fails to match them, it will not be able to cover its costs?
3. If Readme.com is able to establish a market presence and capture enough customers to keep its investors on board, will its low-cost operating system for selling books permit it to earn a normal rate of return in the long run?
4. Will the bookselling market eventually become dominated by a few large firms, including Amazon.com and Barnes & Noble, or will it remain a highly splintered market with a large number of sellers? Over the longer term, what scale size should Readme.com seek to attain?

Points to Analyze

1. In what ways does the bookselling market exhibit characteristics of perfect competition?
2. In what ways does the market have features of imperfect competition?
3. Is there any specific theory of imperfect competition that appears to be a potential "fit" for the bookselling market?
4. Based on the foregoing information, does it appear to you that Readme.com should be concerned about the possible use of limit-pricing strategies by Amazon.com, Barnes & Noble, and other major booksellers? Why or why not?
5. Do there appear to be economies of scale in bookselling? Are diseconomies of scale likely to arise for booksellers when they operate at sufficiently high sales levels? Why or why not?

Casing the Internet

1. **Click on each link to visit the Web sites of both Amazon.com and Barnes & Noble. Now, answer the following questions.**
   a. **What are the similarities between the two Web sites? Are there notable differences?**
   b. **In what ways are the products that these two companies market over the Internet homogeneous? In what respects do the companies market differentiated products?**
2. **Chapter 4 discussed the role that middlemen—market intermediaries between buyers and sellers—play in reducing transaction costs for buyers and sellers. Click here to go to the Web site of Anaconda! Partners. This is a company that markets programs that assist companies in linking their Web sites to those of other firms.**
   a. **Review the basic set of available Anaconda! products. In what sense does it appear that Anaconda! Partners is a market middleman?**
   b. **Why would an Internet seller want to link its Web site to the sites of other companies? That is, how might a client of Anaconda! Partners gain from "creating useful informational or affiliate websites that can earn [it] money," as claimed in the heading above the product descriptions?**
   c. **In your view, are Web links among firms likely to make the markets for products sold by firms over the Internet more or less competitive? Support your position.**

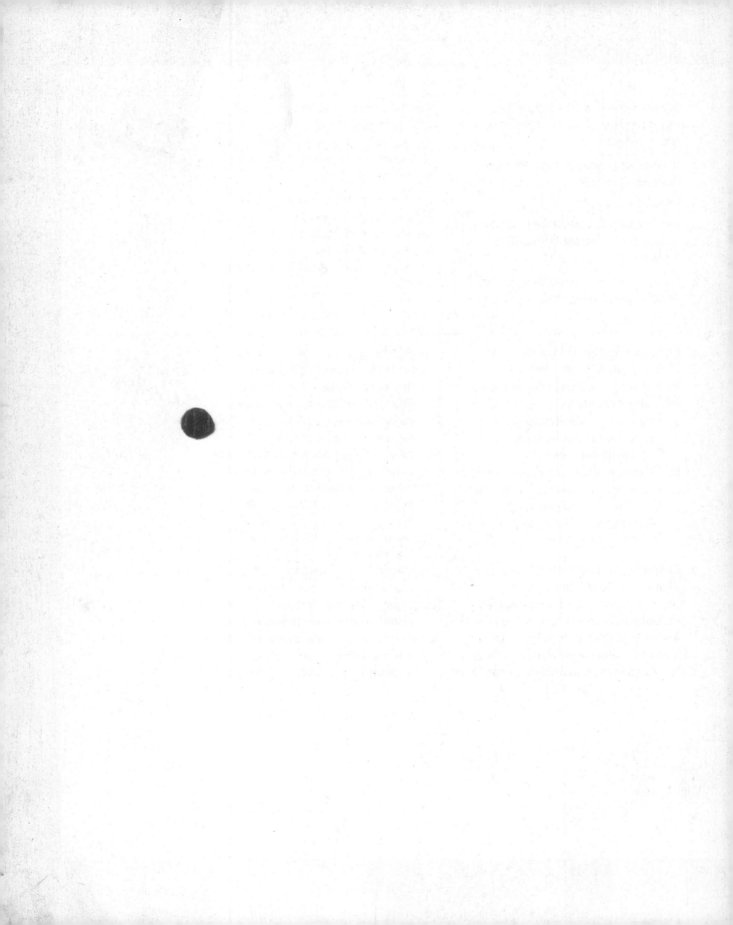

Part 7
Productive Factors, Poverty, Health Care, and the Environment

CHAPTER

27

LABOR DEMAND AND SUPPLY

These identical twins pursued different educational paths. Typically, a twin who goes to college will earn 67 percent more in monthly wages than one who joins the work force immediately upon graduating from high school.

Medical researchers, psychologists, and other scientists often conduct studies of identical twins. This allows them to hold constant heredity, early home life, and other factors. Economists have also learned a lot from identical twins. A study by Orley Ashenfelter and Alan Krueger of Princeton University tracked the earning patterns of more than 250 pairs of identical twins. These researchers found that each additional year of schooling increased wages by nearly 16 percent. A twin who attended four years of college earned monthly wages averaging 67 percent higher than those of the sibling with no college. To understand why additional and specialized training can have such dramatic effects on the wages that people earn, you need to understand the basic model of labor demand and supply.

LEARNING OBJECTIVES

After reading this chapter, you should be able to:

1. Understand why a firm's marginal revenue product curve is its labor demand curve
2. Explain in what sense the demand for labor is a "derived" demand
3. Identify the key factors influencing the elasticity of demand for inputs
4. Describe how equilibrium wage rates are determined for perfectly competitive firms
5. Discuss alternative theories of wage determination
6. Contrast the demand for labor and wage determination by a product market monopolist with outcomes that would arise under perfect competition

Chapter Outline

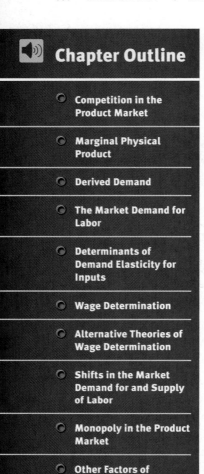

Did You Know That... the top 350 executives in America's biggest corporations are compensated, on the average, $2.5 million each, or about 60 times more than the median family income of a little over $40,000? Recently, the head of the Walt Disney Company, Michael Eisner, was paid more than $100 million in one year. You, in contrast, as a typical college student will probably make between $25,000 and $50,000 a year, or approximately one two-thousandth of Eisner's annual salary. To comprehend why firms pay different employees such vastly different salaries, you must understand how the laws of demand and supply apply to labor.

A firm's demand for inputs can be studied in much the same manner as we studied the demand for output in different market situations. Again, various market situations will be examined. Our analysis will always end with the same commonsense conclusion: A firm will hire employees up to the point beyond which it isn't profitable to hire any more. It will hire employees to the point at which the marginal benefit of hiring a worker will just equal the marginal cost. Basically, in every profit-maximizing situation, it is most profitable to carry out an activity up to the point at which the marginal benefit equals the marginal cost. Remembering that guideline will help you in analyzing decision making at the firm level. We will start our analysis under the assumption that the market for input factors is perfectly competitive. We will further assume that the output market is perfectly competitive. This provides a benchmark against which to compare other situations in which labor markets or product markets are not perfectly competitive.

COMPETITION IN THE PRODUCT MARKET

Let's take as our example a compact disk (CD) manufacturing firm that is in competition with many companies selling the same kind of product. Assume that the laborers hired by our CD manufacturing firm do not need any special skills. This firm sells its product in a perfectly competitive market. A CD manufacturer also buys labor (its variable input) in a perfectly competitive market. A firm that hires labor under perfectly competitive conditions hires only a minuscule proportion of all the workers who are potentially available to the firm. By "potentially available" we mean all the workers in a given geographic area who possess the skills demanded by our perfect competitor. In such a market, it is always possible for the individual firm to pick up extra workers without having to offer a higher wage. Thus the supply of labor to the firm is perfectly elastic at the going wage rate established by the forces of supply and demand in the entire labor market. The firm is a price taker in the labor market.

MARGINAL PHYSICAL PRODUCT

Marginal physical product (MPP) of labor 
The change in output resulting from the addition of one more worker. The MPP of the worker equals the change in total output accounted for by hiring the worker, holding all other factors of production constant.

Look at panel (a) of Figure 27-1. In column 1, we show the number of workers per week that the firm can hire. In column 2, we show total physical product (TPP) per week, the total *physical* production that different quantities of the labor input (in combination with a fixed amount of other inputs) will generate in a week's time. In column 3, we show the additional output gained when a CD manufacturing company adds workers to its existing manufacturing facility. This column, the **marginal physical product (MPP) of labor,** represents the extra (additional) output attributed to employing additional units of the variable input factor. If this firm employs seven workers rather than six, the MPP is 118. The law of diminishing marginal returns predicts that additional units of a variable factor will, after some point, cause the MPP to decline, other things being held constant.

FIGURE 27-1

Marginal Revenue Product

In panel (a), column 4 shows marginal revenue product (MRP), which is the amount of additional revenue the firm receives for the sale of that additional output. Marginal revenue product is simply the amount of money the additional worker brings in—the combination of that worker's contribution to production and the revenue that that production will bring to the firm. For this perfectly competitive firm, marginal revenue is equal to the price of the product, or $6 per unit. At a weekly wage of $498, the profit-maximizing employer will pay for only 12 workers because then the marginal revenue product is just equal to the wage rate or weekly salary.

Panel (a)

(1) Labor Input (workers per week)	(2) Total Physical Product (TPP) CDs per Week	(3) Marginal Physical Product (MPP) CDs per Week	(4) Marginal Revenue (MR = *P* = $6 net) x MPP = Marginal Revenue Product (MRP) ($ per additional worker)	(5) Wage Rate ($ per week) = Marginal Factor Cost (MFC) = Change in Total Costs / Change in Labor
6	882			
		118	$708	$498
7	1,000			
		111	666	498
8	1,111			
		104	624	498
9	1,215			
		97	582	498
10	1,312			
		90	540	498
11	1,402			
		83	498	498
12	1,485			
		76	456	498
13	1,561			

In panel (b), we find the number of workers the firm will want to hire by observing the wage rate that is established by the forces of supply and demand in the entire labor market. We show that this employer is hiring labor in a perfectly competitive labor market and therefore faces a perfectly elastic supply curve represented by *s* at $498 per week. As in all other situations, we basically have a supply and demand model; in this example, the demand curve is represented by MRP, and the supply curve is *s*. Equilibrium occurs at their intersection.

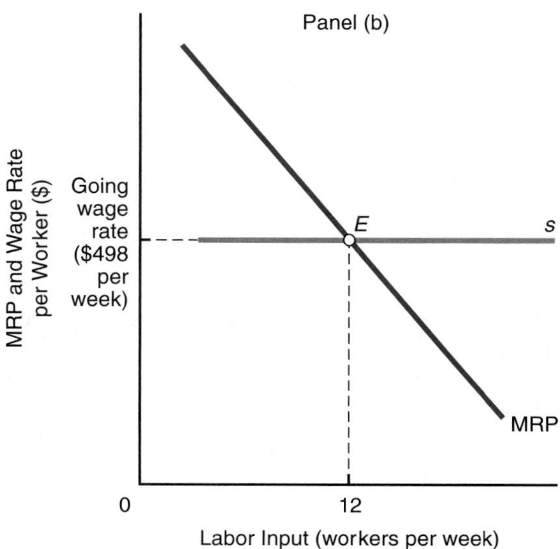

Why the Decline in MPP?

We are assuming all other nonlabor factors of production are held constant. So if our CD manufacturing firm wants to add one more worker to its production line, it has to crowd all the existing workers a little closer together because it does not increase its capital stock (the production equipment). Therefore, as we add more workers, each one has a smaller and smaller fraction of the available capital stock with which to work. If one worker uses one machine, adding another worker usually won't double the output because the machine can run only so fast and for so many hours per day. In other words, MPP declines because of the law of diminishing marginal returns.

Marginal Revenue Product

We now need to translate into a dollar value the physical product that results from hiring an additional worker. This is done by multiplying the marginal physical product by the marginal revenue of the firm. Because our CD firm is selling its product in a perfectly competitive market, marginal revenue is equal to the price of the product. If employing seven workers rather than six yields an MPP of 118 and the marginal revenue is \$6 per CD, the **marginal revenue product (MRP)** is \$708 (118 × \$6). The MRP is shown in column 4 of panel (a) of Figure 27-1. *The marginal revenue product represents the incremental worker's contribution to the firm's total revenues.*

Marginal revenue product (MRP)

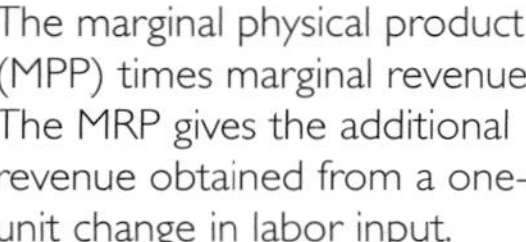

The marginal physical product (MPP) times marginal revenue. The MRP gives the additional revenue obtained from a one-unit change in labor input.

When a firm operates in a competitive product market, the marginal physical product times the product price is also sometimes referred to as the *value of marginal product (VMP).* Because price and marginal revenue are the same for a perfectly competitive firm, the VMP is also the MRP for such a firm.

In column 5 of panel (a) of Figure 27-1, we show the wage rate, or *marginal factor cost,* of each worker. The marginal cost of workers is the extra cost incurred in employing an additional unit of that factor of production. We call that cost the **marginal factor cost (MFC).** Otherwise stated,

Marginal factor cost (MFC) 

The cost of using an additional unit of an input. For example, if a firm can hire all the workers it wants at the going wage rate, the marginal factor cost of labor is the wage rate.

$$\text{Marginal factor cost} \equiv \frac{\text{change in total cost}}{\text{change in amount of resource used}}$$

Because each worker is paid the same competitively determined wage of \$498 per week, the MFC is the same for all workers. And because the firm is buying labor in a perfectly competitive labor market, the wage rate of \$498 per week really represents the supply curve of labor to the firm. That curve is perfectly elastic because the firm can purchase all labor at the same wage rate, considering that it is a minuscule part of the entire labor-purchasing market. (Recall the definition of perfect competition.) We show this perfectly elastic supply curve as *s* in panel (b) of Figure 27-1.

EXAMPLE

Does Attractiveness Lead to Higher Marginal Revenue Product?

Economist Daniel Hamermesh of the University of Texas, Austin, and Jeff Biddle of Michigan State University discovered that "plain-looking" people earn 5 to 10 percent less than people of "average" looks, who in turn earn 5 percent less than those who are considered "good-looking." Surprisingly, their research showed that the "looks effect" on wages was greater for men than for women. This wage differential related to appearance is not, contrary to popular belief, evident only in modeling, acting, or working directly with the public. Looks seem to account for higher earnings in jobs such as bricklaying, factory work, and telemarketing.

According to Hamermesh and Biddle, part of the wage differential may be created by the fact that attractiveness leads to higher marginal revenue product. More attractive individuals may have higher self-esteem, which in turn causes them to be more productive on the job.

For Critical Analysis

What are some of the other possible reasons that more attractive people tend to earn more?

General Rule for Hiring

Virtually every optimizing rule in economics involves comparing marginal benefits with marginal cost. The general rule, therefore, for the hiring decision of a firm is this:

> The firm hires workers up to the point at which the additional cost associated with hiring the last worker is equal to the additional revenue generated by that worker.

In a perfectly competitive market, this is the point at which the wage rate just equals the marginal revenue product. If the firm hired more workers, the additional wages would not be covered by additional increases in total revenue. If the firm hired fewer workers, it would be forfeiting the contributions that those workers could make to total profits.

Therefore, referring to columns 4 and 5 in panel (a) of Figure 27-1, we see that this firm would certainly employ at least seven workers because the MRP is $708 while the MFC is only $498. The firm would continue to employ workers up to the point at which MFC = MRP because as workers are added, they contribute more to revenue than to cost.

The MRP Curve: Demand for Labor

The Marginal Revenue Product of Labor

Gain more experience working with the marginal revenue product (MRP) curve.

We can also use panel (b) of Figure 27-1 to find how many workers our firm should hire. First, we draw a straight line across from the going wage rate, which is determined by demand and supply in the labor market. The straight line is labeled *s* to indicate that it is the supply curve of labor for the *individual* firm purchasing labor in a perfectly competitive labor market. That firm can purchase all the labor it wants of equal quality at $498 per worker. This perfectly elastic supply curve, *s,* intersects the marginal revenue product curve at 12 workers per week. At the intersection, *E,* the wage rate is equal to the marginal revenue product. Equilibrium for the firm is obtained when the firm's demand curve for labor, which turns out to be its MRP curve, intersects the firm's supply curve for labor, shown as *s.* The firm in our example would not hire the thirteenth worker, who will add only $456 to revenue but $498 to cost. If the price of labor should fall to, say, $456 per worker per week, it would become profitable for the firm to hire an additional worker; there is an increase in the quantity of labor demanded as the wage decreases.

DERIVED DEMAND

We have identified an individual firm's demand for labor curve, which shows the quantity of labor that the firm will wish to hire at each wage rate, as its MRP curve. Under conditions of perfect competition in both product and labor markets, MRP is determined by multiplying MPP times the product's price. This suggests that the demand for labor is a **derived demand.** That is to say that our CD firm does not want to purchase the services of labor just for the services themselves. Factors of production are rented or purchased not because they give any intrinsic satisfaction to the firms' owners but because they can be used to manufacture output that is expected to be sold for profit.

Derived Demand 

Input factor demand derived from demand for the final product being produced.

FIGURE 27-2

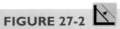

Demand for Labor, a Derived Demand

The demand for labor is derived from the demand for the final product being produced. Therefore, the marginal revenue product curve will shift whenever the price of the product changes. If we start with the marginal revenue product curve MRP at the going wage rate of $498 per week, 12 workers will be hired. If the price of CDs goes down, the marginal product curve will shift to MRP_1, and the number of workers hired will fall to 10. If the price of CDs goes up, the marginal revenue product curve will shift to MRP_2, and the number of workers hired will increase to 15.

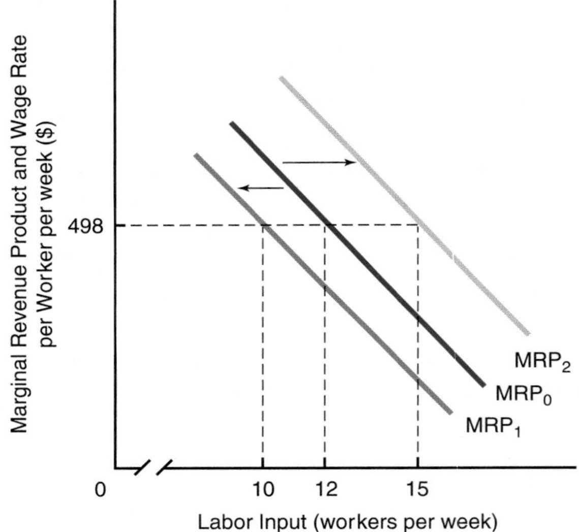

We know that an increase in the market demand for a given product raises the product's price (all other things held constant), which in turn increases the marginal revenue product, or demand for the resource. Figure 27-2 illustrates the effective role played by changes in product demand in a perfectly competitive product market. The MRP curve shifts whenever there is a change in the price of the final product that the workers are producing. Suppose, for example, that the market price of CDs declines. In that case, the MRP curve will shift downward to the left from MRP_0 to MRP_1. We know that MRP $\equiv$ MPP $\times$ MR. If marginal revenue (here the output price) falls, so does the demand for labor. At the same going wage rate, the firm will hire fewer workers. This is because at various levels of labor use, the marginal revenue product of labor is now lower. At the initial equilibrium, therefore, the price of labor (here the MFC) becomes greater than MRP. Thus the firm would reduce the number of workers hired. Conversely, if the marginal revenue (output price) rises, the demand for labor will also rise, and the firm will want to hire more workers at each and every possible wage rate.

We just pointed out that MRP $\equiv$ MPP $\times$ MR. Clearly, then, a change in marginal productivity, or in the marginal physical product of labor, will shift the MRP curve. If the marginal productivity of labor decreases, the MRP curve, or demand curve, for labor will shift inward to the left. Again, this is because at every quantity of labor used, the MRP will be lower. A lower quantity of labor will be demanded at every possible wage rate.

EXAMPLE

"If a Regular Job Doesn't Work Out, Perhaps *Saturday Night Live* Is an Option"

At many firms, the most productive employees are those who can think fast on their feet. Put yourself in the position of an employee of the Chicago-based advertising firm APL/Columbian Advertising. After you pitch carefully prepared proposals to a big client, the client cuts you off and says he hates them. Drawing on comic improvisation techniques that were included in your company's basic employee-training program, you and your colleagues quickly rethink the entire marketing plan and keep your client.

A number of firms, such as the investment company PricewaterhouseCoopers and the advertising company Ogilvy and Mather, send their employees for special training at Second City, the comedy company whose alumni include comic actors Bill Murray and John Belushi, or at Improv Olympic, the rival firm that launched the career of Mike Myers, another standup comedian and actor. Second City is getting so much interest from companies that want to turn wallflowers into rapid-fire communicators that it now has training centers in Chicago, New York, and Toronto and plans to open new centers in Los Angeles and Cleveland. Classes at Second City begin with exercises such as variations on the children's running game called Duck Duck Goose and impromptu skits in which students must carry on conversations using only gibberish. Then students proceed into development of off-the-cuff skits. To the businesses that send their employees to these classes, the idea behind training in stand-up comedy is to prepare their workers to do the kind of speedy thinking that they will have to do each day on the job. This, the companies hope, will raise their employees' productivity.

For Critical Analysis

If companies are correct that comedic training makes their employees more productive, and if more marketing students get such training, what will happen to the demand for these students' skills, other things being equal?

THE MARKET DEMAND FOR LABOR

The downward-sloping portion of each individual firm's marginal revenue product curve is also its demand curve for the one variable factor of production—in our example, labor. When we go to the entire market for a particular type of labor in a particular industry, we find that quantity of labor demanded will vary as the wage rate changes. Given that the market demand curve for labor is made up of the individual firm's downward-sloping demand curves for labor, we can safely infer that the market demand curve for labor will look like *D* in panel (b) of Figure 27-3: It will slope downward. That market demand curve for labor in the CD industry shows the quantities of labor demanded by all of the firms in the industry at various wage rates.

FIGURE 27-3

Derivation of the Market Demand Curve for Labor

The market demand curve for labor is not simply the horizontal summation of each individual firm's demand curve for labor. If wage rates fall from \$20 to \$10, all 200 firms will increase employment and therefore output, causing the price of the product to fall. This causes the marginal revenue product curve of each firm to shift inward, as from d_0 to d_1 in panel (a). The resulting market demand curve, *D*, in panel (b) is therefore less elastic around prices from \$10 to \$20 than it would be if output price remained constant.

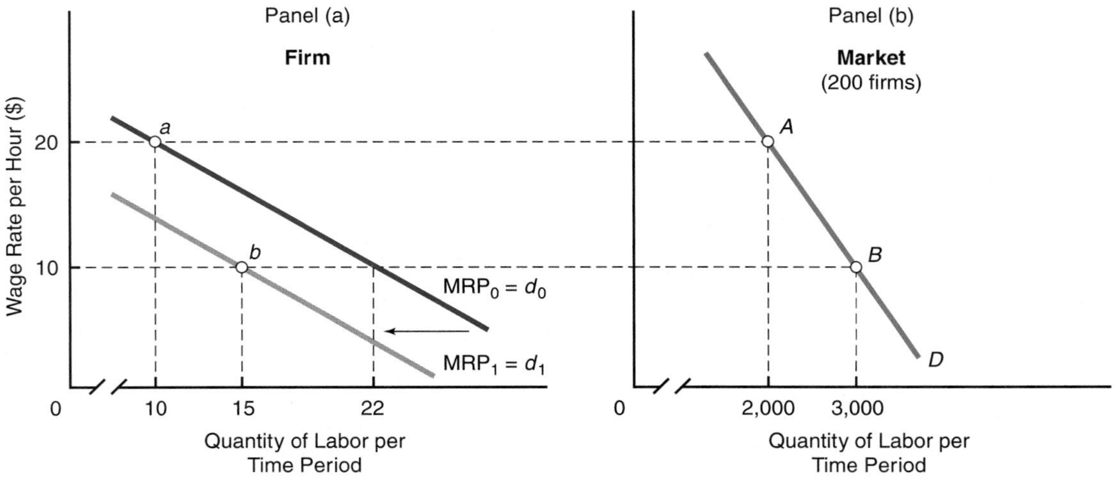

It is important to note that the market demand curve for labor is not a simple horizontal summation of the labor demand curves of all individual firms. Remember that the demand for labor is a derived demand. Even if we hold labor productivity constant, the demand for labor still depends on both the wage rate and the price of the final output. Assume that we start at a wage rate of $20 per hour and employment level 10 in panel (a) of Figure 27-3. If we sum all such employment levels—point *a* in panel (a)—across 200 firms, we get a market quantity demanded of 2,000—point *A* in panel (b)—at the wage rate of $20. A decrease in the wage rate to $10 per hour induces individual firms' employment level to increase toward a quantity demanded of 22. As all 200 firms simultaneously increase employment, however, there is a shift in the product supply curve such that output increases. Hence the price of the product must fall. The fall in the output price in turn causes a downward shift of each firm's MRP curve (d_0) to MRP_1 (d_1) in panel (a). Thus each firm's employment of labor increases to 15 rather than to 22 at the wage rate of $10 per hour. A summation of all such 200 employment levels gives us 3,000—point *B*—in panel (b).

INTERNATIONAL POLICY EXAMPLE

Labor Demand Curves Slope Downward—Except in France

In France, the unemployment rate has exceeded 10 percent for several years now. In an effort to do something about the problem, the French government cut the legal workweek from 39 hours to 35 hours for both hourly and salaried workers. Only senior executives are exempted from the restriction. To enforce the law, the government has issued thousands of citations charging companies with working their employees too many hours. Legal penalties, levied on the chief executive officers of offending companies, include fines up to $1 million and jail terms up to two years.

This has induced some French corporations to install electronic time clocks in hallways. Workers swipe ID cards to record arrival and departure times and coffee and lunch breaks. To allow for some flexibility in the policy, the government permits workers to build up hourly "work credits" in weeks when they exceed the 35-hour threshold. The maximum allowable credit is 15 hours. Managers are required to contact workers who overstep that limit and assist them in drawing up a plan to reduce the backlog. Workaholics who exceed the 15-hour limit by wide margins receive special counseling services to help them figure out how to reduce their time on the job.

This policy has an interesting implication. Lower-paid workers at companies are often blue-collar workers and salaried white-collar clerical staff. The law restricts the hours that these people can work for their relatively lower wages. But the highest-paid senior managers of a company can burn the midnight oil and work as many hours as they wish every week. Thus in France there is now a positive relationship between the wage rate and the quantity of hours that a firm employs workers. In this sense, the law has effectively produced an upward-sloping labor demand curve.

For Critical Analysis

What effect is the French workweek regulation likely to have on the ability of French companies to compete in the face of ever-tougher global competition?

DETERMINANTS OF DEMAND ELASTICITY FOR INPUTS 

Just as we were able to discuss the price elasticity of demand for different commodities in Chapter 20, we can discuss the price elasticity of demand for inputs. The price elasticity of demand for labor is defined in a manner similar to the price elasticity of demand for goods: the percentage change in quantity demanded divided by the percentage change in the price of labor. When the numerical value of this ratio is less than 1, demand is inelastic; when it is 1, demand is unit-elastic; and when it is greater than 1, demand is elastic.

There are four principal determinants of the price elasticity of demand for an input. The price elasticity of demand for a variable input will be greater:

1. The greater the price elasticity of demand for the final product
2. The easier it is for a particular variable input to be substituted for by other inputs
3. The larger the proportion of total costs accounted for by a particular variable input
4. The longer the time period being considered

Consider some examples. An individual radish farmer faces an extremely elastic demand for radishes, given the existence of many competing radish growers. If the farmer's laborers tried to obtain a significant wage increase, the farmer couldn't pass on the resultant higher costs to radish buyers. So any wage increase to the individual radish farmer would lead to a large reduction in the quantity of labor demanded.

Clearly, the easier it is for a producer to switch to using another factor of production, the more responsive that producer will be to an increase in an input's price. If plastic and aluminum can easily be substituted in the production of, say, car bumpers, then a price rise in aluminum will cause automakers to reduce greatly their quantity of aluminum demanded.

When a particular input's costs account for a very large share of total costs, any increase in that input's price will affect total costs relatively more. If labor costs are 80 percent of total costs, a company will cut back on employment more aggressively than if labor costs were only 8 percent of total costs, for any given wage increase.

Finally, over longer periods, firms have more time to figure out ways to economize on the use of inputs whose prices have gone up. Furthermore, over time, technological change will allow for easier substitution in favor of relatively cheaper inputs and against inputs whose prices went up. At first, a pay raise obtained by a strong telephone company union may not result in many layoffs, but over time, the telephone company will use new technology to replace many of the now more expensive workers.

CONCEPTS IN BRIEF

- The change in total output due to a one-unit change in one variable input, holding all other inputs constant, is called the marginal physical product (MPP). When we multiply marginal physical product times marginal revenue, we obtain the marginal revenue product (MRP).
- A firm will hire workers up to the point at which the additional cost of hiring one more worker is equal to the additional revenues generated. For the individual firm, therefore, its MRP of labor curve is also its demand for labor curve.
- The demand for labor is a derived demand, derived from the demand for final output. Therefore, if the price of final output changes, this will cause a shift in the MRP curve (which is also the firm's demand for labor curve).
- Input price elasticity of demand depends on final product elasticity, the ease of other input substitution, the relative importance of the input's cost in total costs, and the time allowed for adjustment.

WAGE DETERMINATION

Having developed the demand curve for labor (and all other variable inputs) in a particular industry, let's turn to the labor supply curve. By adding supply to the analysis, we can come up with the equilibrium wage rate that workers earn in an industry. We can think in terms of a supply curve for labor that slopes upward in a particular industry. At higher wage rates, more workers will want to enter that particular industry. The individual firm, however, does

FIGURE 27-4

The Equilibrium Wage Rate and the CD Industry

The industry demand curve for labor is *D*. We put in a hypothetical upward-sloping labor supply curve for the CD industry, *S*. The intersection is at point *E*, giving an equilibrium wage rate of $498 per week and an equilibrium quantity of labor demanded of Q_1. At a wage above $498 per week, there will be an excess quantity of workers supplied. At a wage below $498 per week, there will be an excess quantity of workers demanded.

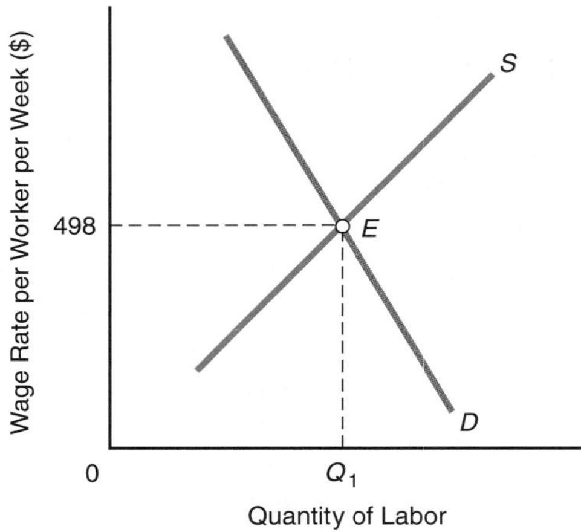

The Equilibrium Wage Rate

Practice thinking through the interaction between labor demand and labor supply.

not face the entire *market* supply curve. Rather, in a perfectly competitive case, the individual firm is such a small part of the market that it can hire all the workers that it wants at the going wage rate. We say, therefore, that the industry faces an upward-sloping supply curve but that the individual *firm* faces a perfectly elastic supply curve for labor.

The demand curve for labor in the CD industry is *D* in Figure 27-4, and the supply curve of labor is *S*. The equilibrium wage rate of $498 a week is established at the intersection of the two curves. The quantity of workers both supplied and demanded at that rate is Q_1. If for some reason the wage rate fell to $400 a week, in our hypothetical example, there would be an excess number of workers demanded at that wage rate. Conversely, if the wage rate rose to $600 a week, there would be an excess quantity of workers supplied at that wage rate. In either case, competition would quickly force the wage back to the equilibrium level.

We have just found the equilibrium wage rate for the entire CD industry. The individual firm must take that equilibrium wage rate as given in the competitive model used here because the individual firm is a very small part of the total demand for labor. Thus each firm purchasing labor in a perfectly competitive market can purchase all of the input it wants at the going market price.

EXAMPLE

Labor Supply Curves for Individuals Eventually Bend Backward

Figure 27-4 depicts an upward-sloping market labor supply curve, which is consistent with evidence that the total quantity of labor supplied by all workers increases with a rise in the market wage. Imagine, however, that you find a job with a company that emerges from initial obscurity to become a market leader. As its fortunes improve, your effective hourly wage rises and rises and then rises some more. It may be stretching your imagination, but mightn't you reach a point where you would prefer to spend more of your time in leisure activities instead of working? That is, isn't there some wage rate high enough to induce you to work *fewer* hours instead of more hours?

In case you can't imagine yourself in this kind of situation, think about this real-life example. Microsoft's wage payments to its employees have included stock in the company. Current estimates are that people who have been with Microsoft since 1994 have earned options on company stock valued at more than $3 million per person. Old-timers who have been with the company since it first went public in 1986 have benefited from a share price rise of more than 700 percent. Some who have held stock in the company all that time are estimated to hold shares valued in excess of $100 million each. All told, about a third of Microsoft's permanent employees are millionaires.

Some are having trouble getting motivated to keep putting in long hours at work. The senior vice-president who supervised Windows 95 and played a key role in developing Internet Explorer switched to part-time status. Another vice-president recently took a year's leave to spend his time sharpening his bowling skills. For most of us, higher wages induce us to substitute *away* from leisure to more time on the job. For people like these Microsoft employees, however, wages are sufficiently high that an *income effect* predominates. Their wages are so high that they prefer to work *less*.

For Critical Analysis

In most occupations, wages are not sufficiently high for workers to become millionaires (at least not very quickly). Does this observation help explain why market labor supply curves slope upward?

ALTERNATIVE THEORIES OF WAGE DETERMINATION

The relatively straightforward analysis of the supply and demand of labor just presented may not fully explain the equilibrium level of wages under certain circumstances. There are two important alternative theories of wage determination that may apply to at least some parts of the economy: efficiency wages and insiders versus outsiders. We analyze those two theories now.

Efficiency Wages

Let's say that in the CD industry, employers can hire as many workers as they want at the equilibrium weekly wage rate of $498. Associated with that weekly wage rate is a specified amount of employment in each firm. Within each firm, though, there is turnover. Some workers quit to go on to other jobs. Turnover costs are significant. Workers have to be trained. What if a firm, even though it could hire workers at $498 a week, offered employment at $600 a week? Several things might occur. First, current employees would have less desire to look elsewhere to find better jobs. There would be less turnover. Second, those workers who applied for openings might be of higher quality, being attracted by the higher wage rate. Third, workers on the job might actually become more productive because they do not want to lose their jobs. They know that alternative competitive wages are $498 a week.

The higher-than-competitive wage rates offered by such a firm have been designated **efficiency wages.** The underlying assumption is that firms operate more efficiently if they pay their workers a higher wage rate. Doing so, goes the efficiency wage argument, gives workers an incentive to be more productive, thereby making firms more cost-efficient.

Efficiency wages 
Wages set above competitive levels to increase labor productivity and profits by enhancing the efficiency of the firm through lower turnover, ease of attracting higher-quality workers, and better efforts by workers.

Insiders Versus Outsiders

A related view of the labor market involves the notion of insiders within a firm. The insiders are those current employees who have the "inside track" and can maintain their positions because the firm would have to incur costs to replace them. These employee insiders are therefore able to exercise some control over the terms under which new employees (outsiders) are hired by the firm. They keep other potential workers out by not allowing them to offer themselves for work at a lower real wage rate than that being earned by the insiders. As pointed out earlier, the costs of hiring and firing workers are significant.

Insider-outsider theory
A theory of labor markets in which workers who are already employed have an influence on wage bargaining in such a way that outsiders who are willing to work for lower real wages cannot get a job.

Indeed, the cost of firing one worker may sometimes be relatively high: termination wages, retraining payments, and litigation if the worker believes termination was unjustified. All such costs might contribute to the development of insider-dominated labor markets. They contain significant barriers to entry by outsiders.

So the **insider-outsider theory** predicts that wages may remain higher than the standard supply and demand model would predict even though outsiders are willing to work at lower real wages.

EXAMPLE

What Corporations Have in Common with Street Gangs: A Quest for the Boss's Job

Although efficiency wage theory and the insider-outsider theory may explain wages that are somewhat above a competitive level, they have a harder time explaining really big differences in wages within a firm's management structure. CEOs tend to make many times more than vice-presidents do. Senior vice-presidents, in turn, earn double what a regular vice-president is paid.

According to one theory, which Edward Lazear of Stanford University and Sherwin Rosen of the University of Chicago call the *tournament theory*, corporations create these big salary differentials not in an attempt to reward recipients but rather to create a structure of powerful incentives to get people in the organization to work harder. Pay is based on *relative* performance, relative to one's peers within the management organization. The pay of the vice-president is not what motivates that vice-president; it is the pay of the CEO, to whose job the vice-president aspires. Thus vice-presidents and others under them are involved in a series of tournaments. At each level, the winner moves up to the next higher level. All aspire to the highest level, that of the CEO.

Steven Levitt of the University of Chicago and Sudhir Venkatesh of the Harvard Society of Fellows found a similar pattern of earnings among members of an inner-city gang that deals in crack cocaine. The typical street-corner crack vendor, at the lowest rung on the ladder within the gang, earns as little as $200 per month, well below what could be earned in a minimum-wage job. "Warriors" who fight during periods of intergang warfare earn about $2,000 per month. A sizable 20 percent of the gang's revenue is split among a small number of leaders, with the head of the gang earning $100,000 per year.

For Critical Analysis

If luck plays an unusually large role in an underling's rise to the top of a corporation or a gang, will the pay differential between CEOs or gang chiefs and the next highest group have to be relatively larger or smaller compared with a situation in which luck is not important?

FAQ

Doesn't the average American stay employed with a company for a relatively long time?

Not unless you consider about $3\frac{1}{2}$ years a long time. This is the average time that a typical U.S. worker now stays with a company before switching jobs. Just a few years ago, the average worker stuck with the same job closer to four years. That employment with a single firm is so relatively brief casts some doubt on the insider-outsider theory's relevance for most U.S. labor markets. In the United States, the theory probably works best for unionized industries and government agencies—and at least some colleges, where tenured professors often appear to be the ultimate "insiders."

SHIFTS IN THE MARKET DEMAND FOR AND SUPPLY OF LABOR

Just as we discussed shifts in the supply curve and the demand curve for various products in Chapter 3, we can discuss the effects of shifts in supply and demand in labor markets.

Reasons for Labor Demand Curve Shifts

Many factors can cause the demand curve for labor to shift. We have already discussed a number of them. Clearly, because the demand for labor or any other variable input is a derived demand, the labor demand curve will shift if there is a shift in the demand for the final product. There are two other important determinants of the position of the demand curve for labor: changes in labor's productivity and changes in the price of related factors of production (substitutes and complements).

Labor Markets

Practice thinking through factors that shift the market demand for and supply of labor.

Changes in Demand for Final Product. The demand for labor or any other variable input is derived from the demand for the final product. The marginal revenue product is equal to marginal physical product times marginal revenue. Therefore, any change in the price of the final product will change MRP. This happened when we derived the market demand for labor. The general rule of thumb is as follows:

> A change in the demand for the final product that labor (or any other variable input) is producing will shift the market demand curve for labor in the same direction.

Changes in Labor Productivity. The second part of the MRP equation is MPP, which relates to labor productivity. We can surmise, then, that, other things being equal,

> A change in labor productivity will shift the market labor demand curve in the same direction.

Labor productivity can increase because labor has more capital or land to work with, because of technological improvements, or because labor's quality has improved. Such considerations explain why the real standard of living of workers in the United States is higher than in most countries. American workers generally work with a larger capital stock, have more natural resources, are in better physical condition, and are better trained than workers in many countries. Hence the demand for labor in America is, other things held constant, greater. Conversely, labor is relatively more scarce in the United States than it is in many other countries. One result of relatively greater demand and relatively smaller supply is a relatively higher wage rate.

Change in the Price of Related Factors. Labor is not the only resource used. Some resources are substitutes and some are complements. If we hold output constant, we have the following general rule:

> A change in the price of a substitute input will cause the demand for labor to change in the same direction. This is typically called the *substitution effect.*

Note, however, that if the cost of production falls sufficiently, the firm will find it more profitable to produce and sell a larger output. If this so-called *output effect* is great enough, it will override the substitution effect just mentioned, and the firm will end up employing not only more of the relatively cheaper variable input but also more labor. This is exactly what happened for many years in the American automobile industry. Auto companies employed more machinery (capital), but employment continued to increase in spite of rising wage rates. The reason: Technological improvement caused the marginal physical productivity of labor to rise faster than its wage rate.

With respect to complements, we are referring to inputs that must be used jointly. Assume now that capital and labor are complementary. In general, we predict the following:

> A change in the price of a complementary input will cause the demand for labor to change in the opposite direction.

If the cost of machines goes up but they must be used with labor, fewer machines will be purchased and therefore fewer workers will be used.

Determinants of the Supply of Labor

There are a number of reasons why labor supply curves will shift in a particular industry. For example, if wage rates for factory workers in the CD industry remain constant while wages for factory workers in the computer industry go up dramatically, the supply curve of factory workers in the CD industry will shift inward to the left as these workers shift to the computer industry.

Changes in working conditions in an industry can also affect its labor supply curve. If employers in the CD industry discover a new production technique that makes working conditions much more pleasant, the supply curve of labor to the CD industry will shift outward to the right.

Job flexibility also determines the position of the labor supply curve. For example, in an industry in which workers are allowed more flexibility, such as the ability to work at home via computer, the workers are likely to work more hours. That is to say, their supply curve will shift outward to the right. Some industries in which firms offer *job sharing,* particularly to people raising families, have found that the supply curve of labor has shifted outward to the right.

CONCEPTS IN BRIEF

- The individual competitive firm faces a perfectly elastic supply curve—it can buy all the labor it wants at the going market wage rate. The industry supply curve of labor slopes upward.
- By plotting an industrywide supply curve for labor and an industrywide demand curve for labor on the same coordinate system, we obtain the equilibrium wage rate in an industry.
- Efficiency wage theory predicts that wages paid above market wages may lead to high productivity because of lower turnover rates and better work effort by existing workers.
- The labor demand curve can shift because (1) the demand for the final product shifts, (2) labor productivity changes, or (3) the price of a related (substitute or complementary) factor of production changes.

MONOPOLY IN THE PRODUCT MARKET

So far we've considered only a perfectly competitive situation, both in selling the final product and in buying factors of production. We will continue our assumption that the firm purchases its factors of production in a perfectly competitive factor market. Now, however, we will assume that the firm sells its product in an *imperfectly* competitive output market. In other words, we are considering the output market structures of monopoly, oligopoly, and monopolistic competition. In all such cases, the firm, be it a monopolist, an oligopolist, or a monopolistic competitor, faces a downward-sloping demand curve for its product. Throughout the rest of this chapter, we will simply refer to a monopoly output situation for ease of analysis. The analysis holds for all industry structures that are less than perfectly competitive. In any event, the fact that our firm now faces a downward-sloping demand curve for its product means that if it wants to sell more of its product (at a uniform price), it has to lower the price, *not just on the last unit, but on all preceding units.* The *marginal revenue* received from selling an additional unit is continuously falling (and is less than price) as the firm attempts to sell more and more. This is certainly different from our earlier discussions in this chapter in which the firm could sell all it wanted at a constant price. Why? Because the firm we discussed until now was a perfect competitor.

Constructing the Monopolist's Input Demand Curve

Labor Demand for a Monopoly Firm
Practice working with a monopolist's demand for labor.

In reconstructing our demand schedule for an input, we must account for the facts that (1) the marginal *physical* product falls because of the law of diminishing returns as more workers are added and (2) the price (and marginal revenue) received for the product sold also falls as more is produced and sold. That is, for the monopolist, we have to account for both the diminishing marginal physical product and the diminishing marginal revenue. Marginal revenue is always less than price for the monopolist. The marginal revenue curve is always below the downward-sloping demand curve.

Marginal revenue for the perfect competitor is equal to the price of the product because all units can be sold at the going market price. In our CD example, we assumed that the perfect competitor could sell all it wanted at $6 per compact disc. A one-unit change in sales always led to a $6 change in total revenues. Hence marginal revenue was always equal to $6 for that perfect competitor.

The monopolist, however, cannot simply calculate marginal revenue by looking at the price of the product. To sell the additional output from an additional unit of input, the monopolist has to cut prices on all previous units of output. As output is increasing, then, marginal revenue is falling. The underlying concept is, of course, the same for both the perfect competitor and the monopolist. We are asking exactly the same question in both cases: When an additional worker is hired, what is the benefit? In either case, the benefit is obviously the change in total revenues due to the one-unit change in the variable input, labor. In our discussion of the perfect competitor, we were able simply to look at the marginal physical product and multiply it by the *constant* per-unit price of the product because the price of the product never changed (for the perfect competitor, P = MR).

A single monopolist ends up hiring fewer workers than all of the competitive firms added together. To see this, we must consider the marginal revenue product for the monopolist which varies with each one-unit change in the monopolist's labor input. This is what we do in panel (a) of Figure 27-5 on page 680, where column 5, headed "Marginal Revenue Product," gives the monopolistic firm a quantitative notion of how additional workers and additional production generates additional revenues. The marginal revenue product curve for this monopolist has been plotted in panel (b) of the figure. To emphasize the lower elasticity of the monopolist's MRP curve, MRP_m, the sum of the MRP curves is for a perfectly competitive industry in Figure 27-1, labeled $\Sigma\text{MRP}_c = D$, the labor demand curve under perfect competition, has been plotted on the same graph.

Why does MRP_m represent the monopolist's input demand curve? As always, our profit-maximizing monopolist will continue to hire labor as long as additional profits result. Profits are made as long as the additional cost of more workers is outweighed by

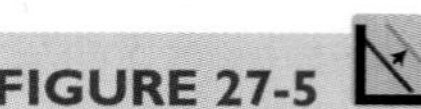

FIGURE 27-5

A Monopolist's Marginal Revenue Product

The monopolist hires just enough workers to make marginal revenue product equal to the going wage rate. If the going wage rate is \$498 per week, as shown by the labor supply curve, *s*, the monopolist would want to hire approximately 10 workers per week. That is the profit-maximizing amount of labor. The MRP curve for the perfect competitor from Figure 27-1 is also plotted (MRP_c). The monopolist's MRP curve will always be less elastic than it would be if marginal revenue were constant.

Panel (a)

(1) Labor Input (workers per week)	(2) Marginal Physical Product (MPP) CDs per week	(3) Price of Product (*P*)	(4) Marginal Revenue (*MR*)	(5) Marginal Revenue Product (MRP_m) = (2) x (4)
8	110	\$8.00	\$6.00	\$660.00
9	104	7.80	5.60	582.40
10	96	7.60	5.20	499.20
11	88	7.40	4.80	422.40
12	77	7.20	4.40	338.80
13	65	7.00	4.00	260.00

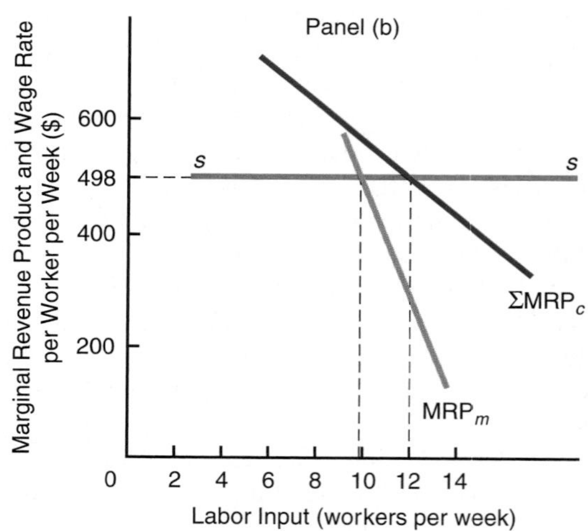

the additional revenues made from selling the output of those workers. When the wage rate equals these additional revenues, the monopolist stops hiring. That is, it stops hiring when the wage rate is equal to the marginal revenue product because additional workers would add more to cost than to revenue.

Why the Monopolist Hires Fewer Workers

Because we have used the same numbers as in Figure 27-1, we can see that the monopolist hires fewer worker-weeks than firms in a perfect competitive market would. That is to say, if we could magically change the CD industry in our example from one in which there is perfect competition in the output market to one in which there is monopoly in the output market, the amount of employment would fall. Why? Because the monopolist must take account of the declining product price that must be charged in order to sell a larger number of CDs. Remember that every firm hires up to the point at which marginal benefit equals marginal cost. The marginal benefit to the monopolist of hiring an additional worker is not simply the additional output times the price of the product. Rather, the monopolist faces a reduction in the price charged on all units sold in order to be able to sell more. So the monopolist ends up hiring fewer workers than all of the perfect competitors taken together, assuming that all other factors remain the same for the two hypothetical examples. But this should not come as a surprise. In considering product markets, by implication we saw that a monopolized CD industry would produce less output than a competitive one. Therefore, the monopolized CD industry would want fewer workers.

OTHER FACTORS OF PRODUCTION

The analysis in this chapter has been given in terms of the demand for the variable input labor. The same analysis holds for any other variable factor input. We could have talked about the demand for fertilizer or the demand for the services of tractors by a farmer instead of the demand for labor and reached the same conclusions. The entrepreneur will hire or buy any variable input up to the point at which its price equals the marginal revenue product.

A further question remains: How much of each variable factor should the firm use when all the variable factors are combined to produce the product? We can answer this question by looking at either the profit-maximizing side of the question or the cost-minimizing side.*

Profit Maximization Revisited

If a firm wants to maximize profits, how much of each factor should be hired (or bought)? As we just saw, the firm will never hire a factor of production unless the marginal benefit from hiring that factor is at least equal to the marginal cost. What is the marginal benefit? As we have pointed out several times, the marginal benefit is the change in total revenues due to a one-unit change in use of the variable input. What is the marginal cost? In the case of a firm buying in a competitive market, it is the price of the variable factor—the wage rate if we are referring to labor.

The profit-maximizing combination of resources for the firm will be where, in a perfectly competitive situation,

$$\text{MRP of labor} = \text{price of labor (wage rate)}$$
$$\text{MRP of land} = \text{price of land (rental rate per unit)}$$
$$\text{MRP of capital} = \text{price of capital (cost per unit of service)}$$

*Many economic problems involving maximization of profit or other economic variables have *duals,* or precise restatements, in terms of *minimization* rather than maximization. The problem "How do we maximize our output, given fixed resources?" for example, is the dual of the problem "How do we minimize our cost, given fixed output?" Noneconomists sometimes confuse their discussions of economic issues by mistakenly believing that a problem and its dual are two problems rather than one. Asking, for example, "How can we maximize our profits while minimizing our costs?" makes about as much sense as asking, "How can we cross the street while getting to the other side?"

The marginal revenue product of each of a firm's resources must be exactly equal to its price. If the MRP of labor were \$20 and its price were only \$15, the firm would be under-employing labor.

Cost Minimization

From the cost minimization point of view, how can the firm minimize its total costs for a given output? Assume that you are an entrepreneur attempting to minimize costs. Consider a hypothetical situation in which if you spend \$1 more on labor, you would get 20 more units of output, but if you spend \$1 more on machines, you would get only 10 more units of output. What would you want to do in such a situation? Most likely you would wish to hire more workers or sell off some of your machines, for you are not getting as much output per last dollar spent on machines as you are per last dollar spent on labor. You would want to employ factors of production so that the marginal products per last dollar spent on each are equal. Thus the least-cost, or cost minimization, rule will be as follows:

> To minimize total costs for a particular rate of production, the firm will hire factors of production up to the point at which the marginal physical product per last dollar spent on each factor of production is equalized.

That is,

$$\frac{\text{MPP of labor}}{\text{Price of labor (wage rate)}} = \frac{\text{MPP of capital}}{\text{price of capital (cost per unit of service)}} = \frac{\text{MPP of land}}{\text{price of land (rental rate per unit)}}$$

All we are saying here is that the profit-maximizing firm will always use *all* resources in such combinations that cost will be minimized for any given output rate. This is commonly called the *least-cost combination of resources.* There is an exact relationship between the profit-maximizing combination of resources and the least-cost combination of resources. In other words, either rule can be used to yield the same cost-minimizing rate of use of each variable resource.*

INTERNATIONAL EXAMPLE

Why Are European Businesses Using More Robots and Fewer Workers than U.S. Businesses?

What a strange world we live in, you might say. European countries are experiencing the highest levels of unemployment since the Great Depression. Typical unemployment rates exceed 10 percent throughout the European Union; they are over 10 percent in France and Italy and well over 13 percent in Spain. Compare this with the below 5 percent unemployment rate in the United States, and you can tell that Europe is in trouble. One would expect, therefore, that European firms could easily replace capital with labor and that there would be general pressure toward lower wages. The opposite has occurred. For example, in Germany, department stores use robots in shoe storerooms to seek out the shoes that a salesperson wants. In Denmark, milk warehouses have gone robotic. All in all, the market for automated systems in Europe has grown by more than 10 percent a year, a much greater rate than in the United States. The reason is that businesses in Europe have concluded that it is cheaper to use robots than people. In Germany, an industrial robot costs about \$10 an hour to operate. An

*This can be proved as follows: Profit maximization requires that the price of every input must equal that input's marginal revenue product (the general case). Let i be the input. Then $P_i = \text{MRP}_i$. But MRP_i is defined as marginal revenue times marginal physical product of the input. Therefore, for every input i, $P_i = \text{MR} \times \text{MPP}_i$. If we divide both sides by MPP_i, we get $P_i/\text{MPP}_i = \text{MR}$. If we take the reciprocal, we obtain $\text{MPP}_i/P_i = 1/\text{MR}$, which must be true for each and every input. That is another way of stating our cost minimization rule.

industrial worker may cost as much as $37 an hour. And while compensation to workers has continued to rise in Germany and elsewhere since the early 1990s, the operating costs of robots have fallen.

There are many reasons why wages remain so high in spite of massive unemployment in Europe. First of all, minimum wages there may be as much as 50 percent higher than in the United States. And social security contributions that employers have to pay for each worker often equal or even exceed the wages that the worker takes home. In addition, a firm must pay significant severance penalties if it fires a worker. Finally, many workers will not take low-paying jobs in some European countries because they are actually better off receiving unemployment and welfare benefits.

For Critical Analysis

Why have robots not taken over many jobs in the United States?

CONCEPTS IN BRIEF

- When a firm sells its output in a monopoly market, marginal revenue is less than price.
- Just as the MRP is the perfectly competitive firm's input demand curve, the MRP is also the monopolist's demand curve.
- For a less than perfectly competitive firm, the profit-maximizing combination of factors will occur when each factor is used up to the point at which its MRP is equal to its unit price.
- To minimize total costs for a given output, the profit-maximizing firm will hire each factor of production up to the point at which the marginal physical product per last dollar spent on each factor is equal to the marginal physical product per last dollar spent on each of the other factors of production.

NETNOMICS

Banking on the Web as an Employee Communication Tool

According to Pitney Bowes, Inc., each day the average American worker sends and receives 201 messages. An increasing number of these messages are e-mail transmissions. To help its 150,000 employees in 100 countries keep all their interoffice memos and other miscellaneous messages organized, Citibank provides Citiweb. This is a company Web site managed by a dozen full-time employees. About half of the company's employees reach Citiweb using the Internet, and the remainder access it through Citibank's proprietary network.

The site provides bank employees with special e-mail facilities. Citiweb also includes a search engine, automated distribution lists, employee forms and job postings, newsletters from business units within the bank, information about savings plans and benefits, a company events calendar, and internal and external news feeds. In addition, the site has special Citibank billboards, chat rooms, and software tools. Although employees can use Citweb to do on-line personal shopping for items such as flowers and health and beauty aids, they also use it to process corporate purchases of computers and other office equipment.

Citibank reports that the site has raised employee productivity by eliminating the need to maintain distribution lists, print newsletters, or send information in the mail. In addition, Citiweb offers Internet-based training programs that employees can use to develop additional skills. Furthermore, Citibank encourages its employees to use the site to help test new on-line banking services, which helps the bank's software developers identify program bugs before the bank offers the services to the general public.

ISSUES & APPLICATIONS

Taking This Course (and Others, of Course) Should Pay Off, at Least in the Near Term

Concepts Applied

- Demand for Labor
- Value of Marginal Product
- Derived Demand
- Substitute Inputs

Often students start to doubt whether they have done the right thing by going on for technical certification or a college degree after high school. If you are one of those students going through some natural soul-searching, stop! There are currently big payoffs to education beyond high school. Whether these sizable relative gains will persist in future years cannot be predicted with certainty, but right now postsecondary education has definite rewards.

An Education-Oriented Labor Market

Take a look at Table 27-1 and at Figure 27-6. Table 27-1 provides estimates going back to 1940 of the breakdown of U.S. employment for high school dropouts, high school graduates, people with some college, and college graduates. As you can see, in 1940, high school dropouts accounted for just over two-thirds of employed workers in the United States. In 1998, they comprised less than 10 percent of the employed workforce. People with any training beyond high school accounted for a share of less than 13 percent of total employment in 1940, but today that share exceeds 57 percent. Today, some college education greatly improves the odds of being employed.

Figure 27-6 shows a ratio-scale plot of the wages of a typical college graduate relative to the wages of a typical high school graduate. The wages of college graduates relative to high school graduates have remained substantially higher, reaching historical levels in recent years. The "higher education wage premium" earned by people who study beyond high school is real and sizeable.

Will the Education Advantage Last?

It is tempting to conclude that people with less education will forever be left behind. This is not necessarily true, however, as reference to Figure 27-6 indicates. Between the 1940s and the 1980s, college graduates' wages relative to those of high school graduates cycled

TABLE 27-1
Full-Time-Equivalent Employment Share, by Education Level

Year	High School Dropouts (%)	High School Graduates(%)	Some College (%)	College Graduates (%)
1940	67.9	19.2	6.5	6.4
1950	58.6	24.4	9.2	7.8
1960	49.5	27.7	12.2	10.6
1970	35.9	34.7	15.6	13.8
1980	20.7	36.1	22.8	20.4
1990	11.4	33.0	30.2	24.4
1998	9.4	33.2	28.3	29.1

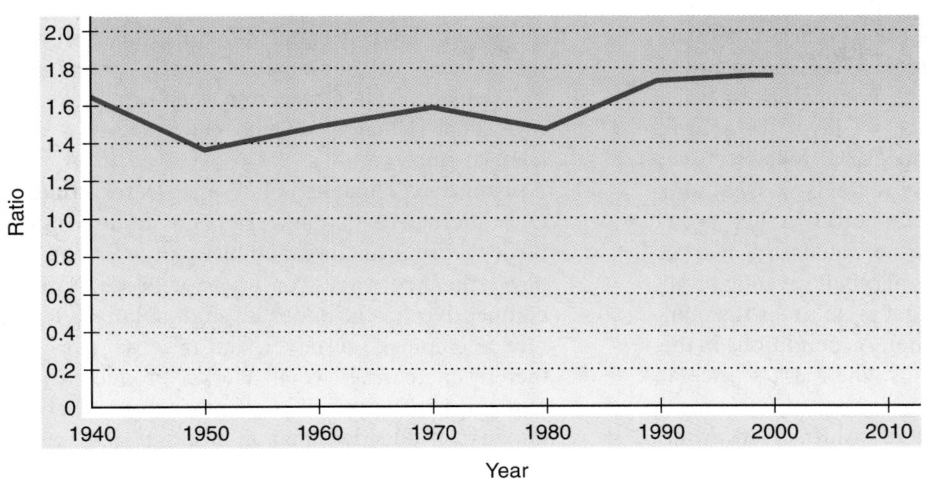

FIGURE 27-6
Wages of College Graduates Relative to Wages of High School Graduates
The ratio of college graduates' average wages to the average wages of high school graduates declined after World War II before rising over the next two decades and then falling off slightly between 1970 and 1980. Since 1980, however, this ratio has risen noticeably.
Source: Lawrence Katz, "Technological Change, Computerization, and the Wage Structure," paper presented at the U.S. Department of Commerce conference "Understanding the Digital Economy," Washington, D.C., May 1999.

up and down. There is nothing to guarantee that a similar downward movement may not take place again.

Indeed, recent software developments may eventually make a difference. One in particular is called electronic performance support systems (EPSS). This software automates many job-related mental tasks and provides quick instructions to help users make the human judgments that are still required for many jobs. For instance, many banks now provide their customer support staff with EPSS software that guides them when they receive calls complaining about features of their credit card accounts. Once the bank's customer service representative enters the caller's account number into a computer, the EPSS software immediately reviews the caller's customer records and evaluates whether the account holder has been profitable for the bank. If so, a green light flashes to cue the bank's customer service representative to satisfy the customer, and directions appear on the screen for, say, upgrading the customer's credit card. If a red light flashes, the bank's employee knows to be unsympathetic. This requires no special skills for the employee beyond an ability to talk with callers. In addition, little training is required to do the job, because the program does most of the work.

Thus EPSS software, a form of capital good, may begin to help replace college-educated employees with others who have less education. Ultimately, the higher education wage premium accruing to college graduates may begin to decline.

FOR CRITICAL ANALYSIS

1. If EPSS software becomes a common feature at most American companies, how do you think the employment distribution in Table 27-1 will change over the next decade or two?
2. What are some pitfalls in trying to forecast how the higher education wage premium may vary in future years?

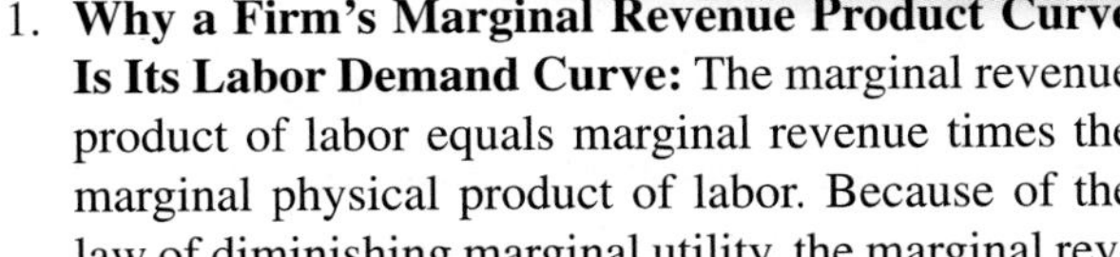

SUMMARY DISCUSSION OF LEARNING OBJECTIVES

1. **Why a Firm's Marginal Revenue Product Curve Is Its Labor Demand Curve:** The marginal revenue product of labor equals marginal revenue times the marginal physical product of labor. Because of the law of diminishing marginal utility, the marginal revenue product curve slopes downward. To maximize profits, a firm hires labor to the point where the marginal factor cost of labor—the addition to total input costs resulting from employing an additional unit of labor. For firms that hire labor in competitive labor markets, the market wage rate is the marginal factor cost of labor, so profit maximization requires hiring

labor to the point where the wage rate equals marginal revenue product, which is a point on the marginal revenue product schedule. Thus the marginal revenue product curve gives combinations of wage rates and desired employment of labor for a firm, which means that it is the firm's labor demand curve.

2. **The Demand for Labor as a Derived Demand:** For firms that are perfect competitors in their product markets, marginal revenue equals the market price of their output, so the marginal revenue product of labor equals the product price times the marginal physical product of labor. As conditions in the product market vary and cause the market price at which firms sell their output to change, their marginal revenue product curves shift. Hence the demand for labor by perfectly competitive firms is derived from the demand for the final products these firms produce.
3. **Key Factors Affecting the Elasticity of Demand for Inputs:** The price elasticity of the demand for an input, such as labor, is equal to the percentage change in the quantity of the input demanded divided by the percentage change in the price of the input, such as the wage rate. The price elasticity of demand for a particular input is relatively high when any one of the following is true: (i) the price elasticity of demand for the final product is relatively high; (ii) it is relatively easy to substitute other inputs in the production process; (iii) the proportion of total costs accounted for by the input is relatively large; or (iv) the firm has a longer time period to adjust to the change in the input's price.
4. **How Equilibrium Wage Rates at Perfectly Competitive Firms Are Determined:** For perfectly competitive firms, the market labor demand curve is the sum of the individual labor demand curves for all firms, which in turn are the firms' marginal revenue product curves. At the equilibrium wage rate, the quantity of labor demanded by all firms is equal to the quantity of labor supplied by all workers in the marketplace. At this wage rate, each firm looks to its own labor demand curve to determine how much labor to employ.
5. **Alternative Theories of Wage Determination:** One alternative to the basic derived-demand-for-labor theory is an approach that proposes that firms pay efficiency wages, or wages sufficiently above competitive levels to attract high-quality workers, reduce employee turnover, and raise worker effort, thereby increasing overall worker productivity and reducing production costs. Another approach, called the insider-outsider theory, proposes that current employees are insiders who are able to influence conditions under which prospective employers are hired, which can make the costs of hiring new workers higher, thereby pushing wages above competitive levels.
6. **Contrasting the Demand for Labor and Wage Determination Under Monopoly with Outcomes Under Perfect Competition:** If a firm that is a monopolist in its product market competes with firms of other industries for labor in a competitive labor market, it takes the market wage rate as given. Its labor demand curve, however, lies to the left of the labor demand curve for the industry that would have arisen if the industry included a number of perfectly competitive firms. The reason is that marginal revenue is less than price for a monopolist, so the marginal revenue product of the monopolist is lower than under competition. Thus at the competitively determined wage rate, a monopolized industry employs fewer workers than the industry otherwise would if it were perfectly competitive.

Key Terms and Concepts

Derived demand (669)
Efficiency wages (675)
Insider-outsider theory (676)
Marginal factor cost (MFC) (668)
Marginal physical product (MPP) of labor (666)
Marginal revenue product (MRP) (668)

Problems

Answers to the odd-numbered problems appear at the back of the book.

27-1. The following table depicts the output of a firm that manufactures computer printers. The printers sell for $100 each.

Labor Input (workers per week)	Total Physical Output (printers per week)
10	200
11	218
12	234
13	248
14	260
15	270
16	278

Calculate the marginal physical product and marginal revenue product for this firm.

27-2. Suppose that the firm in Problem 27-1 has chosen to hire 15 workers. What is the maximum wage the firm would be willing to pay?

27-3. The weekly wages paid by computer printer manufacturers in a perfectly competitive market is $1,200. Using the information provided in the table that accompanies Problem 27-1, how many workers will the profit-maximizing employer hire?

27-4. Suppose that there is an increase in the demand for personal computer systems. Explain the likely effects on marginal revenue product, marginal factor cost, and the number of workers hired by the firm in Problem 27-1.

27-5. Explain what happens to the elasticity of demand for labor in a given industry after each of the following events.

a. A new manufacturing technique makes capital easier to substitute for labor.

b. There is an increase in the number of substitutes for the final product that labor produces.

c. After a drop in the prices of capital inputs, labor accounts for a larger portion of a firm's factor costs.

27-6. Explain how the following events would affect the demand for labor.

a. A new education program administered by the company increases the efficiency of labor.

b. The firm completes a new plant with a larger workspace and new machinery.

27-7. The following table depicts the product market and labor market a portable stereo manufacturer faces.

Labor Input (workers per day)	Total Physical Product	Product Price ($)
10	100	50
11	109	49
12	116	48
13	121	47
14	124	46
15	125	45

Given the information in the table, calculate the firm's marginal physical product, total revenue, and marginal revenue product.

27-8. The firm in Problem 27-7 competes in a perfectly competitive labor market, and the market wage it faces is $100. How many workers will the profit-maximizing employer hire?

27-9. The current market wage rate is $10, the rental rate of land is $1,000, and the rental rate of capital is $500. Production managers at a firm find that under their current allocation of factors of production, the marginal revenue product of labor is 100, the marginal revenue product of land is $10,000, and the marginal revenue product of capital is $4,000. Is the firm maximizing profit? Why or why not?

27-10. The current wage rate is $10, and the rental rate of capital is $500. Production managers at a firm find that the marginal physical product of labor is 200 and the marginal physical product of capital is 20,000. Is the firm maximizing profits for the given cost outlay? Why or why not?

Economics on the Net

How the Minimum Wage Affects the Poor Federal, state, and local minimum-wage laws can affect employment levels around the United States. This Internet application helps you think through the full effects of these laws on many of the poorest individuals that the laws are intended to benefit.

Title: Will Increasing the Minimum Wage Help the Poor?

Navigation: Click here to start at Federal Reserve Bank of Cleveland's home page. Click on Publications. Scroll down, and click on Economic Commentary. Select 1999. Select the article titled "Will Increasing the Minimum Wage Help the Poor?"

Application In this chapter, you read about the market determination of wage rate. Read the article titled "Will Increasing the Minimum Wage Help the Poor?" Then answer the following questions.

1. What type of market control is a minimum wage? What is the primary rationale for increasing the minimum wage rate?
2. Based on the article, will an increase in the minimum wage help the poor? Do you agree? Why or why not?

For Group Discussion and Analysis: Identify the positive economic analysis and the normative issues in this article. What is the consensus view of the economists surveyed on the effect of a minimum wage increase? What alternatives to an increase in the minimum wage can the group propose?

CHAPTER

28

UNIONS AND LABOR MARKET MONOPOLY POWER

These union demonstrators are part of a dwindling fraction of the labor force. In the private sector of the U.S. economy, only about one worker in 10 belongs to a union. Why has union membership declined?

In the early 1960s, one out of every four American workers was a union member. Today, only about one in 10 belongs to a union. Union strike activity also has waned. Why were there so many union members four decades ago? Why has union membership declined since? Has there been a corresponding decline in the importance of unionized industries in the U.S. economy? Is there any likelihood that the American labor movement that spawned unions could revive in the future? Before you can answer these questions, you need to know about monopoly power in the market for labor.

LEARNING OBJECTIVES

After reading this chapter, you should be able to:

1. **Outline the essential history of the American labor union movement**
2. **Discuss the current status of labor unions in the United States**
3. **Describe the basic economic goals and strategies of labor unions**
4. **Evaluate the potential effects of labor unions on wages and productivity**
5. **Explain how a monopsonist determines how much labor to employ and what wage rate to pay**
6. **Compare wage and employment decisions by a monopsonistic firm with the choices made by firms in industries with alternative market structures**

Chapter Outline

Did You Know That... in 1971, some 2.5 million workers were involved in strikes, but in the past few years, fewer than 250,000 have been involved? More than 12 times the number of workdays were lost to strikes in the 1950s than are lost to them today. The labor landscape has been changing in the United States. That does not mean that concerted activity on the part of groups of workers is insignificant in our economy, though. Some workers are able to earn more than they would in a competitive labor market because they have obtained a type of monopoly power. These are members of effective **labor unions,** workers' organizations that seek to secure economic improvements for their members. In forming unions, a certain monopoly element enters into the supply of labor equation. That is because we can no longer talk about a perfectly competitive labor supply situation when active and effective unions bargain as a single entity with management. The entire supply of a particular group of workers is controlled by a single source. Later in the chapter, we will examine the converse—a single employer who is the sole user of a particular group of workers.

THE AMERICAN LABOR MOVEMENT

Labor unions 
Worker organizations that seek to secure economic improvements for their members; they also seek to improve the safety, health, and other benefits (such as job security) of their members.

Craft unions 
Labor unions composed of workers who engage in a particular trade or skill, such as baking, carpentry, or plumbing.

The American labor movement started with local **craft unions.** These were groups of workers in individual trades, such as shoemaking, printing, or baking. Initially, in the United States, laborers struggled for the right to band together to bargain as a unit. In the years between the Civil War and the Great Depression (1861–1930s), the Knights of Labor, an organized group of both skilled and unskilled workers, demanded an eight-hour workday, equal pay for women and men, and the replacement of free enterprise with the socialist system. In 1886, a dissident group from the Knights of Labor formed the American Federation of Labor (AFL) under the leadership of Samuel Gompers. Until World War I, the government supported business's opposition to unions by offering the use of police personnel to break strikes. During World War I, the image of the unions improved and membership increased to more than 5 million. But after the war, the government decided to stop protecting labor's right to organize. Membership began to fall.

Then came the Great Depression. Franklin Roosevelt's National Industrial Recovery Act of 1933 gave labor the federal right to bargain collectively, but that act was declared unconstitutional. The 1935 National Labor Relations Act (NLRA), otherwise known as the Wagner Act, took its place. The NLRA guaranteed workers the right to start unions, to engage in **collective bargaining** (bargaining between management and representatives of all union members), and to be members in any union that was started.

INTERNATIONAL EXAMPLE

European Merchant Guilds: The Original Craft Unions

The origin of today's modern craft unions is found in a type of association that flourished in continental Europe and England during the Middle Ages. Around the eleventh century, merchants started traveling from market to market in a caravan to protect themselves from bandits. The members of the caravan elected a leader whose rules they pledged to obey. The name of such a caravan was *Gilde* in the Germanic countries of Europe. When the members of the caravan returned home, they frequently stayed in close association. They soon found it beneficial to seek exclusive rights to a particular trade from a feudal lord or, later, from the city government itself. Soon merchant guilds obtained a monopoly over an industry and its related commerce in a city. A guild supervised the crafts and the wholesale and retail selling of commodities manufactured in that city. Nonmember merchants were not allowed to sell goods at retail and were subject to many restrictions from which members of the guild were exempt.

For Critical Analysis

Analyze the medieval guild in terms of the insider-outsider theory presented in Chapter 27.

Collective bargaining 
Bargaining between the management of a company or of a group of companies and the management of a union or a group of unions for the purpose of setting a mutually agreeable contract on wages, fringe benefits, and working conditions for all employees in all the unions involved.

Industrial Unions

In 1938, the Congress of Industrial Organizations (CIO) was formed by John L. Lewis, the president of the United Mine Workers. Prior to the formation of the CIO, most labor organizations were craft unions. The CIO was composed of **industrial unions** with membership from an entire industry such as steel or automobiles. In 1955, the CIO and the AFL merged. Organized labor's failure to grow at a continuing rapid rate caused leadership in both associations to seek the merger.

Three important industrial unions declared in 1995 that they, too, planned eventually to merge. Sometime soon the United Auto Workers, the United Steelworkers of America, and the International Association of Machinists will have formed a single industrial union with nearly 2 million members.

Industrial unions 
Labor unions that consist of workers from a particular industry, such as automobile manufacturing or steel manufacturing.

Congressional Control over Labor Unions

Since the Great Depression, Congress has occasionally altered the relationship between labor and management through significant legislation. One of the most important pieces of legislation was the Taft-Hartley Act of 1947 (the Labor Management Relations Act). Among other things, it allows individual states to pass their own **right-to-work laws.** A right-to-work law makes it illegal for union membership to be a requirement for continued employment in any establishment.

More specifically, the Taft-Hartley Act makes a **closed shop** illegal; a closed shop requires union membership before employment can be obtained. A **union shop,** however, is legal; a union shop does not require membership as a prerequisite for employment, but it can, and usually does, require that workers join the union after a specified amount of time on the job. (Even a union shop is illegal in states with right-to-work laws.)

Jurisdictional disputes, sympathy strikes, and secondary boycotts are also made illegal by the Taft-Hartley Act as well. A **jurisdictional dispute** involves two or more unions fighting (and striking) over which should have control in a particular jurisdiction. For example, should a carpenter working for a steel manufacturer be part of the steelworkers' union or the carpenters' union? A **sympathy strike** occurs when one union strikes in sympathy with another union's cause or strike. For example, if the retail clerks' union in an area is striking grocery stores, Teamsters may refuse to deliver products to those stores in sympathy with the retail clerks' demands for higher wages or better working conditions. A **secondary boycott** is the boycotting of a company that deals with a struck company. For example, if union workers strike a baking company, the boycotting of grocery stores that continue to sell that company's products is a secondary boycott. The secondary boycott brings pressure on third parties to force them to stop dealing with an employer who is being struck.

In general, the Taft-Hartley Act outlawed unfair labor practices of unions, such as make-work rules and forcing unwilling workers to join a particular union. Perhaps the most famous aspect of the Taft-Hartley Act is its provision that the president can obtain a court

Right-to-work laws 
Laws that make it illegal to require union membership as a condition of continuing employment in a particular firm.

Closed shop 
A business enterprise in which employees must belong to the union before they can be hired and must remain in the union after they are hired.

Union shop 
A business enterprise that allows the hiring of nonunion members, conditional on their joining the union by some specified date after employment begins.

Jurisdictional dispute 
A dispute involving two or more unions over which should have control of a particular jurisdiction, such as a particular craft or skill or a particular firm or industry.

Sympathy strike 
A strike by a union in sympathy with another union's strike or cause.

Secondary boycott
(From page 691)
A boycott of companies or products sold by companies that are dealing with a company being struck.

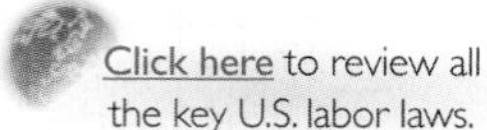
Click here to review all the key U.S. labor laws.

injunction that will stop a strike for an 80-day cooling-off period if the strike is expected to imperil the nation's safety or health.

The Current Status of Labor Unions

You can see from Figure 28-1 that organized labor's heyday occurred from the 1940s through the 1970s. Since then, union membership has fallen almost every year. Currently, it is hovering around 15 percent of the civilian labor force. If you remove labor unions in the public sector—federal, state, and local government workers—private-sector union membership in the United States is only about 11 percent of the civilian labor force.

Part of the explanation for the decline in union membership has to do with the shift away from manufacturing. Unions were always strongest in blue-collar jobs. In 1948, workers in goods-producing industries, transportation, and utilities constituted 51.2 percent of private nonagricultural employment. Today, that number is only 25 percent. Manufacturing jobs account for only 16 percent of all employment. In addition, persistent illegal immigration has weakened the power of unions. Much of the unskilled and typically nonunionized work in the United States is done by foreign-born workers, some of whom are undocumented. They are unlikely targets for union organizers.

The deregulation of certain industries has also led to a decline in unionism. More intense competition in formally regulated industries, such as the airlines, has led to a movement toward nonunionized labor. Undoubtedly, increased global competetion has also played a role. Finally, increased labor force participation by women has led to a decline in

FIGURE 28-1
Decline in Union Membership
Numerically, union membership in the United States has increased dramatically since the 1930s, but as a percentage of the labor force, union membership peaked around 1960 and has been falling ever since. Most recently, the absolute number of union members has also diminished.
Sources: L. Davis et al., *American Economic Growth* (New York: HarperCollins, 1972), p. 220; U.S. Department of Labor, Bureau of Labor Statistics.

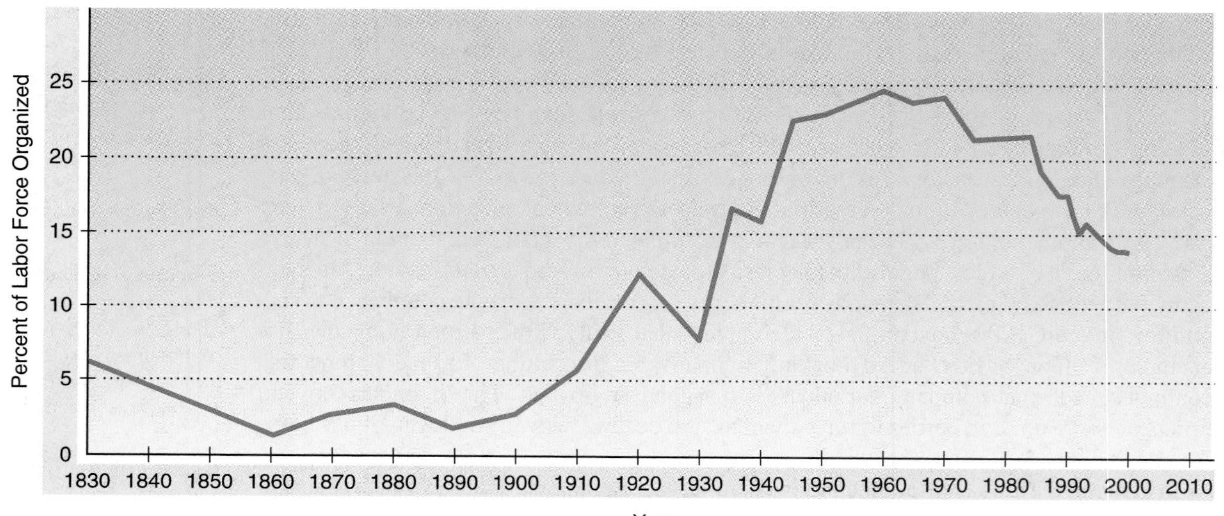

union importance. Women have traditionally been less inclined to join unions than their male counterparts.

INTERNATIONAL EXAMPLE

Europe's Management-Labor Councils

Unionization rates are much higher in the European Union (EU) than in the United States, averaging 48 percent. Perhaps more important, most EU countries have institutionalized the concept of *management-labor councils.* In Germany, legislation dating back to the early 1950s created such councils, requiring that management and labor reach decisions jointly and unanimously. German management-labor councils use up a significant amount of management time. At H. C. Asmussen, a small German distilling company with 300 workers, there are five work councils, some of which meet weekly.

On a pan-European basis, an EU directive has forced 1,500 of the European Union's largest companies to set up Europe-wide worker-management consultative committees. In the United States, no such legislation exists, although there is a management desire to create more "quality circles" (to improve quality and to reduce costs) that involve workers and management. These are often used as a threat to unions or even a substitute for them. In fact, some American unions have succeeded in getting the federal government, through the National Labor Relations Board, to disband such quality circles.

For Critical Analysis

Why do you think American unions might be against quality circles involving management and workers?

CONCEPTS IN BRIEF

- The American Federation of Labor (AFL), composed of craft unions, was formed in 1886 under the leadership of Samuel Gompers. Membership increased until after World War I, at which time the government temporarily stopped protecting labor's right to organize.
- During the Great Depression, legislation was passed that allowed for collective bargaining. The National Labor Relations Act of 1935 guaranteed workers the right to start unions. The Congress of Industrial Organizations (CIO), composed of industrial unions, was formed during the Great Depression.

UNIONS AND COLLECTIVE BARGAINING CONTRACTS

Unions can be regarded as setters of minimum wages. Through collective bargaining, unions establish minimum wages below which no individual worker can offer his or her services. Each year, collective bargaining contracts covering wages as well as working conditions and fringe benefits for about 8 million workers are negotiated. Union negotiators act as agents for all members of the bargaining unit. They bargain with management about the provisions of a labor contract. Once union representatives believe that they have an acceptable collective contract, they will submit it to a vote of the union members. If approved by the members, the contract sets wage rates, maximum workdays, working conditions, fringe benefits, and other matters, usually for the next two or three years. Typically, collective bargaining contracts between management and the union apply also to nonunion members who are employed by the firm or the industry.

Strike: The Ultimate Bargaining Tool

Whenever union-management negotiations break down, union negotiators may turn to their ultimate bargaining tool, the threat or the reality of a strike. The first recorded strike in U.S. history occurred shortly after the Revolutionary War, when Philadelphia printers walked out in 1786 over a demand for a weekly minimum wage of $6. Strikes make headlines, but in less than 4 percent of all labor-management disputes does a strike occur before the contract is signed. In the other 96 percent of cases, contracts are signed without much public fanfare.

The purpose of a strike is to impose costs on recalcitrant management to force its acceptance of the union's proposed contract terms. Strikes disrupt production and interfere with a company's or an industry's ability to sell goods and services. The strike works both ways, though, because workers draw no wages while on strike (though they may be partly compensated out of union strike funds). Striking union workers may also be eligible to draw state unemployment benefits.

Strikebreakers
Temporary or permanent workers hired by a company to replace union members who are striking.

The impact of a strike is closely related to the ability of striking unions to prevent nonstriking (and perhaps nonunion) employees from continuing to work for the targeted company or industry. Therefore, steps are usually taken to prevent others from working for the employer. **Strikebreakers** can effectively destroy whatever bargaining power rests behind a strike. Numerous methods have been used to prevent strikebreakers from breaking strikes. Violence has been known to erupt, almost always in connection with attempts to prevent strikebreaking.

EXAMPLE

Taking On the Teamsters: The "Big" UPS Strike

As unionization rates have fallen, so have the number of labor strikes. As you can see in Figure 28-2, the highest number of strikes took place in 1953 and peaked again in the late 1960s and the mid-1970s. Strike activity has declined sharply since then.

Major strikes used to have significant disruptive effects on the overall economy, but that is rarely the case today. The last strike to bring at least part of the economy to a halt was the 1997 Teamsters strike against United Parcel Service (UPS). For several weeks, mail-order companies, college book publishers, and hundreds of thousands of other firms scrambled to replace UPS shipments with alternatives. Federal Express and Airborne Express in particular gained handsomely from the Teamsters strike against UPS.

FIGURE 28-2
The Declining Number of Labor Strikes
Since about 1974, the number of labor walkouts each year has declined steadily. The power of unions seems to be on the wane.
Source: U.S. Bureau of Labor Statistics.

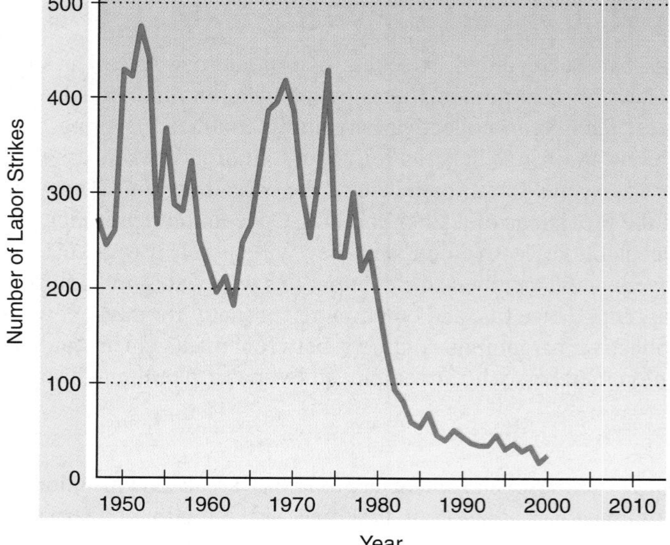

Many media pundits concluded that the strike yielded a big victory for the Teamsters and for organized labor as a whole. The Economic Policy Foundation, however, calculated that the typical UPS worker lost about $1,850 in income as a result of the strike. It calculated that relative to the final prestrike contract offer by UPS, a typical worker would require five years to come out ahead on net after the strike. Furthermore, after the strike the average part-time worker at UPS actually earned slightly *less* relative to what he or she would have earned under the company's prestrike offer. Finally, the higher costs that the new contract imposed on UPS pushed up shipping costs for manufacturing industries that are more heavily unionized, thereby raising prices of manufactured goods and reducing the quantity demanded by consumers. This tends to push down manufacturing wages. So in a sense the Teamsters' gain at UPS translated into a loss for union members in other industries.

For Critical Analysis

In what way may the Teamsters' "victory" have *helped* organized labor?

UNION GOALS 

We have already pointed out that one of the goals of unions is to set minimum wages. In many situations, any wage rate set higher than a competitive market clearing wage rate will reduce total employment in that market. This can be seen in Figure 28-3. We have a competitive market for labor. The market demand curve is *D*, and the market supply curve is *S*. The market clearing wage rate will be W_e; the equilibrium quantity of labor will be Q_e. If the union establishes by collective bargaining a minimum wage rate that exceeds W_e, an excess quantity of labor will be supplied (assuming no change in the labor demand schedule). If the minimum wage established by union collective bargaining is W_U, the quantity supplied would be Q_S; the quantity demanded would be Q_D. The difference is the excess quantity supplied, or surplus. Hence the following point becomes clear:

> One of the major roles of a union that establishes a wage rate above the market clearing wage rate is to ration available jobs among the excess number of workers who wish to work in unionized industries.

Note also that the surplus of labor is equivalent to a shortage of jobs at wage rates above equilibrium.

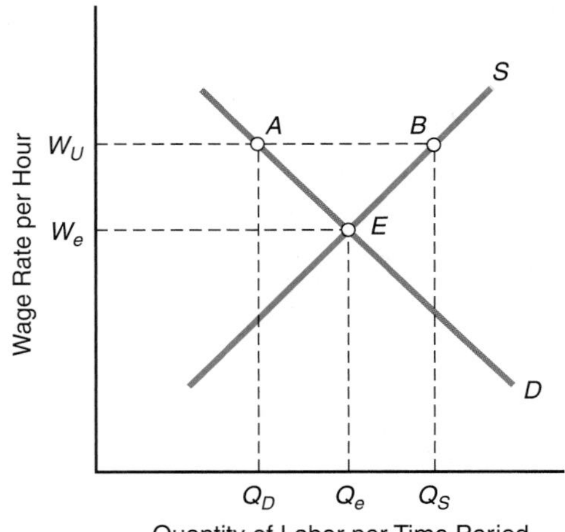

FIGURE 28-3

Unions Must Ration Jobs

If the union succeeds in obtaining wage rate W_U, the quantity of labor demanded will be Q_D, but the quantity of labor supplied will be Q_S. The union must ration a limited number of jobs to a greater number of workers; the surplus of labor is equivalent to a shortage of jobs at that wage rate.

The union may use a system of seniority, a lengthening of the apprenticeship period to discourage potential members from joining, and other such rationing methods. This has the effect of shifting the supply of labor curve to the left in order to support the higher wage, W_U.

There is a trade-off here that any union's leadership must face: Higher wages inevitably mean a reduction in total employment—a smaller number of positions. (Moreover, at higher wages, more workers will seek to enter the industry, thereby adding to the surplus that occurs because of the union contract.) Facing higher wages, management may replace part of the workforce with machinery.

Goals of Unions
Further review union goals and strategies.

Union Strategies

If we view unions as monopoly sellers of a service, we can identify three different wage and employment strategies that they use: ensuring employment for all members of the union, maximizing aggregate income workers, and maximizing wage rates for some workers.

Employing All Members in the Union. Assume that the union has Q_1 workers. If it faces a labor demand curve such as D in Figure 28-4, the only way it can "sell" all of those workers' services is to accept a wage rate of W_1. This is similar to any other demand curve. The demand curve tells the maximum price that can be charged to sell any particular quantity of a good or service. Here the service happens to be labor.

Maximizing Member Income. If the union is interested in maximizing the gross income of its members, it will normally want a smaller membership than Q_1—namely, Q_2 workers, all employed and paid a wage rate of W_2. The aggregate income to all members of the union is represented by the wages of only the ones who work. Total income earned by union members is maximized where the price elasticity of demand is numerically equal to 1. That occurs where marginal revenue equals zero. In Figure 28-4, marginal revenue equals zero at a quantity of labor Q_2. So we know that if the union obtains a wage rate equal to W_2, and therefore Q_2 workers are demanded, the total income to the union membership will be maximized. In other words, $Q_2 \times W_2$ (the shaded area) will be greater than any other combination of wage rates and quantities of union workers demanded. It is, for example, greater than $Q_1 \times W_1$. Note that in this situation, if the union started out with Q_1 members, there

FIGURE 28-4
What Do Unions Maximize?
Assume that the union wants to employ all its Q_1 members. It will attempt to get wage rate W_1. If the union wants to maximize total wage receipts (income), it will do so at wage rate W_2, where the elasticity of the demand for labor is equal to 1. (The shaded area represents the maximum total income that the union would earn at W_2.) If the union wants to maximize the wage rate for a given number of workers, say, Q_3, it will set the wage rate at W_3.

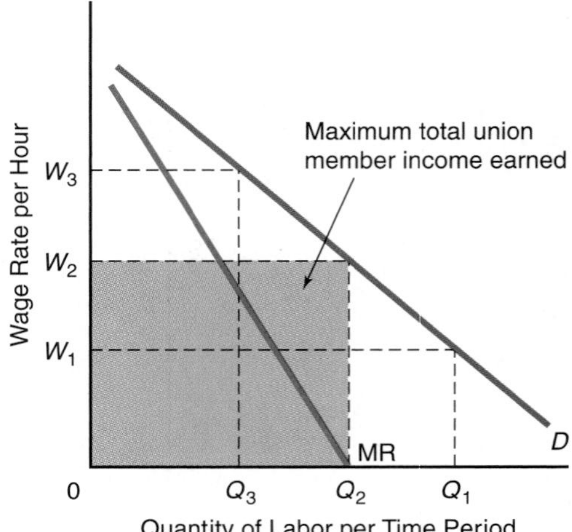

would be $Q_1 - Q_2$ members out of *union* work at the wage rate W_2. (Those out of union work either remain unemployed or go to other industries, which has a depressing effect on wages in nonunion industries due to the increase in supply of nonunion workers there.)

Maximizing Wage Rates for Certain Workers. Assume that the union wants to maximize the wage rates for some of its workers—perhaps those with the most seniority. If it wanted to keep a quantity of Q_3 workers employed, it would seek to obtain a wage rate of W_3. This would require deciding which workers should be unemployed and which workers should work and for how long each week or each year they should be employed.

Limiting Entry over Time

One way to raise wage rates without specifically setting wages is for unions to limit the size of their membership to the size of their employed workforce when the union was first organized. No workers are put out of work at the time the union is formed. Over time, as the demand for labor in the industry increases, there is no net increase in union membership, so larger wage increases are obtained than would otherwise be the case. We see this in Figure 28-5. Union members freeze entry into their union, thereby obtaining a wage rate of $16 per hour instead of allowing a wage rate of $15 per hour with no restriction on labor supply.

Altering the Demand for Union Labor

Another way in which unions can increase wages is to shift the demand curve for labor outward to the right. This approach compares favorably with the supply restriction approach because it increases both wage rates and employment level. The demand for union labor can be increased by increasing worker productivity, increasing the demand for union-made goods, and decreasing the demand for non-union-made goods.

Increasing Worker Productivity. Supporters of unions have argued that unions provide a good system of industrial jurisprudence. The presence of unions may induce workers to feel that they are working in fair and just circumstances. If so, they work harder, increasing

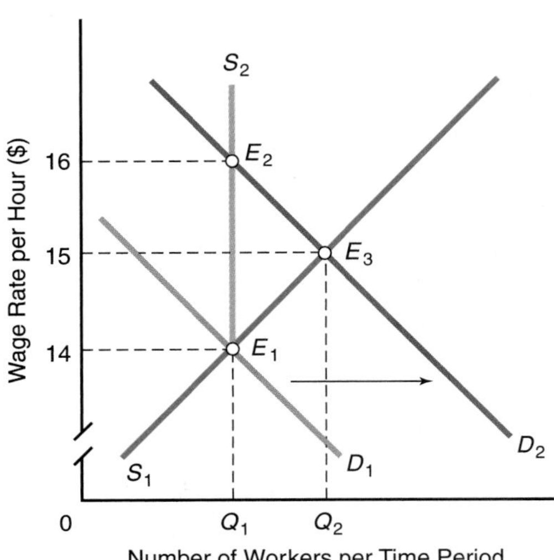

FIGURE 28-5

Restricting Supply over Time

When the union was formed, it didn't affect wage rates or employment, which remained at $14 and Q_1 (the equilibrium wage rate and quantity). However, as demand increased—that is, as the demand schedule shifted outward to D_2 from D_1—the union restricted membership to its original level of Q_1. The new supply curve is S_1S_2, which intersects D_2 at E_2, or at a wage rate of $16. Without the union, equilibrium would be at E_3 with a wage rate of $15 and employment of Q_2.

labor productivity. Productivity is also increased when unions resolve differences and reduce conflicts between workers and management, thereby providing a smoother administrative environment.

Increasing Demand for Union-Made Goods. Because the demand for labor is a derived demand, a rise in the demand for products produced by union labor will increase the demand for union labor itself. One way in which unions attempt to increase the demand for union-labor-produced products is by advertising "Look for the union label."

Decreasing the Demand for Non-Union-Made Goods. When the demand for goods that are competing with (or are substitutes for) union-made goods is reduced, consumers shift to union-made goods, increasing the demand. A good example is when various unions campaign against imports; restrictions on imported cars are supported by the United Auto Workers as strongly as the Textile Workers Unions support restrictions on imported textile goods. The result is greater demand for goods "made in the USA," which in turn presumably increases the demand for American union (and nonunion) labor.

HAVE UNIONS RAISED WAGES?

We have seen that unions are able to raise the wages of their members if they are successful at limiting the supply of labor in a particular industry. They are also able to raise wages above what wages would otherwise be to the extent that they can shift the demand for union labor outward to the right. This can be done using the methods we have just discussed, including collective bargaining agreements that require specified workers for any given job—for example, by requiring a pilot, a copilot, and an engineer in the cockpit of a jet airplane even if an engineer is not needed on short flights. Economists have done extensive research to determine the actual increase in union wages relative to nonunion wages. They have found that in certain industries, such as construction, and in certain occupations, such as commercial airline pilot, the union wage differential can be 50 percent or more. That is to say, unions have been able in some industries and occupations to raise wage rates 50 percent or more above what they would be in the absence of unions.

In addition, the union wage differential appears to increase during recessions. This is because unions often, through collective bargaining, have longer-term contracts than nonunion workers so that they do not have to renegotiate wage rates, even when overall demand in the economy falls.

On average, unions appear to be able to raise the wage rates of their members relative to nonunion members by 10 to 20 percent. Note, though, that when unions increase wages beyond what productivity increases would permit, some union members will be laid off. A redistribution of income from low- to high-seniority union workers is not equivalent to higher wages for *all* union members.

CAN UNIONS INCREASE PRODUCTIVITY?

Featherbedding
Any practice that forces employers to use more labor than they would otherwise or to use existing labor in an inefficient manner.

A traditional view of union behavior is that unions decrease productivity by artificially shifting the demand curve for union labor outward through excessive staffing and make-work requirements. For example, some economists have traditionally felt that unions tend to bargain for excessive use of workers, as when requiring an engineer on all flights. This is referred to as **featherbedding.** Many painters' unions, for example, resisted the use of paint sprayers and required that their members use only brushes. They even specified the maximum width of the brush. Moreover, whenever a union strikes, productivity drops, and this reduction in productivity in one sector of the economy can spill over into other sectors.

This traditional view against unions has been countered by a view that unions can actually increase productivity. Some labor economists contend that unions act as a collective voice for their members. In the absence of a collective voice, any dissatisfied worker either simply remains at a job and works in a disgruntled manner or quits. But unions, as a collective voice, can listen to worker grievances on an individual basis and then apply pressure on the employer to change working conditions and other things. The individual worker does not run the risk of being singled out by the employer and harassed. Also, the individual worker doesn't have to spend time trying to convince the employer that some change in the working arrangement should be made. Given that unions provide this collective voice, worker turnover in unionized industries should be less, and this should contribute to productivity. Indeed, there is strong evidence that worker turnover is reduced when unions are present. Of course, this evidence may also be consistent with the fact that wage rates are so attractive to union members that they will not quit unless working conditions become truly intolerable.

THE BENEFITS OF LABOR UNIONS 

It should by now be clear that there are two opposing views about unions. One portrays them as monopolies whose main effect is to raise the wage rate of high-seniority members at the expense of low-seniority members. The other contends that they can increase labor productivity through a variety of means. Harvard economists Richard B. Freeman and James L. Medoff argue that the truth is somewhere in between. They came up with the following conclusions:

1. Unionism probably raises social efficiency, thereby contradicting the traditional monopoly interpretation of what unions do. Even though unionism reduces employment in the unionized sector, it does permit labor to develop and implement workplace practices that are more valuable to workers. In some settings, unionism is associated with increased productivity.
2. Unions appear to reduce wage inequality.
3. Unions seem to reduce profits.
4. Internally, unions provide a political voice for all workers, and unions have been effective in promoting general social legislation.
5. Unions tend to increase the stability of the workforce by providing services, such as arbitration proceedings and grievance procedures.

Freeman and Medoff take a positive view of unionism. But their critics point out that they may have overlooked the fact that many of the benefits that unions provide do not require that unions engage in restrictive labor practices, such as the closed shop. Unions could still do positive things for workers without restricting the labor market.

CONCEPTS IN BRIEF

- When unions raise wage rates above market clearing prices, they face the problem of rationing a restricted number of jobs to a more than willing supply of workers.
- Unions may pursue any one of three goals: (1) to employ all members in the union, (2) to maximize total income of the union's workers, or (3) to maximize wages for certain, usually high-seniority, workers.

- Unions can increase the wage rate of members by engaging in practices that shift the union labor supply curve inward or shift the demand curve for union labor outward (or both).
- Some economists believe that unions can increase productivity by acting as a collective voice for their members, thereby freeing members from the task of convincing their employers that some change in working arrangements should be made. Unions may reduce turnover, thus improving productivity.

MONOPSONY: A BUYER'S MONOPOLY 

Let's assume that a firm is a perfect competitor in the product market. The firm cannot alter the price of the product it sells, and it faces a perfectly elastic demand curve for its product. We also assume that the firm is the only buyer of a particular input. Although this situation may not occur often, it is useful to consider. Let's think in terms of a factory town, like those dominated by textile mills or in the mining industry. One company not only hires the workers but also owns the businesses in the community, owns the apartments that workers live in, and hires the clerks, waiters, and all other personnel. This buyer of labor is called a **monopsonist,** the single buyer.

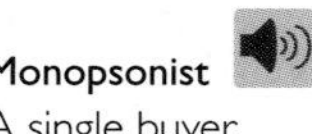
Monopsonist
A single buyer.

What does an upward-sloping supply curve mean to a monopsonist in terms of the costs of hiring extra workers? It means that if the monopsonist wants to hire more workers, it has to offer higher wages. Our monopsonist firm cannot hire all the labor it wants at the going wage rate. If it wants to hire more workers, it has to raise wage rates, including the wage of all its current workers (assuming a non-wage-discriminating monopsonist). It therefore has to take account of these increased costs when deciding how many more workers to hire.

EXAMPLE

Monopsony in College Sports

How many times have you read stories about colleges and universities violating National Collegiate Athletic Association (NCAA) rules? If you keep up with the sports press, these stories about alleged violations occur every year. About 600 four-year colleges and universities belong to the NCAA, which controls more than 20 sports. In effect, the NCAA operates an intercollegiate cartel that is dominated by universities that operate big-time athletic programs. It operates as a cartel with monopsony (and monopoly) power in four ways:

1. It regulates the number of student athletes that universities can recruit.
2. It often fixes the prices that the university charges for tickets to important intercollegiate sporting events.
3. It sets the prices (wages) and the conditions under which the universities can recruit these student athletes.
4. It enforces its regulations and rules with sanctions and penalties.

The NCAA rules and regulations expressly prohibit bidding for college athletes in an overt manner. Rather, the NCAA requires that all athletes be paid only for tuition, fees, room, board, and books. Moreover, the NCAA limits the number of athletic scholarships that can be given by a particular university. These rules are ostensibly to prevent the richest universities from "hiring" the best student athletes.

Not surprisingly, from the very beginning of the NCAA, individual universities and colleges have attempted to cheat on the rules in order to attract better athletes. The original agreement among the colleges was to pay no wages. Almost immediately after this agreement was put into effect, colleges switched to offering athletic scholarships, jobs, free room and board, travel expenses, and other enticements. It was not unusual for athletes to be paid $10 an hour to rake leaves when the going wage rate for such work was only $5 an hour. Finally, the NCAA had to agree to permit wages up to a certain amount per year.

If all universities had to offer exactly the same money wages and fringe benefits, the academically less distinguished colleges in metropolitan areas (with a large potential number of ticket-buying fans) would have the most inducement to violate the NCAA agreements (to compensate for the lower market value of their degrees). They would figure out all sorts of techniques to get the best student athletes. Indeed, such schools have in fact cheated more than other universities and colleges, and their violations have been detected and punished with a greater relative frequency than those of other colleges and universities.

For Critical Analysis

College and university administrators argue that the NCAA rules are necessary to "keep business out of higher education." How can one argue that college athletics is related to academics?

Marginal Factor Cost

The monopsonist faces an upward-sloping supply curve of the input in question because as the only buyer, it faces the entire market supply curve. Each time the monopsonist buyer of labor, for example, wishes to hire more workers, it must raise wage rates. Thus the marginal cost of another unit of labor is rising. In fact, the marginal cost of increasing its workforce will always be greater than the wage rate. This is because in the situation in which the monopsonist pays the same wage rate to everyone in order to obtain another unit of labor, the higher wage rate has to be offered not only to the last worker but also to all its other workers. We call the additional cost to the monopsonist of hiring one more worker the marginal factor cost (MFC).

The marginal factor cost for the last worker is therefore his or her wages plus the increase in the wages of all other existing workers. As we pointed out in Chapter 27, marginal factor cost is equal to the change in total variable cost due to a one-unit change in the one variable factor of production—in this case, labor. In Chapter 27, marginal factor cost was simply the competitive wage rate because the employer could hire all workers at the same wage rate.

Derivation of a Marginal Factor Cost Curve

Panel (a) of Figure 28-6 on page 702 shows the quantity of labor purchased, the wage rate per hour, the total cost of the quantity of labor supplied per hour, and the marginal factor cost per hour for the additional labor bought.

We translate the columns from panel (a) to the graph in panel (b) of the figure. We show the supply curve as *S*, which is taken from columns 1 and 2. (Note that this is the same as the *average* factor cost curve; hence you can view Figure 28-6 as showing the relationship between average factor cost and marginal factor cost.) The marginal factor cost curve (MFC) is taken from columns 1 and 4. The MFC curve must be above the supply curve whenever the supply curve is upward-sloping. If the supply curve is upward-sloping, the firm must pay a higher wage rate in order to attract a larger amount of labor. This higher wage rate must be paid to all workers; thus the increase in total costs due to an increase in the labor input will exceed the wage rate. Note that in a perfectly competitive input market, the supply curve is perfectly elastic and the marginal factor cost curve is identical to the supply curve.

Monopsony
Gain further understanding of marginal factor cost for a monopsonist.

FIGURE 28-6

Derivation of a Marginal Factor Cost Curve

The supply curve, *S,* in panel (b) is taken from columns 1 and 2 of panel (a). The marginal factor cost curve (MFC) is taken from columns 1 and 4. It is the increase in the total wage bill resulting from a one-unit increase in labor input.

Panel (a)

(1) Quantity of Labor Supplied to Management	(2) Required Hourly Wage Rate	(3) Total Wage Bill (3) = (1) x (2)	(4) Marginal Factor Cost (MFC) = Change in (3) / Change in (1)
0	—	—	
			$1.00
1	$1.00	$1.00	
			3.00
2	2.00	4.00	
			3.20
3	2.40	7.20	
			4.00
4	2.80	11.20	
			6.80
5	3.60	18.00	
			7.20
6	4.20	25.20	

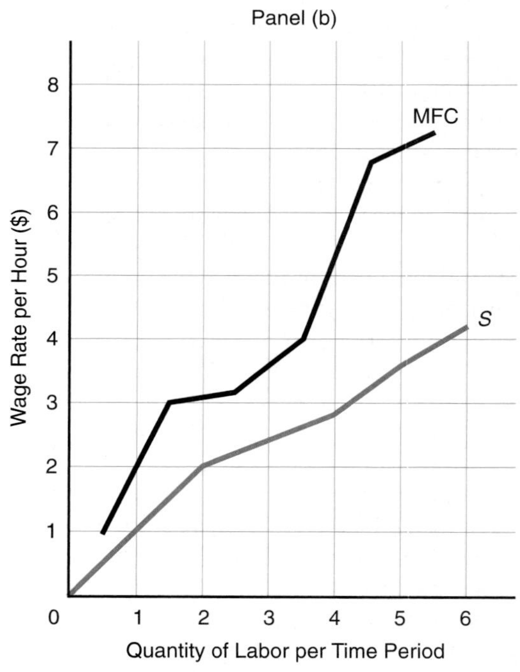

Employment and Wages Under Monopsony

To determine the number of workers that a monopsonist desires to hire, we compare the marginal benefit to the marginal cost of each hiring decision. The marginal cost is the marginal factor cost curve, and the marginal benefit is the marginal revenue product curve. In Figure 28-7, we assume competition in the output market and monopsony in the input market. A monopsonist finds its profit-maximizing quantity of labor demanded at *E,* where the marginal revenue product is just equal to the marginal factor cost.

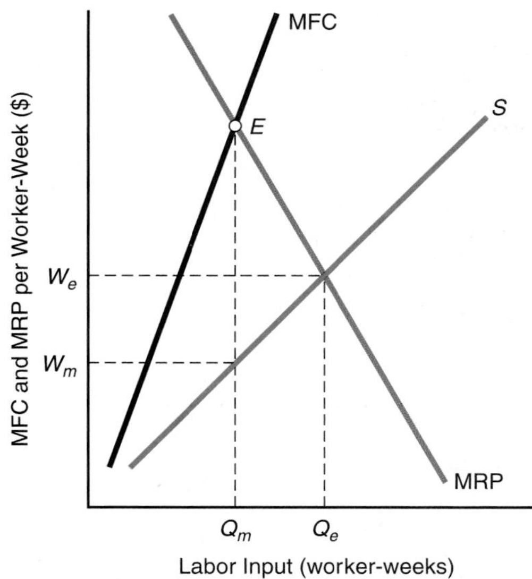

FIGURE 28-7

Marginal Factor Cost Curve for a Monopsonist

The monopsonist firm looks at a marginal cost curve, MFC, that slopes upward and is above its labor supply curve, *S*. The marginal benefit of hiring additional workers is given by the firm's MRP curve. The intersection of MFC with MRP, at point *E*, determines the number of workers hired. The firm hires Q_m workers but has to pay them only W_m in order to attract them. Compare this with the competitive solution, in which the wage rate would have to be W_e and the quantity of labor would be Q_e.

How much is the firm going to pay these workers? In a nonmonopsonistic situation it would face a given wage rate in the labor market, but because it is a monopsonist, it faces the entire supply curve, *S*.

A monopsonist faces an *upward-sloping* supply curve for labor. Firms do not usually face the market supply curve; most firms can hire all the workers they want at the going wage rate and thus usually face a perfectly elastic supply curve for each factor of production. The market supply curve, however, slopes upward.

The monopsonist therefore sets the wage rate so that it will get exactly the quantity, Q_m, supplied to it by its "captive" labor force. We find that wage rate is W_m. There is no reason to pay the workers any more than W_m because at that wage rate, the firm can get exactly the quantity it wants. The actual quantity used is established at the intersection of the marginal factor cost curve and the marginal revenue product curve for labor—that is, at the point at which the marginal revenue from expanding employment just equals the marginal cost of doing so.

Notice that the profit-maximizing wage rate paid to workers (W_m) is lower than the marginal revenue product. That is to say that workers are paid a wage that is less than their contribution to the monopsonist's revenues. This is sometimes referred to as **monopsonistic exploitation** of labor. The monopsonist is able to do this because each individual worker has little power in bargaining for a higher wage. The organization of workers into a union, though, creates a monopoly supplier of labor, which gives the union some power to bargain for higher wages.

Monopsonistic exploitation 
Exploitation due to monopsony power. It leads to a price for the variable input that is less than its marginal revenue product. Monopsonistic exploitation is the difference between marginal revenue product and the wage rate.

What happens when a monopsonist meets a monopolist? This is the situation called **bilateral monopoly,** defined as a market structure in which a single buyer faces a single seller. An example is a state education employer facing a single teachers' union in the labor market. Another example is a professional players' union facing an organized group of team owners. Such bilateral monopoly situations have indeed occurred in professional baseball and football. To analyze bilateral monopoly, we would have to look at the interaction of both sides, buyer and seller. The price outcome turns out to be indeterminate.

Bilateral monopoly 
A market structure consisting of a monopolist and a monopsonist.

We have studied the pricing of labor in various situations, including perfect competition in both the output and input markets and monopoly in both the output and input markets. Figure 28-8 on page 704 shows four possible situations graphically.

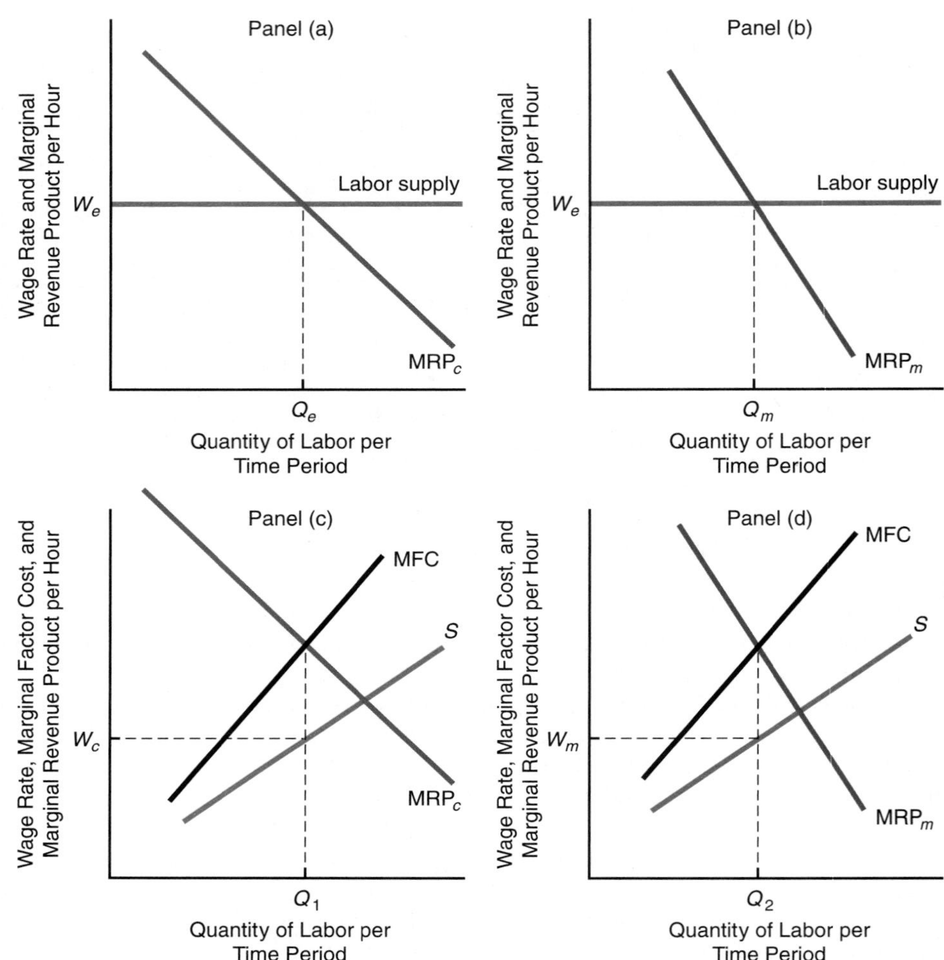

FIGURE 28-8
Summary of Pricing and Employment Under Various Market Conditions
In panel (a), the firm operates in perfect competition in both input and output markets. It purchases labor up to the point where the going rate W_e is equal to MRP_c. It hires quantity Q_e of labor. In panel (b), the firm is a perfect competitor in the input market but has a monopoly in the output market. It purchases labor up to the point where W_e is equal to MRP_m. It hires a smaller quantity of labor, Q_m, than in panel (a). In panel (c), the firm is a monopsonist in the input market and a perfect competitor in the output market. It hires labor up to the point where MFC = MRP_c. It will hire quantity Q_1 and pay wage rate W_c. Panel (d) shows a situation in which the firm is both a monopolist in the market for its output and a monopsonist in its labor market. It hires the quantity of labor Q_2 at which MFC = MRP_m and pays the wage rate W_m.

FAQ

Isn't the gender pay gap evidence of employer exploitation of women?

The fact that the average weekly wages of females continue to equal only about three-fourths of average male wages does not necessarily imply that employers exploit female workers. Although wage discrimination against women by some employers undoubtedly occurs, other factors contribute to the gender wage gap. One is that women tend to interrupt their careers to have children and continue in many households to bear the brunt of home responsibilities. Another is that even though there are growing ranks of highly trained female college graduates, the elimination of traditional welfare programs has increased the workforce participation of poorly educated women who have few marketable skills. Francine Blau and Lawrence Kahn of Cornell University have found that after accounting for education, experience, and occupations, women now earn wages no more than 12 percent less than men. Thus the gender wage gap may be somewhat overstated by direct wage comparisons.

EXAMPLE

Will Internet Job-Hunting Services Finally Make Monopsony an Irrelevant Economic Concept?

The classic example of monopsony is the "company town"—a small community in which a single firm is the dominant employer. In extreme examples, companies have owned and managed all housing, stores, and health care facilities in such towns. In these unusual situations, the companies had both monopoly and monopsony power.

Of course, the age of the automobile and commuting brought an end to most company towns. It did not necessarily bring a complete end to monopsony power for some businesses, however. For instance, imagine being a licensed practical nurse in a remote area with relatively few doctors and a single hospital largely managed by those same doctors. Avoiding some monopsonistic exploitation could prove difficult, and it might be hard for you to obtain information about alternative job openings for nurses, say, in home health care or in nursing care facilities within commuting distance of your home.

Today, however, the opportunities for a nurse in this situation are likely to brighten considerably if she logs on to her Internet service provider and types in "www." followed by "careermosaic.com," "careerpath.com," or "nationjob.com." These and other Web sites post job listings sent by company recruiters and help wanted ads from all over. Some sites have facilities for job hunters to post their résumés, and others even collect data from job seekers and then e-mail them potential matches given their talents and locational preferences. Increasingly, the Internet is blurring the distinctions among "local," "regional," and "national" labor markets, making it harder for any firm to exercise much monopsony power.

For Critical Analysis

If a local hospital faces little or no competition from other hospitals, is it possible for it to exploit its nursing employees even if it has no monopsony power?

CONCEPTS IN BRIEF

- A monopsonist is a single buyer. The monopsonist faces an upward-sloping supply curve of labor.
- Because the monopsonist faces an upward-sloping supply curve of labor, the marginal factor cost of increasing the labor input by one unit is greater than the wage rate. Thus the marginal factor cost curve always lies above the supply curve.
- A monopsonist will hire workers up to the point at which marginal factor cost equals marginal revenue product. Then the monopsonist will find what minimal wage is necessary to attract that number of workers. This is taken from the supply curve.

NETNOMICS

Working at Home: A Return to Sweatshops or a New Kind of Liberation?

By the 1890s, many American city-dwellers, adults and children alike, worked in what became known as "sweatshops." These were factories set up in large rooms in urban buildings. Women who worked for textile firms sometimes brought sewing work back to their tenement apartments and had their children assist them. In this way, some homes became extensions of the sweatshops. Today, some labor leaders are expressing concern about the potential for homes to become sweatshops of a different sort, largely as a result of widespread access to the Internet. Already, about 9 million U.S. workers are classified as "telecommuters." These are workers who work out of their homes, interacting with their employers via Internet links, e-mail and fax transmissions, and telephone communications. In addition, a growing number of people and their families now operate on-line businesses out of their homes.

One concern of labor leaders is that some telecommuters or home business operators may begin to pass a portion of their work along to their spouses and children, thereby violating child labor laws. More broadly, however, they fear that companies may increasingly *promote* telecommuting as a way to move work out of traditional plants, shops, and offices that unions have been able to organize. This, they believe, could make it easier for employers to exploit their workers. Certainly, a movement toward more telecommuting will not make it easier for unions to grow.

It is true that companies themselves are beginning to promote telecommuting. Many are cutting back on space. Increasingly, workers share offices and phones with two or three other people. In addition, companies are swayed by studies showing that many people are actually more productive at home, where there are fewer distractions.

Nevertheless, there are many factors pushing more people toward *choosing* to work at home. For one thing, it is easier for a father to make an afternoon transition to "quality time" with his child—say, finding time to take her to softball practice or gymnastics—if he is already at home, where he can e-mail a memo to his boss before departing with his daughter for the diamond or the gym. Likewise, it is easier for a mother to pick her son up at preschool on time each afternoon if she can download sales data from her company's Web site to analyze at home instead of having to stay late at the office to get the work done. Indeed, for some people, the biggest danger associated with using the Internet and e-mail to get their work done may be their computer's location under the same roof as their refrigerator. The waistlines of compulsive snackers may not benefit from the work-at-home revolution made possible by the Internet.

ISSUES & APPLICATIONS

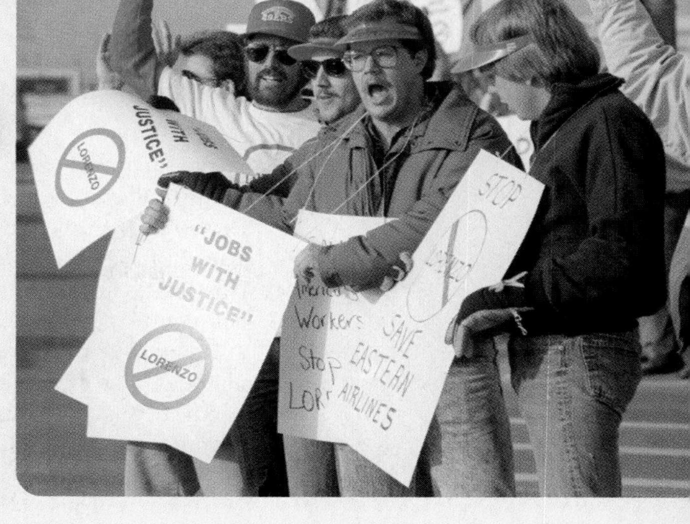

Is Profit Sharing Making Unions Obsolete?

Many economists have contended that the best wage-setting arrangement entails automatic adjustments of wages to firm profitability. Some proponents of profit sharing argue that it can help stabilize employment, because effective wage reductions would accompany profit declines, thereby reducing firms' wage costs and consequent layoffs. Some also contend that increased profit sharing could actually raise overall employment by effectively reducing the net cost of employing each additional unit of labor.

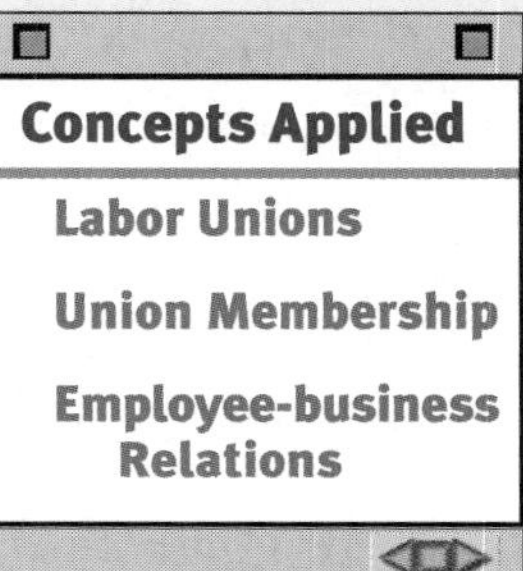
Concepts Applied

Labor Unions

Union Membership

Employee-business Relations

The Rise of Profit Sharing

Panel (a) of Figure 28-9 displays estimates of the proportion of workers employed under contracts with profit-sharing clauses in the nine countries with the largest numbers of workers covered by such contracts. France leads the list, with over a fourth of its workers covered by profit-sharing schemes, which is well above Japan's 15 percent profit-sharing coverage rate. Somewhat contradictory to proponents' arguments, France is infamous for strikes and other manifestations of labor disgruntlement. Labor produc-

FIGURE 28-9

Profit-Sharing Arrangements

Panel (a) indicates the proportion of workers covered by contracts containing profit-sharing arrangements in countries where profit sharing is most prevalent. Panel (b) shows that in the United States, profit sharing has been on the rise in the form of deferred profit-sharing pension plans.

Sources: Organization for Economic Cooperation and Development; John Duca, "The New Labor Paradigm: More Market-Responsive Rules of Work and Pay," Federal Reserve Bank of Dallas *Southwest Economy,* May-June 1998; author's estimates.

Panel (a)

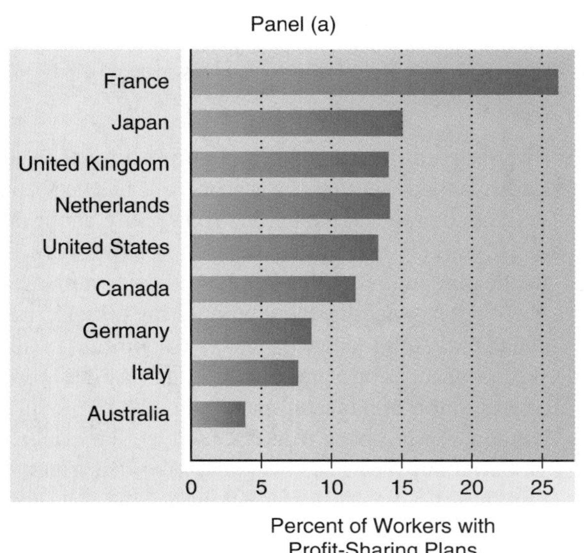

Panel (b)

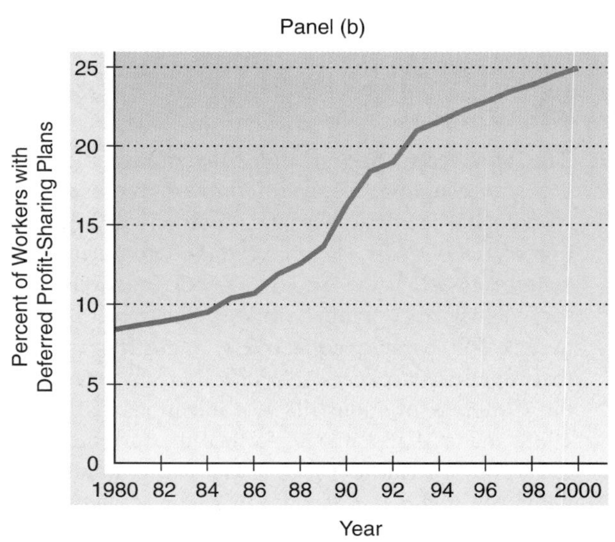

tivity growth in France also lags behind many other countries, and it suffers from a double-digit unemployment rate. Is France a "special case"? The answer is yes. French laws *require* firms with over 50 employees to offer government-designed profit-sharing plans. Hence government edict determines the structure of French profit-sharing plans. This makes it less likely that French workers and firms benefit as much from profit sharing.

Nevertheless, governmental policies also influence the degree of profit sharing in other countries. For example, in Britain, profit-based bonuses are tax-free up to a threshold income level, and in the United States, over 10 percent of workers covered under profit-sharing plans are employed by businesses that receive special tax credits for offering the programs. The Japanese government also gives favored tax treatment to certain profit-sharing schemes. Thus profit sharing is at present not a fully market-determined process. It remains to be seen how widespread profit-sharing arrangements may become in the absence of governmental stimulus.

Panel (b) of Figure 28-9 shows that the proportion of U.S. workers covered by deferred profit-sharing pension plans has risen steadily since 1980. Today, an estimated one in four workers is covered by deferred profit-sharing pension plans. Some of these workers and others also participate in employee stock ownership plans, or ESOPs. Workers in ESOPs receive shares of their companies' stocks as a form of payment. Because firms' rates of profitability influence increases in share prices and stock dividends, this is another way that firms can share profits with workers.

Does a Profit Inducement Lower the Incentive to Unionize?

If you look back at Figure 28-1 on page 692, you will note that the proportion of U.S. workers in unions began its most recent sustained decline during the 1980s. As panel (b) of Figure 28-9 indicates, this is also when profit sharing became more common. Undoubtedly, increased competition in the U.S. marketplace has influenced both patterns.

FOR CRITICAL ANALYSIS

1. If a worker's effective wage falls because of a decline in an employer's profitability, does this give the worker a greater incentive to go on strike or to increase his or her productivity?
2. Is profit sharing necessarily incompatible with unionization?

SG

SUMMARY DISCUSSION OF LEARNING OBJECTIVES

1. **The American Labor Union Movement:** The first U.S. labor unions were craft unions, representing workers in specific trades, and the American Federation of Labor (AFL) emerged in the late nineteenth century. In 1935, the National Labor Relations Act (or Wagner Act) granted workers the right to form unions and bargain collectively. Industrial unions that represent workers of specific industries formed the Congress of Industrial Organizations (CIO) in 1938, and in 1955 a merger formed the current AFL-CIO. The Taft-Hartley Act of 1947 placed limitations on unions' rights to organize, strike, and boycott.
2. **The Current Status of U.S. Labor Unions:** In the mid-twentieth century, nearly one out of every four workers belonged to a union. Today only about one in 10 workers is a union member. A key reason for the decline in union membership rates is undoubtedly the relative decline in manufacturing jobs as a percentage of total employment. In addition, in less skilled occupations that would otherwise be attractive to union organizers, many workers are undocumented, foreign-born workers. Greater domestic and global competition has probably also had a part in bringing about a decline in unions.

3. **Basic Goals and Strategies of Labor Unions:** A key goal of most unions is to achieve higher wages. Often this entails bargaining for wages above competitive levels, which produces surplus labor. Thus a major task of many unions is to ration available jobs among the excess number of individuals who desire to work at the wages established by collective bargaining agreements. One strategy that unions often use to address this trade-off between wages and the number of jobs is to maximize the total income of members. If the focus of union objectives is the well-being of current members only, the union may bargain for limits on entry of new workers and seek to maximize the wages only of current union members. Another way for unions to try to push up wages is to try to increase worker productivity and lobby consumers to increase their demands for union-produced goods and reduce their demands for goods produced by nonunionized industries.
4. **Effects of Labor Unions on Wages and Productivity:** Economists have found that wages of unionized workers are typically higher than those of workers who are not union members. This is especially true during recessions, when the wages of nonunionized workers decline while those of unionized workers covered by collective bargaining agreements remain unchanged. On average, union wages are 10 to 20 percent higher than wages of nonunionized workers. It is less clear how unions affect worker productivity. On the one hand, some collective bargaining rules specifying how jobs are performed appear to reduce productivity. On the other hand, unionization reduces job turnover, which may enhance productivity.
5. **How a Monopsonist Determines How Much Labor to Employ and What Wage Rate to Pay:** A monopsony is the only firm that buys a particular input, such as labor. For a monopsonist in a labor market, paying a higher wage to attract an additional unit of labor increases its total factor costs for all other labor employed. For this reason, the marginal factor cost of labor is always higher than the wage rate, so the marginal factor cost schedule lies above the labor supply schedule. The labor market monopsonist employs labor to the point where the marginal factor cost of labor equals the marginal revenue product of labor. It then pays the workers it hires the wage at which they are willing to work, as determined by the labor supply curve that lies below the marginal factor cost curve. As a result, the monopsonist pays workers a wage that is less than their marginal revenue product, thereby engaging in monopsonistic exploitation of labor.
6. **Comparing a Monopsonist's Wage and Employment Decisions with Choices by Firms in Industries with Other Market Structures:** Firms that are perfect competitors or monopolies in their product markets but hire workers in perfectly competitive labor markets take the wage rate as market-determined, meaning that their individual actions are unable to influence the market wage rate. A product market monopolist tends to employ fewer workers than would be employed if the monopolist's industry were perfectly competitive, but the product market monopolist nonetheless cannot affect the market wage rate. By contrast, a monopsonist is the only employer of labor, so it searches for the wage rate that maximizes its profit. This wage rate is less than the marginal revenue product of labor, so monopsonistic exploitation results. In a situation in which a firm is both a product market monopolist and a labor market monopsonist, the firm's demand for labor is also lower than it would be if the firm's product market were competitive, and hence the firm hires fewer workers as well.

Key Terms and Concepts

Bilateral monopoly (703)
Closed shop (691)
Collective bargaining (691)
Craft unions (690)
Featherbedding (698)
Industrial unions (691)
Jurisdictional dispute (691)
Labor unions (690)
Monopsonist (700)
Monopsonistic exploitation (703)
Right-to-work laws (691)
Secondary boycott (691)
Strikebreakers (694)
Sympathy strike (691)
Union shop (691)

Problems

Answers to the odd-numbered problems appear at the back of the book.

28-1. Discuss three aspects of collective bargaining that society might deem desirable.

28-2. Give three reasons why a government might seek to limit the power of a union.

28-3. What effect do strikebreakers have on the collective bargaining power of a union or other collective bargaining arrangement?

28-4. Suppose that the objective of a union is to maximize the total dues paid to the union by its membership. Explain the union strategy, in terms of the wage level and employment level, under the following two scenarios.

a. Union dues are a percentage of total earnings of the union membership.
b. Union dues are paid as a flat amount per union member employed.

28-5. Explain why, in economic terms, the total income of union membership is maximized when marginal revenue is zero.

28-6. Explain the impact of each of the following events on the market for union labor.

a. Union-produced commercials convince consumers to buy domestically manufactured clothing instead of imported clothing.
b. The union sponsors periodic training programs that instruct union laborers about the most efficient use of machinery and tools.

28-7. In the short run, a tool manufacturer has a fixed amount of capital. Labor is a variable input. The cost and output structure that the firm faces is depicted in the following table:

Labor Supplied	Total Physical Product	Required Hourly Wage Rate ($)
10	100	5
11	109	6
12	116	7
13	121	8
14	124	9
15	125	10

Derive, at each level of labor supplied, the firm's total wage bill and marginal factor cost.

28-8. Suppose that for the firm in Problem 28-7, the goods market is perfectly competitive. The market price of the product the firm produces is $4 at each quantity supplied by the firm. What is the amount of labor that this profit-maximizing firm will hire, and what wage rate will it pay?

28-9. A firm finds that the price of its product changes with the rate of output. In addition, the wage it pays its workers varies with the amount of labor it employs. The price and wage structure that the firm faces is depicted in the following table.

Labor Supplied	Total Physical Product	Required Hourly Wage Rate ($)	Product Price ($)
10	100	5	3.11
11	109	6	3.00
12	116	7	2.95
13	121	8	2.92
14	124	9	2.90
15	125	10	2.89

This firm maximizes profits. How many units of labor will it hire? What wage will it pay?

28-10. What is the amount of monopsonistic exploitation that takes place at the firm examined in Problem 28-9?

Economics on the Net

Evaluating Union Goals As discussed in this chapter, unions can pursue any of a number of goals. The AFL-CIO's homepage provides links to the Web sites of several unions, and reviewing these sites can help you determine the objectives these unions have selected.

Title: American Federation of Labor–Congress of Industrial Organizations

Navigation: Click here to visit the AFL-CIO's homepage.

Application Perform the indicated operations, and answer the following questions:

1. Click on About the AFL-CIO. Then click on AFL-CIO's Mission. Does the AFL-CIO claim to represent the interests of all workers or just workers in specific firms or industries? Can you discern what broad wage and employment strategy the AFL-CIO pursues?
2. Click on Partners and Links. Explore two or three of these Web sites. Do these unions appear to represent the interests of all workers or just workers in specific firms or industries? What general wage and employment strategies do these unions appear to pursue?

For Group Study and Analysis Divide up all the unions affiliated with the AFL-CIO among groups, and have each group explore the Web sites listed under Partners and Links at the AFL-CIO Web site. Have each group report on the wage and employment strategies that appear to prevail for the unions it examined.

CHAPTER 29

RENT, INTEREST, AND PROFITS

State lotteries advertise their "jackpots" regularly. Most winnings, though, are paid out over 20 years. Is it correct to add up the yearly payments and call the total the jackpot?

A few years ago, a retired electrician from Streamwood, Illinois, purchased $5 in Wisconsin lottery tickets that entered him in a Powerball lottery jointly operated by 20 states. The states sold a total of 138 million Powerball tickets, and the electrician beat odds of 80 million to one to win a single-ticketholder jackpot. Even though he could have received a total of $195 million paid in equal installments over 25 years, the retiree opted for immediate receipt of a lump-sum payment of $104 million. Why did this man choose $104 million immediately instead of $195 million to be received over the course of 25 years? To understand the answer to this question, you must learn about interest rates and the present value of future sums, which are key topics of this chapter.

LEARNING OBJECTIVES

After reading this chapter, you should be able to:

1. Understand the concept of economic rent
2. Evaluate the role of economic rent in the allocation of resources
3. Explain how market interest rates are determined
4. Discuss how the interest rate performs a key role in allocating resources
5. Calculate the present discounted value of a payment to be received at a future date
6. Describe the fundamental role of economic profits

Did You Know That... in America, presumably one of the most industrialized countries in the world, compensation for labor services makes up over 70 percent of national income every year? But what about the other 30 percent? It consists of compensation to the owners of the other factors of production that you read about in Part 1: land, capital, and entrepreneurship. Somebody who owns real estate downtown may earn monthly commercial rents that are higher for one square foot than you might pay to rent a whole apartment. Land is a factor of production, and it has a market clearing price. Businesses also have to use capital. Compensation for that capital is interest, and it, too, has a market clearing level. Finally, some of you may have entrepreneurial ability that you offer to the marketplace. Your compensation is called profit. In this chapter, you will also learn about the sources and functions of profit.

Chapter Outline

- Rent
- Economic Rent to Labor
- Interest
- Profits

RENT

When you hear the term *rent,* you are accustomed to having it mean the payment made to property owners for the use of land or dwellings. The term *rent* has a different meaning in economics. **Economic rent** is payment to the owner of a resource in excess of its opportunity cost—the payment that would be necessary to call forth production of that amount of the resource.

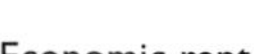

Economic rent
A payment for the use of any resource over and above its opportunity cost.

Economists originally used the term *rent* to designate payment for the use of land. What was thought to be important about land was that its supply is completely inelastic. Hence the supply curve for land is a vertical line; no matter what the prevailing market price for land, the quantity supplied will remain the same.

Determining Land Rent

The concept of economic rent is associated with the British economist David Ricardo (1772–1823). He looked at two plots of land on which grain was growing, one of which happened to be more fertile than the other. The owners of these two plots sold the grain that came from their land, but the one who owned the more fertile land grew more grain and therefore made more profits. According to Ricardo, the owner of the fertile land was receiving economic rents that were due not to the landowner's hard work or ingenuity but rather to an accident of nature. Ricardo asked his readers to imagine another scenario, that of walking up a hill that starts out flat with no rocks and then becomes steeper and rockier. The value of the land falls as one walks up the hill. If a different person owns the top of the hill than the bottom, the highland owner will receive very little in payment from, say, a farmer who wants to cultivate land for wheat production.

Here is how Ricardo analyzed economic rent for land. He first simplified his model by assuming that all land is equally productive. Then Ricardo assumed that the quantity of land in a country is *fixed.* Graphically, then, in terms of supply and demand, we draw the supply curve of land vertically (zero price elasticity). In Figure 29-1 on the next page, the supply curve of land is represented by *S.* If the demand curve is D_1, it intersects the supply curve, *S,* at price P_1. The entire amount of revenues obtained, $P_1 \times Q_1$, is labeled "Economic rent." If the demand for land increased to D_2, the equilibrium price would rise to P_2. Additions to economic rent are labeled "More economic rent." Notice that the quantity of land remains insensitive to the change in price. Another way of stating this is that the supply curve is perfectly inelastic.

FIGURE 29-1

Economic Rent

If indeed the supply curve of land were completely price inelastic in the long run, it would be depicted by S. At the quantity in existence, Q_1, any and all revenues are economic rent. If demand is D_1, the price will be P_1; if demand is D_2, price will rise to P_2. Economic rent would be $P_1 \times Q_1$ and $P_2 \times Q_1$, respectively.

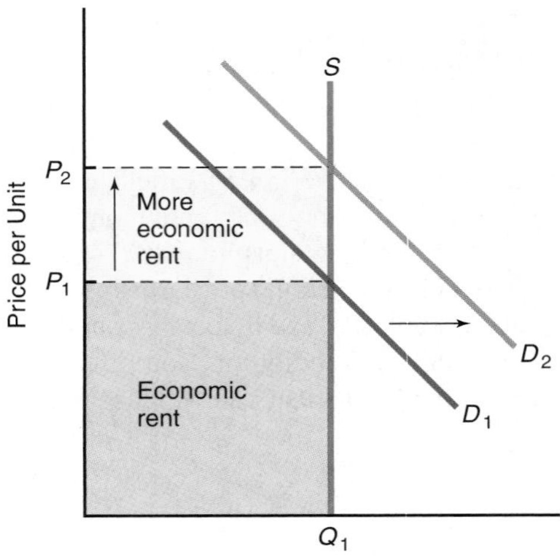

ECONOMIC RENT TO LABOR

Land and natural resources are not the only factors of production to which the analysis of economic rent can be applied. In fact, the analysis is probably more often applicable to labor. Here is a list of people who provide different labor services, some of whom probably receive large amounts of economic rent:

Professional sports superstars
Rock stars
Movie stars
World-class models
Successful inventors and innovators
World-famous opera stars

Just apply the definition of economic rent to the phenomenal earnings that these people make. They would undoubtedly work for much, much less than they earn. Therefore, much of their earnings constitutes economic rent (but not all, as we shall see). Economic rent occurs because specific resources cannot be replicated exactly. No one can duplicate today's most highly paid entertainment figures, and therefore they receive economic rent.

Economic Rent and the Allocation of Resources 

If an extremely highly paid movie star would make the same number of movies at half his or her current annual earnings, does that mean that 50 percent of his or her income is unnecessary? To answer the question, consider first why the superstar gets such a high income. The answer can be found in Figure 29-1. Substitute *entertainment activities of the superstars* for the word *land.* The high "price" received by the superstar is due to the demand for his or her services. If Leonardo Di Caprio announces that he will work for a measly $1 million a movie and do two movies a year, how is he going to know which production company values his services the most highly? Di Caprio and other movie stars let the market decide where their resources should be used. In this sense, we can say the following:

Economic rent allocates resources to their highest-valued use.

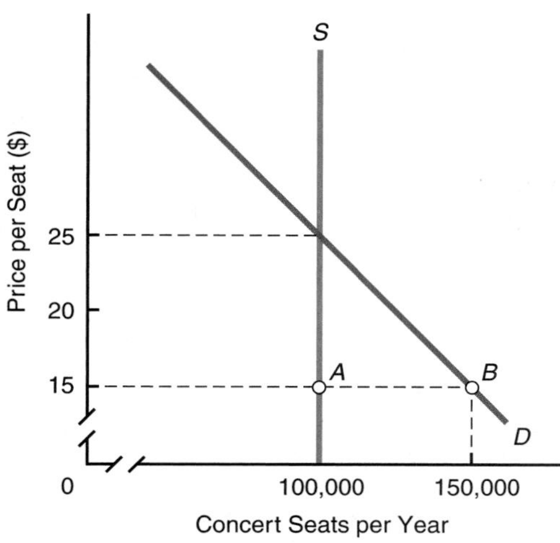

FIGURE 29-2

The Allocative Function of Rent

If the performer agrees to give five concerts a year "at any price" and there are 20,000 seats in each concert hall, the supply curve of concerts, *S*, is vertical at 100,000 seats per year. The demand curve is given by *D*. The performer wants a price of only $15 to be charged. At that price, the quantity of seats demanded per year is 150,000. The excess quantity demanded is equal to the horizontal distance between points *A* and *B*, or 50,000 seats per year.

Otherwise stated, economic rent directs resources to the people who can most efficiently use them.

A common counterexample involves rock stars who claim that promoters try to overprice their tickets. Consequently, the artists agree to perform, say, five concerts with all tickets being sold at the same price, $15. Assume that a star performs these concerts in halls with 20,000 seats. A total of 100,000 individuals per year will be able to see this particular performer. This is represented by point *A* in Figure 29-2. By assumption, this performer is still receiving some economic rent because we are assuming that the supply curve of concerts is vertical at 100,000 seats per year. At a price per ticket of $15, however, the annual quantity of seats demanded will be 150,000, represented by point *B*. The difference between points *A* and *B* is the excess quantity of tickets demanded at the below-market-clearing price of $15 a seat. The *additional* economic rent that could be earned by this performer by charging the clearing price of $25 per seat in this graph would serve as the rationing device that would make the quantity demanded equal to the quantity supplied.

In such situations, part of the economic rent that could have been earned is dissipated—it is captured, for example, by radio station owners in the form of promotional gains when they are allowed to give away a certain number of tickets on the air (even if they have to pay $15 per ticket) because the tickets are worth $25. Ticket holders who resell tickets at higher prices ("scalpers") also capture part of the rent. Conceivably, at 100,000 seats per year, this performer could charge the market clearing price of $25 per ticket and give away to charity the portion of the economic rent ($10 per ticket) that would be dissipated. In such a manner, the performer could make sure that the recipients of the rent are worthy in his or her own esteem.

EXAMPLE

Do Entertainment Superstars Make Super Economic Rents?

Superstars certainly do well financially. Table 29-1 on the next page shows the earnings of selected individuals in the entertainment industry as estimated by *Forbes* magazine. Earnings are totaled for a two-year period. How much of these earnings can be called economic rent? The question is not easy to answer, because an entertainment newcomer would almost certainly work for much less than he or she earns, thereby making high

TABLE 29-1
Superstar Earnings

Name	Occupation	Earnings (two years, millions of dollars)
Jerry Seinfeld	Actor, comedian	267
Larry David	Producer	242
Steven Spielberg	Director, producer, studio owner	175
Oprah Winfrey	Talk show host	125
James Cameron	Director, producer	115
Tim Allen	Actor, comedian	77
Michael Crichton	Writer, producer	65
Harrison Ford	Actor	58
Rolling Stones	Rock group	57
Master P	Rapper, actor	57

Source: Forbes, 2000.

economic rents. The same cannot necessarily be said for entertainers who have been raking in millions for years. They probably have very high accumulated wealth and also a more jaded outlook about their work. It is therefore not clear how much they would work if they were not offered those huge sums of money.

For Critical Analysis

Even if some superstar entertainers would work for less, what forces cause them to make so much income anyway?

Taxing Away Economic Rent

Some people have argued in favor of imposing high taxes on economic rent. For example, drug companies that have developed *successful* patented drugs make large amounts of economic rent during the life of the patent. That is to say, the marginal cost of production is much less than the price charged. If the government taxed this economic rent completely, those successful drugs already on the market would in fact stay on the market. But there would be long-run consequences. Drug companies would invest fewer resources in discovering new successful drugs. So economic rent is typically a *short-run* phenomenon. In the long run, it constitutes a source of reward for risk taking in society. This is true not only in the drug business but also in entertainment and professional sports.

- Economic rent is defined as payment for a factor of production that is completely inelastic in supply. It is payment for a resource over and above what is necessary to keep that resource in existence at its current level in the long run.
- Economic rent serves an allocative function by guiding available supply to the most efficient use.

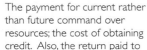

Interest 
The payment for current rather than future command over resources; the cost of obtaining credit. Also, the return paid to owners of capital.

INTEREST

The term **interest** is used to mean two different things: (1) the price paid by debtors to creditors for the use of loanable funds and (2) the market return earned by (nonfinancial) capital as a factor of production. Owners of capital, whether directly or indirectly, obtain interest income. Often businesses go to credit markets to obtain so-called money capital in order to invest in physical capital from which they hope to make a satisfactory return. In other words, in our complicated society, the production of capital goods often occurs because of the existence of credit markets in which borrowing and lending take place. For the moment, we will look only at the credit market.

Interest and Credit

When you obtain credit, you actually obtain money to have command over resources today. We can say, then, that interest is the payment for current rather than future command over resources. Thus interest is the payment for obtaining credit. If you borrow $100 from me, you have command over $100 worth of goods and services today. I no longer have that command. You promise to pay me back $100 plus interest at some future date. The interest that you pay is usually expressed as a percentage of the total loan, calculated on an annual basis. If at the end of one year you pay me back $110, the annual interest is $10 ÷ $100, or 10 percent. When you go out into the marketplace to obtain credit, you will find that the interest rate charged differs greatly. A loan to buy a house (a mortgage) may cost you 7 to 10 percent annual interest. An installment loan to buy an automobile may cost you 9 to 14 percent annual interest. The federal government, when it wishes to obtain credit (issue U.S. Treasury securities), may have to pay only 3 to 8 percent annual interest. Variations in the rate of annual interest that must be paid for credit depend on the following factors.

1. *Length of loan.* In some (but not all) cases, the longer the loan will be outstanding, other things being equal, the greater will be the interest rate charged.
2. *Risk.* The greater the risk of nonrepayment of the loan, other things being equal, the greater the interest rate charged. Risk is assessed on the basis of the creditworthiness of the borrower and whether the borrower provides collateral for the loan. Collateral consists of any asset that will automatically become the property of the lender should the borrower fail to comply with the loan agreement.
3. *Handling charges.* It takes resources to set up a loan. Papers have to be filled out and filed, credit references have to be checked, collateral has to be examined, and so on. The larger the amount of the loan, the smaller the handling (or administrative) charges as a percentage of the total loan. Therefore, we would predict that, other things being equal, the larger the loan, the lower the interest rate.

What Determines Interest Rates?

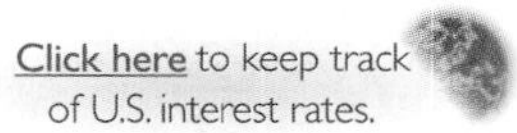

Click here to keep track of U.S. interest rates.

The overall level of interest rates can be described as the price paid for loanable funds. As with all commodities, price is determined by the interaction of supply and demand. Let's first look at the supply of loanable funds and then at the demand for them.

The Supply of Loanable Funds. The supply of loanable funds (credit available) depends on individuals' willingness to save.* When you save, you exchange rights to current consumption for rights to future consumption. The more current consumption you give up, the more valuable is a marginal unit of present consumption in comparison with future consumption.

*Actually, the supply of loanable funds also depends on business and government saving and on the behavior of the monetary authorities and the banking system. For simplicity of discussion, we ignore these components here.

Recall from our discussion of diminishing marginal utility that the more of something you have, the less you value an additional unit. Conversely, the less of something you have, the more you value an additional unit. Thus when you give up current consumption of a good—that is, have less of it—you value an additional unit more. The more you save today, the more utility you attach to your last unit of today's consumption. So to be induced to save more—to consume less—you have to be offered a bigger and bigger reward to match the marginal utility of current consumption you will give up by saving. Because of this, if society wants to induce people to save more, it must offer a higher rate of interest. Hence we expect that the supply curve of loanable funds will slope upward. At higher rates of interest, savers will be willing to offer more current consumption to borrowers, other things being constant.* When the income of individuals increases or when there is a change in individual preferences toward more saving, the supply curve of loanable funds will shift outward to the right, and vice versa.

The Demand for Loanable Funds. There are three major sources of the demand for loanable funds:

1. Households that want loanable funds for the purchase of services and nondurable goods, as well as consumer durables such as automobiles and homes
2. Businesses that want loanable funds to make investments
3. Governments that want loanable funds, usually to cover deficits—the excess of government spending over tax revenues

We will ignore the government's demand for loanable funds and consider only consumers and businesses.

Loans are taken out both by consumers and by businesses. It is useful for us to separate the motives underlying the demand for loans by these two groups of individuals. We will therefore treat consumption loans and investment loans separately. In the discussion that follows, we will assume that there is no inflation—that is, that there is no persistent increase in the overall level of prices.

Consumer Demand for Loanable Funds In general, consumers demand loanable funds because they tend to prefer earlier consumption to later consumption. That is to say, people subjectively value goods obtained immediately more than the same goods of the same quality obtained later on. Consider that sometimes an individual household's present income falls below the average income level expected over a lifetime. Individuals may go to the credit market to borrow whenever they perceive a temporary dip in their current income—assuming that they expect their income to go back to normal later on. Furthermore, by borrowing, they can spread out purchases more evenly during their lifetimes. In so doing, they're able to increase their lifetime total utility.

Consumers' demand for loanable funds will be inversely related to the cost of borrowing—the rate of interest. Why? For the same reason that all demand curves slope downward: A higher rate of interest means a higher cost of borrowing, and a higher cost of borrowing must be

---

*A complete discussion would include the income effect: At higher interest rates, households receive a higher yield on savings, permitting them to save less to achieve any given target.

POLICY EXAMPLE

Should Payday Lenders Be Regulated?

Payday lenders are companies that typically offer an individual a small amount of cash, from $100 to $300, in exchange for a personal check. The lender holds on to the check until the individual receives his or her next paycheck and then cashes the check. Payday lending is a booming business. Since 1995, the number of payday lenders in Indiana has increased from 11 to more than 60, and payday loans in that state rose from $13 million to $98 million. Check Into Cash opened its first payday store in 1993 and now has a chain of 432 stores in 16 states, including more than 30 in Illinois.

Payday lenders provide their services for a fee that typically ranges from 15 to 25 percent of the face value of the check. That is, they charge interest on loans that they effectively make to individuals who use their services. When the interest rates on these loans are converted to an annual percentage interest rate, the numbers can be shocking. For instance, a *Chicago Sun-Times* survey of Illinois payday loan lenders found the average annual interest rate charged by the lenders to be 569 percent.

The Consumer Federation of America calls payday lending "legal loan-sharking" and argues that payday lenders prey on the poor while making exorbitant profits. It calls for regulating the interest rates charged by payday lenders. But the key reason that payday lenders charge high rates is that the risk of bad checks is very high. There is also a big benefit to consumers: The ability to borrow $500 reduces the likelihood that someone who is poor will suffer a "spell of hardship," such as not having enough money for food. Thus for someone who cannot obtain a speedy loan any other way, the only thing worse than borrowing $200 at an annual interest rate exceeding 500 percent might be not being able borrow $200 at all.

For Critical Analysis

Payday lenders like to compare payday loans to taxicab transportation, which may be cost-effective for short distances but not for long-distance travel. Does this analogy seem reasonable to you?

weighed against alternative uses of limited income. At higher costs of borrowing, consumers will forgo some current consumption.

Business Demand for Loanable Funds Businesses demand loanable funds to make investments that they believe will increase productivity or profit. Whenever a business believes that by making an investment, it can increase revenues (net of other costs) by more than the cost of capital, it will make the investment. Businesses compare the interest rate they must pay in the loanable funds market with the rate of return they think they can earn by investing. This comparison helps them decide whether to invest.

In any event, we hypothesize that the demand curve for loanable funds by firms for investment purposes will be negatively sloped. At higher interest rates, fewer investment projects will make economic sense to businesses because the cost of capital (loanable funds) will exceed the net revenues derivable from the capital investment. Conversely, at lower rates of interest, more investment projects will be undertaken because the cost of capital will be less than the expected rate of return on the capital investment.

The Equilibrium Rate of Interest

When we add together the demand for loanable funds by households and businesses (and government in more complex models), we obtain a demand curve for loanable funds, as given in Figure 29-3 (p. 720). The supply curve is S. The equilibrium rate of interest is i_e.

FIGURE 29-3

The Supply of and Demand for Loanable Funds

We draw *D* as the demand curve for all loanable funds by households and businesses (and governments). It slopes downward. *S* is the supply curve of credit, or loanable funds. It slopes upward. The intersection of *S* and *D* gives the equilibrium rate of interest at i_e.

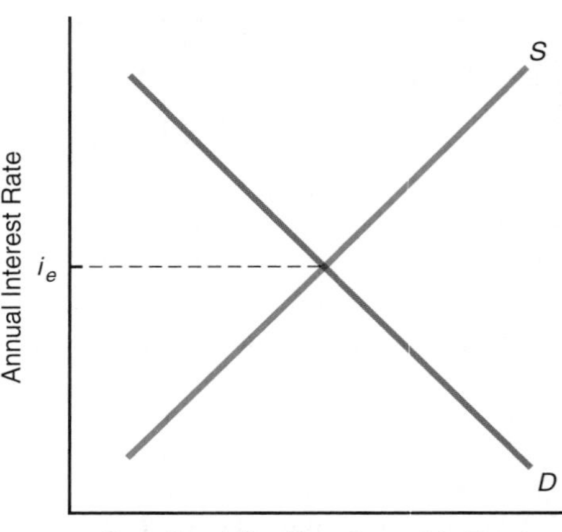

INTERNATIONAL EXAMPLE

Combating Japanese Loan Sharks with "Instant Cash Loans"

Japan has a reputation for trying to keep foreign competition away from its shores. In 1978, however, Japan's Ministry of Finance invited U.S. finance companies to open up shop in the country. Its hope was that American financiers would have the wherewithal to compete with one of Japan's most notorious industries, loan-shark operations, many of which had links to organized crime.

A number of U.S. finance companies, including Household International, Inc., Beneficial Corporation, and Associates First Capital, gave it a try. Initially, it was tough to convince Japanese residents to borrow yen from U.S. companies. Two factors ultimately worked in these companies' favor, however. One was that Japanese banks were so protected from competition in lending to corporations that they did not even try to compete for many individual and small-business customers in the 1980s. Another was that when Japan's banks had problems during the recession that hit East Asia in the late 1990s, even customers who had previously been bank borrowers had trouble getting loans. Many of these former bank customers began to turn to the U.S. finance companies.

Today, finance companies offer credit in the form of "instant cash loans," many of which borrowers can access using electronic dispensers that shoot out currency, typically in the form of 10,000-yen bills (about $100 each). The total volume of finance company credit outstanding in Japan now exceeds $60 billion. Associates First Capital alone has been increasing its lending in Japan at a rate in excess of 20 percent per year, and it now has 600 branches across the country. Associates and other U.S. finance companies typically charge 30 percent interest for loans. The companies pay a rate of 6 percent to raise funds to lend.

For Critical Analysis

There is a lot of competition among U.S. finance companies to extend instant cash loans in Japan. What factors might explain the high interest rate on these loans?

Real Versus Nominal Interest Rates

Nominal rate of interest
The market rate of interest expressed in today's dollars.

We have been assuming that there is no inflation. In a world of inflation—a persistent rise in an average of all prices—the **nominal rate of interest** will be higher than it would be in a world with no inflation. Basically, nominal, or market, rates of interest rise to take account of the anticipated rate of inflation. If, for example, there is no inflation and no inflation is expected, the nominal rate of interest might be 5 percent for home mortgages. If the rate of inflation goes to 10 percent a year and stays there, everybody will anticipate that inflation rate. The nominal rate of interest will rise to about 15 percent to take account of the anticipated rate of inflation. If the interest rate did not rise to 15 percent, the principal plus interest earned at 5 percent would be worth less in the future because inflation would have eroded its purchasing power. We can therefore say that the nominal, or market, rate of interest is approximately equal to the real rate of interest plus the anticipated rate of inflation, or

$$i_n = i_r + \text{anticipated rate of inflation}$$

where i_n equals the nominal rate of interest and i_r equals the real rate of interest. In short, you can expect to see high nominal rates of interest in periods of high inflation rates. The **real rate of interest** may not necessarily be high, though. We must first correct the nominal rate of interest for the anticipated rate of inflation before determining whether the real interest rate is in fact higher than normal.

Real rate of interest 
The nominal rate of interest minus the anticipated rate of inflation.

FAQ

Aren't high nominal interest rates always an indication that real interest rates are high?

No, in many instances real interest rates are relatively low in countries with high nominal rates of interest. The reason for double- and triple-digit interest rates in some countries—such as interest rates exceeding 100 percent in Russia in the early 1990s and above 40 percent in Brazil more recently—has often been that people anticipated high rates of inflation. Real interest rates in double digits are very rare.

The Allocative Role of Interest

In Chapter 4, we talked about the price system and the role that prices play in the allocation of resources. Interest is a price that allocates loanable funds (credit) to consumers and to businesses. Within the business sector, interest allocates loanable funds to different firms and therefore to different investment projects. Investment, or capital, projects with rates of return higher than the market rate of interest in the credit market will be undertaken, given an unrestricted market for loanable funds. For example, if the expected rate of return on the purchase of a new factory in some industry is 15 percent and loanable funds can be acquired for 11 percent, the investment project may proceed. If, however, that same project had an expected rate of return of only 9 percent, it would not be undertaken. In sum, the interest rate allocates loanable funds to industries whose investments yield the highest returns—where resources will be the most productive.

It is important to realize that the interest rate performs the function of allocating money capital (loanable funds) and that this ultimately allocates real physical capital to various firms for investment projects.

Interest Rates and Present Value 

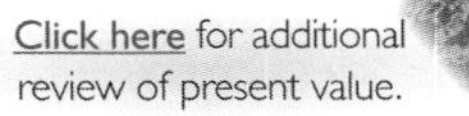

Click here for additional review of present value.

Businesses make investments in which they often incur large costs today but don't make any profits until some time in the future. Somehow they have to be able to compare their investment cost today with a stream of future profits. How can they relate present cost to future benefits?

Interest rates are used to link the present with the future. After all, if you have to pay \$110 at the end of the year when you borrow \$100, that 10 percent interest rate gives you a measure of the premium on the earlier availability of goods and services. If you want to have things today, you have to pay the 10 percent interest rate in order to have current purchasing power.

The question could be put this way: What is the present value (the value today) of \$110 that you could receive one year from now? That depends on the market rate of interest, or the rate of interest that you could earn in some appropriate savings institution, such as in a

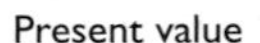

Present value
The value of a future amount expressed in today's dollars; the most that someone would pay today to receive a certain sum at some point in the future.

savings account. To make the arithmetic simple, let's assume that the rate of interest is 10 percent. Now you can figure out the **present value** of \$110 to be received one year from now. You figure it out by asking the question, How much money must I put aside today at the market interest rate of 10 percent to receive \$110 one year from now? Mathematically, we represent this equation as

$$(1 + .1)PV_1 = \$110$$

where PV_1 is the sum that you must set aside now.

Let's solve this simple equation to obtain PV_1:

$$PV_1 = \frac{\$110}{1.1} = \$100$$

That is to say, \$100 will accumulate to \$110 at the end of one year with a market rate of interest of 10 percent. Thus the present value of \$110 one year from now, using a rate of interest of 10 percent, is \$100. The formula for present value of any sums to be received one year from now thus becomes

$$PV_1 = \frac{FV_1}{1 + i}$$

Click here to calculate present value on the Internet.

where

PV_1 = present value of a sum one year hence
FV_1 = future sum of money paid or received one year hence
i = market rate of interest

Present Values for More Distant Periods. The present-value formula for figuring out today's worth of dollars to be received at a future date can now easily be seen. How much would have to be put in the same savings account today to have \$110 two years from now if the account pays a rate of 10 percent per year compounded annually?

After one year, the sum that would have to be set aside, which we will call PV_2, would have grown to $PV_2 \times 1.1$. This amount during the second year would increase to $PV_2 \times 1.1 \times 1.1$, or $PV_2 \times (1.1)^2$. To find the PV_2 that would grow to \$110 over two years, let

$$PV_2 \times (1.1)^2 = \$110$$

and solve for PV_2:

$$PV_2 = \frac{\$110}{(1.1)^2} = \$90.91$$

Thus the present value of \$110 to be paid or received two years hence, discounted at an interest rate of 10 percent per year compounded annually, is equal to \$90.91. In other words, \$90.91 put into a savings account yielding 10 percent per year compounded interest would accumulate to \$110 in two years.

Discounting
The method by which the present value of a future sum or a future stream of sums is obtained.

The General Formula for Discounting. The general formula for **discounting** becomes

$$PV_t = \frac{FV_t}{(1 + i)^t}$$

Year	Compounded Annual Interest Rate				
	3%	5%	8%	10%	20%
1	.971	.952	.926	.909	.833
2	.943	.907	.857	.826	.694
3	.915	.864	.794	.751	.578
4	.889	.823	.735	.683	.482
5	.863	.784	.681	.620	.402
6	.838	.746	.630	.564	.335
7	.813	.711	.583	.513	.279
8	.789	.677	.540	.466	.233
9	.766	.645	.500	.424	.194
10	.744	.614	.463	.385	.162
15	.642	.481	.315	.239	.0649
20	.554	.377	.215	.148	.0261
25	.478	.295	.146	.0923	.0105
30	.412	.231	.0994	.0573	.00421
40	.307	.142	.0460	.0221	.000680
50	.228	.087	.0213	.00852	.000109

TABLE 29-2

Present Value of a Future Dollar

This table shows how much a dollar received at the end of a certain number of years in the future is worth today. For example, at 5 percent a year, a dollar to be received 20 years in the future is worth 37.7 cents; if received in 50 years, it isn't even worth a dime today. To find out how much $10,000 would be worth a certain number of years from now, just multiply the figures in the table by 10,000. For example, $10,000 received at the end of 10 years discounted at a 5 percent rate of interest would have a present value of $6,140.

where t refers to the number of periods in the future the money is to be paid or received.

Table 29-2 gives the present value of $1 to be received in future years at various interest rates. The interest rate used to derive the present value is called the **rate of discount.**

Rate of discount 
The rate of interest used to discount future sums back to present value.

POLICY EXAMPLE

Should the "Pre-Death" Business Be Regulated?

Many Americans with terminal illnesses have life insurance policies that they would like to sell in order to use the proceeds while they are alive. To satisfy this demand, viatical ("provisions for a journey") companies make a present value calculation to determine how much they will pay to the person who is going to die. A terminally ill person with a life insurance policy may have an expected life of, say, four years. If the life insurance policy is sold to a viatical business, the latter must estimate the present value of receiving the payoff from the life insurance policy in four years. The company also has to determine an appropriate discount rate. The viatical business, which started around 1988, has enjoyed a rate of return of around 20 percent a year. Cries in favor of state regulation of the business are now heard virtually everywhere. After all, dying people may be too willing to sell their life insurance policies at a low price because they do not have enough information. Already, state insurance commissioners have agreed that terminally ill patients with six months to live should be paid at least 80 percent of the face value of their policies.

For Critical Analysis

What alternatives do terminally ill life insurance policy holders have? (Hint: How could they use the policy as collateral?)

CONCEPTS IN BRIEF

- Interest is the price paid for the use of capital. It is also the cost of obtaining credit. In the credit market, the rate of interest paid depends on the length of the loan, the risk, and the handling charges, among other things.
- The interest rate is determined by the intersection of the supply curve of credit, or loanable funds, and the demand curve for credit, or loanable funds. The major sources for the demand for loanable funds are households, businesses, and governments.
- Nominal, or market, interest rates include a factor to take account of the anticipated rate of inflation. Therefore, during periods of high anticipated inflation, nominal interest rates will be relatively high.
- Payments received or costs incurred in the future are worth less than those received or incurred today. The present value of any future sum is lower the further it occurs in the future and the greater the discount rate used.

PROFITS

In Chapter 2, we identified entrepreneurship, or entrepreneurial talent, as a factor of production. Profit is the reward that this factor earns. You may recall that entrepreneurship involves engaging in the risk of starting new businesses. In a sense, then, nothing can be produced without an input of entrepreneurial skills.

Until now, we have been able to talk about the demand for and supply of labor, land, and capital. We can't talk as easily about the demand for and supply of entrepreneurship. For one thing, we have no way to quantify entrepreneurship. What measure should we use? We do know that entrepreneurship exists. We cannot, however, easily present a supply and demand analysis to show the market clearing price per unit of entrepreneurship. We must use a different approach, focusing on the reward for entrepreneurship—profit. First we will determine what profit is *not*. Then we will examine the sources of true, or economic, profit. Finally, we will look at the functions of profits in a market system.

Distinguishing Between Economic Profit and Business, or Accounting, Profit

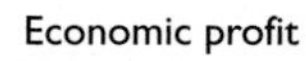
Economic profit 
The difference between total revenues and the opportunity cost of all factors of production.

Accounting profit 
Total revenues minus total explicit costs.

In our discussion of rent, we had to make a distinction between the common notions of rent and the economist's concept of economic rent. We must do the same thing when we refer to profit. We always have to distinguish between **economic profit** and **accounting profit.** The accountant calculates profit for a business as the difference between total explicit revenues and total explicit costs. Consider an extreme example. You are given a large farm as part of your inheritance. All of the land, fertilizer, seed, machinery, and tools has been fully paid for by your deceased relative. You take over the farm and work on it diligently with half a dozen workers. At the end of the year, you sell the output for $1 million. Your accountant then subtracts your actual ("explicit") expenses, mainly the wages you paid.

The difference is called profit, but it is not economic profit. Why? Because no accounting was taken of the *implicit* costs of using the land, seed, tools, and machinery. The only explicit cost considered was the workers' wages. But as long as the land could be rented out, the seed could be sold, and the tools and machinery could be leased, there was an opportunity cost to using them. To derive the economic profit that you might have earned last year from the farm, you must subtract from total revenues the full opportunity cost of all factors of production used (which will include both implicit and explicit costs).

In summary, then, accounting profit is used mainly to define taxable income and, as such, may include some returns to both the owner's labor and capital. Economic profit, by contrast, represents a return over and above the opportunity cost of all resources (including a normal return on, or payment for, the owner's entrepreneurial abilities).

When viewed in this light, it is possible for economic profit to be negative, even if accounting profit is positive. Turning to our farming example again, what if the opportunity cost of using all of the resources turned out to be $1.1 million? The economic profit would have been a *negative* $100,000. You would have suffered economic losses.

In sum, the businessperson's accounting definition and the economist's economic definition of profit usually do not coincide. Economic profit is a residual. It is whatever remains after all economic, or opportunity, costs have been taken into account.

Explanations of Economic Profit

Alternative sources of profit are numerous. Let us examine a few of them: restrictions on entry, innovation, and reward for bearing uninsurable risks.

Restrictions on Entry. We pointed out in Chapter 24 that monopoly profits—a special form of economic profits—are possible when there are barriers to entry, and these profits are often called monopoly rents by economists. Entry restrictions exist in many industries, including taxicabs, cable television franchises, and prescription drugs and eyeglasses. Basically, monopoly profits are built into the value of the business that owns the particular right to have the monopoly.

Innovation. A number of economists have maintained that economic profits are created by innovation, which is defined as the creation of a new organizational strategy, a new marketing strategy, or a new product. This source of economic profit was popularized by Harvard economics professor Joseph Schumpeter (1883–1950). The innovator creates new economic profit opportunities through innovation. The successful innovator obtains a temporary monopoly position, garnering temporary economic profits. When other firms catch up, those temporary economic profits disappear.

Reward for Bearing Uninsurable Risks

There are risks in life, including those involved in any business venture. Many of these risks can be insured, however. You can insure against the risk of losing your house to fire, flood, hurricane, or earthquake. You can do the same if you own a business. You can insure against the risk of theft also. Insurance companies are willing to sell you such insurance because they can predict relatively accurately what percentage of a class of insured assets will suffer losses each year. They charge each insured person or business enough to pay for those fully anticipated losses and to make a normal rate of return.

But there are risks that cannot be insured. If you and a group of your friends get together and pool your resources to start a new business, no amount of statistical calculations can accurately predict whether your business will still be running a year from now or 10 years from now. Consequently, you can't, when you start your business, buy insurance against losing money, bad management, miscalculations about the size of the market, aggressive competition by big corporations, and the like. Entrepreneurs therefore incur uninsurable risks. According to a theory of profits advanced by economist Frank H. Knight (1885–1973), this is the origin of economic profit.

The Function of Economic Profit

In a market economy, the expectation of profits induces firms to discover new products, new production techniques, and new marketing techniques—literally all the new ways to make higher profits. Profits in this sense spur innovation and investment.

Profits also cause resources to move from lower-valued to higher-valued uses. Prices and sales are dictated by the consumer. If the demand curve is close to the origin, there will be few sales and few profits, if any. The lack of profits therefore means that there is insufficient demand to cover the opportunity cost of production. In the quest for higher profits, businesses will take resources out of areas in which lower than normal rates of return are being made and put them into areas in which there is an expectation of higher profits. The profit reward is an inducement for an industry to expand when demand and supply conditions warrant it. Conversely, the existence of economic losses indicates that resources in the particular industry are not valued as highly as they might be elsewhere. These resources therefore move out of that industry, or at least no further resources are invested in it. Therefore, resources follow the businessperson's quest for higher profits. Profits allocate resources, just as wages and interest do.

CONCEPTS IN BRIEF

- Profit is the reward for entrepreneurial talent, a factor of production.
- It is necessary to distinguish between accounting profit and economic profit. Accounting profit is measured by the difference between total revenues and all explicit costs. Economic profit is measured by the difference between total revenues and the total of all opportunity costs of all factors of production.
- Theories of why profits exist include restriction on entry, innovation, and payment to entrepreneurs for taking uninsurable risks.
- The function of profits in a market economy is to allocate scarce resources. Resources will flow to wherever profits are highest.

ISSUES & APPLICATIONS

Copyright 2000–Wisconsin Department of Revenue–Lottery Division

Accepting Millions of Dollars in Lottery Winnings Is Harder than You Might Imagine

When 67-year-old Frank Capaci won the 1998 Wisconsin Powerball jackpot, he opted for a lump-sum payment of $104 million instead of $195 million paid in annual installments of $7.8 million over 25 years. Was this his best choice? One argument for taking a lump-sum amount was his age. But his 63-year-old wife probably had a longer life expectancy. In addition, they might have had children and grandchildren about whom they cared deeply. Assuming that he cared about his loved ones, wouldn't Capaci want them to be guaranteed receipt of $7.8 million per year even after his death?

Concepts Applied

- **Present Value**
- **Interest Rates**

Determining the Value of Lottery Payments

Put yourself in Frank Capaci's place. The Powerball lottery administrators notified him that he could either receive $104 million instantly or $7.8 million every year for 25 years. What Capaci had to do was compare the present value of $7.8 million per year for a total of 25 years with an immediate $104 million lump sum.

Look back at Table 29-2 on page 723. How could Capaci calculate the present value of 25 years' worth of lottery payments? The answer is that he could use the present-value figures in Table 29-2 to convert each year's $7.8 million payment into present-value terms. For instance, at an interest rate of 5 percent, the present value of $7.8 million received a year later would be .952 times $7.8 million, or $7,425,600. The present value of $7.8 million two years later would be .907 times $7.8 million, or $7,074,600. Using the 5 percent column of Table 29-2 in this way (after filling in years 11–14, 16–19, and 21–24 in the table), he could calculate 25 years' worth of present values of annual payments of $7.8 million. Then he could sum these to come up with a grand total present value of the payments to compare with the $104 million lump sum he was offered.

A Retired Electrician Who Understood Interest and Present Value

The same calculations can be performed at each interest rate in Table 29-2. Table 29-3 gives the resulting present-value sums (rounded to the nearest hundred thousand dollars) for the 25 years of annual payments. As you can see, the present value of these payments was $115.4 million at an interest rate of 5 percent. At an interest rate of 8 percent, however, the present value of the payments was only $90.3 million.

TABLE 29-3
Present Values of Lottery Payments at Different Interest Rates

	Interest Rate				
	3%	5%	8%	10%	20%
Present Value ($ million)	139.9	115.4	90.3	77.9	46.3

Thus, if Frank Capaci cared about his loved ones as much as he did himself, he knew that one key issue was what he expected market interest returns to be over the next 25 years. At the time he won the lottery, most bonds were offering annual returns ranging from 7 to 8 percent. Much higher average (though riskier) annual returns were available in the stock market. Thus if Frank Capaci saved his lump-sum payment by holding a mix of bonds and stocks, he could feel reasonably certain that he and his loved ones would be better off than if he accepted 25 years' worth of payments instead. (Capaci did not indicate an intention to spend all the money quickly. He said that he planned to buy a Harley-Davidson motorcycle.)

Of Course, There Are Always Complications

Other factors surely influenced Frank Capaci's decision. For instance, if he decided to leave all his wealth to his wife, then there would be no inheritance taxes on that sum. Annual payments would be subject to inheritance taxes.

FOR CRITICAL ANALYSIS

1. Why was the present value of the annual lottery payments higher at lower interest rates?
2. Initial press accounts said that Capaci won a $195 million jackpot. Were they accurate?

SUMMARY DISCUSSION OF LEARNING OBJECTIVES

1. **The Concept of Economic Rent:** Owners of a resource in fixed supply, meaning that the resource supply curve is perfectly inelastic, are paid economic rent. Originally, this term was used to refer to payment for the use of land or any other natural resource that is considered to be in fixed supply. More generally, however, economic rent is a payment for use of any resource that exceeds the opportunity cost of the resource.
2. **Economic Rent and Resource Allocation:** Owners of any productive factors with inelastic supply earn economic rent because competition among potential users of those factors bids up the prices of these factors. Hence people who provide labor services that are difficult for others to provide, such as sports superstars, movie stars, and the like, typically receive earnings well in excess of the earnings that would otherwise have been sufficient to induce them to provide their services. Nevertheless, the economic rents that they earn reflect the maximum market valuation of their value, so economic rent allocates resources to their highest-valued use.
3. **How Market Interest Rates Are Determined:** Interest is a payment for the ability to use resources today instead of in the future. The equilibrium rate of interest is determined by the intersection of the demand for loanable funds (the demand for credit) with the supply of loanable funds (the supply of credit). Other factors that influence interest rates are the length of the term of a loan, the loan's risk, and handling charges. The nominal interest rate includes a factor that takes into account the anticipated inflation rate. Therefore, during periods of high anticipated inflation, current market (nominal) interest rates are high.
4. **The Key Role the Interest Rate Performs in Allocating Resources:** The rate of interest is a price that induces lenders to allocate loanable funds to consumers and to businesses. Comparing the market interest rate with the rate of return on prospective capital investment projects enables owners of loanable funds to determine the highest-valued uses of the funds. Thus the interest rate allocates loanable funds to industries whose investments yield the highest returns, thereby ensuring that available resources will be put to their most productive uses.
5. **Calculating the Present Discounted Value of a Payment to Be Received at a Future Date:** The present value of a future payment is the value of the future amount expressed in today's dollars, and it is equal to the most that someone would pay today to receive that amount in the future. The method by which the present value of a future sum is calculated is called *discounting*. This method implies that the

present value of a sum to be received a year from now is equal to the future amount divided by 1 plus the appropriate rate of interest, which is called the *rate of discount.*

6. **The Fundamental Role of Economic Profits:** A positive economic profit of a firm is a return over and above the opportunity cost of all resources, including a payment for the entrepreneurial abilities of the firms' owners. Hence economic profit reflects implicit opportunity costs of directing entrepreneurial resources to one line of business instead of a different line of business. A firm earning positive accounting profit, in which total revenues exceed explicit, out-of-pocket expenses, can still earn negative economic profits. This occurs if the accounting profit fails to cover the opportunity cost of entrepreneurship allocated to that business. In response to a negative economic profit in one business, an owner has an incentive to redirect resources to a different business, thereby allocating them to their highest-valued use.

Key Terms and Concepts

Accounting profit (724)
Discounting (722)
Economic profit (724)
Economic rent (713)
Interest (716)
Nominal rate of interest (720)
Present value (722)
Rate of discount (723)
Real rate of interest (721)

Problems

Answers to odd-numbered problems appear at the back of the book.

29-1. Which of the following would you expect to have a high level of economic rent, and which would you expect to have a low level of economic rent? Explain why for each.

a. Bob has a highly specialized medical skill that is in great demand.

b. Sally has never attended school. She is 25 years old and is an internationally known supermodel.

c. Tim is a high school teacher and sells insurance part time.

29-2. Though he has retired from hockey, Wayne Gretzky still earns a sizable annual income from endorsements. Explain why, in economic terms, his level of economic rent is still so high.

29-3. Michael Jordan once retired from basketball to play baseball. As a result, his annual dollar income dropped from the millions to the thousands. Eventually Jordan quit baseball and returned to basketball. What can be said about the role of economic rents in his situation?

29-4. A British pharmaceutical company spent several years and considerable funds on the development of a treatment for HIV patients. Now, with the protection afforded by patent rights, the company has the potential to reap enormous gains. The government, in response, has threatened to tax away any rents the company may earn. Is this an advisable policy? Why or why not?

29-5. Explain how the following events would likely affect the relevant interest rate.

a. A major bond-rating agency has improved the risk rating of a developing nation.

b. To regulate and protect the public, the government has passed legislation that requires a considerable increase in the reporting paperwork when a bank makes a loan.

c. At the time of graduation, you elect to pay off your student loan in five years instead of 10.

29-6. Explain how each of the following would affect the rate of interest.

a. Because of expected higher future prices of durable goods, consumers borrow money to buy these items today.

b. Pessimistic views on business prospects lead businesses to postpone capital expenditures.

29-7. Suppose that the government enacts a binding ceiling on interest rates. What is the impact of this legislation on the market for loanable funds and on the economy in general?

29-8. Suppose that the rate of interest in Japan is only 2 percent, while the comparable rate in the United States is 4 percent. Japan's rate of inflation is .5 percent, while the U.S. inflation rate is 3 percent. Which economy has the higher real interest rate?

29-9. You expect to receive a payment of $104 one year from now. Your discount rate is 4 percent. What is the present value of the payment to be received? Suppose that the discount rate is 5 percent. What is the present value of the payment to be received?

29-10. An individual leaves a college faculty, where she was earning $40,000 a year, to begin a new venture. She invests her savings of $10,000, which were earning 10 percent annually. She then spends $20,000 on office equipment, hires two students at $30,000 a year each, rents office space for $12,000, and has other variable expenses of $40,000. At the end of the year, her revenues were $200,000. What are her accounting profit and her economic profit for the year?

Economics on the Net

Interest Rates in Mexico As discussed in this chapter, there are many different types of interest rates in the United States. Indeed, any nation has a number of different market interest rates. In this application, you will contemplate various interest rates in Mexico.

Title: The Bank of Mexico

Navigation: Click here to begin at the Bank of Mexico's homepage. Select "Economic and Financial Indicators," then "Financial Markets and Interest Rates". Scroll down to "Information Structures" and then click on the daily "Money Market Representative Interest Rates".

Application Record the most recent 28-day TIIE rate, bank funding rate, and government funding rate.

Next, click here to visit the Federal Reserve Web site. Select the most recent release, and find the U.S. prime lending rate.

1. On the Bank of Mexico's site, back up to the main "Economic and Financial Indicators" page. Click on "Prices" and select to view the monthly Main Price Index. Record the percent change in the Consumer Price Index for the most recent month with respect to the same month of the previous year. What was the annual rate of inflation for Mexico over the past year? Using the three one-month rates you collected, which are quoted in annual terms, calculate the real rate of each.

For Group Discussion and Analysis Based on the data you collected, why do you think the U.S. prime lending rate is lower than the TIIE rate? Does this necessarily mean that U.S. prime customers are less risky than the Mexican government? (Hint: Discuss the how anticipated changes in exchange rates likely affect the amount of interest charged.)

CHAPTER

30

INCOME, POVERTY, AND HEALTH CARE

These workers are cleaning up in the South Shore neighborhood of Chicago, where many residents are officially listed as earning below the poverty line. Yet during the 1990s, consumer spending increased more in South Shore than in any other part of Chicago. Can you explain this anomaly?

A few years ago, a Chicago group called Social Compact sought to evaluate the opportunities for regenerating neighborhoods on the south side of the city. It focused on a largely African-American neighborhood called South Shore, where U.S. government data indicated that 27 percent of residents were mired in poverty. To the group's surprise, it found that spending in parts of the South Shore economy was actually booming. Over the previous 10-year period, South Shore residents had increased their use of electricity by double the average rate of growth of the rest of Chicago. Supermarket sales in the area placed the stores among the top Chicago outlets. Insurers reported that sales of homeowners' insurance policies were increasing twice as fast as elsewhere in the city. What is the right way to measure "poverty"? This is one of the questions you will contemplate as you read this chapter.

LEARNING OBJECTIVES

After reading this chapter, you should be able to:

1. **Describe how to use a Lorenz curve to represent a nation's income distribution**
2. **Identify the key determinants of income differences across individuals**
3. **Discuss theories of desired income distribution**
4. **Distinguish among alternative approaches to measuring and addressing poverty**
5. **Recognize the major reasons for rising health care costs**
6. **Describe alternative approaches to paying for health care**

Chapter Outline

- Income
- Determinants of Income Differences
- Theories of Desired Income Distribution
- Poverty and Attempts to Eliminate It
- Health Care

Did You Know That... 20 percent of the world's people consume 86 percent of its goods and services? This highest-income portion of the population also uses more than half the world's annual energy output and devours close to half its meat and fish. Even as a billion of the world's poorest individuals struggle to meet their basic dietary requirements, Americans spend \$8 billion a year on cosmetics, and Europeans spend \$50 billion a year on cigarettes. Why is it that some people can earn more income and spend more than others? Why is the **distribution of income** the way it is? Economists have devised various theories to explain income distribution. We will present some of these theories in this chapter. We will also present some of the more obvious institutional reasons why income is not distributed equally in the United States and examine what might be done about health care problems.

INCOME

Distribution of income

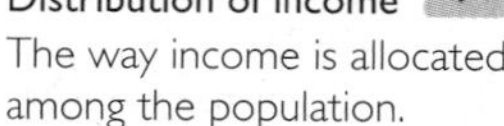

The way income is allocated among the population.

Income provides each of us with the means of consuming and saving. Income can be derived from a payment for labor services or a payment for ownership of one of the other factors of production besides labor—land, physical capital, and entrepreneurship. In addition, individuals obtain spendable income from gifts and government transfers. (Some individuals also obtain income by stealing, but we will not treat this matter here.) Right now, let us examine how money income is distributed across classes of income earners within the United States.

Lorenz curve

A geometric representation of the distribution of income. A Lorenz curve that is perfectly straight represents complete income equality. The more bowed a Lorenz curve, the more unequally income is distributed.

Measuring Income Distribution: The Lorenz Curve

We can represent the distribution of money income graphically with what is known as the **Lorenz curve,** named after a U.S.-born statistician, Max Otto Lorenz, who proposed it in 1905. The Lorenz curve shows what portion of total money income is accounted for by different proportions of the nation's households. Look at Figure 30-1. On the horizontal axis, we measure the *cumulative* percentage of households, lowest-income households first. Starting at the left corner, there are zero households; at the right corner, we have 100 percent

FIGURE 30-1

The Lorenz Curve

The horizontal axis measures the cumulative percentage of households, with lowest-income households first, from 0 to 100 percent. The vertical axis measures the cumulative percentage of money income from 0 to 100. A straight line at a 45-degree angle cuts the box in half and represents a line of complete income equality, along which 25 percent of the families get 25 percent of the money income, 50 percent get 50 percent, and so on. The Lorenz curve, showing actual money income distribution, is not a straight line but rather a curved line as shown. The difference between complete money income equality and the Lorenz curve is the inequality gap.

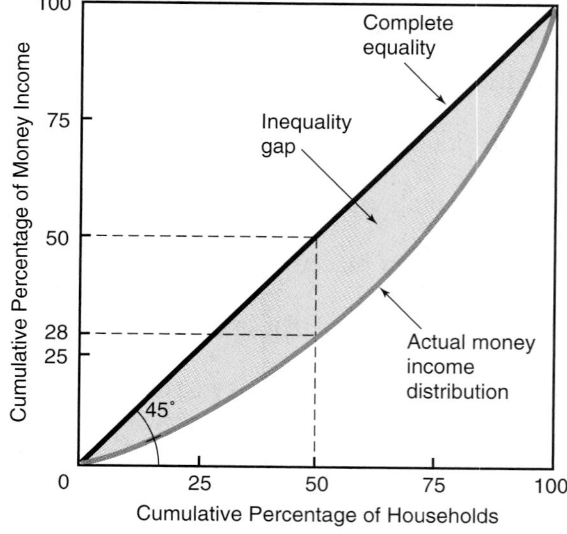

of households; and in the middle, we have 50 percent of households. The vertical axis represents the cumulative percentage of money income. The 45-degree line represents complete equality: 50 percent of the households obtain 50 percent of total income, 60 percent of the households obtain 60 percent of total income, and so on. Of course, in no real-world situation is there such complete equality of income; no actual Lorenz curve would be a straight line. Rather, it would be some curved line, like the one labeled "Actual money income distribution" in Figure 30-1. For example, the bottom 50 percent of households in the United States receive about 28 percent of total money income.

In Figure 30-2, we again show the actual money income distribution Lorenz curve, and we also compare it to the distribution of money income in 1929. Since that year, the Lorenz curve has become less bowed; that is, it has moved closer to the line of complete equality.

Criticisms of the Lorenz Curve. In recent years, economists have placed less and less emphasis on the shape of the Lorenz curve as an indication of the degree of income inequality in a country. There are five basic reasons why the Lorenz curve has been criticized:

1. The Lorenz curve is typically presented in terms of the distribution of *money* income only. It does not include **income in kind,** such as government-provided food stamps, education, or housing aid, and goods or services produced and consumed in the home or on the farm.
2. The Lorenz curve does not account for differences in the size of households or the number of wage earners they contain.
3. It does not account for age differences. Even if all families in the United States had exactly the same *lifetime* incomes, chances are that young families would have lower incomes, middle-aged families would have relatively high incomes, and retired families would have low incomes. Because the Lorenz curve is drawn at a moment in time, it could never tell us anything about the inequality of *lifetime* income.
4. The Lorenz curve ordinarily reflects money income *before* taxes.
5. It does not measure unreported income from the underground economy, a substantial source of income for some individuals.

Income in kind 

Income received in the form of goods and services, such as housing or medical care; to be contrasted with money income, which is simply income in dollars, or general purchasing power, that can be used to buy *any* goods and services.

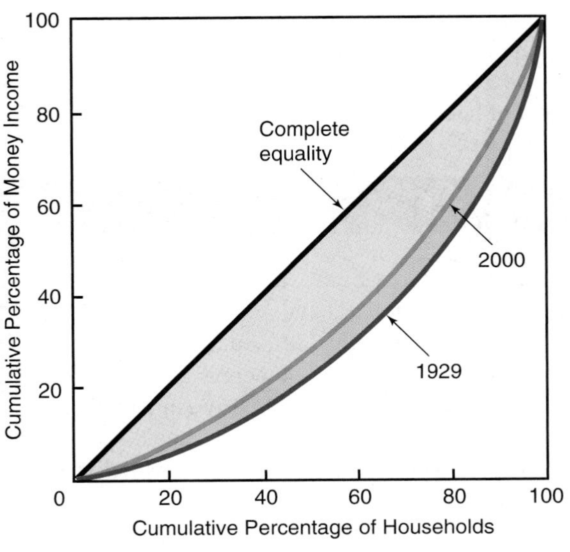

FIGURE 30-2

Lorenz Curves of Income Distribution, 1929 and 2000

Since 1929, the Lorenz curve has moved slightly inward toward the straight line of perfect income equality.

Source: U.S. Department of Commerce.

TABLE 30-1
Percentage Share of Money Income for Households Before Direct Taxes

Income Group	1998	1975	1960	1947
Lowest fifth	3.6	4.4	4.8	5.1
Second fifth	9.0	10.5	12.2	11.8
Third fifth	15.0	17.1	17.8	16.7
Fourth fifth	23.2	24.8	24.0	23.2
Highest fifth	49.2	43.2	41.3	43.3

Source: U.S. Bureau of the Census.
Note: Figures may not sum to 100 percent due to rounding.

Income Distribution in the United States

Click here to view the most recent data on U.S. income distribution. Click on the most recent year next to "Money Income in the United States."

We could talk about the percentage of income earners within specific income classes—those earning between $20,001 and $30,000 per year, those earning between $30,001 and $40,000 per year, and so on. The problem with this type of analysis is that we live in a growing economy. Income, with some exceptions, is going up all the time. If we wish to make comparisons of the relative share of total income going to different income classes, we cannot look at specific amounts of money income. Instead, we talk about a distribution of income over five groups. Then we can talk about how much the bottom fifth (or quintile) makes compared with the top fifth, and so on. In Table 30-1, we see the percentage share of income for households before direct taxes. The table groups households according to whether they are in the lowest 20 percent of the income distribution, the second lowest 20 percent, and so on. We see that in 1998, the lowest 20 percent had a combined money income of 3.6 percent of the total money income of the entire population. This is a little less than the lowest 20 percent had at the end of World War II. Accordingly, the conclusion has been drawn that there have been only slight changes in the distribution of money income. Indeed, considering that the definition of money income used by the U.S. Bureau of the Census includes only wage and salary income, income from self-employment, interest and dividends, and such government transfer payments as Social Security and unemployment compensation, we have to agree that the distribution of money income has not changed. *Money* income, however, understates *total* income for individuals who receive in-kind transfers from the government in the form of food stamps, public housing, education, and so on. In particular, since World War II, the share of total income—money income plus in-kind benefits—going to the bottom 20 percent of households has probably more than doubled.

INTERNATIONAL EXAMPLE

Relative Income Inequality Throughout the Richest Countries

The United States wins again—it has, according to the World Bank, the greatest amount of income inequality of any of the major industrialized countries. Look at Figure 30-3. There you see the ratio of income of the richest 20 percent of households to the poorest 20 percent of households. Should something be done about such income inequality?

Public attitudes toward the government's role in reducing income inequality differ dramatically in the United States and elsewhere. Whereas fewer than 30 percent of Americans believe that government should reduce income differentials, between 60 and 80 percent of Britons, Germans, Italians, and Austrians believe it is the government's job.

FIGURE 30-3

Relative Income Inequality in the World

The United States has greater income inequality than other developed countries.

Source: World Bank.

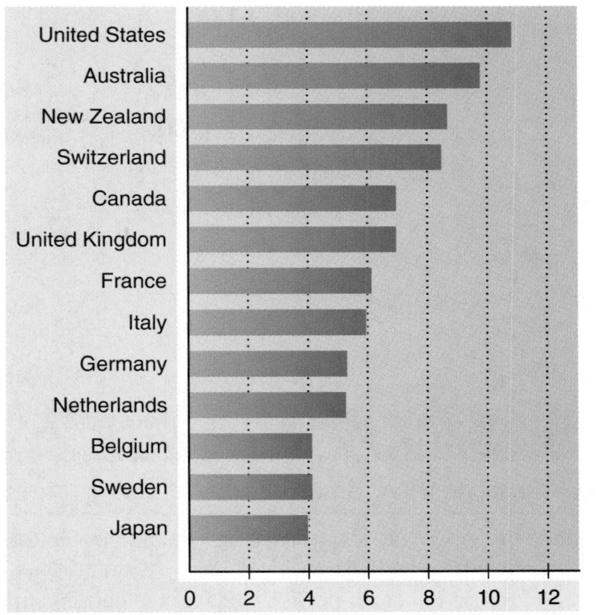

For Critical Analysis

Does it matter whether the same families stay in the lowest fifth of income earners over time? Otherwise stated, do we need to know anything about mobility across income groups?

The Distribution of Wealth

We have been referring to the distribution of income in the United States. We must realize that income—a flow—can be viewed as a return on wealth (both human and nonhuman)—a stock. A discussion of the distribution of income in the United States is not the same thing as a discussion of the distribution of wealth. A complete concept of wealth would include tangible objects, such as buildings, machinery, land, cars, and houses—nonhuman wealth—as well as people who have skills, knowledge, initiative, talents, and so on—human wealth. The total of human and nonhuman wealth in the United States makes up our nation's capital stock. (Note that the terms *wealth* and *capital* are often used only with reference to nonhuman wealth.) The capital stock consists of anything that can generate utility to individuals in the future. A fresh ripe tomato is not part of our capital stock. It has to be eaten before it turns rotten, and once it has been eaten, it can no longer generate satisfaction.

Figure 30-4 (p. 736) shows that the richest 10 percent of U.S. households hold about two-thirds of all wealth. The problem with those data, gathered by the Federal Reserve System, is that they do not include many important assets. The first of these is workers' claims on private pension plans, which equal at least $4 trillion according to economist Lawrence B. Lindsey. If you add the value of these pensions, household wealth increases by almost a quarter, meaning that the majority of U.S. households belong to middle-income households (popularly known as the *middle class*). Also omitted is future Social Security liabilities, estimated at about $13 trillion. Again, most of this is "owned" by the middle class.

FIGURE 30-4
Measured Total Wealth Distribution
The top 10 percent of households have 69 percent of all *measured* wealth.

Source: Board of Governors of the Federal Reserve.

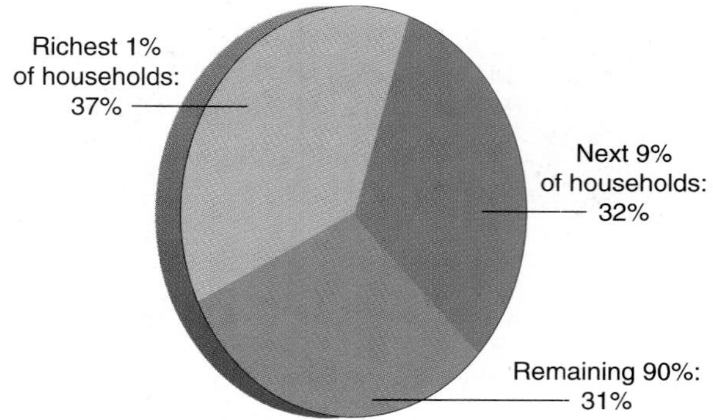

POLICY EXAMPLE

Should the Government Encourage Marriage?

Since the end of 1970s, the average income of the top fifth of male income earners has risen by about 4 percent. During the same period, the average earnings of men in the bottom fifth fell by 44 percent. A key reason for this disparity is that poor men today are less likely to be married. In 1979, almost three out of every five of the men among the poorest 20 percent of income earners were married. Today, however, only about two out of five are married.

The reason this drop in marriage rates among lowest-income men makes such a big difference is that the incomes of women have risen. Today, about 65 percent of women with poor husbands work, up only slightly from 61 percent in 1979. The wages of these women have increased by about two-thirds, however. If the poorest males were marrying at the same rate as before, fewer lower-income households would have suffered big drops in their average earnings. Marriage has only added to the gains experienced by the households of the highest-income men. In 1979, just over half of the women with the highest-income husbands worked. Today, three-fourths of these women work, and their average wages have risen by more than 70 percent. This has further enriched the households of the highest-income males.

Based on these data, some economists argue that the government should develop policies that encourage higher marriage rates among the poorest individuals. At a minimum, they recommend eliminating policies that discourage marriage, such as taxing married couples at higher rates than single individuals at the same income levels.

For Critical Analysis

Some poor men are probably less likely to be married because their sharp income drop has hurt their marriage prospects. What, if anything, can or should the government do about this?

CONCEPTS IN BRIEF

- The Lorenz curve graphically represents the distribution of income. If it is a straight line, there is complete equality of income. The more it is bowed, the more inequality of income exists.
- The distribution of wealth is not the same as the distribution of income. Wealth includes assets such as houses, stocks, and bonds. Although the apparent distribution of wealth seems to be more concentrated at the top, the data used are not very accurate, and most summary statistics fail to take account of workers' claims on private and public pensions, which are substantial.

DETERMINANTS OF INCOME DIFFERENCES 

We know that there are income differences—that is not in dispute. A more important question is why these differences in income occur, for if we know why income differences occur, perhaps we can change public policy, particularly with respect to helping people in the lowest income classes climb the income ladder. What is more, if we know the reasons for income differences, we can ascertain whether any of these determinants have changed over time. We will look at four income difference determinants: age, marginal productivity, inheritance, and discrimination.

Age

Age turns out to be a determinant of income because with age comes, usually, more education, more training, and more experience. It is not surprising that within every class of income earners, there seem to be regular cycles of earning behavior. Most individuals earn more when they are middle-aged than when they are younger or older. We call this the **age-earnings cycle.**

Age-earnings cycle 
The regular earnings profile of an individual throughout his or her lifetime. The age-earnings cycle usually starts with a low income, builds gradually to a peak at around age 50, and then gradually curves down until it approaches zero at retirement.

The Age-Earnings Cycle. Every occupation has its own age-earnings cycle, and every individual will probably experience some variation from the average. Nonetheless, we can characterize the typical age-earnings cycle graphically in Figure 30-5. Here we see that at age 18, earnings from wages are relatively low. Earnings gradually rises until they peak at about age 50. Then they fall until retirement, when they become zero (that is, currently earned wages become zero, although retirement payments may then commence). The reason for such a regular cycle in earnings is fairly straightforward.

When individuals start working at a young age, they typically have no work-related experience. Their ability to produce is less than that of more seasoned workers—that is, their productivity is lower. As they become older, they obtain more training and accumulate more experience. Their productivity rises, and they are therefore paid more. They also generally start to work longer hours. As the age of 50 approaches, the productivity of individual workers usually peaks. So, too, do the number of hours per week that are worked. After this peak in the age-earnings cycle, the detrimental effects of aging—decreases in stamina, strength, reaction time, and the like—usually outweigh any increases in training

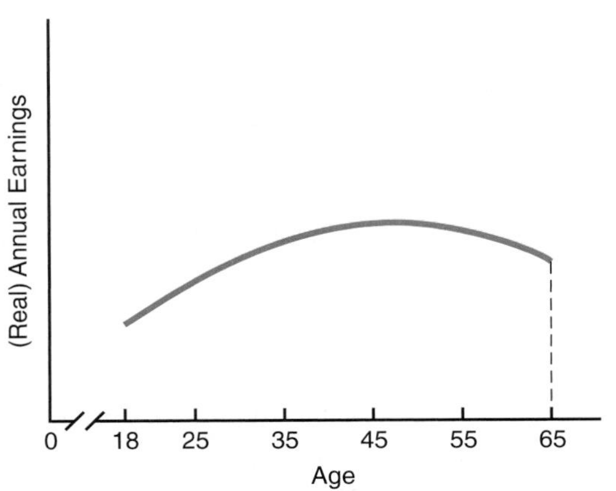

FIGURE 30-5 

Typical Age-Earnings Profile

Within every class of income earners there is usually a typical age-earnings profile. Earnings from wages are lowest when starting work at age 18, reach their peak at around age 50, and then taper off until retirement around age 65, when they become zero for most people. The rise in earnings up to age 50 is usually due to increased experience, longer working hours, and better training and schooling. (We abstract from economywide productivity changes that would shift the entire curve upward.)

or experience. Also, hours worked usually start to fall for older people. Finally, as a person reaches retirement, both productivity and hours worked diminish rather drastically.

Note that general increases in overall productivity for the entire workforce will result in an upward shift in the typical age-earnings profile given in Figure 30-5. Thus even at the end of the age-earnings cycle, when just about to retire, the worker would not receive a really low wage compared with the starting wage 45 years earlier. The wage would be higher due to factors that contribute to rising real wages for everyone, regardless of the stage in the age-earnings cycle.

Now we have some idea why specific individuals earn different incomes at different times in their lives, but we have yet to explain why different people are paid different amounts of money for their labor. One way to explain this is to recall the marginal productivity theory developed in Chapter 27.

Marginal Productivity

When trying to determine how many workers a firm would hire, we had to construct a marginal revenue product curve. We found that as more workers were hired, the marginal revenue product fell due to diminishing marginal returns. If the forces of demand and supply established a certain wage rate, workers would be hired until their marginal physical product times marginal revenue (which equals the marketing price under perfect competition) was equal to the going wage rate. Then the hiring would stop. This analysis suggests what workers can expect to be paid in the labor market: They can each expect to be paid their marginal revenue product (assuming that there are low-cost information flows and that the labor and product markets are competitive).

In a competitive situation, with mobility of labor resources (at least on the margin), workers who are being paid less than their marginal revenue product will be bid away to better employment opportunities. Either they will seek better employment themselves, or other employers will offer them a higher wage rate. This process will continue until each worker is being paid his or her marginal revenue product.

You may balk at the suggestion that people are paid their marginal revenue product because you may personally know individuals whose MRP is more or less than what they are being paid. Such a situation may, in fact, exist because we do not live in a world of perfect information or in a world with perfectly competitive input and output markets. Employers cannot always find the most productive employees available. It takes resources to research the past records of potential employees, their training, their education, and their abilities. Nonetheless, competition creates a tendency toward equality of wages and MRP.

Determinants of Marginal Productivity. If we accept marginal revenue product theory, we have a way to find out how people can earn higher incomes. If they can increase their marginal physical product, they can expect to be paid more. Some of the determinants of marginal physical product are talent, education, experience, and training. Most of these are means by which marginal physical product can be increased. Let's examine them in greater detail.

Talent This factor is the easiest to explain but difficult to acquire if you don't have it. Innate abilities and attributes can be very strong, if not overwhelming, determinants of a person's potential productivity. Strength, coordination, and mental alertness are facets of nonacquired human capital and thus have some bearing on the ability to earn income. Someone who is extremely tall has a better chance of being a basketball player than someone who is short. A person born with a superior talent for abstract thinking has a better chance of earning a relatively high income as a mathematician or a physicist than someone who is not born with that knack.

Experience Additional experience at particular tasks is another way to increase productivity. Experience can be linked to the well-known *learning curve* that applies when the same task is done over and over. The worker repeating a task becomes more efficient: The worker can do the same task in less time or in the same amount of time but better. Take an example of a person going to work on an automobile assembly line. At first she is able to fasten only three bolts every two minutes. Then the worker becomes more adept and can fasten four bolts in the same time plus insert a rubber guard on the bumper. After a few more weeks, another task can be added. Experience allows this individual to improve her productivity. The more effectively people learn to do something, the quicker they can do it and the more efficient they are. Hence we would expect experience to lead to higher productivity. And we would expect people with more experience to be paid more than those with less experience. More experience, however, does not guarantee a higher wage rate. The *demand* for a person's services must also exist. Spending a long time to become a first-rate archer in modern society would probably add very little to a person's income. Experience has value only if the output is demanded by society.

Training Training is similar to experience but is more formal. Much of a person's increased productivity is due to on-the-job training. Many companies have training programs for new workers. On-the-job training is perhaps responsible for as much of an increase in productivity as is formal education beyond grade school.

EXAMPLE

Economists, Aging, and Productivity

Do the actions of professional economists fit the model that predicts a decrease in productivity after some peak at around age 50? Yes, according to University of Texas economist Daniel Hamermesh. One measure of productivity of economics professors is the number of articles they publish in professional journals. Whereas the over-50 economists constitute 30 percent of the profession, they contribute a mere 6 percent of the articles published in leading economics journals. Whereas 56 percent of economists between ages 36 and 50 submit articles on a regular basis, only 14 percent of economists over 50 do so.

For Critical Analysis

Why should we predict that an economist closer to retirement will submit fewer professional journal articles for publication than a younger economist?

Investment in Human Capital. Investment in human capital is just like investment in any other thing. If you invest in yourself by going to college, rather than going to work after high school and earning more current income, you will presumably be rewarded in the future with a higher income or a more interesting job (or both). This is exactly the motivation that underlies the decision of many college-bound students to obtain a formal higher education. Undoubtedly there would be students going to school even if the rate of return on formal education were zero or negative. But we do expect that the higher the rate of return on investing in ourselves, the more such investment there will be. U.S. Labor Department data demonstrate conclusively that, on average, high school graduates make more than grade school graduates and that college graduates make more than high school graduates. The estimated annual income of a full-time worker with four years of college in the early 2000s was about $65,000. That person's high school counterpart was estimated to earn only $32,000, which gives a "college premium" of about 57 percent. Generally, the rate of return on investment in human capital is on a par with the rate of return on investment in other areas.

To figure out the rate of return on an investment in a college education, we first have to figure out the marginal costs of going to school. The main cost is not what you have to pay for books, fees, and tuition but rather the income you forgo. *The main cost of education is the income forgone—the opportunity cost of not working.* In addition, the direct expenses of college must be paid for. Not all students forgo all income during their college years. Many work part time. Taking account of those who work part time and those who are supported by state tuition grants and other scholarships, the average rate of return on going to college ranges between 12 and 18 percent. This is not a bad rate. Of course, this type of computation does leave out all the consumption benefits you get from attending college. Also omitted from the calculations is the change in personality after going to college. You undoubtedly come out a different person. Most people who go through college feel that they have improved themselves both culturally and intellectually in addition to having increased their potential marginal revenue product so that they can make more income. How do we measure the benefit from expanding our horizons and our desire to experience different things in life? This is not easy to measure, and such nonmoney benefits from investing in human capital are not included in normal calculations.

Inheritance

It is not unusual to inherit cash, jewelry, stocks, bonds, homes, or other real estate. Yet only about 10 percent of income inequality in the United States can be traced to differences in wealth that was inherited. If for some reason the government confiscated all property that had been inherited, there would be only a modest change in the distribution of income in the United States. In any event, at both federal and state levels of taxation, substantial inheritance taxes are levied on the estates of relatively wealthy deceased Americans (although there are some legally valid ways to avoid certain estate taxes).

Discrimination

Economic discrimination occurs whenever workers with the same marginal revenue product receive unequal pay due to some noneconomic factor such as their race, sex, or age. Alternatively, it occurs when there is unequal access to labor markets. It is possible—and indeed quite obvious—that discrimination affects the distribution of income. Certain groups in our society are not paid wages at rates comparable to those received by other groups, even when we correct for productivity. Differences in income remain between whites and nonwhites and between men and women. For example, the median income of black families is about 60 percent that of white families. The median wage rate of women is about 70 percent that of men. Some people argue that all of these differences are due to discrimination against nonwhites and against women. We cannot simply accept *any* differences in income as due to discrimination, though. What we need to do is discover why differences in income between groups exist and then determine if factors other than discrimination in the labor market can explain them. The unexplained part of income differences can rightfully be considered the result of discrimination.

Access to Education. African Americans and other minorities have faced discrimination in the acquisition of human capital. The amount and quality of schooling offered black Americans has generally been inferior to that offered whites. Even if minorities attend school as long as whites, their scholastic achievement can be lower because they are typically allotted fewer school resources than their white counterparts. Nonwhite urban individuals are more likely to live in lower-income areas, which have fewer resources to allocate to education due to the lower tax base. One study showed that nonwhite urban males receive between 23 and 27 percent less income than white urban males because of lower-quality education. This would mean that even if employment discrimination were substantially reduced, we would still expect to see a difference between white and nonwhite income because of the low quality of schooling received by the nonwhites and the resulting lower level of productivity. We say, therefore, that among other things, African Americans and certain other minority groups, such as Hispanics, suffer from too small an investment in human capital. Even when this difference in human capital is taken into account, however, there still appears to be an income differential that cannot be explained. The unexplained income differential between whites and blacks is often attributed to discrimination in the labor market. Because no better explanation is offered, we will stick with the notion that discrimination in the labor market does indeed exist.

EXAMPLE

Removing Racial Barriers: The Colorful but Color-Blind Internet

When a white customer asks an African-American salesman if a different salesperson can assist her, the salesman may suspect that his race may have cost him a sale. Likewise, when a white banker turns down an African-American loan applicant, there is always the chance that race made a difference. To explain why race or other factors might affect people's economic choices, economists have developed the *cultural affinity hypothesis.* It indicates that lenders find it less costly to evaluate applicants who share their own backgrounds. This hypothesis could also help explain why applicants for loans might prefer to apply at banks that are owned and managed by people who share their characteristics or why customers might prefer to do business with certain salespersons rather than others.

Documenting or explaining differential interactions on the basis of different characteristics does nothing for people who feel that their racial, ethnic, or gender status causes them to lose out on earnings. For many African-American entrepreneurs, the Internet is increasingly providing a means to avoid such lost opportunities. For instance, Autonetwork.com is a booming Web site that offers auto broker services and leasing information, but there is no reason for anyone looking for a good deal on an auto lease to know—or care—that the site is owned by an African-American man who earns more than $200,000 per year in advertising revenue alone from operating the site. Likewise, all a college student who wants to do better in biology class cares about is whether Cyberstudy101.com can help him, without regard to the fact that this successful on-line business was the brainchild of an African-American woman.

For Critical Analysis

Some on-line businesses advertise that they are owned by people of a particular race, ethnicity, or gender and offer products aimed at people who share that characteristic. Could the cultural affinity hypothesis help explain this phenomenon?

The Doctrine of Comparable Worth. Discrimination against women can occur because of barriers to entry in higher-paying occupations and because of discrimination in the acquisition of human capital, just as has occurred for African Americans. Consider the distribution of highest-paying and lowest-paying occupations. The lowest-paying jobs are dominated by females, both white and nonwhite. For example, the proportion of women in secretarial, clerical, janitorial, and food service jobs ranges from 70 percent (food service) to 97 percent (secretarial). Proponents of the **comparable-worth doctrine** feel that female secretaries, janitors, and food service workers should be making salaries comparable to those of male truck drivers or construction workers, assuming that the levels of skill and responsibility in these jobs are comparable. These advocates also believe that a comparable-worth policy would benefit the economy overall. They contend that adjusting the wages of workers in female-dominated jobs upward would create a move toward more efficient and less discriminatory labor markets.

Comparable-worth doctrine 
The belief that women should receive the same wages as men if the levels of skill and responsibility in their jobs are equivalent.

THEORIES OF DESIRED INCOME DISTRIBUTION

We have talked about the factors affecting the distribution of income, but we have not yet mentioned the normative issue of how income *ought* to be distributed. This, of course, requires a value judgment. We are talking about the problem of economic justice. We can never completely resolve this problem because there are always going to be conflicting values. It is impossible to give all people what each thinks is just. Nonetheless, two particular normative standards for the distribution of income have been popular with economists. These are income distribution based on productivity and income distribution based on equality.

Productivity

The *productivity standard* for the distribution of income can be stated simply as "To each according to what he or she produces." This is also called the *contributive standard* because it is based on the principle of rewarding according to the contribution to society's total output. It is also sometimes referred to as the *merit standard* and is one of the oldest concepts of justice. People are rewarded according to merit, and merit is judged by one's ability to produce what is considered useful by society.

However, just as any standard is a value judgment, so is the productivity standard. It is rooted in the capitalist ethic and has been attacked vigorously by some economists and philosophers, including Karl Marx, who felt that people should be rewarded according to need and not according to productivity.

We measure a person's productive contribution in a capitalist system by the market value of that person's output. We have already referred to this as the marginal revenue product theory of wage determination.

Do not immediately jump to the conclusion that in a world of income distribution determined by productivity, society will necessarily allow the aged, the infirm, and the disabled to die of starvation because they are unproductive. In the United States today, the productivity standard is mixed with a standard based on people's "needs" so that the aged, the disabled, the involuntarily unemployed, the very young, and other unproductive (in the market sense of the word) members of the economy are provided for through private and public transfers.

Equality

The *egalitarian principle* of income distribution is simply "To each exactly the same." Everyone would have exactly the same amount of income. This criterion of income distribution has been debated as far back as biblical times. This system of income distribution has been considered equitable, meaning that presumably everybody is dealt with fairly and equally. There are problems, however, with an income distribution that is completely equal.

Some jobs are more unpleasant or more dangerous than others. Should the people undertaking these jobs be paid exactly the same as everyone else? Indeed, under an equal distribution of income, what incentive would there be for individuals to take risky, hazardous, or unpleasant jobs at all? What about overtime? Who would be willing to work overtime without additional pay? There is another problem: If everyone earned the same income, what incentive would there be for individuals to invest in their own human capital—a costly and time-consuming process?

Just consider the incentive structure within a corporation. Recall from Chapter 27 that much of the pay differential between, say, the CEO and all of the vice-presidents is meant to create competition among the vice-presidents for the CEO's job. The result is higher productivity. If all incomes were the same, much of this competition would disappear, and productivity would fall.

There is some evidence that differences in income lead to higher rates of economic growth. Future generations are therefore made better off. Elimination of income differences may reduce the rate of economic growth and cause future generations to be poorer than they otherwise might have been.

CONCEPTS IN BRIEF

- Most people follow an age-earnings cycle in which they earn relatively small incomes when they first start working, increase their incomes until about age 50, and then slowly experience a decrease in their real incomes as they approach retirement.
- If we accept the marginal revenue product theory of wages, workers can expect to be paid their marginal revenue product. However, full adjustment is never obtained, so some workers may be paid more or less than their MRP.
- Marginal physical productivity depends on talent, education, experience, and training.
- Going to school and receiving on-the-job training can be considered an investment in human capital. The main cost of education is the opportunity cost of not working.
- Discrimination is most easily observed in various groups' access to high-paying jobs and to quality education. Minorities and women are disproportionately underrepresented in high-paying jobs. Also, minorities sometimes do not receive access to higher education of the same quality offered to majority-group members.
- Proponents of the comparable-worth doctrine contend that disparate jobs can be compared by examining efforts, skill, and educational training and that wages should therefore be paid on the basis of this comparable worth.
- Two normative standards for income distribution are income distribution based on productivity and income distribution based on equality.

POVERTY AND ATTEMPTS TO ELIMINATE IT

Throughout the history of the world, mass poverty has been accepted as inevitable. However, this nation and others, particularly in the Western world, have sustained enough economic growth in the past several hundred years so that *mass* poverty can no longer be said to be a problem for these fortunate countries. As a matter of fact, the residual of poverty in the United States strikes us as bizarre, an anomaly. How can there still be so much poverty in a nation of such abundance? Having talked about the determinants of the distribution of income, we now have at least some ideas of why some people are destined to remain low-income earners throughout their lives.

FIGURE 30-6
Official Number of Poor in the United States
The number of individuals classified as poor fell steadily from 1959 through 1969. From 1970 to 1981, the number stayed about the same. It then increased during the 1981–1982 recession, dropped off for a while, rose in the early 1990s, and then fell.
Source: U.S. Department of Labor.

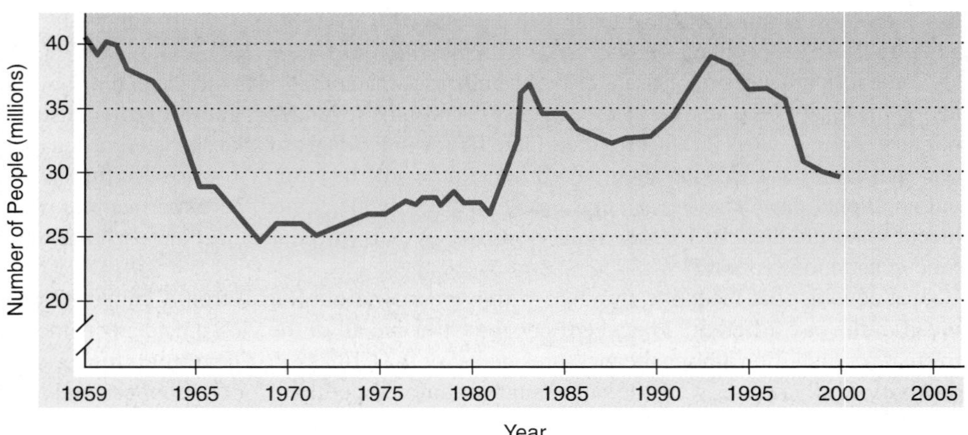

There are methods of transferring income from the relatively well-to-do to the relatively poor, and as a nation we have been using them for a long time. Today, we have a vast array of welfare programs set up for the purpose of redistributing income. However, we know that these programs have not been entirely successful. Are there alternatives to our current welfare system? Is there a better method of helping the poor? Before we answer these questions, let's look at the concept of poverty in more detail and at the characteristics of the poor. Figure 30-6 shows that those classified as poor fell steadily from 1959 to 1969, then leveled off until the recession of 1981–1982. The number started to rise dramatically, fell back during the late 1980s, rose again after the recession in the early 1990s, and has been falling slowly since then.

INTERNATIONAL EXAMPLE

Poverty Rates in the European Union

For years, politicians throughout much of the European Union have proclaimed their unwillingness to adopt the more laissez-faire, "let the chips fall where they may" economic model that prevails in the United States. They are convinced that the result is too much poverty. But they were shocked to discover in an article published in the newspaper *Le Monde* in 1997 that the poverty rate for the European Union was more than 17 percent—fully 57 million people out of a population of 330 million. Whereas the poverty rate in the United States has hovered between 13 and 15 percent of the population since the 1970s, the rate in Europe has increased over the same period from 10 percent to the current 17 percent. One-third of the officially poor in the European Union work, one-third are retired, and one-third are unemployed.

For Critical Analysis

What problems might there be in comparing poverty rates across nations?

Defining Poverty 

The threshold income level, which is used to determine who falls into the poverty category, was originally based on the cost of a nutritionally adequate food plan designed by the U.S. Department of Agriculture for emergency or temporary use. The threshold was determined by multiplying the food plan cost by 3 on the assumption that food expenses comprise approximately one-third of a poor family's income. Annual revisions of the threshold level were based only on price changes in the food budget. In 1969, a federal interagency committee looked at the calculations of the threshold and decided to set new standards, with adjustments made on the basis of changes in the Consumer Price Index. For example, in 2000, the official poverty level for an urban family of four was around $17,000. It goes up each year to reflect whatever inflation has occurred.

FAQ

Don't nations with higher average incomes also have higher average life expectancies?

On net, the answer is yes. In Africa, one of the lowest-income regions of the world, more than three-fourths of deaths were of people under the age of 50. In Europe, by contrast, only 15 percent of people die before reaching 50. Nevertheless, higher-income nations also experience a greater incidence of so-called "diseases of affluence"—heart disease, strokes, and cancer—that are associated with high-fat, low-exercise lifestyles. Deaths from circulatory diseases and cancer have increased steadily as the world's population has become relatively more affluent, even as deaths from infectious and parasitic diseases have fallen off. As a result, worldwide deaths from diseases of affluence now exceed deaths from infectious and parasitic diseases by several million per year.

Absolute Poverty

Because the low-income threshold is an absolute measure, we know that if it never changes in real terms, we will reduce poverty even if we do nothing. How can that be? The reasoning is straightforward. Real incomes in the United States have been growing at a compounded annual rate of almost 2 percent per capita for at least the past century and at about 2.5 percent since World War II. If we define the poverty line at a specific real level, more and more individuals will make incomes that exceed that poverty line. Thus in absolute terms, we will eliminate poverty (assuming continued per capita growth and no change in income distribution).

Click here to learn about the World Bank's programs intended to combat global poverty.

Relative Poverty

Be careful with this analysis, however. Poverty can also be defined in relative terms; that is, it is defined in terms of the income levels of individuals or families relative to the rest of the population. As long as the distribution of income is not perfectly equal, there will always be some people who make less income than others, even if their relatively low income is high by historical standards. Thus in a relative sense, the problem of poverty will always exist, although it can be reduced. In any given year, for example, the absolute poverty level *officially* decided on by the U.S. government is far above the average income in many countries in the world.

Transfer Payments as Income

The official poverty level is based on pretax income, including cash but not in-kind subsidies—food stamps, housing vouchers, and the like. If we correct poverty levels for such benefits, the percentage of the population that is below the poverty line drops dramatically. Some economists argue that the way the official poverty level is calculated makes no sense in a nation that redistributed over $850 billion in cash and noncash transfers in 2000.

Furthermore, some of the nation's official poor partake in the informal, or underground, sectors of the economy without reporting their income from these sources. And some of the officially defined poor obtain benefits from owning their own home (40 percent of all poor households do own their own homes). Look at Figure 30-7 (p. 746) for two different views of what has happened to the relative position of this nation's poor. The graph shows the ratio of the top fifth of the nation's households to the bottom fifth of the nation's households. If

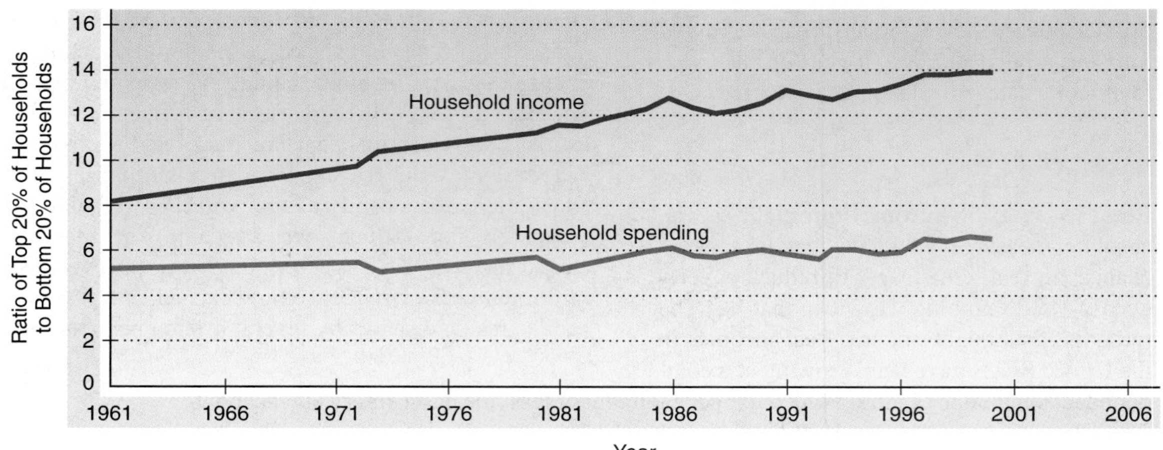

FIGURE 30-7

Relative Poverty: Comparing Household Incomes and Household Spending

This graph shows, on the vertical axis, the ratio of the top 20 percent of income-earning households to the bottom 20 percent. If measured household income is used, there appears to be increasing income inequality, particularly during the early to mid-1980s. If we look at household *spending*, though, inequality appears to remain constant.

Sources: U.S. Bureau of Labor Statistics; U.S. Bureau of the Census.

we look only at measured income, it appears that the poor are getting relatively poorer compared to the rich (the top line). If we compare household spending (consumption), a different picture emerges. The nation's poorest households are in fact holding their own.

Attacks on Poverty: Major Income Maintenance Programs

There are a variety of income maintenance programs designed to help the poor. We examine a few of them here.

Social Security. For the retired, the unemployed, and the disabled, social insurance programs provide income payments in prescribed situations. The best known is Social Security, which includes what has been called old-age, survivors', and disability insurance (OASDI). As discussed in Chapter 6, this is essentially a program of compulsory saving financed from compulsory payroll taxes levied on both employers and employees. Workers pay for Social Security while working and receive the benefits after retirement. The benefit payments are usually made to people who have reached retirement age. When the insured worker dies, benefits accrue to the survivors, including widows and children. Special benefits provide for disabled workers. Over 90 percent of all employed persons in the United States are covered by OASDI. Social Security was originally proposed as a social insurance program that workers paid for themselves and under which they received benefits that varied with the size of past contributions. Today, it is simply an intergenerational income transfer that is only vaguely related to past earnings. It transfers income from Americans who work—the young through the middle-aged—to those who do not work—older retired persons.

In 2000, more than 52 million people were receiving OASDI checks averaging about $742 a month. Benefit payments from OASDI redistribute income to some degree. However, benefit payments are not based on recipient need. Participants' contributions give them the right to benefits even if they would be financially secure without them. Social Security is not really an insurance program because people are not guaranteed that the benefits they receive will be in line with the contributions they have made. It is not a personal savings account. The benefits are legislated by Congress. In the future, Congress may not be as sympathetic toward older people as it is today. It could (and probably will have to) legislate for lower real levels of benefits instead of higher ones.

Supplemental Security Income (SSI) and Temporary Assistance to Needy Families (TANF). Many people who are poor but do not qualify for Social Security benefits are assisted through other programs. The federally financed and administered Supplemental Security Income (SSI) program was instituted in 1974. The purpose of SSI is to establish a nationwide minimum income for the aged, the blind, and the disabled. SSI has become one of the fastest-growing transfer programs in America. Whereas in 1974 less than $8 billion was spent, the prediction for 2001 is $35.4 billion. Americans currently eligible for SSI include children and individuals claiming mental disabilities, including drug addicts and alcoholics.

Temporary Assistance to Needy Families (TANF) is a state-administered program, financed in part by federal grants. The program provides aid to families in need. TANF replaced Aid to Families with Dependant Children (AFDC). TANF is intended to be temporary. Projected expenditures for TANF are $21.4 billion in 2001.

Food Stamps. Food stamps are government-issued coupons that can be used to purchase food. The food stamp program was started in 1964, seemingly, in retrospect, mainly to shore up the nation's agricultural sector by increasing demand for food through retail channels. In 1964, some 367,000 Americans were receiving food stamps. In 2000, the estimate is over 28 million recipients. The annual cost has jumped from $860,000 to more than $30 billion. In 2000, almost one in every nine citizens (including children) was using food stamps. The food stamp program has become a major part of the welfare system in the United States. The program has also become a method of promoting better nutrition among the poor.

The Earned Income Tax Credit Program (EITC). In 1975, the EITC was created to provide rebates of Social Security taxes to low-income workers. Over one-fifth of all tax returns claim an earned-income tax credit. In some states, such as Mississippi, as well as the District of Columbia, nearly half of all families are eligible for EITC. The program works as follows: Households with a reported income of less than $25,300 (exclusive of welfare payments) receive EITC benefits up to $2,528. There is a catch, though. Those with earnings between $8,425 and $11,000 get a flat $2,528. But families earning between $11,000 and $25,300 get penalized 17.68 cents for every dollar they earn above $11,000. This constitutes a punitive tax. Thus the EITC discourages work by a low- or moderate-income earner more than it rewards work. In particular, it discourages low-income earners from taking on a second job. The General Accounting Office estimates that hours worked by working wives in EITC-beneficiary households have consequently decreased by 10 percent. The average EITC recipient works 1,300 hours compared to a normal work year of 2,000 hours.

No Apparent Reduction in Poverty Rates

In spite of the numerous programs in existence and the hundreds of billions of dollars transferred to the poor, the officially defined rate of poverty in the United States has shown no long-run tendency to decline. From 1945 until the early 1970s, the percentage of Americans in poverty fell steadily every year. It reached a low of around 11 percent in 1973, shot back up beyond 15 percent in 1983, fell steadily to 13.1 percent in 1990, and has stayed about that ever since. Why this has happened is a real puzzlement. Since the War on Poverty was launched under President Lyndon B. Johnson in 1965, nearly $4 trillion has been transferred to the poor, and yet more Americans are poor today than ever before.This fact created the political will to pass the Welfare Reform Act of 1996, putting limits on people's use of welfare. The goal is now to get people off welfare and onto "workfare."

- If poverty is defined in absolute terms, economic growth eventually decreases the number of officially defined poor. If poverty is defined relatively, however, we will never eliminate it.
- Major attacks on poverty have been social insurance programs in the form of Social Security, Supplemental Security Income, Aid to Families with Dependent Children, the earned-income tax credit, and food stamps.
- Although the relative lot of the poor measured by household income seems to have worsened, household spending by the bottom 20 percent of households compared to the top 20 percentile has shown little change since the 1960s.

HEALTH CARE

It may seem strange to be reading about health care in a chapter on the distribution of income and poverty. Yet health care is in fact intimately related to those two topics. For example, sometimes people become poor because they do not have adequate health insurance (or have none at all), fall ill, and deplete all of their wealth on care. Moreover, sometimes individuals remain in certain jobs simply because their employer's health care package seems so good that they are afraid to change jobs and risk not being covered by health care insurance in the process. Finally, as you will see, much of the cause of the increased health care spending in America can be attributed to a change in the incentives that Americans face.

America's Health Care Situation

Spending for health care is estimated to account for 14 percent of the total annual income created in the U.S. economy. You can see from Figure 30-8 that in 1965, about 6 percent of annual income was spent on health care, but that percentage has been increasing ever since. Per capita spending on health care is greater in the United States than anywhere else in the world today. On a per capita basis, we spend more than twice as much as citizens of Luxembourg, Austria, Australia, Japan, and Denmark. We spend almost three times as much on a per capita basis as citizens of Spain and Ireland.

Why Have Health Care Costs Risen So Much? There are numerous explanations for why health care costs have risen so much. At least one has to do with changing demographics: The U.S. population is getting older.

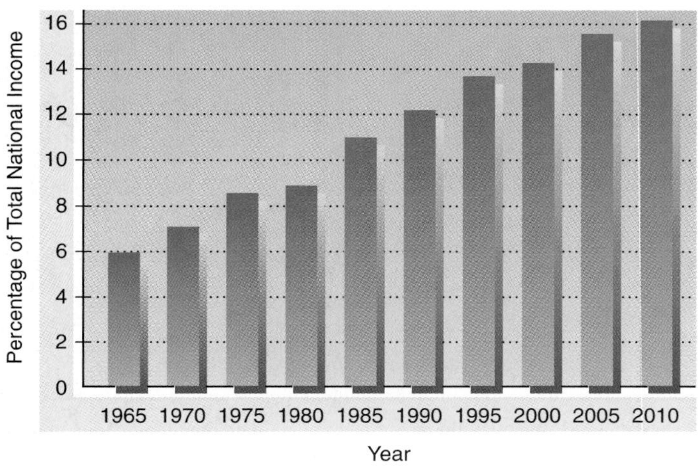

FIGURE 30-8
Percentage of Total National Income Spent on Health Care in the United States
The portion of total national income spent on health care has risen steadily since 1965.
Sources: U.S. Department of Commerce; U.S. Department of Health and Human Services; Deloitte and Touche LLP; VHA, Inc.

The Age–Health Care Expenditure Equation The top 5 percent of health care users incur over 50 percent of all health costs. The bottom 70 percent of health care users account for only 10 percent of health care expenditures. Not surprisingly, the elderly make up most of the top users of health care services. Nursing home expenditures are made primarily by people older than 70. The use of hospitals is also dominated by the aged.

The U.S. population is aging steadily. More than 12 percent of the current 275 million Americans are over 65. It is estimated that by the year 2035, senior citizens will comprise about 22 percent of our population. This aging population stimulates the demand for health care. The elderly consume more than four times the per capita health care services than the rest of the population uses. In short, whatever the demand for health care services is today, it is likely to be considerably higher in the future as the U.S. population ages.

New Technologies Another reason that health care costs have risen so dramatically is high technology. A CT (computerized tomography) scanner costs around $1 million. An MRI (magnetic resonance imaging) scanner can cost over $2 million. A PET (positron emission tomography) scanner costs around $4 million. All of these machines became increasingly available in the 1980s, 1990s, and 2000s and are desired throughout the country. Typical fees for procedures using them range from $300 to $500 for a CT scan to as high as $2,000 for a PET scan. The development of new technologies that help physicians and hospitals prolong human life is an ongoing process in an ever-advancing industry. New procedures at even higher prices can be expected in the future.

Third-Party Financing Currently, government spending on health care constitutes over 40 percent of total health care spending (of which the *federal* government pays about 70 percent). Private insurance accounts for a little over 35 percent of payments for health care. The remainder—less than 20 percent—is paid directly by individuals. Figure 30-9 on the next page shows the change in the payment scheme for medical care in the United States since 1930. Medicare and Medicaid are the main sources of hospital and other medical benefits to 35 million Americans, most of whom are over 65. Medicaid—the joint state-federal program—provides long-term health care, particularly for people living in nursing homes. Medicare, Medicaid, and private insurance companies are considered **third parties** in the medical care equation. Caregivers and patients are the two primary parties. When third parties step in to pay for medical care, the quantity demanded for those services increases. For example, when

Third parties 
Parties who are not directly involved in a given activity or transaction. For example, in the relationship between caregivers and patients, fees may be paid by third parties (insurance companies, government).

FIGURE 30-9 

Third Party Versus Out-of-Pocket Health Care Payments

Out-of-pocket payments for health care services have been falling steadily since the 1930s. In contrast, third-party payments for health care have risen to the point that they account for over 80 percent of all such outlays today.

Sources: Health Care Financing Administration; U.S. Department of Health and Human Services.

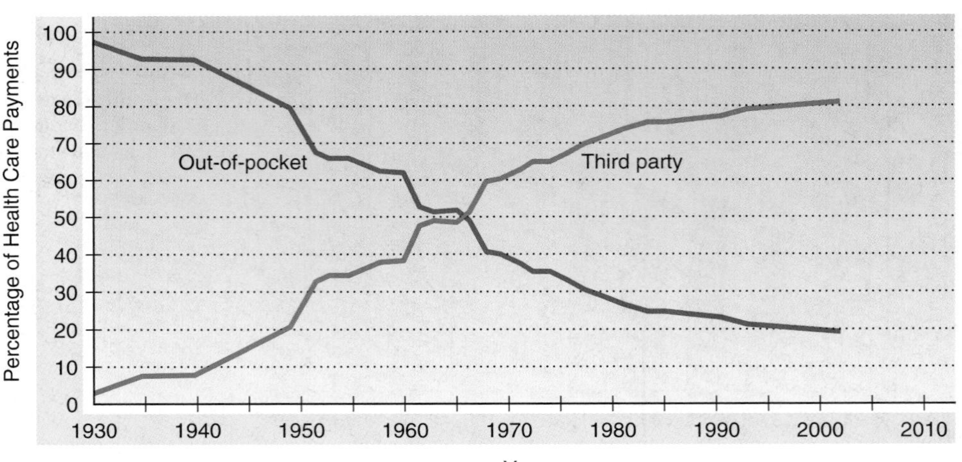

Medicare and Medicaid went into effect in the 1960s, the volume of federal government–reimbursed medical services increased by more than 65 percent.

The availability of third-party payments for costly medical care has generated increases in the availability of hospital beds. Between 1974 and 2000, the number of hospital beds increased by over 50 percent. Present occupancy rates are only around 65 percent.

Price, Quantity Demanded, and the Question of Moral Hazard. While some people may think that the demand for health care is insensitive to price changes, theory clearly indicates otherwise. Look at Figure 30-10. There you see a hypothetical demand curve for health care services. To the extent that third parties—whether government or private insurance—pay for health care, the out-of-pocket cost, or net price, to the individual will drop. In an extreme example, all medical expenses are paid for by third parties so that the price is zero in Figure 30-10 and the quantity demanded is many times what it would be at a higher price.

One of the issues here has to do with the problem of moral hazard. Consider two individuals with two different health insurance policies. The first policy pays for all medical expenses, but in the second the individual has to pay the first $1,000 a year (this amount is known as the *deductible*). Will the behavior of the two individuals be different? Generally, the answer is yes. The individual with no deductible may be more likely to seek treatment for health problems after they develop rather than try to avoid them and will generally expect medical attention on a more regular basis. In contrast, the individual who faces the

FIGURE 30-10

The Demand for Health Care Services

At price P_1, the quantity of health care services demanded per year would hypothetically be Q_1. If the price falls to zero (third-party payment with zero deductible), the quantity demanded expands to Q_2.

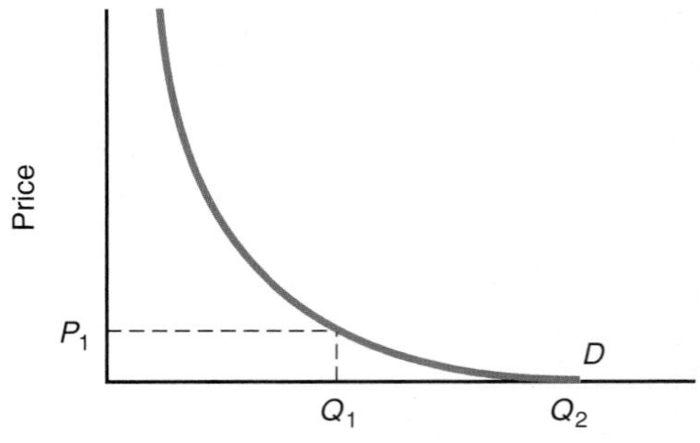

first $1,000 of medical expenses each year will tend to engage in more wellness activities and will be less inclined to seek medical care for minor problems. The moral hazard here is that the individual with the zero deductible for medical care expenses may engage in a lifestyle that is less healthful than will the individual with the $1,000 deductible.

Moral Hazard as It Affects Physicians and Hospitals. The issue of moral hazard also has a direct effect on the behavior of physicians and hospital administrators. Due to third-party payments, patients rarely have to worry about the expense of operations and other medical procedures. As a consequence, both physicians and hospitals order more procedures. Physicians are typically reimbursed on the basis of medical procedures; thus they have no financial interest in trying to keep hospital costs down. Indeed, many have an incentive to raise costs.

Such actions are most evident with terminally ill patients. A physician may order a CT scan and other costly procedures for a terminally ill patient. The physician knows that Medicare or some other type of insurance will pay. Then the physician can charge a fee for analyzing the CT scan. Fully 30 percent of Medicare expenditures are for Americans who are in the last six months of their lives.

Rising Medicare expenditures are one of the most serious problems facing the federal government today. The number of beneficiaries has increased from 19.1 million in 1966 (first year of operation) to an estimated 40 million in 2000. Figure 30-11 shows that federal spending on Medicare has been growing at over 10 percent a year, adjusted for inflation.

Is National Health Insurance the Answer?

Proponents of a national health care system believe that the current system relies too heavily on private insurers. They argue in favor of a Canadian-style system. In Canada, the government sets the fees that are paid to each doctor for seeing a patient and prohibits private practice. The Canadian government also imposes a cap on the incomes that any doctor can receive in a given year. The Canadian federal government provides a specified amount of funding to hospitals, leaving it to them to decide how to allocate the funds. If we were to follow the

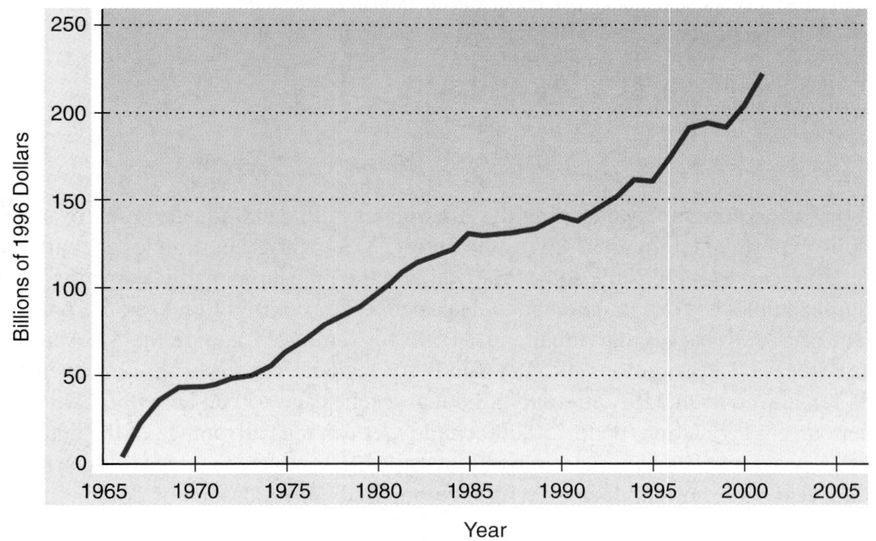

FIGURE 30-11

Federal Medicare Spending

Federal spending on Medicare has increased about 10 percent a year, after adjusting for inflation, since its inception in 1966. (All figures expressed in constant 1996 dollars.)

Sources: Economic Report of the President; U.S. Bureau of Labor Statistics.

Canadian model, the average American would receive fewer health services than at present. Hospital stays would be longer, but there would be fewer tests and procedures.

Alternatives to a national health care policy involve some type of national health insurance, perhaps offered only to people who qualify on the basis of low annual income. A number of politicians have offered variations on such a program. The over 40 million Americans who have no health insurance at some time during each year would certainly benefit. The share of annual national income that goes to health care expenditures would rise, however. Also, federal government spending might increase by another $30 billion to $50 billion (or more) per year to pay for the program.

INTERNATIONAL EXAMPLE

While Americans Complain About Health Care Expenses, Canadians Wait in Line

In Chapter 4, you learned about several ways to ration goods and services. Although government programs and some private programs engage in nonprice rationing in the United States, the primary rationing device continues to be the price mechanism. A disadvantage of this approach is that some people may not wish to pay market prices for the best-quality care. A large number of U.S. residents do not have health insurance at some time each year.

In Canada, the government provides a "single-payer" national health system under which all citizens are promised "free care." In recent years, proponents of a national U.S. health care system have held up the Canadian system as a model for the United States to emulate. Within the past few years, dramatic events highlighted the pitfalls of the Canadian system. For instance, a pregnant woman died of a brain hemorrhage when her doctors could not locate a neurosurgical facility that had room for her. After months of postponed appointments, a woman suffering from stomach pains died of cancer that might have been treatable if detected earlier. Other patients with suspected cancers had to sign waiting lists *to get on to* true waiting lists for magnetic resonance imaging (MRI) devices.

Offering free health care encourages patients to seek as much care as they can get. Of course, a government that promises care must incur costs to provide it. These costs have put a severe strain on Canadian federal and provincial governments. To cope with rising costs, Canadian officials have closed hospitals and limited the hours that physicians can treat patients. They have depended on *rationing by queues*. For people who can get treatment in Canada, the quality of care is very good. The problem is that people typically have to wait in line to get it—and some die waiting.

For Critical Analysis

What identifiable groups stand to gain from allowing market prices to ration health care? Do any specific groups gain from health care rationing by queues?

Countering the Moral Hazard Problem: A Medical Savings Account

Medical savings account (MSA) 
A tax-exempt health care account into which individuals would pay on a regular basis and out of which medical care expenses could be paid.

As an alternative to completely changing the American health care industry, Congress has legislated the experimental **medical savings account (MSA)** program. Employers with 50 or fewer employees, as well as the self-employed and the uninsured, can set up a tax-free MSA. Eligible employees can make an annual tax-deductible contribution to an MSA up to a maximum of $2,250 for an individual and $4,500 for family. Money in the MSA accumulates tax-free, and distributions of MSA funds for medical expenses are also exempt. Any funds remaining in an MSA after an individual reaches age 65 can be withdrawn tax-free. Under current legislation, up to 750,000 employees can take advantage of the demonstration MSA program. The benefits can be impressive. A single person depositing around $1,500 each year with no withdrawals will have hundreds of thousands of dollars in the account after 40 years.

Combating Moral Hazard. A major benefit of an MSA is that the moral hazard problem is reduced. Individuals ultimately pay for their own minor medical expenses. They do not have the incentive to seek medical care as frequently for minor problems. In addition, they have an incentive to engage in wellness activities. Finally, for those using an MSA, the physician-patient relationship remains intact, for third parties (insurance companies or the government) do not intervene in paying or monitoring medical expenses. Patients with MSAs will not allow physicians to routinely order expensive tests for every minor ache or pain because they get to keep any money saved in the MSA.

Critics' Responses. Some critics argue that because individuals get to keep whatever they don't spend from their MSAs, they will forgo necessary visits to medical care facilities and may develop more serious medical problems as a consequence. Other critics argue that MSAs will sabotage managed care plans. Under managed care plans, deductibles are either reduced or eliminated completely. In exchange, managed health care plan participants are extremely limited in physician choice. Just the opposite would occur with MSAs—high deductibles and unlimited choice of physicians.

CONCEPTS IN BRIEF

- Health care costs have risen because (1) our population has been getting older and the elderly use more health care services, (2) new technologies and medicine cost more, and (3) third-party financing—private and government-sponsored health insurance—reduces the incentive for individuals to reduce their spending on health care services.
- National health insurance has been proposed as an answer to our current problems, but it does little to alter the reasons why health care costs continue to rise.
- An alternative to a national health care program might be medical savings accounts, which allow individuals to set aside money that is tax exempt, to be used only for medical care. Whatever is left over becomes a type of retirement account.

NETNOMICS

Cyberdocs Versus Cyberquacks

It is estimated that more than 30 million people per year log on to the Internet to look for information or assistance with a medical or personal problem. Doctors, psychologists, and health care firms have noticed. Since 1997, at least $250 million in venture capital has been invested in Net-related health care sites. The nation's largest health maintenance organization, Kaiser Permanente, now has a Web site that allows its 9.2 million members to register for office visits, send e-mail questions to nurses and pharmacists, learn about the results of lab tests, and refill prescriptions. Former U.S. Surgeon General C. Everett Koop operates a consumer health site called drkoop.com, and the Mayo Clinic's Health Oasis Web site receives hundreds of thousands of visitors each month. Anyone today can access Web sites offering a wide array of medical research and news, as well as links to databases that explain diseases and drugs in laymen's terms. Some offer on-line chats with physicians and nurses, personal medical pages with customized data, and risk assessment services that rate a person's health based on lifestyle and medical information. A growing number of sites sell health-related products ranging from vitamins to health insurance.

Some medical experts hope that the Web will ultimately link physicians, patients, and insurers much like human nerve cells link to form the body's nervous system. Creating a

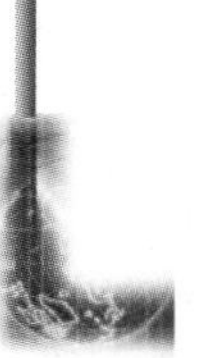

Net-based "electronic nervous system" for the health care industry, they argue, could help avoid wasting funds on unnecessary and duplicated medical treatments, thereby saving about a third of the more than $1 trillion that Americans spend on health care.

Nevertheless, there are hazards to Net-based health advice and care. Recall the lemons problem discussed in Chapter 23: If consumers do not know the details about the quality of a product, they may be willing to pay no more than the price of a low-quality product, even if a higher-quality product is available at a higher price. There are now at least 15,000 health-related Web sites, and undoubtedly some charge consumers for bad or misleading information. A few cyberspace health practitioners undoubtedly market low-priced "home remedies" that do little, if anything, to cure real diseases. To combat this problem, the non-profit Health on the Net Foundation certifies and monitors health-related Web sites. The U.S. Department of Health and Human Services has even set up a Web site, www.healthfinder.gov, which is aimed at helping consumers distinguish legitimate sites from those that practice cyberquackery.

ISSUES & APPLICATIONS

Why Is Measuring Poverty So Hard?

When officers of financial firms in Chicago formed Social Compact and launched their study of opportunities for bringing about economic renewal in official poverty-stricken portions of the city, they were surprised to see how well African-American South Side was doing. In addition, figures that Social Compact compiled in its study of low-income Chicago neighborhoods led to a particularly startling conclusion: People in some of the neighborhoods appeared to be spending more than official income data showed that they were earning.

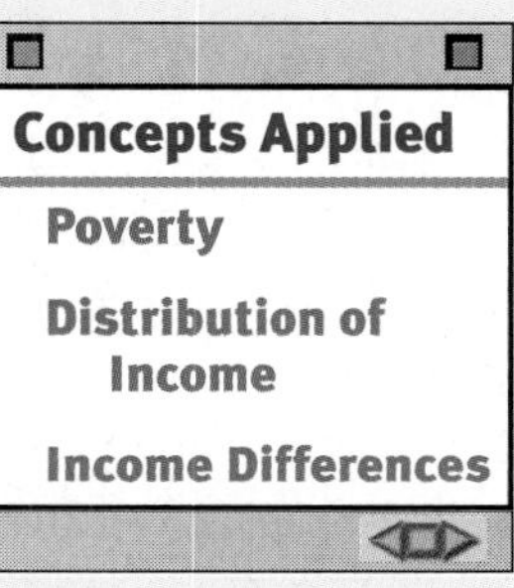

Problems in Relying on Incomes to Measure Poverty

Many economists are not surprised that spending has increased in poor neighborhoods. Studies of the earnings and spending of Americans who, according to government figures, earn between $10,000 and $20,000 per year find that overall they spend 40 percent more than their reported incomes. People who report earning less than $10,000 per year spend more than 150 percent more than their reported incomes.

What explains these discrepancies? One possible explanation, of course, is measurement errors. Perhaps people aren't really spending that much more than they report earnings. Nevertheless, study after study indicates the same pattern. A second, and more likely, explanation is that many low-income people report less income than they actually earn. Again, there may be reporting errors. Nevertheless, a plausible inference is that a lot of low-income people want to avoid paying taxes on the little income they do earn. So they do not report all their income.

Consumption as a Measure of Poverty

As you learned in this chapter, the government officially defines poverty on the basis of income levels. A number of economists have questioned this method for years, because incomes are not particularly useful measures of well-being. A person's reported income typically does not include earnings from informal work, and it does not take into account the value of health and education subsidies received from the government. This has led some economists to propose defining poverty in terms of *consumption* levels.

To do this, economists such as Dale Jorgenson of Harvard University and Robert Triest of the Federal Reserve Bank of Boston have used the federal government's Survey of Consumer Expenditures to fill in blanks and pick up details missed by income surveys. For instance, data from consumption surveys reveal when a low-income household can get by relatively well because it lives in a comfortable house inherited from parents. In addition, they indicate general improvements in standard of living, such as increased ownership of washing machines and automatic dishwashers. Of course, some consumption patterns have ambiguous implications. For example, if people consume less beef, is it because they are worse off and cannot afford to buy as much, or is it because they are better off and want to switch to a more healthful diet?

An Old Problem Rears Its Ugly Head

One of the biggest problems with consumption-based measures of poverty, however, has to do with tracking changes in the cost of living over time. Economists have found that there are significant measurement problems in determining changes in consumer prices. It turns out that depending on how economists measure price changes over time, they reach different conclusions about whether the poverty problem is worsening or improving. It seems that no matter where economists turn in their quest to define poverty, measurement problems abound.

FOR CRITICAL ANALYSIS

1. Why might similar households with identical incomes consume different amounts?
2. How might economists define an official "poverty" level of consumption?

SUMMARY DISCUSSION OF LEARNING OBJECTIVES

1. **Using a Lorenz Curve to Represent a Nation's Income Distribution:** A Lorenz curve is a diagram that illustrates the distribution of income geometrically by measuring the percentage of households in relation to the cumulative percentage of income earnings. A perfectly straight Lorenz curve depicts perfect income equality, because at each percentage of households measured along a straight-line Lorenz curve, those households earn exactly the same percentage of income. The more bowed a Lorenz curve, the more unequally income is distributed.
2. **Key Determinants of Income Differences Across Individuals:** Because of the age-earnings cycle, in which people typically begin working at relatively low incomes when young, age is an important factor influencing income differences. So are marginal productivity differences, which arise from differences in talents, experience, and training due to different human capital investments. Discrimination likely plays a role as well, and economists attribute some of the unexplained portions of income differences across people to factors that relate to discrimination.
3. **Theories of Desired Income Distribution:** Economists agree that determining how income ought to be distributed is a normative issue influenced by alternative notions of economic justice. Nevertheless, two theories of desired income distribution receive considerable attention. One is the productivity standard (also called the contributive or merit standard), according to which each person receives income according to the value of what the person produces. The other is the egalitarian principle of income distribution, which proposes that each person should receive exactly the same income.
4. **Alternative Approaches to Measuring and Addressing Poverty:** One approach to defining poverty is to define an absolute poverty standard, such as a specific and unchanging income level. If an absolute measure of poverty is used and the economy experiences persistent real growth, poverty eventually will disappear. Another approach defines poverty in terms of income levels relative to the rest of the population. Under this definition, poverty exists as long as the distribution of incomes is unequal. Official poverty measures are often based on pretax income and fail to take transfer payments into account. Currently, the U.S. government seeks to address poverty via income maintenance programs such as Social Security, Supplemental Security Income, Temporary Assistance to Needy Families, food stamps, and the Earned Income Tax Credit program.
5. **Major Reasons for Rising Health Care Costs:** Spending on health care as a percentage of total U.S. spending has increased during recent decades. One reason is that the U.S. population is aging, and older people typically experience more health problems. Another contributing factor is the adoption of higher-priced technologies for diagnosing and treating health problems. In addition, third-party financing of health care expenditures by private and government insurance programs gives covered individuals an incentive to purchase more health care than they would if they paid all expenses out of pocket. Moral hazard problems can also arise, because consumers

may be more likely to seek treatment for insured health problems after they develop instead of trying to avoid them, and doctors and hospitals may order more procedures than they otherwise would require.

6. **Alternative Approaches to Paying for Health Care:** An alternative approach to funding health care would be to rely less on private insurers and more on governmental funding of care for all citizens. Under such a system, the government typically sets fees and establishes limits on access to care. Another approach would be to establish a national health insurance program that is income-based, in which only lower-income people would qualify for government assistance in meeting their health care expenses. Another option is provide incentives for people to save some of their income in medical savings accounts, from which they can draw funds to pay for health care expenses in the future.

Key Terms and Concepts

Age-earnings cycle (737)
Comparable-worth doctrine (742)
Distribution of income (732)
Income in kind (733)
Lorenz curve (732)
Medical savings account (MSA) (752)
Third parties (749)

Problems

Answers to the odd-numbered problems appear at the back of the book.

30-1. Consider the accompanying graph, which depicts Lorenz curves for countries X, Y, and Z.

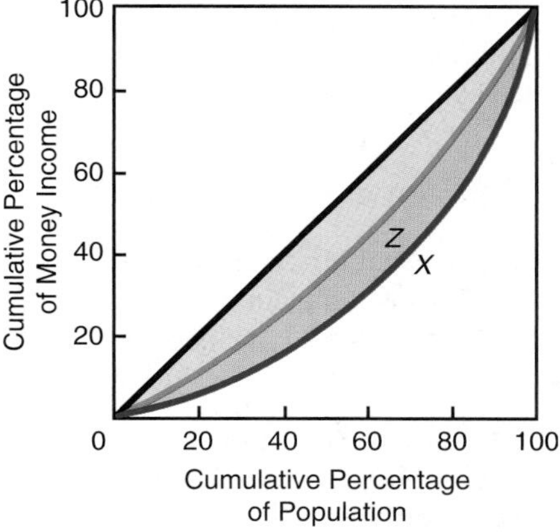

a. Which country has the least income inequality?
b. Which country has the most income inequality?
c. Countries Y and Z are identical in all but one respect: population distribution. The share of the population made up of children below working age is much higher in country Z. Recently, however, birthrates have declined in country Z and risen in country Y. Assuming that the countries remain identical in all other respects, would you expect that in 20 years the Lorenz curves for the two countries will be closer together or farther apart?

30-2. Consider the following income distribution estimates from the 1990s. Use graph paper or a hand-drawn diagram to draw rough Lorenz curves for each country. Which has the most nearly equal distribution, based on your diagram?

Country	Poorest 40%	Next 30%	Next 20%	Richest 10%
Bolivia	13	21	26	40
Chile	13	20	26	41
Uruguay	22	26	26	26

30-3. Estimates indicate that during the 1990s, the poorest 40 percent of the population earned about 15 percent of total income in Argentina. In Brazil, the poorest 40 percent earned about 10 percent of total income. The next-highest 30 percent of income earners in Argentina received roughly 25 percent of total income. By contrast, in Brazil, the next-highest 30 percent of income earners received approximately 20 percent of total income. Can you determine, without drawing a diagram (though you can if you wish), which country's Lorenz curve was bowed out farther to the right?

30-4. A retired 72-year-old man currently draws Social Security and a small pension from his previous employment. He is in very good health and would like to take on a new challenge, and he decides to go back to work. He determines that under the rules of Social Security and his pension plan, if he were to work full time, he would face a marginal tax rate of 110 percent for the last hour he works each week. What does this mean?

30-5. In what ways might policies aimed at achieving complete income equality across all households be incompatible with economic efficiency?

30-6. Some economists have argued that if the government wishes to subsidize health care, it should instead provide predetermined sums of money (based on the type of health care problems experienced) directly to patients, who then would be free to choose their health care providers. Whether or not you agree, can you provide an economic rationale for this approach to governmental health care funding?

30-7. Suppose that a government agency guarantees to pay all of an individual's future health care expenses after the end of this year, so that the effective price of health care for the individual will be zero from that date onward. In what ways might this well-intended policy induce the individual to consume "excessive" health care services in future years?

30-8. Suppose that a group of doctors establishes a joint practice in a remote area. This group provides the only health care available to people in the local community, and its objective is to maximize total economic profits for the group's members. Draw a diagram illustrating how the price and quantity of health care will be determined in this community.

30-9. A government agency determines that the entire community discussed in Problem 30-8 qualifies for a special program in which the government will pay for a number of health care services that most residents previously had not consumed. Many residents immediately make appointments with the community physicians' group. Given the information in Problem 30-8, what is the likely effect on the profit-maximizing price and the equilibrium quantity of health care services provided by the physicians' group in this community?

30-10. A government agency notifies the physicians' group in Problem 30-8 that to continue providing services in the community, the group must document its activities. The resulting paperwork expenses raise the cost of each unit of health care services that the group provides. What is the likely effect on the profit-maximizing price and the equilibrium quantity of health care services provided by the physicians' group in this community?

Economics on the Net

Measuring Poverty Many economists believe that there are problems with the current official measure of poverty. In this application, you will learn about some of these problems and will be able to examine an alternative poverty measure that one group of economists has proposed.

Title: Joint Center for Poverty Research (JCPR)

Navigation: Click here to visit the JCPR's homepage. Click on Publications. Select the complete listing of policy briefs. Click on the Policy Brief titled "Measuring Poverty—A New Approach."

Application Read the article; then answer the following questions.

1. How is the current official poverty income level calculated? What is the main problem with this way of calculating the threshold income for classifying impoverished households?
2. What is the alternative conceptual measure of poverty that the authors propose? How does it differ from the current measure?

For Group Study and Analysis Discuss the two measures of poverty discussed in the article. What people would no longer be classified as living in poverty under the proposed measure of poverty? What people would join the ranks of those classified as among the impoverished in America? How might adopting the new measure of poverty affect efforts to address the U.S. poverty problem?

CHAPTER

31

ENVIRONMENTAL ECONOMICS

These tourists are on a Nepalese tiger safari. They are willing to pay large sums of money to observe tigers in the wild. Can you use this fact to devise a policy to preserve Asian tigers?

It is estimated that at the beginning of the twentieth century, there were more than 100,000 tigers that roamed Asia. Today there are at most 7,300. Furthermore, despite concerted international efforts—bans on hunting, government-operated tiger reserves, and restraints on trade in tiger body parts—over more than three decades, the number of tigers continues to dwindle. Can economists contribute to continuing efforts to save the tiger? To understand what economics can add to wildlife conservation efforts, as well as to broader efforts to prevent environmental degradation, you must first learn about environmental economics. You will be looking at the costs and benefits of every action, including those already undertaken and those proposed to solve any problem of global dimension.

LEARNING OBJECTIVES

After reading this chapter, you should be able to:

1. Distinguish between private costs and social costs
2. Understand market externalities and possible ways to correct externalities
3. Describe how economists can conceptually determine the optimal quantity of pollution
4. Explain the roles of private and common property rights in alternative approaches to addressing the problem of pollution
5. Discuss how the assignment of property rights may influence the fates of endangered species
6. Contrast the benefits and costs of recycling scarce resources

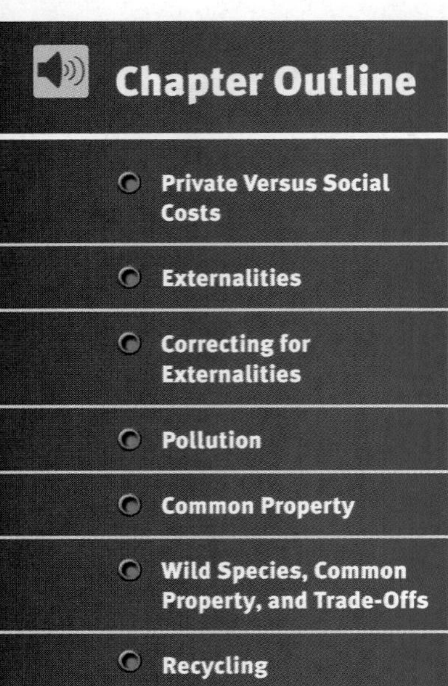

Chapter Outline
Private Versus Social Costs
Externalities
Correcting for Externalities
Pollution
Common Property
Wild Species, Common Property, and Trade-Offs
Recycling

Did You Know That... within three months after the Pilgrims landed at Plymouth Rock, half of them had died from malnutrition and illness because of the harsh conditions they encountered? Some of the surviving Pilgrims gave up and returned with the *Mayflower* when it sailed back across the Atlantic. The remaining Pilgrims struggled with famine. After three years of enduring conditions bordering on starvation, and after some Pilgrims became so desperate that they took to stealing from the others, the colonists began to reconsider a key method they had adopted in an effort to promote their new society. This was the practice of "farming in common," which entailed pooling what they produced and then rationing this "common property" in equal allotments. Following much thought and discussion, the colonists decided instead to parcel the *land* equally among families, who could then either consume or trade all fruits of their labors. This change in the Pilgrims' incentive structure worked wonders. Soon they had such bountiful harvests that they decided to have a day of thanksgiving—the forerunner of the modern American Thanksgiving holiday.

How to design incentives for people to use common property in ways that is in the interest of society as a whole is an important economic problem. Certainly, it is in the interest of today's societies and of future generations to find a mix of incentives that induce human beings to protect our most important form of common property, our environment. It should not surprise you that the economic way of thinking about the environment has to do with costs.

For example, are you willing to give up driving your car in order to have a cleaner environment? Or would you pay $4 for a gallon of gas to help clean up the environment? In a phrase, how much of your current standard of living are you willing to give up to help the environment? The economic way of looking at ecological issues is often viewed as anti-ecological. But this is not so. Economists want to help citizens and policymakers opt for informed policies that have the maximum possible *net* benefits (benefits minus costs). As you will see, every decision in favor of "the environment" involves a trade-off.

PRIVATE VERSUS SOCIAL COSTS

Human actions often give rise to unwanted side effects—the destruction of our environment is one. Human actions generate pollutants that go into the air and the water. The question that is often asked is, Why can individuals and businesses continue to create pollution without necessarily paying directly for the negative consequences?

Until now, we've been dealing with situations in which the costs of an individual's actions are borne directly by the individual. When a business has to pay wages to workers, it knows exactly what its labor costs are. When it has to buy materials or build a plant, it knows quite well what these will cost. An individual who has to pay for car repairs or a theater ticket knows exactly what the cost will be. These costs are what we term *private costs*. **Private costs** are borne solely by the individuals who incur them. They are *internal* in the sense that the firm or household must explicitly take account of them.

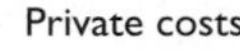

Private costs Costs borne solely by the individuals who incur them. Also called *internal costs*.

What about a situation in which a business dumps the waste products from its production process into a nearby river or in which an individual litters a public park or beach? Obviously, a cost is involved in these actions. When the firm pollutes the water, people downstream suffer the consequences. They may not want to swim in or drink the polluted water. They may also be unable to catch as many fish as before because of the pollution. In the case of littering, the people who come along after our litterer has cluttered the park or the beach are the ones who bear the costs. The cost of these actions is borne by people other than those who commit the actions. The creator of the cost is not the sole bearer. The costs are not internalized by the individual or firm; they are external. When we add *external* costs to *internal,* or private, costs, we get **social costs.** Pollution problems—indeed, all problems pertaining to the environment—may be viewed as situations in which social costs exceed private costs. Because some economic participants don't pay the full social costs of their actions but rather only the smaller private costs, their actions are socially "unacceptable." In such situations in which there is a divergence between social and private costs, we therefore see "too much" steel production, automobile driving, and beach littering, to pick only a few of the many possible examples.

Social costs

The full costs borne by society whenever a resource use occurs. Social costs can be measured by adding private, or internal, costs to external costs.

The Costs of Polluted Air

Why is the air in cities so polluted from automobile exhaust fumes? When automobile drivers step into their cars, they bear only the private costs of driving. That is, they must pay for the gas, maintenance, depreciation, and insurance on their automobiles. But they cause an additional cost, that of air pollution, which they are not forced to take account of when they make the decision to drive. Air pollution is a cost because it causes harm to individuals—burning eyes, respiratory ailments, and dirtier clothes, cars, and buildings. The air pollution created by automobile exhaust is a cost that individual operators of automobiles do not yet bear directly. The social cost of driving includes all the private costs plus at least the cost of air pollution, which society bears. Decisions made only on the basis of private costs lead to too much automobile driving or, alternatively, to too little money spent on the reduction of automobile pollution for a given amount of driving. Clean air is a scarce resource used by automobile drivers free of charge. They will use more of it than they would if they had to pay the full social costs.

EXTERNALITIES

When a private cost differs from a social cost, we say that there is an **externality** because individual decision makers are not paying (internalizing) all the costs. (We briefly covered this topic in Chapter 5.) Some of these costs remain external to the decision-making process. Remember that the full cost of using a scarce resource is borne one way or another by all who live in the society. That is, society must pay the full opportunity cost of any activity that uses scarce resources. The individual decision maker is the firm or the customer, and external costs and benefits will not enter into that individual's or firm's decision-making processes.

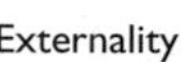

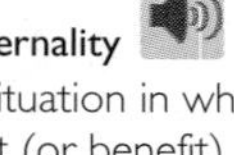

Externality

A situation in which a private cost (or benefit) diverges from a social cost (or benefit); a situation in which the costs (or benefits) of an action are not fully borne (or gained) by the two parties engaged in exchange or by an individual engaging in a scarce-resource-using activity.

We might want to view the problem as it is presented in Figure 31-1 on the next page. Here we have the market demand curve, *D,* for the product X and the supply curve, S_1, for product X. The supply curve, S_1, includes only internal, or private, costs. The intersection of the demand and supply curves as drawn will be at price P_1 and quantity Q_1 (at E_1). We now assume that the production of good X involves externalities that the private firms did not take into account. Those externalities could be air pollution, water pollution, scenery destruction, or anything of that nature.

We know that the social costs of producing product X exceed the private costs. We show this by drawing curve S_2. It is above the original supply curve S_1 because it includes the full social costs of producing the product. If firms could be made to bear these costs, the price would be P_2 and the quantity Q_2 (at E_2). The inclusion of external costs in the decision-making process leads to a higher-priced product and a decline in quantity produced. Thus we see that when social costs are not being fully borne by the creators of those costs, the quantity produced is "excessive," because the price is too low.

FIGURE 31-1

Reckoning with Full Social Costs

The supply curve, S_1, is equal to the horizontal summation (Σ) of the individual marginal cost curves above the respective minimum average variable costs of all the firms producing good X. These individual marginal cost curves include only internal, or private, costs. If the external costs were included and added to the private costs, we would have social costs. The supply curve would shift upward to S_2. In the uncorrected situation, the equilibrium price would be P_1 and the equilibrium quantity would be Q_1. In the corrected situation, the equilibrium price would rise to P_2 and the equilibrium quantity would fall to Q_2.

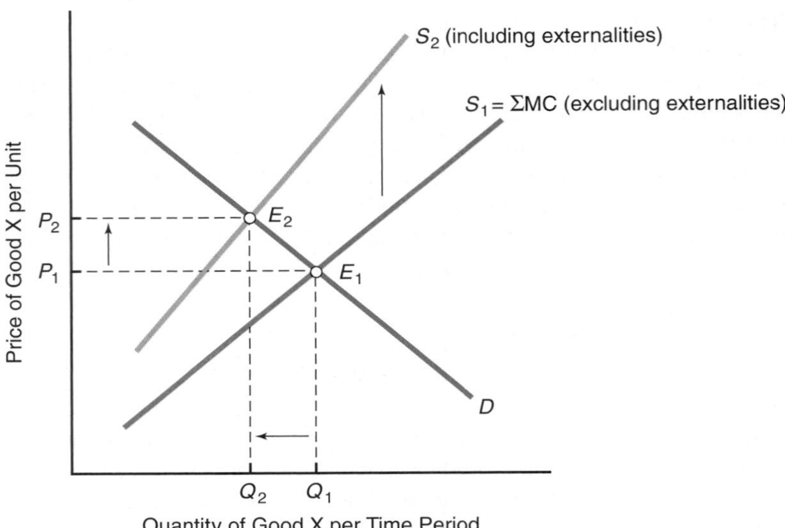

CORRECTING FOR EXTERNALITIES

We can see here a method for reducing pollution and environmental degradation. Somehow the signals in the economy must be changed so that decision makers will take into account *all* the costs of their actions. In the case of automobile pollution, we might want to devise some method by which motorists are taxed according to the amount of pollution they cause. In the case of a firm, we might want to devise a system whereby businesses are taxed according to the amount of pollution for which they are responsible. In this manner, they would have an incentive to install pollution abatement equipment.

The Polluters' Choice

Facing an additional private cost for polluting, firms will be induced to (1) install pollution abatement equipment or otherwise change production techniques so as to reduce the amount of pollution, (2) reduce pollution-causing activity, or (3) simply pay the price to pollute. The relative costs and benefits of each option for each polluter will determine which one or combination will be chosen. Allowing the choice is the efficient way to decide who pollutes and who doesn't. In principle, each polluter faces the full social cost of its actions and makes a production decision accordingly.

Is a Uniform Tax Appropriate?

It may not be appropriate to levy a *uniform* tax according to physical quantities of pollution. After all, we're talking about external costs. Such costs are not necessarily the same everywhere in the United States for the same action.

Essentially, we must establish the amount of the *economic damages* rather than the amount of the physical pollution. A polluting electrical plant in New York City will cause much more damage than the same plant in remote Montana. There are already innumerable demands on the air in New York City, so the pollution from smokestacks will not be cleansed away naturally. Millions of people will breathe the polluted air and thereby incur the costs of sore throats, sickness, emphysema, and even early death. Buildings will become dirtier faster because of the pollution, as will cars and clothes. A given quantity of pollution will cause more harm in concentrated urban environments than it will in less dense rural environments. If we were to establish some form of taxation to align private costs with social costs and to force people to internalize externalities, we would somehow have to come up with a measure of *economic* costs instead of *physical* quantities. But the tax, in any event, would fall on the private sector and modify private-sector economic agents' behavior. Therefore, because the economic cost for the same physical quantity of pollution would be different in different locations according to population density, the natural formation of mountains and rivers, and so forth, so-called optimal taxes on pollution would vary from location to location. (Nonetheless, a uniform tax might make sense when administrative costs, particularly the cost of ascertaining the actual economic costs, are relatively high.)

POLICY EXAMPLE

Should Car Antitheft Devices Be Subsidized?

Externalities exist for many activities. Consider the theft of automobiles. About 1.5 million cars are stolen in the United States every year. If you own an expensive car, you run a risk of having it stolen when you park on the street. Enter an antitheft device called Lojack, first used in 1986. A tiny transmitter is hidden in each Lojack-equipped car. When a car is stolen, in any of 20 major cities, the police can turn on the transmitter. About 95 percent of Lojack-equipped stolen cars are recovered and sustain less damage than other recovered stolen cars. Researchers Ian Ayres and S. D. Levitt of the National Bureau of Economic Research estimate that positive externalities are worth 15 times more than the benefit received by the Lojack-equipped car owner—when there are lots of Lojacks in the area, thieves leave the area, meaning that they don't steal non-Lojack-equipped cars either. One auto theft is eliminated annually for every three Lojacks installed in central cities.

For Critical Analysis

Who might want to subsidize Lojacks?

CONCEPTS IN BRIEF

- Private costs are costs that are borne directly by consumers and producers when they engage in any resource-using activity.
- Social costs are private costs plus any other costs that are external to the decision maker. For example, the social costs of driving include all the private costs plus any pollution and congestion caused.
- When private costs differ from social costs, externalities exist because individual decision makers are not internalizing all the costs that society is bearing.
- When social costs exceed private costs, we say that there are externalities.

POLLUTION

The term *pollution* is used quite loosely and can refer to a variety of by-products of any activity. Industrial pollution involves mainly air and water but can also include noise and such concepts as aesthetic pollution, as when a landscape is altered in a negative way. For the most part, we will be analyzing the most common forms, air and water pollution.

When asked how much pollution there should be in the economy, many people will respond, "None." But if we ask those same people how much starvation or deprivation of consumer products should exist in the economy, many will again say, "None." Growing and distributing food or producing consumer products creates pollution, however. In effect, therefore, there is no correct answer to how much pollution should be in an economy because when we ask how much pollution there *should* be, we are entering the realm of normative economics. We are asking people to express values. There is no way to disprove somebody's value system scientifically. One way we can approach a discussion of the "correct" amount of pollution would be to set up the same type of marginal analysis we used in our discussion of a firm's employment and output decisions. That is to say, we should pursue measures to reduce pollution only up to the point at which the marginal benefit from further reduction equals the marginal cost of further reduction.

Click here to see a review of possible economic effects of alternative pollution reduction scenarios.

Look at Figure 31-2. On the horizontal axis, we show the degree of cleanliness of the air. A vertical line is drawn at 100 percent cleanliness—the air cannot become any cleaner. Consider the benefits of obtaining a greater degree of air cleanliness. These benefits are represented by the marginal benefit curve, which slopes downward because of the law of diminishing marginal utility.

When the air is very dirty, the marginal benefit from air that is a little cleaner appears to be relatively high, as shown on the vertical axis. As the air becomes cleaner and cleaner, however, the marginal benefit of a little bit more air cleanliness falls.

Consider the marginal cost of pollution abatement—that is, the marginal cost of obtaining cleaner air. In the 1960s, automobiles had no pollution abatement devices. Eliminating only 20 percent of the pollutants emitted by internal-combustion engines entailed a relatively small cost per unit of pollution removed. The cost of eliminating the next 20 percent rose, though. Finally, as we now get to the upper limits of removal of pollutants from the emissions of internal-combustion engines, we find that the elimination of one more percentage point of the amount of pollutants becomes astronomically expensive. To go from 97 percent cleanliness to 98 percent cleanliness involves a marginal cost that is many times greater than going from 10 percent cleanliness to 11 percent cleanliness.

It is realistic, therefore, to draw the marginal cost of pollution abatement as an upward-sloping curve, as shown in Figure 31-2. (The marginal cost curve slopes up because of the law of diminishing returns.)

FIGURE 31-2

The Optimal Quantity of Air Pollution

As we attempt to get a greater degree of air cleanliness, the marginal cost rises until even the slightest attempt at increasing air cleanliness leads to a very high marginal cost, as can be seen at the upper right of the graph. Conversely, the marginal benefit curve slopes downward: The more pure air we have, the less we value an additional unit of pure air. Marginal cost and marginal benefit intersect at point *E*. The optimal degree of air cleanliness is something less than 100 percent at Q_0. The price that we should pay for the last unit of air cleanup is no greater than P_0, for that is where marginal cost equals marginal benefit.

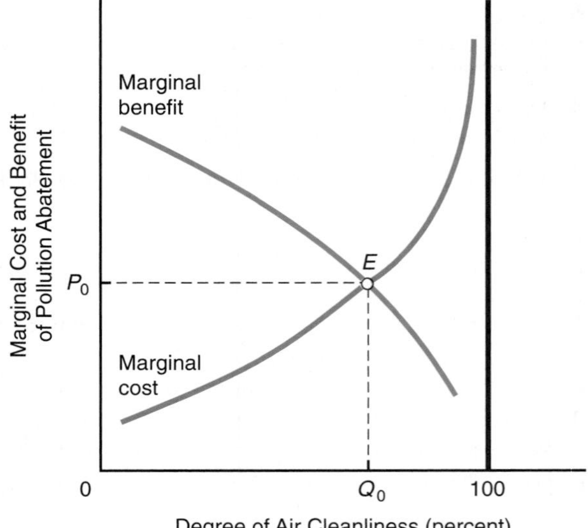

The Optimal Quantity of Pollution

The **optimal quantity of pollution** is defined as the level of pollution at which the marginal benefit equals the marginal cost of obtaining clean air. This occurs at the intersection of the marginal benefit curve and the marginal cost curve in Figure 31-2, at point *E,* which is analytically exactly the same as for every other economic activity. If we increased pollution control by one more unit greater than Q_0, the marginal cost of that small increase in the degree of air cleanliness would be greater than the marginal benefit to society.

Optimal quantity of pollution 
The level of pollution for which the marginal benefit of one additional unit of clean air just equals the marginal cost of that additional unit of clean air.

As is usually the case in economic analysis, the optimal quantity of just about anything occurs when marginal cost equals marginal benefit. That is, the optimal quantity of pollution occurs at the point at which the marginal cost of reducing (or abating) pollution is just equal to the marginal benefit of doing so. The marginal cost of pollution abatement rises as more and more abatement is achieved (as the environment becomes cleaner and cleaner, the *extra* cost of cleansing rises). The state of technology is such that early units of pollution abatement are easily achieved (at low cost), but attaining higher and higher levels of environmental quality becomes progressively more difficult (as the extra cost rises to prohibitive levels). At the same time, the marginal benefits of a cleaner and cleaner environment fall; the marginal benefit of pollution abatement declines as the concept of a cleaner and cleaner environment moves from human life-support requirements to recreation to beauty to a perfectly pure environment. The point at which the increasing marginal cost of pollution abatement equals the decreasing marginal benefit of pollution abatement defines the (theoretical) optimal quantity of pollution.

Click here to learn about a market-oriented government program for reducing pollution.

Recognizing that the optimal quantity of pollution is not zero becomes easier when we realize that it takes scarce resources to reduce pollution. It follows that a trade-off exists between producing a cleaner environment and producing other goods and services. In that sense, nature's ability to cleanse itself is a resource that can be analyzed like any other resource, and a cleaner environment must take its place with other societal wants.

INTERNATIONAL POLICY EXAMPLE

Will Anyone Be Able to Tell If Abiding by the Kyoto Protocol Affects Global Temperatures?

In December 1997, the United States government tentatively agreed at a United Nations meeting held in Kyoto, Japan, to reduce nationwide emissions of greenhouse gases by 7 percent below 1990 levels. This goal would be achieved by reducing the combustion of fossil fuels sufficiently to diminish emission levels in 2010 to 41 percent below where they would end up at current rates of emission growth. Although any estimates of the overall economic effects of the agreement are fraught with uncertainties, economists estimated that abiding by the agreement could reduce U.S. GDP growth by as much as 2.3 percentage points per year.

Scientists using a climate model developed at the National Center for Atmospheric Research also had trouble coming up with very precise estimates of the likely effect of the proposed emissions reduction on global temperatures. Their best estimate was that such a reduction in emissions might reduce planetary warming by 0.19 degree Celsius (0.32 degree Fahrenheit) over a 50-year period—a barely discernible reduction in the earth's potential warming trend. Another problem is that the networks of surface thermometers that scientists use to monitor the earth's overall average temperature are unable to differentiate such a small temperature change from normal year-to-year variations. Even accounting for improved temperature-measuring capabilities 50 years in the future, measuring the ultimate environmental impact of implementing the Kyoto Protocol on Greenhouse Emissions might prove impossible. Consequently, determining the marginal social benefit of emissions reductions, at least from a global-warming standpoint, may be impracticable.

For Critical Analysis

If the effects of greenhouse emission abatement on global temperatures are too hard to measure, how else might the marginal benefit of emission abatement be determined?

Aren't carbon emissions polluting the atmosphere?

Not all of them. The earth's oceans absorb a third of all emissions of carbon emitted by autos, trucks, and other motorized vehicles. Recent studies indicate that as much as another fourth of all carbon emissions may be absorbed by the "North American carbon sink," consisting of the continent's forests and plants. This is more than the carbon output of the United States and Canada resulting from the burning of fossil fuels. Thus it is actually conceivable that North America may be contributing to a net reduction in the world's carbon levels. This further complicates measuring the marginal benefit of emission abatement limitations intended to slow global warming.

CONCEPTS IN BRIEF

- The marginal cost of cleaning up the environment rises as we get closer to 100 percent cleanliness. Indeed, it rises at an increasing rate.
- The marginal benefit of environmental cleanliness falls as we have more of it.
- The optimal quantity of pollution is the quantity at which the marginal cost of cleanup equals the marginal benefit of cleanup.
- Pollution abatement is a trade-off. We trade off goods and services for cleaner air and water, and vice versa.

COMMON PROPERTY

Private property rights Exclusive rights of ownership that allow the use, transfer, and exchange of property.

Common property Property that is owned by everyone and therefore by no one. Air and water are examples of common property resources.

In most cases, you do not have **private property rights**—exclusive ownership rights—to the air surrounding you, nor does anyone else. Air is a **common property**—nonexclusive—resource. Therein lies the crux of the problem. When no one owns a particular resource, no one has any incentive (conscience aside) to consider misuse of that resource. If one person decides not to pollute the air, there normally will be no significant effect on the total level of pollution. If one person decides not to pollute the ocean, there will still be approximately the same amount of ocean pollution—provided, of course, that the individual was previously responsible for only a small part of the total amount of ocean pollution.

Basically, pollution occurs where we have poorly defined private property rights, as in air and common bodies of water. We do not, for example, have a visual pollution problem in people's attics. That is their own property, which they choose to keep as clean as they want, given their preferences for cleanliness as weighed against the costs of keeping the attic neat and tidy.

Where private property rights exist, individuals have legal recourse to any damages sustained through the misuse of their property. When private property rights are well defined, the use of property—that is, the use of resources—will generally involve contracting between the owners of those resources. If you own land, you might contract with another person who wants to use your land for raising cows. The contract would most likely be written in the form of a lease agreement.

INTERNATIONAL POLICY EXAMPLE

Dead Dogs in the Hills of Italy

Each September, about 110 miles north of Rome, a truffle hunt breaks out across 1,000 square miles of public land. Some 1,833 licensed "hunters" try their luck at finding truffles (a rare and hence expensive edible fungus), which grow wild on the buried roots of various trees. Truffle hunters use trained dogs to sniff out the hidden treasure. Each year, some of those dogs do not survive the truffle-hunting season. They are poisoned by bits of meat laced with strychnine—placed there by other truffle hunters seeking to reduce competition. In a recent year, more than 50 dogs died this way. The number of dogs poisoned turns out to be directly related to the market price of white Italian truffles. Several years ago, owing to a dry summer, the truffle crop dropped in half, the market price skyrocketed—and the number of dogs poisoned doubled from the previous year. Clearly, if the public land on which the truffles grow were not common property, the situation would be different.

For Critical Analysis

Assume that you owned all of the land in which Italian truffles grew. What system would you use for harvesting each year's crop?

Voluntary Agreements and Transaction Costs

Is it possible for externalities to be internalized via voluntary agreement? Take a simple example. You live in a house with a nice view of a lake. The family living below you plants a tree. The tree grows so tall that it eventually starts to cut off your view. In most cities, no one has property rights to views; therefore, you cannot usually go to court to obtain relief. You do have the option of contracting with your neighbor, however.

Voluntary Agreements: Contracting. You have the option of paying your neighbors (contracting) to cut back the tree. You could start out with an offer of a small amount and keep going up until your neighbors agree or until you reach your limit. Your limit will equal the value you place on having an unobstructed view of the lake. Your neighbors will be willing if the payment is at least equal to the reduction in their intrinsic property value due to a stunted tree. Your offering the payment makes your neighbors aware of the social cost of their actions. The social cost here is equal to the care of the tree plus the cost suffered by you from an impeded view of the lake.

In essence, then, your offer of money income to your neighbors indicates to them that there is an opportunity cost to their actions. If they don't comply, they forfeit the money that you are offering them. The point here is that *opportunity cost always exists, whoever has property rights.* Therefore, we would expect under some circumstances that voluntary contracting will occur to internalize externalities.* The question is, When will voluntary agreements occur?

Transaction Costs. One major condition for the outcome just outlined is that the **transaction costs**—all costs associated with making and enforcing agreements—must be low relative to the expected benefits of reaching an agreement. (We already looked at this

Transaction costs 
All costs associated with making, reaching, and enforcing agreements.

*This analysis is known as the *Coase theorem,* named after its originator, Nobel laureate Ronald Coase, who demonstrated that negative or positive externalities do not necessarily require government intervention in situations in which property rights are defined and enforceable and transaction costs are relatively low.

topic briefly in Chapter 4.) If we expand our example to a much larger one such as air pollution, the transaction costs of numerous homeowners trying to reach agreements with the individuals and companies that create the pollution are relatively high. Consequently, we don't expect voluntary contracting to be an effective way to internalize the externality of air pollution.

Changing Property Rights

In considering the problem of property rights, we can approach it by assuming that initially in a society, many property rights to resources are not defined. But this situation does not cause a problem so long as no one cares to use the resources for which there are no property rights or so long as enough of these resources are available that people can have as much as they want at a zero price. Only when and if a use is found for a resource or the supply of a resource is inadequate at a zero price does a problem develop. The problem requires that something be done about deciding property rights. If not, the resource will be wasted and possibly even destroyed. Property rights can be assigned to individuals who will then assert control; or they may be assigned to government, which can maintain and preserve the resource, charge for its use, or implement some other rationing device. What we have seen with common property such as air and water is that governments have indeed attempted to take over the control of those resources so that they cannot be wasted or destroyed.

Another way of viewing the pollution problem is to argue that property rights are "sacred" and that there are property rights in every resource that exists. We can then say that each individual does not have the right to act on anything that is not his or her property. Hence no individual has the right to pollute because that amounts to using property that the individual does not specifically own.

Clearly, we must fill the gap between private costs and social costs in situations in which property rights are not well defined or assigned. There are three ways to fill this gap: taxation, subsidization, and regulation. Government is involved in all three. Unfortunately, government does not have perfect information and may not pick the appropriate tax, subsidy, or type of regulation. We also have to consider cases in which taxes are hard to enforce or subsidies are difficult to give out to "worthy" recipients. In such cases, outright prohibition of the polluting activity may be the optimal solution to a particular pollution problem. For example, if it is difficult to monitor the level of a particular type of pollution that even in small quantities can cause severe environmental damage, outright prohibition of activities that cause such pollution may be the only alternative.

Are There Alternatives to Pollution-Causing Resource Use?

Some people cannot understand why, if pollution is bad, we still use pollution-causing resources such as coal and oil to generate electricity. Why don't we forgo the use of such polluting resources and opt for one that apparently is pollution free, such as solar energy? The plain fact is that the cost of generating solar power in most circumstances is much higher than generating that same power through conventional means. We do not yet have the technology that allows us the luxury of driving solar-powered cars. Moreover, with current technology, the solar panels necessary to generate the electricity for the average town would cover massive sections of the countryside, and the manufacturing of those solar panels would itself generate pollution.

WILD SPECIES, COMMON PROPERTY, AND TRADE-OFFS

One of the most distressing common property problems concerns endangered species, usually in the wild. No one is too concerned about not having enough dogs, cats, cattle, sheep, and horses. The reason is that virtually all of those species are private property. Spotted owls, bighorn mountain sheep, condors, and the like are typically common property. No one has a vested interest in making sure that they perpetuate in good health.

Click here to contemplate the issue of endangered species.

The federal government passed the Endangered Species Act in an attempt to prevent species from dying out. Initially, few individuals were affected by the rulings of the Interior Department regarding which species were listed as endangered. Eventually, however, as more and more species were put on the endangered list, a trade-off became apparent. Nationwide, the trade-off was brought to the public's attention when the spotted owl was declared an endangered species in the Pacific Northwest. Ultimately, thousands of logging jobs were lost when the courts upheld the ban on logging in the areas presumed to be the spotted owl's natural habitat. Then another small bird, the marbled murrelet, was found in an ancient forest, causing the Pacific Lumber Company to cut back its logging practices. In 1995, the U.S. Supreme Court ruled that the federal government did have the right to regulate activities on private land in order to save endangered species.

The issues are not straightforward. Today, the earth has only 0.02 percent of all of the species that have ever lived, and nearly all the 99.08 percent of extinct species became extinct *before* humans appeared. Every year, 1,000 to 3,000 new species are discovered and classified. Estimates of how many species are actually dying out vary from a high of 50,000 a year (based on an assumption that undiscovered insect species are dying off before being discovered) to a low of one every four years.

INTERNATIONAL POLICY EXAMPLE

Preventing Overfishing by Trading Quotas

Under the European Union's Common Fisheries Policy, countries are allocated quotas for the amounts of different kinds of fish that their fishermen can catch in various areas of the sea. In most European nations, governments control the allocation of fishing rights under these quotas. When a fisherman retires or dies, his quota goes into a pool to be reallocated. In the United Kingdom, however, fishermen can buy, sell, or lease their quotas. It turns out that this has had beneficial side effects for fish conservation.

The reason is that because many fishermen would like to catch more fish than their quotas permit them to catch, there is always a temptation to exceed quota limits. If a British fisherman thinks that he is more efficient at hauling in fish than another fisherman, he can buy or lease the other fisherman's quota. If he is right, he earns higher profits than he would by overfishing and trying to sell his excess catch (which the fishermen call "black fish") illegally in the black market.

Indeed, many British fishermen might be pleased if the European Union were to cut quotas in a further effort to repopulate stocks of fish. Their current incomes would fall, but the market value of their quotas would rise. The values of quotas are already relatively high. When a tragic accident recently led to the sinking of a fishing boat off the coast of Scotland, the deceased owner's quotas for herring, mackerel, and other fish sold for about $10 million.

For Critical Analysis

How does the existence of a market for quotas help keep the stocks of fish off the shores of Europe from dwindling?

CONCEPTS IN BRIEF

- A common property resource is one that no one owns—or, otherwise stated, that everyone owns.
- Common property exists when property rights are indefinite or nonexistent.
- When no property rights exist, pollution occurs because no one individual or firm has a sufficient economic incentive to care for the common property in question, be it air, water, or scenery.
- Private costs will not equal social costs when common property is at issue unless only a few individuals are involved and they are able to contract among themselves.

RECYCLING 

Recycling 
The reuse of raw materials derived from manufactured products.

As part of the overall ecology movement, there has been a major push to save scarce resources via recycling. **Recycling** involves reusing paper products, plastics, glass, and metals rather than putting them into solid waste dumps. Many cities have instituted mandatory recycling programs.

The benefits of recycling are straightforward. Fewer *natural* resources are used. But some economists argue that recycling does not necessarily save *total* resources. For example, recycling paper products may not necessarily save trees, according to A. Clark Wiseman, an economist for Resources for the Future in Washington, D.C. He argues that an increase in paper recycling will eventually lead to a reduction in the demand for virgin paper and thus for trees. Because most trees are planted specifically to produce paper, a reduction in the demand for trees will mean that certain land now used to grow trees will be put to other uses. The end result may be smaller rather than larger forests, a result that is probably not desired in the long run.

Recycling's Invisible Costs

The recycling of paper can also pollute. Used paper has ink on it that has to be removed during the recycling process. According to the National Wildlife Federation, the product of 100 tons of deinked (bleached) fiber generates 40 tons of sludge. This sludge has to be disposed of, usually in a landfill. A lot of recycled paper companies, however, are beginning to produce unbleached paper. In general, recycling does create waste that has to be disposed of.

There is another issue involved in the use of resources: Recycling requires human effort. The labor resources involved in recycling are often many times more costly than the potential savings in scarce resources not used. That means that net resource use, counting all resources, may sometimes be greater with recycling than without it.

Landfills

One of the arguments in favor of recycling is to avoid a solid waste "crisis." Some people believe that we are running out of solid waste dump sites in the United States. This is perhaps true in and near major cities, and indeed the most populated areas of the country might ultimately benefit from recycling programs. In the rest of the United States, however, the data do not seem to indicate that we are running out of solid waste landfill sites. Throughout the United States, the disposal price per ton of city garbage has actually fallen. Prices vary, of course, for the 200 million tons of trash disposed of each year. In San Jose, California, it costs $50 a ton to dump, whereas in Morris County, New Jersey, it costs $131 a ton.

Currently, municipal governments can do three things with solid waste: burn it, bury it, or recycle it. The amount of solid waste dumped in landfills is dropping, even as total trash output rises. Consider, though, that the total garbage output of the United States for the entire twenty-first century could be put in a square landfill 35 miles on a side that is 100 yards deep. Recycling to reduce solid waste disposal may end up costing society more resources simply because putting such waste into a landfill may be a less costly alternative.

INTERNATIONAL POLICY EXAMPLE

Can Citizens Recycle Too Much? The Case of Germany

Recycling is popular throughout the European Union, but the Germans have raised it to an art form—a very expensive art form. Germany has a law requiring that manufacturers or retailers take back their packaging or ensure that 80 percent of it is collected rather than thrown away. What is collected must be recycled or reused. The law covers about 40 percent of the country's garbage. The problem is that German consumers responded more enthusiastically than anticipated. The administrative costs of the program run by the company in charge of recycling Germany's trash, Duales System Deutschland, have ballooned to more than $2 billion, and these funds are raised through licensing fees paid by manufacturers and retailers, who pass some of these additional costs on to consumers in the form of higher prices. Public dissatisfaction has encouraged competition to emerge. The Lahn-Dill district in the German state of Hessen recently implemented a new waste-processing program that can handle nearly as many recyclables at about half the expense. One of Lahn-Dill's biggest cost-saving features is a simple rule common in the United States: requiring citizens themselves to sort through their garbage and place recyclables in a separate container.

For Critical Analysis

How is it possible that German citizens might have recycled "too much" of their trash?

Should We Save Scarce Resources?

Periodically, the call for recycling focuses on the necessity of saving scarce resources because "we are running out." There is little evidence to back up this claim because virtually every natural resource has fallen in price (corrected for inflation) over the past century. In 1980, the late Julian Simon made a $1,000 bet with well-known environmentalist Paul Erlich. Simon bet $200 per resource that any five natural resources that Erlich picked would decline in price (corrected for inflation) by the end of the 1980s. Simon won. (When Simon asked Erlich to renew the bet for $20,000 for the 1990s, Erlich declined.) During the 1980s and 1990s, the price of virtually every natural resource fell (corrected for inflation), and so did the price of every agricultural commodity. The same was true for every forest product. Though few people remember the dire predictions of the 1970s, many noneconomists throughout the world argued at that time that the world's oil reserves were vanishing. If this were true, the pretax, inflation-corrected price of gasoline would not be the same today as it was in the 1950s (which it is).

In spite of predictions in the early 1980s by World Watch Institute president Lester Brown, real food prices did not rise. Indeed, the real price of food fell by more than 30 percent for the major agricultural commodities during the 1980s and even more during the 1990s. A casual knowledge of supply and demand tells you that because the demand for food did not decrease, supply must have increased faster than demand.

With respect to the forests, at least in the United States and Western Europe, there are more forests today than there were 100 years ago. In this country, the major problems of deforestation seem to be on land owned by the United States Forest Service for which private timber companies are paid almost $1 billion a year in subsidies to cut down trees.

EXAMPLE

Earning Profits from Conserving Natural Wonders

In Virginia's Shenandoah Valley, 230 miles southwest of Washington, D.C., stands a 215-foot-tall rock arch called Natural Bridge. A tributary of the James River flows beneath. A 347-foot cavern lies inside a park surrounding Natural Bridge. The 1,600-acre park receives about 300,000 visitors per year. This park has been in private hands since 1774, when Thomas Jefferson paid King George III 20 shillings for it. Today, the park belongs to Natural Bridge of Virginia, Inc., a private company controlled by a Washington, D.C., real estate developer who purchased it in 1988 for $6.6 million. The reason he paid so much is that the park earns a tidy annual profit, estimated at about $5 million. A park visitor pays $8 to see the bridge and another $7 for a tour of a cave and a wax museum. A visitor also can buy souvenirs at park shops, purchase food at one or more of its three on-site restaurants, and pay to stay in one of the park's 180 guest rooms. To attract these profit-generating visitors, the company pays close attention to details. It pays botanists to plant and care for native plants, and it stocks the river with rainbow trout. The park is kept free of graffiti; the last known person to carve his initials into Natural Bridge was a young surveyor by the name of George Washington.

Some economists have argued that lands currently owned by the government and administered by state and national park services might receive better long-term care if they were privately owned and administered instead. Natural Bridge is one example of a part of the environment that the profit motive is helping to preserve.

For Critical Analysis

Why does the profit motive encourage environmental conservation efforts at a private park?

CONCEPTS IN BRIEF

- Recycling involves reusing paper, glass, and other materials rather than putting them into solid waste dumps. Recycling does have a cost both in the resources used for recycling and in the pollution created during recycling, such as the sludge from deinking paper for reuse.
- Landfills are an alternative to recycling. Expansion of these solid waste disposal sites is outpacing demand increases.
- Resources may not be getting scarcer. The inflation-corrected price of most resources has been falling for decades.

NETNOMICS

Will the Internet Make Most Languages Obsolete?

Linguistics is the study of languages and their structure. By their nature, languages are common property. They are nonexclusive resources. In some instances, of course, we may use language for communicating only with ourselves, such as when we take notes for later reference. For the most part, however, we use language to communicate with others.

Today, the Internet is emerging as one of the world's key communications media. Roughly 80 percent of all information stored on the world's computers is in English. The same proportion of Internet transmissions—e-mail messages, file transfers, and the like—are in English. This has added to existing incentives for non-English speakers around the globe to learn English. Berlitz International, the world's largest language school, reports that 70 percent of the 5 million language lessons it gives each year are for English. Many experts today argue that English is now such an intrinsic part of the global communications revolution that its dominance is unassailable. This has led some to worry about loss of national identities as English "replaces" other languages. A former French president went so far as to call the Internet "a major risk for humanity."

In fact, there are good economic reasons to believe that global use of the Internet could actually *improve* the odds that many languages will survive the onslaught from English. Because they rely on one-way transmissions, broadcast media such as television and radio force languages to compete. For instance, the time that a European transmission of a *Star Wars* movie dubbed in Danish takes on a given bandwidth could instead be devoted to transmission of the original English version, which more people could understand, thereby increasing the chances that advertisers will reach more customers. In cyberspace, however, transmissions in various languages do not compete directly. Promoters of a Danish rock festival can post Internet advertisements for the festival in English, but they can also post them in Danish, as well as German Norwegian, Swedish, and any other language whose speakers might be interested.

Ultimately, the languages that survive will do so because of gains in specialization. People will continue to use their native language when they want to communicate with others who share that tongue, whether across a shared fence, in local newspapers, or via Internet chat rooms. They will use other languages, such as English today, primarily for formal communications with others around the globe. In the process, the "professional" version of English itself could begin to diverge from traditional English. Someday, English speakers may even have to know two languages: the English they read and speak at home and the "techie English" they use in their Web-based communications.

ISSUES & APPLICATIONS

What Mix of Economic Incentives Will Save the Tiger?

The tiger's worldwide population has declined by almost 93 percent during the past 100 years. Trying to understand why this has occurred, and determining how to stop it from continuing, requires thinking about economic incentives.

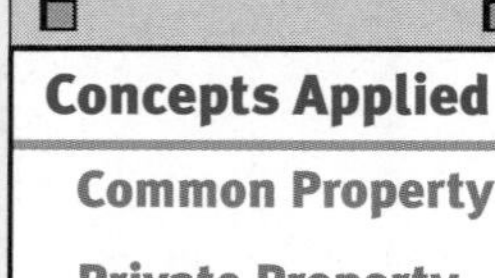

Concepts Applied
Common Property
Private Property
Trade-Offs

The Private Incentives All Point Toward Tiger Extinction

If you have ever viewed tigers at a zoo, you probably noticed that the zoo's operators designed the exhibit so that both space and iron bars separated you from the tigers. There is a reason for this. Tigers are natural predators. They are very good at killing other animals, including humans. In their natural habitats in nations such as India, Indonesia, and Nepal, wild tigers frequently attack and kill both livestock and the animals' owners. This gives people who live near tigers powerful incentives to kill the giant felines, either in acts of self-defense or as "preemptive strikes." Furthermore, several highly prized traditional East Asian medicines use powder from the bones of tigers as a prime ingredient. As a result, tiger bones command high prices on the black market, providing yet another incentive to destroy these creatures. In the private marketplace, private benefits derive mainly from tiger deaths, not tiger population enhancement.

Are There Market Solutions for Repopulating Tigers?

Nearly anyone who has seen a tiger, however, would agree that they are beautiful animals. Society, therefore, might determine that the species is a form of common property that should be preserved. The issue is how best to change human incentives. So far bans on hunting and set-asides of public lands have not succeeded.

There are at least four possible changes that might promote tiger repopulation. All entail giving people incentives.

1. *Private property rights:* South Africa already has adopted a private property law to protect the rhinoceros. Conservationists who own private reserves naturally wish to keep the animals on their reserves alive. They are also often more successful than governments, who face competing demands for public moneys, at raising funds specifically aimed at supporting and caring for animals on their lands.
2. *Promoting trourism:* In 1995, Nepal's government gave a local group land management rights in a tiger habitat adjoining a national park. Local residents build nature trails for elephant-back safaris and a viewing tower with hotel accommodations for overnight guests. Income generated from tiger-based tourism helps fund education and health care for local residents—giving them strong incentives to protect the tigers on their reserve.

3. *Limited hunting:* Selling rights to hunt endangered animals to people who have always dreamed of big game hunting may seem counterproductive—after all, the hunters kill the animals, don't they? Nevertheless, South Africa has turned this into a trade-off that ultimately helps white rhinos. Fees paid by white rhino hunters, amounting to hundreds of thousands of dollars a year, are used to help preserve the species as a whole. The same approach could work for tigers.
4. *Legalized farming:* Unlike some animals, tigers breed readily in captivity. Farmers could breed tigers for eventual sale of their bones. This would drive down the price of tiger bones, greatly reducing the incentive for illegal poaching.

FOR CRITICAL ANALYSIS

1. Which people would stand to lose the most from legalized tiger farming?
2. Which of these proposals might help protect endangered aquatic species?

SG

SUMMARY DISCUSSION OF LEARNING OBJECTIVES

1. **Private Costs Versus Social Costs:** Private, or internal, costs are borne solely by individuals who use resources. Social costs are the full costs that society bears whenever resources are used. Pollution problems and other problems related to the environment arise when individuals take into account only private costs instead of the broader social costs arising from their use of resources.
2. **Market Externalities and Ways to Correct Them:** A market externality is a situation in which a private cost (or benefit) differs from the social cost (or benefit) associated with a market transaction between two parties or from use of a scarce resource. Correcting an externality arising from differences between private and social costs, such as pollution, requires forcing individuals to take all the social costs of their actions into account. This might be accomplished by taxing those who create externalities, such as polluters.
3. **Determining the Optimal Amount of Pollution:** The marginal benefit of pollution abatement, or the additional benefit to society from reducing pollution, declines as the quality of the environment improves. At the same time, however, the marginal cost of pollution abatement, or the additional cost to society from reducing pollution, increases as more and more resources are devoted to bringing about an improved environment. The optimal quantity of pollution is the amount of pollution for which the marginal benefit of pollution abatement just equals the marginal cost of pollution abatement. Beyond this level of pollution, the additional cost of cleaning the environment exceeds the additional benefit.
4. **Private and Common Property Rights and the Pollution Problem:** Private property rights are exclusive individual rights of ownership that permit the use and exchange of a resource. Common property is owned by everyone and therefore by no single individual. A pollution problem often arises because air and many water resources are common property, and private property rights relating to them are not well defined. Therefore, no one has an individual incentive to take the long-run pernicious effects of excessive pollution into account. This is a common rationale for using taxes, subsidies, or regulations to address the pollution problem.
5. **Endangered Species and the Assignment of Property Rights:** Many members of such species as dogs, pigs, and horses are the private property of human beings. Thus people have economic incentives—satisfaction derived from pet ownership, the desire for pork as a food product, a preference for animal-borne transport—to protect members of these species. By contrast, most members of species such as spotted owls, condors, or tigers are common property, so no specific individuals have incentives to keep these species in good health. One way to address the endangered species problem is government involvement via taxes, subsidies, or regulations. Another is to find a way to assign private property rights to at least some members of species that are endangered.
6. **Benefits and Costs of Recycling:** Recycling entails reusing paper, glass, and other materials instead of putting them in solid waste dumps. Recycling has a clear benefit of limiting the use of natural resources. It also entails costs, however. One cost might be lost benefits of forests, because a key incentive for perpetuating forests is the future production of paper and other wood-based products. Recycling also requires the use of labor, and the costs of these human resources can exceed the potential savings in scarce resources not used because of recycling.

Key Terms and Concepts

Common property (766)
Externality (761)
Optimal quantity of pollution (765)
Private costs (760)
Private property rights (766)
Recycling (770)
Social costs (761)
Transaction costs (767)

Problems

Answers to the odd-numbered problems appear at the back of the book.

31-1. The market price of insecticide is initially $10 per unit. To address a negative externality in this market, the government decides to charge producers of insecticide for the privilege of polluting during the production process. A fee that fully takes into account the social costs of pollution is determined, and once it is put into effect, the market supply curve for insecticide shifts upward by $4 per unit. The market price of insecticide also increases, to $12 per unit. What is the fee that the government is charging insecticide manufacturers?

31-2. A tract of land is found to contain a plant from which drug companies can extract a newly discovered cancer-fighting medicine. This variety of plant does not grow anywhere else in the world. Initially, the many owners of lots within this tract, who had not planned to use the land for anything other than its current use as a scenic locale for small vacation homes, announced that they would put all their holdings up for sale to drug companies. Because the land is also home to an endangered lizard species, however, a government agency decides to limit the number of acres in this tract that drug companies can purchase and use for their drug-producing operations. The government declares that the remaining portion of the land must be left in its current state. What will happen to the market price of the acreage that is available for extraction of cancer-fighting medicine? What will happen to the market price of the land that the government declares to be usable only for existing vacation homes?

31-3. When a government charges firms for the privilege of polluting, a typical result is a rise in the market price of the good or service produced by those firms. Consequently, consumers of the good or service usually have to pay a higher price to obtain it. Why might this be socially desirable?

31-4. Most wild Asian tigers are the common property of the humans and governments that control the lands they inhabit. Why does this pose a significant problem for maintaining the wild tiger population in the future?

31-5. In several African countries where the rhinoceros was once a prevalent species, the animal is now nearly extinct. In most of these nations, rhinoceros horns are used as traditional ingredients in certain medicines. Why might making rhinoceros farming legal do more to promote preservation of the species than imposing stiff penalties on people who are caught engaging in rhinoceros hunting?

31-6. Why is it possible for recycling of paper or plastics to use up more resources than the activity saves?

31-7. Examine the following marginal costs and marginal benefits associated with water cleanliness in a given locale.

Quantity of Clean Water (%)	Marginal Cost ($)	Marginal Benefit ($)
0	3,000	200,000
20	15,000	120,000
40	50,000	90,000
60	85,000	85,000
80	100,000	40,000
100	Infinite	0

a. What is the optimal degree of water cleanliness?

b. What is the optimal degree of water pollution?

c. Suppose that a company creates a food additive that offsets most of the harmful effects of drinking polluted water. As a result, the marginal benefit of water cleanliness declines by $40,000 at each degree of water cleanliness at or less than 80 percent. What is the optimal degree of water cleanliness after this change?

31-8. Examine the following marginal costs and marginal benefits associated with air cleanliness in a given locale:

Quantity of Clean Air (%)	Marginal Cost ($)	Marginal Benefit ($)
0	50,000	600,000
20	150,000	360,000
40	200,000	200,000
60	300,000	150,000
80	400,000	120,000
100	Infinite	0

a. What is the optimal degree of air cleanliness?
b. What is the optimal degree of air pollution?
c. Suppose that a state provides subsidies for a company to build plants that contribute to air pollution. Cleaning up this pollution causes the marginal cost of air cleanliness to rise by$210,000 at each degree of water cleanliness. What is the optimal degree of air cleanliness after this change?

31-9. The following table displays hypothetical annual total costs and total benefits of conserving wild tigers at several possible worldwide tiger population levels.

Population of Wild Tigers	Total Cost ($ million)	Total Benefit ($ million)
0	0	40
2,000	5	90
4,000	15	130
6,000	30	160
8,000	55	185
10,000	90	205
12,000	140	215

a. Calculate the marginal costs and benefits.
b. Given the data, what is the socially optimal world population of wild tigers?
c. Suppose that tiger farming is legalized and that this has the effect of reducing the marginal cost of tiger conservation by $15 million for each 2,000-tiger population increment in the table. What is the new socially optimal population of wild tigers?

Economics on the Net

Economic Analysis at the Environmental Protection Agency In this chapter, you learned how to use economic analysis to think about environmental problems. Does the U.S. government use economic analysis? This application helps you learn the extent to which the government uses economics in its environmental policymaking.

Title: The Environmental Protection Agency: Environmental Economics Research at the EPA

Navigation: Click here to visit the EPA's homepage. Click on Browse EPA Topics, then Economics, and finally on Economy and the Environment. Select Other Information, then Environmental Economics in Plain English. Click on Regulatory Economic Analysis at the EPA and view the table of contents. Read the Introduction.

Application Read this section of the article; then answer the following questions:

1. According to the article, what are the key objectives of the EPA? What role does cost-benefit analysis appear to play in the EPA's efforts? Does the EPA appear to take other issues into account in its policymaking?

2. Back up to Table of Contents, and in Section 1: Introduction, click on Statutory Authorities for Economic Analysis. In what ways does this discussion help clarify your answers in item 1?

For Group Study and Analysis Have a class discussion of the following question: Should the EPA apply economic analysis in all aspects of its policymaking? If not, why not? If so, in what manner should economic analysis be applied?

TYING IT ALL TOGETHER

Part 7 Case Problem

Case Background

Modular Systems, Inc. (MSI), manufacturers and sells four products for personal computers: modems, diskette drives, CD-ROM drives, and DVD drives. Until now its workforce has not been unionized. Recently, however, professional union organizers from two unions have held meetings with a large portion of MSI's employees.

The Derived Demands for Labor at a Firm That Sells Multiple Products MSI has separate plants for each of the four products it produces, and its workforce is divided among these four facilities. Workers rarely move from one plant to another. The markets for modems and diskette drives contain large numbers of buyers and sellers, and MSI competes for labor with a number of other manufacturers of modems and diskette drives.

MSI is the only producer and seller of a new external, wireless-connection CD-ROM drive. It competes with many other manufacturers of CD-ROM drives for workers, however. MSI is also the only producer and seller of a new external, wireless-connection DVD drive. The employees that have developed and now manufacture this product have highly specialized skills, and they have found that many potential employers regard them as overspecialized. Consequently, those who have interviewed for jobs with other DVD drive manufacturers have not received job offers. For these workers, MSI is their only good match for jobs, at least in the near term. Recently, some workers in the company's DVD drive facility staged a work slowdown to express their displeasure with what they perceive to be low pay for their highly specialized skills in developing MSI's new DVD drive product offering. They are particularly unhappy that they earn lower wages than workers in MSI's other three facilities. They are also disgruntled about recent company layoffs of a few workers who have had trouble finding jobs in any industry because of the region's faltering economic climate.

MSI is located in a union shop state. In contrast to the experience of much of the rest of the country, the state's economy has faltered in recent months, which has reduced the overall demand for labor on the part of most other employers in the state.

One complication arose when the two union organizers conducted their visits with MSI's employees in successive weeks. The second visitor disputed the first organizer's claim that her union is the "better fit" for MSI's workers and hence should have the first opportunity to conduct a unionization vote.

Determining the Appropriate Company Response MSI's owners and managers were shocked by the recent work slowdown in the DVD drive facility. They decide that the company should contemplate the following options:

1. No response whatsoever
2. Attempting to convince employees that wages are stagnant because of the recent weakening in economic conditions within the state

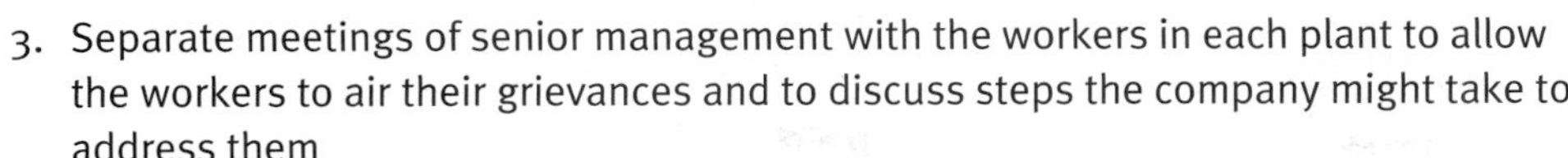

3. Separate meetings of senior management with the workers in each plant to allow the workers to air their grievances and to discuss steps the company might take to address them
4. Turning each facility into a separate company owned by an umbrella corporation, in the hope that workers in at least two of the current facilities would vote not to unionize the new companies
5. Moving its operations to a right-to-work state
6. Making a dramatic change in how the company compensates its workers, including one or all of the following: (a) improving worker health benefits; (b) offering company-subsidized child care at each of its manufacturing facilities; (c) offering employee stock ownership plans, bonus plans, and other forms of company profit sharing

Points to Analyze

1. In which of the markets for its products is MSI more likely to be a perfectly competitive firm? In which is it more likely to be a monopolist?
2. In which of its facilities is it more likely that MSI employees supply their time and skills in perfectly competitive labor markets? In monopsonistic labor markets?
3. Could MSI's management make a case that weak economic conditions help explain relatively low wages? Could the workers contend that this argument is contrived?
4. Workers are equally productive, and the per-unit price of each of the company's products happens to be the same. List each facility according to which is likely to employ the largest number of workers and which is likely to employ the fewest number.
5. What are the advantages and disadvantages of moving MSI's production facilities to a right-to-work state?
6. Which of the options for changing the company's compensation of its workers is most likely to help address the concerns of the DVD-drive workers? Why?

Casing the Internet

1. **Click here to go to the AFL-CIO's homepage. Click on "Partners and Links." Explore several of these Web sites; then answer the following questions.**
   a. **Does it appear that these unions are engaged in actively recruiting new members?**
   b. **Do you see any potential jurisdictional disputes that could arise as a result of efforts by these various unions to increase their memberships?**
2. **Click here to go to the homepage of the National Right to Work Legal Defense Foundation, Inc.**
   a. **Click on "About the Foundation," and then click on "Right to Work Frequently Asked Questions." Read this page. Do you see any regional concentration among the states that have right-to-work laws?**
   b. **In states without right-to-work laws, how much flexibility do workers have to avoid paying union dues and associated fees?**

Part 8
Global Economics

CHAPTER

32

COMPARATIVE ADVANTAGE AND THE OPEN ECONOMY

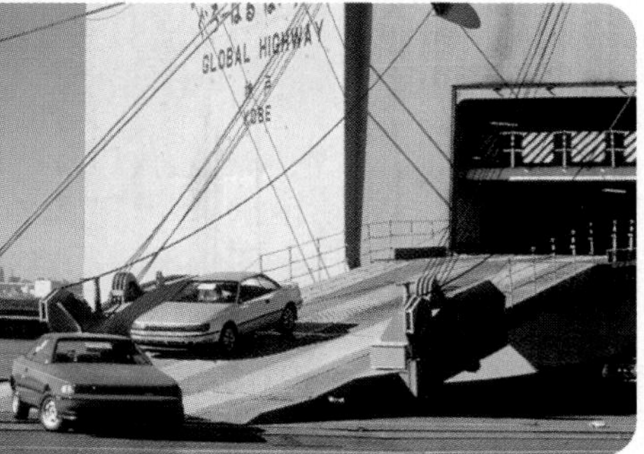

These cars built in Japan are being unloaded in Baltimore. Who would lose and who would gain if imports of Japanese cars were outlawed?

An American businessman visiting an emerging economy came upon a team of about 100 workers using shovels to move earth next to a stream. His guide told him that several days earlier, a local government agency had assigned the people to build a dam. Later, the businessman told a local official about a U.S. company that was offering discounts on earth-moving machines. "With such a machine," the businessman boasted, "one worker could build that dam in a single afternoon." The official replied, "Of course. But think of all the unemployment that importing such a machine would create." The businessman then said, "Oh, I thought you were building a dam. If it's jobs you want to create, take away the workers' shovels and give them spoons!"

In this chapter, you will learn that U.S. exports to other nations do not necessarily cause workers in those nations to lose their jobs or earn lower pay. Nor do American imports of goods from other nations necessitate *net* job losses or pay cuts in the United States. Nevertheless, workers in certain industries often unite with owners and managers to oppose free trade. In this chapter, you will learn the elements of international trade, as well as the arguments for and against free trade.

LEARNING OBJECTIVES

After reading this chapter, you should be able to:

1. **Discuss the worldwide importance of international trade**
2. **Explain why nations can gain from specializing in production and engaging in international trade**
3. **Distinguish between comparative advantage and absolute advantage**
4. **Understand common arguments against free trade**
5. **Describe ways that nations restrict foreign trade**
6. **Identify key international agreements and organizations that adjudicate trade disputes among nations**

Chapter Outline

Did You Know That... most U.S. imports come from a few developed countries? In fact, about two-thirds of imported goods and services are produced in nations that economists classify as high-wage countries. Only 10 percent of U.S. imports come from countries classified as low-wage nations. The remainder of U.S. imports are produced in middle-income countries located mainly in Latin America and Southeast Asia.

The workers residing in nations from which Americans import most of their goods earn relatively high wages. Recent studies indicate that manufacturing wages paid to workers who live and work in twenty-five nations that engage in the most trade with the United States have have risen steadily. In 1975, manufacturing workers in these top U.S. trading partners earned 65 percent of the U.S. compensation level. Today, the wages of these workers have reached 95 percent of the U.S. compensation level.

Without international trade, many people who work to produce goods for sale to other nations would have to find other employment. Some might even have trouble finding work. Nevertheless, other people in these countries would undoubtedly stand to gain from restricting international trade. Learning about international trade will help you understand why this is so.

THE WORLDWIDE IMPORTANCE OF INTERNATIONAL TRADE

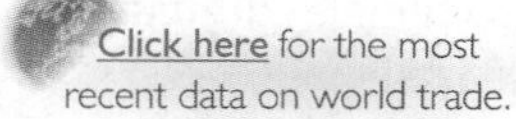
Click here for the most recent data on world trade.

Look at panel (a) of Figure 32-1. Since the end of World War II, world output of goods and services (world gross domestic product, or GDP) has increased almost every year until the present, when it is almost six times what it was. Look at the top line in panel (a). World trade has increased to more than 13 times what it was in 1950.

The United States figured prominently in this expansion of world trade. In panel (b) of Figure 32-1, you see imports and exports expressed as a percentage of total annual yearly income (GDP). Whereas imports added up to barely 4 percent of annual national income in 1950, today they account for over 12 percent. International trade has definitely become more important to the economy of the United States. Trade may become even more important in the United States as other countries start to loosen their trade restrictions.

INTERNATIONAL EXAMPLE

The Importance of International Trade in Various Countries

Whereas both imports and exports in the United States each account for more than 10 percent of total annual national income, in some countries the figure is much greater (see Table 32-1). Consider that Luxembourg must import practically everything!

Another way to understand the worldwide importance of international trade is to look at trade flows on the world map in Figure 32-2 on page 786. You can see that the United States trades more with Europe than with other parts of the world.

For Critical Analysis

How can Luxembourg have a strong economy if it imports so many goods and services?

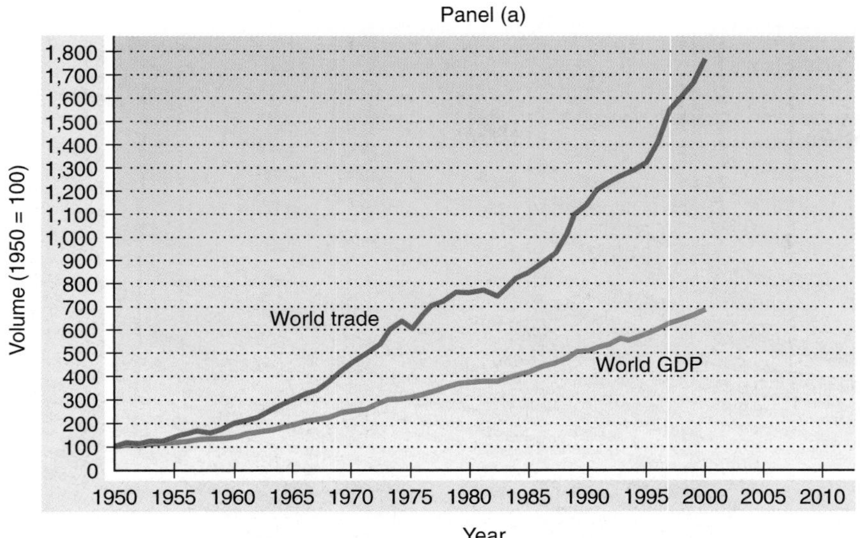

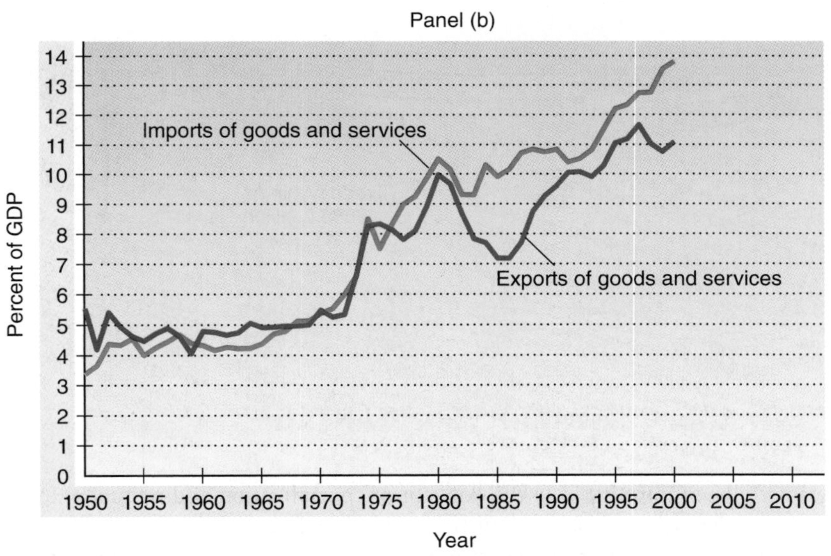

FIGURE 32-1

The Growth of World Trade

In panel (a), you can see the growth in world trade in relative terms because we use an index of 100 to represent real world trade in 1950. By the early 2000s, that index had increased to over 1,700. At the same time, the index of world GDP (annual world income) had gone up to only around 700. World trade is clearly on the rise: Both imports and exports, expressed as a percentage of annual national income (GDP) in panel (b), have been rising.

Sources: Steven Husted and Michael Melvin, *International Economics,* 3d ed. (New York: HarperCollins, 1995), p. 11, used with permission; World Trade Organization; Federal Reserve System; U.S. Department of Commerce.

Country	Imports as a Percentage of Annual National Income
Luxembourg	95.0
Netherlands	58.0
Norway	30.0
Canada	23.5
Germany	23.0
United Kingdom	21.0
China	19.0
France	18.4
Japan	6.8

Source: International Monetary Fund.

TABLE 32-1

Importance of Imports in Selected Countries

Residents of some nations spend much of their incomes on imported goods and services.

FIGURE 32-2
World Trade Flows
International merchandise trade amounts to over $3 trillion worldwide. The percentage figures show the proportion of trade flowing in the various directions.
Source: World Trade Organization (data are for 2000).

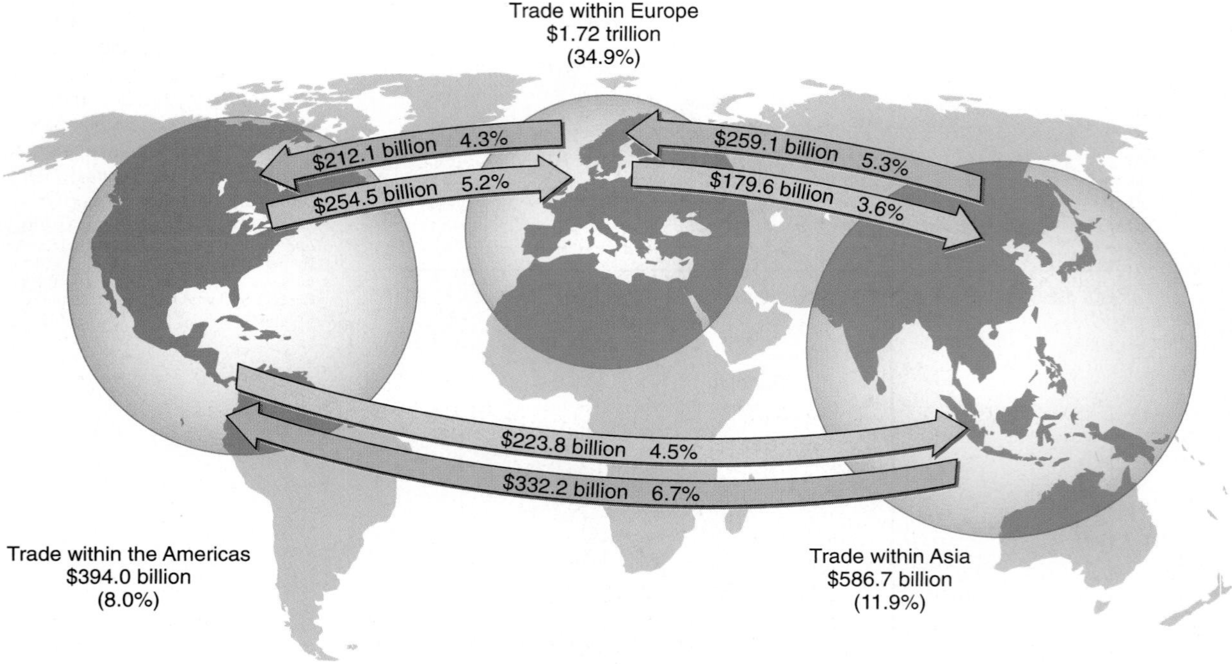

WHY WE TRADE: COMPARATIVE ADVANTAGE ANDMUTUAL GAINS FROM EXCHANGE

You have already been introduced to the concept of specialization and mutual gains from trade in Chapter 2. These concepts are worth repeating because they are essential to understanding why the world is better off because of more international trade. The best way to understand the gains from trade among nations is first to understand the output gains from specialization between individuals.

The Output Gains from Specialization 

Suppose that a creative advertising specialist can come up with two pages of ad copy (written words) an hour or generate one computerized art rendering per hour. At the same time, a computer artist can write one page of ad copy per hour or complete one computerized art rendering per hour. Here the ad specialist can come up with more pages of ad copy per hour than the computer specialist and seemingly is just as good as the computer specialist at doing computerized art renderings. Is there any reason for the creative specialist and the computer specialist to "trade"? The answer is yes, because such trading will lead to higher output.

Consider the scenario of no trading. Assume that during each eight-hour day, the ad specialist and the computer whiz devote half of their day to writing ad copy and half to computerized art rendering. The ad specialist would create eight pages of ad copy (4 hours × 2) and four computerized art renderings (4 × 1). During that same period, the computer specialist would create four pages of ad copy (4 × 1) and four computerized art renderings (4 × 1). Each day, the combined output for the ad specialist and the computer specialist would be 12 pages of ad copy and eight computerized art renderings with no decline in art renderings.

Click here for data on U.S. trade with all other nations of the world.

If the ad specialist specialized only in writing ad copy and the computer whiz specialized only in creating computerized art renderings, their combined output would rise to 16 pages of ad copy (8 × 2) and eight computerized art renderings (8 × 1). Overall, production would increase by four pages of ad copy per day.

The creative advertising employee has a comparative advantage in writing ad copy, and the computer specialist has a comparative advantage in doing computerized art renderings. **Comparative advantage** derives from the ability to produce something at a lower opportunity cost than other producers, as we pointed out in Chapter 2.

Comparative advantage 
The ability to produce a good or service at a lower opportunity cost than other producers.

Specialization Among Nations

To demonstrate the concept of comparative advantage for nations, let's take the example of France and the United States. In Table 32-2, we show the comparative costs of production of wine and beer in terms of worker-days. This is a simple two-country, two-commodity world in which we assume that labor is the only factor of production. As you can see from the table, in the United States, it takes one worker-day to produce 1 liter of wine, and the same is true for 1 liter of beer. In France, it takes one worker-day to produce 1 liter of wine but two worker-days for 1 liter of beer. In this sense, Americans appear to be just as good at producing wine as the French and actually have an **absolute advantage** in producing beer.

Absolute advantage 
The ability to produce more output from given inputs of resources than other producers can.

Trade will still take place, however, which may seem paradoxical. How can trade take place if we can seemingly produce both goods at least as cheaply as the French can? Why don't we just produce both ourselves? To understand why, let's assume first that there is no trade and no specialization and that the workforce in each country consists of 200 workers. These 200 workers are, by assumption, divided equally in the production of wine and beer. We see in Table 32-3 on the next page that 100 liters of wine and 100 liters of beer are produced per day in the United States. In France, 100 liters of wine and 50 liters of beer are produced per day. The total daily world production in our two-country world is 200 liters of wine and150 liters of beer.

Now the countries specialize. What can France produce more cheaply? Look at the comparative costs of production expressed in worker-days in Table 32-2. What is the cost of producing 1 liter more of wine? One worker-day. What is the cost of producing 1 liter more of beer? Two worker-days. We can say, then, that in terms of the value of beer given up, in France the opportunity cost of producing wine is lower than in the United States. France will specialize in the activity that has the lower opportunity cost. In other words, France will specialize in its comparative advantage, which is the production of wine.

TABLE 32-2
Comparative Costs of Production

Product	United States (worker-days)	France (worker-days)
Wine (1 liter)	1	1
Beer (1 liter)	1	2

TABLE 32-3
Daily World Output Before Specialization
It is assumed that 200 workers are available in each country.

	United States		France		
Product	Workers	Output (liters)	Workers	Output (liters)	World Output (liters)
Wine	100	100	100	100	200
Beer	100	100	100	50	150

According to Table 32-4, after specialization, the United States produces 200 liters of beer and France produces 200 liters of wine. Notice that the total world production per day has gone up from 200 liters of wine and 150 liters of beer to 200 liters of wine and 200 liters of beer per day. This was done without any increased use of resources. The gain, 50 "free" liters of beer, results from a more efficient allocation of resources worldwide. World output is greater when countries specialize in producing the goods in which they have a comparative advantage and then engage in foreign trade. Another way of looking at this is to consider the choice between two ways of producing a good. Obviously, each country would choose the less costly production process. One way of "producing" a good is to import it, so if in fact the imported good is cheaper than the domestically produced good, we will "produce" it by importing it. Not everybody, of course, is better off when free trade occurs. In our example, U.S. wine makers and French beer makers are worse off because those two *domestic* industries have disappeared.

TABLE 32-4
Daily World Output After Specialization
It is assumed that 200 workers are available in each country.

	United States		France		
Product	Workers	Output (liters)	Workers	Output (liters)	World Output (liters)
Wine	—	—	200	200	200
Beer	200	200	—	—	200

Some people are worried that the United States (or any country, for that matter) might someday "run out of exports" because of overaggressive foreign competition. The analysis of comparative advantage tells us the contrary. No matter how much other countries compete for our business, the United States (or any other country) will always have a comparative advantage in something that it can export. In 10 or 20 years, that something may not be what we export today, but it will be exportable nonetheless because we will have a comparative advantage in producing it.

Why Do People Trade?
Practice applying the concepts of comparative and absolute advantage.

Other Benefits from International Trade: The Transmission of Ideas

Beyond the fact that comparative advantage results in an overall increase in the output of goods produced and consumed, there is another benefit to international trade. International trade bestows benefits on countries through the international transmission of ideas. According to economic historians, international trade has been the principal means by which new goods, services, and processes have spread around the world. For example, coffee was initially grown in Arabia near the Red Sea. Around A.D. 675, it began to be roasted and consumed as a beverage. Eventually, it was exported to other parts of the world, and the Dutch started cultivating it in their colonies during the seventeenth century and the French in the eighteenth century. The lowly potato is native to the Peruvian Andes. In the sixteenth century, it was brought to Europe by Spanish explorers. Thereafter, its cultivation and consumption spread rapidly. It became part of the American agricultural scene in the early eighteenth century.

All of the *intellectual property* that has been introduced throughout the world is a result of international trade. This includes new music, such as rock and roll in the 1950s and hip-hop and grunge in the 1990s. It includes the software applications that are common for computer users everywhere.

New processes have been transmitted through international trade. One of those involves the Japanese manufacturing innovation that emphasized redesigning the system rather than running the existing system in the best possible way. Inventories were reduced to just-in-time levels by reengineering machine setup methods. Just-in-time inventory control is now common in American factories.

INTERNATIONAL EXAMPLE

International Trade and the Alphabet

Even the alphabetic system of writing that appears to be the source of most alphabets in the world today was spread through international trade. According to some scholars, the Phoenicians, who lived on the long, narrow strip of Mediterranean coast north of Israel from the ninth century B.C. to around 300 B.C., created the first true alphabet. Presumably, they developed the alphabet to keep international trading records on their ships rather than having to take along highly trained scribes.

For Critical Analysis

Before alphabets were used, how might have people communicated in written form?

THE RELATIONSHIP BETWEEN IMPORTS AND EXPORTS

The basic proposition in understanding all of international trade is this:

In the long run, imports are paid for by exports.*

The reason that imports are ultimately paid for by exports is that foreigners want something in exchange for the goods that are shipped to the United States. For the most part, they want goods made in the United States. From this truism comes a remarkable corollary:

Any restriction of imports ultimately reduces exports.

Click here to view the most recent trade statistics for the United States.

This is a shocking revelation to many people who want to restrict foreign competition to protect domestic jobs. Although it is possible to protect certain U.S. jobs by restricting foreign competition, it is impossible to make *everyone* better off by imposing import restrictions. Why? Because ultimately such restrictions lead to a reduction in employment in the export industries of the nation.

*We have to modify this rule by adding that in the short run, imports can also be paid for by the sale (or export) of real and financial assets, such as land, stocks, and bonds, or through an extension of credit from other countries.

INTERNATIONAL EXAMPLE

The Importation of Priests into Spain

Imports affect not only goods but also services and the movement of labor. In Spain, some 3,000 priests retire each year, but barely 250 young men are ordained to replace them. Over 70 percent of the priests in Spain are now over the age of 50. The Spanish church estimates that by 2005, the number of priests will have fallen to half the 20,441 who were active in Spain in 1990. The Spanish church has had to seek young seminarians from Latin America under what it calls Operation Moses. It is currently subsidizing the travel and training of an increasing number of young Latin Americans to take over where native Spaniards have been before.

For Critical Analysis

How might the Catholic church in Spain induce more native Spaniards to become priests?

INTERNATIONAL COMPETITIVENESS

"The United States is falling behind." "We need to stay competitive internationally." These and similar statements are often heard in government circles when the subject of international trade comes up. There are two problems with this issue. The first has to do with a simple definition. What does "global competitiveness" really mean? When one company competes against another, it is in competition. Is the United States like one big corporation, in competition with other countries? Certainly not. The standard of living in each country is almost solely a function of how well the economy functions *within that country,* not relative to other countries.

Another problem arises with respect to the real world. According to the Institute for Management Development in Lausanne, Switzerland, the United States continues to lead the pack in overall productive efficiency, ahead of Japan, Germany, and the rest of the European Union. According to the report, America's top-class ranking is due to the sustained U.S. economic recovery following its 1990–1991 recession, widespread entrepreneurship, and a decade of economic restructuring. Other factors include America's sophisticated financial system and large investments in scientific research.

Don't productivity improvements in other countries erode the competitive position of the United States?

International trade is not a zero-sum game: If China becomes more productive, this does not mean that the United States is now less productive. A more productive China will certainly have more products to market to American consumers. It will also have higher-quality products to sell at lower prices than before, which benefits consumers in the United States who buy Chinese goods. Furthermore, China's national income will rise as a result of its productivity improvement. Consequently, it will become a bigger potential market for U.S. exports. Thus other nations can experience economic success without in any way reducing the ability of U.S. firms to produce efficiently and compete with foreign producers.

CONCEPTS IN BRIEF

- Countries can be better off materially if they specialize in producing goods for which they have a comparative advantage.
- It is important to distinguish between absolute and comparative advantage; the former refers to the ability to produce a unit of output with fewer physical units of input; the latter refers to producing output that has the lowest opportunity cost for a nation.
- Different nations will always have different comparative advantages because of differing opportunity costs due to different resource mixes.

ARGUMENTS AGAINST FREE TRADE 

Numerous arguments are raised against free trade. They mainly point out the costs of trade; they do not consider the benefits or the possible alternatives for reducing the costs of free trade while still reaping benefits.

The Infant Industry Argument

A nation may feel that if a particular industry were allowed to develop domestically, it could eventually become efficient enough to compete effectively in the world market. Therefore, if some restrictions were placed on imports, domestic producers would be given the time needed to develop their efficiency to the point where they would be able to compete in the domestic market without any restrictions on imports. In graphic terminology, we would expect that if the protected industry truly does experience improvements in production techniques or technological breakthroughs toward greater efficiency in the future, the supply curve will shift outward to the right so that the domestic industry can produce larger quantities of each and every price. National policymakers often conclude that this **infant industry argument** has some merit in the short run. They have used it to protect a number of industries in their infancy around the world.

Infant industry argument 
The contention that tariffs should be imposed to protect from import competition an industry that is trying to get started. Presumably, after the industry becomes technologically efficient, the tariff can be lifted.

Such a policy can be abused, however. Often the protective import-restricting arrangements remain even after the infant has matured. If other countries can still produce more cheaply, the people who benefit from this type of situation are obviously the stockholders (and specialized factors of production that will earn economic rents) in the industry that is still being protected from world competition. The people who lose out are the consumers, who must pay a price higher than the world price for the product in question. In any event, it is very difficult to know beforehand which industries will eventually survive. In other words, we cannot predict very well the specific infant industries that policymakers might deem worthy of protection. Note that when we speculate about which industries "should" be protected, we are in the realm of *normative economics.* We are making a value judgment, a subjective statement of what *ought to be.*

EXAMPLE

An Infant Industry Blossoms Due to Protection from Foreign Imports: Marijuana

Marijuana was made illegal in the United States in the 1930s, but just as for many other outlawed drugs, a market for it remained. Until about 25 years ago, virtually all the marijuana consumed in the United States was imported. Today, earnings from the burgeoning and increasingly high-tech "pot" industry are estimated at $35 billion a year, making it the nation's biggest cash crop (compared to corn at $15 billion). Starting with President Richard Nixon in the 1970s, the federal government has ended up protecting the domestic marijuana industry from imports by declaring a war on drugs. Given virtually no foreign competition, the American marijuana industry expanded and invested millions in developing both more productive and more potent seeds as well as more efficient growing technologies. Domestic marijuana growers now dominate the high end of a market in which consumers pay $300 to $500 an ounce for a reengineered home-grown product. New growing technologies allow domestic producers, using high-intensity sodium lights, carbon dioxide, and advances in genetics, to produce a kilogram of the potent sinsemilla variety every two months in a space no bigger than a phone booth.

For Critical Analysis

What has spurred domestic producers to develop highly productive indoor growing methods?

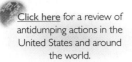

Click here for a review of antidumping actions in the United States and around the world.

Countering Foreign Subsidies and Dumping

Another strong argument against unrestricted foreign trade has to do with countering other nations' subsidies to their own producers. When a foreign government subsidizes its producers, our producers claim that they cannot compete fairly with these subsidized foreigners. To the extent that such subsidies fluctuate, it can be argued that unrestricted free trade will seriously disrupt domestic producers. They will not know when foreign governments are going to subsidize their producers and when they are not. Our competing industries will be expanding and contracting too frequently.

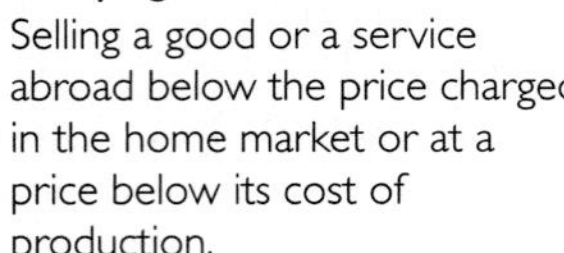

Dumping
Selling a good or a service abroad below the price charged in the home market or at a price below its cost of production.

The phenomenon called *dumping* is also used as an argument against unrestricted trade. **Dumping** is said to occur when a producer sells its products abroad below the price that is charged in the home market or at a price below its cost of production. When a foreign producer is accused of dumping, further investigation usually reveals that the foreign nation is in the throes of a recession. The foreign producer does not want to slow down its production at home. Because it anticipates an end to the recession and doesn't want to hold large inventories, it dumps its products abroad at prices below home prices. U.S. competitors may also allege that it sells its output at prices below its costs in an effort to cover at least part of its variable costs of production. Dumping does disrupt international trade. It also creates instability in domestic production and therefore may impair commercial well-being at home.

INTERNATIONAL POLICY EXAMPLE

Who's Dumping on Whom?

Claims of dumping are handled on a case-by-case basis under international rules. Only a few firms in an industry have to lodge a claim to justify a dumping investigation. Under international law, antidumping rules permit governments to impose *duties*—special taxes on imported goods—on the products sold by firms of offending nations. Take a look at Figure 32-3. As you can see, in the early 1990s, developed nations filed an

FIGURE 32-3
Claims to the World Trade Organization for Antidumping Relief
In recent years, developing nations have filed at least as many claims seeking antidumping relief as the number filed by developed nations.
Source: World Trade Organization.

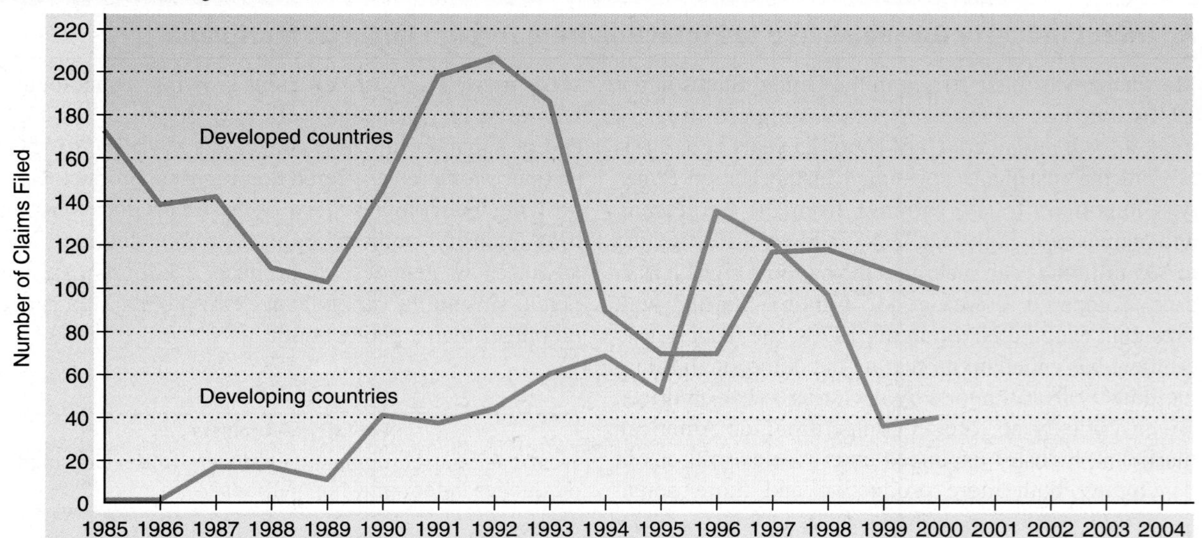

increasing number of claims seeking antidumping relief. The biggest filer of dumping claims during this period was the United States, which launched cases mainly against companies based in South America and Asia. The United States began to cut back on dumping claims beginning in the mid-1990s. Nevertheless, dumping claims by emerging economies—notably Argentina, Brazil, Mexico, and South Africa—rose precipitously. Whom did these emerging economies accuse of dumping? Firms in the United States, of course.

For Critical Analysis

Why did dumping claims by emerging nations fall as their economies expanded after the early 1990s?

Protecting American Jobs

Perhaps the argument used most often against free trade is that unrestrained competition from other countries will eliminate American jobs because other countries have lower-cost labor than we do. (Less restrictive environmental standards in other countries might also lower their private costs relative to ours.) This is a compelling argument, particularly for politicians from areas that might be threatened by foreign competition. For example, a representative from an area with shoe factories would certainly be upset about the possibility of constituents' losing their jobs because of competition from lower-priced shoe manufacturers in Brazil and Italy. But of course this argument against free trade is equally applicable to trade between the states.

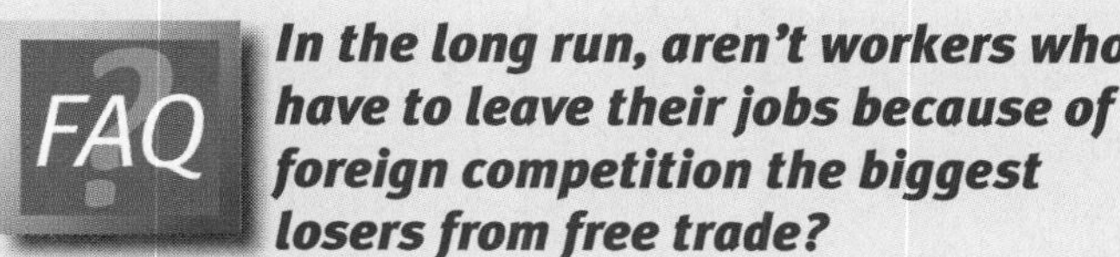

In the long run, aren't workers who have to leave their jobs because of foreign competition the biggest losers from free trade?

Some economists would argue that this is the opposite of the truth. Americans who leave their jobs rather than take wage cuts to match lower labor costs of new foreign competitors are presumably the ones who cared the least about their jobs in the first place. From this perspective, the biggest losers in the U.S. workplace are the Americans who value their jobs highly enough to keep them and absorb the full effects of the wage cuts. Because these workers presumably lack skills that they need to switch to jobs in industries with a comparative advantage over foreign producers, they are more likely to be "stuck" in low-paying jobs.

Economists David Gould, G. L. Woodbridge, and Roy Ruffin examined the data on the relationship between increases in imports and the rate of unemployment. Their conclusion was that there is no causal link between the two. Indeed, in half the cases they studied, when imports increased, unemployment fell.

Another issue has to do with the cost of protecting American jobs by restricting international trade. The Institute for International Economics examined just the restrictions on foreign textiles and apparel goods. U.S. consumers pay $9 billion a year more to protect jobs in those industries. That comes out to $50,000 a year for each job saved in an industry in which the average job pays only $20,000 a year. Similar studies have yielded similar results: Restrictions on the imports of Japanese cars have cost $160,000 *per year* for every job saved in the auto industry. Every job preserved in the glass industry has cost $200,000 each and every year. Every job preserved in the U.S. steel industry has cost an astounding $750,000 per year.

Click here to learn about the domestic costs of trade restrictions.

Emerging Arguments Against Free Trade

In recent years, two new antitrade arguments have been advanced. One of these focuses on environmental concerns. For instance, many environmentalists have raised concerns that genetic engineering of plants and animals could lead to accidental production of new diseases. These worries have induced the European Union to restrain trade in such products.

Another argument against free trade arises from national defense concerns. Major espionage successes by China in the late 1990s led some U.S. strategic experts to propose sweeping restrictions on exports of new technology.

Free trade proponents counter that at best these are arguments for the judicial regulation of trade. They continue to argue that by and large, broad trade restrictions mainly harm the interests of the nations that impose them.

CONCEPTS IN BRIEF

- The infant industry argument against free trade contends that new industries should be protected against world competition so that they can become technologically efficient in the long run.
- Unrestricted foreign trade may allow foreign governments to subsidize exports or foreign producers to engage in dumping—selling products in other countries below their cost of production. To the extent that foreign export subsidies and dumping create more instability in domestic production, they may impair our well-being.

WAYS TO RESTRICT FOREIGN TRADE

There are many ways in which international trade can be stopped or at least stifled. These include quotas and taxes (the latter are usually called *tariffs* when applied to internationally traded items). Let's talk first about quotas.

Quotas

Quota system A government-imposed restriction on the quantity of a specific good that another country is allowed to sell in the United States. In other words, quotas are restrictions on imports. These restrictions are usually applied to one or several specific countries.

Under the **quota system,** individual countries or groups of foreign producers are restricted to a certain amount of trade. An import quota specifies the maximum amount of a commodity that may be imported during a specified period of time. For example, the government might not allow more than 50 million barrels of foreign crude oil to enter the United States in a particular year.

Consider the example of quotas on textiles. Figure 32-4 presents the demand and the supply curves for imported textiles. In an unrestricted import market, the equilibrium quantity imported is 900 million yards at a price of $1 per yard (expressed in constant-quality units). When an import quota is imposed, the supply curve is no longer *S*. Rather, the supply

Trade Restrictions and Their Effects
See how trade restrictions work.

FIGURE 32-4
The Effect of Quotas on Textile Imports
Without restrictions, 900 million yards of textiles would be imported each year into the United States at the world price of $1.00 per yard. If the federal government imposes a quota of only 800 million yards, the effective supply curve becomes vertical at that quantity. It intersects the demand curve at a new equilibrium price of $1.50 per yard.

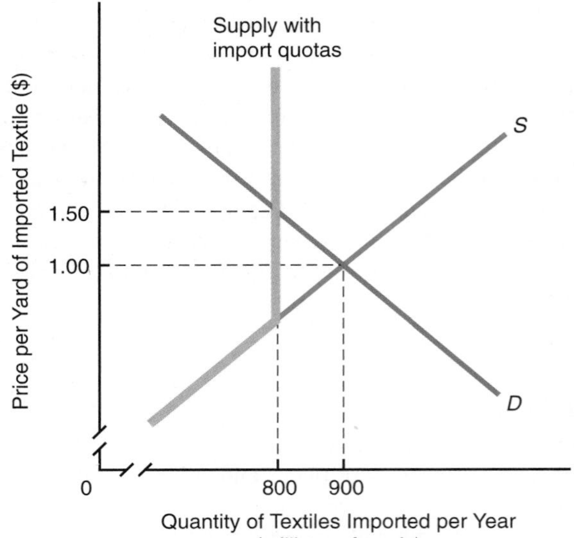

curve becomes vertical at some amount less than the equilibrium quantity—here, 800 million yards per year. The price to the American consumer increases from $1.00 to $1.50. Thus the output restriction induced by the textile quota also has the effect of influencing the price that domestic suppliers can charge for their goods. This benefits domestic textile producers by raising their revenues and therefore their profits.

INTERNATIONAL POLICY EXAMPLE

The U.S. Textile Industry: A Quota Agency of Its Very Own

Recently, American textile companies decided that they did not want so much foreign competition. Under normal circumstances, an industry might have to band together with others to lobby Congress for new laws imposing tariffs or quotas. Since the 1970s, however, the U.S. textile industry has had a special arrangement known as CITA—the Committee for the Implementation of Textile Agreements. CITA is comprised of appointees from the U.S. departments of Commerce, Labor, State, and Treasury, along with the chief textile negotiator of the Office of the President.

CITA holds no open meetings. Yet in a recent four-year period, CITA reduced or threatened to reduce quotas on specific types of textile imports. For instance, it placed limits on men's underwear from the Dominican Republic, cotton nightwear from Jamaica, and wool coats from Honduras. The annual benefit of CITA quotas for U.S. textile firms has been estimated to be as high as $12 billion in additional profits. In 2005, the United States is committed to international treaties that will phase out most textile quotas. Until then, however, CITA's quotas will be the law of the land.

For Critical Analysis

How are CITA quotas on textile imports likely to affect the prices that American consumers pay for underwear, nightwear, and coats?

Voluntary Quotas. Quotas do not have to be explicit and defined by law. They can be "voluntary." Such a quota is called a **voluntary restraint agreement (VRA).** In the early 1980s, the United States asked Japan voluntarily to restrain its exports to the United States. The Japanese government did so, limiting itself to exporting 2.8 million Japanese automobiles. Today, there are VRAs on machine tools and textiles.

Voluntary restraint agreement (VRA) 
An official agreement with another country that "voluntarily" restricts the quantity of its exports to the United States.

The opposite of a VRA is a **voluntary import expansion (VIE).** Under a VIE, a foreign government agrees to have its companies import more foreign goods from another country. The United States almost started a major international trade war with Japan in 1995 over just such an issue. The U.S. government wanted Japanese automobile manufacturers voluntarily to increase their imports of U.S.-made automobile parts. Ultimately, Japanese companies did make a token increase in the imports of U.S. auto parts.

Voluntary import expansion (VIE) 
An official agreement with another country in which it agrees to import more from the United States.

Tariffs

We can analyze tariffs by using standard supply and demand diagrams. Let's use as our commodity laptop computers, some of which are made in Japan and some of which are made domestically. In panel (a) of Figure 32-5 on the next page, you see the demand and supply of Japanese laptops. The equilibrium price is $1,000 per constant-quality unit, and the equilibrium quantity is 10 million per year. In panel (b), you see the same equilibrium price of $1,000, and the *domestic* equilibrium quantity is 5 million units per year.

Click here to take a look at the U.S. State Department's reports on economic policy and trade practices.

Now a tariff of $500 is imposed on all imported Japanese laptops. The supply curve shifts upward by $500 to S_2. For purchasers of Japanese laptops, the price increases to $1,250. The quantity demanded falls to 8 million per year. In panel (b), you see that at the

FIGURE 32-5

The Effect of a Tariff on Japanese-Made Laptop Computers

Without a tariff, the United States buys 10 million Japanese laptops per year at an average price of \$1,000, as shown in panel (a). American producers sell 5 million domestically made laptops, also at \$1,000 each, as shown in panel (b). A \$500-per-laptop tariff will shift the Japanese import supply curve to S_2 in panel (a), so that the new equilibrium is at E_2, with price \$1,250 and quantity sold reduced to 8 million per year. The demand curve for American-made laptops (for which there is no tariff) shifts to D_2 in panel (b). Domestic sales increase to 6.5 million per year.

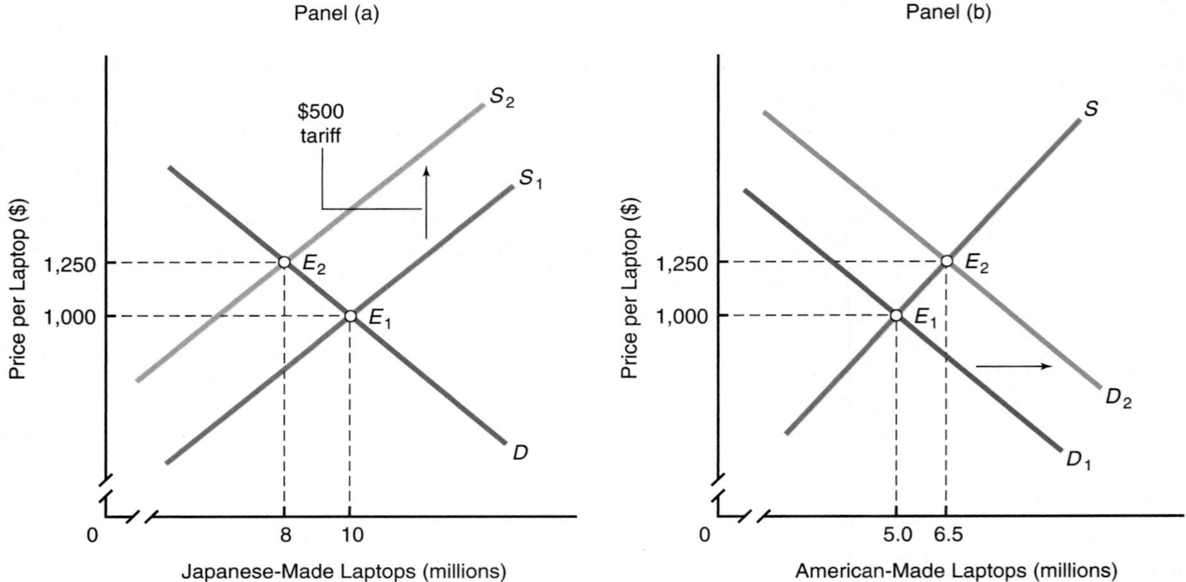

higher price of imported Japanese laptops, the demand curve for American-made laptops shifts outward to the right to D_2. The equilibrium price increases to \$1,250, but the equilibrium quantity increases to 6.5 million units per year. So the tariff benefits domestic laptop producers because it increases the demand for their products due to the higher price of a close substitute, Japanese laptops. This causes a redistribution of income from American consumers of laptops to American producers of laptops.

Tariffs in the United States. In Figure 32-6, we see that tariffs on all imported goods have varied widely. The highest rates in the twentieth century occurred with the passage of the Smoot-Hawley Tariff in 1930.

POLICY EXAMPLE

Did the Smoot-Hawley Tariff Worsen the Great Depression?

By 1930, the unemployment rate had almost doubled in a year. Congress and President Hoover wanted to do something that would help stimulate U.S. production and reduce unemployment. The result was the Smoot-Hawley Tariff, which set tariff schedules for over 20,000 products, raising duties on imports by an average of 52 percent. This attempt to improve the domestic economy at the expense of foreign economies backfired. Each trading partner of the United States in turn imposed its own high tariffs, including the United Kingdom, the Netherlands, France, and Switzerland. The result was a massive reduction in international trade by an incredible 64 percent in three years. Some believe that the ensuing world Great Depression was partially caused by such tariffs.

For Critical Analysis

The Smoot-Hawley Tariff has been labeled a "beggar thy neighbor" policy. Explain why.

Current Tariff Laws. The Trade Expansion Act of 1962 gave the president the authority to reduce tariffs by up to 50 percent. Subsequently, tariffs were reduced by about 35 percent. In 1974, the Trade Reform Act allowed the president to reduce tariffs further. In 1984, the Trade and Tariff Act resulted in the lowest tariff rates ever. All such trade agreement obligations of the United States were carried out under the auspices of the **General Agreement on Tariffs and Trade (GATT),** which was signed in 1947. Member nations of GATT account for more

General Agreement on Tariffs and Trade (GATT) 
An international agreement established in 1947 to further world trade by reducing barriers and tariffs.

FIGURE 32-6
Tariff Rates in the United States Since 1820
Tariff rates in the United States have bounced around like a football; indeed, in Congress, tariffs are a political football. Import-competing industries prefer high tariffs. In the twentieth century, the highest tariff we had was the Smoot-Hawley Tariff of 1930, which was almost as high as the "tariff of abominations" in 1828.
Source: U.S. Department of Commerce.

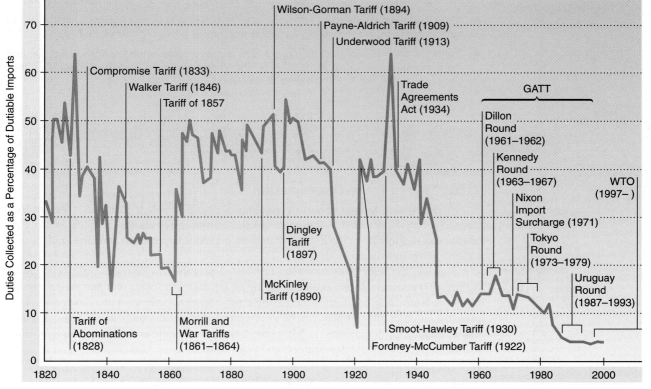

Duties Collected as a Percentage of Dutiable Imports
70
60
50
40
30
20
10
0
Wilson-Gorman Tariff (1894)
Payne-Aldrich Tariff (1909)
Underwood Tariff (1913)
Compromise Tariff (1833)
Walker Tariff (1846)
Tariff of 1857
Trade Agreements Act (1934)
GATT
Dillon Round (1961–1962)
Kennedy Round (1963–1967)
WTO (1997–)
Nixon Import Surcharge (1971)
Dingley Tariff (1897)
Tokyo Round (1973–1979)
McKinley Tariff (1890)
Uruguay Round (1987–1993)
Tariff of Abominations (1828)
Morrill and War Tariffs (1861–1864)
Smoot-Hawley Tariff (1930)
Fordney-McCumber Tariff (1922)
1820
1840
1860
1880
1900
1920
1940
1960
1980
2000
Year

than 85 percent of world trade. As you can see in Figure 32-6 on page 797, there have been a number of rounds of negotiations to reduce tariffs since the early 1960s. The latest round was called the Uruguay Round because that is where the meetings were held.

The World Trade Organization (WTO)

World Trade Organization (WTO)
The successor organization to GATT, it handles all trade disputes among its 135 member nations.

The Uruguay Round of the General Agreement on Tariffs and Trade (GATT) was ratified by 117 nations at the end of 1993. A year later, in a special session of Congress, the entire treaty was ratified. On January 1, 1995, the new **World Trade Organization (WTO)** replaced GATT. As of 2000, the WTO had 135 member nations, plus 32 observer governments, all but two of which have applied for membership. WTO decisions have concerned such topics as the European Union's "banana wars," in which the EU's policies were determined to favor unfairly many former European colonies in Africa, the Caribbean, and the Pacific at the expense of banana-exporting countries in Latin America. Now those former colonies no longer have a privileged position in European markets.

On a larger scale, the WTO fostered the most important and far-reaching global trade agreement ever covering financial institutions, including banks, insurers, and investment companies. The more than 100 signatories to this new treaty have legally committed themselves to giving foreigners more freedom to own and operate companies in virtually all segments of the financial services industry.

CONCEPTS IN BRIEF

- One means of restricting foreign trade is a quota system. Beneficiaries of quotas are the importers who get the quota rights and the domestic producers of the restricted good.
- Another means of restricting imports is a tariff, which is a tax on imports only. An import tariff benefits import-competing industries and harms consumers by raising prices.
- The main international institution created to improve trade among nations is the General Agreement on Tariffs and Trade (GATT). The latest round of trade talks under GATT, the Uruguay Round, led to the creation of the World Trade Organization.

NETNOMICS

WTO: "Wired Trade Organization"?

Across the span of human history, technological change has helped advance international trade. Speedier transoceanic transport fed the growth of cross-border trade in the eighteenth and nineteenth centuries. Air transport played a key role in spurring trade among nations in the twentieth century.

Likewise, the telecommunications revolution promises to provide a big boost in the twenty-first century. Books and compact disks are easier to locate and purchase from afar using the Internet. In addition to increasing cross-border trade in such physical goods, however, the Internet also promises to be an avenue for increased trade in services. Anything that is tradable in digital form is fair game. Examples include architectural designs, information about new medical treatments and surgical techniques, and banking, insurance, and brokerage services.

Electronic commerce is emerging as a big problem for the WTO. WTO rules work differently for tariffs versus quotas. In most nations, goods are subjected to tariffs. By contrast, many nations have chosen to apply quotas to services by placing restrictions on access to national markets.

The Internet and digital technology are blurring the distinctions between traded goods and traded services, however. Under current interpretation, a recording by a top rap artist that crosses a national border while resident on a CD is a good subject to tariffs. Is the same recording sent over the Internet in digital form a service under WTO rules? Or is it no different from a CD and thus subject to the WTO's tariff guidelines? Likewise, if an architectural firm ships detailed drawings to a customer in another country, the drawings are treated as goods, and tariffs apply. But what if the firm sends the drawings to its client in the form of an e-mail attachment?

These examples illustrate how WTO rules concerning how to define goods and services might exert significant effects on the choice between physical and digital methods of trade. National authorities are already having trouble keeping track of the proliferation of Internet-based service offerings. If quotas on cross-border Internet services are difficult for national authorities to enforce, people will have a strong incentive to shift even more trade to the Internet.

ISSUES & APPLICATIONS

Does Importing Goods Hurt Low-Wage Workers at Home?

Once the U.S. economy got past the 1990–1991 recession, it entered a lengthy period of simultaneous low inflation and low unemployment. For many Americans, the 1990s were a time of higher real wages, increased fringe benefits, and soaring stock values.

Rising Earnings Inquality

Not all Americans shared in these gains, however. Since the 1970s, the real pay of male workers among the 10 percent at the top of the U.S. income distribution has risen by over 10 percent, but the real compensation received by the 10 percent at the bottom has not increased by much. Female workers in the bottom 10 percent of the U.S. income distribution have done a little better than their male counterparts: Their earnings have risen by just under 5 percent. Women in the top 10 percent have made considerable strides, however. These high-income women have seen their earnings increase by nearly 30 percent.

Some politicians and union leaders blamed this growing U.S. earnings inequality on international trade. In the early 1970s, they point out, only one-sixth of U.S. imports of manufactured goods came from emerging economies. Today, the proportion is about one-third. There must be a simple line of causation, they claim. Extrapolating from these data, they conclude that to keep from losing his job to foreign workers, the pay of an "average Joe" is falling. The "average Jane," they contend, has barely been holding her own in the face of this same competition from abroad.

FIGURE 32-7

U.S. Manufacturing Wages and Trade with Developing Countries

In recent decades, wages earned by workers in manufacturing in nations that trade with the United States have increased relative to the wages of U.S. manufacturing workers. Some observers argue that the implied relative decline in U.S. manufacturing wages is due in part to increased trade with developing countries.

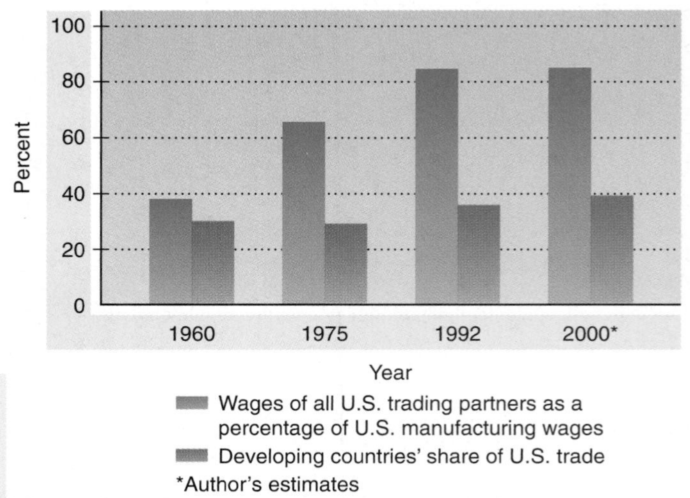

Is Free Trade the Culprit?

Take a look at Figure 32-7. It shows that American consumers have slightly increased the share of products they buy from developing countries. It also shows that the wages of all U.S. trading partners, including emerging economies, have increased relative to the wages of American manufacturing workers. One interpretation of these data is that the politicians and union leaders are correct: By purchasing more goods from emerging nations, American consumers end up reducing the wages of American workers relative to low-wage workers in those countries. Thus, goes the argument, Americans are losing out from freer trade, and the United States should put up barriers against imports from emerging nations.

As you have learned in this chapter, however, the story is not nearly this simple. The whole point of free trade is that it induces nations to specialize in producing goods for which they have a comparative advantage. Thus when trade barriers are removed—as many of them were in the United States during the 1970s and 1980s—resources naturally shift into industries in nations with a comparative advantage. They shift away from industries that lack a comparative advantage. Although this change undoubtedly works in favor of the U.S. economy as a whole, in the short run it can also work to the disadvantage of people with fewer marketable skills. One result can be a relative decline in the real earnings of lower-paid workers, at least in the near term.

FOR CRITICAL ANALYSIS

1. Do the data in Figure 32-7 necessarily indicate that U.S. manufacturing wages are declining? (Hint: A ratio can rise even if both the numerator and denominator increase, if the numerator increases faster.)
2. If American industries are losing out to foreign competition, what are some policy alternatives to dealing with the plight faced by lower-wage U.S. workers, aside from telling all American consumers that they cannot buy products from emerging nations?

SG

SUMMARY DISCUSSION OF LEARNING OBJECTIVES

1. **The Worldwide Importance of International Trade:** Total trade among nations has been growing faster than total world GDP. The growth of U.S. exports and imports relative to U.S. GDP parallels this global trend. Exports and imports now equal more than 10 percent of total national production. In some countries, trade accounts for much higher shares of total economic activity.
2. **Why Nations Can Gain from Specializing in Production and Engaging in Trade:** A country has a comparative advantage in producing a good if it can produce that good at a lower opportunity cost, in terms of forgone production of a second good, than another nation. If the other nation has a comparative advantage in producing the second good, both nations can gain by specializing in producing the goods in which they have a comparative advantage and engaging in international trade. Together they can then produce and consume more than they would have produced and consumed in the absence of specialization and trade.
3. **Comparative Advantage Versus Absolute Advantage:** Whereas a nation has a comparative advantage in producing a good when it can produce the good at lower opportunity cost relative to the opportunity cost of producing the good in another nation, a nation has an absolute advantage when it can produce more output with a given set of inputs than can be produced in the other country. Nevertheless, trade can still take place if both nations have a comparative advantage in producing goods that they can agree to exchange. The reason is that it can still benefit the nation with an absolute advantage to specialize in production.
4. **Arguments Against Free Trade:** One argument against free trade is that temporary import restrictions might permit an "infant industry" to develop to the point where it could compete without such

restrictions. Another argument concerns dumping, in which foreign companies allegedly sell some of their output in domestic markets at prices below the prices in the companies' home markets or even below the companies' costs of production. In addition, some environmentalists contend that nations should restrain foreign trade to prevent exposing their countries to environmental hazards to plants, animals, or even humans. Finally, some contend that countries should limit exports of technologies that could pose a threat to their national defense.

5. **Ways That Nations Restrict Foreign Trade:** One way to restrain trade is to impose a quota, or a limit on imports of a good. This action restricts the supply of the good in the domestic market, thereby pushing up the equilibrium price of the good. Another way to reduce trade is to place a tariff on imported goods. This reduces the supply of foreign-made goods and increases the demand for domestically produced goods, which brings about a rise in the price of the good.
6. **Key International Agreements and Organizations That Adjudicate Trade Disputes:** From 1947 to 1995, nations agreed to abide by the General Agreement on Trades and Tariffs (GATT), which laid an international legal foundation for relaxing quotas and reducing tariffs. Since 1995, the World Trade Organization (WTO) has adjudicated trade disputes that arise between or among nations.

Key Terms and Concepts

Absolute advantage (787)
Comparative advantage (787)
Dumping (792)
General Agreement on Tariffs and Trade (GATT) (797)
Infant industry argument (791)
Quota system (794)
Voluntary import expansion (VIE) (795)
Voluntary restraint agreement (VRA) (795)
World Trade Organization (WTO) (798)

Problems

Answers to the odd-numbered problems appear at the back of the book.

32-1. The following hypothetical example depicts the number of calculators and books that Norway and Sweden can produce with one unit of labor.

Country	Calculators	Books
Norway	2	1
Sweden	4	1

If each country has 100 workers and the country splits its labor force evenly between the two industries, how much of each good can the nations produce individually and jointly? Which nation has an absolute advantage in calculators, and which nation has an absolute advantage in books?

32-2. Suppose that the two nations in Problem 32-1 do not trade.

a. What would be the price of books in terms of calculators for each nation?

b. What is the opportunity cost of producing one calculator in each nation?

c. What is the opportunity cost of producing one book in each nation?

32-3. Consider the nations in Problem 32-1 when answering the following questions.

a. Which has a comparative advantage in calculators and which in books?

b. What is total or joint output if the two nations specialize in the good for which they have a comparative advantage?

32-4. Illustrate the production possibilities frontiers for the two nations in Problem 32-1 in a graph with books depicted on the vertical axis and calculators on the horizontal axis. What is the significance of the differing slopes of the PPFs for these two nations?

32-5. Suppose that the two nations in Problem 32-1 trade with each other at a rate where one book exchanges for three calculators. Using this rate of exchange, explain, in economic terms, whether their exchange is a zero-sum game, a positive-sum game, or a negative-sum game. (Hint: Review Chapter 25 if necessary to answer this question.)

32-6. The marginal physical product of a worker in an advanced nation (MPP_A) is 100 and the wage (W_A) is $25. The marginal physical product of a worker in a developing nation (MPP_D) is 15 and the wage (W_D) is $5. As a cost-minimizing business manager in the developing nation, would you be enticed to move your business to the developing nation to take advantage of the lower wage?

32-7. You are a policymaker of a major exporting nation. Your main export good has a price elasticity of demand of −.50. Is there any economic reason why you would voluntarily agree to export restraints?

32-8. The following table depicts the bicycle industry before and after a nation has imposed quota restraints.

	Before Quota	After Quota
Quantity imported	1,000,000	900,000
Price paid	$50	$60

Draw a diagram illustrating conditions in the imported bicycle market before and after the quota, and answer the following questions.

a. What are the total expenditures of consumers before and after the quota?

b. What is the price elasticity of demand for bicycles?

c. Who benefits from the imposition of the quota?

32-9. The following diagrams illustrate the markets for imported Korean-made and U.S. manufactured televisions before and after a tariff is imposed on imported TVs.

a. What was the amount of the tariff?

b. What was the total revenue of Korean television exports before the tariff? After the tariff?

c. What is the tariff revenue earned by the U.S. government?

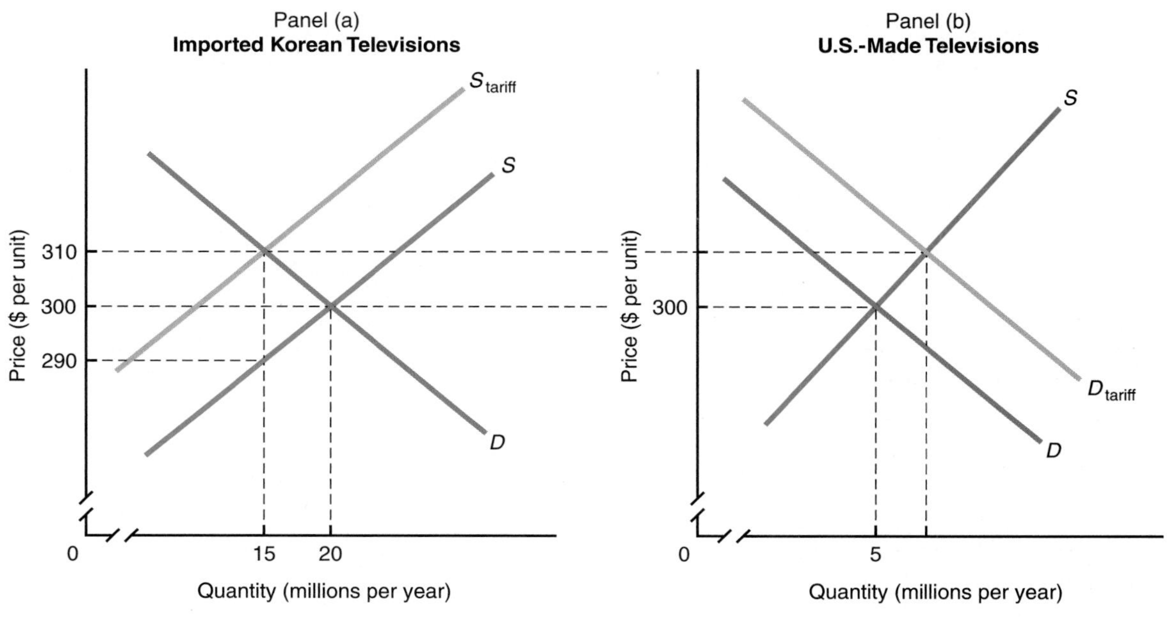

32-10. Base your answers to the following questions on the graph accompanying Problem 32-9.

a. What was the revenue of U.S. television manufacturers before the tariff was imposed?

b. What is their total revenue after the tariff?

c. Who has gained from the tariff and who has it made worse off?

Economics on the Net

How the World Trade Organization Settles Trade Disputes A key function of the WTO is to adjudicate trade disagreements that arise among nations. This application helps you learn about the process that the WTO follows when considering international trade disputes.

Title: The World Trade Organization: Settling Trade Disputes

Navigation: Click here to begin at the WTO's homepage. Select the A-Z List of Topics. Then click on Disputes, and click on How Does the WTO Settle Disputes?

Application Read the first article. Then answer the following questions.

1. As the article discusses, settling trade disputes often takes at least a year. What aspects of the WTO's dispute settlement process take the longest time?

2. Does the WTO actually "punish" a country it finds has broken international trading agreements? If not, who does impose sanctions?

For Group Study and Analysis Read the Beyond the Agreements section, which lists areas that the WTO is currently exploring for future action. Have a class discussion of the pros and cons of WTO involvement in each of these areas. Which are most important for promoting world trade? Which are least important?

CHAPTER

33

EXCHANGE RATES AND THE BALANCE OF PAYMENTS

During the Asian currency crisis, the Thai government launched a campaign to keep the national currency, the baht, from falling in value. The government asked Thais to turn in their foreign currencies in exchange for baht. Why?

In 1997, an international payments crisis swept Southeast Asia. Investors from around the world began selling off their holdings of bonds and stocks denominated in the Thai baht, Indonesian rupiah, and Malaysian ringgit. The prime minister of Malaysia, Mahathir Mohamad, said that the crisis was caused by currency speculators—individuals and firms that seek to profit solely from the activity of buying currencies at low values and selling them at higher values. During the summer of 1997, a number of currency speculators earned sizable profits by conjecturing that Southeast Asian nations, including Malaysia, could not maintain the value of their currencies. According to Mahathir, these were ill-gotten gains. Speculative currency trading, Mahathir contended, "is unnecessary, unproductive, and immoral." Are currency speculators really unproductive individuals engaged in an unnecessary and immoral business? To evaluate this question, you must first learn more about international payments and exchange rates.

LEARNING OBJECTIVES

After reading this chapter, you should be able to:

1. Distinguish between the balance of trade and the balance of payments
2. Identify the key accounts within the balance of payments
3. Outline how exchange rates are determined in the markets for foreign exchange
4. Discuss factors that can induce changes in equilibrium exchange rates
5. Understand how policymakers can go about attempting to fix exchange rates
6. Explain alternative approaches to limiting exchange rate variability

Chapter Outline

- The Balance of Payments and International Capital Movements
- Determining Foreign Exchange Rates
- The Gold Standard and the International Monetary Fund
- Fixed Versus Floating Exchange Rates

Did You Know That... every day, around the clock, over $1 trillion in foreign currencies is traded? Along with that trading come news headlines, such as "The dollar weakened today," "The dollar is clearly overvalued," "The dollar is under attack," and "Members of the Group of Seven acted to prevent the dollar from rising." If you are confused by such newspaper headlines, join the crowd. Surprisingly, though, if you regard the dollar, the pound, the euro, the yen, and the baht as assets that are subject to the laws of supply and demand, the world of international finance can be quickly demystified. Perhaps the first step is to examine the meaning of the terms used with respect to U.S. international financial transactions during any one-year period.

THE BALANCE OF PAYMENTS AND INTERNATIONAL CAPITAL MOVEMENTS

Governments typically keep track of each year's economic activities by calculating the gross domestic product—the total of expenditures on all newly produced final domestic goods and services—and its components. In the world of international trade also, a summary information system has been developed. It relates to the balance of trade and the balance of payments. The **balance of trade** refers specifically to exports and imports of goods as discussed in Chapter 32. When international trade is in balance, the value of exports equals the value of imports. When the value of imports exceeds the value of imports, we are running a deficit in the balance of trade. When the value of exports exceeds the value of imports, we are running a surplus.

Balance of trade 
The difference between exports and imports of goods.

Balance of payments 
A system of accounts that measures transactions of goods, services, income, and financial assets between domestic households, businesses, and governments and residents of the rest of the world during a specific time period.

The **balance of payments** is a more general concept that expresses the total of all economic transactions between a nation and the rest of the world, usually for a period of one year. Each country's balance of payments summarizes information about that country's exports, imports, earnings by domestic residents on assets located abroad, earnings on domestic assets owned by foreign residents, international capital movements, and official transactions by central banks and governments. In essence, then, the balance of payments is a record of all the transactions between households, firms, and the government of one country and the rest of the world. Any transaction that leads to a *payment* by a country's residents (or government) is a deficit item, identified by a negative sign (−) when we examine the actual numbers that might be in Table 33-1. Any transaction that leads to a *receipt* by a country's residents (or government) is a surplus item and is identified by a plus sign (+) when actual numbers are considered. Table 33-1 gives a listing of the surplus and deficit items on international accounts.

Accounting Identities

Accounting identities 
Values that are equivalent by definition.

Accounting identities—definitions of equivalent values—exist for financial institutions and other businesses. We begin with simple accounting identities that must hold for families and then go on to describe international accounting identities.

If a family unit is spending more than its current income, such a situation necessarily implies that the family unit must be doing one of the following:

1. Reducing its money holdings, or selling stocks, bonds, or other assets
2. Borrowing
3. Receiving gifts from friends or relatives

TABLE 33-1
Surplus (+) and Deficit (−) Items on the International Accounts

Surplus Items (+)	Deficit Items (−)
Exports of merchandise	Imports of merchandise
Private and governmental gifts from foreigners	Private and governmental gifts to foreigners
Foreign use of domestically owned transportation	Use of foreign-owned transportation
Foreign tourists' expenditures in this country	Tourism expenditures abroad
Foreign military spending in this country	Military spending abroad
Interest and dividend receipts from foreign entities	Interest and dividends paid to foreigners
Sales of domestic assets to foreigners	Purchases of foreign assets
Funds deposited in this country by foreigners	Funds placed in foreign depository institutions
Sales of gold to foreigners	Purchases of gold from foreigners
Sales of domestic currency to foreigners	Purchases of foreign currency

4. Receiving public transfers from a government, which obtained the funds by taxing others (a transfer is a payment, in money or in goods or services, made without receiving goods or services in return)

We can use this information to derive an identity: If a family unit is currently spending more than it is earning, it must draw on previously acquired wealth, borrow, or receive either private or public aid. Similarly, an identity exists for a family unit that is currently spending less than it is earning: It must be increasing its money holdings or be lending and acquiring other financial assets, or it must pay taxes or bestow gifts on others. When we consider businesses and governments, each unit in each group faces its own identities or constraints. Ultimately, net lending by households must equal net borrowing by businesses and governments.

Disequilibrium. Even though our individual family unit's accounts must balance, in the sense that the identity discussed previously must hold, sometimes the item that brings about the balance cannot continue indefinitely. *If family expenditures exceed family income and this situation is financed by borrowing, the household may be considered to be in disequilibrium because such a situation cannot continue indefinitely.* If such a deficit is financed by drawing on previously accumulated assets, the family may also be in disequilibrium because it cannot continue indefinitely to draw on its wealth; eventually, it will become impossible for that family to continue such a lifestyle. (Of course, if the family members are retired, they may well be in equilibrium by drawing on previously acquired assets to finance current deficits; this example illustrates that it is necessary to understand circumstances fully before pronouncing an economic unit in disequilibrium.)

Equilibrium. Individual households, businesses, and governments, as well as the entire group of households, businesses, and governments, must eventually reach equilibrium. Certain economic adjustment mechanisms have evolved to ensure equilibrium. Deficit households must eventually increase their income or decrease their expenditures. They will find that they have to pay higher interest rates if they wish to borrow to finance their deficits. Eventually, their credit sources will dry up, and they will be forced into equilibrium. Businesses, on occasion, must lower costs or prices—or go bankrupt—to reach equilibrium.

TABLE 33-2
U.S. Balance of Payments Account, 2000 (in billions of dollars)

Current Account			
(1)	Exports of goods	+711.6	
(2)	Imports of goods	−1,135.3	
(3)	Balance of trade		−423.7
(4)	Exports of services	+311.2	
(5)	Imports of services	−213.4	
(6)	Balance of services		+97.8
(7)	Balance on goods and services [(3) + (6)]		−325.9
(8)	Net unilateral transfers	−34.2	
(9)	Balance on current account		−360.1
Capital Account			
(10)	U.S. private capital going abroad	−642.2	
(11)	Foreign private capital coming into the United States	+987.1*	
(12)	Balance on capital account [(10) + (11)]		+344.9
(13)	Balance on current account plus balance on capital account [(9) + (12)]		−15.2
Official Reserve Transactions Account			
(14)	Official transactions balance		+15.2
(15)	Total (balance)		.00

Sources: U.S. Department of Commerce, Bureau of Economic Analysis; U.S. Department of the Treasury.

*Includes a $26 billion statistical discrepancy, probably unaccounted capital inflows, many of which relate to the illegal drug trade.

An Accounting Identity Among Nations. When nations trade or interact, certain identities or constraints must also hold. Nations buy goods from people in other nations; they also lend to and present gifts to people in other nations. If a nation interacts with others, an accounting identity ensures a balance (but not an equilibrium, as will soon become clear). Let's look at the three categories of balance of payments transactions: current account transactions, capital account transactions, and official reserve account transactions.

Current Account Transactions

During any designated period, all payments and gifts that are related to the purchase or sale of both goods and services constitute the current account in international trade. The four major types of current account transactions are the exchange of merchandise, the exchange of services, unilateral transfers, and net investment income.

Merchandise Trade Exports and Imports. The largest portion of any nation's balance of payments current account is typically the importing and exporting of merchandise goods. During 2000, for example, as can be seen in lines 1 and 2 of Table 33-2, the United States exported $711.6 billion of merchandise and imported $1,135.3 billion. The balance of merchandise trade is defined as the difference between the value of merchandise exports and the value of merchandise imports. For 2000, the United States had a balance of merchandise trade deficit because the value of its merchandise imports exceeded the value of its merchandise exports. This deficit amounted to $423.7 billion (line 3).

Service Exports and Imports. The balance of (merchandise) trade has to do with tangible items—you can feel them, touch them, and see them. Service exports and imports have to do with invisible or intangible items that are bought and sold, such as shipping, insurance, tourist expenditures, and banking services. Also, income earned by foreigners on U.S. investments and income earned by U.S. residents on foreign investments are part of service imports and exports. As can be seen in lines 4 and 5 of Table 33-2, in 2000, service exports were $311.2 billion and service imports were $213.4 billion. Thus the balance of services was about $97.8 billion in 2000 (line 6). Exports constitute receipts or inflows into the United States and are positive; imports constitute payments abroad or outflows of money and are negative.

When we combine the balance of merchandise trade with the balance of services, we obtain a balance of goods and services equal to −$325.9 billion in 2000 (line 7).

Unilateral Transfers. U.S. residents give gifts to relatives and others abroad, the federal government grants gifts to foreign nations, foreigners give gifts to U.S. residents, and some foreign governments have granted money to the U.S. government. In the current account, we see that net unilateral transfers—the total amount of gifts given by U.S. residents minus the total amount received by U.S. residents from abroad—came to −$34.2 billion in 2000 (line 8). The fact that there is a minus sign before the number for unilateral transfers means that U.S. residents gave more to foreigners than foreigners gave to U.S. residents.

Balancing the Current Account. The balance on current account tracks the value of a country's exports of goods and services (including military receipts plus income on investments abroad) and transfer payments (private and government) relative to the value of that country's imports of goods and services and transfer payments (private and government). In 2000, it was −$360.1 billion.

> If the sum of net exports of goods and services plus unilateral transfers plus net investment income exceeds zero, a current account surplus is said to exist; if this sum is negative, a current account deficit is said to exist. A current account deficit means that we are importing more than we are exporting. Such a deficit must be paid for by the export of money or money equivalent, which means a capital account surplus.

Click here for latest U.S. balance-of-payments figures.

Capital Account Transactions

In world markets, it is possible to buy and sell not only goods and services but also real and financial assets. This is what the capital accounts are concerned with in international transactions. Capital account transactions occur because of foreign investments—either by foreign residents investing in the United States or by U.S. residents investing in other countries. The purchase of shares of stock on the London stock market by a U.S. resident causes an outflow of funds from the United States to Britain. The building of a Japanese automobile factory in the United States causes an inflow of funds from Japan to the United States. Any time foreign residents buy U.S. government securities, that is an inflow of funds from other countries to the United States. Any time U.S. residents buy foreign government securities, there is an outflow of funds from the United States to other countries. Loans to and from foreign residents cause outflows and inflows.

The United States has large trade deficits. Does this mean we have a weak economy?

It is true that the current account in the United States has been in deficit continuously since the early 1980s, but this was also true during the 1880s. So it is not a new phenomenon. (Note also that we were a creditor nation from 1914 to 1985.) Figure 33-1 shows that whenever the United States is in deficit in its current account, it is in surplus in its capital account. The United States does not have a trade deficit because its economy is weak and it cannot compete in world markets. Rather, the United States is a good place to invest capital because we have strong prospects for growth. As long as foreign residents wish to invest more in the United States than U.S. residents wish to invest abroad, there will *always* be a current account deficit. The U.S. is better off, not worse off, because of it.

Line 10 of Table 33-2 indicates that in 2000, the value of private and government capital going out of the United States was −\$642.2 billion, and line 11 shows that the value of private and government capital coming into the United States (including a statistical discrepancy) was \$987.1 billion. U.S. capital going abroad constitutes payments or outflows and is therefore negative. Foreign capital coming into the United States constitutes receipts or inflows and is therefore positive. Thus there was a positive net capital movement of \$344.9 billion into the United States (line 12). This is also called the balance on capital account.

There is a relationship between the current account and the capital account, assuming no interventions by the finance ministries or central banks of nations.

In the absence of interventions by finance ministries or central banks, the current account and the capital account must sum to zero. Stated differently, the current account deficit must equal the capital account surplus when governments or central banks do not engage in foreign exchange interventions. In this situation, any nation experiencing a current account deficit, such as the United States, must also be running a capital account surplus.

Official Reserve Account Transactions

The third type of balance of payments transaction concerns official reserve assets, which consist of the following:

1. Foreign currencies
2. Gold
3. **Special drawing rights (SDRs),** which are reserve assets that the International Monetary Fund created to be used by countries to settle international payment obligations
4. The reserve position in the International Monetary Fund
5. Financial assets held by an official agency, such as the U.S. Treasury Department

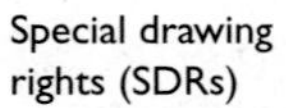

Special drawing rights (SDRs)
Reserve assets created by the International Monetary Fund for countries to use in settling international payment obligations.

To consider how official reserve account transactions occur, look again at Table 33-2. The surplus in the U.S. capital account was \$344.9 billion. But the deficit in the U.S. current account was −\$360.1 billion, so the United States had a net deficit on the combined accounts (line 13) of −\$15.2 billion. In other words, the United States obtained less in foreign money in all its international transactions than it used. How is this deficiency made up? By our central bank drawing down its existing balances of foreign moneys, shown by the +\$15.2 billion in official transactions shown on line 14 in Table 33-2. There is a plus sign on line 14 because this represents an *inflow* of foreign exchange into our international transactions.

The balance (line 15) in Table 33-2 is zero, as it must be with double-entry bookkeeping. The U.S. balance of payments deficit is measured by the official transactions figure on line 14.

FIGURE 33-1

The Relationship Between the Current Account and the Capital Account

To some extent, the capital account is the mirror image of the current account. We can see this in the years since 1970. When the current account was in surplus, the capital account was in deficit. When the current account was in deficit, the capital account was in surplus. Indeed, virtually the only time foreigners can invest in America is when the current account is in deficit.

Sources: International Monetary Fund; *Economic Indicators.*

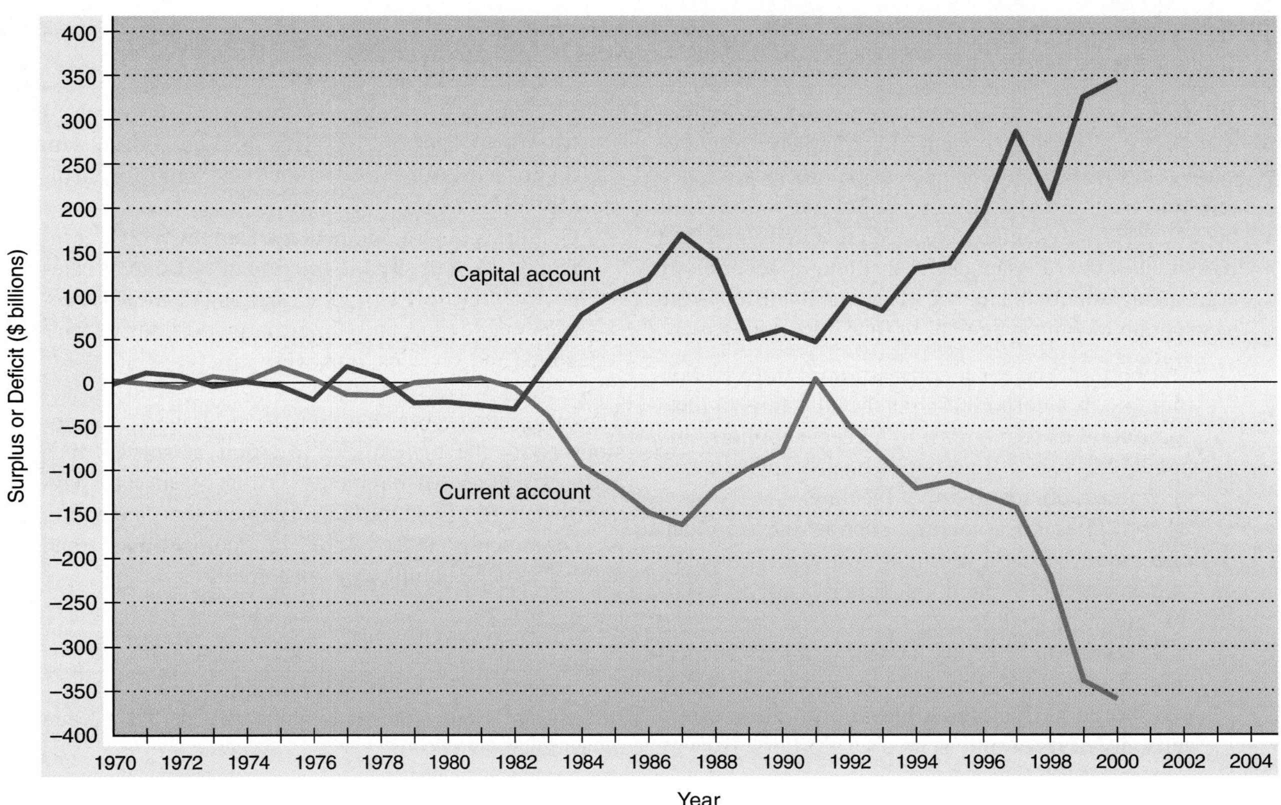

What Affects the Balance of Payments?

A major factor affecting any nation's balance of payments is its rate of inflation relative to that of its trading partners. Assume that the rates of inflation in the United States and in Japan are equal. Now suppose that all of a sudden, the U.S. inflation rate increases. The Japanese will find that U.S. products are becoming more expensive, and U.S. firms will export fewer of them to Japan. At the current exchange rate, U.S. residents will find Japanese products relatively cheaper, and they will import more. The converse will occur if the U.S. inflation rate suddenly falls relative to that of Japan. All other things held constant, whenever the U.S. rate of inflation exceeds that of its trading partners, we expect to see a larger deficit in the U.S. balance of trade and payments. Conversely, when the U.S. rate of inflation is less than that of its trading partners, other things being constant, we expect to see a smaller deficit in the U.S. balance of trade and payments.

Another important factor that sometimes influences a nation's balance of payments is its relative political stability. Political instability causes *capital flight.* Owners of capital in countries anticipating or experiencing political instability will often move assets to countries that are politically stable, such as the United States. Hence the U.S. capital account balance, and so its balance of payments, is likely to increase whenever political instability looms in other nations in the world.

POLICY EXAMPLE

Does "Competitiveness" Apply to Countries as Well as Corporations?

Although a nation's balance of payments bears similarities to the accounting system of a company, deficit or surplus measures in the balance of payments are much different from a corporation's bottom line—that is, its net of expenditures relative to receipts. Economist Paul Krugman of the Massachusetts Institute of Technology argues that a nation's balance of payments differs from a corporate income statement in four important ways:

1. The bottom line for a corporation is truly its bottom line. If a corporation persistently fails to meet commitments to pay its employees, suppliers, and bondholders, it will go out of business. Countries, in contrast, do not go out of business.
2. Bottom lines for a country, such as the merchandise trade balance, do not necessarily indicate "weakness" or "strength." A deficit is not necessarily "good" or "bad."
3. U.S. residents typically consume about 90 percent of the goods and services produced within U.S. borders. Even the largest corporation rarely sells any of its output to its own workers. By way of contrast, the "exports" of a company such as Microsoft Corporation—its sales to people who do not work for the company—account for virtually all its sales.
4. Countries do not compete the same way that companies do. A negligible fraction of Netscape's sales go to Microsoft Corporation, for instance. Countries may export and import large portions of their goods and services, however.

Thus we must be very cautious about drawing conclusions about the meaning of a deficit or surplus in a nation's balance of payments. Using balance of payments statistics to support an argument that one nation is economically more viable or "competitive" than another may be completely misguided.

For Critical Analysis

Under what circumstances might a nation find a trade deficit to be beneficial?

CONCEPTS IN BRIEF

- The balance of payments reflects the value of all transactions in international trade, including goods, services, financial assets, and gifts.
- The merchandise trade balance gives us the difference between exports and imports of tangible items. Merchandise trade transactions are represented by exports and imports of tangible items.
- Included in the current account along with merchandise trade are service exports and imports relating to commerce in intangible items, such as shipping, insurance, and tourist expenditures. The current account also includes income earned by foreign residents on U.S. investments and income earned by U.S. residents on foreign investments.
- Unilateral transfers involve international private gifts and federal government grants or gifts to foreign nations.
- When we add the balance of merchandise trade and the balance of services and take account of net unilateral transfers and net investment income, we come up with the balance on the current account, a summary statistic.

- There are also capital account transactions that relate to the buying and selling of financial and real assets. Foreign capital is always entering the United States, and U.S. capital is always flowing abroad. The difference is called the balance on capital account.
- Another type of balance of payments transaction concerns the official reserve assets of individual countries, or what is often simply called official transactions. By standard accounting convention, official transactions are exactly equal to a nation's balance of payments but opposite in sign.
- A nation's balance of payments can be affected by its relative rate of inflation and by its political stability relative to other nations.

DETERMINING FOREIGN EXCHANGE RATES

When you buy foreign products, such as a Japanese-made laptop computer, you have dollars with which to pay the Japanese manufacturer. The Japanese manufacturer, however, cannot pay workers in dollars. The workers are Japanese, they live in Japan, and they must have yen to buy goods and services in that country. There must therefore be some way of exchanging dollars for yen that the computer manufacturer will accept. That exchange occurs in a **foreign exchange market,** which in this case specializes in exchanging yen and dollars. (When you obtain foreign currencies at a bank or an airport currency exchange, you are participating in the foreign exchange market.)

Foreign exchange market
A market in which households, firms, and governments buy and sell national currencies.

The particular **exchange rate** between yen and dollars that prevails—the dollar price of the yen—depends on the current demand for and supply of yen and dollars. In a sense, then, our analysis of the exchange rate between dollars and yen will be familiar, for we have used supply and demand throughout this book. If it costs you 1 cent to buy 1 yen, that is the foreign exchange rate determined by the current demand for and supply of yen in the foreign exchange market. The Japanese person going to the foreign exchange market would need 100 yen to buy 1 dollar.

Exchange rate
The price of one nation's currency in terms of the currency of another country.

We will continue our example in which the only two countries in the world are Japan and the United States. Now let's consider what determines the demand for and supply of foreign currency in the foreign exchange market.

Demand for and Supply of Foreign Currency

You wish to purchase a Japanese-made laptop computer direct from the manufacturer. To do so, you must have Japanese yen. You go to the foreign exchange market (or your U.S. bank). Your desire to buy the Japanese laptop computer therefore causes you to offer (supply) dollars to the foreign exchange market. Your demand for Japanese yen is equivalent to your supply of U.S. dollars to the foreign exchange market.

> Every U.S. transaction involving the importation of foreign goods constitutes a supply of dollars and a demand for some foreign currency, and the opposite is true for export transactions.

In this case, the import transaction constitutes a demand for Japanese yen.

In our example, we will assume that only two goods are being traded, Japanese laptop computers and U.S. microprocessors. The U.S. demand for Japanese laptop computers creates a supply of dollars and demand for yen in the foreign exchange market. Similarly, the Japanese demand for U.S. microprocessors creates a supply of yen and a demand for dollars in the foreign exchange market. Under a system of **flexible exchange rates,** the supply of and demand for dollars and yen in the foreign exchange market will determine the

Flexible exchange rates
Exchange rates that are allowed to fluctuate in the open market in response to changes in supply and demand. Sometimes called *floating exchange rates.*

equilibrium foreign exchange rate. The equilibrium exchange rate will tell us how many yen a dollar can be exchanged for—that is, the dollar price of yen—or how many dollars (or fractions of a dollar) a yen can be exchange for—the yen price of dollars.

The Equilibrium Foreign Exchange Rate

To determine the equilibrium foreign exchange rate, we have to find out what determines the demand for and supply of foreign exchange. We will ignore for the moment any speculative aspect of buying foreign exchange. That is, we assume that there are no individuals who wish to buy yen simply because they think that their price will go up in the future.

Click here for recent data on the exchange value of the U.S. dollar relative to the major currencies of the world.

The idea of an exchange rate is no different from the idea of paying a certain price for something you want to buy. If you like coffee, you know you have to pay about 75 cents a cup. If the price went up to $2.50, you would probably buy fewer cups. If the price went down to 5 cents, you might buy more. In other words, the demand curve for cups of coffee, expressed in terms of dollars, slopes downward following the law of demand. The demand curve for yen slopes downward also, and we will see why.

Let's think more closely about the demand schedule for yen. Let's say that it costs you 1 cent to purchase 1 yen; that is the exchange rate between dollars and yen. If tomorrow you had to pay $1\frac{1}{4}$ cents ($.0125) for the same yen, the exchange rate would have changed. Looking at such an increase with respect to the yen, we would say that there has been an **appreciation** in the value of the yen in the foreign exchange market. But another way to view this increase in the value of the yen is to say that there has been a **depreciation** in the value of the dollar in the foreign exchange market. The dollar used to buy 100 yen; tomorrow, the dollar will be able to buy only 80 yen at a price of $1\frac{1}{4}$ cents per yen. If the dollar price of yen rises, you will probably demand fewer yen. Why? The answer lies in looking at the reason you and others demand yen in the first place.

Appreciation 
An increase in the exchange value of one nation's currency in terms of the currency of another nation.

Depreciation 
A decrease in the exchange value of one nation's currency in terms of the currency of another nation.

Appreciation and Depreciation of Japanese Yen. Recall that in our example, you and others demand yen to buy Japanese laptop computers. The demand curve for Japanese laptop computers, we will assume, follows the law of demand and therefore slopes downward. If it costs more U.S. dollars to buy the same quantity of Japanese laptop computers, presumably you and other U.S. residents will not buy the same quantity; your quantity demanded will be less. We say that your demand for Japanese yen is *derived from* your demand for Japanese laptop computers. In panel (a) of Figure 33-2, we present the hypothetical demand schedule for Japanese laptop computers by a representative set of U.S. consumers during a typical week. In panel (b), we show graphically the U.S. demand curve for Japanese yen in terms of U.S. dollars taken from panel (a).

An Example of Derived Demand. Let us assume that the price of a Japanese laptop computer in Japan is 100,000 yen. Given that price, we can find the number of yen required to purchase up to 500 Japanese laptop computers. That information is given in panel (c) of Figure 33-2. If one laptop computer requires 100,000 yen, 500 laptop computers require 50 million yen. Now we have enough information to determine the derived demand curve for Japanese yen. If 1 yen costs 1 cent, a laptop computer would cost $1,000 (100,000 yen per computer $\times$ 1 cent per yen = $1,000 per computer). At $1,000 per computer, the representative group of U.S. consumers would, we see from panel (a) of Figure 33-2, demand 500 laptop computers.

From panel (c), we see that 50 million yen would be demanded to buy the 500 laptop computers. We show this quantity demanded in panel (d). In panel (e), we draw the derived demand curve for yen. Now consider what happens if the price of yen goes up to $1\frac{1}{4}$ cents

Panel (a)
Demand Schedule for Japanese Laptop Computers in the United States per Week

Price per Unit	Quantity Demanded
$1,500	100
1,250	300
1,000	500
750	700

Panel (b)
American Demand Curve for Japanese Laptop Computers

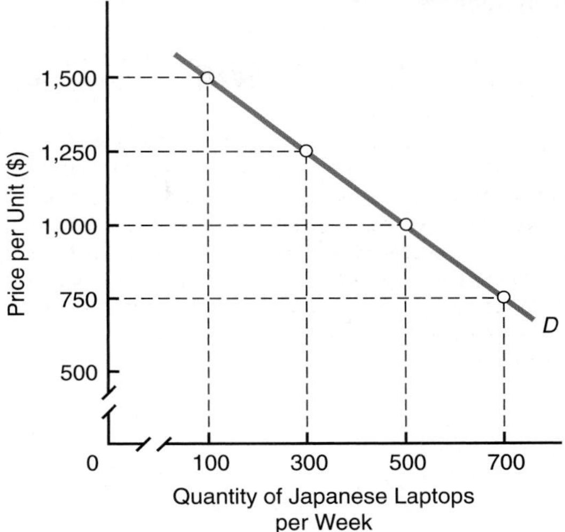

Panel (c)
Yen Required to Purchase Quantity Demanded (at P = 100,000 yen per computer)

Quantity Demanded	Yen Required (millions)
100	10
300	30
500	50
700	70

Panel (d)
Derived Demand Schedule for Yen in the United States with Which to Pay for Imports of Laptops

Dollar Price of One Yen	Dollar Price of Computers	Quantity of Computers Demanded	Quantity of Yen Demanded per Week (millions)
$ .0150	$1,500	100	10
.0125	1,250	300	30
.0100	1,000	500	50
.0075	750	700	70

Panel (e)
American Derived Demand for Yen

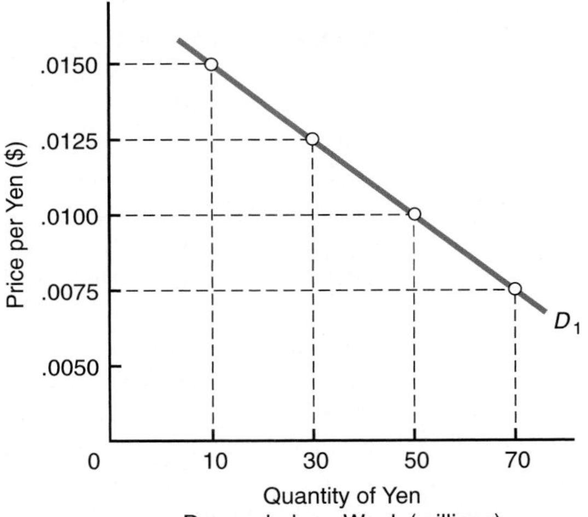

FIGURE 33-2

Deriving the Demand for Yen

In panel (a), we show the demand schedule for Japanese laptop computers in the United States, expressed in terms of dollars per computer. In panel (b), we show the demand curve, *D,* which slopes downward. In panel (c), we show the number of yens required to purchase up to 700 laptop computers. If the price per laptop computer in Japan is 100,000 yen, we can now find the quantity of yen needed to pay for the various quantities demanded. In panel (d), we see the derived demand for yen in the United States in order to purchase the various quantities of computers given in panel (a). The resultant demand curve, D_1, is shown in panel (e). This is the American derived demand for yen.

FIGURE 33-3
The Supply of Japanese Yen
If the market price of a U.S.-produced microprocessor is $200, then at an exchange rate of $.0100 per yen (1 cent per yen), the price of the microprocessor to a Japanese consumer is 20,000 yen. If the exchange rate rises to $.0125 per yen, the Japanese price of the microprocessor falls to 16,000 yen. This induces an increase in the quantity of microprocessors demanded by Japanese consumers and consequently an increase in the quantity of yen supplied in exchange for dollars in the foreign exchange market. By contrast, if the exchange rate falls to $.0075 per yen, the Japanese price of the microprocessor rises to 26,667 yen. This causes a decrease in the quantity of microprocessors demanded by Japanese consumers. As a result, there is a decline in the quantity of yen supplied in exchange for dollars in the foreign exchange market.

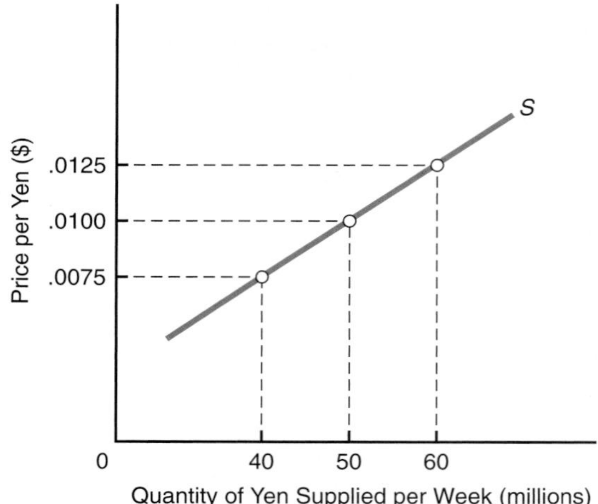

($.0125). A Japanese laptop computer priced at 100,000 yen in Japan would now cost $1,250. From panel (a), we see that at $1,250 per computer, 300 laptop computers will be imported from Japan into the United States by our representative group of U.S. consumers. From panel (c), we see that 300 computers would require 30 million yen to be purchased; thus in panels (d) and (e), we see that at a price of $1\frac{1}{4}$ cents per yen, the quantity demanded will be 30 million yen.

We continue similar calculations all the way up to a price of $1\frac{1}{2}$ cents ($.0150) per yen. At that price, a Japanese laptop computer costing 100,000 yen in Japan would cost $1,500, and our representative U.S. consumers would import only 100 laptop computers.

Downward-Sloping Derived Demand. As can be expected, as the price of yen rises, the quantity demanded will fall. The only difference here from the standard demand analysis developed in Chapter 3 and used throughout this text is that the demand for yen is derived from the demand for a final product—Japanese laptop computers in our example.

Supply of Japanese Yen. Assume that Japanese laptop manufacturers buy U.S. microprocessors. The supply of Japanese yen is a derived supply in that it is derived from the Japanese demand for U.S. microprocessors. We could go through an example similar to the one for laptop computers to come up with a supply schedule of Japanese yen in Japan. It slopes upward. Obviously, the Japanese want dollars to purchase U.S. goods. Japanese residents will be willing to supply more yen when the dollar price of yen goes up, because they can then buy more U.S. goods with the same quantity of yen. That is, the yen would be worth more in exchange for U.S. goods than when the dollar price for yen was lower.

An Example. Let's take an example. Suppose a U.S.-produced microprocessor costs $200. If the exchange rate is 1 cent per one yen, a Japanese resident will have to come up with 20,000 yen (= $200 at $.0100 per yen) to buy one microprocessor. If, however, the exchange rate goes up to $1\frac{1}{4}$ cents for yen, a Japanese resident must come up with only 16,000 yen (= $200 at $.0125 per yen) to buy a U.S. microprocessor. At a lower price (in yen) of U.S. microprocessors, the Japanese will demand a larger quantity. In other words, as the price of Japanese yen goes up in terms of dollars, the quantity of U.S. microprocessors demanded will go up, and hence the quantity of Japanese yen supplied will go up.

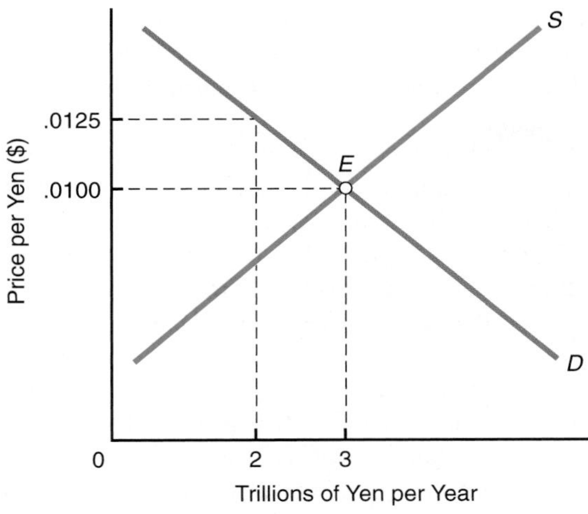

FIGURE 33-4

Total Demand for and Supply of Japanese Yen

The market supply curve for Japanese yen results from the total demand for U.S. microprocessors. The demand curve, *D,* slopes downward like most demand curves, and the supply curve *S,* slopes upward. The foreign exchange price, or the U.S. dollar price of yen, is given on the vertical axis. The number of yen is represented on the horizontal axis. If the foreign exchange rate is \$.0125—that is, if it takes $1\frac{1}{4}$ cents to buy 1 yen—Americans will demand 2 trillion yen. The equilibrium exchange rate is at the intersection of *D* and *S.* The equilibrium exchange rate is \$.0100 (1 cent). At this point, 3 trillion yen are both demanded and supplied each year.

Therefore, the supply schedule of yen, which is derived from the Japanese demand for U.S. goods, will slope upward.*

We could easily work through a detailed numerical example to show that the supply curve of Japanese yen slopes upward. Rather than do that, we will simply draw it as upward-sloping in Figure 33-3 on the previous page. In our hypothetical example, assuming that there are only representative groups of laptop computer consumers in the United States and microprocessor consumers in Japan, the equilibrium exchange rate will be set at 1 cent per yen, or 100 yen to 1 dollar.

Total Demand for and Supply of Japanese Yen. Let us now look at the total demand for and supply of Japanese yen. We take all demanders of Japanese laptop computer and U.S. microprocessors and put their demands for and supplies of yen together into one diagram. Thus we are showing the total demand for and total supply of Japanese yen. The horizontal axis in Figure 33-4 represents a quantity of foreign exchange—the number of yen per year. The vertical axis represents the exchange rate—the price of foreign currency (yen) expressed in dollars (per yen). The foreign currency price of \$.0125 per yen means it will cost you $1\frac{1}{4}$ cents to buy 1 yen. At the foreign currency price of \$.0100 per yen, you know that it will cost you 1 cent to buy 1 yen. The equilibrium is again established at 1 cent for 1 yen.

This equilibrium is not established because U.S. residents like to buy yen or because the Japanese like to buy dollars. Rather, the equilibrium exchange rate depends on how many microprocessors the Japanese want and how many Japanese laptop computers U.S. residents want (given their respective incomes, their tastes, and the relative price of laptop computers and microprocessors).†

*Actually, the supply schedule of foreign currency will be upward-sloping if we assume that the demand for U.S. imported microprocessors on the part of the Japanese is price elastic. If the demand schedule for microprocessors is inelastic, the supply schedule will be negatively sloped. In the case of unit elasticity of demand, the supply schedule for yen will be a vertical line. Throughout the rest of this chapter, we will assume that demand is price elastic. Remember that the price elasticity of demand tells us whether or not total expenditures by microprocessor purchasers in Japan will rise or fall when the Japanese yen drops in value. In the long run, it is quite realistic to think that the price elasticity of demand for imports is numerically greater than 1 anyway.

†Remember that we are dealing with a two-country world in which we are considering only the exchange of U.S. microprocessors and Japanese laptop computers. In the real world, more than just goods and services are exchanged among countries. Some U.S. residents buy Japanese financial assets; some Japanese residents buy U.S. financial assets. We are ignoring such transactions for the moment.

A Shift in Demand. Assume that a successful advertising campaign by U.S. computer importers has caused U.S. demand for Japanese laptop computers to rise. U.S. residents demand more laptop computers at all prices. Their demand curve for Japanese laptop computers has shifted outward to the right.

The increased demand for Japanese laptop computers can be translated into an increased demand for yen. All U.S. residents clamoring for laptop computers will supply more dollars to the foreign exchange market while demanding more Japanese yen to pay for the computers. Figure 33-5 presents a new demand schedule, D_2, for Japanese yen; this demand schedule is to the right of the original demand schedule. If the Japanese do not change their desire for U.S. microprocessors, the supply schedule for Japanese yen will remain stable.

A new equilibrium will be established at a higher exchange rate. In our particular example, the new equilibrium is established at an exchange rate of $.0120 per yen. It now takes 1.2 cents to buy 1 Japanese yen, whereas formerly it took 1 cent. This will be translated into an increase in the price of Japanese laptop computers to U.S. residents and as a decrease in the price of U.S. microprocessors to the Japanese. For example, a Japanese laptop computer priced at 100,000 yen that sold for $1,000 in the United States will now be priced at $1,200. Conversely, a U.S. microprocessor priced at $50 that previously sold for 5,000 yen in Japan will now sell for 4,167 yen.

A Shift in Supply. We just assumed that the U.S. demand for Japanese laptop computers had shifted due to a successful ad compaign. Because the demand for Japanese yen is a derived demand by U.S. residents for laptop computers, this is translated into a shift in the demand curve for yen. As an alternative exercise, we might assume that the supply curve of Japanese yen shifts outward to the right. Such a supply shift could occur for many reasons, one of which is a relative rise in the Japanese price level. For example, if the price of all Japanese-manufactured computer components went up 100 percent in yen, U.S. microprocessors would become relatively cheaper. That would mean that Japanese residents would want to buy more U.S. microprocessors. But remember that when they want to buy more U.S. microprocessors, they supply more yen to the foreign exchange market.

Thus we see in Figure 33-6 that the supply curve of Japanese yen moves from S to S_1. In the absence of restrictions—that is, in a system of flexible exchange rates—the new

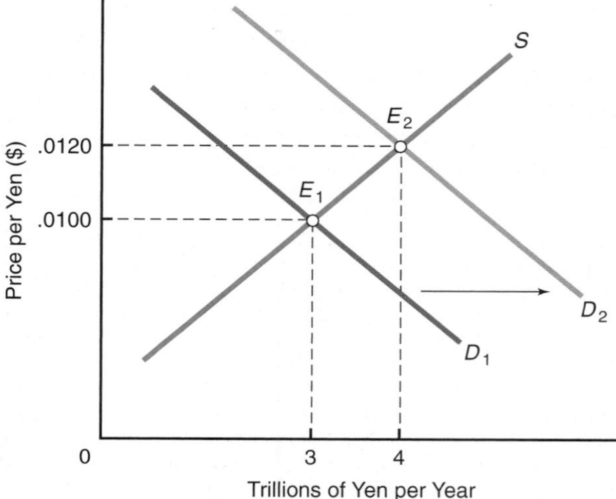

FIGURE 33-5

A Shift in the Demand Schedule

The demand schedule for Japanese laptop computers shifts to the right, causing the derived demand schedule for yen to shift to the right also. We have shown this as a shift from D_1 to D_2. We have assumed that the Japanese supply schedule for yen has remained stable—that is, Japanese demand for American microprocessors has remained constant. The old equilibrium foreign exchange rate was $.0100 (1 cent). The new equilibrium exchange rate will be E_2; it will now cost $.0120 (1.2 cents) to buy 1 yen. The higher price of yen will be translated into a higher U.S. dollar price for Japanese laptop computers and a lower Japanese yen price for American microprocessors.

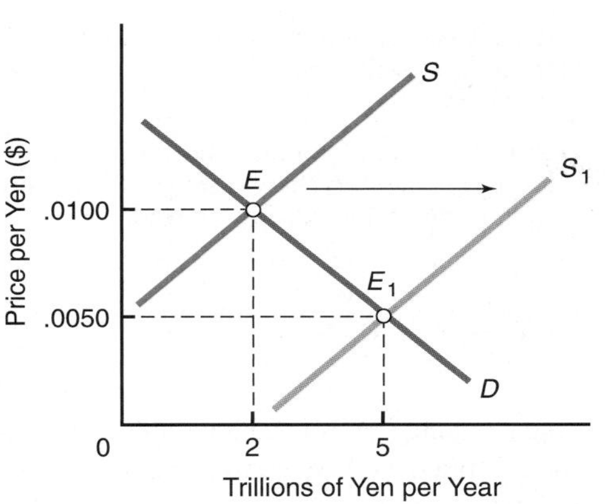

FIGURE 33-6

A Shift in the Supply of Japanese Yen

There has been a shift in the supply curve for Japanese yen. The new equilibrium will occur at E_1, meaning that $.0050 ($\frac{1}{2}$ cent), rather than $.0100 (1 cent), will now buy 1 yen. After the exchange rate adjustment, the amount of yen demanded and supplied will increase to 5 trillion per year.

equilibrium exchange rate will be 1 yen equals $.0050, or $\frac{1}{2}$ cent equals 1 yen. The quantity of yen demanded and supplied will increase from 2 trillion per year to 5 trillion per year. We say, then, that in a flexible international exchange rate system, shifts in the demand for and supply of foreign currencies will cause changes in the equilibrium foreign exchange rates. Those rates will remain in effect until supply or demand shifts.

Market Determinants of Exchange Rates

The foreign exchange market is affected by many other variables in addition to changes in relative price levels, including the following:

1. *Changes in real interest rates.* If the United States interest rate, corrected for people's expectations of inflation, abruptly increases relative to the rest of the world, international investors elsewhere will increase their demand for dollar-denominated assets, thereby increasing the demand for dollars in foreign exchange markets. An increased demand for dollars in foreign exchange markets, other things held constant, will cause the dollar to appreciate and other currencies to depreciate.
2. *Changes in productivity.* Whenever one country's productivity increases relative to another's, the former country will become more price competitive in world markets. At lower prices, the quantity of its exports demanded will increase. Thus there will be an increase in the demand for its currency.
3. *Changes in consumer preferences.* If Germany's citizens suddenly develop a taste for U.S.-made automobiles, this will increase the derived demand for U.S. dollars in foreign exchange markets.
4. *Perceptions of economic stability.* As already mentioned, if the United States looks economically and politically more stable relative to other countries, more foreign residents will want to put their savings into U.S. assets than in their own domestic assets. This will increase the demand for dollars.

CONCEPTS IN BRIEF

- The foreign exchange rate is the rate at which one country's currency can be exchanged for another's.
- The demand for foreign exchange is a derived demand; it is derived from the demand for foreign goods and services (and financial assets). The supply of foreign exchange is derived from foreign residents' demands for domestic goods and services.

- The demand curve of foreign exchange slopes downward, and the supply curve of foreign exchange slopes upward. The equilibrium foreign exchange role occurs at the intersection of the demand and supply curves for a currency.
- A shift in the demand for foreign goods will result in a shift in the demand for foreign exchange, thereby changing the equilibrium foreign exchange rate. A shift in the supply of foreign currency will also cause a change in the equilibrium exchange rate.

THE GOLD STANDARD AND THE INTERNATIONAL MONETARY FUND

The current system of more or less freely floating exchange rates is a recent development. We have had, in the past, periods of a gold standard, fixed exchange rates under the International Monetary Fund, and variants of these two.

The Gold Standard

Until the 1930s, many nations were on a gold standard. The value of their domestic currency was tied directly to gold. Nations operating under this gold standard agreed to redeem their currencies for a fixed amount of gold at the request of any holder of that currency. Although gold was not necessarily the means of exchange for world trade, it was the unit to which all currencies under the gold standard were pegged. And because all currencies in the system were linked to gold, exchange rates between those currencies were fixed. Indeed, the gold standard has been offered as the prototype of a fixed exchange rate system. The heyday of the gold standard was from about 1870 to 1914.

There was (and always is) a relationship between the balance of payments and changes in domestic money supplies throughout the world. Under a gold standard, the international financial market reached equilibrium through the effect of gold flows on each country's money supply. When a nation suffered a deficit in its balance of payments, more gold would flow out than in. Because the domestic money supply was based on gold, an outflow of gold to foreign residents caused an automatic reduction in the domestic money supply. This caused several things to happen. Interest rates rose, thereby attracting foreign capital and reducing any deficit in the balance of payments. At the same time, the reduction in the money supply was equivalent to a restrictive monetary policy, which caused national output and prices to fall. Imports were discouraged and exports were encouraged, thereby again improving the balance of payments.

Two problems plagued the gold standard. One was that by varying the value of its currency in response to changes in the quantity of gold, a nation gave up control of its domestic monetary policy. Another was that the world's commerce was at the mercy of gold discoveries. Throughout history, each time new veins of gold were found, desired expenditures on goods and services increased. If production of goods and services failed to increase, however, prices of goods and services increased, so inflation resulted.

International Monetary Fund (IMF) An international agency, founded to administer the Bretton Woods agreement and to lend to member countries that experienced significant balance of payments deficits, that now functions primarily as a lender of last resort for national governments.

Bretton Woods and the International Monetary Fund

In 1944, as World War II was ending, representatives from the world's capitalist countries met in Bretton Woods, New Hampshire, to create a new international payment system to replace the gold standard, which had collapsed during the 1930s. The Bretton Woods Agreement Act was signed on July 31, 1945, by President Harry Truman. It created a new permanent institution, the **International Monetary Fund (IMF),** to administer the agreement and to lend to member countries that were experiencing significant balance of payments deficits. The arrangements thus provided are now called the old IMF system or the Bretton Woods system.

Member governments were obligated to intervene to maintain the value of their currencies in foreign exchange markets within 1 percent of the declared **par value**—the officially determined value. The United States, which owned most of the world's gold stock, was similarly obligated to maintain gold prices within a 1 percent margin of the official rate of $35 an ounce. Except for a transitional arrangement permitting a onetime adjustment of up to 10 percent in par value, members could alter exchange rates thereafter only with the approval of the IMF.

Par value 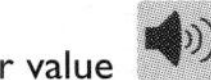
The officially determined value of a currency.

On August 15, 1971, President Richard Nixon suspended the convertibility of the dollar into gold. On December 18, 1971, the United States officially devalued the dollar—that is, lowered its official value—relative to the currencies of 14 major industrial nations. Finally, on March 16, 1973, the finance ministers of the European Economic Community (now the European Union) announced that they would let their currencies float against the dollar, something Japan had already begun doing with its yen. Since 1973, the United States and most other trading countries have had either freely floating exchange rates or managed ("dirty") floating exchange rates, in which their governments or central banks intervene from time to time to try to influence market exchange rates.

FIXED VERSUS FLOATING EXCHANGE RATES

The United States went off the Bretton Woods system of fixed exchange rates in 1973. As Figure 33-7 indicates, many other nations of the world have been less willing to permit the values of their currencies to vary in the foreign exchange markets.

Fixing the Exchange Rate

How did nations fix their exchange rates in years past? How do many countries accomplish this today? Figure 33-8 on the next page shows the market for baht, the currency of Thailand. At the initial equilibrium point E_1, U.S. residents had to give up $0.40 to obtain 1 baht. Suppose now that there is an increase in the supply of baht for dollars, perhaps because Thai residents wish to buy more U.S. goods. Other things being equal, the result would be a movement to point E_2 in Figure 33-8. The dollar value of the baht would fall to $0.30.

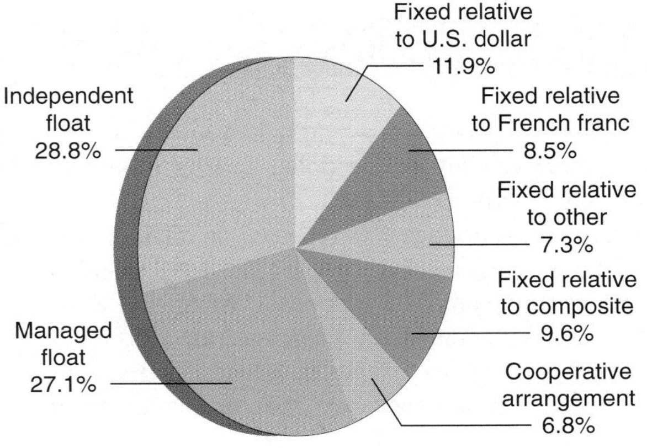

FIGURE 33-7
Current Foreign Exchange Rate Arrangements
Currently, 56 percent of the member nations of the International Monetary Fund have an independent float or managed float exchange rate arrangement. Among countries with a fixed exchange rate, nearly one in three uses a fixed U.S. dollar exchange rate. Fixing the exchange rate relative to a composite or basket of currencies is the next most common arrangement.
Source: International Monetary Fund.

FIGURE 33-8

A Fixed Exchange Rate

This figure illustrates how the Bank of Thailand could fix the dollar-baht exchange rate in the face of an increase in the supply of baht caused by a rise in the demand for U.S. goods by Thai residents. In the absence of any action by the Bank of Thailand, the result would be a movement from point E_1 to point E_2. The dollar value of the baht would fall from $0.40 to $0.30. The Bank of Thailand can prevent this exchange rate change by purchasing baht with dollars in the foreign exchange market, thereby raising the demand for baht. At the new equilibrium point E_3, the baht's value remains at $0.40.

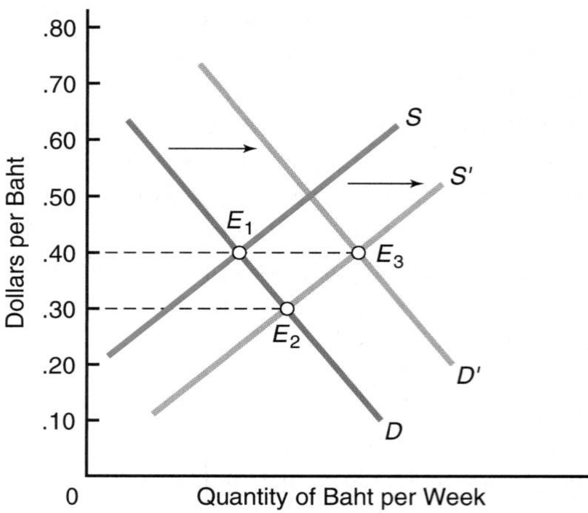

To prevent a baht depreciation from occurring, however, the Bank of Thailand, the central bank, could increase the demand for baht in the foreign exchange market by purchasing baht with dollars. The Bank of Thailand can do this using dollars that it had on hand as part of its *foreign exchange reserves.* All central banks hold reserves of foreign currencies. Because the U.S. dollar is a key international currency, the Bank of Thailand and other central banks typically hold billions of dollars in reserve so that they can, if they wish, make transactions such as the one in this example. Note that a sufficiently large purchase of baht could, as shown in Figure 33-8, cause the demand curve to shift rightward to achieve the new equilibrium point E_3, at which the baht's value remains at $0.40. Provided that it has enough dollar reserves on hand, the Bank of Thailand could maintain—effectively fix—the exchange rate in the face of the sudden fall in the demand for baht.

This is the manner in which the Bank of Thailand fixed the dollar-baht exchange rate until 1997. This basic approach—varying the amount of the national currency demanded at any given exchange rate in foreign exchange markets when necessary—is also the way that *any* central bank seeks to keep its nation's currency value unchanged in light of changing market forces.

Central banks can keep exchange rates fixed as long as they have enough foreign exchange reserves available to deal with potentially long-lasting changes in the demand for or supply of their nation's currency.

INTERNATIONAL POLICY EXAMPLE

Can Foreign Exchange Rates Be Fixed Forever?

Trying to keep the exchange rate fixed in the face of foreign exchange market volatility can be a difficult policy to pursue. Consider Thailand's experience. At the beginning of 1997, the Bank of Thailand was holding $40 billion in foreign exchange reserves. Within 10 months, those reserves had fallen to $3 billion. Whatever the Bank of Thailand promised about not devaluing, it no longer had credibility. Not surprisingly, the baht's value relative to the dollar fell by more than 25 percent in July 1997 alone.

The Thai experience was repeated on a larger scale throughout Southeast Asia in 1997 and 1998 as efforts by the central banks of Indonesia, Malaysia, South Korea, and Vietnam to fix exchange rates ultimately collapsed, leading to sizable devaluations. Even the previously stalwart exchange rate arrangements of

Singapore, Taiwan, and Hong Kong became increasingly less credible. These nations learned an old lesson: Trying to protect residents from foreign exchange risks works only as long as foreign exchange market traders believe that central banks have the financial wherewithal to keep exchange rates unchanged. Otherwise, a fixed exchange rate policy can ultimately prove unsustainable.

For Critical Analysis

Why do you think governments attempt to maintain the foreign exchange value of their domestic currencies?

Pros and Cons of a Fixed Exchange Rate 

Why might a nation such as Thailand wish to keep the value of its currency from fluctuating? One reason is that changes in the exchange rate can affect the market values of assets that are denominated in foreign currencies. This can increase the financial risks that a nation's residents face, thereby forcing them to incur costs to avoid these risks.

Foreign Exchange Risk. The possibility that variations in the market value of assets can take place as a result of changes in the value of a nation's currency is called the **foreign exchange risk** that residents of a country face because their nation's currency value can vary. For instance, if companies in Thailand had many loans denominated in dollars but earned nearly all their revenues in baht from sales within Thailand, a decline in the dollar value of the baht would mean that Thai companies would have to allocate a larger portion of their earnings to make the same *dollar* loan payments as before. Thus a fall in the baht's value would increase the operating costs of these companies, thereby reducing their profitability and raising the likelihood of eventual bankruptcy.

Foreign exchange risk 
The possibility that changes in the value of a nation's currency will result in variations in market values of assets.

Limiting foreign exchange risk is a classic rationale for adopting a fixed exchange rate. Nevertheless, a country's residents are not defenseless against foreign exchange risk. They can **hedge** against such risk, meaning that they can adopt strategies intended to offset the risk arising from exchange rate variations. For example, a company in Thailand that has significant euro earnings from sales in Germany but sizable loans from U.S. investors could arrange to convert its euro earnings into dollars via special types of foreign exchange contracts called *currency swaps.* The Thai company could thereby avoid holdings of baht and shield itself—*hedge*—against variations in the baht's value.

Hedge 
A financial strategy that reduces the chance of suffering losses arising from foreign exchange risk.

The Exchange Rate as a Shock Absorber. If fixing the exchange rate limits foreign exchange risk, why do so many nations allow the exchange rates to float? The answer must be that there are potential drawbacks associated with fixing exchange rates. One is that exchange rate variations can actually perform a valuable service for a nation's economy. Consider a situation in which residents of a nation speak only their own nation's language, which is so difficult that hardly anyone else in the world takes the trouble to learn it. As a result, the country's residents are very *immobile:* They cannot trade their labor skills outside of their own nation's borders.

Now think about what happens if this nation chooses to fix its exchange rate. Imagine a situation in which other countries begin to sell products that are close substitutes for the products its people specialize in producing, causing a sizable drop in worldwide demand for the nation's goods. Over a short-run period in which prices and wages cannot adjust, the result will be a sharp decline in production of goods and services, a fall-off in national income, and higher unemployment. Contrast this situation with one in which the exchange rate floats. In this case, a sizable decline in outside demand for the nation's products will cause it to experience a trade deficit, which will lead to a significant drop in the demand for the nation's currency. As a result, the nation's currency will experience a sizable depreciation, making the goods that the nation offers to sell abroad much less expensive in other countries. People abroad who continue to consume the nation's products will increase their purchases, and the nation's exports will increase. Its production will begin to recover somewhat, as will its residents' incomes. Unemployment will begin to fall

This example illustrates how exchange rate variations can be beneficial, especially if a nation's residents are relatively immobile. It can be much more difficult, for example, for a Polish resident who has never studied Portuguese to make a move to Lisbon, even if she is highly qualified for available jobs there. If many residents of Poland face similar linguistic or cultural barriers, Poland could be better off with a floating exchange rate even if its residents must incur significant costs hedging against foreign exchange risk as a result.

Splitting the Difference: Dirty Floats and Target Zones

In recent years, national policymakers have tried to soften the choice of either adopting a fixed exchange rate or allowing exchange rates full flexibility in the foreign exchange markets by "splitting the difference" between the two extremes.

Dirty float
Active management of a floating exchange rate on the part of a country's government, often in cooperation with other nations.

A Dirty Float. One way to split the difference is to let exchange rates float most of the time but "manage" exchange rate movements part of the time. U.S. policymakers have occasionally engaged in what is called a **dirty float,** the management of flexible exchange rates. The management of flexible exchange rates has usually come about through international policy cooperation. For example, the Group of Five (G-5) nations—France, Germany, Japan, the United Kingdom, and the United States—and the Group of Seven (G-7) nations—the G-5 nations plus Italy and Canada—have for some time shared information on their economic policy objectives and procedures. They do this through regular meetings between economic policy secretaries, ministers, and staff members. One of their principal objectives has been to "smooth out" foreign exchange rates.

Is it possible for these groups to "manage" foreign exchange rates? Some economists do not think so. For example, economists Michael Bordo and Anna Schwartz studied the foreign exchange intervention actions coordinated by the Federal Reserve and the U.S. Treasury during the second half of the 1980s. Besides showing that such interventions were sporadic and variable, Bordo and Schwartz came to an even more compelling conclusion: Exchange rate interventions were trivial relative to the total trading of foreign exchange on a daily basis. For example, in April 1989, total foreign exchange trading amounted to \$129 billion per day, yet the American central bank purchased only \$100 million in deutsche marks and yen during that entire month (and did so on a single day). For all of 1989, Fed purchases of marks and yen were only \$17.7 billion, or the equivalent of less than 13 percent of the amount of an average day's trading in April of that year. Their conclusion is that neither the U.S. central bank nor the central banks of the other G-7 nations can influence exchange rates in the long run.

Crawling peg
An exchange rate arrangement in which a country pegs the value of its currency to the exchange value of another nation's currency but allows the par value to change at regular intervals.

Crawling Pegs. Another approach to splitting the difference between fixed and floating exchange rates is called a **crawling peg.** This is an automatically adjusting target for the value of a nation's currency. For instance, a central bank might announce that it wants the value of its currency relative to the U.S. dollar to decline at an annual rate of 5 percent, a rate of depreciation that it feels is consistent with long-run market forces. The central bank would then try to buy or sell foreign exchange reserves in sufficient quantities to be sure that the currency depreciation takes place gradually, thereby reducing the foreign exchange risk faced by the nation's residents.

In this way, a crawling peg functions like a floating exchange rate in the sense that the exchange rate can change over time. But it is like a fixed exchange rate in the sense that the central bank always tries to keep the exchange rate close to a target value. In this way, a crawling peg has elements of both kinds of exchange rate systems.

Target Zones. A third way to try to split the difference between fixed and floating exchange rates is to adopt an exchange rate **target zone.** Under this policy, a central bank announces that there are specific upper and lower *bands,* or limits, for permissible values for the exchange rate. Within those limits, which define the exchange rate target zone, the central bank permits the exchange rate to move flexibly. The central bank commits itself, however, to intervene in the foreign exchange markets to ensure that its nation's currency value will not rise above the upper band or fall below the lower band. For instance, if the exchange rate approaches the upper band, the central bank must sell foreign exchange reserves in sufficient quantities to prevent additional depreciation of its nation's currency. If the exchange rate approaches the lower band, the central bank must purchase sufficient amounts of foreign exchange reserves to halt any further currency appreciation.

Target zone

A range of permitted exchange rate variations between upper and lower exchange rate bands that a central bank defends by selling or buying foreign exchange reserves.

Starting in 1999, officials from the European Union attempted to get the United States, Japan, and several other countries' governments to agree to target zones for the exchange rate between the newly created euro and the dollar, yen, and some other currencies. Officials in the United States were not in favor. So far no target zones have been created, and the euro has floated freely—mostly downward.

CONCEPTS IN BRIEF

- The International Monetary Fund was developed after World War II as an institution to maintain fixed exchange rates in the world. Since 1973, however, fixed exchange rates have disappeared in most major trading countries. For these nations, exchange rates are largely determined by the forces of demand and supply in foreign exchange markets.
- Many other nations, however, have tried to fix their exchange rates, with varying degrees of success. Although fixing the exchange rate helps protect a nation's residents from foreign exchange risk, this policy makes less mobile residents susceptible to greater volatility in income and employment. It can also expose the central bank to sporadic currency crises arising from unpredictable changes in world capital flows.
- Countries have experimented with exchange rate systems between the extremes of fixed and floating exchange rates. Under a dirty float, a central bank permits the value of its nation's currency to float in foreign exchange markets but intervenes from time to time to influence the exchange rate. Under a crawling peg, a central bank tries to push its nation's currency value in a desired direction. Pursuing a target zone policy, a central bank aims to keep the exchange rate between upper and lower bands, intervening only when the exchange rate approaches either limit.

Making Foreign Exchange Markets More Efficient

The buying and selling of foreign exchange can involve considerable transaction costs. This is particularly true for companies that do not engage in large orders. The Internet has allowed for increased efficiency in this market, at least measured by real-time access and lower implicit commission rates for such transactions.

Back in 1993, a company called E-FOREX was founded to take advantage of Internet technology to develop a new marketplace for foreign exchange. In October 1995, E-FOREX completed its first Internet-based foreign exchange trade. Initially, E-FOREX was conceived as an on-line brokerage company, similar to E*Trade for stocks. Starting in 1996, though, E-FOREX began to license its Internet platforms to other financial institutions. Banks, brokers, and asset managers, for companies, pension plans, and governments, are using E-FOREX to trade today.

Consider a client that wishes to convert U.S. dollars to pay a 13 million yen invoice from its Japanese parts supplier. Even though a foreign exchange trading company would charge only a $50 commission on such a trade, it would also impose a large "spread" between the buying and selling price of yen. E-FOREX charges no commission but makes its profit on a small spread. In this transaction, the savings would be over $500 to the client. Throughout a year's worth of transactions, these savings might become considerable.

With large quantities of dollars, yen, euros, baht, and other currencies being traded over the Internet, security is a major issue. E-FOREX incorporates the latest 128-bit encryption technology and uses digital certificates from Versign as well as firewalls, which prevent outsiders from entering the secure system.

To avoid disaster, if one computer system fails, E-FOREX, similar to other Internet-based brokerage companies, operates two or more systems for routers and database servers. In addition, a remote backup data center supports those systems redundantly. In the event of a service interruption at any facility, no data are lost.

Finally, E-FOREX provides so-called 100 percent double-blind dealing. The party who takes the other side of a client's trade does not know who the client is, and vice versa. This increases foreign exchange efficiency because no clients can guess at the direction of trades and skew rates to earn trading profits in excess of a normal profit.

Issues & Applications

Are Currency Speculators Unproductive?

When the exchange value of the pound sterling plummeted more than 30 years ago, British politicians blamed the fall on "gnomes of Zurich"—currency speculators based in Switzerland. More recently, when Mahathir Mohamad, the Malaysian prime minister, decried currency speculators as "immoral," he particularly had in mind a speculator named George Soros, the chief executive of Quantum Fund, a firm that sought to earn speculative trading profits for its clients.

Concepts Applied
Exchange Rates
Foreign Exchange Market Equilibrium

Speculative Attacks

In Mahathir's view, Quantum Fund reaped millions of dollars in trading profits at the expense of Malaysia when Soros correctly speculated that Malaysia could not maintain a fixed exchange rate for the Malaysian ringgit relative to the U.S. dollar. Quantum Fund and other individuals and firms conducted large numbers of currency trades with an aim to profit from a decline in the ringgit's value, thereby engaging in what economists call a *speculative attack* on the Malaysian currency.

Perhaps not surprisingly, Mahathir has argued that speculative currency trading is "excessive." He points to the trend highlighted in Figure 33-9: The growth of total foreign exchange trading has far outpaced the growth of total world trade in goods and services. Much of the growth in foreign exchange trading arises from increased purchases and sales of currencies by speculators. Much of this trading, Mahathir concludes, is "unnecessary" and "unproductive."

Some economists and policymakers agree with this assessment. They worry that foreign exchange markets may experience excessive volatility because of the activities of currency

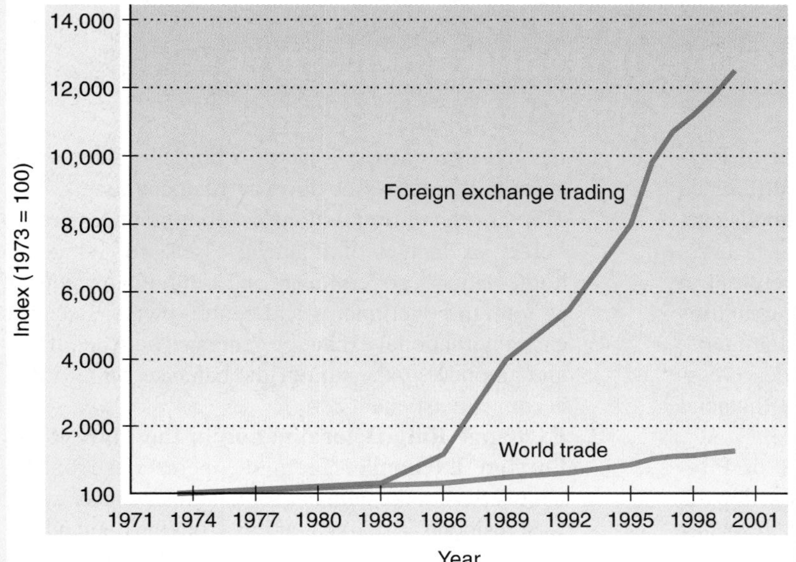

FIGURE 33-9

Foreign Exchange Trading and World Trade Since 1973

This figure displays index measures (1973 = 100) of the dollar volumes of total world trade and foreign exchange trading. At least a portion of the much faster growth of foreign exchange trading undoubtedly reflects an increase in speculative currency trading.

Sources: Bank for International Settlements; World Trade Organization.

speculators. To address this concern, Nobel laureate James Tobin has proposed taxing foreign exchange transactions to reduce the incentive to engage in currency speculation. In 1999, a United Nations study proposed imposing this "Tobin tax" and transferring the proceeds to the less developed nations of the world.

The Economic Role of Currency Speculators

There are, however, reasons to argue that the activities of currency speculators have social value. Firms such as Quantum Fund devote considerable time to studying the economic and political factors that play a fundamental role in determining exchange rates. This helps the firms seek out economic imbalances that are ultimately likely to force exchange rates to move into line with these fundamental factors at some point in the future. For currency speculators, such imbalances—such as, in the case of Malaysia in 1997, a fixed exchange rate that conflicts with the nation's economic policies—offer profitable opportunities. It is arguable that these imbalances could eventually pose serious economic problems in nations that experience them. By forcing countries to deal with imbalances sooner rather than later, speculative attacks may help prevent national policymakers from following misguided policies.

Speculative currency trading also plays an important economic role by making foreign exchange markets more liquid. Suppose that currency speculation were inhibited, for instance, by high taxes on foreign exchange transactions or by regulations requiring anyone who buys a foreign-currency-denominated asset to keep it for a specified period, regardless of changes in economic conditions. In such a situation, there might not be a strong incentive to hold the currency at all. This could make it hard for someone who wants to engage in the cross-border exchange of a real good or service to find willing buyers or sellers of currency required to finance the transaction. Thus the activities of currency speculators may contribute to the liquidity of foreign exchange markets and thereby contribute to the growth of world trade in goods and services. Stopping currency speculation could hinder or even reverse global growth of international trade.

FOR CRITICAL ANALYSIS

1. Why might it be desirable for a country's government to alter policies that are contributing to national economic imbalances sooner rather than later?
2. If defenders of currency speculators are correct, does Figure 33-9 indicate that foreign exchange markets have become more or less liquid in recent years?

SUMMARY DISCUSSION OF LEARNING OBJECTIVES

1. **The Balance of Trade Versus the Balance of Payments:** The balance of trade is the difference between exports of goods and imports of goods during a given period. The balance of payments is a system of accounts for all transactions between a nation's residents and the residents of other countries of the world. In addition to exports and imports, therefore, the balance of payments includes cross-border exchanges of services, income, and financial assets within a given time interval.
2. **The Key Accounts Within the Balance of Payments:** There are three important accounts within the balance of payments. The current account measures net exchanges of goods and services, transfers, and income flows across a nation's borders. The capital account measures net flows of financial assets. The official reserve transactions account tabulates cross-border exchanges of financial assets involving the home nation's governments and central bank as well as foreign governments and central banks. Because each international exchange generates both an inflow and an outflow, the sum of the balances on all three accounts must equal zero.
3. **Exchange Rate Determination in the Market for Foreign Exchange:** From the perspective of the United States, the demand for a nation's currency by U.S. residents is derived largely from the demand for imports from that nation. Likewise, the supply of a

nation's currency is derived mainly from the supply of U.S. exports to that country. The equilibrium exchange rate is the rate of exchange between the dollar and the other nation's currency at which the quantity of the currency demanded is equal to the quantity supplied.

4. **Factors That Can Induce Changes in Equilibrium Exchange Rates:** The equilibrium exchange rate changes in response to changes in the demand for or supply of another nation's currency. Changes in desired flows of exports or imports, real interest rates, productivity in one nation relative to productivity in another nation, tastes and preferences of consumers, and perceptions of economic stability are key factors that can affect the positions of the demand and supply curves in foreign exchange markets. Thus changes in these factors can induce variations in equilibrium exchange rates.
5. **How Policymakers Can Attempt to Keep Exchange Rates Fixed:** If the current price of another nation's currency in terms of the home currency starts to fall below the level where the home country wants it to remain, the home country's central bank can use reserves of the other nation's currency to purchase the home currency in foreign exchange markets. This raises the demand for the home currency and thereby pushes up the currency's value in terms of the other nation's currency. In this way, the home country can keep the exchange rate fixed at a desired value, as long as it has sufficient reserves of the other currency to use for this purpose.
6. **Alternative Approaches to Limiting Exchange Rate Variability:** Today, many nations permit their exchange rates to vary in foreign exchange markets. Others pursue policies that limit the variability of exchange rates. Some engage in a dirty float, in which they manage exchange rates, often in cooperation with other nations. Some establish crawling pegs, in which the target value of the exchange rate is adjusted automatically over time. And some establish target zones, with upper and lower limits on the extent to which exchange rates are allowed to vary.

Key Terms and Concepts

Accounting identities (806)
Appreciation (814)
Balance of payments (806)
Balance of trade (806)
Crawling peg (824)
Depreciation (814)
Dirty float (824)
Exchange rate (813)
Flexible exchange rates (813)
Foreign exchange market (813)
Foreign exchange risk (823)
Hedge (823)
International Monetary Fund (IMF) (820)
Par value (821)
Special drawing rights (SDRs) (810)
Target zone (825)

Problems

Answers to the odd-numbered problems appear at the back of the book.

33-1. Over the course of a year, a nation tracked its foreign transactions and arrived at the following amounts:

Merchandise exports	500
Service Exports	75
Net unilateral exports	10
Domestic assets abroad (capital outflows)	−200
Foreign assets at home (capital inflows)	300
Changes in official reserves	−35
Merchandise imports	600
Service imports	50

What is this nation's balance of trade, current account balance, and capital account balance?

33-2. Whenever the United States reaches record levels on its current account deficit, Congress flirts with the idea of restricting imported goods. Would trade restrictions like those studied in Chapter 32 be an appropriate response?

33-3. Explain how the following events would affect the market for the Mexican peso.

a. Improvements in Mexican production technology yield superior guitars, and many musicians desire these guitars.

b. Perceptions of political instability surrounding regular elections in Mexico make international investors nervous about future business prospects in Mexico.

33-4. On Wednesday, the exchange rate between the euro and the U.S. dollar was $1.07 per euro. On Thursday, it was $1.05. Did the euro appreciate or depreciate against the dollar? By how much?

33-5. On Wednesday, the exchange rate between the euro and the U.S. dollar was $1.07 per euro and the exchange rate between the Canadian dollar and the U.S. dollar was U.S. $.68 per Canadian dollar. What is the exchange rate between the Canadian dollar and the euro?

33-6. Suppose that signs of an improvement in the Japanese economy lead international investors to resume lending to the Japanese government and businesses. Policymakers, however, are worried about how this will influence the yen. How would this event affect the market for the yen? How should the central bank, the Bank of Japan, respond to this event if it wants to maintain the value of the yen?

33-7. Briefly explain the differences between a flexible exchange rate system, a fixed exchange rate system, a dirty float, and a target zone.

33-8. Explain how each of the following would affect Canada's balance of payments.

a. Canada's rate of inflation falls below that of the United States, its main trading partner.

b. The possibility of Quebec's separating from the federation frightens international investors.

33-9. Suppose that under a gold standard, the U.S. dollar is pegged to gold at a rate of $35 per ounce and the pound sterling is pegged to gold at a rate of £17.50 per ounce. Explain how the gold standard constitutes an exchange rate arrangement. What is the exchange rate between the U.S. dollar and the pound sterling?

33-10. Suppose that under the Bretton Woods System, the dollar is pegged to gold at a rate of $35 per ounce and the pound sterling is pegged to the dollar at a rate of $2 = £1. If the dollar is devalued against gold and the pegged rate is changed to $40 per ounce, what does this imply for the exchange value of the pound?

Economics on the Net

Daily Exchange Rates It is an easy matter to keep up with changes in exchange rates every day using the Web site of the Federal Reserve Bank of New York. In this application, you will learn how hard it is to predict exchange rate movements, and you will get some practice thinking about what factors can cause exchange rates to change.

Title: The Federal Reserve Bank of New York: Foreign Exchange 12 Noon Rates

Navigation: Click here to visit the Federal Reserve Bank of New York's homepage. Select Statistics. Click on Foreign Exchange 12 Noon Rates.

Application

1. For each currency listed, how many dollars does it take to purchase a unit of the currency in the spot foreign exchange market?
2. For each day during a given week (or month), choose a currency from those listed and keep track of its value relative to the dollar. Based on your tabulations, try to predict the value of the currency at the end of the week *following* your data collections. Use any information you may have, or just do your best without any additional information. How far off did your prediction turn out to be?

For Group Study and Analysis Each day, you can also click on a report titled "Foreign Exchange 10 a.m. Rates," which shows exchange rates for a subset of countries listed in the noon report. Assign each country in the 10 A.M. report to a group. Ask the group to determine whether the currency's value appreciated or depreciated relative to the dollar between 10 A.M. and noon. In addition, ask each group to discuss what kinds of demand or supply shifts could have caused the change that occurred during this interval.

TYING IT ALL TOGETHER

Part 8 Case Problem

Case Background

The president of a small, less developed Latin American nation has big problems. The annual inflation rate is running above 100 percent, the value of the country's currency is dropping like a rock, and foreign savers are rushing to sell off their shares in investment within the country. The president has appointed a working group of economists to study alternative approaches to achieving the president's goal of fixing the nation's exchange rate relative to the U.S. dollar.

A Currency Board Versus Dollarization It does not take long for the working group to narrow down the choices. One means of establishing a truly fixed rate of exchange for a nation's currency is by establishing a currency board. This is an institution that issues currency fully backed by reserves of a foreign currency. That is, the currency board pledges to redeem its domestic currency for a foreign "hard currency," such as the U.S. dollar, at a fixed rate of exchange. With full backing of outstanding currency, the government board can fulfill this pledge.

Establishing a currency board would preclude a couple of activities associated with central banking. Most obviously, this nation could no longer conduct an independent monetary policy if it cannot vary the quantity of its currency that is in circulation. In the event of unexpected outflows of funds—such as the one the country has recently experienced—there would be pressure for the nation's currency to depreciate. To prevent this from occurring, the currency board would simply sell some of its foreign reserves. The second central-banking activity that a currency board often cannot undertake is lending to liquidity-constrained banks and other financial institutions to thwart a bank run or similar financial crisis. Some nations, such as Argentina, have preserved this central-banking role for their currency boards by permitting the currency board to hold some domestic securities. In the event of a liquidity crunch, the currency board can lend financial institutions funds from that available pool of domestic assets.

In addition, there can be an explicit cost of operating a currency board. Financial instruments of developing nations often yield higher returns than those of a developed country such as the United States. Because a currency board would hold dollar-denominated reserves instead of domestic securities, the government of this Latin American country would have to forgo some interest earnings that it normally could use to help fund public expenditures.

An even more dramatic way to achieve a permanently fixed exchange rate is dollarization, which entails the abandonment of the nation's own currency in favor of making the U.S. dollar the country's only legal currency. In this event, there really would be no exchange rate, of course; the currency circulating in the Latin American nation would be the U.S. currency. But the rate of exchange of home currency for U.S. currency would be, as the president wishes, one for one, so in this sense dollarization is the most extreme form of a fixed exchange rate.

In a fully dollarized economy, the nation's monetary policymaker's job would simply be to facilitate the replacement of worn-out dollars. To get to the point of complete dollarization, the nation would obtain the dollars by issuing dollar-denominated debts, and the interest it would have to pay on these debts would be an explicit cost of dollarization. As with a currency board, this forgone interest income could be used to help fund public expenditures. Another cost would be the expense of transporting new dollars and coins from the United States when setting up the system and when old U.S. currency eventually wears out and has to be replaced.

Points to Analyze

1. What is the fundamental difference between a fixed-exchange-rate policy as implemented by a central bank as compared with a fixed exchange rate policy as pursued by a currency board? Why might foreign savers perceive that the latter is less risky than the former?
2. Is there any point in retaining a central bank if there is a currency board? If the economy is dollarized?
3. Why might adopting a currency board or dollarization help stabilize cross-border flows of funds and international trade in goods and services?
4. Why are foreign savers likely to believe that dollarization is a more credible commitment to stable terms of international exchange than a currency board would be?
5. Suppose that the nation decides to dollarize its economy. Who in this country would pay for this change? (Hint: Who pays for the public expenditures that in the past have been partly funded with government revenues from interest on domestic security holdings?)
6. Is an irrevocably fixed exchange rate more desirable than a floating exchange rate? Why?

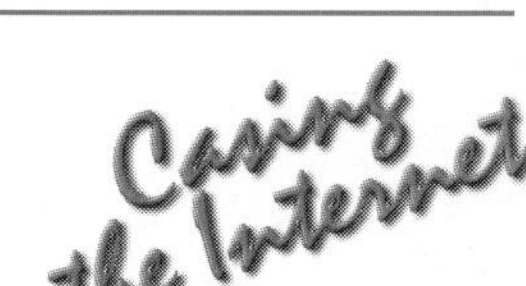

1. **Click here to learn more about how currency boards have functioned. Click on "Introduction." Read the article, and then answer the following questions:**
   a. **What are the key features of an "orthodox" currency board?**
   b. **In what ways have Argentina and Bulgaria's currency board arrangements differed from those of an orthodox currency board?**
   c. **The article lists a number of countries that have used currency board arrangements in the past and present. Make a list of nations that have had either good or poor experience with currency boards. What factors appear to influence how well a currency board works?**
2. **Click here to go to the Web site of the Hong Kong Monetary Authority. Answer the following questions:**
   a. **Click on "THE HKMA," and after you read the page, at the top click on "Advisory Committee". Read about the Exchange Fund Advisory Committee. In the context of our case description of a currency board, what exactly is the Hong Kong "Exchange Fund"?**
   b. **Back up to the homepage, and under "Monetary Stability" click on "Currency Board System". Why does the Hong Kong Monetary Authority refer to its system as "Linked Exchange Rate System"?**

Answers to Odd-Numbered Problems

CHAPTER 1

1-1. This issue involves choice and therefore can be approached using the economic way of thinking. In the case of health care, an individual typically has an unlimited desire for good health. The individual has a limited budget and limited time, however. She must allocate her budget across other desirable goods, such as housing and food, and must allocate their time across waiting in the doctor's office, work, leisure, and sleep. Hence choices must be made in light of limited resources.

1-3. Sally is displaying rational behavior if all of these activities are in her self-interest. For example, Sally likely derives intrinsic value from volunteer and extracurricular activities and may believe that these activities, along with good grades, improve her prospects of finding a job after she completes her studies. Hence these activities are in her self-interest even though they take away some study time.

1-5. Suppose that you desire to earn an A (90 percent) in economics and merely to pass (60 percent) in French. If your model indicates that you earn 15 percentage points on each exam for every hour you spend studying, you would spend 6 hours ($6 \times 15 = 90$) studying economics and 4 hours ($4 \times 15 = 60$) studying French.

1-7. Positive economic analysis deals with the outcome of economics models, whereas normative analysis includes social values in the choice as well.

1-9. a. An increase in the supply of laptop computers, perhaps because of the entry of new computer manufacturers into the market, pushes their price back down.

b. Another factor, such as higher hotel taxes at popular vacation destinations, makes vacation travel more expensive.

c. Some other factor, such as a fall in wages that workers earn, discourages people from working additional hours.

APPENDIX A

A-1. a. Independent: price; dependent: quantity

b. Independent: work-study hours; dependent: credit hours

c. Independent: hours of study; dependent: economics grade

A-3. a. Above x axis; left of y axis

b. Below x axis; right of y axis

c. Above x axis; on y axis

A-5.

y	x
−20	−4
−10	−2
0	0
10	2
20	4

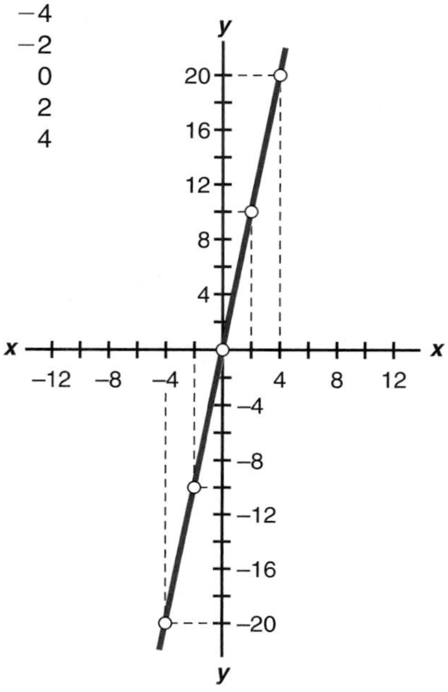

y
20
16
12
8
4
x
−12 −8 −4 4 8 12
x
−4
−8
−12
−16
−20
y

A-7. 5

A-9. a. Positive
b. Positive
c. Negative

CHAPTER 2

2-1. Each additional 10 points earned in economics costs 10 additional points in biology, so this PPC illustrates *constant* opportunity costs.

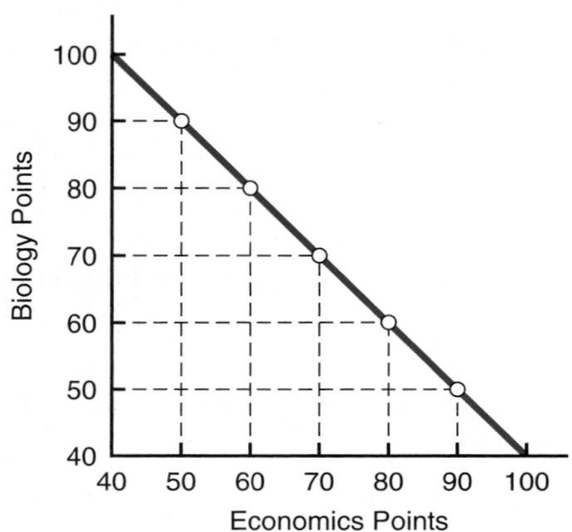

2-3. The \$4,500 paid for tuition, room and board, and books consists of explicit costs, not opportunity costs. The \$3,000 in lost wages is a forgone opportunity, as is the 3 percent interest that could have been earned on the \$4,500. Hence the total opportunity cost is equal to \$3,000 + (\$4,500 × 0.03) = \$3,000 + \$135 = \$3,135.

2-5.

a.

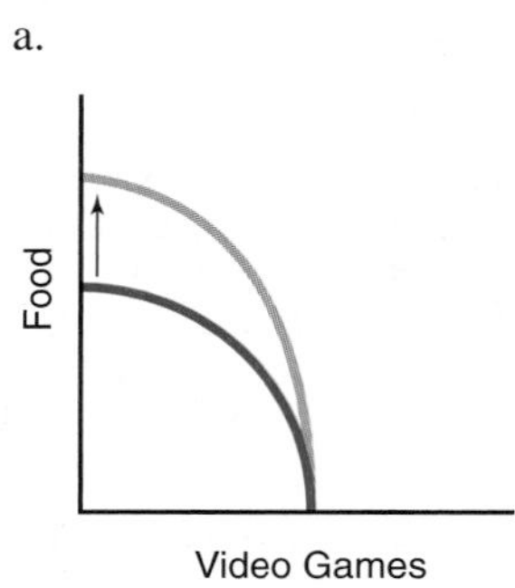

b.

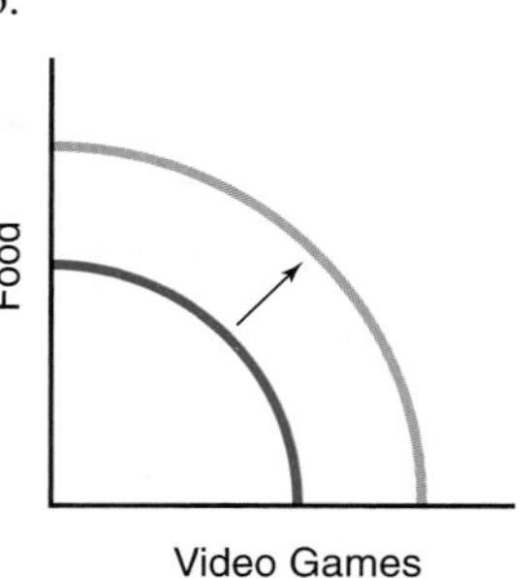

c.

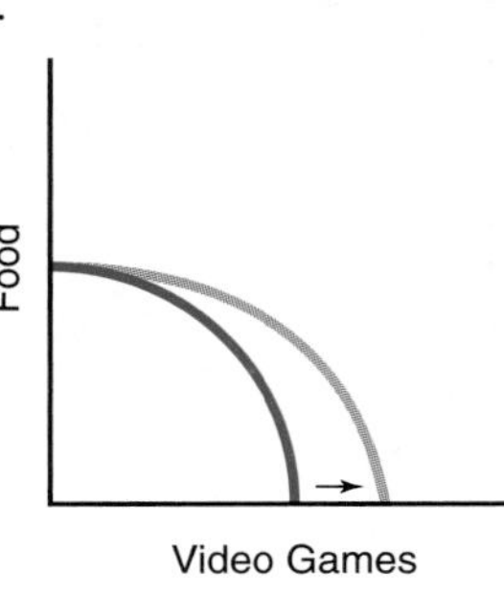

d.

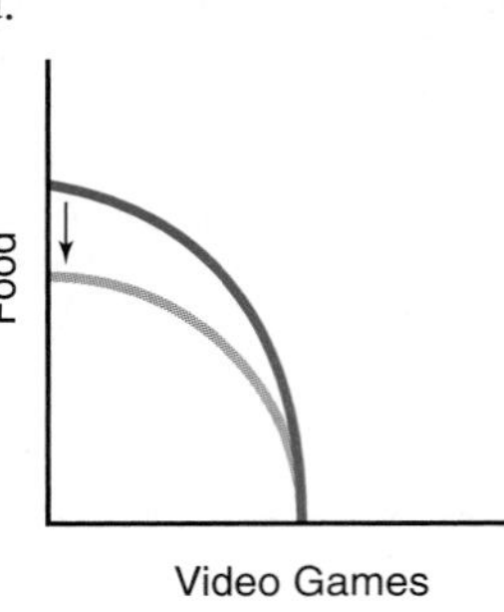

2-7. Because it takes you less time to do laundry, you have an absolute advantage in laundry. Neither you nor your roommate has an absolute advantage in meal preparation. You require two hours to fold a basket of laundry, so your opportunity cost of folding a basket of laundry is two meals. Your roommate's opportunity cost of folding a basket of laundry is three meals. Hence you have a comparative advantage in laundry, and your roommate has a comparative advantage in meal preparation.

2-9. If countries produce the goods for which they have a comparative advantage and trade for those for which they are at a comparative disadvantage, the distribution of resources is more efficient in each nation, yielding gains for both. Artificially restraining trade that would otherwise yield such gains thereby imposes social losses on the residents of both nations.

2-11. a. If the two nations have the same production possibilities, they face the same opportunity costs of producing consumption goods and capital goods. Thus at present neither has a comparative advantage in producing either good.
b. Because country B produces more capital goods today, it will be able to produce more of both goods in the future. Consequently, country B's PPC will shift outward by a greater amount next year.
c. Country B now has a comparative advantage in producing capital goods, and country A now has a comparative advantage in producing consumer goods.

CHAPTER 3

3-1. The equilibrium price is \$11 per CD, and the equilibrium quantity is 80 million CDs. At a price of \$10 per CD, the quantity of CDs demanded is 90 million, and the quantity of CDs supplied is 60 million. Hence there is a shortage of 30 million CDs at a price of \$10 per CD.

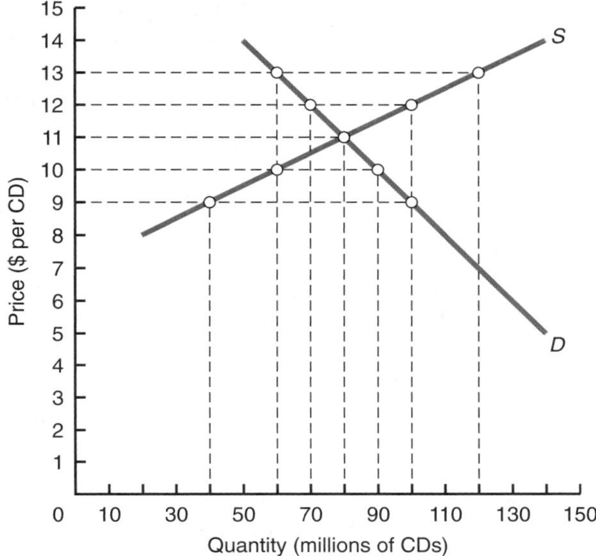

3-3. a. This fall in the price of an input used to produce rock music CDs causes the supply of these CDs to increase. The results are a decline in the market price of rock music CDs and an increase in the equilibrium quantity of rock music CDs.

b. Because CD players and CDs are complements in consumption, a decrease in the price of CD players causes the demand for rock music CDs to increase. This results in an increase in the market price of rock music CDs and an increase in the equilibrium quantity of these CDs.

c. Because cassette tapes and CDs are substitutes in consumption, an increase in the price of cassette tapes increases the demand for rock music CDs. This causes an increase in the market price of rock music CDs and an increase in the equilibrium quantity of rock music CDs.

d. As long as a CD is a normal good, an increase in the income of the typical rock music CD consumer results in an increase in the demand for rock music CDs, which causes the market price of rock music CDs to rise and the equilibrium quantity of these CDs to increase.

e. This shift in preferences would cause a decrease in the demand for rock music CDs, so the market price of these CDs would decline, and the equilibrium quantity of rock music CDs would decrease.

3-5. The imposition of this tax would decrease the supply of Roquefort cheese, which would cause the supply curve to shift leftward. The market price would increase, and equilibrium quantity would fall.

3-7. a. Because memory chips are an input in the production of laptop computers, a decrease in the price of memory chips causes an increase in the supply of laptop computers. The market supply curve shifts to the right, causing the market price to fall and the equilibrium quantity to increase.

b. A decrease in the price of memory chips used in desktop personal computers causes the supply of desktop computers to increase, thereby bringing about a decline in the market price of desktop computers, which are substitutes for laptop computers. This causes a decrease in the demand for laptop computers. The market demand curve shifts leftward, which causes declines in the market price and equilibrium quantity of laptop computers.

c. An increase in the number of manufactures of laptop computers causes an increase in the supply of laptop computers. The market supply curve shifts rightward. The market price of laptop computers declines, and the equilibrium quantity of laptop computers increases.

d. Because computer peripherals are complements, decreases in their prices induce an increase in the demand for laptop computers. Thus the market demand curve shifts to the right, and the market price and equilibrium quantity of laptop computers increase.

3-9. a. The demand for tickets declines, and there will be a surplus of tickets.

b. The demand for tickets rises, and there will be a shortage of tickets.

c. The demand for tickets increases, and there will be a shortage of tickets.

d. The demand for tickets falls, and there will be a surplus of tickets.

CHAPTER 4

4-1. To the band, its producer, and consumers, the market price of the CD provides an indication of the popularity of the band's music; for instance, if the market price rises relative to other CDs, this signals that the band should continue to record its music for sale.

4-3. The market rental rate is $500 per apartment, and 2,000 apartments are rented at this price. At a ceiling price of $450 per month, students wishing to live off campus wish to rent 2,500 apartments, but apartment owners are willing to supply only 1,800 apartments. Thus there is a shortage of 700 apartments at the ceiling price.

4-5. At the above-market price of sugar in the U.S. sugar market, U.S. businesses that use sugar as an input in their products (such as chocolate manufacturers) face higher costs, which shifts the market supply curve leftward. This pushes up the market price of chocolate products and reduces the equilibrium quantity. U.S. sugar producers also sell surplus sugar in foreign sugar markets, which causes the supply curve to shift rightward in foreign markets. This reduces the market price of foreign sugar and raises the equilibrium quantity in the international market.

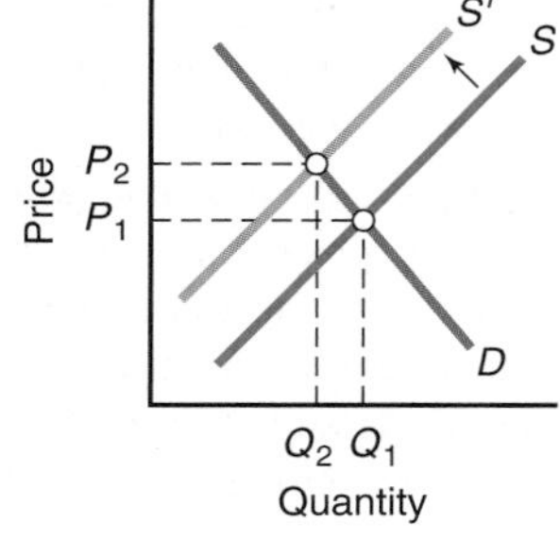

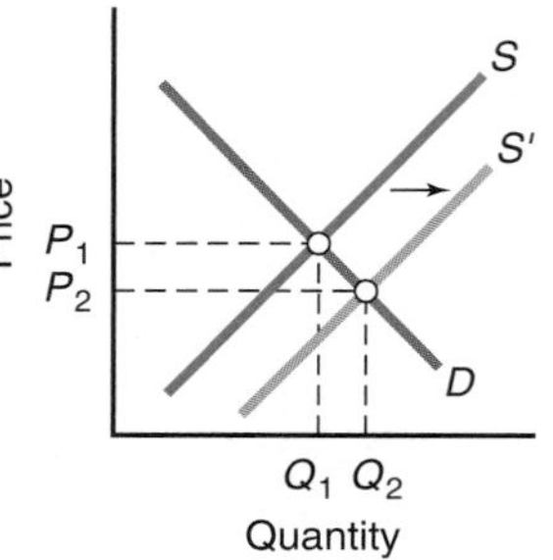

4-7. The market price is $400, and the equilibrium quantity of seats is 1,600. If airlines cannot sell tickets to more than 1,200 passengers, passengers are willing to pay $600 per seat, but airlines are willing to sell each ticket for $200.

4-9. Before the price support program, total revenue for farmers was $5 million. After the program, total revenue is $10 million. The cost of the program for taxpayers is $5 million.

CHAPTER 5

5-1. a. As shown in the figure, if the social costs associated with groundwater contamination were reflected in the costs incurred by pesticide manufacturers, the supply schedule would be S' instead of S, and the market price would be higher. The equilibrium quantity of pesticides produced would be lower.

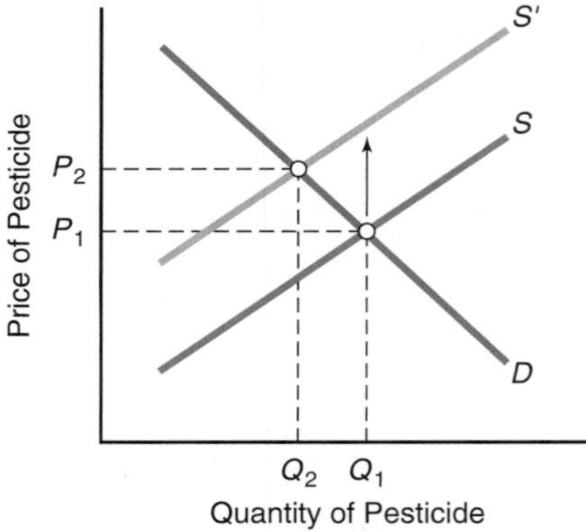

b. The government could tax the production and sale of pesticides, thereby shifting the supply curve upward and to the left.

5-3 a. As shown in the figure, if the social benefits associated with bus ridership were taken into account, the demand schedule would be D' instead of D, and the market price would be higher. The equilibrium quantity of bus rides would be higher.

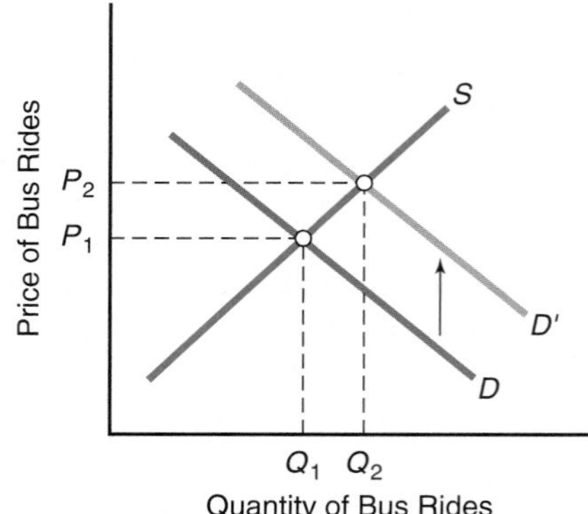

b. The government could pay commuters a subsidy to ride the bus, thereby shifting the demand curve upward and to the right. This would increase the market price and equilibrium number of bus rides.

5-5. The problem is that although most people around the lighthouse will benefit from its presence, there is no incentive for people to contribute voluntarily if they believe that others ultimately will pay for it. That is, the city is likely to face a free-rider problem in its efforts to raise its share of the funds required for the lighthouse.

5-7. Because the marginal tax rate increases as workers' earnings decline, this tax system is regressive.

5-9. Seeking to increase budget allocations in future years and to make workers' jobs more interesting is similar to the goals of firms in private markets. Achieving these goals via majority rule and regulatory coercion, however, are aspects that are specific to the public sector.

CHAPTER 6

6-1. 50 percent

6-3. No more than $9 per hour

6-5. a. Equilibrium price = $500; society's total expense = $40 million
b. 100,000 tests
c. Producers' per-unit cost = $700; society's total expense = $70 million
d. Government's per-unit subsidy = $600; total subsidy = $60 million

CHAPTER 19

19-1. The campus pizzeria indicates by its pricing policy that it recognizes the principle of diminishing marginal utility. Because the marginal utility of the second pizza is typically lower than the first, the customer is likely to value the second less and is therefore less willing to pay full price for it.

19-3. The total utility of the third, fourth, and fifth cheeseburger is 48, 56, and 60, respectively. The marginal utility of the first and second cheeseburger is 20 and 16, respectively. The total utility of the first, second, and third bag of french fries is 8, 14, and 18, respectively. The marginal utility of the fourth and fifth bag of french fries is 2 and 0, respectively.

19-5. When total utility is rising, the only thing we can say for certain about marginal utility is that it is positive.

19-7. The student should compare the marginal utility per tuition dollar spent at the two universities. Assuming that a "unit" of college is a degree, the student should divide the notional value of an education at each university by the total tuition it would take to earn a degree at each institution. The university with the higher marginal utility per tuition dollar is the one the student should attend.

19-9. The new utility-maximizing combination is four cheeseburgers and two orders of french fries. The substitution effect is shown by the increase in the relatively less expensive good, cheeseburgers, relative to french fries. The income effect is illustrated by greater total consumption.

CHAPTER 20

20-1. $\dfrac{(200 - 150)/(350/2)}{(9 - 10)/(19/2)} = 2.7$

20-3. $\dfrac{(100 - 200)/(300/2)}{(2 - 1)/(3/2)} = 1.0$

20-5. a. Nearly perfectly elastic
b. Nearly perfectly inelastic
c. Nearly perfectly inelastic
d. Nearly perfectly inelastic

20-7. Within the first range, demand is elastic. As price falls, therefore, total revenue rises, and the total revenue curve is increasing. Within the second range, demand is at first elastic and then inelastic. When price falls, therefore, total revenue and the total revenue curve are initially rising. Eventually total revenue and the total revenue curve reach the maximum point, which corresponds to the point of unit elasticity. Beyond this point, total revenue declines.

20-9. Goods X and Y are substitutes; goods X and Z are complements; therefore, goods Y and Z are substitutes.

20-11. Income elasticity of demand is measured as the percentage change in demand divided by the percentage change in income. A negative income elasticity of demand indicates that as income rises, demand falls. This type of good is defined in Chapter 3 as an inferior good. A positive income elasticity of demand therefore indicates that the good is a normal good, as defined in Chapter 3. Hence we can conclude that a hot dog is an inferior good and that lobster is a normal good.

CHAPTER 21

21-1. a. Physical capital
b. Financial capital
c. Financial capital
d. Physical capital

21-3. The dividends of a corporation result from the corporation's profits, which are subject to corporate income taxation. The dividends are then paid out to shareholders, who must pay taxes on them as personal income. The profits of a partnership or proprietorship are subject only to individual income tax.

21-5. a. The owner of WebCity faces both tax rates if the firm is a corporation, but if it is a proprietorship, the owner faces only the 30 percent personal income tax rate.
b. If WebCity is a corporation, the $100,000 in corporate earnings is taxed at a 20 percent rate, so after-tax dividends are $80,000, and these are taxed at the personal income tax rate of 30 percent, leaving $56,000 in after-tax income for the owner. Hence the firm should be organized as a proprietorship so that the after-tax earnings are $70,000.
c. In this case, incorporation raises earnings to $150,000, which are taxed at a rate of 20 percent, yielding after-tax dividends of $120,000 that are taxed at the personal rate of 30 percent. This leaves an after-tax income for the owner of $84,000, which is higher than the after-tax earnings of $70,000 if WebCity is a proprietorship that earns lower pretax income taxed at the personal rate.
d. After-tax profits rise from $56,000 to $84,000, or by $28,000.
e. This policy change would only increase the incentive to incorporate.
f. A corporate structure provides limited liability for owners, which can be a major advantage. Furthermore, owners may believe that the corporate structure will yield higher pretax earnings.

21-7. a. For both, trading 100 shares with FSB entails paying the $25 flat fee plus the volume fee of $10, or $35. Including the opportunity cost of 30 minutes, Lucinda's cost of trading with WebTrader instead is $65 higher, and Ralph's is $35 higher. Both should execute their trades with FSB.
b. For both, trading 500 shares with FSB entails paying the $25 flat fee plus the volume fee of $50, or $75. Including the opportunity cost of 30 minutes, Lucinda's cost of trading with WebTrader instead is $35 higher, but Ralph's is $5 lower. Lucinda should execute her trade with FSB, but Ralph should do so with WebTrader.
c. For both, trading 1,000 shares with FSB entails paying the $25 flat fee plus the volume fee of $100, or $125. Including the opportunity cost of 30 minutes, Lucinda's cost of trading with WebTrader instead is $15 lower, and Ralph's is $55 lower. Both should execute their trades with WebTrader.
d. In general, larger trades will be executed with WebTrader, because FSB's total fees rise with the number of share trades that the broker executes, but the total cost of having WebTrader execute trades does not.
e. A person with a higher opportunity cost of time is more likely to have FSB execute trades.

21-9. a. Adverse selection
b. Asymmetric information
c. Moral hazard

21-11. You should point out to your classmate that stock prices tend to follow a random walk. That is, yesterday's price is the best guide to today's price, and there are no predictable trends that can be used to "beat" the market.

CHAPTER 22

22-1. Explicit costs are $12,000 in rent, $1,000 in office supplies, $20,000 for office staff, and $4,000 in telephone expenses, for a total of $37,000. Implicit costs are the forgone $40,000 salary and the 5 percent interest on the $5,000 savings ($250), for a total of $40,250.

22-3. The short run is a time period in which the academic cannot enter the job market and find employment elsewhere. This is the nine-month period from August 15 through May 15. The academic can find employment elsewhere after the contract has been fulfilled, so the short run is nine months and the long run is greater than nine months.

22-5.

Input of Labor (workers per month)	Total Output of DVD Drives	Marginal Physical Product
0	0	—
100	25	0.25
200	60	0.35
300	85	0.25
400	105	0.20
500	115	0.10
600	120	0.05

22-7. Variable costs are equal to total costs, $5 million, less fixed costs, $2 million. Variable costs are therefore equal to $3 million. Average variable costs are equal to total variable costs divided by the number of units produced. Average variable costs therefore equal $3 million divided by 10,000, or $300.

22-9. Increasing marginal cost occurs as the firm moves from producing 50 cable modems to 75 cable modems.`

Output (cable modems per month)	Total Cost of Output ($ thousands)	Marginal Costs ($ thousands)
0	10	—
25	60	2.0
50	95	1.4
75	150	2.2
100	220	2.8
125	325	4.2
150	465	5.6

22-11. a. Diseconomies of scale
b. Plant size E

CHAPTER 23

23-1. a. The single dominant firm can affect price. Therefore, this is not a competitive industry.
b. The output of each firm is not homogeneous, so this is not a competitive industry.
c. Firms cannot easily enter the industry, so this is not a competitive industry.

23-3. During the course of a week, the barber cuts hair for $15 \times 5 = 75$ people. His total revenue for a week is $75 \times \$6 = \$450$. Because this is a competitive market, marginal revenue equals market price, $6.

23-5. The profit-maximizing rate of output is where marginal cost equals marginal revenue, which occurs at 8 pizzas.

Total Output and Sales of Pizzas	Total Cost ($)	Marginal Cost ($)	Marginal Revenue ($)
0	5	0	10
1	9	4	10
2	11	2	10
3	12	1	10
4	14	2	10
5	18	4	10
6	24	6	10
7	32	8	10
8	42	10	10
9	54	12	10
10	68	14	10

23-7. Even though the price of pizzas, and hence marginal revenue, falls to only $5, this covers average variable cost. Thus the shop should stay open.

23-9. Because firms experience diseconomies of scale, they will increase their output at the current market price level. This causes the market supply schedule to shift rightward. The market price declines, and some firms begin to earn negative economic profits and leave the industry. This causes the supply schedule to shift back to the left and the market price to rise somewhat. In the final long-run equilibrium, the market price is equal to the minimum long-run average cost, and each surviving firm produces output at the minimum point of its long-run average cost curve.

CHAPTER 24

24-1. Because the objective of each cartel member is to maximize economic profits, there is an incentive for an individual member to cheat. Preventing members from cheating becomes harder and harder as the number of members grows. Hence the large number of coffee growers that exists today makes it unlikely that the cartel will be effective in the long run.

24-3. a. The total revenue and total profits of the dry cleaner are as follows.

Output (suits cleaned)	Price per Suit ($)	Total Costs ($)	Total Revenue ($)	Total Profit ($)
0	8.00	3.00	0	−3.00
1	7.50	6.00	7.50	1.50
2	7.00	8.50	14.00	5.50
3	6.50	10.50	19.50	9.00
4	6.00	11.50	24.00	12.50
5	5.50	13.50	27.50	14.00
6	5.00	16.00	30.00	14.00
7	4.50	19.00	31.50	12.50
8	4.00	24.00	32.00	8.00

b. The profit-maximizing rate of output is 5 or 6 units.

24-5. This statement is not true. Profit maximization occurs at the output rate where marginal revenue and marginal cost are equal. This rate of output may well occur before the point of minimum average total cost.

24-7. In a perfectly competitive market, price is $4.50 and quantity is 8,000. Because the monopolist produces less and charges a higher price than under perfect competition, price exceeds marginal cost at the profit-maximizing level of output. The difference between the price and marginal cost is the per-unit cost to society of a monopolized industry.

24-9. If price varies positively with total revenue, the monopolist is operating on the inelastic portion of the demand curve. This corresponds to the range where marginal revenue is negative. The monopolist cannot therefore be at the point where its profits are maximized. In other words, the monopolist is not producing where marginal cost equals marginal revenue.

24-11. Because marginal cost have risen, the monopolist will be operating at a lower rate of output and charging a higher price.

CHAPTER 25

25-1. a. There are many rival fast food restaurants that sell heterogeneous products. Both features of this industry are consistent with the theory of monopolistic competition.

b. There is a large number of colleges and universities, but each specializes in different academic areas and hence produces heterogeneous products, as in the theory of monopolistic competition.

25-3.

Output	Price ($)	Total Costs ($)	Total Revenue ($)	Marginal Cost ($)	Marginal Revenue ($)
0	6.00	2.00	0	—	—
1	5.75	5.00	5.75	3.00	5.75
2	5.50	7.50	11.00	2.50	5.25
3	5.25	9.50	15.75	2.00	4.75
4	5.00	10.50	20.00	1.00	4.25
5	4.75	12.50	23.75	2.00	3.75
6	4.50	15.00	27.00	2.50	3.25
7	4.00	18.00	28.00	3.00	1.00

25-5. The market price is $5.00 per unit, and the firm's economic profits equal $9.50.

25-7. a. Zero-sum game
b. Positive-sum game
c. Negative-sum game

25-9. This is an oligopoly structure that is consistent with the kinked demand curve. If the store's marginal cost curve shifts only slightly, it probably will not choose to vary its prices.

CHAPTER 26

26-1. If cable service is an industry that enjoys diminishing long-run average total costs, the city may wish to have a single, large firm that produces at a lower long-run average cost and to regulate the firm's activity.

26-3. If the firm were allowed to operate as a monopolist, it would produce at the level where marginal cost equals marginal revenue, which occurs at 2 units. Price is $90 at this level of output, so monopoly profit is $180 − $175 = $5.

26-5. Average cost pricing occurs where long-run average total cost equals demand, which is at 3 units. Price is $85, so profit is zero at this level.

26-7. Economic regulation seeks to keep prices low. Social regulation seeks to improve the working conditions of the firm and minimize adverse spillovers of production.

26-9. If European regulation is designed to protect domestic farm interests, it is an example of the capture hypothesis. If there are legitimate health concerns, it is an example of share-the-pains, share-the-gains hypothesis.

CHAPTER 27

27-1.

Labor Input (workers per week)	Total Physical Output (printers per week)	Marginal Physical Product ($)	Marginal Revenue Product ($)
10	200	—	—
11	218	18	1,800
12	234	16	1,600
13	248	14	1,400
14	260	12	1,200
15	270	10	1,000
16	278	8	800

27-3. The profit-maximizing employer will hire 14 workers, as this is the level where marginal revenue product equals marginal factor cost.

27-5. a. The greater the substitutability of capital, the more elastic the demand for labor.
b. Because the demand for labor is a derived demand, the greater the elasticity of demand for the final product, the greater the elasticity of demand for labor.
c. The larger the portion of factor costs accounted for by labor, the larger the price elasticity of demand for labor.

27-7.

Labor Input (workers per day)	Total Physical	Product Price ($)	Marginal Physical Product	Total Revenue ($)	Marginal Revenue Product ($)
10	100	50	—	5,000	—
11	109	49	9	5,341	341
12	116	48	7	5,568	227
13	121	47	5	5,687	119
14	124	46	3	5,704	17
15	125	45	1	5,625	−79

27-9. To maximize profits, a firm should hire inputs up to the point where marginal revenue product per dollar spent is equalized across all factors. This is not true in this example, so the firm is not maximizing profits. The firm should reduce the number of capital units it uses and increase its use of labor and land.

CHAPTER 28

28-1. Individual workers can air grievances to the collective voice, who then takes the issue to the employer. The individual does not run the risk of being singled out by an employer. The individual employee does not waste work time trying to convince employers that changes are needed in the workplace.

28-3. Because strikebreakers can replace union employees, they diminish the collective bargaining power of a union.

28-5. When marginal revenue is zero, the price elasticity of demand is equal to unity. At this point, total revenue is neither rising nor falling. Hence it is at a maximum point.

28-7.

Labor Supplied	Total Physical Product	Required Hourly Wage Rate ($)	Total Wage Bill ($)	Marginal Factor Cost ($)
10	100	5	50	—
11	109	6	66	16
12	116	7	84	18
13	121	8	104	20
14	124	9	126	22
15	125	10	150	24

28-9.

Labor Supplied	Total Physical Product	Required Hourly Wage Rate ($)	Product Price ($)	Total Revenue ($)	Marginal Revenue Product ($)
10	100	5	3.11	311	—
11	109	6	3.00	327	16.00
12	116	7	2.95	342.20	15.20
13	121	8	2.92	353.32	11.12
14	124	9	2.90	359.60	6.28
15	125	10	2.89	361.25	1.65

At 11 units of labor, the marginal revenue product is $16. This is equal to the marginal factor cost at this level of employment, as seen in the answer to Problem 28-7. The firm will therefore hire 11 units of labor and pay a wage of $6 an hour.

CHAPTER 29

29-1. a. Bob earns a high economic rent. With a specialized skill that is in great demand, his income is likely to be high and his opportunity cost relatively low.

b. Sally earns a high economic rent. As a supermodel, her income is likely to be high and, without any education, her opportunity cost relatively low.

c. If Tim were to leave teaching, not a relatively high-paying occupation, he could sell insurance full time. Hence his opportunity cost is high relative to his income, and his economic rent is low.

29-3. The economic rents that Michael Jordan would enjoy as a basketball player relative to those he enjoyed as a baseball player surely played a large role in his decision to return to basketball. Hence they help direct his talent (resources) into their most efficient use.

29-5. a. The debt issued by this country will not appear as risky to individuals, and they would therefore not require as high an interest rate. The interest rate will decline.

b. Increases in reporting requirements increase the cost of issuing a loan. The lender will increase rates to compensate for this. The interest rate will rise.

c. By shortening the length of the loan, the interest rate will decline.

29-7. The binding ceiling generates a shortage of loanable funds. Overall there is a decrease in loanable funds activity and a decrease in capital improvement projects.

29-9. The present value is $PV_1 = \$104/1.04 = \$100$. With a 5 percent discount rate, the present value is $\$104/1.05 = \$99.05$.

CHAPTER 30

30-1. a. X

b. Z

c. Closer

30-3. Brazil's

30-5. To achieve complete equality of incomes, such policies would remove individual gains from maximizing the economic value of resources and minimizing production costs. Enacting policies aimed at complete income equality could therefore significantly reduce overall efficiency in an economy.

30-7. First, a moral hazard problem will exist, because government action would reduce the individual's incentive to continue a healthy lifestyle, thereby increasing the likelihood of greater health problems that will require future treatment. Second, an individual who currently has health problems will have an incentive to substitute future care that will be available at a zero price for current care that the individual must purchase at a positive price. Finally, in future years the patient will no longer have an incentive to contain health care expenses, nor will health care providers have an incentive to minimize their costs.

30-9. The profit-maximizing price and the equilibrium quantity of health care services will increase.

CHAPTER 31

31-1. $4 per unit

31-3. At the previous, lower market price, consumers failed to pay a price that reflected the social costs, including those relating to pollution, of resources that the firms use to produce the good or service.

31-5. Penalizing rhino hunting discourages most people from engaging in the activity, which reduces the supply of rhino horns and drives up their market price. This in turn makes illegal poaching a more lucrative activity, which can lead to an increase in illegal hunting of the few remaining rhinos. If raising rhinos as stock animals were legalized, more rhino horns would be produced-via an increase in the number of rhinos on farms-and the market price of rhino horns would decline. This would reduce the incentive for poaching wild rhinos.

31-7. a. 60 percent

b. 40 percent

c. 40 percent

31-9. a.

Population of Wild Tigers	Marginal Cost	Marginal Benefit
0	—	—
2,000	5	50
4,000	10	40
6,000	15	30
8,000	25	25
10,000	35	20
12,000	50	10

b. 8,000 tigers
c. 6,000 tigers

CHAPTER 32

32-1. Norway can produce 100 calculators and 50 books, while Sweden can produce 200 calculators and 50 books. Their total output, therefore, is 300 calculators and 100 books. Sweden has an absolute advantage in calculators. Neither country has an absolute advantage in books.

32-3. a. Norway has a comparative advantage in the production of books and Sweden has a comparative advantage in the production of calculators.
b. If they specialize, total production is 400 calculators and 100 books.

32-5. Without trade, Norway would have to forgo 1/2 book to obtain 1 calculator. With trade, however, Norway can obtain 1 calculator for 1/3 book. Without trade, Sweden would have to forgo 4 calculators to obtain 1 book. With trade, however, Sweden can obtain 1 book for 3 calculators. By trading, both nations can obtain the good at a price that is less than the opportunity cost of producing it. They are both better off with trade, so this is a positive-sum game.

32-7. A price elasticity of demand less than unity indicates inelastic demand, and therefore price and total revenue move in the same direction. If the nation restricts its exports, the price of the product rises and so does total revenue, even though the nation is selling fewer units.

32-9. a. Because the supply curve shifts by the amount of the tariff, the diagram indicates that the tariff is $20 per television.
b. Total revenue was $6 billion before the tariff and $4.35 billion after the tariff.
c. The tariff revenue earned by the U.S. government is $20 × 15 million, or $300 million.

CHAPTER 33

33-1. The trade balance is a deficit of 100, the current account balance is a deficit of 65, and the capital account balance is a surplus of 100.

33-3. a. The increase in demand for Mexican-made guitars increases the demand for the Mexican peso, and the peso appreciates.
b. International investors will move their capital out of Mexico. The increase in the supply of the peso in the foreign exchange market will cause the peso to depreciate.

33-5. The Canadian dollar–euro rate is found by dividing the U.S. dollar–euro rate by the U.S. dollar–Canadian dollar rate. Thus the Canadian dollar–euro rate = 1.07/0.68 = 1.57.

33-7. A flexible exchange rate system allows the exchange value of a currency to be determined freely in the foreign exchange market with no intervention by the government. A fixed exchange rate pegs the value of the currency, and the authorities responsible for the value of the currency intervene in foreign exchange markets to maintain this value. A dirty float involves occasional intervention by the exchange authorities. A target zone allows the exchange value to fluctuate, but only within a given range of values.

33-9. When the U.S. dollar is pegged to gold at a rate of $35 and the pound sterling at a rate of $17.50, an implicit value between the dollar and the pound is established. The exchange value is $35/£17.50 = $2 per pound.

Glossary

Absolute advantage The ability to produce more units of a good or service using a given quantity of labor or resource inputs. Equivalently, the ability to produce the same quantity of a good or service using fewer units of labor or resource inputs. *Can also be viewed as* the ability to produce more output from given inputs of resources than other producers can.

Accounting identities Values that are equivalent by definition.

Accounting profit Total revenues minus total explicit costs.

Action time lag The time between recognizing an economic problem and implementing policy to solve it. The action time lag is quite long for fiscal policy, which requires congressional approval.

Active (discretionary) policymaking All actions on the part of monetary and fiscal policymakers that are undertaken in response to or in anticipation of some change in the overall economy.

Adverse selection The likelihood that individuals who seek to borrow money may use the funds that they receive for unworthy, high-risk projects.

Age-earnings cycle The regular earnings profile of an individual throughout his or her lifetime. The age-earnings cycle usually starts with a low income, builds gradually to a peak at around age 50, and then gradually curves down until it approaches zero at retirement.

Aggregate demand The total of all planned expenditures for the entire economy.

Aggregate demand curve A curve showing planned purchase rates for all final goods and services in the economy at various price levels, all other things held constant.

Aggregate demand shock Any shock that causes the aggregate demand curve to shift inward or outward.

Aggregates Total amounts or quantities; aggregate demand, for example, is total planned expenditures throughout a nation.

Aggregate supply The total of all planned production for the economy.

Aggregate supply shock Any shock that causes the aggregate supply curve to shift inward or outward.

Anticipated inflation The inflation rate that we believe will occur; when it does, we are in a situation of fully anticipated inflation.

Antitrust legislation Laws that restrict the formation of monopolies and regulate certain anticompetitive business practices.

Appreciation An increase in the exchange value of one nation's currency in terms of the currency of another nation.

Asset demand Holding money as a store of value instead of other assets such as certificates of deposit, corporate bonds, and stocks.

Assets Amounts owned; all items to which a business or household holds legal claim.

Asymmetric information Possession of information by one party in a financial transaction but not by the other party.

Automated clearinghouse (ACH) A computer-based clearing and settlement facility that replaces check transactions by interchanging credits and debits electronically.

Automated teller machine (ATM) network A system of linked depository institution computer terminals that are activated by magnetically encoded bank cards.

Automatic, or **built-in, stabilizers** Special provisions of certain federal programs that cause changes in desired aggregate expenditures without the action of Congress and the president. Examples are the federal tax system and unemployment compensation.

Autonomous consumption The part of consumption that is independent of (does not depend on) the level of disposable income. Changes in autonomous consumption shift the consumption function.

Average fixed costs Total fixed costs divided by the number of units produced.

Average physical product Total product divided by the variable input.

Average propensity to consume (APC) Consumption divided by disposable income; for any given level of income, the proportion of total disposable income that is consumed.

Average propensity to save (APS) Saving divided by disposable income; for any given level of income, the proportion of total disposable income that is saved.

Average tax rate The total tax payment divided by total income. It is the proportion of total income paid in taxes.

Average total costs Total costs divided by the number of units produced; sometimes called average per-unit total costs.

Average variable costs Total variable costs divided by the number of units produced.

Balance of payments A system of accounts that measures transactions of goods, services, income, and financial assets between domestic households, businesses, and governments and residents of the rest of the world during a specific time period.

Balance of trade The difference between exports and imports of goods.

Balance sheet A statement of the assets and liabilities of any business entity, including financial institutions and the Federal Reserve System. Assets are what is owned; liabilities are what is owed.

Bank runs Attempts by many of a bank's depositors to convert checkable and time deposits into currency out of fear for the bank's solvency.

Barter The direct exchange of goods and services for other goods and services without the use of money.

Base year The year that is chosen as the point of reference for comparison of prices in other years.

Bilateral monopoly A market structure consisting of a monopolist and a monopsonist.

Black market A market in which goods are traded at prices above their legal maximum prices or in which illegal goods are sold.

Bond A legal claim against a firm, usually entitling the owner of the bond to receive a fixed annual coupon payment, plus a lump-sum payment at the bond's maturity date. Bonds are issued in return for funds lent to the firm.

Budget constraint All of the possible combinations of goods that can be purchased (at fixed prices) with a specific budget.

Business fluctuations The ups and downs in overall business activity, as evidenced by changes in national income, employment, and the price level.

Capital consumption allowance Another name for depreciation, the amount that businesses would have to save in order to take care of the deterioration of machines and other equipment.

Capital controls Legal restrictions on the ability of a nation's residents to hold and trade assets denominated in foreign currencies.

Capital gain The positive difference between the purchase price and the sale price of an asset. If a share of stock is bought for $5 and then sold for $15, the capital gain is $10.

Capital goods Producer durables; nonconsumable goods that firms use to make other goods.

Capital loss The negative difference between the purchase price and the sale price of an asset.

Capture hypothesis A theory of regulatory behavior that predicts that the regulators will eventually be captured by the special interests of the industry being regulated.

Cartel An association of producers in an industry that agree to set common prices and output quotas to prevent competition.

Central bank A banker's bank, usually an official institution that also serves as a country's treasury's bank. Central banks normally regulate commercial banks.

Certificate authority A group charged with supervising the terms governing how buyers and sellers can legitimately make digital cash transfers.

Certificate of deposit (CD) A time deposit with a fixed maturity date offered by banks and other financial institutions.

***Ceteris paribus* [KAY-ter-us PEAR-uh-bus] assumption** The assumption that nothing changes except the factor or factors being studied.

Checkable deposits Any deposits in a thrift institution or a commercial bank on which a check may be written.

Clearing House Interbank Payment System (CHIPS) A large-value wire transfer system linking about 100 banks that permits them to transmit large sums of money related primarily to foreign exchange and Eurodollar transactions.

Closed shop A business enterprise in which employees must belong to the union before they can be hired and must remain in the union after they are hired.

Collateral An asset pledged to guarantee the repayment of a loan.

Collective bargaining Bargaining between the management of a company or of a group of companies and the management of a union or a group of unions for the purpose of setting a mutually agreeable contract on wages, fringe benefits, and working conditions for all employees in all the unions involved.

Collective decision making How voters, politicians, and other interested parties act and how these actions influence nonmarket decisions.

Common property Property that is owned by everyone and therefore by no one. Air and water are examples of common property resources.

Comparable-worth doctrine The belief that women should receive the same wages as men if the levels of skill and responsibility in their jobs are equivalent.

Comparative advantage The ability to produce a good or service at a lower opportunity cost compared to other producers.

Complements Two goods are complements if both are used together for consumption or enjoyment—for example, coffee and cream. The more you buy of one, the more you buy of the other. For complements, a change in the price of one causes an opposite shift in the demand for the other.

Concentration ratio The percentage of all sales contributed by the leading four or leading eight firms in an industry; sometimes called the *industry concentration ratio*.

Constant dollars Dollars expressed in terms of real purchasing power using a particular year as the base or standard of comparison, in contrast to current dollars.

Constant returns to scale No change in long-run average costs when output increases.

Constant-cost industry An industry whose total output can be increased without an increase in long-run per-unit costs; an industry whose long-run supply curve is horizontal.

Consumer optimum A choice of a set of goods and services that maximizes the level of satisfaction for each consumer, subject to limited income.

Consumer Price Index (CPI) A statistical measure of a weighted average of prices of a specified set of goods and services purchased by wage earners in urban areas.

Consumption Spending on new goods and services out of a household's current income. Whatever is not consumed is saved. Consumption includes such things as buying food and going to a concert. *Can also be viewed as* the use of goods and services for personal satisfaction.

Consumption function The relationship between amount consumed and disposable income. A consumption function tells us how much people plan to consume at various levels of disposable income.

Consumption goods Goods bought by households to use up, such as food, clothing, and movies.

Contraction A business fluctuation during which the pace of national economic activity is slowing down.

Cooperative game A game in which the players explicity cooperate to make themselves better off. As applied to firms, it involves companies colluding in order to make higher than competitive rates of return.

Corporation A legal entity that may conduct business in its own name just as an individual does; the owners of a corporation, called shareholders, own shares of the firm's profits and enjoy the protection of limited liability.

Cost-of-living adjustments (COLAs) Clauses in contracts that allow for increases in specified nominal values to take account of changes in the cost of living.

Cost-of-service regulation Regulation based on allowing prices to reflect only the actual cost of production and no monopoly profits.

Cost-push inflation Inflation caused by a continually decreasing short-run aggregate supply curve.

Craft unions Labor unions composed of workers who engage in a particular trade or skill, such as baking, carpentry, or plumbing.

Crawling peg An exchange rate arrangement in which a country pegs the value of its currency to the exchange value of another nation's currency but allows the par value to change at regular intervals.

Creative response Behavior on the part of a firm that allows it to comply with the letter of the law but violate the spirit, significantly lessening the law's effects.

Credit risk The risk of loss that might occur if one party to an exchange fails to honor the terms under which the exchange was to take place.

Cross price elasticity of demand (E_{xy}) The percentage change in the demand for one good (holding its price constant) divided by the percentage change in the price of a related good.

Crowding-out effect The tendency of expansionary fiscal policy to cause a decrease in planned investment or planned consumption in the private sector; this decrease normally results from the rise in interest rates.

Crude quantity theory of money and prices The belief that changes in the money supply lead to proportional changes in the price level.

Cyclical unemployment Unemployment resulting from business recessions that occur when aggregate (total) demand is insufficient to create full employment.

Debit card A plastic card that allows the bearer to transfer funds to a merchant's account, provided that the bearer authorizes the transfer by providing personal identification.

Decreasing-cost industry An industry in which an increase in output leads to a reduction in long-run per-unit costs, such that the long-run industry supply curve slopes downward.

Deflation The situation in which the average of all prices of goods and services in an economy is falling.

Demand A schedule of how much of a good or service people will purchase at any price during a specified time period, other things being constant.

Demand curve A graphical representation of the demand schedule; a negatively sloped line showing the inverse relationship between the price and the quantity demanded (other things being equal).

Demand-pull inflation Inflation caused by increases in aggregate demand not matched by increases in aggregate supply.

Demerit good A good that has been deemed socially undesirable through the political process. Heroin is an example.

Dependent variable A variable whose value changes according to changes in the value of one or more independent variables.

Depository institutions Financial institutions that accept deposits from savers and lend those deposits out at interest.

Depreciation Reduction in the value of capital goods over a one-year period due to physical wear and tear and also to obsolescence; also called *capital consumption allowance. Can also be viewed as* a decrease in the exchange value of one nation's currency in terms of the currency of another nation.

Depression An extremely severe recession.

Deregulation The elimination or phasing out of regulations on economic activity.

Derived demand Input factor demand derived from demand for the final product being produced.

Development economics The study of factors that contribute to the economic development of a country.

Digital cash Funds contained on computer software, in the form of secure programs stored on microchips and other computer devices.

Diminishing marginal utility The principle that as more of any good or service is consumed, its extra benefit declines. Otherwise stated, increases in total utility from the consumption of a good or service become smaller and smaller as more is consumed during a given time period.

Direct expenditure offsets Actions on the part of the private sector in spending income that offset government fiscal policy actions. Any increase in government spending in an area that competes with the private sector will have some direct expenditure offset.

Direct relationship A relationship between two variables that is positive, meaning that an increase in one variable is associated with an increase in the other and a decrease in one variable is associated with a decrease in the other.

Dirty float Active management of a floating exchange rate on the part of a country's government, often in cooperation with other nations.

Discounting The method by which the present value of a future sum or a future stream of sums is obtained.

Discount rate The interest rate that the Federal Reserve charges for reserves that it lends to depository institutions. It is sometimes referred to as the rediscount rate or, in Canada and England, as the bank rate.

Discouraged workers Individuals who have stopped looking for a job because they are convinced that they will not find a suitable one.

Diseconomies of scale Increases in long-run average costs that occur as output increases.

Disposable personal income (DPI) Personal income after personal income taxes have been paid.

Dissaving Negative saving; a situation in which spending exceeds income. Dissaving can occur when a household is able to borrow or use up existing assets.

Distribution of income The way income is allocated among the population.

Dividends Portion of a corporation's profits paid to its owners (shareholders).

Division of labor The segregation of a resource into different specific tasks; for example, one automobile worker puts on bumpers, another doors, and so on.

Dominant strategies Strategies that always yield the highest benefit. Regardless of what other players do, a dominant strategy will yield the most benefit for the player using it.

Dumping Selling a good or a service abroad below the price charged in the home market or at a price below its cost of production.

Durable consumer goods Consumer goods that have a life span of more than three years.

Economic goods Goods that are scarce, for which the quantity demanded exceeds the quantity supplied at a zero price.

Economic growth Increases in per capita real GDP measured by its rate of change per year.

Economic profits Total revenues minus total opportunity costs of all inputs used, or the total of all implicit and explicit costs. *Can also be viewed as* the difference between total revenues and the opportunity cost of all factors of production.

Economic rent A payment for the use of any resource over and above its opportunity cost.

Economics The study of how people allocate their limited resources to satisfy their unlimited wants.

Economies of scale Decreases in long-run average costs resulting from increases in output.

Effect time lag The time that elapses between the onset of policy and the results of that policy.

Efficiency wage theory The hypothesis that the productivity of workers depends on the level of the real wage rate.

Efficiency The case in which a given level of inputs is used to produce the maximum output possible. Alternatively, the situation in which a given output is produced at minimum cost.

Efficiency wages Wages set above competitive levels to increase labor productivity and profits by enhancing the efficiency of the firm through lower turnover, ease of attracting higher-quality workers, and better efforts by workers.

Effluent fee A charge to a polluter that gives the right to discharge into the air or water a certain amount of pollution. Also called a *pollution tax*.

Elastic demand A demand relationship in which a given percentage change in price will result in a larger percentage change in quantity demanded. Total expenditures and price changes are inversely related in the elastic region of the demand curve.

Empirical Relying on real-world data in evaluating the usefulness of a model.

Endowments The various resources in an economy, including both physical resources and such human resources as ingenuity and management skills.

Entrepreneurship The factor of production involving human resources that perform the functions of raising capital, organizing, managing, assembling other factors of production, and making basic business policy decisions. The entrepreneur is a risk taker.

Entry deterrence strategy Any strategy undertaken by firms in an industry, either individually or together, with the intent or effect of raising the cost of entry into the industry by a new firm.

Equation of exchange The formula indicating that the number of monetary units times the number of times each unit is spent on final goods and services is identical to the price level times output (or nominal national income).

Equilibrium The situation when quantity supplied equals quantity demanded at a particular price.

Eurodollar deposits Deposits denominated in U.S. dollars but held in banks outside the United States, often in overseas branches of U.S. banks.

Excess reserves The difference between legal reserves and required reserves.

Exchange rate The price of one nation's currency in terms of the currency of another country.

Exclusion principle The principle that no one can be excluded from the benefits of a public good, even if that person hasn't paid for it.

Expansion A business fluctuation in which overall business activity is rising at a more rapid rate than previously or at a more rapid rate than the overall historical trend for the nation.

Expenditure approach A way of computing national income by adding up the dollar value at current market prices of all final goods and services.

Explicit costs Costs that business managers must take account of because they must be paid; examples are wages, taxes, and rent.

Externality A consequence of an economic activity that spills over to affect third parties. Pollution is an externality. *Can also be viewed as* a situation in which a private cost (or benefit) diverges from a social cost (or benefit); a situation in which the costs (or benefits) of an action are not fully borne (or gained) by the two parties engaged in exchange or by an individual engaging in a scarce-resource-using activity.

Featherbedding Any practice that forces employers to use more labor than they would otherwise or to use existing labor in an inefficient manner.

The Fed The Federal Reserve System; the central bank of the United States.

Federal Deposit Insurance Corporation (FDIC) A government agency that insures the deposits held in banks and most other depository institutions; all U.S. banks are insured this way.

Federal funds market A private market (made up mostly of banks) in which banks can borrow reserves from other banks that want to lend them. Federal funds are usually lent for overnight use.

Federal funds rate The interest rate that depository institutions pay to borrow reserves in the interbank federal funds market.

Fedwire A large-value wire transfer system operated by the Federal Reserve that is open to all depository institutions that legally must maintain required reserves with the Fed.

Fiduciary monetary system A system in which currency is issued by the government and its value is based uniquely on the public's faith that the currency represents command over goods and services.

Final goods and services Goods and services that are at their final stage of production and will not be transformed into yet other goods or services. For example, wheat is not ordinarily considered a final good because it is usually used to make a final good, bread.

Financial capital Money used to purchase capital goods such as buildings and equipment.

Financial intermediaries Institutions that transfer funds between ultimate lenders (savers) and ultimate borrowers.

Financial intermediation The process by which financial institutions accept savings from businesses, households, and governments and lend the savings to other businesses, households, and governments.

Financial trading system A mechanism linking buyers and sellers of stocks and bonds.

Firm A business organization that employs resources to produce goods or services for profit. A firm normally owns and operates at least one plant in order to produce.

Fiscal policy The discretionary changing of government expenditures or taxes to achieve national economic goals, such as high employment with price stability.

Fixed costs Costs that do not vary with output. Fixed costs include such things as rent on a building. These costs are fixed for a certain period of time; in the long run, they are variable.

Fixed investment Purchases by businesses of newly produced producer durables, or capital goods, such as production machinery and office equipment.

Flexible exchange rates Exchange rates that are allowed to fluctuate in the open market in response to changes in supply and demand. Sometimes called *floating exchange rates*.

Flow A quantity measured per unit of time; something that occurs over time, such as the income you make per week or per year or the number of individuals who are fired every month.

Foreign exchange market A market in which households, firms, and governments buy and sell national currencies.

Foreign exchange rate The price of one currency in terms of another.

Foreign exchange risk The possibility that changes in the value of a nation's currency will result in variations in market values of assets.

45-degree reference line The line along which planned real expenditures equal real national income per year.

Fractional reserve banking A system in which depository institutions hold reserves that are less than the amount of total deposits.

Free-rider problem A problem that arises when individuals presume that others will pay for public goods so that, individually, they can escape paying for their portion without causing a reduction in production.

Frictional unemployment Unemployment due to the fact that workers must search for appropriate job offers. This takes time, and so they remain temporarily unemployed.

Full employment An arbitrary level of unemployment that corresponds to "normal" friction in the labor market. In 1986, a 6.5 percent rate of unemployment was considered full employment. Today, it is assumed to be 5 percent or possibly even less.

Game theory A way of describing the various possible outcomes in any situation involving two or more interacting individuals when those individuals are aware of the interactive nature of their situation and plan accordingly. The plans made by these individuals are known as *game strategies*.

GDP deflator A price index measuring the changes in prices of all new goods and services produced in the economy.

General Agreement on Tariffs and Trade (GATT) An international agreement established in 1947 to further world trade by reducing barriers and tariffs.

Goods All things from which individuals derive satisfaction or happiness.

Government, or **political, goods** Goods (and services) provided by the public sector; they can be either private or public goods.

Gross domestic income (GDI) The sum of all income—wages, interest, rent, and profits—paid to the four factors of production.

Gross domestic product (GDP) The total market value of all final goods and services produced by factors of production located within a nation's borders.

Gross private domestic investment The creation of capital goods, such as factories and machines, that can yield production and hence consumption in the future. Also included in this definition are changes in business inventories and repairs made to machines or buildings.

Gross public debt All federal government debt irrespective of who owns it.

Hedge A financial strategy that reduces the chance of suffering losses arising from foreign exchange risk.

Horizontal merger The joining of firms that are producing or selling a similar product.

Human capital The accumulated training and education of workers.

Implicit costs Expenses that managers do not have to pay out of pocket and hence do not normally explicitly calculate, such as the opportunity cost of factors of production that are owned; examples are owner-provided capital and owner-provided labor.

Import quota A physical supply restriction on imports of a particular good, such as sugar. Foreign exporters are unable to sell in the United States more than the quantity specified in the import quota.

Incentive-compatible contract A loan contract under which a significant amount of the borrower's assets are at risk, providing an incentive for the borrower to look after the lender's interests.

Incentives Rewards for engaging in a particular activity.

Incentive structure The system of rewards and punishments individuals face with respect to their own actions.

Income approach A way of measuring national income by adding up all components of national income, including wages, interest, rent, and profits.

Income elasticity of demand (E_i) The percentage change in demand for any good, holding its price constant, divided by the percentage change in income; the responsiveness of demand to changes in income, holding the good's relative price constant.

Income in kind Income received in the form of goods and services, such as housing or medical care; to be contrasted with money income, which is simply income in dollars, or general purchasing power, that can be used to buy *any* goods and services.

Income velocity of money The number of times per year a dollar is spent on final goods and services; equal to GDP divided by the money supply.

Income-consumption curve The set of optimum consumption points that would occur if income were increased, relative prices remaining constant.

Increasing-cost industry An industry in which an increase in industry output is accompanied by an increase in long-run per-unit costs, such that the long-run industry supply curve slopes upward.

Independent variable A variable whose value is determined independently of, or outside, the equation under study.

Indifference curve A curve composed of a set of consumption alternatives, each of which yields the same total amount of satisfaction.

Indirect business taxes All business taxes except the tax on corporate profits. Indirect business taxes include sales and business property taxes.

Industrial unions Labor unions that consist of workers from a particular industry, such as automobile manufacturing or steel manufacturing.

Industry supply curve The locus of points showing the minimum prices at which given quantities will be forthcoming; also called the *market supply curve*.

Inefficient point Any point below the production possibilities curve at which resources are being used inefficiently.

Inelastic demand A demand relationship in which a given percentage change in price will result in a less than proportionate percentage change in the quantity demanded. Total expenditures and price are directly related in the inelastic region of the demand curve.

Infant industry argument The contention that tariffs should be imposed to protect from import competition an industry that is trying to get started. Presumably, after the industry becomes technologically efficient, the tariff can be lifted.

Inferior goods Goods for which demand falls as income rises.

Inflation The situation in which the average of all prices of goods and services in an economy is rising.

Inflation-adjusted return A rate of return that is measured in terms of real goods and services, that is, after the effects of inflation have been factored out.

Inflationary gap The gap that exists whenever the equilibrium level of real national income per year is greater than the full-employment level as shown by the position of the long-run aggregate supply curve.

Innovation Transforming an invention into something that is useful to humans.

Inside information Information that is not available to the general public about what is happening in a corporation.

Insider-outsider theory A theory of labor markets in which workers who are already employed have an influence on wage bargaining in such a way that outsiders who are willing to work for lower real wages cannot get a job.

Interest The payment for current rather than future command over resources; the cost of obtaining credit. Also, the return paid to owners of capital.

Interest rate effect One of the reasons that the aggregate demand curve slopes downward is that higher price levels increase the interest rate, which in turn causes businesses and consumers to reduce desired spending due to the higher price of borrowing.

Intermediate goods Goods used up entirely in the production of final goods.

International financial diversification Financing investment projects in more than one country.

International Monetary Fund (IMF) An international agency, founded to administer the Bretton Woods agreement and to lend to member countries that experienced significant balance of payments deficits, that now functions primarily as a lender of last resort for national governments.

Inventory investment Changes in the stocks of finished goods and goods in process, as well as changes in the raw materials that businesses keep on hand. Whenever inventories are decreasing, inventory investment is negative; whenever they are increasing, inventory investment is positive.

Inverse relationship A relationship between two variables that is negative, meaning that an increase in one variable is associated with a decrease in the other and a decrease in one variable is associated with an increase in the other.

Investment Any use of today's resources to expand tomorrow's production or consumption. *Can also be viewed as* the spending by businesses on things such as machines and buildings, which can be used to produce goods and services in the future. The investment part of total output is the portion that will be used in the process of producing goods in the future.

Job leaver An individual in the labor force who quits voluntarily.

Job loser An individual in the labor force whose employment was involuntarily terminated.

Jurisdictional dispute A dispute involving two or more unions over which should have control of a particular jurisdiction, such as a particular craft or skill or a particular firm or industry.

Keynesian short-run aggregate supply curve The horizontal portion of the aggregate supply curve in which there is unemployment and unused capacity in the economy.

Labor Productive contributions of humans who work, involving both mental and physical activities.

Labor force Individuals aged 16 years or older who either have jobs or are looking and available for jobs; the number of employed plus the number of unemployed.

Labor force participation rate The percentage of noninstitutionalized working-age individuals who are employed or seeking employment.

Labor productivity Total real domestic output (real GDP) divided by the number of workers (output per worker).

Labor unions Worker organizations that seek to secure economic improvements for their members; they also seek to improve the safety, health, and other benefits (such as job security) of their members.

Land The natural resources that are available from nature. Land as a resource includes location, original fertility and mineral deposits, topography, climate, water, and vegetation.

Large-value wire transfer system A payment system that permits the electronic transmission of large dollar sums.

Law of demand The observation that there is a negative, or inverse, relationship between the price of any good or service and the quantity demanded, holding other factors constant.

Law of diminishing (marginal) returns The observation that after some point, successive equal-sized increases in a variable factor of production, such as labor, added to fixed factors of production, will result in smaller increases in output.

Law of increasing relative cost The observation that the opportunity cost of additional units of a good generally increases as society attempts to produce more of that good. This accounts for the bowed-out shape of the production possibilities curve.

Law of supply The observation that the higher the price of a good, the more of that good sellers will make available over a specified time period, other things being equal.

Leading indicators Factors that economists find to exhibit changes before changes in business activity.

Legal reserves Reserves that depository institutions are allowed by law to claim as reserves—for example, deposits held at Federal Reserve district banks and vault cash.

Lemons problem The situation in which consumers, who do not know details about the quality of a product, are willing to pay no more than the price of a low-quality product, even if a higher-quality product at a higher price exists.

Liabilities Amounts owed; the legal claims against a business or household by nonowners.

Limited liability A legal concept whereby the responsibility, or liability, of the owners of a corporation is limited to the value of the shares in the firm that they own.

Limit-pricing model A model that hypothesizes that a group of colluding sellers will set the highest common price that they believe they can charge without new firms seeking to enter that industry in search of relatively high profits.

Liquidity The degree to which an asset can be acquired or disposed of without much danger of any intervening loss in *nominal* value and with small transaction costs. Money is the most liquid asset.

Liquidity approach A method of measuring the money supply by looking at money as a temporary store of value.

Liquidity risk The risk of loss that may occur if a payment is not received when due.

Long run The time period in which all factors of production can be varied.

Long-run aggregate supply curve A vertical line representing real output of goods and services after full adjustment has occurred. *Can also be viewed as* representing the real output of the economy under conditions of full employment—the full-employment level of real GDP.

Long-run average cost curve The locus of points representing the minimum unit cost of producing any given rate of output, given current technology and resource prices.

Long-run industry supply curve A market supply curve showing the relationship between prices and quantities forthcoming after firms have been allowed the time to enter into or exit from an industry, depending on whether there have been positive or negative economic profits.

Lorenz curve A geometric representation of the distribution of income. A Lorenz curve that is perfectly straight represents complete income equality. The more bowed a Lorenz curve, the more unequally income is distributed.

Lump-sum tax A tax that does not depend on income or the circumstances of the taxpayer. An example is a $1,000 tax that every family must pay, irrespective of its economic situation.

M1 The money supply, taken as the total value of currency plus checkable deposits plus traveler's checks not issued by banks.

M2 M1 plus (1) savings and small-denomination time deposits at all depository institutions, (2) overnight repurchase agreements at commercial banks, (3) overnight Eurodollars held by U.S. residents other than banks at Caribbean branches of member banks, (4) balances in retail money market mutual funds, and (5) money market deposit accounts (MMDAs).

Macroeconomics The study of the behavior of the economy as a whole, including such economywide phenomena as changes in unemployment, the general price level, and national income.

Majority rule A collective decision-making system in which group decisions are made on the basis of more than 50 percent of the vote. In other words, whatever more than half of the electorate votes for, the entire electorate has to accept.

Marginal cost pricing A system of pricing in which the price charged is equal to the opportunity cost to society of producing one more unit of the good or service in question. The opportunity cost is the marginal cost to society.

Marginal costs The change in total costs due to a one-unit change in production rate.

Marginal factor cost (MFC) The cost of using an additional unit of an input. For example, if a firm can hire all the workers it wants at the going wage rate, the marginal factor cost of labor is the wage rate.

Marginal physical product The physical output that is due to the addition of one more unit of a variable factor of production; the change in total product occurring when a variable input is increased and all other inputs are held constant; also called *marginal product* or *marginal return.*

Marginal physical product (MPP) of labor The change in output resulting from the addition of one more worker. The MPP of the worker equals the change in total output accounted for by hiring the worker, holding all other factors of production constant.

Marginal propensity to consume (MPC) The ratio of the change in consumption to the change in disposable income. A marginal propensity to consume of 0.8 tells us that an additional $100 in take-home pay will lead to an additional $80 consumed.

Marginal propensity to save (MPS) The ratio of the change in saving to the change in disposable income. A marginal propensity to save of 0.2 indicates that out of an additional $100 in take-home pay, $20 will be saved. Whatever is not saved is consumed. The marginal propensity to save plus the marginal propensity to consume must always equal 1, by definition.

Marginal revenue The change in total revenues resulting from a change in output (and sale) of one unit of the product in question.

Marginal revenue product (MRP) The marginal physical product (MPP) times marginal revenue. The MRP gives the additional revenue obtained from a one-unit change in labor input.

Marginal tax rate The change in the tax payment divided by the change in income, or the percentage of additional dollars that must be paid in taxes. The marginal tax rate is applied to the highest tax bracket of taxable income reached.

Marginal utility The change in total utility due to a one-unit change in the quantity of a good or service consumed.

Market All of the arrangements that individuals have for exchanging with one another. Thus we can speak of the labor market, the automobile market, and the credit market.

Market clearing, or **equilibrium, price** The price that clears the market, at which quantity demanded equals quantity supplied; the price where the demand curve intersects the supply curve.

Market demand The demand of all consumers in the marketplace for a particular good or service. The summing at each price of the quantity demanded by each individual.

Market failure A situation in which an unrestrained market operation leads to either too few or too many resources going to a specific economic activity.

Market share test The percentage of a market that a particular firm supplies, used as the primary measure of monopoly power.

Median age The age that divides the older half of the population from the younger half.

Medical savings account (MSA) A tax-exempt health care account into which individuals would pay on a regular basis and out of which medical care expenses could be paid.

Medium of exchange Any asset that sellers will accept as payment.

Merit good A good that has been deemed socially desirable through the political process. Museums are an example.

Microeconomics The study of decision making undertaken by individuals (or households) and by firms.

Minimum efficient scale (MES) The lowest rate of output per unit time at which long-run average costs for a particular firm are at a minimum.

Minimum wage A wage floor, legislated by government, setting the lowest hourly rate that firms may legally pay workers.

Models, or **theories** Simplified representations of the real world used as the basis for predictions or explanations.

Monetarists Macroeconomists who believe that inflation is always caused by excessive monetary growth and that changes in the money supply affect aggregate demand both directly and indirectly.

Monetary rule A monetary policy that incorporates a rule specifying the annual rate of growth of some monetary aggregate.

Money Any medium that is universally accepted in an economy both by sellers of goods and services as payment for those goods and services and by creditors as payment for debts.

Money illusion Reacting to changes in money prices rather than relative prices. If a worker whose wages double when the price level also doubles thinks he or she is better off, the worker is suffering from money illusion.

Money market deposit accounts (MMDAs) Accounts issued by banks yielding a market rate of interest with a minimum balance requirement and a limit on transactions. They have no minimum maturity.

Money market mutual funds Funds of investment companies that obtain funds from the public that are held in common and used to acquire short-maturity credit instruments, such as certificates of deposit and securities sold by the U.S. government.

Money multiplier The reciprocal of the required reserve ratio, assuming no leakages into currency and no excess reserves. It is equal to 1 divided by the required reserve ratio.

Money price The price that we observe today, expressed in today's dollars. Also called the *absolute* or *nominal price*.

Money supply The amount of money in circulation.

Monopolist A single supplier that comprises its entire industry for a good or service for which there is no close substitute.

Monopolistic competition A market situation in which a large number of firms produce similar but not identical products. Entry into the industry is relatively easy.

Monopolization The possession of monopoly power in the relevant market and the willful acquisition or maintenance of that power, as distinguished from growth or development as a consequence of a superior product, business acumen, or historical accident.

Monopoly A firm that has great control over the price of a good. In the extreme case, a monopoly is the only seller of a good or service.

Monopsonist A single buyer.

Monopsonistic exploitation Exploitation due to monopsony power. It leads to a price for the variable input that is less than its marginal revenue product. Monopsonistic exploitation is the difference between marginal revenue product and the wage rate.

Moral hazard The possibility that a borrower might engage in riskier behavior after a loan has been obtained.

Multiplier The ratio of the change in the equilibrium level of real national income to the change in autonomous expenditures; the number by which a change in autonomous investment or autonomous consumption, for example, is multiplied to get the change in the equilibrium level of real national income.

National income (NI) The total of all factor payments to resource owners. It can be obtained by subtracting indirect business taxes from NDP.

National income accounting A measurement system used to estimate national income and its components; one approach to measuring an economy's aggregate performance.

Natural monopoly A monopoly that arises from the peculiar production characteristics in an industry. It usually arises when there are large economies of scale relative to the industry's demand such that one firm can produce at a lower average cost than can be achieved by multiple firms.

Natural rate of unemployment The rate of unemployment that is estimated to prevail in long-run macroeconomic equilibrium, when all workers and employers have fully adjusted to any changes in the economy.

Near moneys Assets that are almost money. They have a high degree of liquidity; they can be easily converted into money without loss in value. Time deposits and short-term U.S. government securities are examples.

Negative-sum game A game in which players as a group lose at the end of the game.

Net domestic product (NDP) GDP minus depreciation.

Net investment Gross private domestic investment minus an estimate of the wear and tear on the existing capital stock. Net investment therefore measures the change in capital stock over a one-year period.

Net public debt Gross public debt minus all government interagency borrowing.

Net worth The difference between assets and liabilities.

New classical model A modern version of the classical model in which wages and prices are flexible, there is pure competition in all markets, and the rational expectations hypothesis is assumed to be working.

New entrant An individual who has never held a full-time job lasting two weeks or longer but is now seeking employment.

New growth theory A theory of economic growth that examines the factors that determine why technology, research, innovation, and the like are undertaken and how they interact.

New Keynesian economics A macroeconomic approach that emphasizes that the prices of some goods and services adjust sluggishly in response to changing market conditions. Thus an unexpected decrease in the price level results in some firms with higher-than-desired prices. A consequence is a reduction in sales for those firms.

Nominal rate of interest The market rate of interest expressed in today's dollars.

Nominal values The values of variables such as GDP and investment expressed in current dollars, also called money values; measurement in terms of the actual market prices at which goods are sold.

Nonaccelerating inflation rate of unemployment (NAIRU) The rate of unemployment below which the rate of inflation tends to rise and above which the rate of inflation tends to fall.

Noncooperative game A game in which the players neither negotiate nor cooperate in any way. As applied to firms in an industry, this is the common situation in which there are relatively few firms and each has some ability to change price.

Nondurable consumer goods Consumer goods that are used up within three years.

Nonincome expense items The total of indirect business taxes and depreciation.

Nonprice rationing devices All methods used to ration scarce goods that are price-controlled. Whenever the price system is not allowed to work, nonprice rationing devices will evolve to ration the affected goods and services.

Normal goods Goods for which demand rises as income rises. Most goods are considered normal.

Normal rate of return The amount that must be paid to an investor to induce investment in a business; also known as the *opportunity cost of capital.*

Normative economics Analysis involving value judgments about economic policies; relates to whether things are good or bad. A statement of what ought to be.

Number line A line that can be divided into segments of equal length, each associated with a number.

Oligopoly A market situation in which there are very few sellers. Each seller knows that the other sellers will react to its changes in prices and quantities.

Open economy effect One of the reasons that the aggregate demand curve slopes downward is that higher price levels result in foreigners' desiring to buy fewer American-made goods while Americans now desire more foreign-made goods, thereby reducing net exports. This is equivalent to a reduction in the amount of real goods and services purchased in the United States.

Open market operations The purchase and sale of existing U.S. government securities (such as bonds) in the open private market by the Federal Reserve System.

Opportunistic behavior Actions that ignore the possible long-run benefits of cooperation and focus solely on short-run gains.

Opportunity cost The highest-valued, next-best alternative that must be sacrificed to obtain something or to satisfy a want.

Opportunity cost of capital The normal rate of return, or the available return on the next-best alternative investment. Economists consider this a cost of production, and it is included in our cost examples.

Optimal quantity of pollution The level of pollution for which the marginal benefit of one additional unit of clean air just equals the marginal cost of that additional unit of clean air.

Origin The intersection of the *y* axis and the *x* axis in a graph.

Par value The officially determined value of a currency.

Partnership A business owned by two or more joint owners, or partners, who share the responsibilities and the profits of the firm and are individually liable for all of the debts of the partnership.

Passive (nondiscretionary) policymaking Policymaking that is carried out in response to a rule. It is therefore not in response to an actual or potential change in overall economic activity.

Patent A government protection that gives an inventor the exclusive right to make, use, or sell an invention for a limited period of time (currently, 20 years).

Payment intermediary An institution that facilitates the transfer of funds between buyer and seller during the course of any purchase of goods, services, or financial assets.

Payment system An institutional structure by which consumers, businesses, governments, and financial institutions exchange payments.

Payoff matrix A matrix of outcomes, or consequences, of the strategies available to the players in a game.

Perfect competition A market structure in which the decisions of individual buyers and sellers have no effect on market price.

Perfectly competitive firm A firm that is such a small part of the total industry that it cannot affect the price of the product it sells.

Perfectly elastic demand A demand that has the characteristic that even the slightest increase in price will lead to zero quantity demanded.

Perfectly elastic supply A supply characterized by a reduction in quantity supplied to zero when there is the slightest decrease in price.

Perfectly inelastic demand A demand that exhibits zero responsiveness to price changes; no matter what the price is, the quantity demanded remains the same.

Perfectly inelastic supply A supply for which quantity supplied remains constant, no matter what happens to price.

Personal income (PI) The amount of income that households actually receive before they pay personal income taxes.

Phillips curve A curve showing the relationship between unemployment and changes in wages or prices. It was long thought to reflect a trade-off between unemployment and inflation.

Physical capital All manufactured resources, including buildings, equipment, machines, and improvements to land that is used for production.

Planning curve The long-run average cost curve.

Planning horizon The long run, during which all inputs are variable.

Plant size The physical size of the factories that a firm owns and operates to produce its output. Plant size can be defined by square footage, maximum physical capacity, and other physical measures.

Point-of-sale (POS) network System in which consumer payments for retail purchases are made by means of direct deductions from their deposit accounts at depository institutions.

Policy irrelevance proposition The new classical and rational expectations conclusion that policy actions have no real effects in the short run if the policy actions are anticipated and none in the long run even if the policy actions are unanticipated.

Positive economics Analysis that is strictly limited to making either purely descriptive statements or scientific predictions; for example, "If A, then B." A statement of what is.

Positive-sum game A game in which players as a group are better off at the end of the game.

Precautionary demand Holding money to meet unplanned expenditures and emergencies.

Present value The value of a future amount expressed in today's dollars; the most that someone would pay today to receive a certain sum at some point in the future.

Price ceiling A legal maximum price that may be charged for a particular good or service.

Price controls Government-mandated minimum or maximum prices that may be charged for goods and services.

Price differentiation Establishing different prices for similar products to reflect differences in marginal cost in providing those commodities to different groups of buyers.

Price discrimination Selling a given product at more than one price, with the price difference being unrelated to differences in cost.

Price elasticity of demand (E_p) The responsiveness of the quantity demanded of a commodity to changes in its price; defined as the percentage change in quantity demanded divided by the percentage change in price.

Price elasticity of supply (E_s) The responsiveness of the quantity supplied of a commodity to a change in its price; the percentage change in quantity supplied divided by the percentage change in price.

Price floor A legal minimum price below which a good or service may not be sold. Legal minimum wages are an example.

Price index The cost of today's market basket of goods expressed as a percentage of the cost of the same market basket during a base year.

Price leadership A practice in many oligopolistic industries in which the largest firm publishes its price list ahead of its competitors, who then match those announced prices. Also called *parallel pricing*.

Price searcher A firm that must determine the price-output combination that maximizes profit because it faces a downward-sloping demand curve.

Price system An economic system in which relative prices are constantly changing to reflect changes in supply and demand for different commodities. The prices of those commodities are signals to everyone within the system as to what is relatively scarce and what is relatively abundant.

Price taker A competitive firm that must take the price of its product as given because the firm cannot influence its price.

Price war A pricing campaign designed to capture additional market share by repeatedly cutting prices.

Price-consumption curve The set of consumer optimum combinations of two goods that the consumer would choose as the price of one good changes, while money income and the price of the other good remain constant.

Principal-agent problem The conflict of interest that occurs when agents—managers of firms—pursue their own objectives to the detriment of the goals of the firms' principals, or owners.

Principle of rival consumption The recognition that individuals are rivals in consuming private goods because one person's consumption reduces the amount available for others to consume.

Principle of substitution The principle that consumers and producers shift away from goods and resources that become priced relatively higher in favor of goods and resources that are now priced relatively lower.

Prisoners' dilemma A famous strategic game in which two prisoners have a choice between confessing and not confessing to a crime. If neither confesses, they serve a minimum sentence. If both confess, they serve a maximum sentence. If one confesses and the other doesn't, the one who confesses goes free. The dominant strategy is always to confess.

Private costs Costs borne solely by the individuals who incur them. Also called *internal costs*.

Private goods Goods that can be consumed by only one individual at a time. Private goods are subject to the principle of rival consumption.

Private property rights Exclusive rights of ownership that allow the use, transfer, and exchange of property.

Producer durables, or **capital goods** Durable goods having an expected service life of more than three years that are used by businesses to produce other goods and services.

Producer Price Index (PPI) A statistical measure of a weighted average of prices of commodities that firms produce and sell.

Product differentiation The distinguishing of products by brand name, color, and other minor attributes. Product differentiation occurs in other than perfectly competitive markets in which products are, in theory, homogeneous, such as wheat or corn.

Production Any activity that results in the conversion of resources into products that can be used in consumption.

Production function The relationship between inputs and maximum physical output. A production function is a technological, not an economic, relationship.

Production possibilities curve (PPC) A curve representing all possible combinations of total output that could be produced assuming (1) a fixed amount of productive resources of a given quality and (2) the efficient use of those resources.

Profit-maximizing rate of production The rate of production that maximizes total profits, or the difference between total revenues and total costs; also, the rate of production at which marginal revenue equals marginal cost.

Progressive taxation A tax system in which as income increases, a higher percentage of the additional income is taxed. The marginal tax rate exceeds the average tax rate as income rises.

Property rights The rights of an owner to use and to exchange property.

Proportional rule A decision-making system in which actions are based on the proportion of the "votes" cast and are in proportion to them. In a market system, if 10 percent of the "dollar votes" are cast for blue cars, 10 percent of the output will be blue cars.

Proportional taxation A tax system in which regardless of an individual's income, the tax bill comprises exactly the same proportion. Also called a *flat-rate tax*.

Proprietorship A business owned by one individual who makes the business decisions, receives all the profits, and is legally responsible for all the debts of the firm.

Public goods Goods to which the principle of rival consumption does not apply; they can be jointly consumed by many individuals simultaneously at no additional cost and with no reduction in quality or quantity.

Purchasing power The value of money for buying goods and services. If your money income stays the same but the price of one good that you are buying goes up, your effective purchasing power falls, and vice versa.

Purchasing power parity Adjustment in exchange rate conversions that takes into account differences in the true cost of living across countries.

Quota system A government-imposed restriction on the quantity of a specific good that another country is allowed to sell in the United States. In other words, quotas are restrictions on imports. These restrictions are usually applied to one or several specific countries.

Random walk theory The theory that there are no predictable trends in securities prices that can be used to "get rich quick."

Rate of discount The rate of interest used to discount future sums back to present value.

Rate of return An economic system in which relative prices are constantly changing to reflect changes in supply and demand for different commodities. The prices of those commodities are signals to everyone within the system as to what is relatively scarce and what is relatively abundant.

Rate-of-return regulation Regulation that seeks to keep the rate of return in the industry at a competitive level by not allowing excessive prices to be charged.

Rational expectations hypothesis A theory stating that people combine the effects of past policy changes on important economic variables with their own judgment about the future effects of current and future policy changes.

Rationality assumption The assumption that people do not intentionally make decisions that would leave them worse off.

Reaction function The manner in which one oligopolist reacts to a change in price, output, or quality made by another oligopolist in the industry.

Real-balance effect The change in expenditures resulting from the real value of money balances when the price level changes, all other things held constant. Also called the wealth effect.

Real business cycle theory An extension and modification of the theories of the new classical economists of the 1970s and 1980s, in which money is neutral and only real, supply-side factors matter in influencing labor employment and real output.

Real-income effect The change in people's purchasing power that occurs when, other things being constant, the price of one good that they purchase changes. When that price goes up, real income, or purchasing power, falls, and when that price goes down, real income increases.

Real rate of interest The nominal rate of interest minus the anticipated rate of inflation.

Real values Measurement of economic values after adjustments have been made for changes in the average of prices between years.

Recession A period of time during which the rate of growth of business activity is consistently less than its long-term trend or is negative.

Recessionary gap The gap that exists whenever the equilibrium level of real national income per year is less than the full-employment level as shown by the position of the long-run aggregate supply curve.

Recognition time lag The time required to gather information about the current state of the economy.

Recycling The reuse of raw materials derived from manufactured products.

Reentrant An individual who used to work full time but left the labor force and has now reentered it looking for a job.

Regressive taxation A tax system in which as more dollars are earned, the percentage of tax paid on them falls. The marginal tax rate is less than the average tax rate as income rises.

Reinvestment Profits (or depreciation reserves) used to purchase new capital equipment.

Relative price The price of one commodity divided by the price of another commodity; the number of units of one commodity that must be sacrificed to purchase one unit of another commodity.

Rent control The placement of price ceilings on rents in particular cities.

Repricing, or **menu, cost of inflation** The cost associated with recalculating prices and printing new price lists when there is inflation.

Repurchase agreement (REPO, or **RP)** An agreement made by a bank to sell Treasury or federal agency securities to its customers, coupled with an agreement to repurchase them at a price that includes accumulated interest.

Required reserve ratio The percentage of total deposits that the Fed requires depository institutions to hold in the form of vault cash or deposits with the Fed.

Required reserves The value of reserves that a depository institution must hold in the form of vault cash or deposits with the Fed.

Reserves In the U.S. Federal Reserve System, deposits held by Federal Reserve district banks for depository institutions, plus depository institutions' vault cash.

Resources Things used to produce other things to satisfy people's wants.

Retained earnings Earnings that a corporation saves, or retains, for investment in other productive activities; earnings that are not distributed to stockholders.

Ricardian equivalence theorem The proposition that an increase in the government budget deficit has no effect on aggregate demand.

Right-to-work laws Laws that make it illegal to require union membership as a condition of continuing employment in a particular firm.

Saving The act of not consuming all of one's current income. Whatever is not consumed out of spendable income is, by definition, saved. *Saving* is an action measured over time (a flow), whereas *savings* are a stock, an accumulation resulting from the act of saving in the past.

Savings deposits Interest-earning funds that can be withdrawn at any time without payment of a penalty.

Say's law A dictum of economist J. B. Say that supply creates its own demand; producing goods and services generates the means and the willingness to purchase other goods and services.

Scarcity A situation in which the ingredients for producing the things that people desire are insufficient to satisfy all wants.

Seasonal unemployment Unemployment resulting from the seasonal pattern of work in specific industries. It is usually due to seasonal fluctuations in demand or to changing weather conditions, rendering work difficult, if not impossible, as in the agriculture, construction, and tourist industries.

Secondary boycott A boycott of companies or products sold by companies that are dealing with a company being struck.

Secular deflation A persistent decline in prices resulting from economic growth in the presence of stable aggregate demand.

Securities Stocks and bonds.

Separation of ownership and control The situation that exists in corporations in which the owners (shareholders) are not the people who control the operation of the corporation (managers). The goals of these two groups are often different.

Services Mental or physical labor or help purchased by consumers. Examples are the assistance of doctors, lawyers, dentists, repair personnel, housecleaners, educators, retailers, and wholesalers; things purchased or used by consumers that do not have physical characteristics.

Share of stock A legal claim to a share of a corporation's future profits; if it is *common stock*, it incorporates certain voting rights regarding major policy decisions of the corporation; if it is *preferred stock*, its owners are accorded preferential treatment in the payment of dividends.

Share-the-gains, share-the-pains theory A theory of regulatory behavior in which the regulators must take account of the demands of three groups: legislators, who established and who oversee the regulatory agency; members of the regulated industry; and consumers of the regulated industry's products or services.

Short run The time period when at least one input, such as plant size, cannot be changed.

Short-run aggregate supply curve The relationship between aggregate supply and the price level in the short run, all other things held constant. If prices adjust gradually in the short run, the curve is positively sloped.

Short-run break-even price The price at which a firm's total revenues equal its total costs. At the break-even price, the firm is just making a normal rate of return on its capital investment. (It is covering its explicit and implicit costs.)

Short-run shutdown price The price that just covers average variable costs. It occurs just below the intersection of the marginal cost curve and the average variable cost curve.

Shortage A situation in which quantity demanded is greater than quantity supplied at a price below the market clearing price.

Signals Compact ways of conveying to economic decision makers information needed to make decisions. A true signal not only conveys information but also provides the incentive to react appropriately. Economic profits and economic losses are such signals.

Slope The change in the *y*-value divided by the corresponding change in the *x* value of a curve; the "incline" of the curve.

Small menu cost theory A hypothesis that it is costly for firms to change prices in response to demand changes because of the cost of renegotiating contracts, printing price lists, and so on.

Smart card A card containing a microprocessor that permits storage of funds via security programming, can communicate with other computers, and does not require on-line authorization for funds transfers.

Social costs The full costs borne by society whenever a resource use occurs. Social costs can be measured by adding private, or internal, costs to external costs.

Social Security contributions The mandatory taxes paid out of workers' wages and salaries. Although half are supposedly paid by employers, in fact the net wages of employees are lower by the full amount.

Special drawing rights (SDRs) Reserve assets created by the International Monetary Fund for countries to use in settling international payment obligations.

Specialization The division of productive activities among persons and regions so that no one individual or one area is totally self-sufficient. An individual may specialize, for example, in law or medicine. A nation may specialize in the production of coffee, computers, or cameras.

Standard of deferred payment A property of an asset that makes it desirable for use as a means of settling debts maturing in the future; an essential property of money.

Stock The quantity of something, measured at a given point in time—for example, an inventory of goods or a bank account. Stocks are defined independently of time, although they are assessed at a point in time.

Store of value The ability to hold value over time; a necessary property of money.

Stored-value card A card bearing magnetic stripes that hold magnetically encoded data, providing access to stored funds.

Strategic dependence A situation in which one firm's actions with respect to price, quality, advertising, and related changes may be strategically countered by the reactions of one or more other firms in the industry. Such dependence can exist only when there are a limited number of major firms in an industry.

Strategy Any rule that is used to make a choice, such as "Always pick heads"; any potential choice that can be made by players in a game.

Strikebreakers Temporary or permanent workers hired by a company to replace union members who are striking.

Structural unemployment Unemployment resulting from a poor match of workers' abilities and skills with current requirements of employers.

Subsidy A negative tax; a payment to a producer from the government, usually in the form of a cash grant.

Substitutes Two goods are substitutes when either one can be used for consumption to satisfy a similar want—for example, coffee and tea. The more you buy of one, the less you buy of the other. For substitutes, the change in the price of one causes a shift in demand for the other in the same direction as the price change.

Substitution effect The tendency of people to substitute cheaper commodities for more expensive commodities.

Supply A schedule showing the relationship between price and quantity supplied for a specified period of time, other things being equal.

Supply curve The graphical representation of the supply schedule; a line (curve) showing the supply schedule, which generally slopes upward (has a positive slope), other things being equal.

Supply-side economics The notion that creating incentives for individuals and firms to increase productivity will cause the aggregate supply curve to shift outward.

Surplus A situation in which quantity supplied is greater than quantity demanded at a price above the market clearing price.

Sweep account A depository institution account that entails regular shifts of funds from transaction deposits that are subject to reserve requirements to savings deposits that are exempt from reserve requirements.

Sympathy strike A strike by a union in sympathy with another union's strike or cause.

Systemic risk The risk that some payment intermediaries may not be able to meet the terms of their credit agreements because of failures by other institutions to settle other transactions.

Target zone A range of permitted exchange rate variations between upper and lower exchange rate bands that a central bank defends by selling or buying foreign exchange reserves.

Tariffs Taxes on imported goods.

Tax bracket A specified interval of income to which a specific and unique marginal tax rate is applied.

Tax incidence The distribution of tax burdens among various groups in society.

Technology Society's pool of applied knowledge concerning how goods and services can be produced.

Terms of exchange The terms under which trading takes place. Usually the terms of exchange are equal to the price at which a good is traded.

Theory of contestable markets A hypothesis concerning pricing behavior that holds that even though there are only a few firms in an industry, they are forced to price their products more or less competitively because of the ease of entry by outsiders. The key aspect of a contestable market is relatively costless entry into and exit from the industry.

Theory of public choice The study of collective decision making.

Third parties Parties who are not directly involved in a given activity or transaction. For example, in the relationship between caregivers and patients, fees may be paid by third parties (insurance companies, government).

Thrift institutions Financial institutions that receive most of their funds from the savings of the public; they include mutual savings banks, savings and loan associations, and credit unions.

Time deposit A deposit in a financial institution that requires notice of intent to withdraw or must be left for an agreed period. Withdrawal of funds prior to the end of the agreed period may result in a penalty.

Tit-for-tat strategic behavior In game theory, cooperation that continues so long as the other players continue to cooperate.

Total costs The sum of total fixed costs and total variable costs.

Total income The yearly amount earned by the nation's resources (factors of production). Total income therefore includes wages, rent, interest payments, and profits that are received, respectively, by workers, landowners, capital owners, and entrepreneurs.

Total revenues The price per unit times the total quantity sold.

Transaction costs All of the costs associated with exchanging, including the informational costs of finding out price and quality, service record, and durability of a product, plus the cost of contracting and enforcing that contract.

Transactions accounts Checking account balances in commercial banks and other types of financial institutions, such as credit unions and mutual savings banks; any accounts in financial institutions on which you can easily write checks without many restrictions.

Transactions approach A method of measuring the money supply by looking at money as a medium of exchange.

Transactions demand Holding money as a medium of exchange to make payments. The level varies directly with nominal national income.

Transfer payments Money payments made by governments to individuals for which in return no services or goods are concurrently rendered. Examples are welfare, Social Security, and unemployment insurance benefits.

Transfers in kind Payments that are in the form of actual goods and services, such as food stamps, subsidized public housing, and medical care, and for which in return no goods or services are rendered concurrently.

Traveler's checks Financial instruments purchased from a bank or a nonbanking organization and signed during purchase that can be used as cash upon a second signature by the purchaser.

Unanticipated inflation Inflation at a rate that comes as a surprise, either higher or lower than the rate anticipated.

Unemployment The total number of adults (aged 16 years or older) who are willing and able to work and who are actively looking for work but have not found a job.

Union shop A business enterprise that allows the hiring of nonunion members, conditional on their joining the union by some specified date after employment begins.

Unit elasticity of demand A demand relationship in which the quantity demanded changes exactly in proportion to the change in price. Total expenditures are invariant to price changes in the unit-elastic region of the demand curve.

Unit of accounting A measure by which prices are expressed; the common denominator of the price system; a central property of money.

Universal banking Environment in which banks face few or no restrictions on their power to offer a full range of financial services and to own shares of stock in corporations.

Unlimited liability A legal concept whereby the personal assets of the owner of a firm can be seized to pay off the firm's debts.

Util A representative unit by which utility is measured.

Utility The want-satisfying power of a good or service.

Utility analysis The analysis of consumer decision making based on utility maximization.

Value added The dollar value of an industry's sales minus the value of intermediate goods (for example, raw materials and parts) used in production.

Variable costs Costs that vary with the rate of production. They include wages paid to workers and purchases of materials.

Vertical merger The joining of a firm with another to which it sells an output or from which it buys an input.

Voluntary exchange An act of trading, done on a voluntary basis, in which both parties to the trade are subjectively better off after the exchange.

Voluntary import expansion (VIE) An official agreement with another country in which it agrees to import more from the United States.

Voluntary restraint agreement (VRA) An official agreement with another country that "voluntarily" restricts the quantity of its exports to the United States.

Wants What people would buy if their incomes were unlimited.

Wealth The stock of assets owned by a person, household, firm, or nation. For a household, wealth can consist of a house, cars, personal belongings, stocks, bonds, bank accounts, and cash.

World index fund A portfolio of bonds issued in various nations whose yields generally move in offsetting directions, thereby reducing the overall risk of losses.

World Trade Organization (WTO) The successor organization to GATT, it handles all trade disputes among its 135 member nations.

***x* axis** The horizontal axis in a graph.

y axis The vertical axis in a graph.

Zero-sum game A game in which any gains within the group are exactly offset by equal losses by the end of the game.

Index